CONTENTS

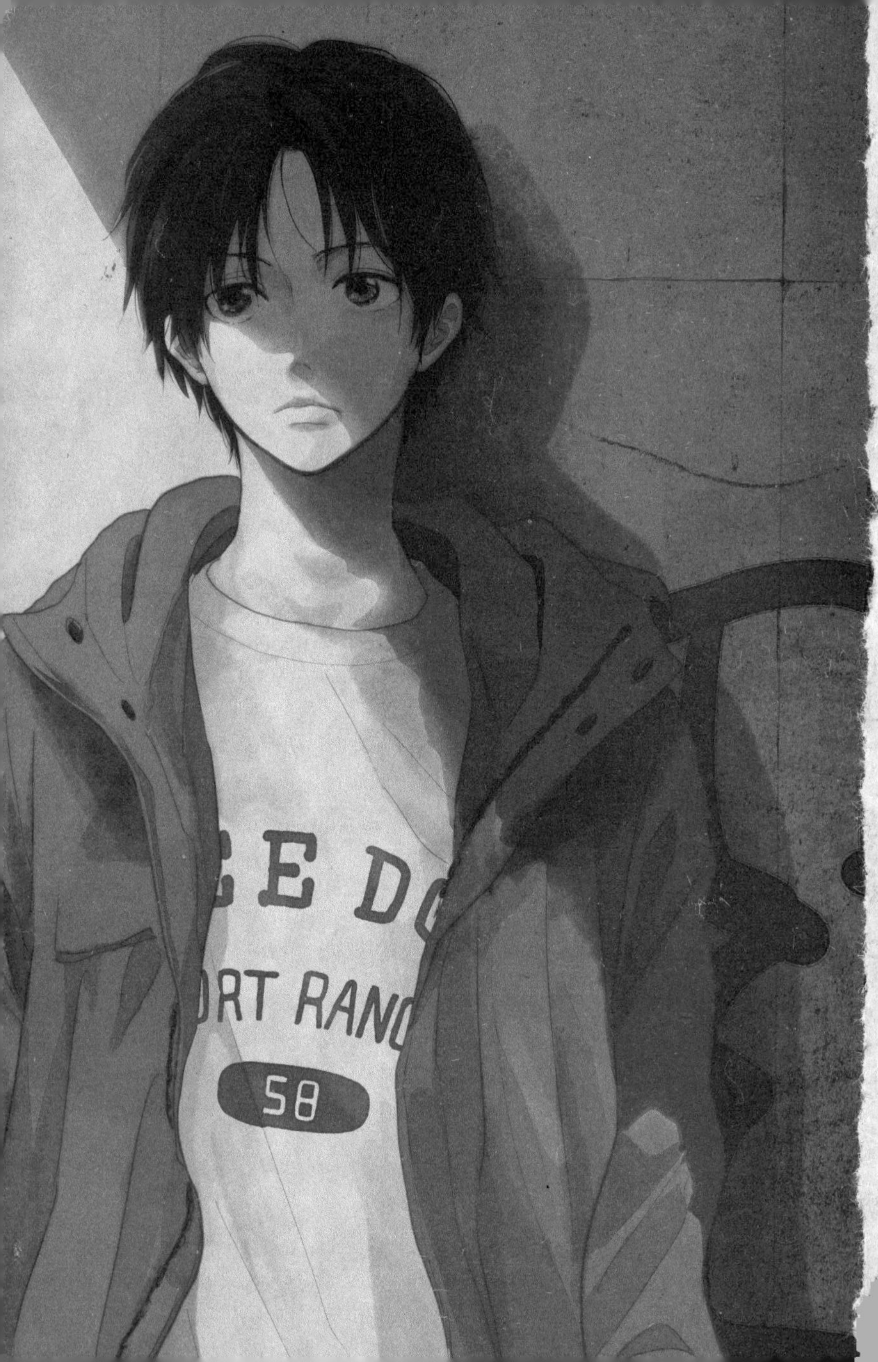
58

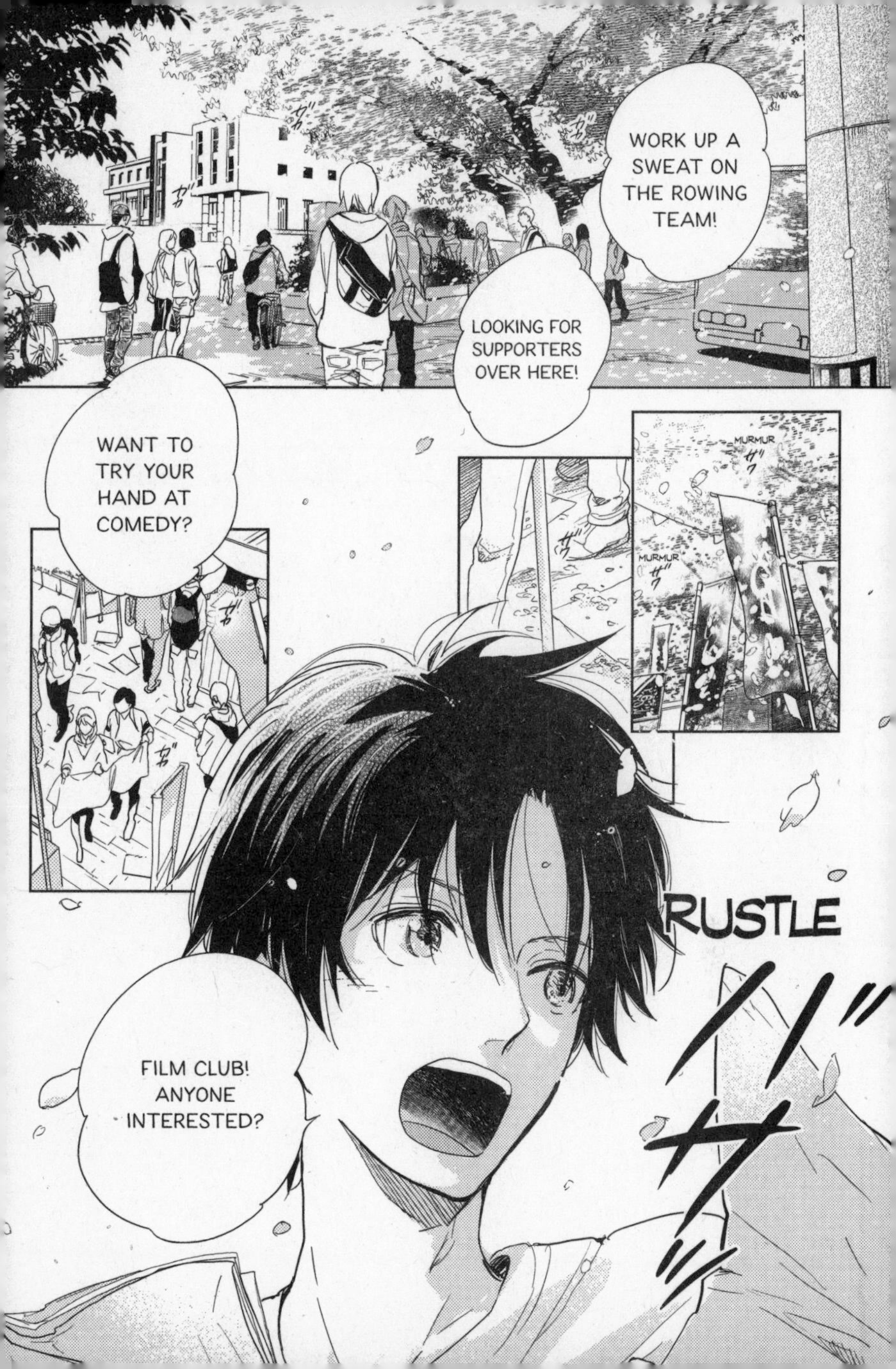

WORK UP A SWEAT ON THE ROWING TEAM!
LOOKING FOR SUPPORTERS OVER HERE!
MURMUR
MURMUR
WANT TO TRY YOUR HAND AT COMEDY?
RUSTLE
FILM CLUB! ANYONE INTERESTED?

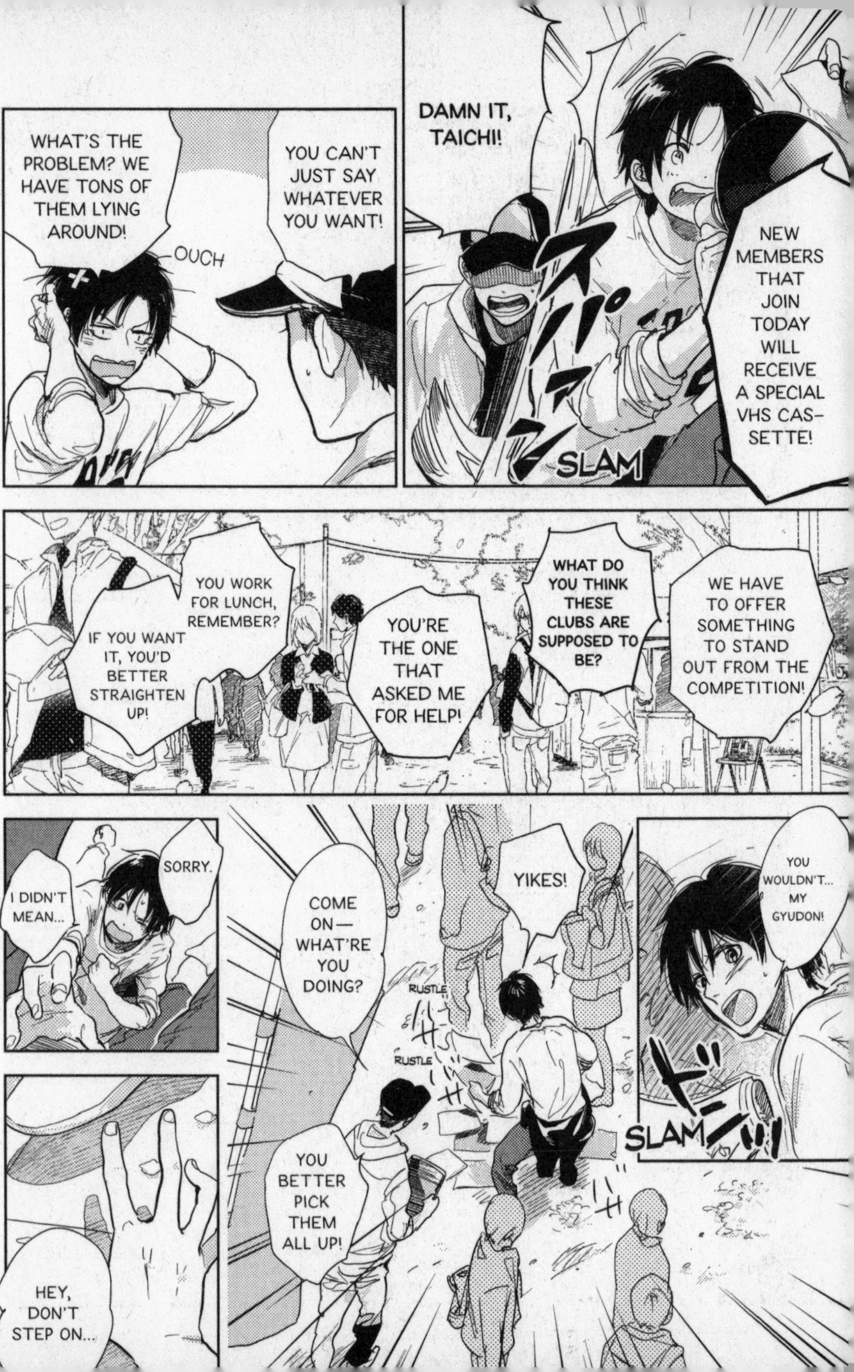

DAMN IT, TAICHI!
NEW MEMBERS THAT JOIN TODAY WILL RECEIVE A SPECIAL VHS CAS-SETTE!
SLAM
YOU CAN'T JUST SAY WHATEVER YOU WANT!
WHAT'S THE PROBLEM? WE HAVE TONS OF THEM LYING AROUND!
OUCH
WE HAVE TO OFFER SOMETHING TO STAND OUT FROM THE COMPETITION!
WHAT DO YOU THINK THESE CLUBS ARE SUPPOSED TO BE?
YOU'RE THE ONE THAT ASKED ME FOR HELP!
YOU WORK FOR LUNCH, REMEMBER?
IF YOU WANT IT, YOU'D BETTER STRAIGHTEN UP!
YOU WOULDN'T... MY GYUDON!
SLAM
YIKES!
COME ON— WHAT'RE YOU DOING?
RUSTLE
RUSTLE
YOU BETTER PICK THEM ALL UP!
SORRY.
I DIDN'T MEAN...
HEY, DON'T STEP ON...

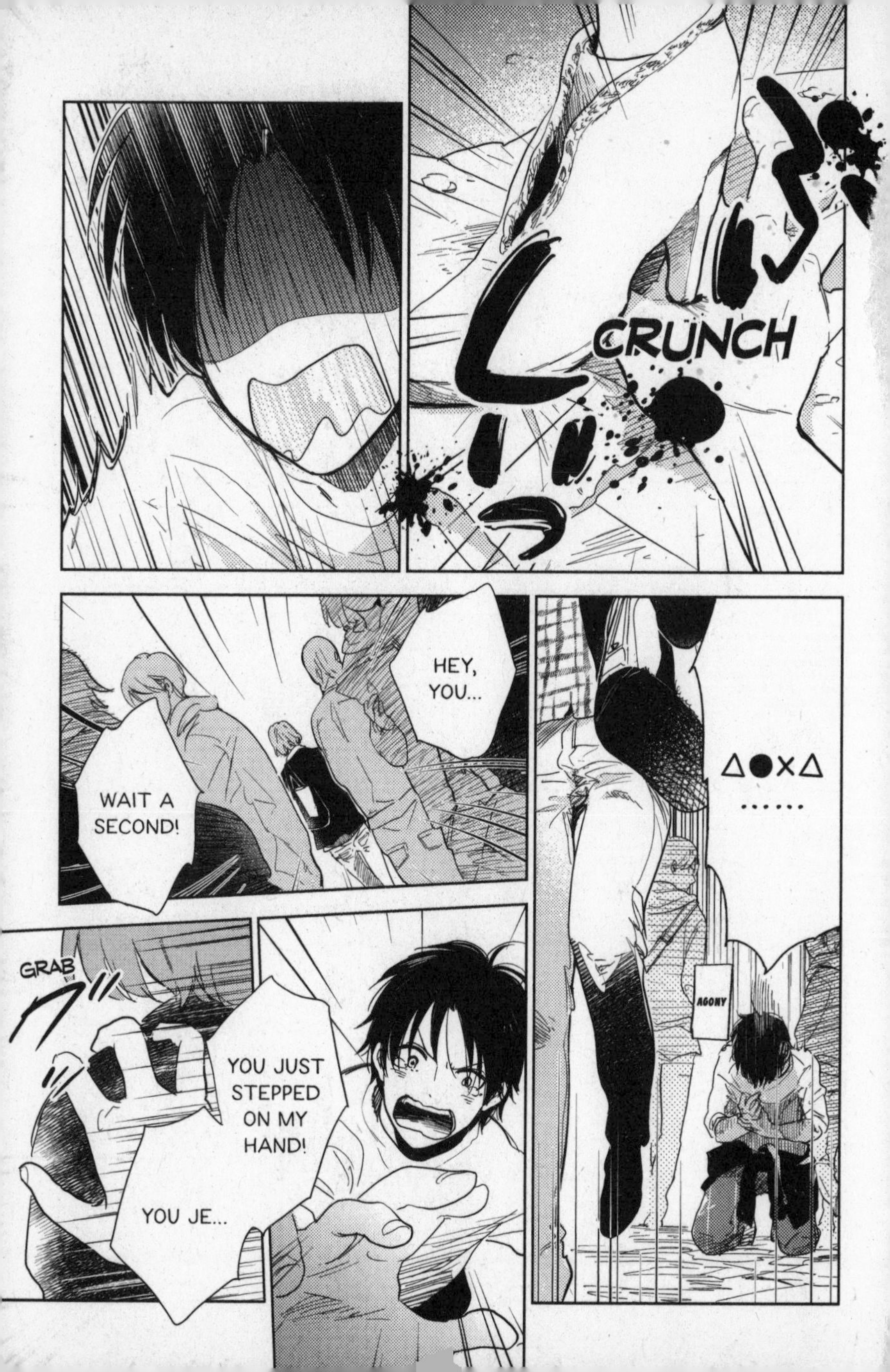
CRUNCH
△●×△
......
AGONY
HEY, YOU...
WAIT A SECOND!
YOU JUST STEPPED ON MY HAND!
YOU JE...
GRAB

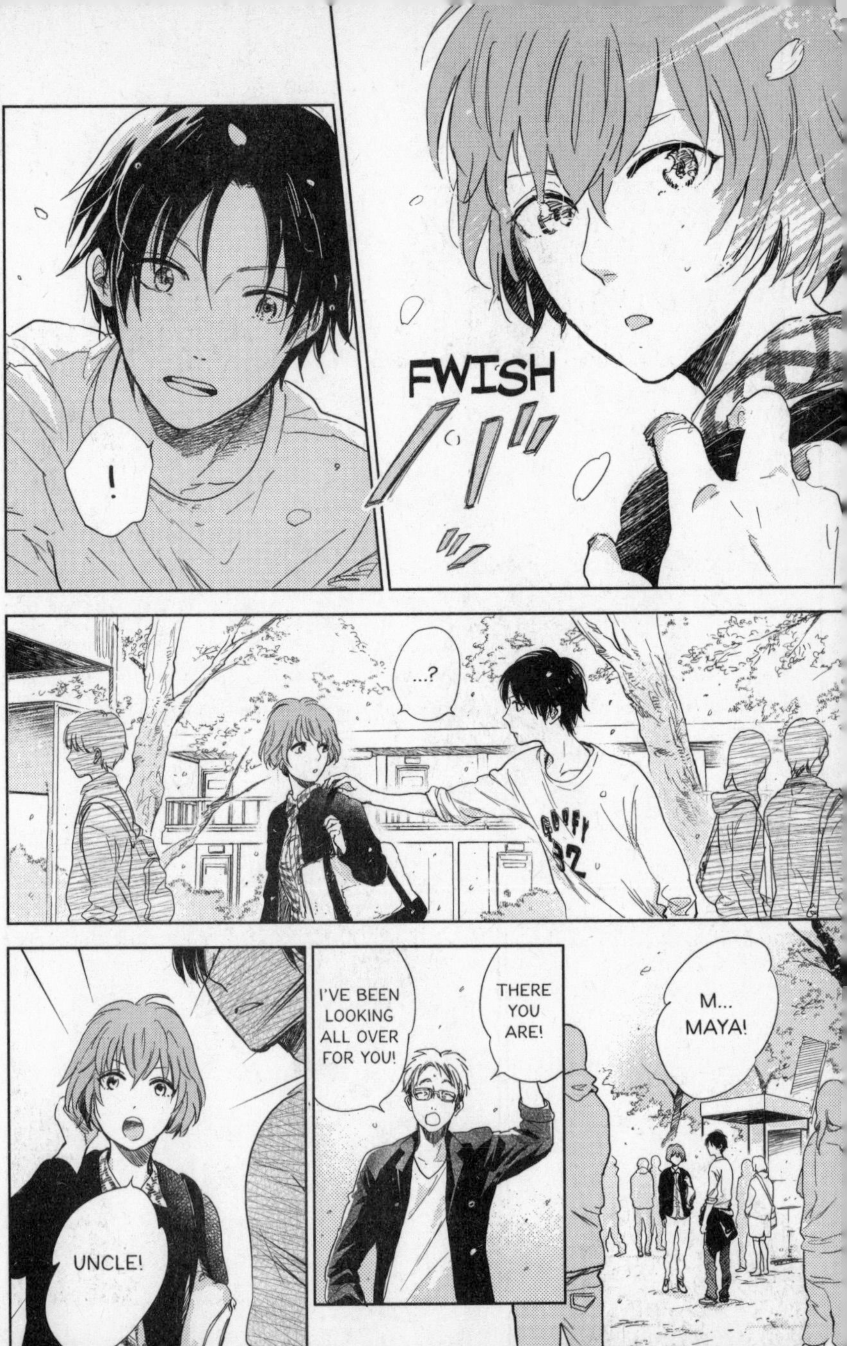
FWISH
!
...?
M... MAYA!
THERE YOU ARE!
I'VE BEEN LOOKING ALL OVER FOR YOU!
UNCLE!

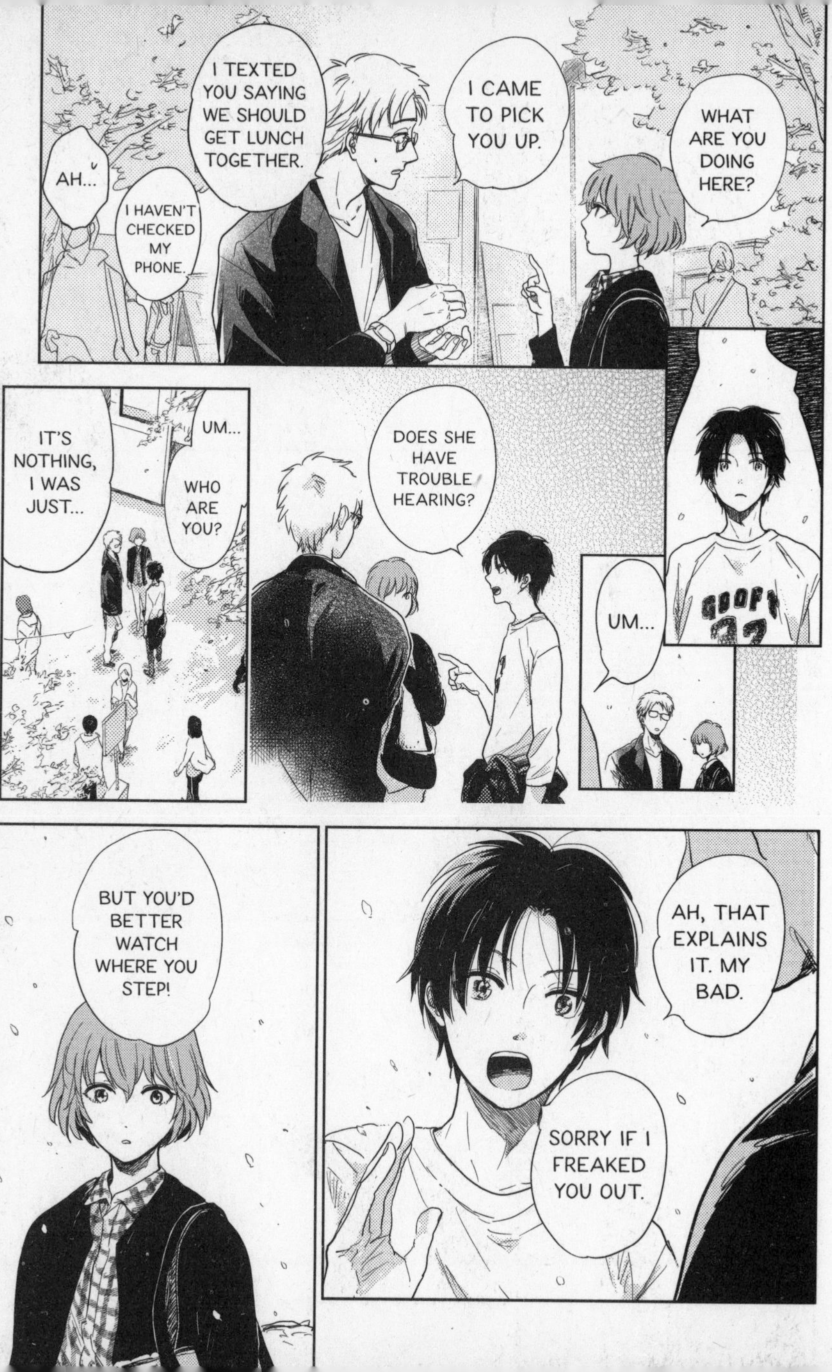
WHAT ARE YOU DOING HERE?
I CAME TO PICK YOU UP.
I TEXTED YOU SAYING WE SHOULD GET LUNCH TOGETHER.
AH...
I HAVEN'T CHECKED MY PHONE.
UM...
DOES SHE HAVE TROUBLE HEARING?
UM...
WHO ARE YOU?
IT'S NOTHING, I WAS JUST...
AH, THAT EXPLAINS IT. MY BAD.
SORRY IF I FREAKED YOU OUT.
BUT YOU'D BETTER WATCH WHERE YOU STEP!

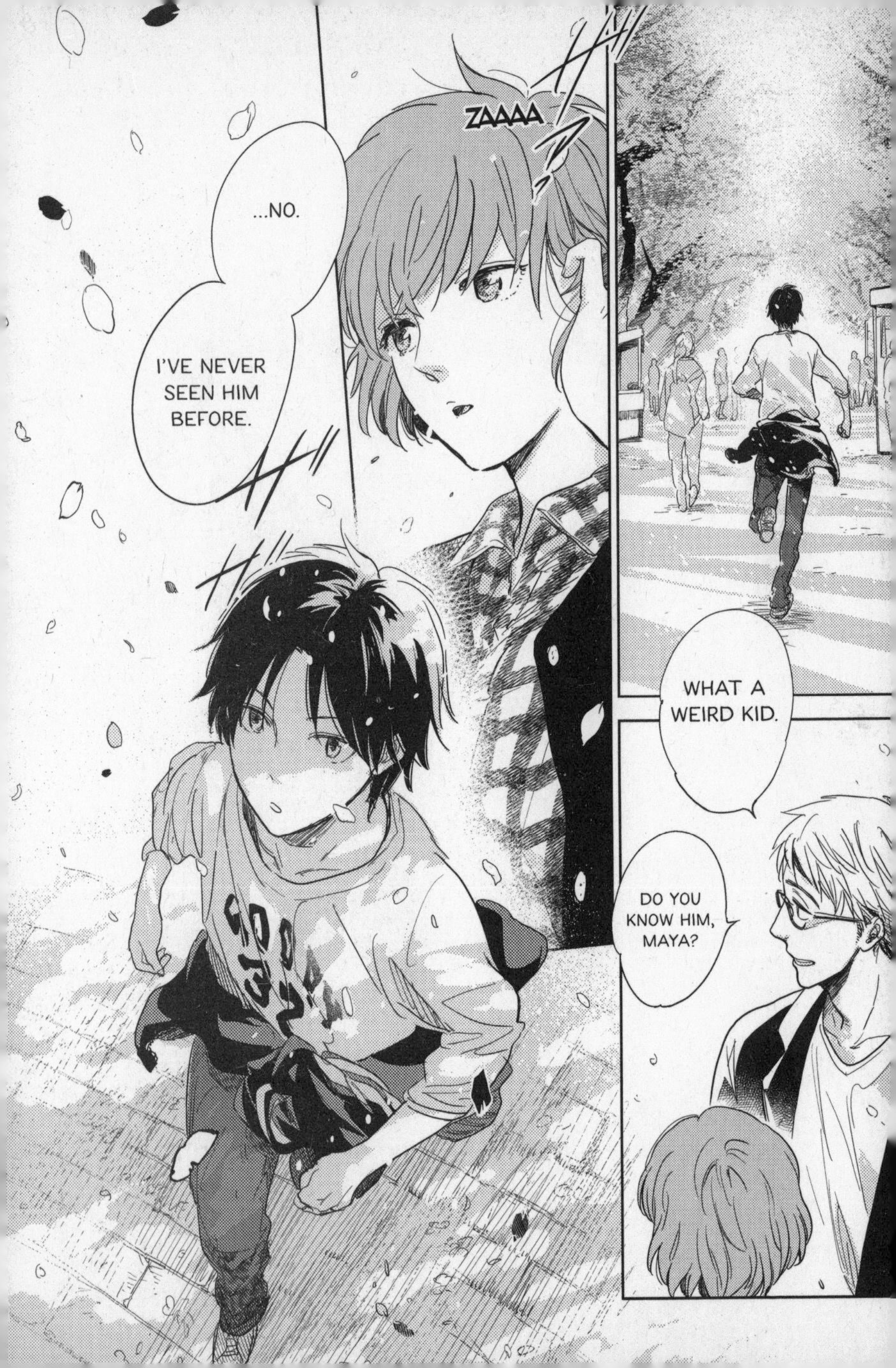
WHAT A WEIRD KID.
DO YOU KNOW HIM, MAYA?
ZAAAA
...NO.
I'VE NEVER SEEN HIM BEFORE.

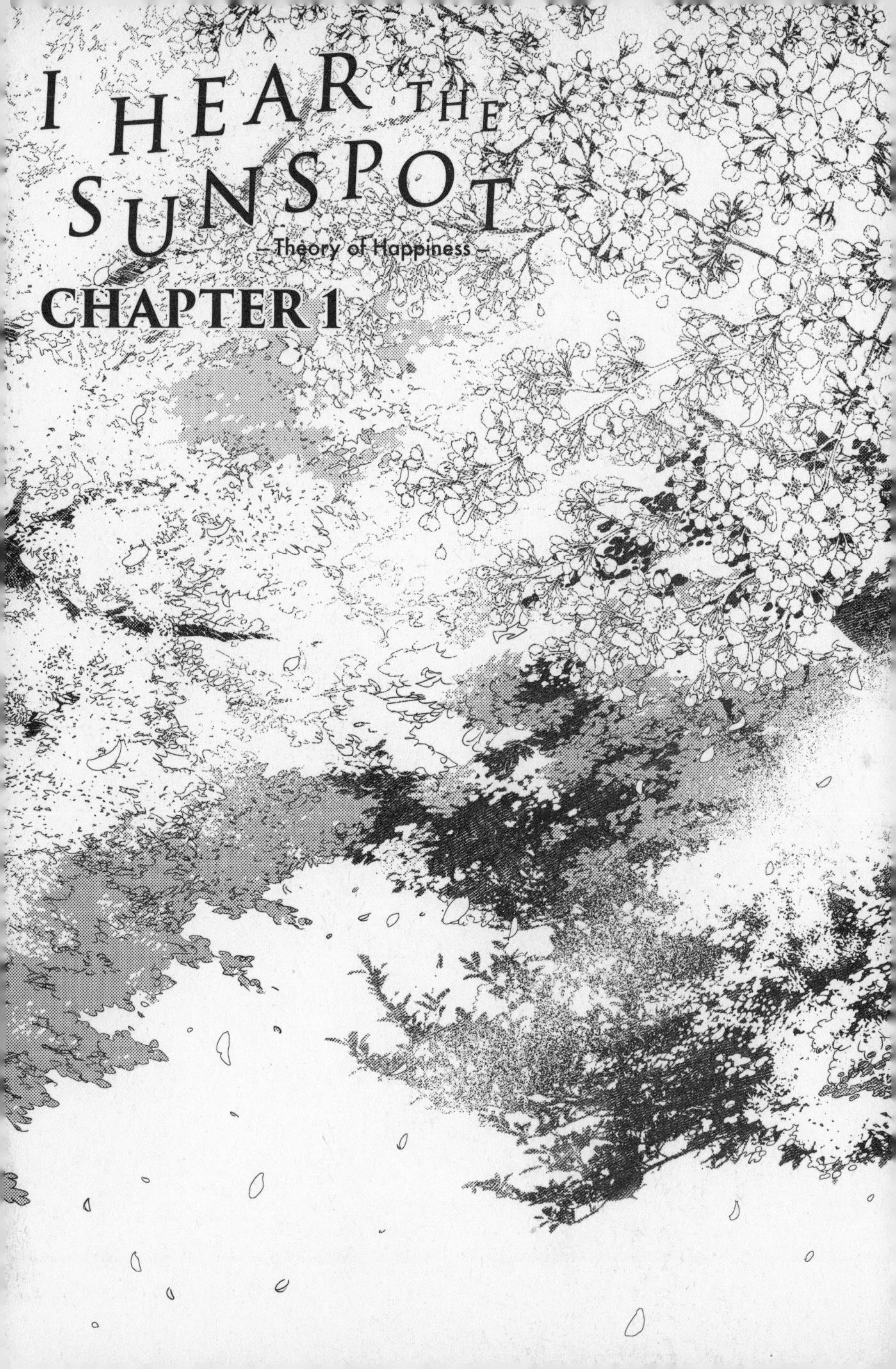
I HEAR THE SUNSPOT
– Theory of Happiness –
CHAPTER 1

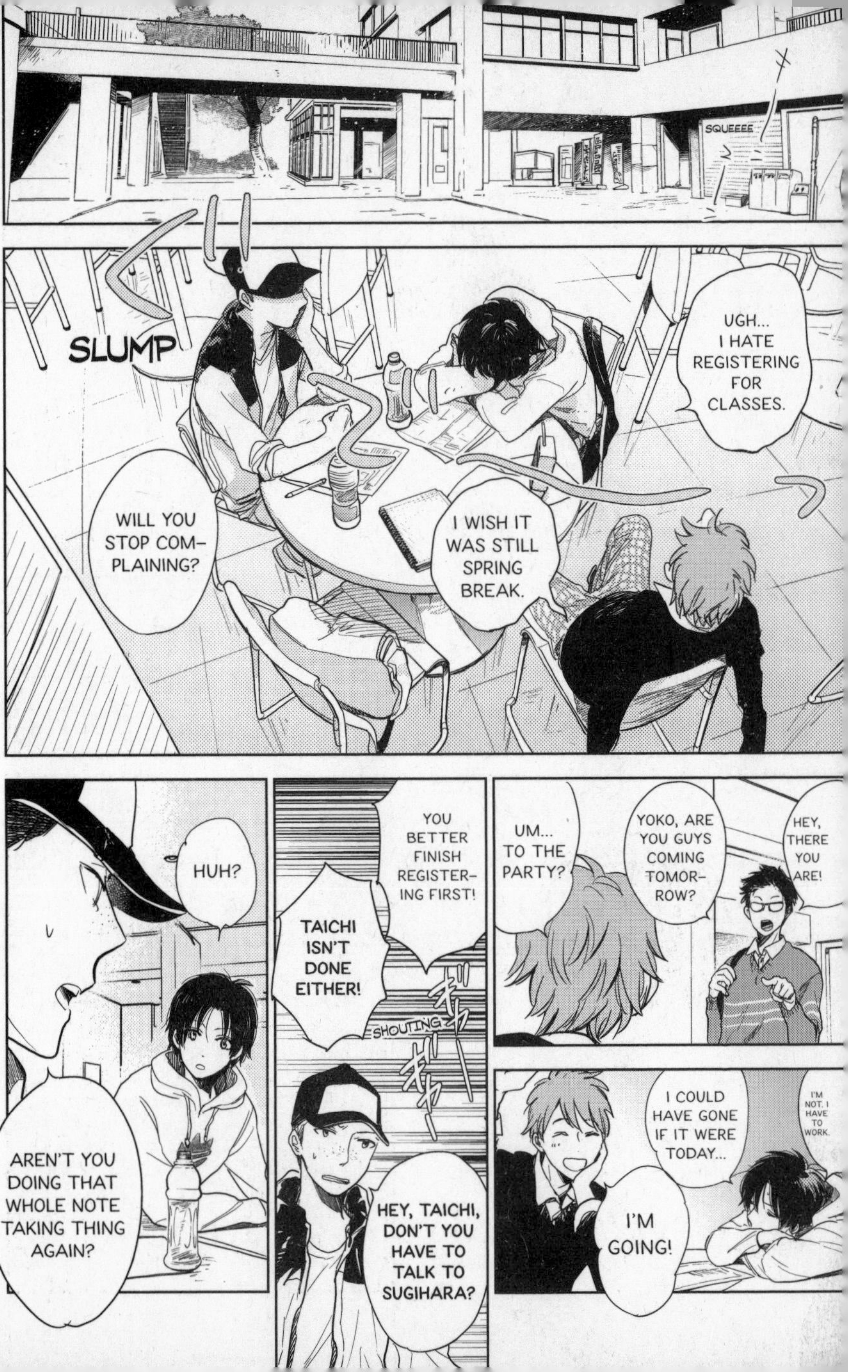
SQUEEEE
UGH... I HATE REGISTERING FOR CLASSES.
I WISH IT WAS STILL SPRING BREAK.
WILL YOU STOP COM-PLAINING?
SLUMP
HEY, THERE YOU ARE!
YOKO, ARE YOU GUYS COMING TOMOR-ROW?
UM... TO THE PARTY?
I'M NOT. I HAVE TO WORK.
I COULD HAVE GONE IF IT WERE TODAY...
I'M GOING!
YOU BETTER FINISH REGISTER-ING FIRST!
TAICHI ISN'T DONE EITHER!
SHOUTING
HEY, TAICHI, DON'T YOU HAVE TO TALK TO SUGIHARA?
HUH?
AREN'T YOU DOING THAT WHOLE NOTE TAKING THING AGAIN?

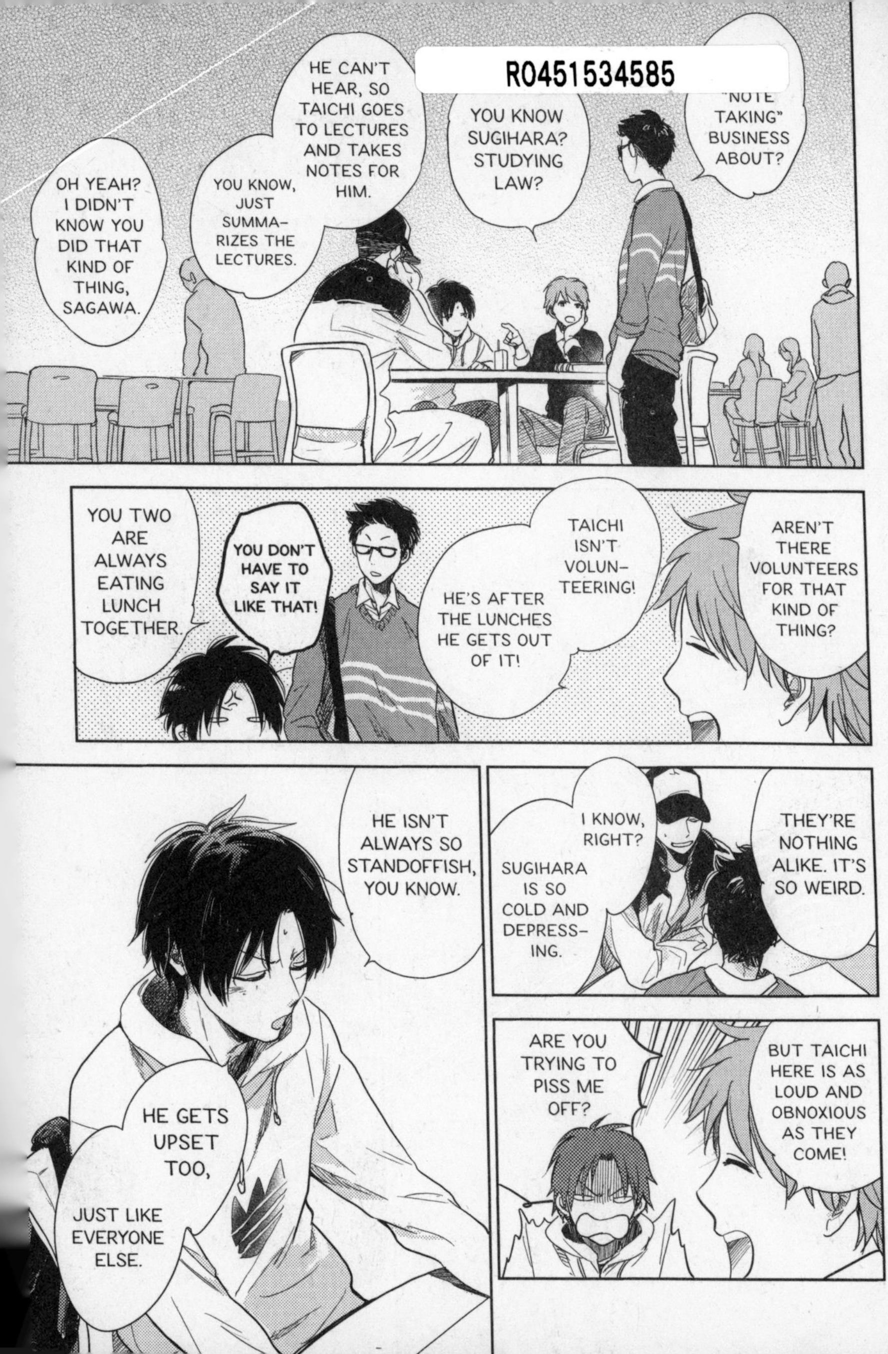
"NOTE TAKING" BUSINESS ABOUT?
YOU KNOW SUGIHARA? STUDYING LAW?
HE CAN'T HEAR, SO TAICHI GOES TO LECTURES AND TAKES NOTES FOR HIM.
YOU KNOW, JUST SUMMA-RIZES THE LECTURES.
OH YEAH? I DIDN'T KNOW YOU DID THAT KIND OF THING, SAGAWA.
AREN'T THERE VOLUNTEERS FOR THAT KIND OF THING?
TAICHI ISN'T VOLUN-TEERING!
HE'S AFTER THE LUNCHES HE GETS OUT OF IT!
YOU DON'T HAVE TO SAY IT LIKE THAT!
YOU TWO ARE ALWAYS EATING LUNCH TOGETHER.
THEY'RE NOTHING ALIKE. IT'S SO WEIRD.
I KNOW, RIGHT?
SUGIHARA IS SO COLD AND DEPRESS-ING.
BUT TAICHI HERE IS AS LOUD AND OBNOXIOUS AS THEY COME!
ARE YOU TRYING TO PISS ME OFF?
HE ISN'T ALWAYS SO STANDOFFISH, YOU KNOW.
HE GETS UPSET TOO,
JUST LIKE EVERYONE ELSE.

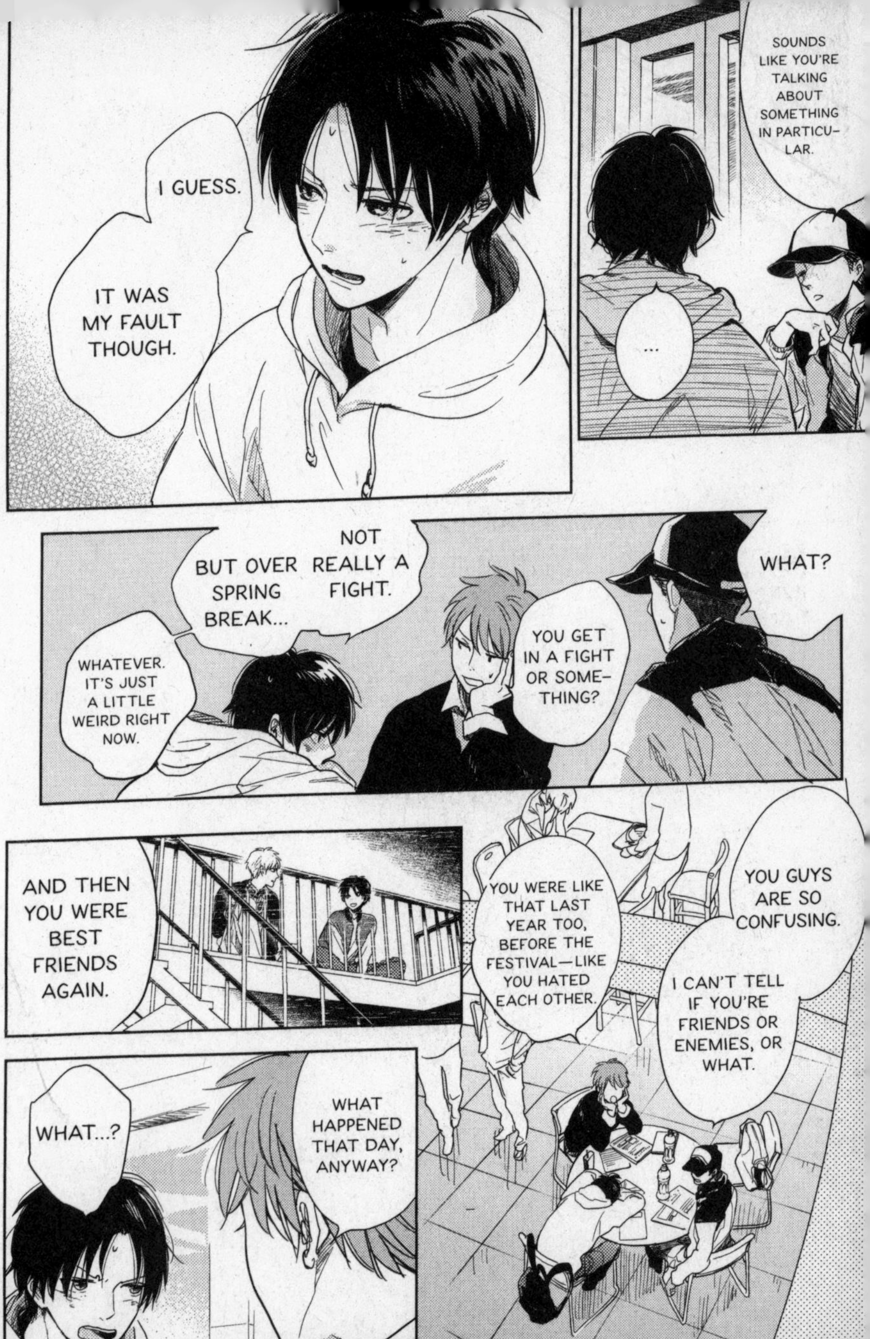
SOUNDS LIKE YOU'RE TALKING ABOUT SOMETHING IN PARTICU-LAR.
...
I GUESS.
IT WAS MY FAULT THOUGH.
WHAT?
YOU GET IN A FIGHT OR SOME-THING?
NOT REALLY A FIGHT.
BUT OVER SPRING BREAK...
WHATEVER. IT'S JUST A LITTLE WEIRD RIGHT NOW.
YOU GUYS ARE SO CONFUSING.
I CAN'T TELL IF YOU'RE FRIENDS OR ENEMIES, OR WHAT.
YOU WERE LIKE THAT LAST YEAR TOO, BEFORE THE FESTIVAL—LIKE YOU HATED EACH OTHER.
AND THEN YOU WERE BEST FRIENDS AGAIN.
WHAT HAPPENED THAT DAY, ANYWAY?
WHAT...?

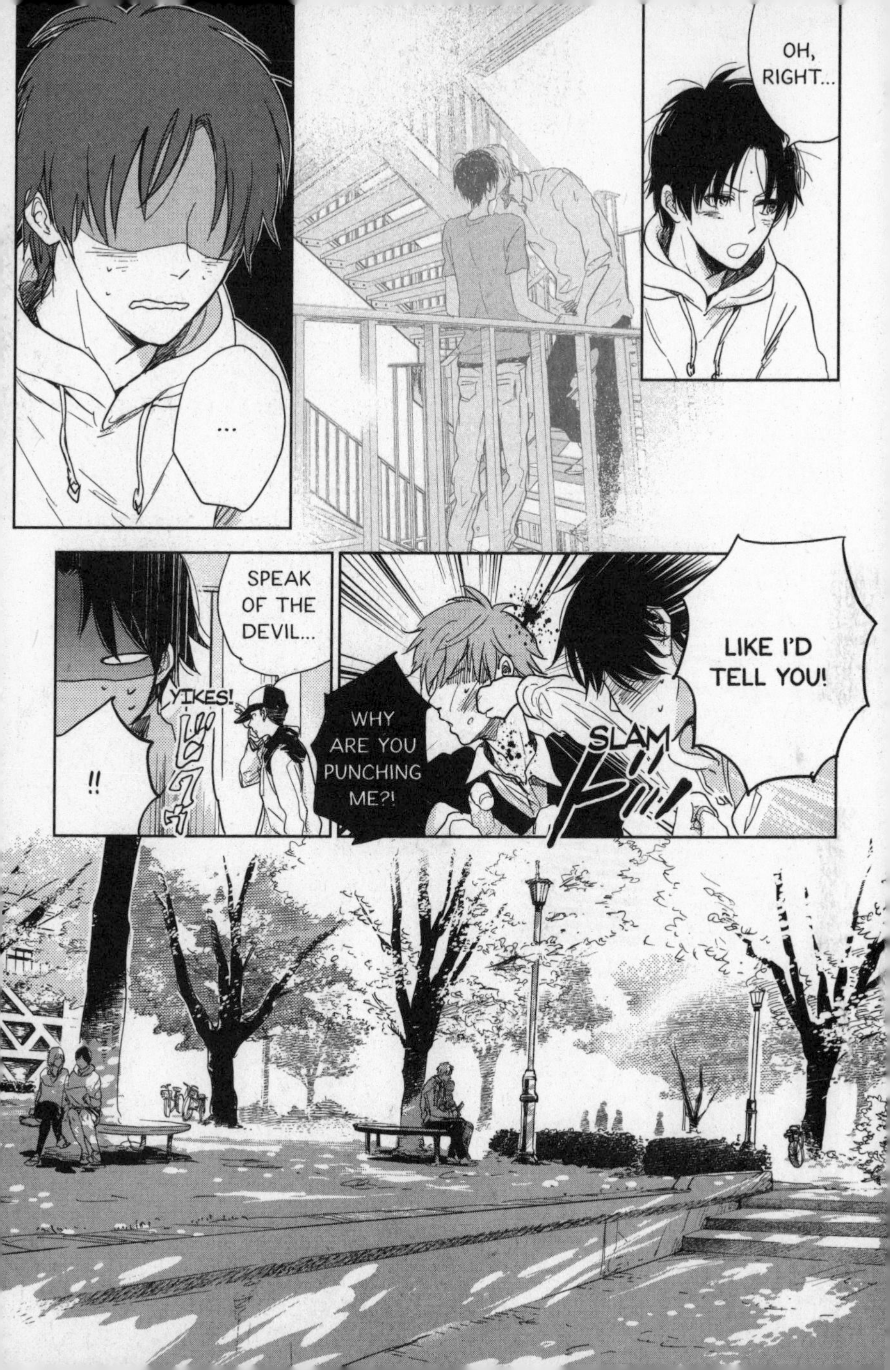
OH, RIGHT...
...
LIKE I'D TELL YOU!
SLAM
WHY ARE YOU PUNCHING ME?!
SPEAK OF THE DEVIL...
YIKES!
!!

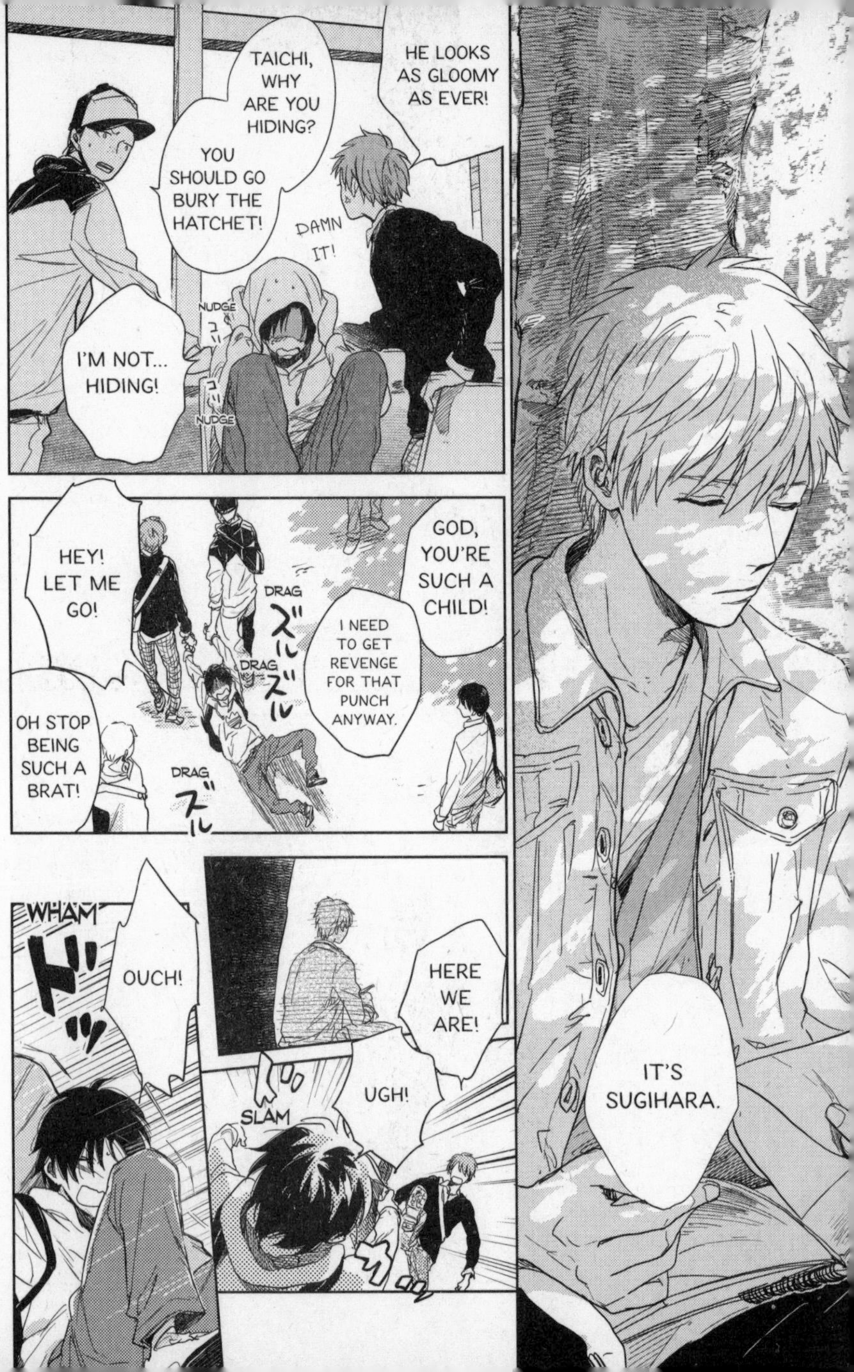
IT'S SUGIHARA.
HE LOOKS AS GLOOMY AS EVER!
TAICHI, WHY ARE YOU HIDING?
YOU SHOULD GO BURY THE HATCHET!
DAMN IT!
NUDGE
I'M NOT... HIDING!
NUDGE
GOD, YOU'RE SUCH A CHILD!
I NEED TO GET REVENGE FOR THAT PUNCH ANYWAY.
DRAG ズル
DRAG ズル
HEY! LET ME GO!
OH STOP BEING SUCH A BRAT!
DRAG ズル
HERE WE ARE!
WHAM ドッ
OUCH!
UGH!
SLAM

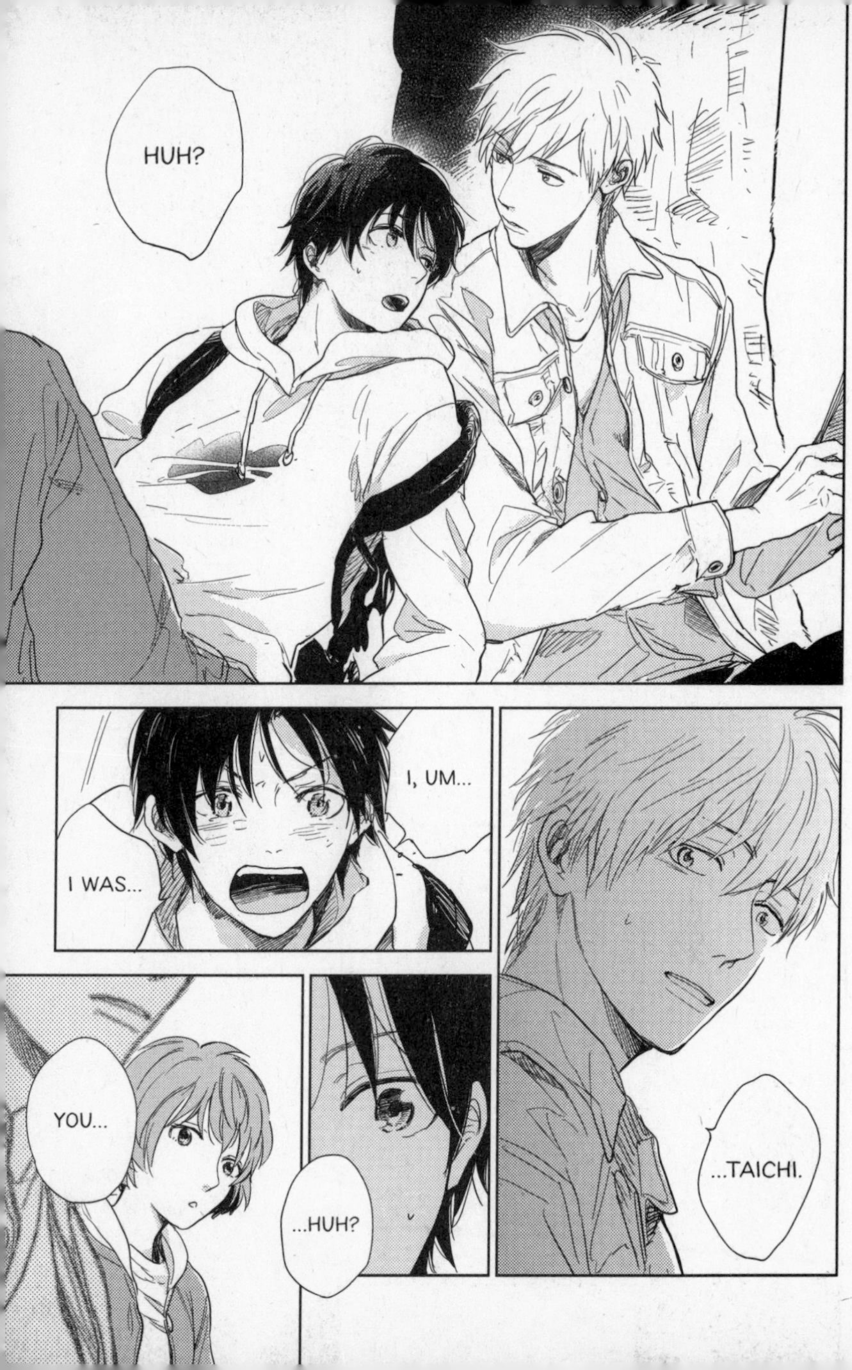
HUH?
...TAICHI.
I, UM...
I WAS...
...HUH?
YOU...

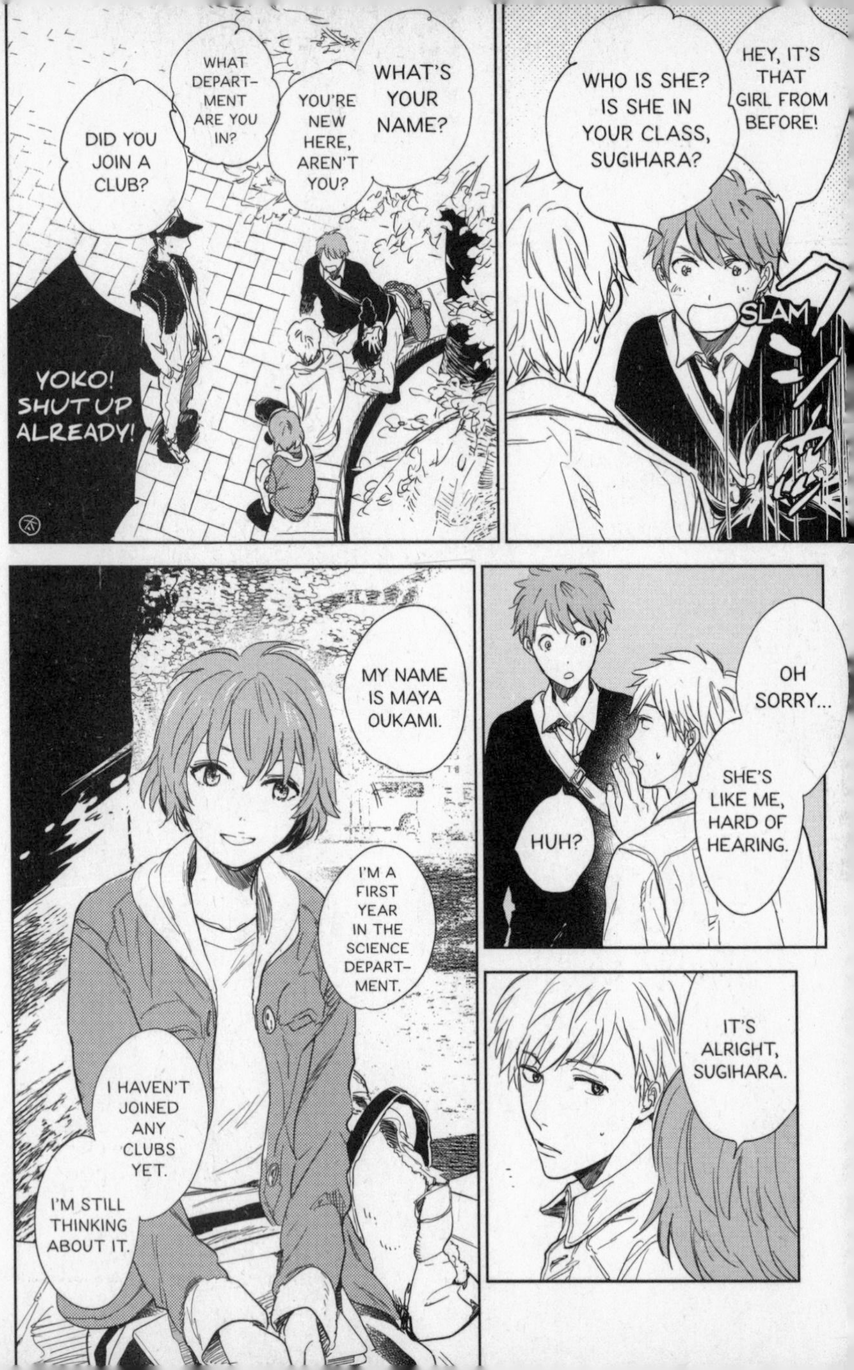
HEY, IT'S THAT GIRL FROM BEFORE!
WHO IS SHE? IS SHE IN YOUR CLASS, SUGIHARA?
SLAM
WHAT'S YOUR NAME?
YOU'RE NEW HERE, AREN'T YOU?
WHAT DEPARTMENT ARE YOU IN?
DID YOU JOIN A CLUB?
YOKO! SHUT UP ALREADY!
OH SORRY...
SHE'S LIKE ME, HARD OF HEARING.
HUH?
IT'S ALRIGHT, SUGIHARA.
MY NAME IS MAYA OUKAMI.
I'M A FIRST YEAR IN THE SCIENCE DEPARTMENT.
I HAVEN'T JOINED ANY CLUBS YET.
I'M STILL THINKING ABOUT IT.

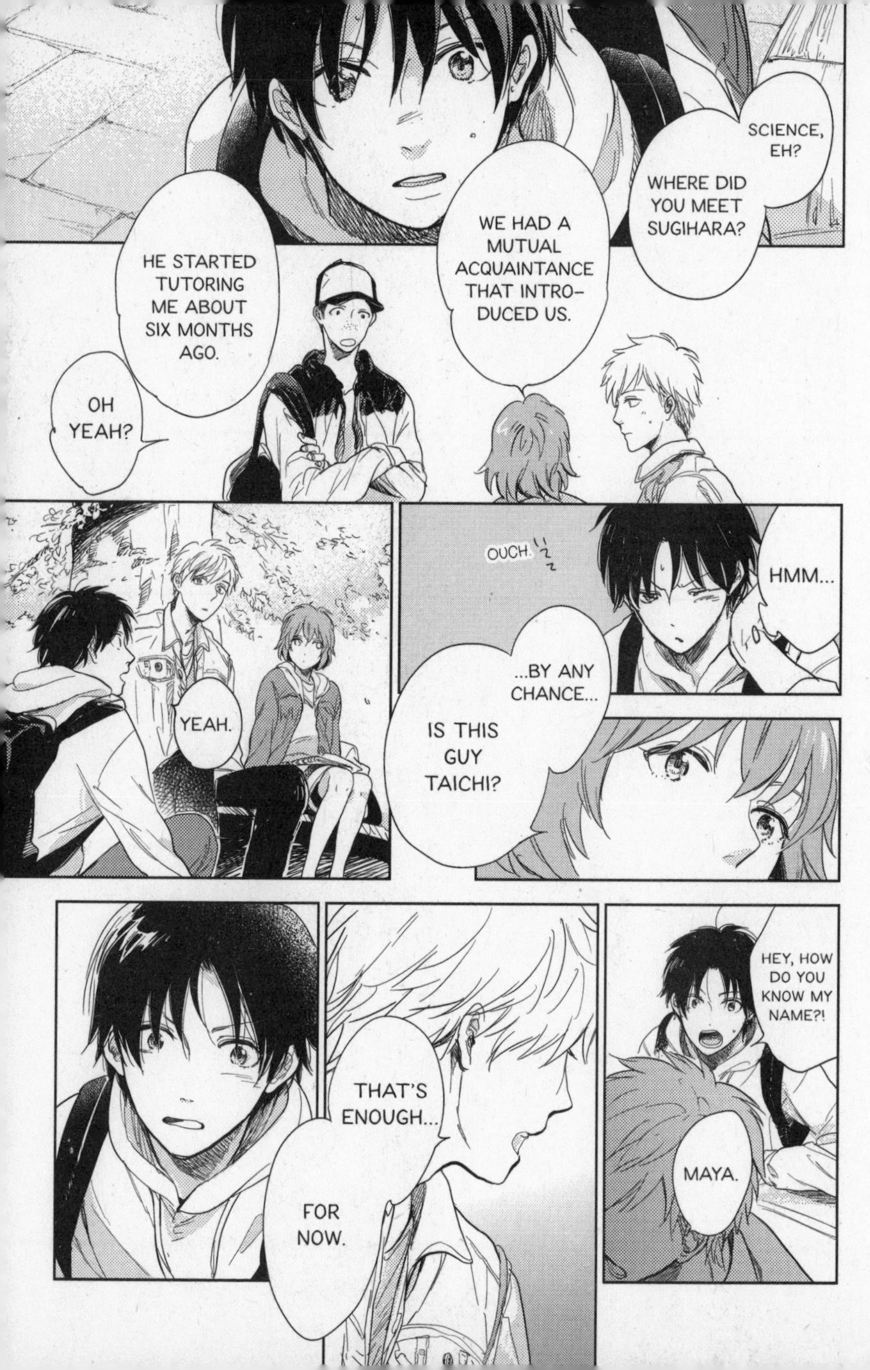
SCIENCE, EH?
WHERE DID YOU MEET SUGIHARA?
WE HAD A MUTUAL ACQUAINTANCE THAT INTRO-DUCED US.
HE STARTED TUTORING ME ABOUT SIX MONTHS AGO.
OH YEAH?
HMM...
OUCH.
...BY ANY CHANCE...
IS THIS GUY TAICHI?
YEAH.
HEY, HOW DO YOU KNOW MY NAME?!
MAYA.
THAT'S ENOUGH...
FOR NOW.

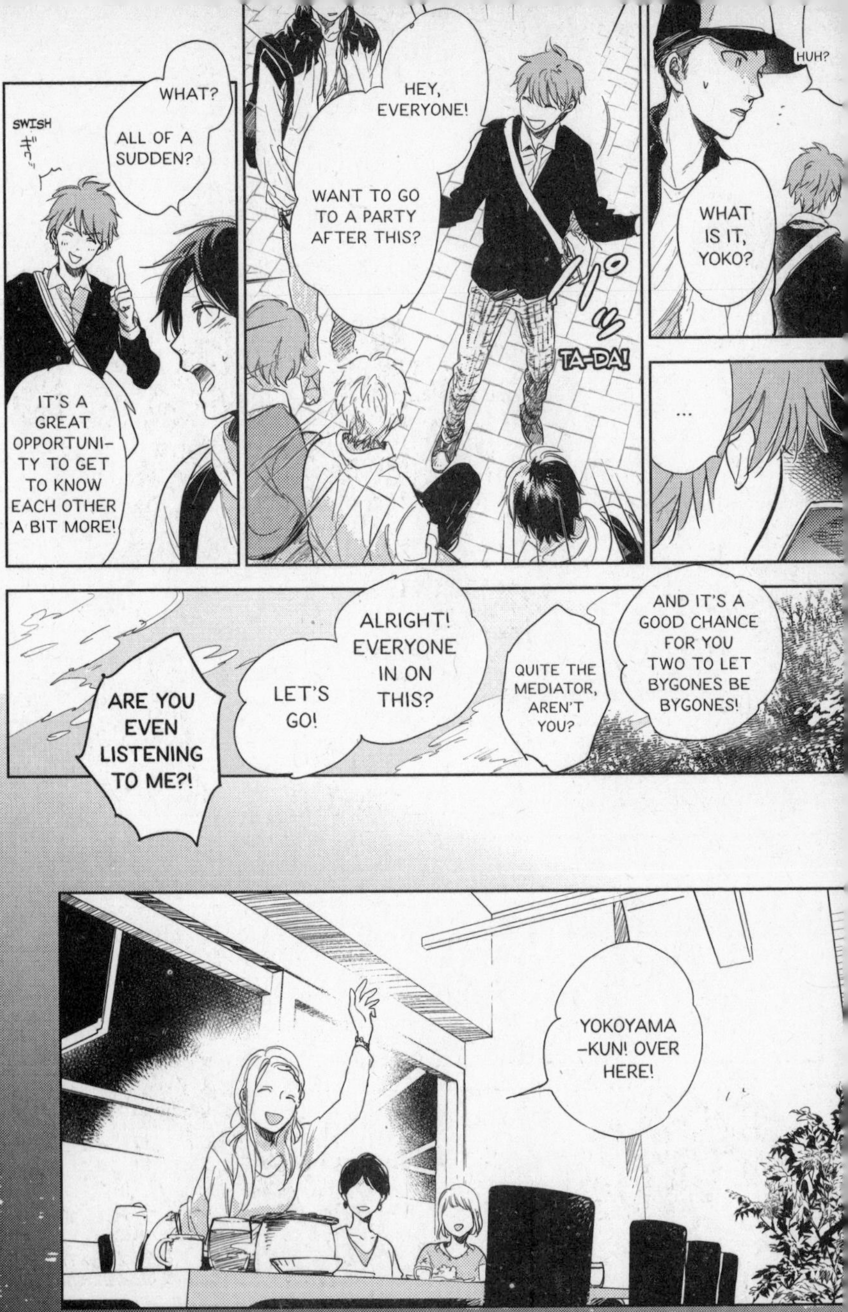
HUH?
WHAT IS IT, YOKO?
...
HEY, EVERYONE!
WANT TO GO TO A PARTY AFTER THIS?
TA-DA!
WHAT? ALL OF A SUDDEN?
SWISH
IT'S A GREAT OPPORTUNITY TO GET TO KNOW EACH OTHER A BIT MORE!
AND IT'S A GOOD CHANCE FOR YOU TWO TO LET BYGONES BE BYGONES!
QUITE THE MEDIATOR, AREN'T YOU?
ALRIGHT! EVERYONE IN ON THIS?
LET'S GO!
ARE YOU EVEN LISTENING TO ME?!
YOKOYAMA-KUN! OVER HERE!

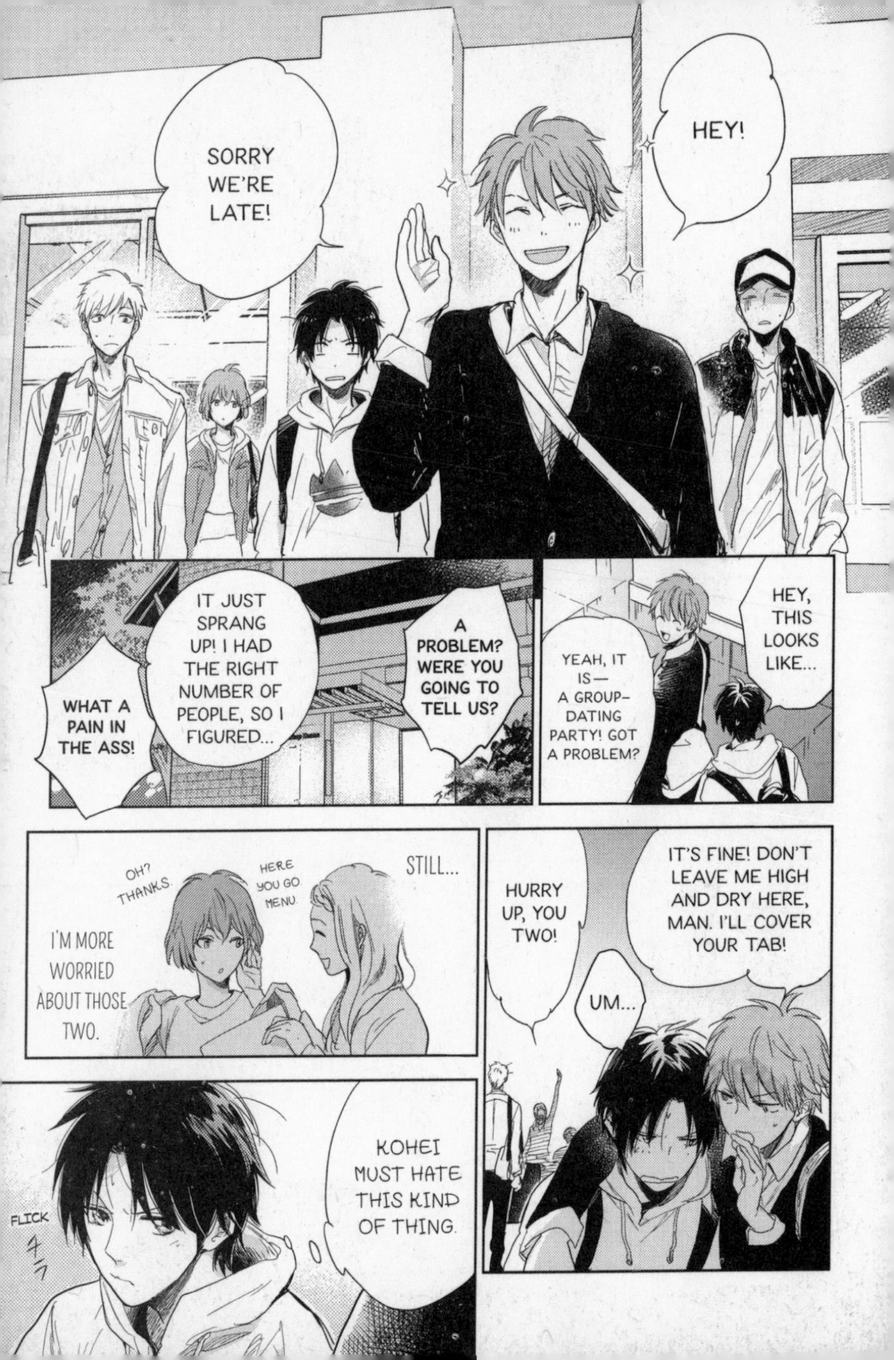
HEY!
SORRY WE'RE LATE!
HEY, THIS LOOKS LIKE...
YEAH, IT IS— A GROUP-DATING PARTY! GOT A PROBLEM?
A PROBLEM? WERE YOU GOING TO TELL US?
IT JUST SPRANG UP! I HAD THE RIGHT NUMBER OF PEOPLE, SO I FIGURED...
WHAT A PAIN IN THE ASS!
IT'S FINE! DON'T LEAVE ME HIGH AND DRY HERE, MAN. I'LL COVER YOUR TAB!
HURRY UP, YOU TWO!
UM...
STILL...
HERE YOU GO. MENU.
OH? THANKS.
I'M MORE WORRIED ABOUT THOSE TWO.
KOHEI MUST HATE THIS KIND OF THING.
FLICK

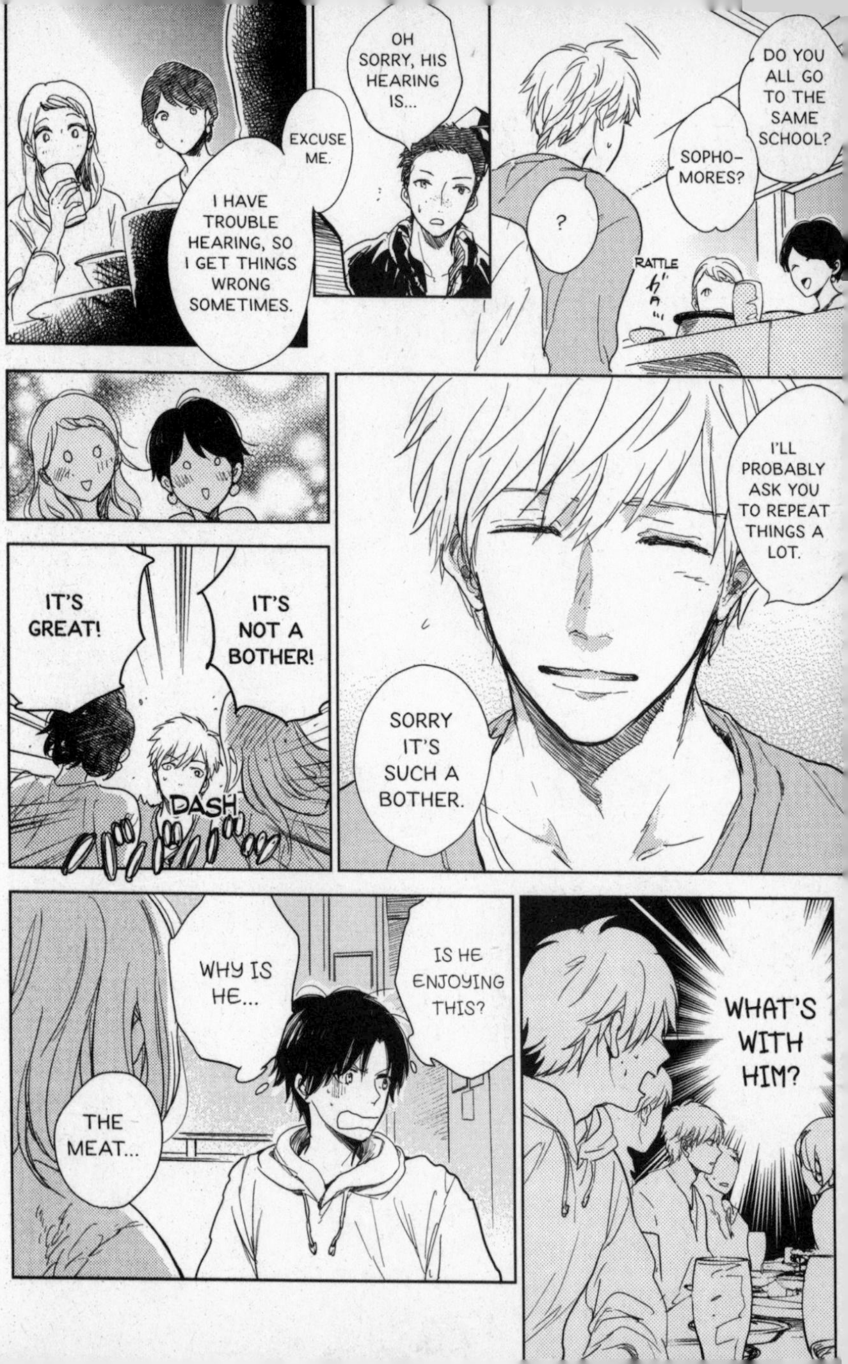
DO YOU ALL GO TO THE SAME SCHOOL?
SOPHO-MORES?
?
RATTLE
OH SORRY, HIS HEARING IS...
EXCUSE ME.
I HAVE TROUBLE HEARING, SO I GET THINGS WRONG SOMETIMES.
I'LL PROBABLY ASK YOU TO REPEAT THINGS A LOT.
SORRY IT'S SUCH A BOTHER.
IT'S NOT A BOTHER!
IT'S GREAT!
DASH
WHAT'S WITH HIM?
IS HE ENJOYING THIS?
WHY IS HE...
THE MEAT...

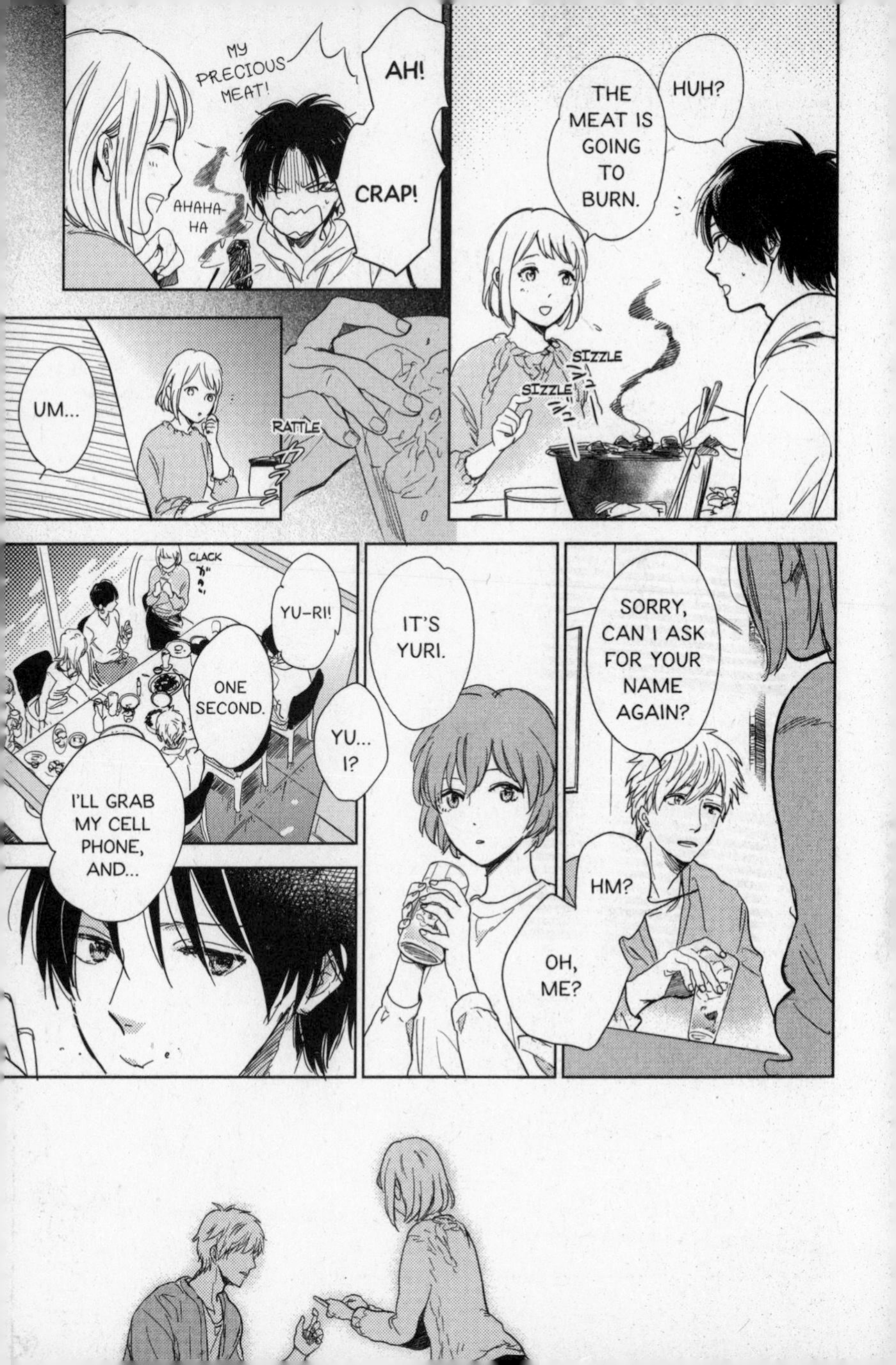
HUH?
THE MEAT IS GOING TO BURN.
SIZZLE
SIZZLE
AH!
MY PRECIOUS MEAT!
CRAP!
AHAHA-HA
UM...
RATTLE
SORRY, CAN I ASK FOR YOUR NAME AGAIN?
HM?
OH, ME?
IT'S YURI.
YU... I?
CLACK
YU-RI!
ONE SECOND.
I'LL GRAB MY CELL PHONE, AND...

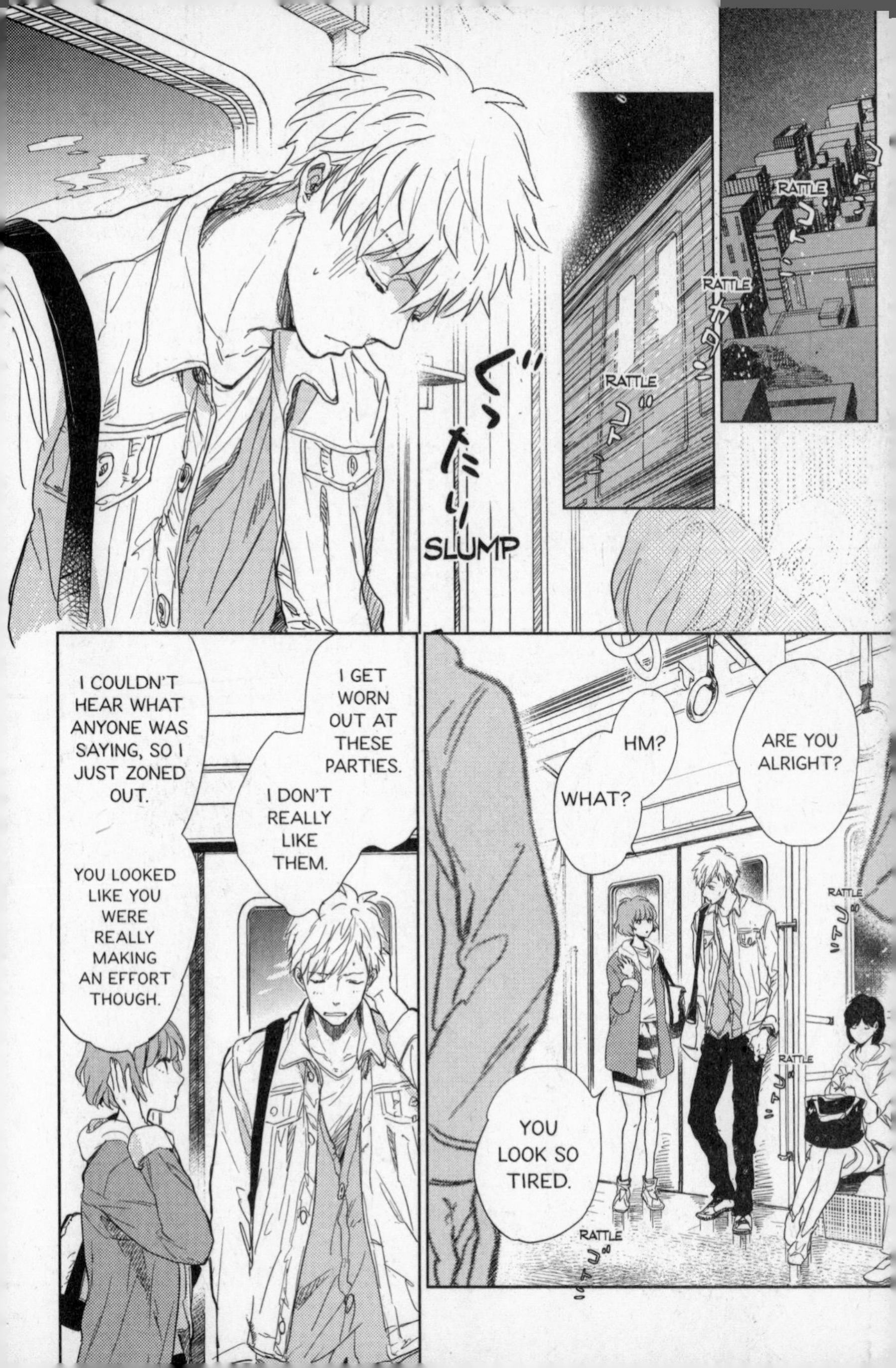
RATTLE
RATTLE
RATTLE
ぐったり
SLUMP
ARE YOU ALRIGHT?
HM?
WHAT?
RATTLE
RATTLE
YOU LOOK SO TIRED.
RATTLE
I GET WORN OUT AT THESE PARTIES.
I DON'T REALLY LIKE THEM.
I COULDN'T HEAR WHAT ANYONE WAS SAYING, SO I JUST ZONED OUT.
YOU LOOKED LIKE YOU WERE REALLY MAKING AN EFFORT THOUGH.

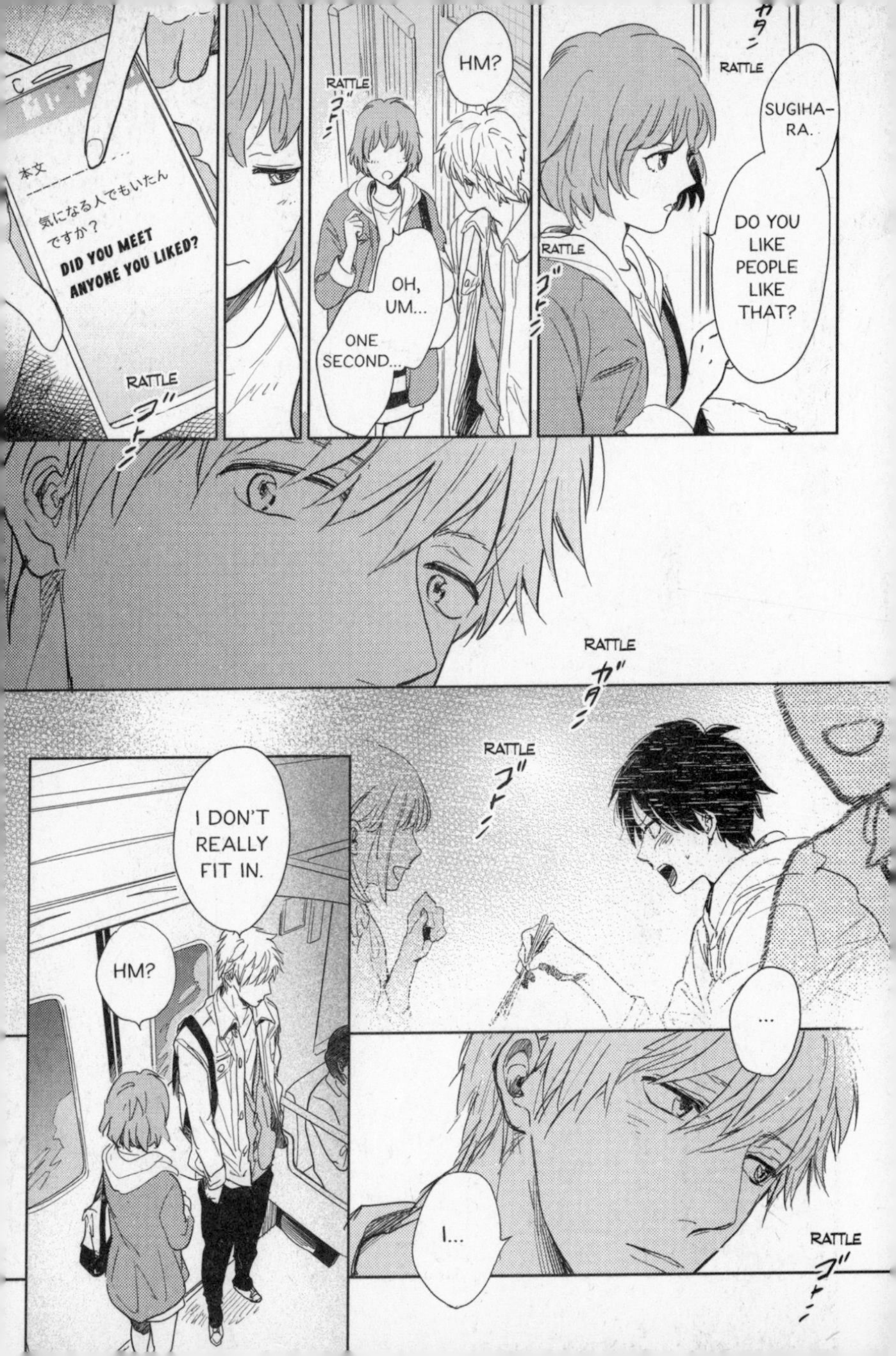

RATTLE
SUGIHARA.
RATTLE
DO YOU LIKE PEOPLE LIKE THAT?
HM?
RATTLE
OH, UM...
ONE SECOND...
本文
気になる人でもいたんですか？
DID YOU MEET ANYONE YOU LIKED?
RATTLE
RATTLE
RATTLE
RATTLE
...
I...
RATTLE
I DON'T REALLY FIT IN.
HM?

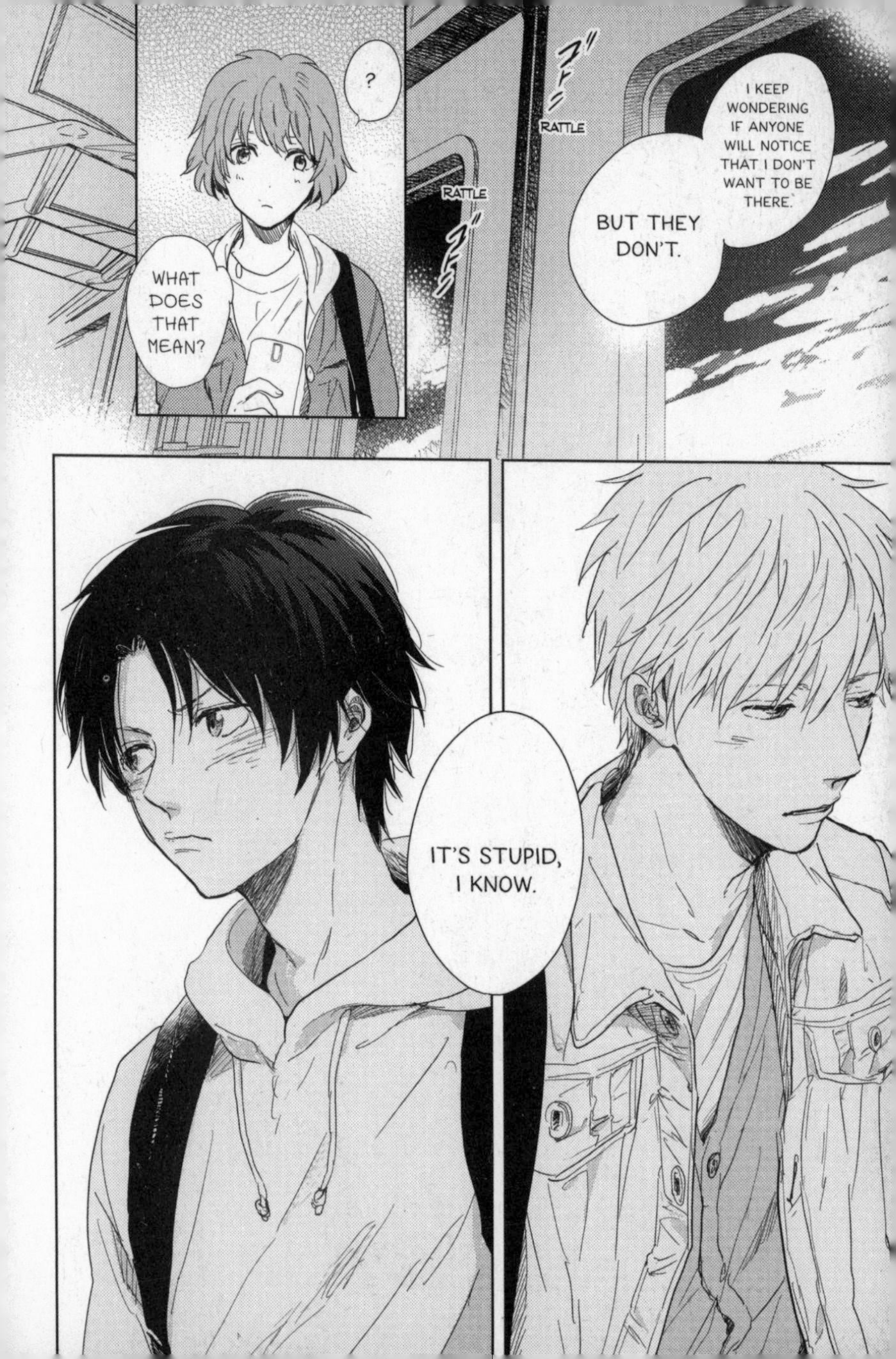
I KEEP WONDERING IF ANYONE WILL NOTICE THAT I DON'T WANT TO BE THERE.
BUT THEY DON'T.
RATTLE
RATTLE
?
WHAT DOES THAT MEAN?
IT'S STUPID, I KNOW.

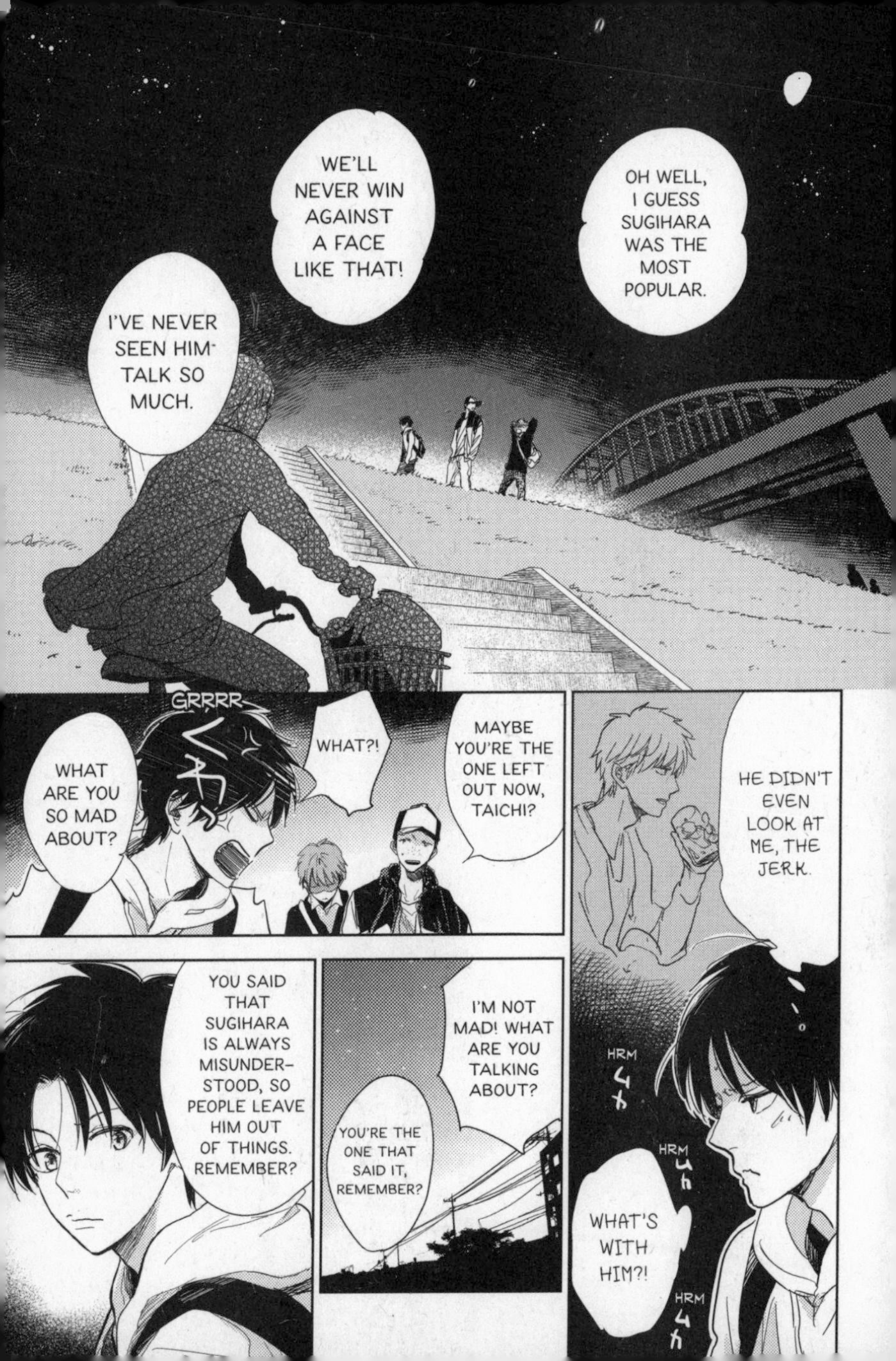
OH WELL, I GUESS SUGIHARA WAS THE MOST POPULAR.
WE'LL NEVER WIN AGAINST A FACE LIKE THAT!
I'VE NEVER SEEN HIM TALK SO MUCH.
HE DIDN'T EVEN LOOK AT ME, THE JERK.
HRM
HRM
WHAT'S WITH HIM?!
HRM
MAYBE YOU'RE THE ONE LEFT OUT NOW, TAICHI?
WHAT?!
GRRRR
WHAT ARE YOU SO MAD ABOUT?
I'M NOT MAD! WHAT ARE YOU TALKING ABOUT?
YOU'RE THE ONE THAT SAID IT, REMEMBER?
YOU SAID THAT SUGIHARA IS ALWAYS MISUNDER-STOOD, SO PEOPLE LEAVE HIM OUT OF THINGS. REMEMBER?

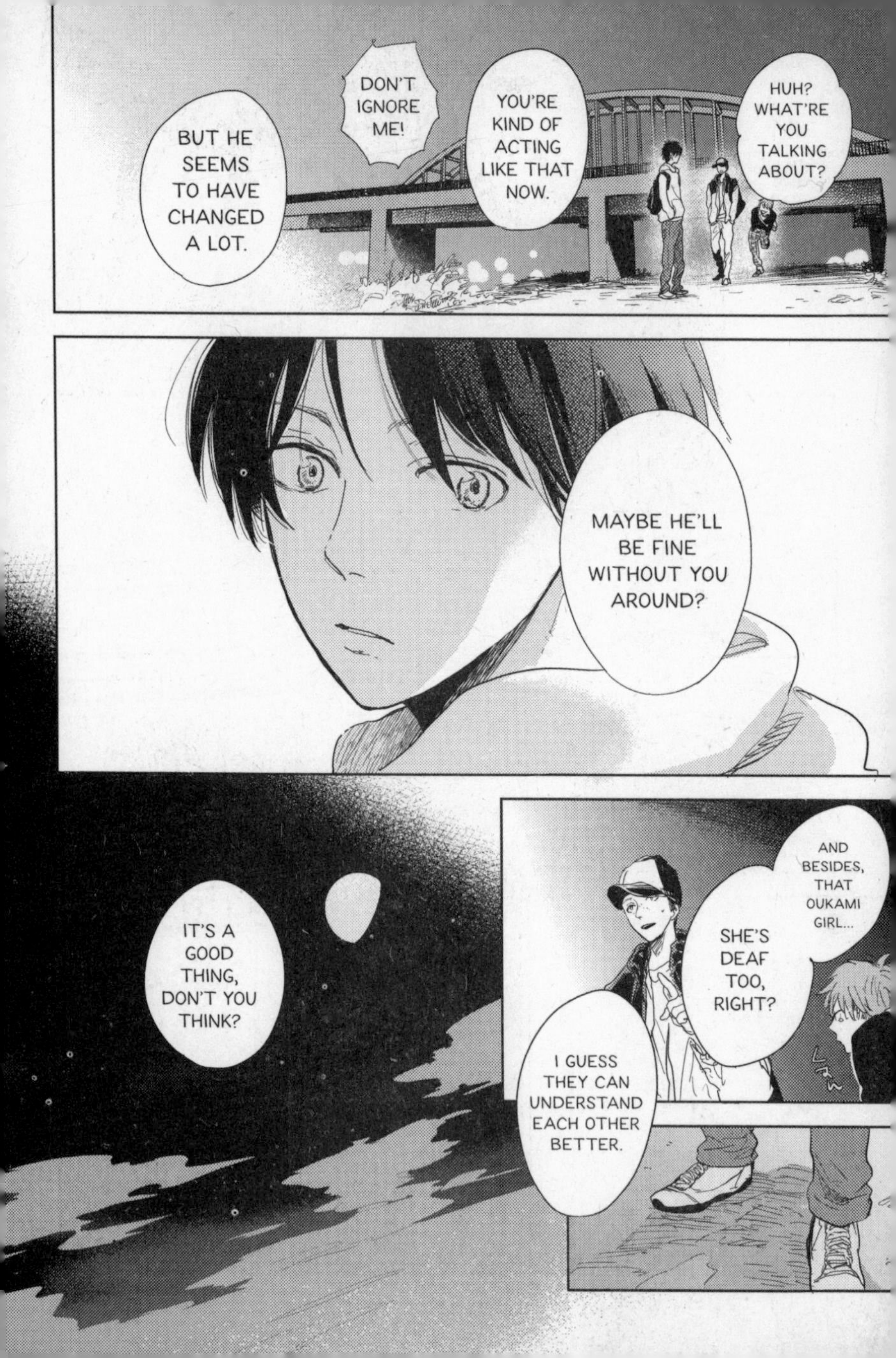
HUH? WHAT'RE YOU TALKING ABOUT?
YOU'RE KIND OF ACTING LIKE THAT NOW.
DON'T IGNORE ME!
BUT HE SEEMS TO HAVE CHANGED A LOT.
MAYBE HE'LL BE FINE WITHOUT YOU AROUND?
AND BESIDES, THAT OUKAMI GIRL...
SHE'S DEAF TOO, RIGHT?
I GUESS THEY CAN UNDERSTAND EACH OTHER BETTER.
IT'S A GOOD THING, DON'T YOU THINK?

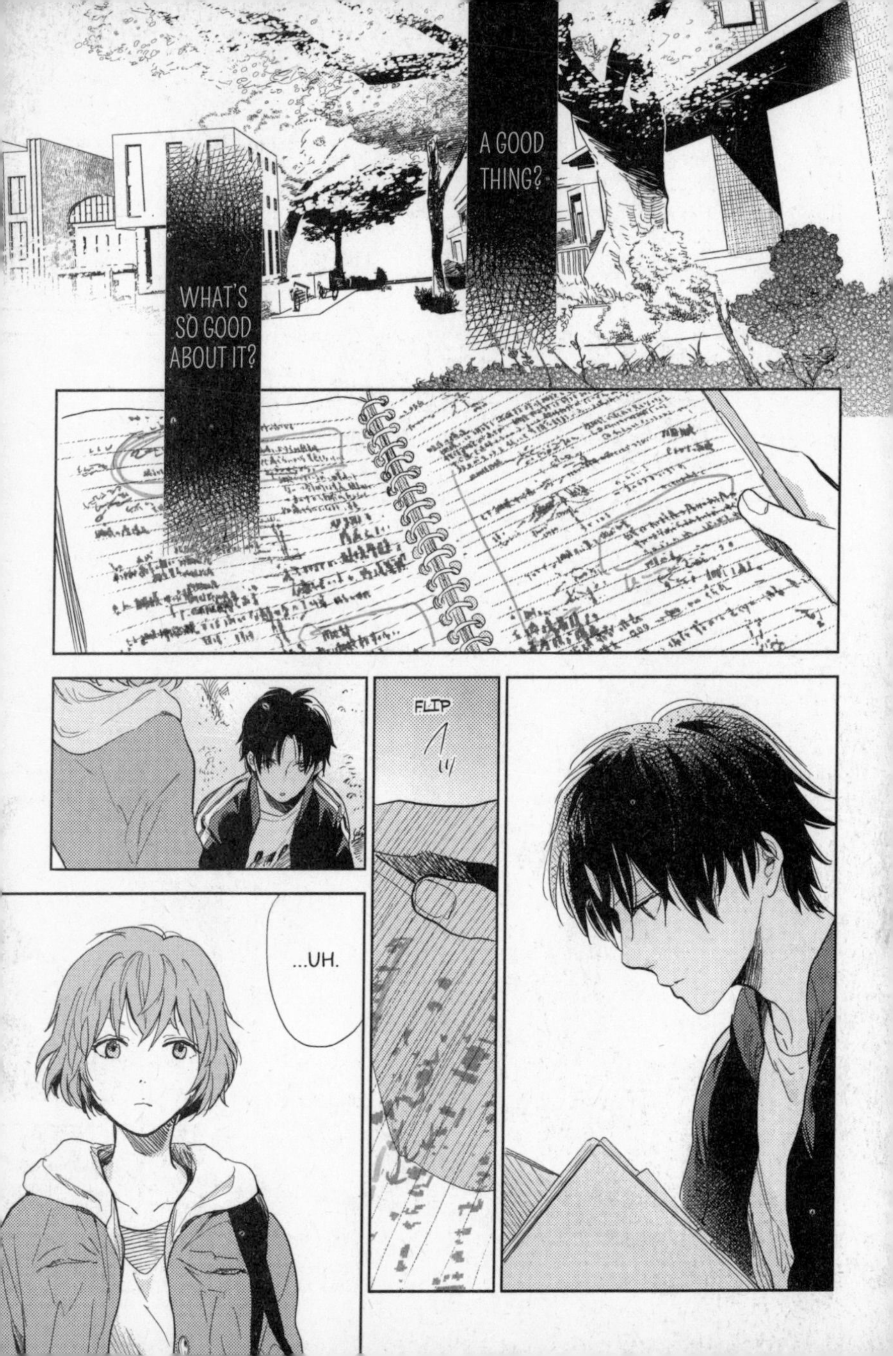
A GOOD THING?
WHAT'S SO GOOD ABOUT IT?
FLIP
...UH.

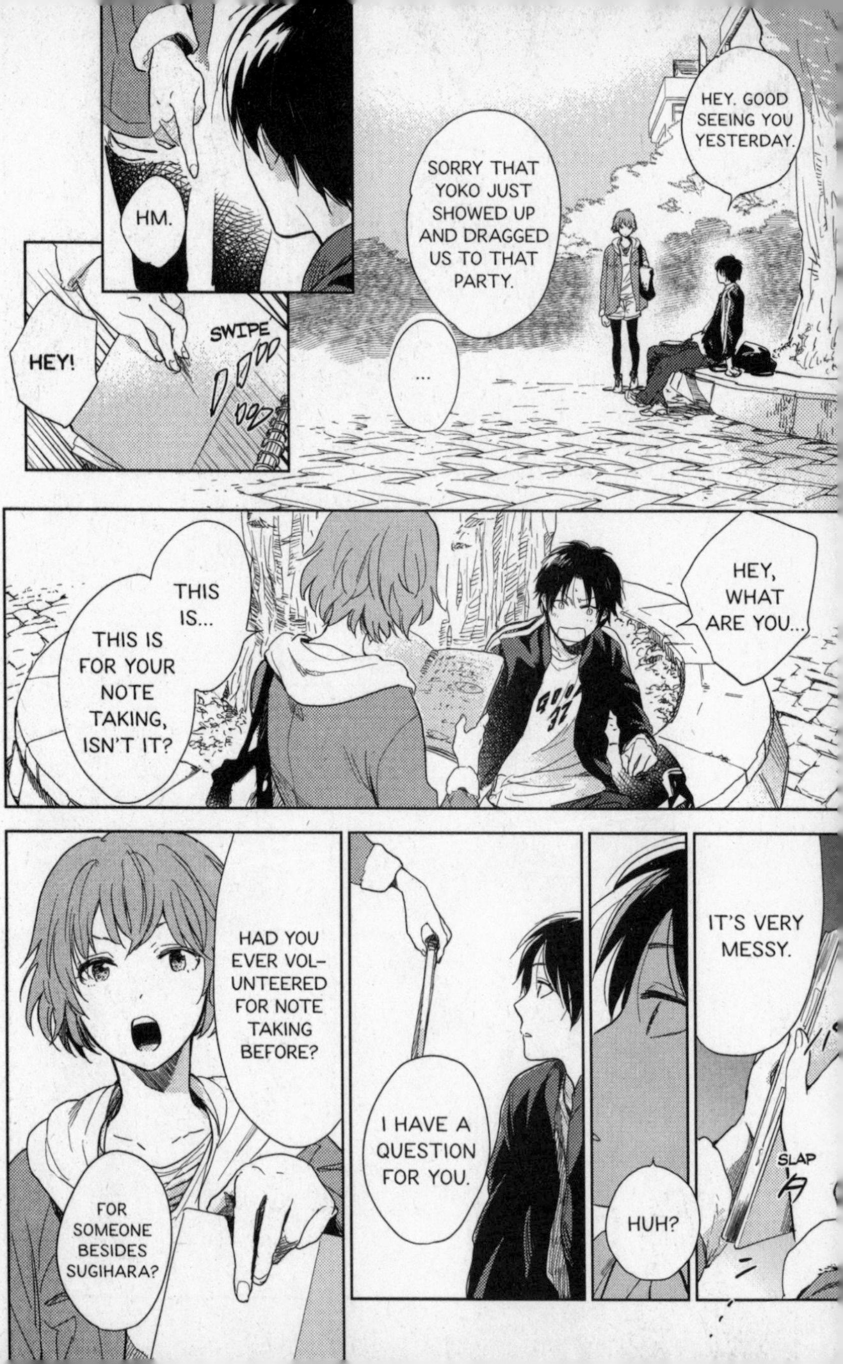

HEY. GOOD SEEING YOU YESTERDAY.
SORRY THAT YOKO JUST SHOWED UP AND DRAGGED US TO THAT PARTY.
...
HM.
SWIPE
HEY!
HEY, WHAT ARE YOU...
THIS IS...
THIS IS FOR YOUR NOTE TAKING, ISN'T IT?
IT'S VERY MESSY.
SLAP
HUH?
I HAVE A QUESTION FOR YOU.
HAD YOU EVER VOL-UNTEERED FOR NOTE TAKING BEFORE?
FOR SOMEONE BESIDES SUGIHARA?

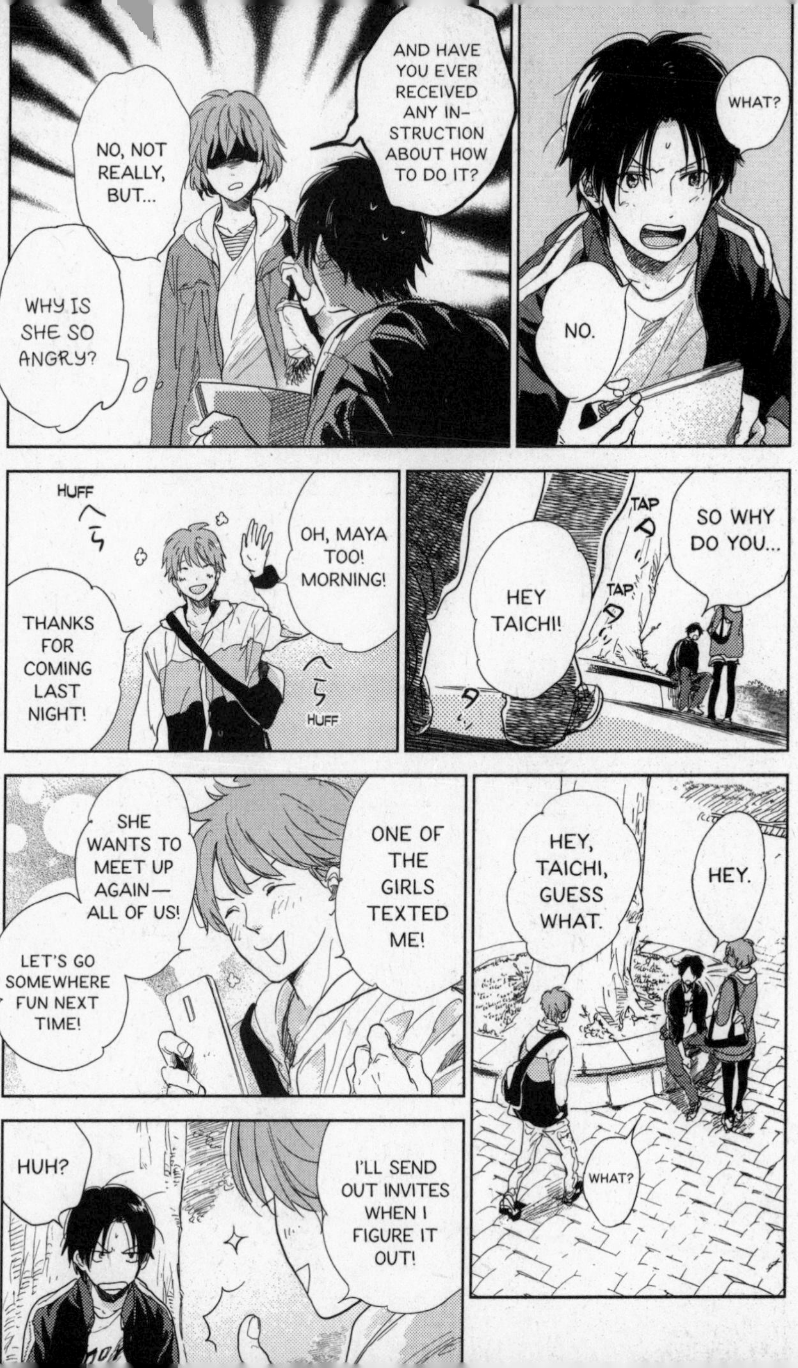
WHAT?
NO.
AND HAVE YOU EVER RECEIVED ANY IN-STRUCTION ABOUT HOW TO DO IT?
NO, NOT REALLY, BUT...
WHY IS SHE SO ANGRY?
SO WHY DO YOU...
TAP
TAP
HEY TAICHI!
HUFF
OH, MAYA TOO! MORNING!
THANKS FOR COMING LAST NIGHT!
HUFF
HEY.
HEY, TAICHI, GUESS WHAT.
WHAT?
ONE OF THE GIRLS TEXTED ME!
SHE WANTS TO MEET UP AGAIN—ALL OF US!
LET'S GO SOMEWHERE FUN NEXT TIME!
I'LL SEND OUT INVITES WHEN I FIGURE IT OUT!
HUH?

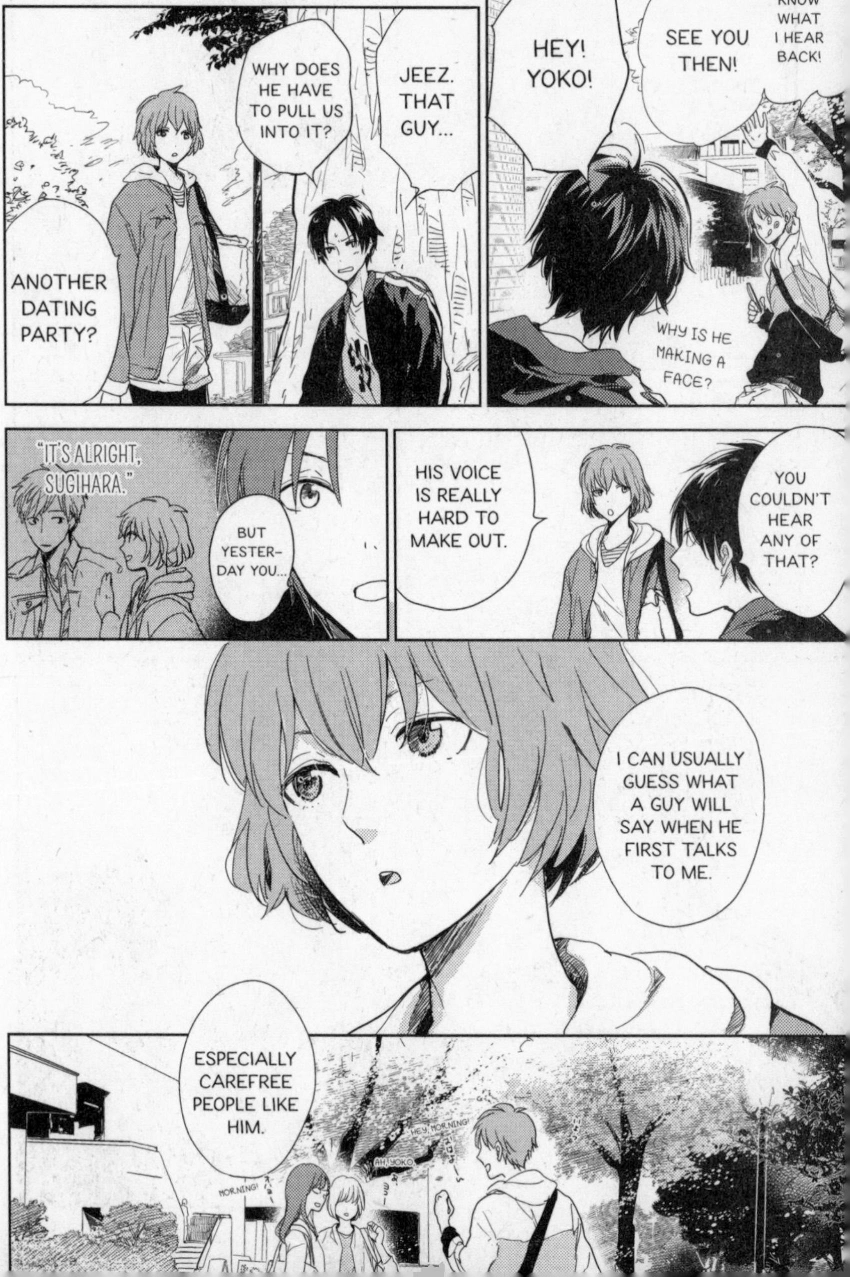
I'LL LET YOU KNOW WHAT I HEAR BACK!
SEE YOU THEN!
HEY! YOKO!
WHY IS HE MAKING A FACE?
JEEZ. THAT GUY...
WHY DOES HE HAVE TO PULL US INTO IT?
ANOTHER DATING PARTY?
YOU COULDN'T HEAR ANY OF THAT?
HIS VOICE IS REALLY HARD TO MAKE OUT.
BUT YESTER-DAY YOU...
"IT'S ALRIGHT, SUGIHARA."
I CAN USUALLY GUESS WHAT A GUY WILL SAY WHEN HE FIRST TALKS TO ME.
ESPECIALLY CAREFREE PEOPLE LIKE HIM.
HEY, MORNING!
AH, YOKO
MORNING!

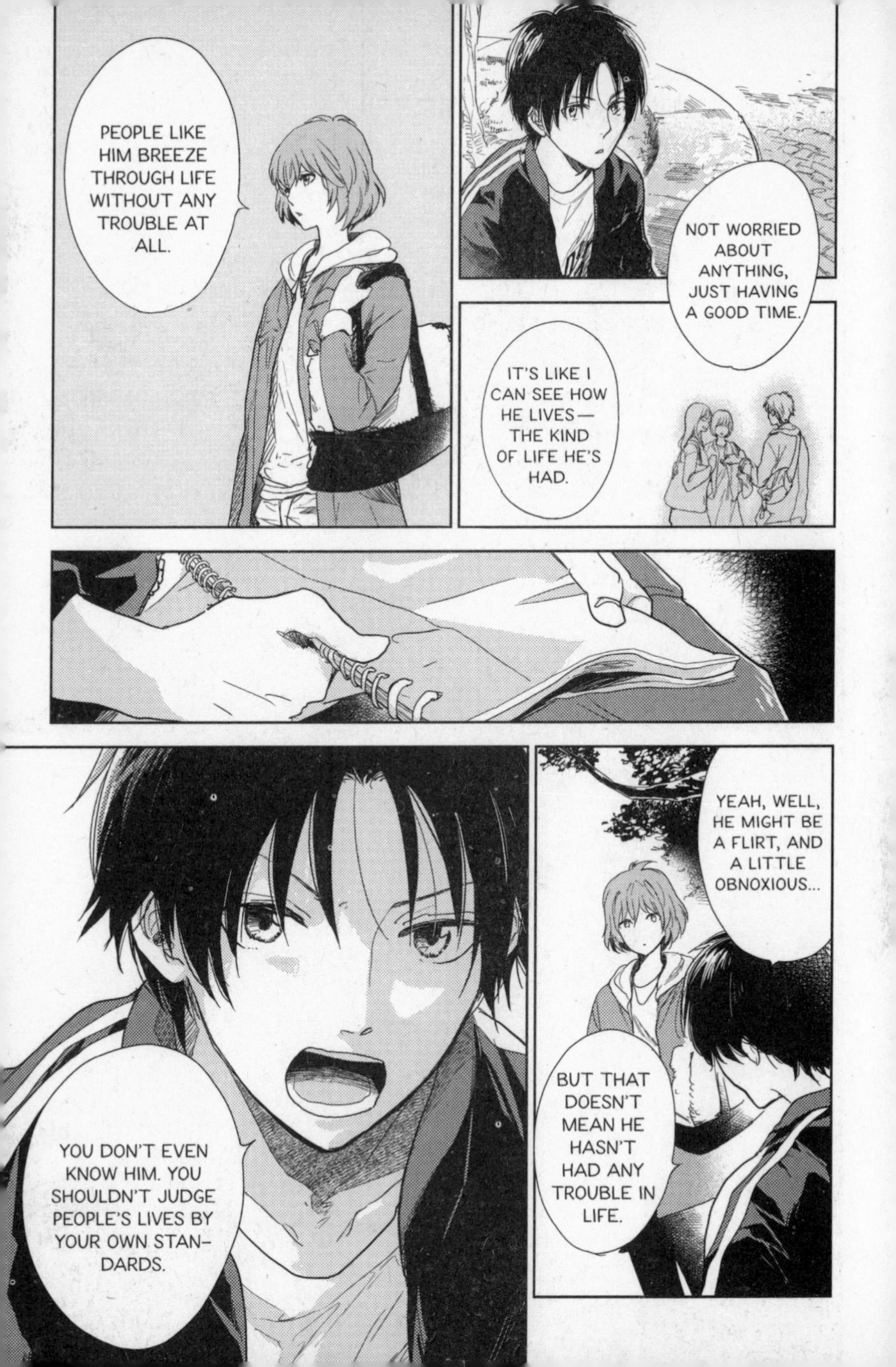
NOT WORRIED ABOUT ANYTHING, JUST HAVING A GOOD TIME.
IT'S LIKE I CAN SEE HOW HE LIVES— THE KIND OF LIFE HE'S HAD.
PEOPLE LIKE HIM BREEZE THROUGH LIFE WITHOUT ANY TROUBLE AT ALL.
YEAH, WELL, HE MIGHT BE A FLIRT, AND A LITTLE OBNOXIOUS...
BUT THAT DOESN'T MEAN HE HASN'T HAD ANY TROUBLE IN LIFE.
YOU DON'T EVEN KNOW HIM. YOU SHOULDN'T JUDGE PEOPLE'S LIVES BY YOUR OWN STAN-DARDS.

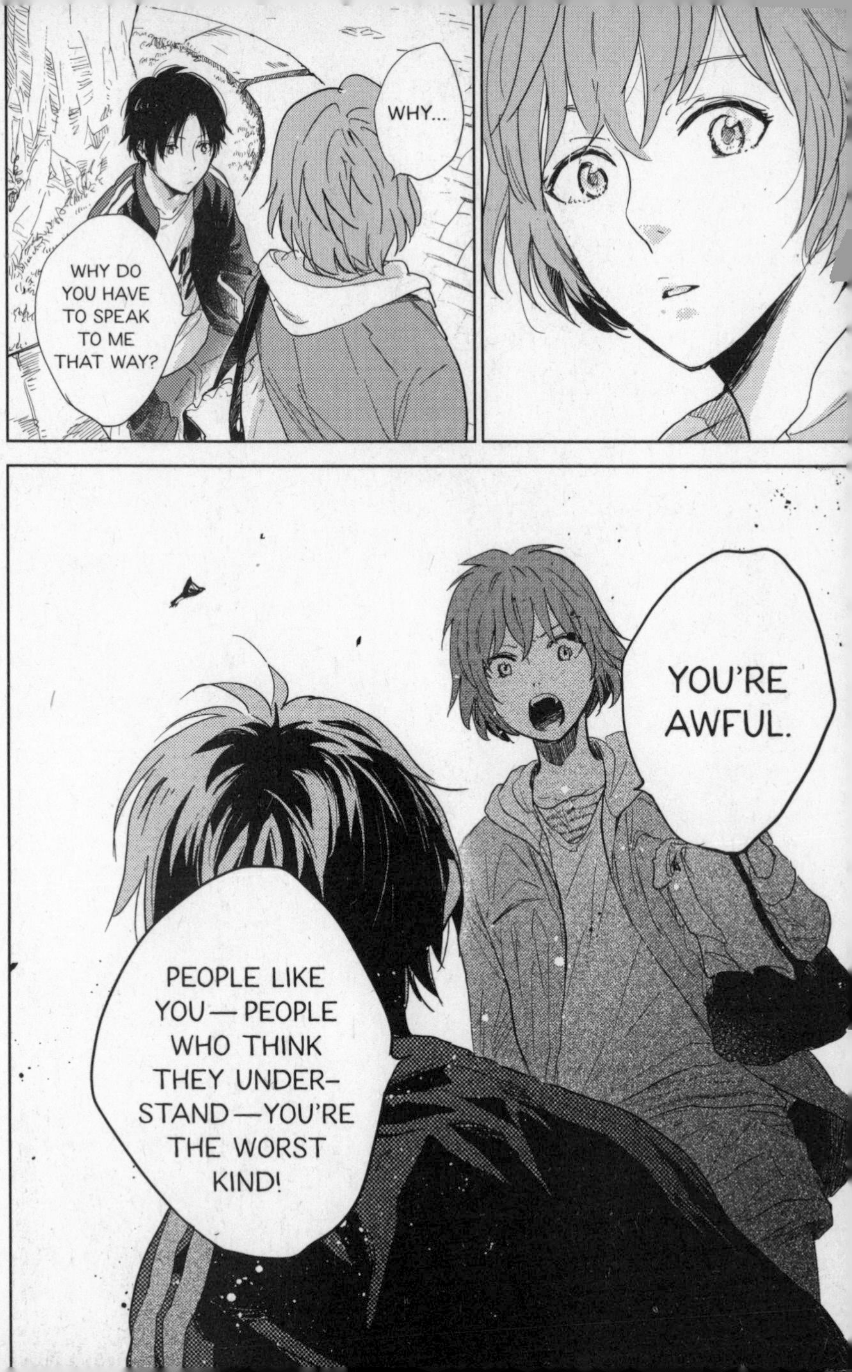
WHY...
WHY DO YOU HAVE TO SPEAK TO ME THAT WAY?
YOU'RE AWFUL.
PEOPLE LIKE YOU—PEOPLE WHO THINK THEY UNDER-STAND—YOU'RE THE WORST KIND!

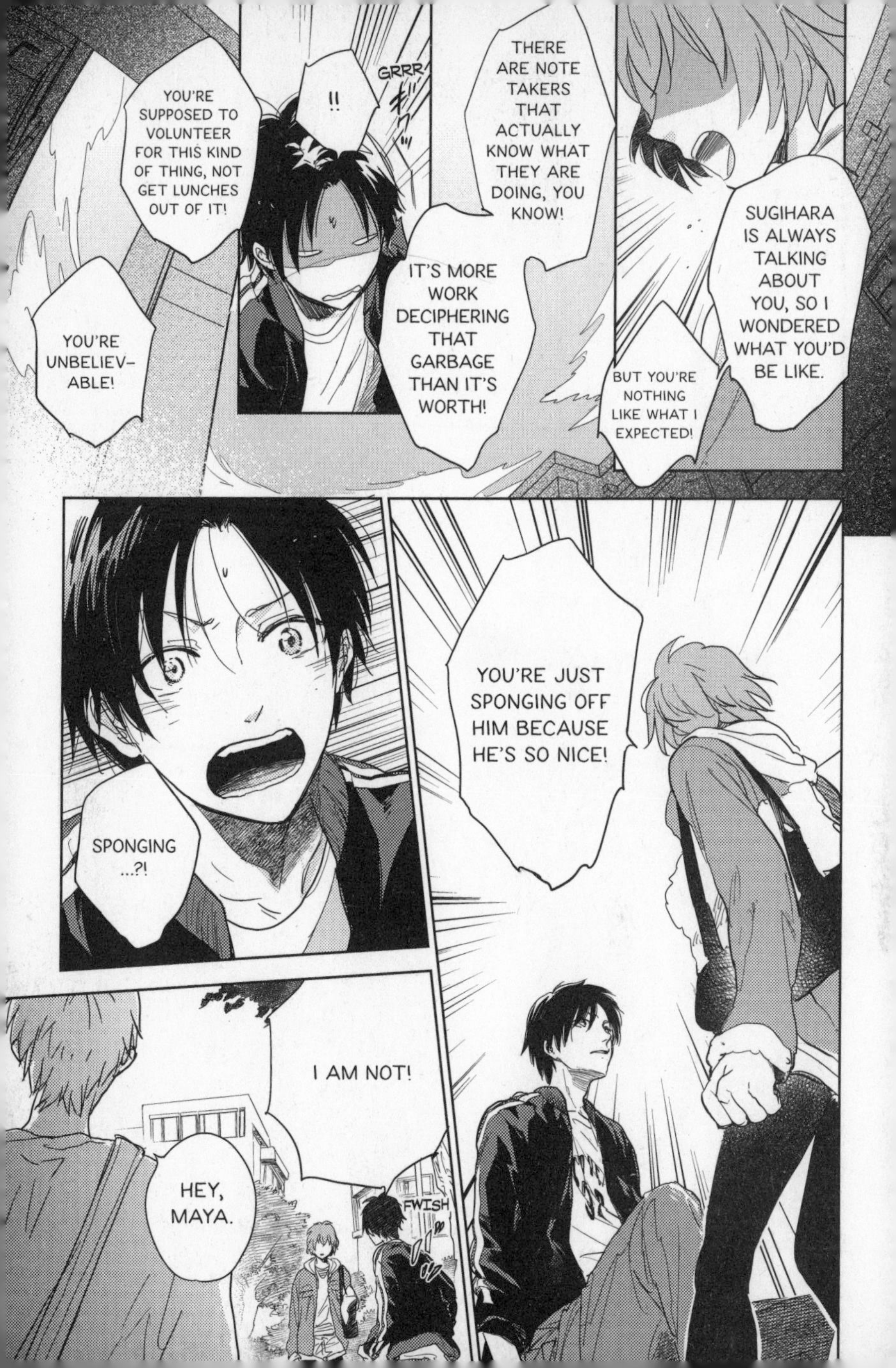
SUGIHARA IS ALWAYS TALKING ABOUT YOU, SO I WONDERED WHAT YOU'D BE LIKE.
BUT YOU'RE NOTHING LIKE WHAT I EXPECTED!
THERE ARE NOTE TAKERS THAT ACTUALLY KNOW WHAT THEY ARE DOING, YOU KNOW!
GRRR
!!
IT'S MORE WORK DECIPHERING THAT GARBAGE THAN IT'S WORTH!
YOU'RE SUPPOSED TO VOLUNTEER FOR THIS KIND OF THING, NOT GET LUNCHES OUT OF IT!
YOU'RE UNBELIEV-ABLE!
YOU'RE JUST SPONGING OFF HIM BECAUSE HE'S SO NICE!
SPONGING ...?!
I AM NOT!
FWISH
HEY, MAYA.

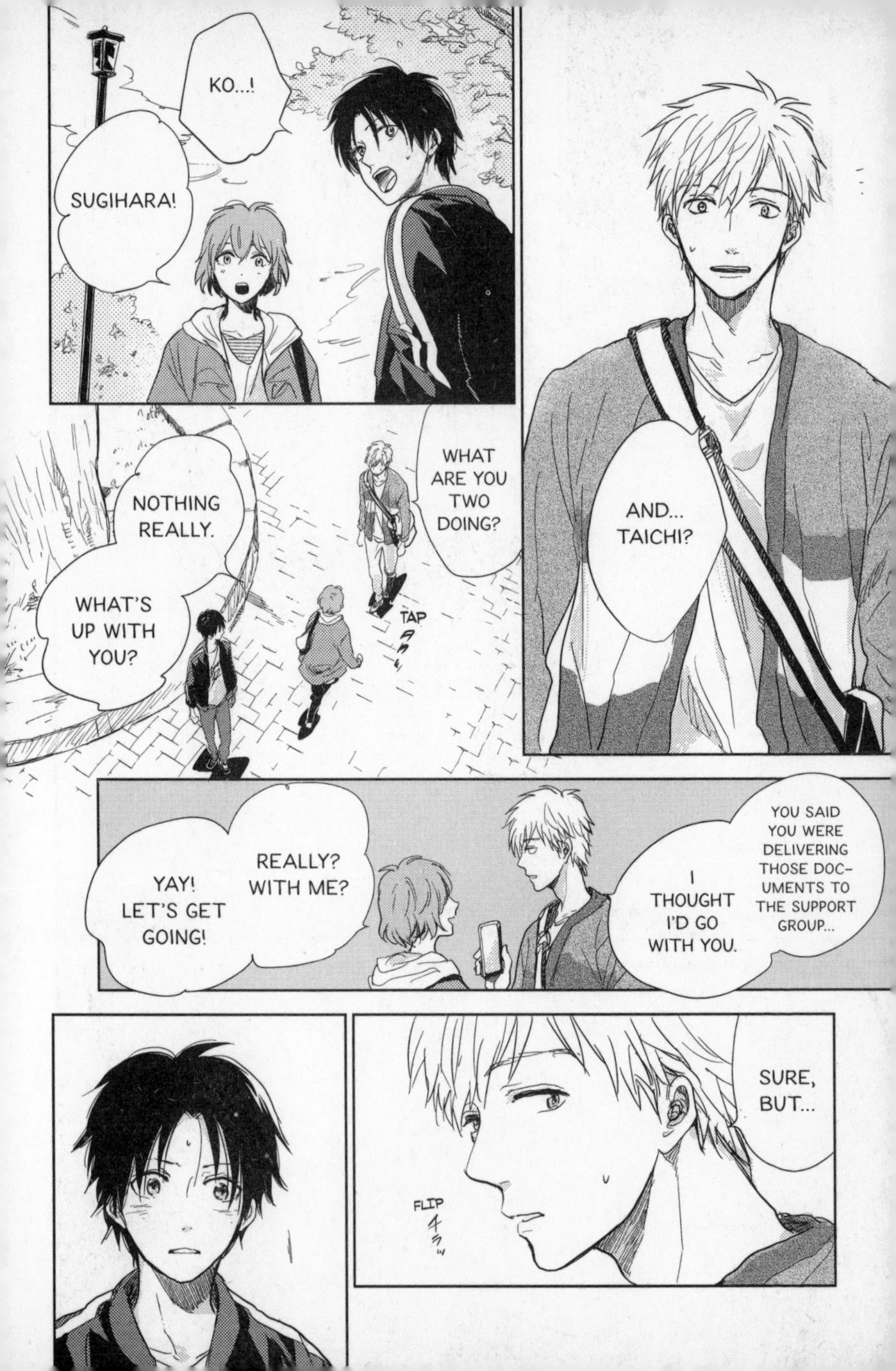
AND... TAICHI?
KO...!
SUGIHARA!
WHAT ARE YOU TWO DOING?
NOTHING REALLY.
WHAT'S UP WITH YOU?
TAP
YOU SAID YOU WERE DELIVERING THOSE DOCUMENTS TO THE SUPPORT GROUP...
I THOUGHT I'D GO WITH YOU.
REALLY? WITH ME?
YAY! LET'S GET GOING!
SURE, BUT...
FLIP

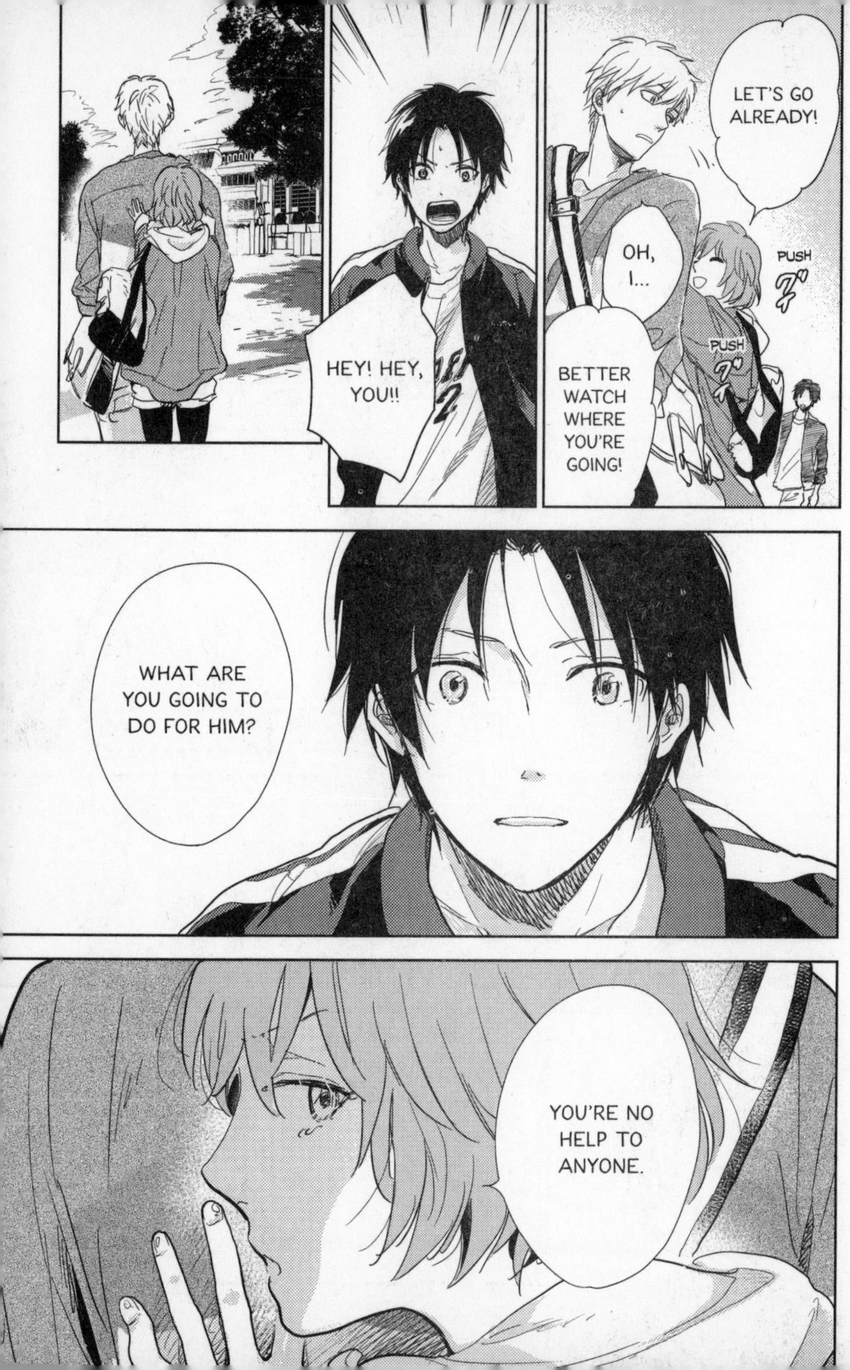
LET'S GO ALREADY!
PUSH
OH, I...
PUSH
BETTER WATCH WHERE YOU'RE GOING!
HEY! HEY, YOU!!
WHAT ARE YOU GOING TO DO FOR HIM?
YOU'RE NO HELP TO ANYONE.

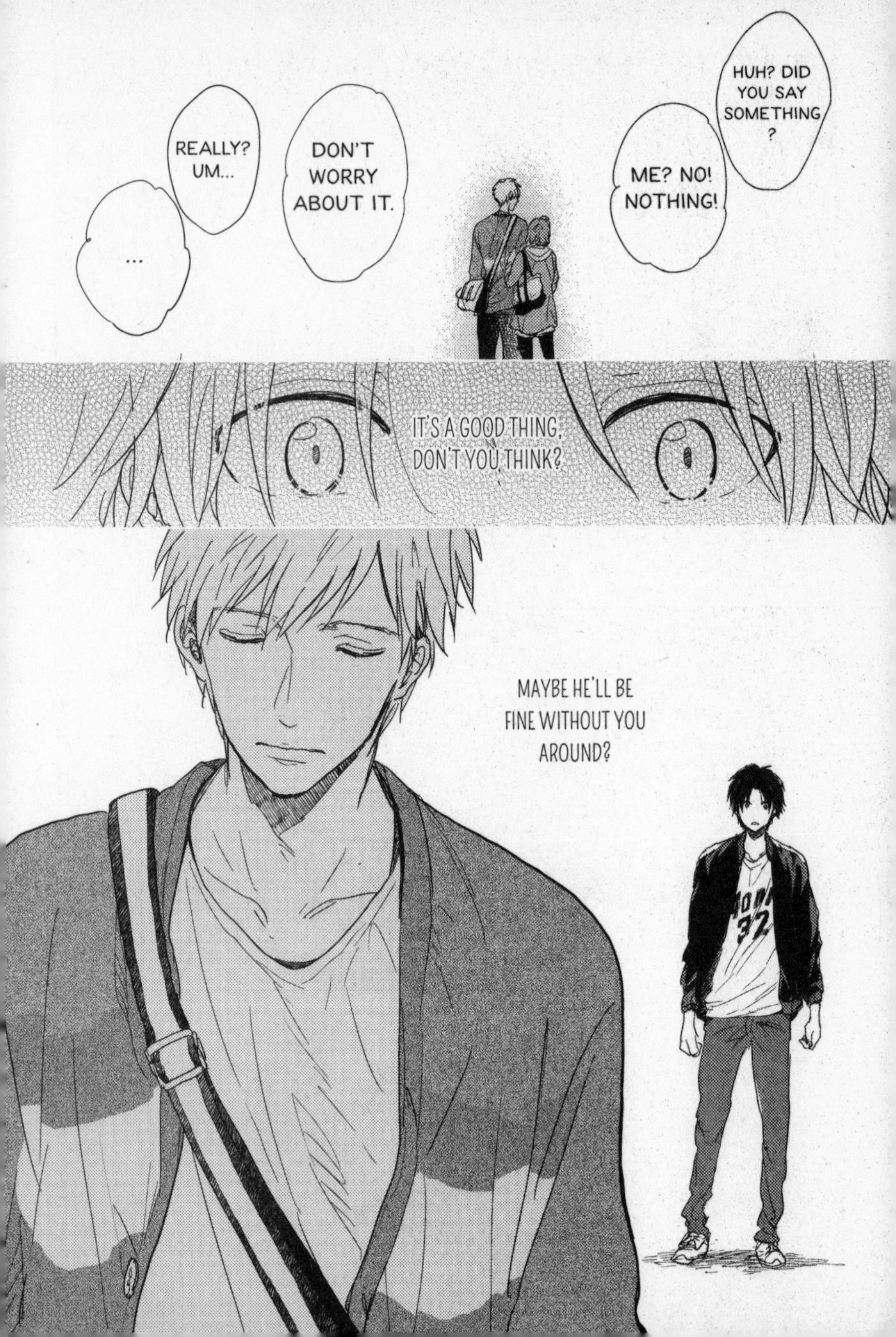
HUH? DID YOU SAY SOMETHING?
ME? NO! NOTHING!
DON'T WORRY ABOUT IT.
REALLY? UM...
...
IT'S A GOOD THING, DON'T YOU THINK?
MAYBE HE'LL BE FINE WITHOUT YOU AROUND?

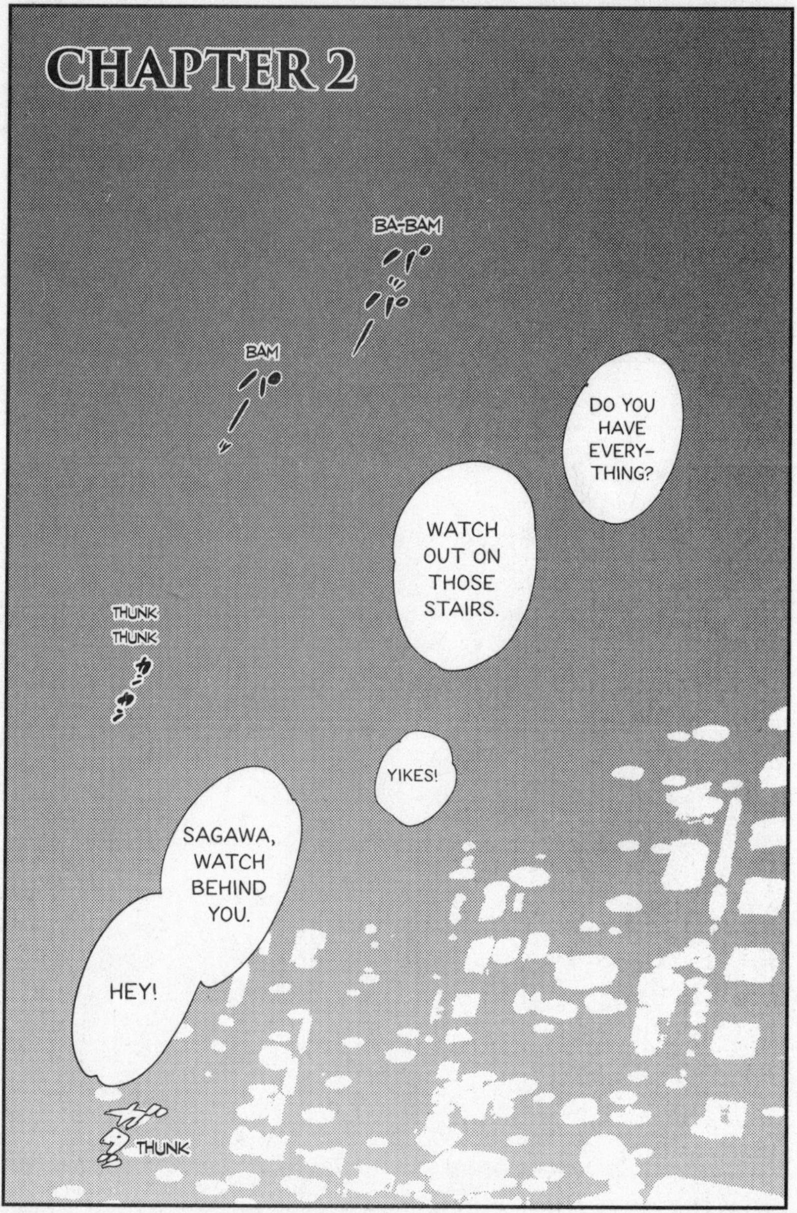
CHAPTER 2
DO YOU HAVE EVERYTHING?
WATCH OUT ON THOSE STAIRS.
BA-BAM
BAM
THUNK THUNK
YIKES!
SAGAWA, WATCH BEHIND YOU.
HEY!
THUNK

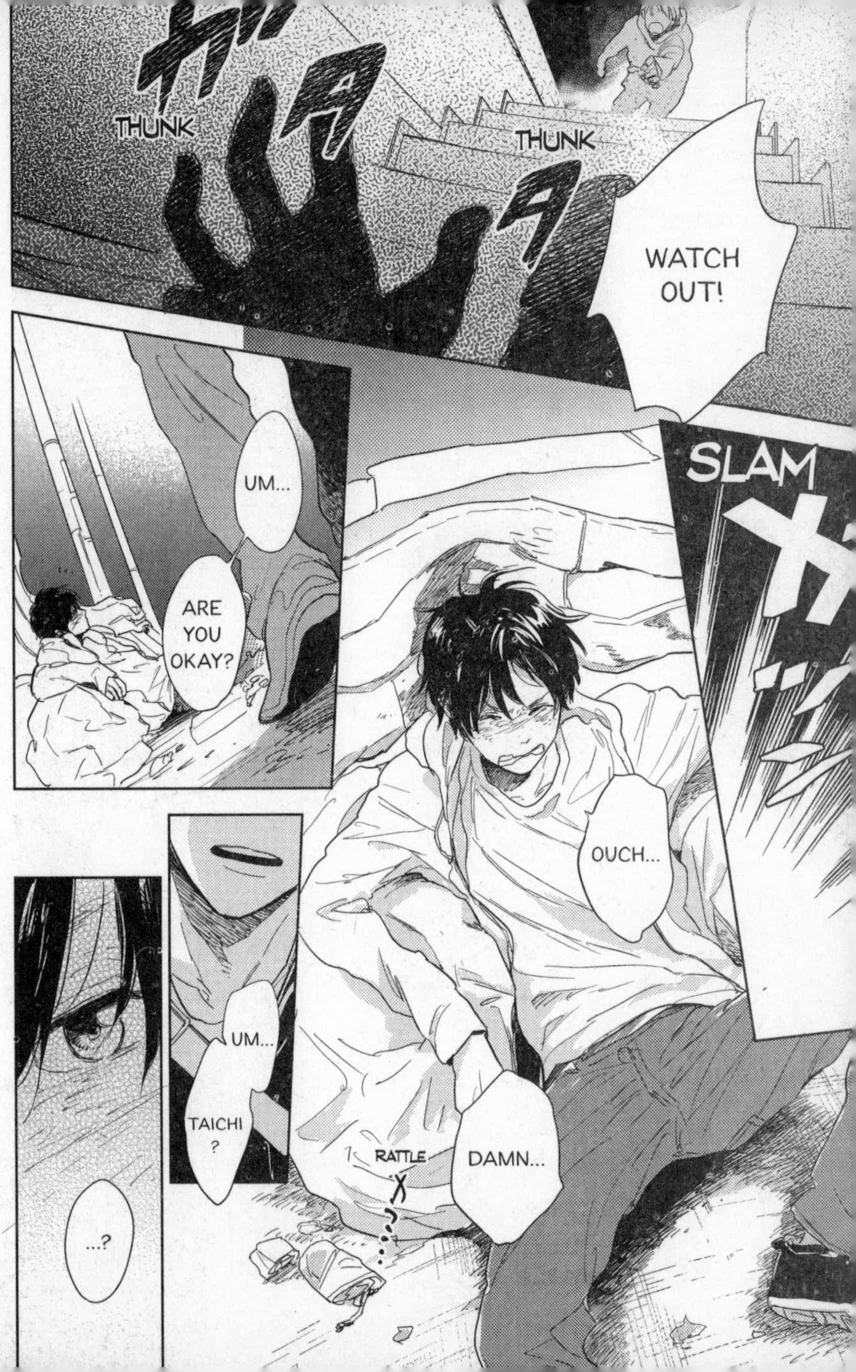
ガタタ
THUNK
THUNK
WATCH OUT!
SLAM
OUCH...
DAMN...
RATTLE
UM...
ARE YOU OKAY?
UM...
TAICHI?
...?

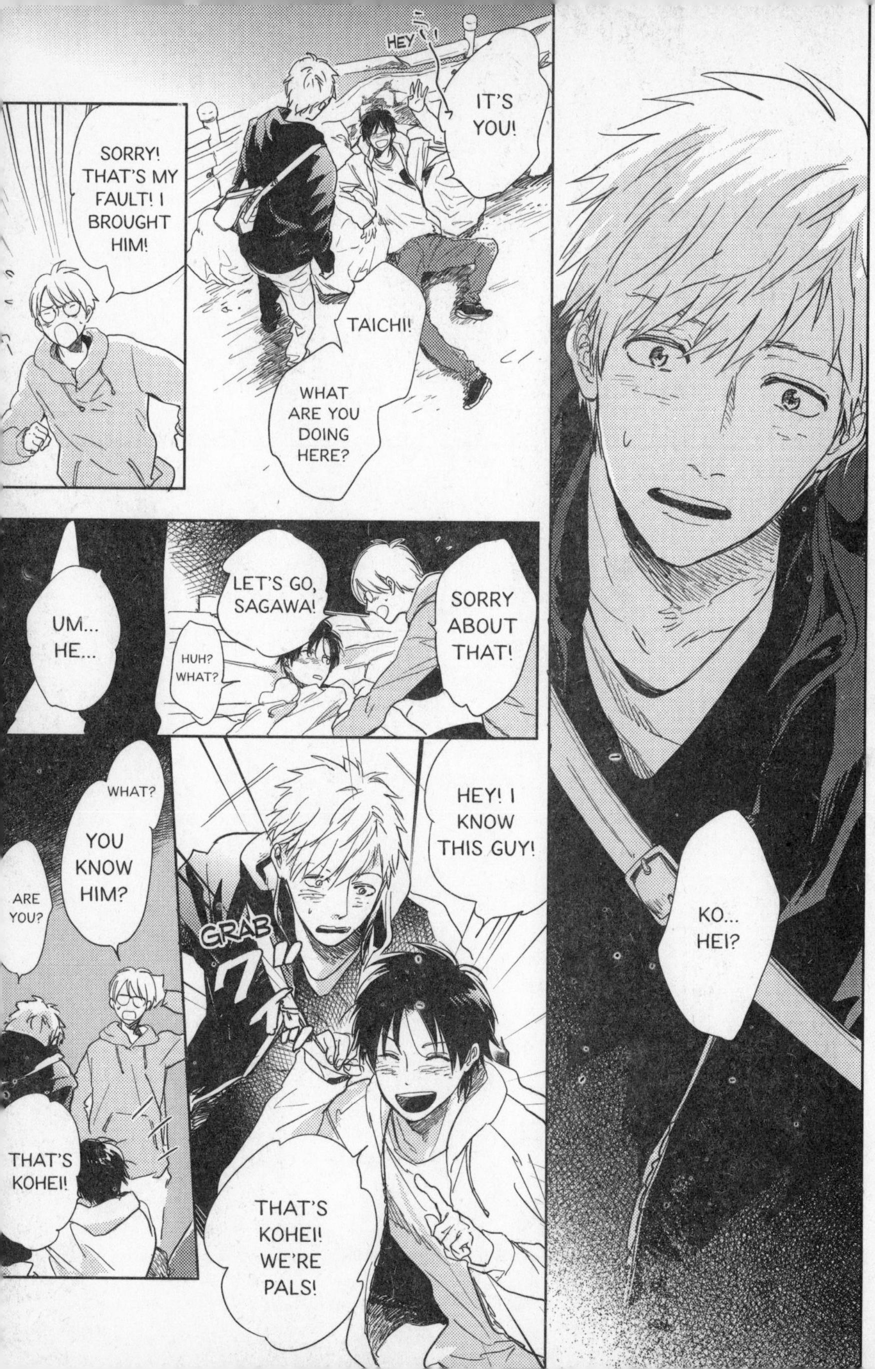

HEY
IT'S YOU!
TAICHI!
WHAT ARE YOU DOING HERE?
SORRY! THAT'S MY FAULT! I BROUGHT HIM!
SORRY ABOUT THAT!
LET'S GO, SAGAWA!
HUH? WHAT?
UM... HE...
HEY! I KNOW THIS GUY!
GRAB
THAT'S KOHEI! WE'RE PALS!
WHAT?
YOU KNOW HIM?
ARE YOU?
THAT'S KOHEI!
KO... HEI?

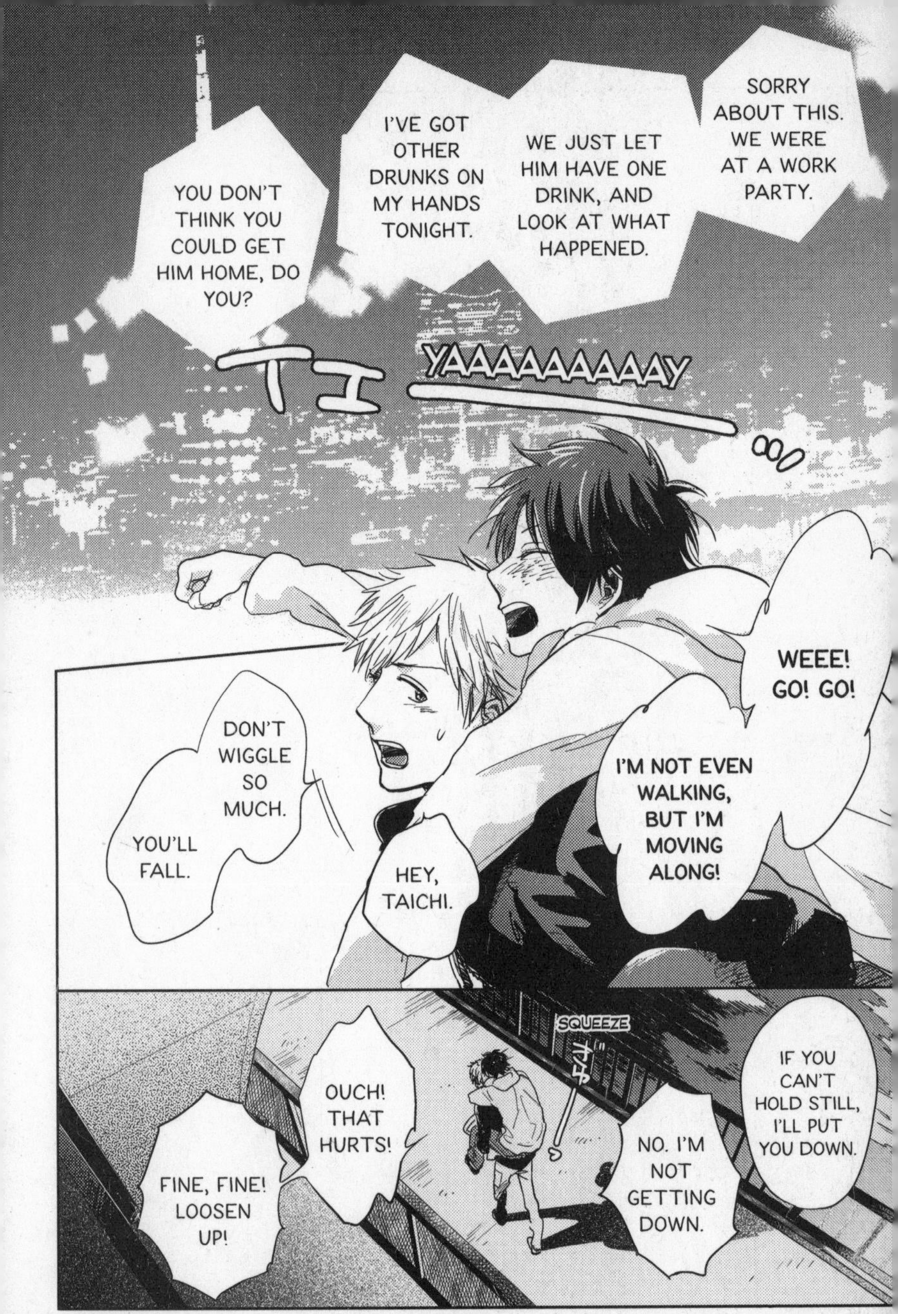
SORRY ABOUT THIS. WE WERE AT A WORK PARTY.
WE JUST LET HIM HAVE ONE DRINK, AND LOOK AT WHAT HAPPENED.
I'VE GOT OTHER DRUNKS ON MY HANDS TONIGHT.
YOU DON'T THINK YOU COULD GET HIM HOME, DO YOU?
YAAAAAAAAAY
WEEE! GO! GO!
I'M NOT EVEN WALKING, BUT I'M MOVING ALONG!
HEY, TAICHI.
DON'T WIGGLE SO MUCH.
YOU'LL FALL.
IF YOU CAN'T HOLD STILL, I'LL PUT YOU DOWN.
SQUEEZE
NO. I'M NOT GETTING DOWN.
OUCH! THAT HURTS!
FINE, FINE! LOOSEN UP!

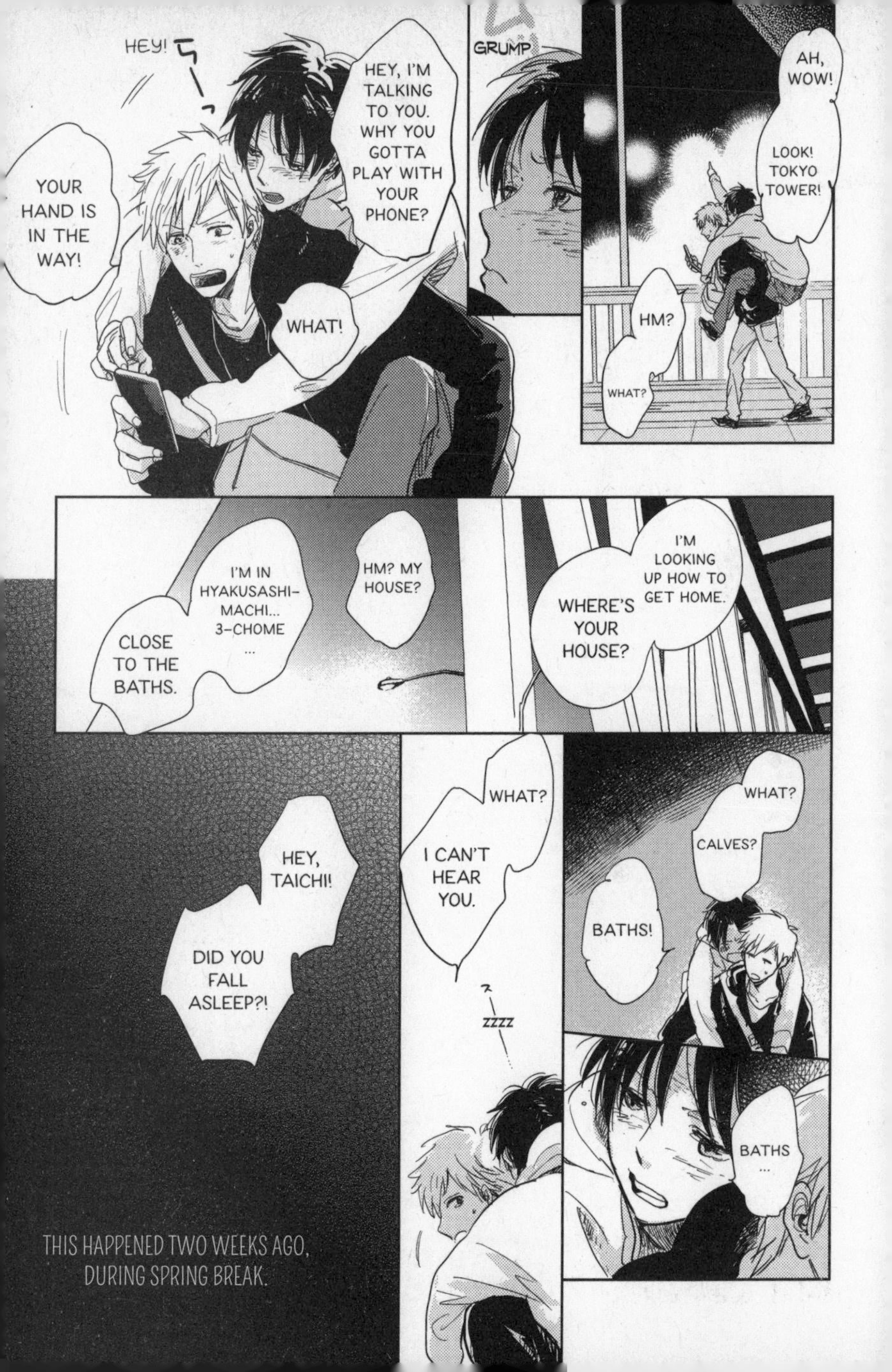
AH, WOW!
LOOK! TOKYO TOWER!
HM?
WHAT?
GRUMP
HEY, I'M TALKING TO YOU. WHY YOU GOTTA PLAY WITH YOUR PHONE?
HEY!
YOUR HAND IS IN THE WAY!
WHAT!
I'M LOOKING UP HOW TO GET HOME.
WHERE'S YOUR HOUSE?
HM? MY HOUSE?
I'M IN HYAKUSASHI-MACHI... 3-CHOME ...
CLOSE TO THE BATHS.
WHAT?
CALVES?
BATHS!
BATHS ...
WHAT?
I CAN'T HEAR YOU.
ZZZZ
HEY, TAICHI!
DID YOU FALL ASLEEP?!
THIS HAPPENED TWO WEEKS AGO, DURING SPRING BREAK.

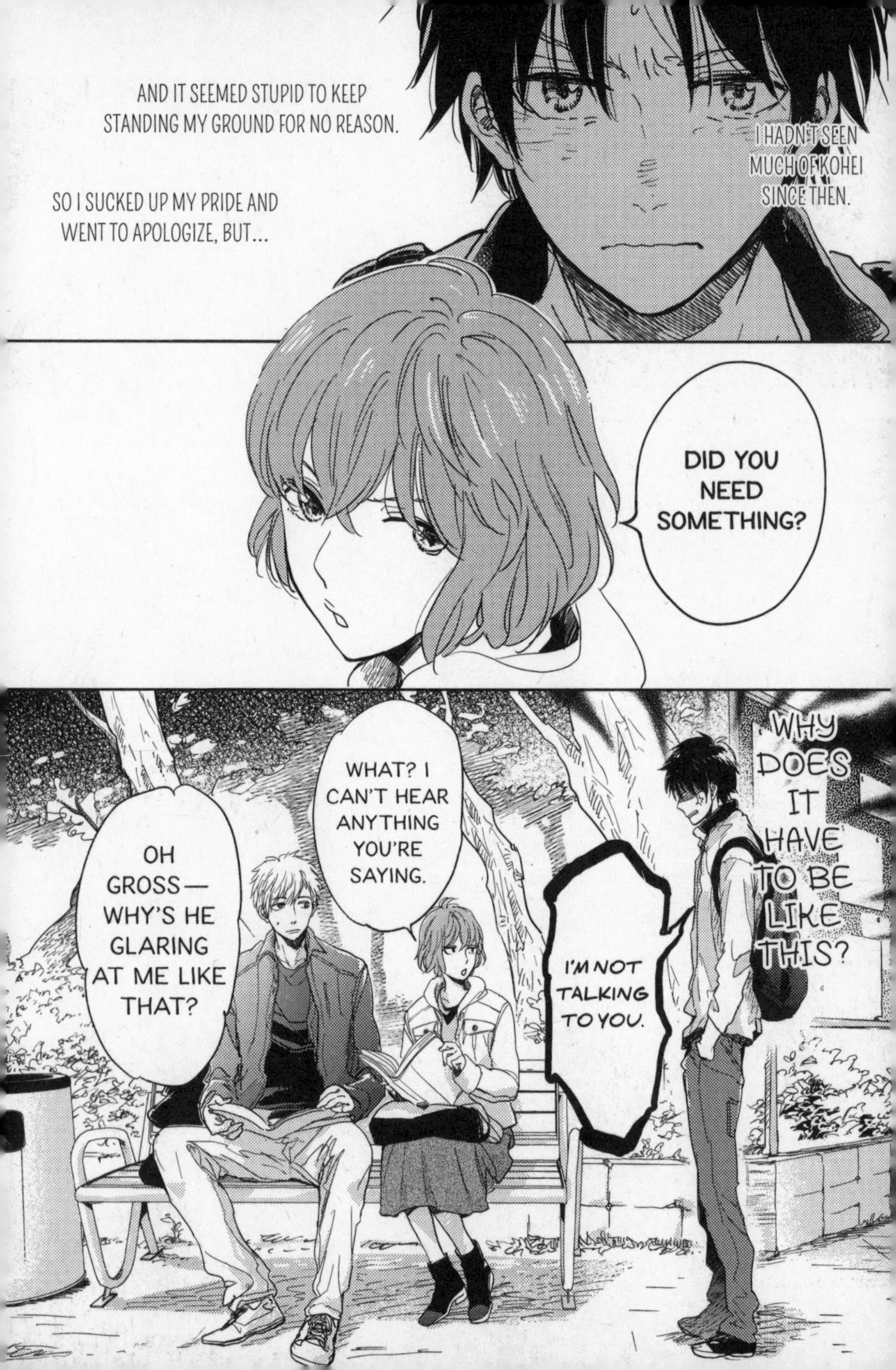
I HADN'T SEEN MUCH OF KOHEI SINCE THEN.
AND IT SEEMED STUPID TO KEEP STANDING MY GROUND FOR NO REASON.
SO I SUCKED UP MY PRIDE AND WENT TO APOLOGIZE, BUT...
DID YOU NEED SOMETHING?
WHY DOES IT HAVE TO BE LIKE THIS?
I'M NOT TALKING TO YOU.
WHAT? I CAN'T HEAR ANYTHING YOU'RE SAYING.
OH GROSS—WHY'S HE GLARING AT ME LIKE THAT?

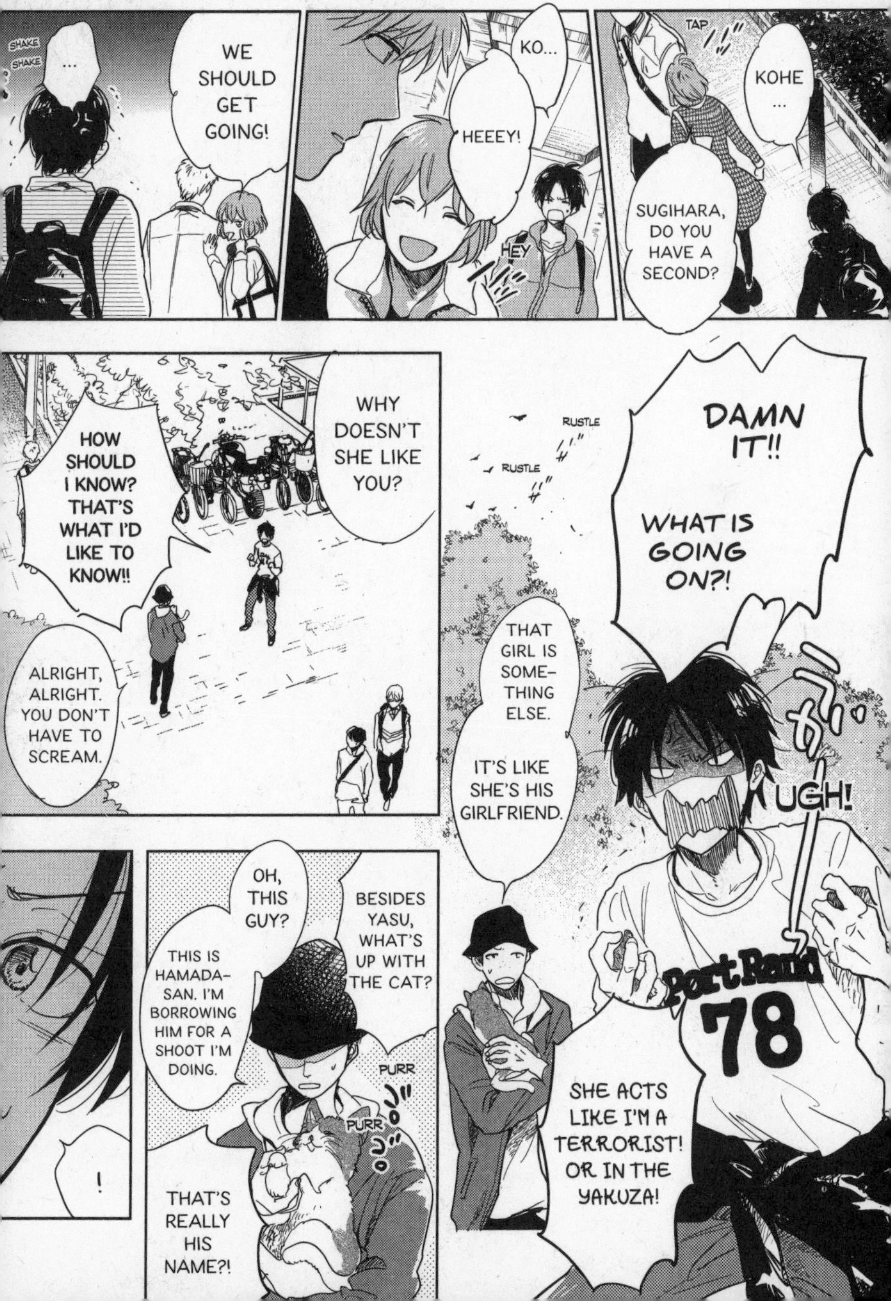
TAP
KOHE ...
SUGIHARA, DO YOU HAVE A SECOND?
KO...
HEEEY!
HEY
WE SHOULD GET GOING!
SHAKE SHAKE
...
DAMN IT!!
WHAT IS GOING ON?!
RUSTLE
RUSTLE
UGH!
THAT GIRL IS SOMETHING ELSE.
IT'S LIKE SHE'S HIS GIRLFRIEND.
SHE ACTS LIKE I'M A TERRORIST! OR IN THE YAKUZA!
Port Rand
78
WHY DOESN'T SHE LIKE YOU?
HOW SHOULD I KNOW? THAT'S WHAT I'D LIKE TO KNOW!!
ALRIGHT, ALRIGHT. YOU DON'T HAVE TO SCREAM.
BESIDES YASU, WHAT'S UP WITH THE CAT?
OH, THIS GUY?
THIS IS HAMADA-SAN. I'M BORROWING HIM FOR A SHOOT I'M DOING.
PURR
PURR
THAT'S REALLY HIS NAME?!
!

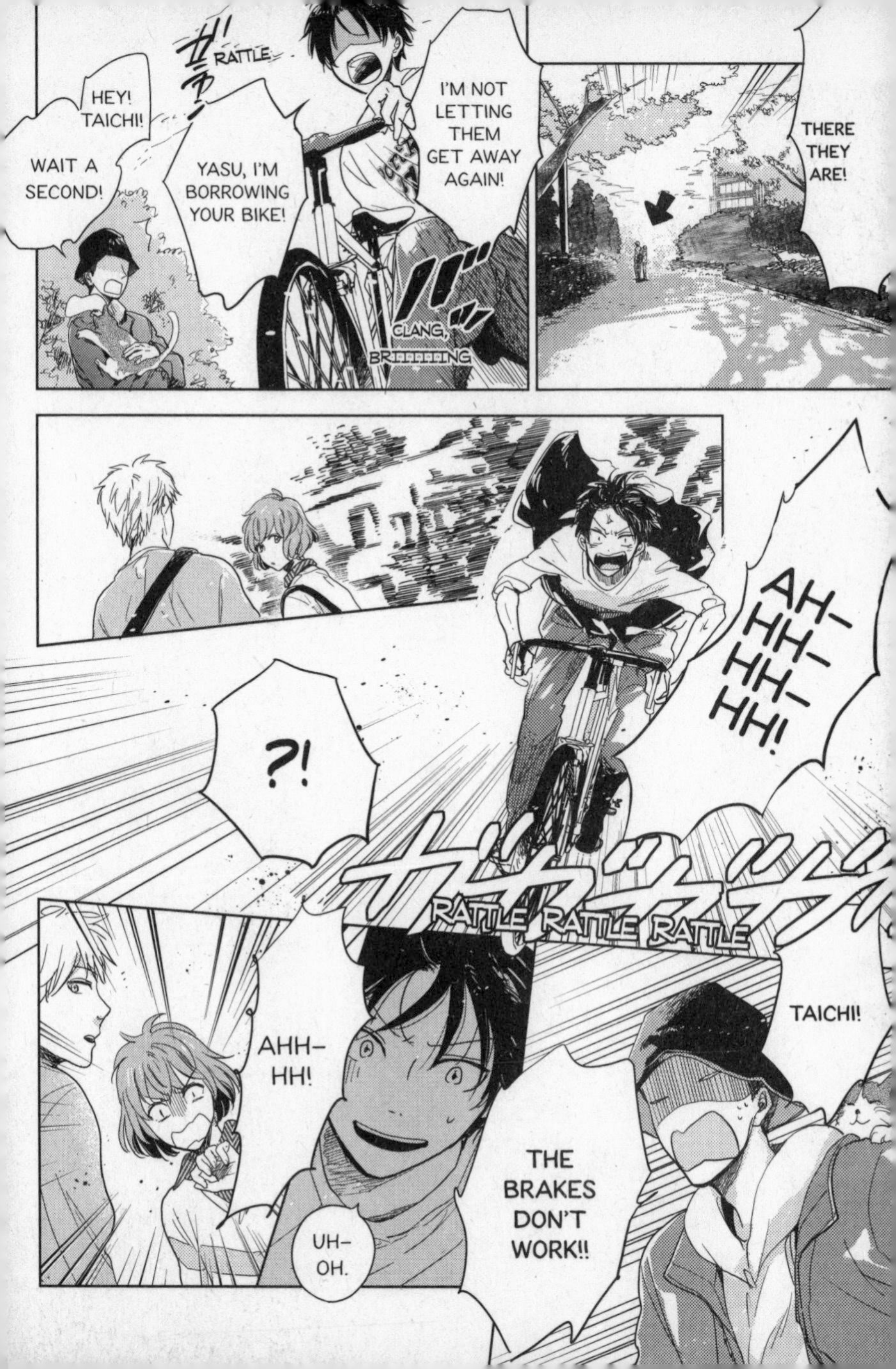
THERE THEY ARE!
I'M NOT LETTING THEM GET AWAY AGAIN!
RATTLE
YASU, I'M BORROWING YOUR BIKE!
HEY! TAICHI!
WAIT A SECOND!
CLANG, BRIIIIIING
AH-HH-HH-HH!
?!
RATTLE RATTLE RATTLE
TAICHI!
THE BRAKES DON'T WORK!!
UH-OH.
AHH-HH!

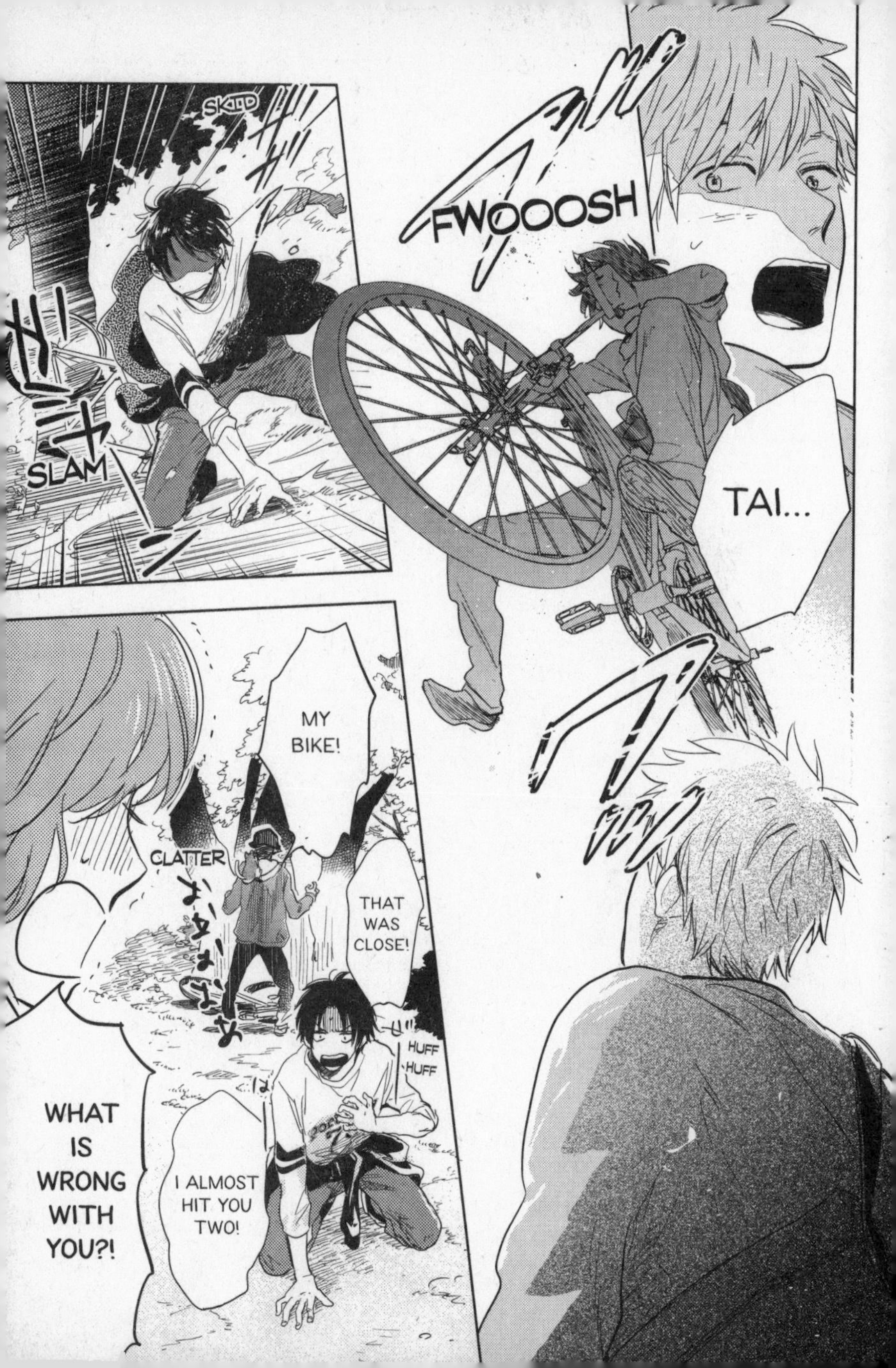
FWOOOSH
TAI...
SKID
SLAM
MY BIKE!
THAT WAS CLOSE!
CLATTER
HUFF HUFF
I ALMOST HIT YOU TWO!
WHAT IS WRONG WITH YOU?!

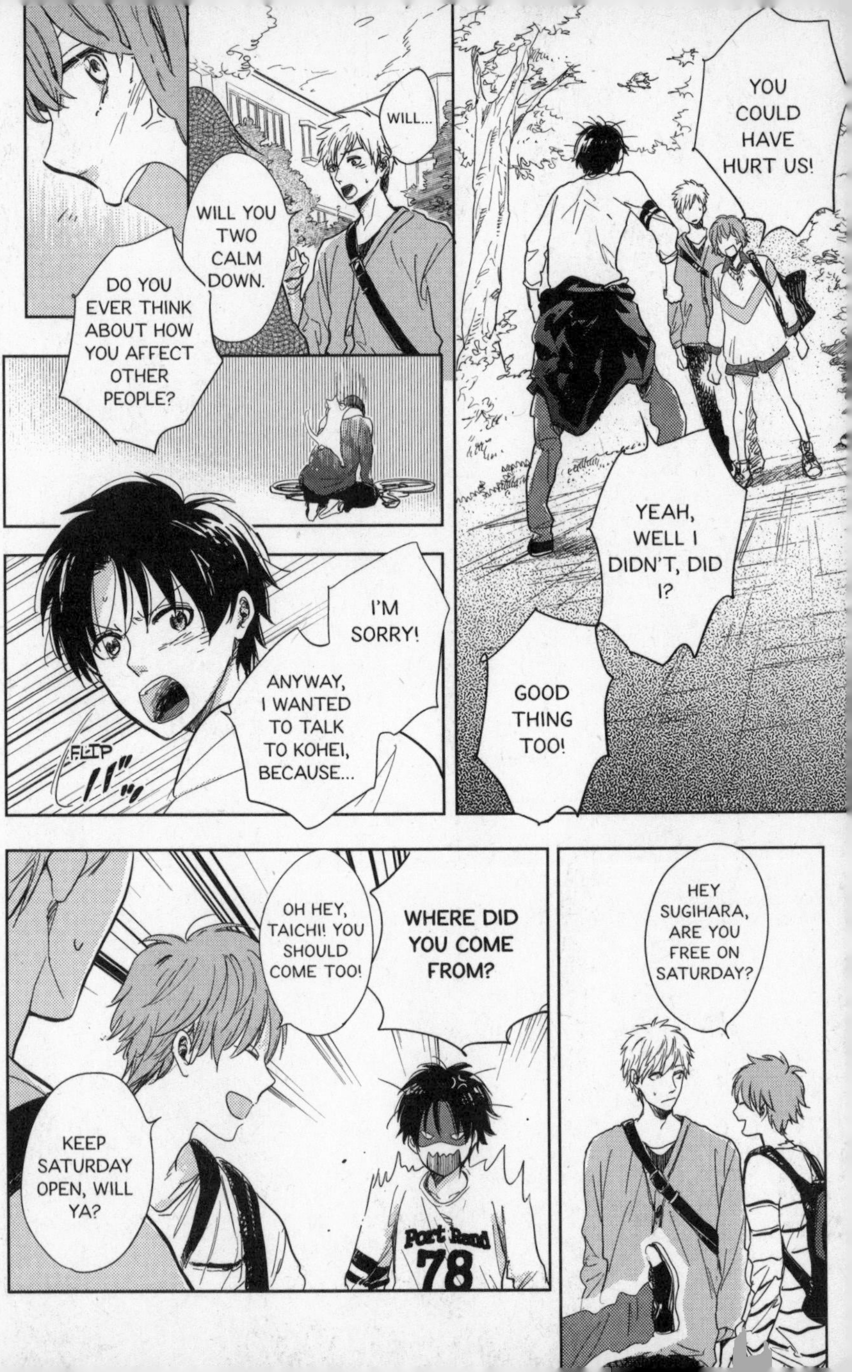
YOU COULD HAVE HURT US!
YEAH, WELL I DIDN'T, DID I?
GOOD THING TOO!
WILL...
WILL YOU TWO CALM DOWN.
DO YOU EVER THINK ABOUT HOW YOU AFFECT OTHER PEOPLE?
I'M SORRY!
ANYWAY, I WANTED TO TALK TO KOHEI, BECAUSE...
FLIP
HEY SUGIHARA, ARE YOU FREE ON SATURDAY?
WHERE DID YOU COME FROM?
OH HEY, TAICHI! YOU SHOULD COME TOO!
KEEP SATURDAY OPEN, WILL YA?

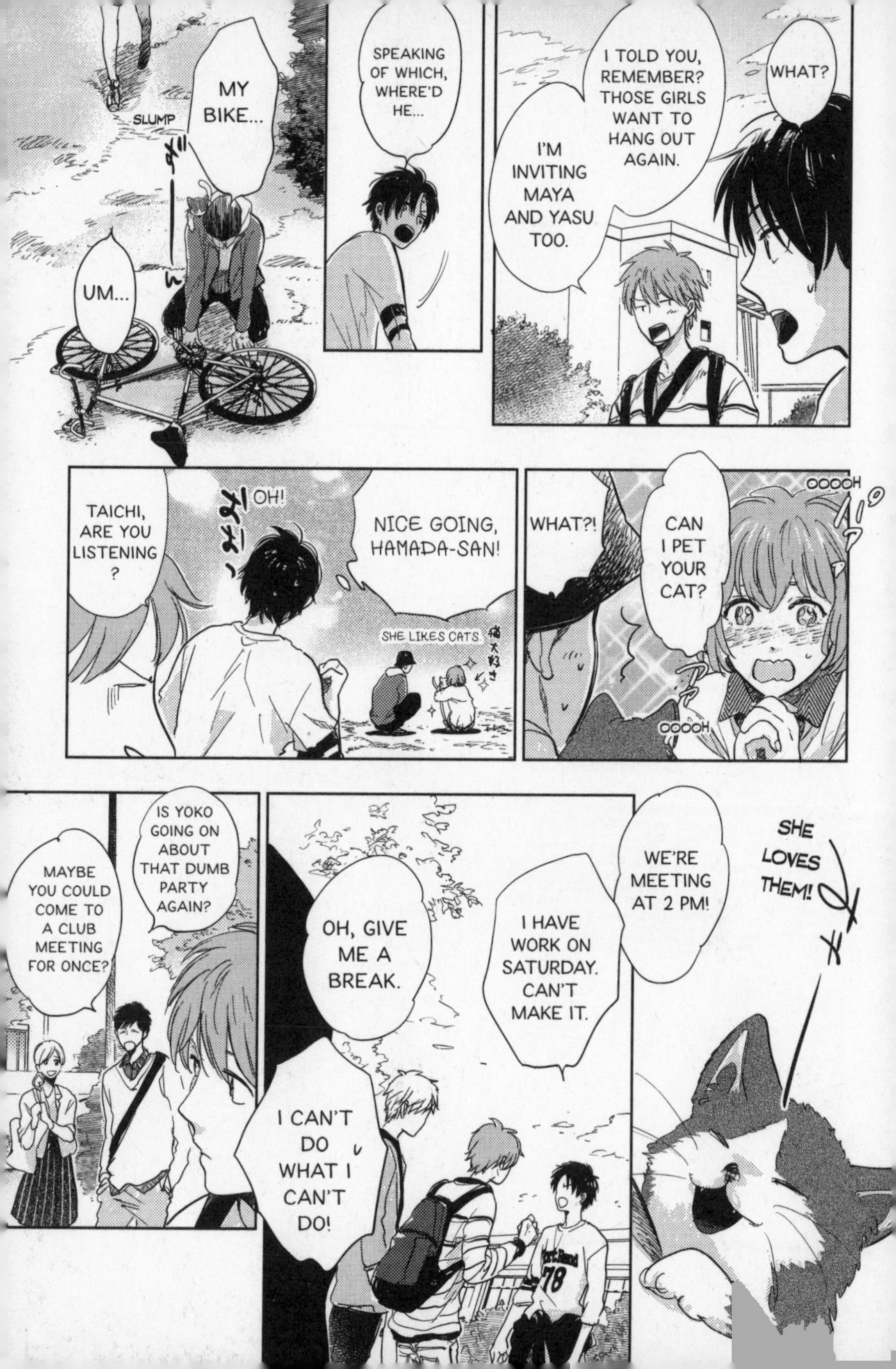
WHAT?
I TOLD YOU, REMEMBER? THOSE GIRLS WANT TO HANG OUT AGAIN.
I'M INVITING MAYA AND YASU TOO.
SPEAKING OF WHICH, WHERE'D HE...
MY BIKE...
SLUMP
UM...
OOOOH
CAN I PET YOUR CAT?
WHAT?!
OOOOH
NICE GOING, HAMADA-SAN!
OH!
TAICHI, ARE YOU LISTENING?
SHE LIKES CATS.
SHE LOVES THEM!
WE'RE MEETING AT 2 PM!
I HAVE WORK ON SATURDAY. CAN'T MAKE IT.
OH, GIVE ME A BREAK.
I CAN'T DO WHAT I CAN'T DO!
IS YOKO GOING ON ABOUT THAT DUMB PARTY AGAIN?
MAYBE YOU COULD COME TO A CLUB MEETING FOR ONCE?

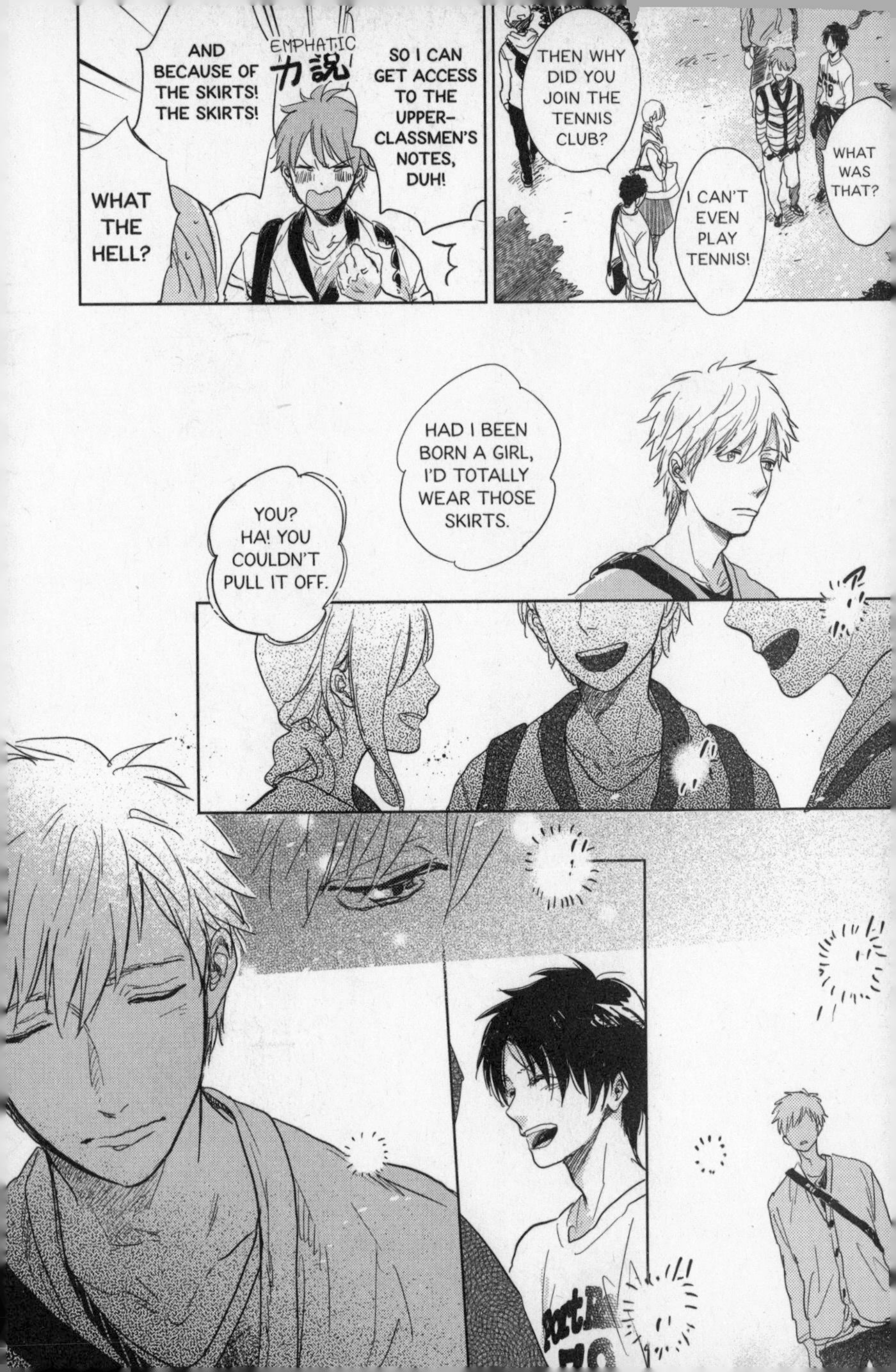
WHAT WAS THAT?
I CAN'T EVEN PLAY TENNIS!
THEN WHY DID YOU JOIN THE TENNIS CLUB?
SO I CAN GET ACCESS TO THE UPPER-CLASSMEN'S NOTES, DUH!
EMPHATIC 力説
AND BECAUSE OF THE SKIRTS! THE SKIRTS!
WHAT THE HELL?
HAD I BEEN BORN A GIRL, I'D TOTALLY WEAR THOSE SKIRTS.
YOU? HA! YOU COULDN'T PULL IT OFF.

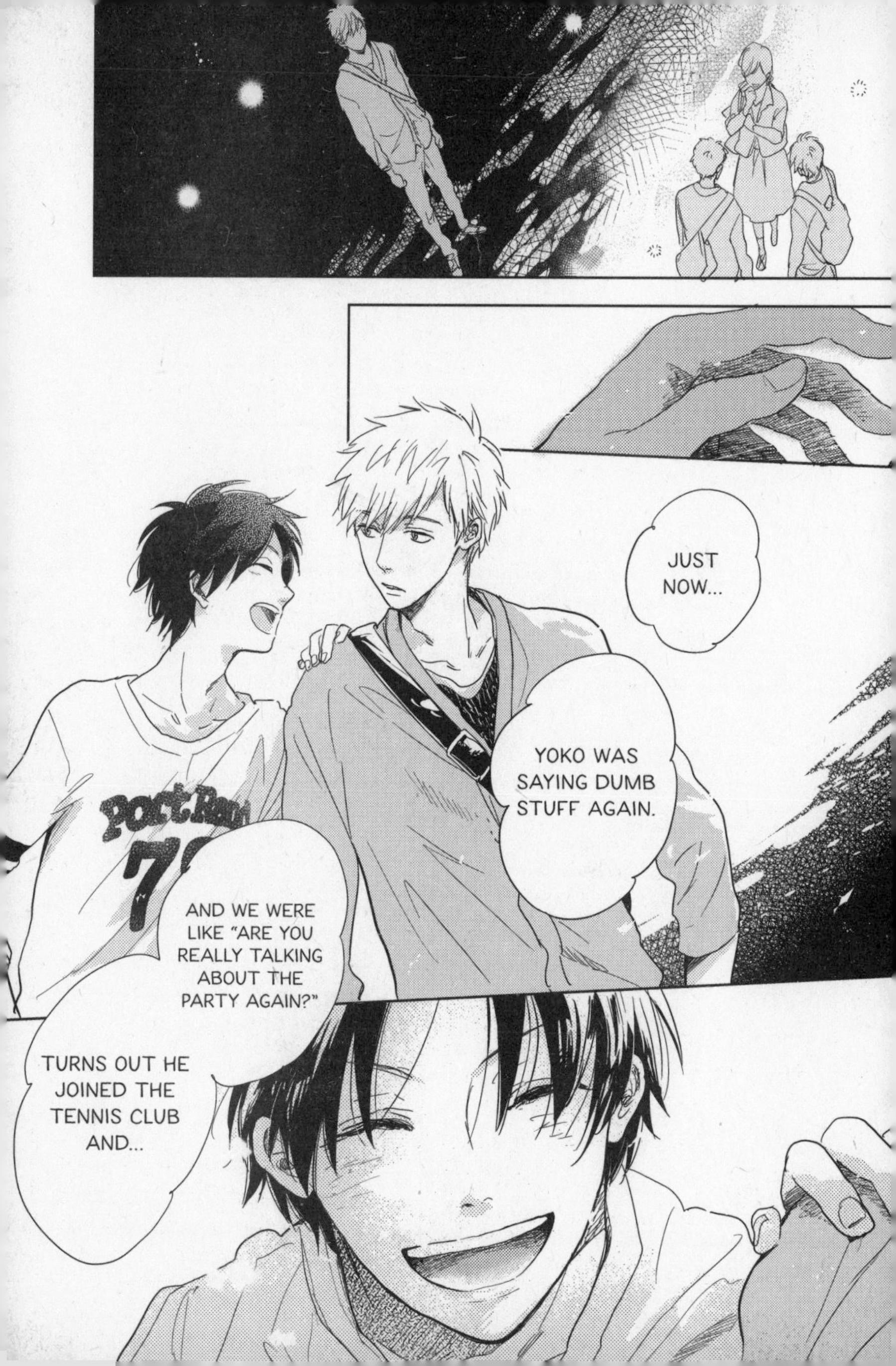
JUST NOW...
YOKO WAS SAYING DUMB STUFF AGAIN.
AND WE WERE LIKE "ARE YOU REALLY TALKING ABOUT THE PARTY AGAIN?"
TURNS OUT HE JOINED THE TENNIS CLUB AND...

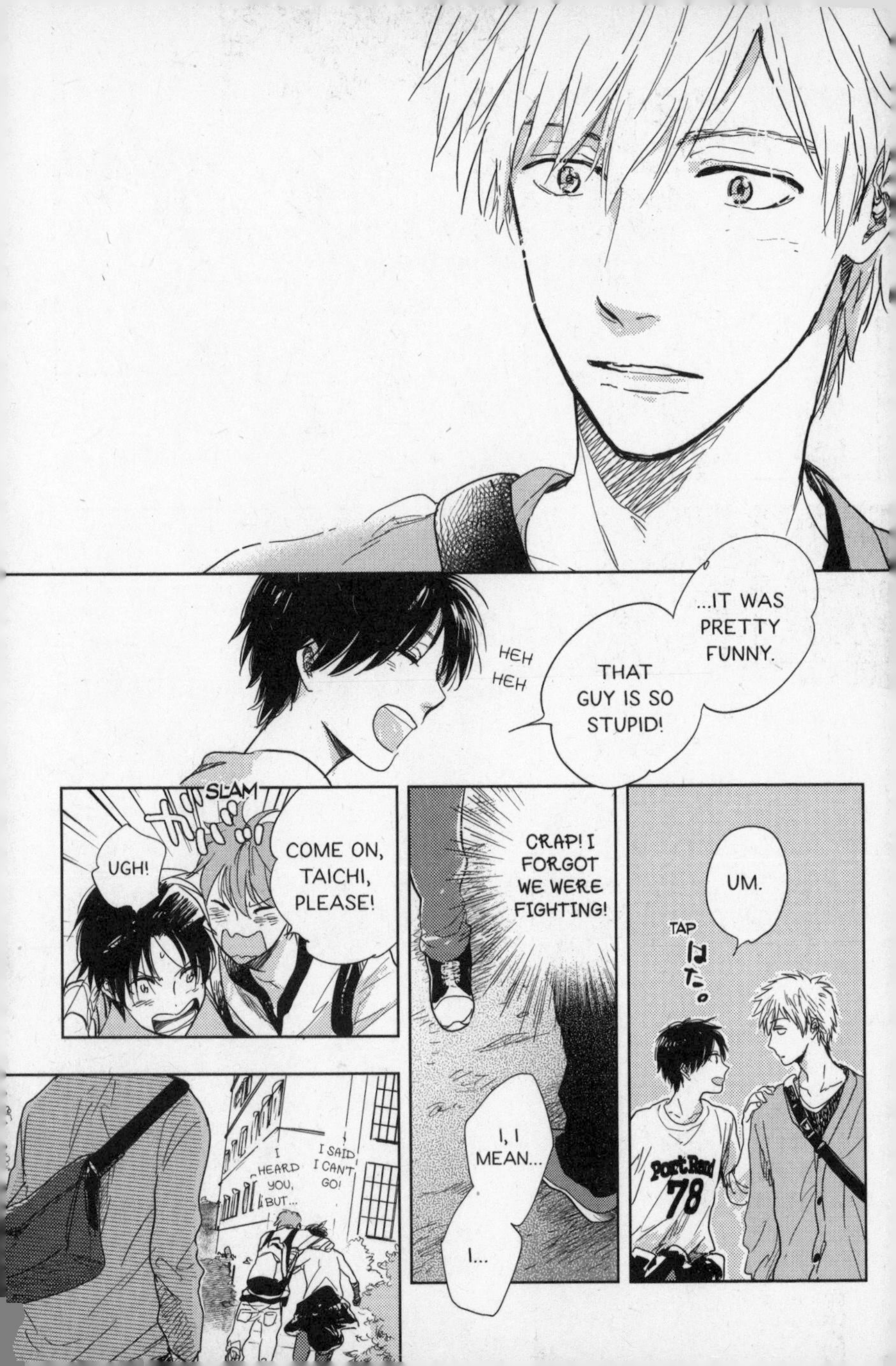
...IT WAS PRETTY FUNNY.
THAT GUY IS SO STUPID!
HEH HEH
UM.
TAP
はっ。
CRAP! I FORGOT WE WERE FIGHTING!
I, I MEAN...
I...
SLAM
COME ON, TAICHI, PLEASE!
UGH!
I SAID I CAN'T GO!
I HEARD YOU, BUT...
Port Rand
78

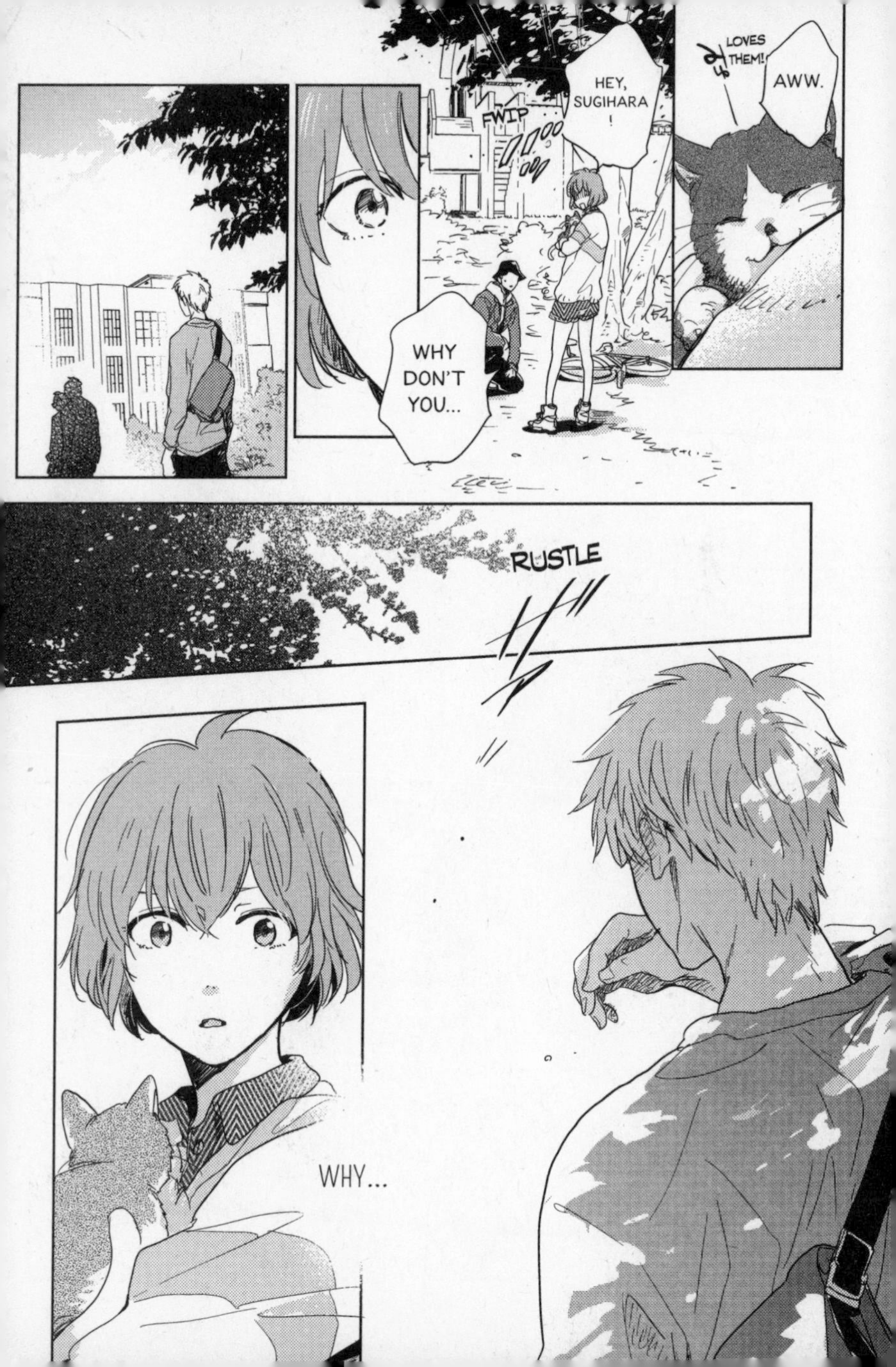
AWW.
LOVES THEM!
HEY, SUGIHARA!
FWIP
WHY DON'T YOU...
RUSTLE
WHY...

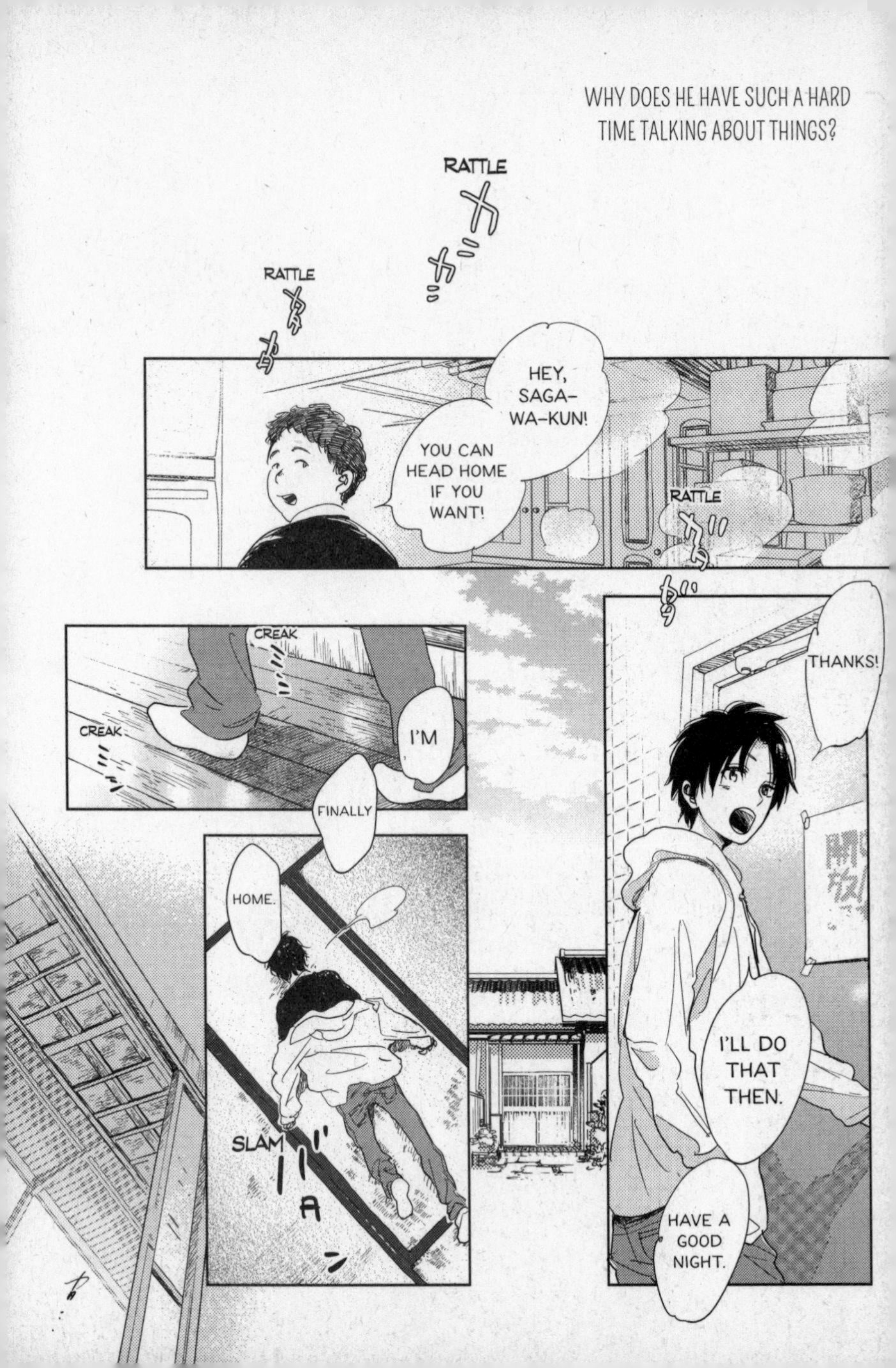
WHY DOES HE HAVE SUCH A HARD TIME TALKING ABOUT THINGS?
RATTLE
RATTLE
HEY, SAGA-WA-KUN!
YOU CAN HEAD HOME IF YOU WANT!
RATTLE
THANKS!
I'LL DO THAT THEN.
HAVE A GOOD NIGHT.
CREAK
CREAK
I'M
FINALLY
HOME.
SLAM

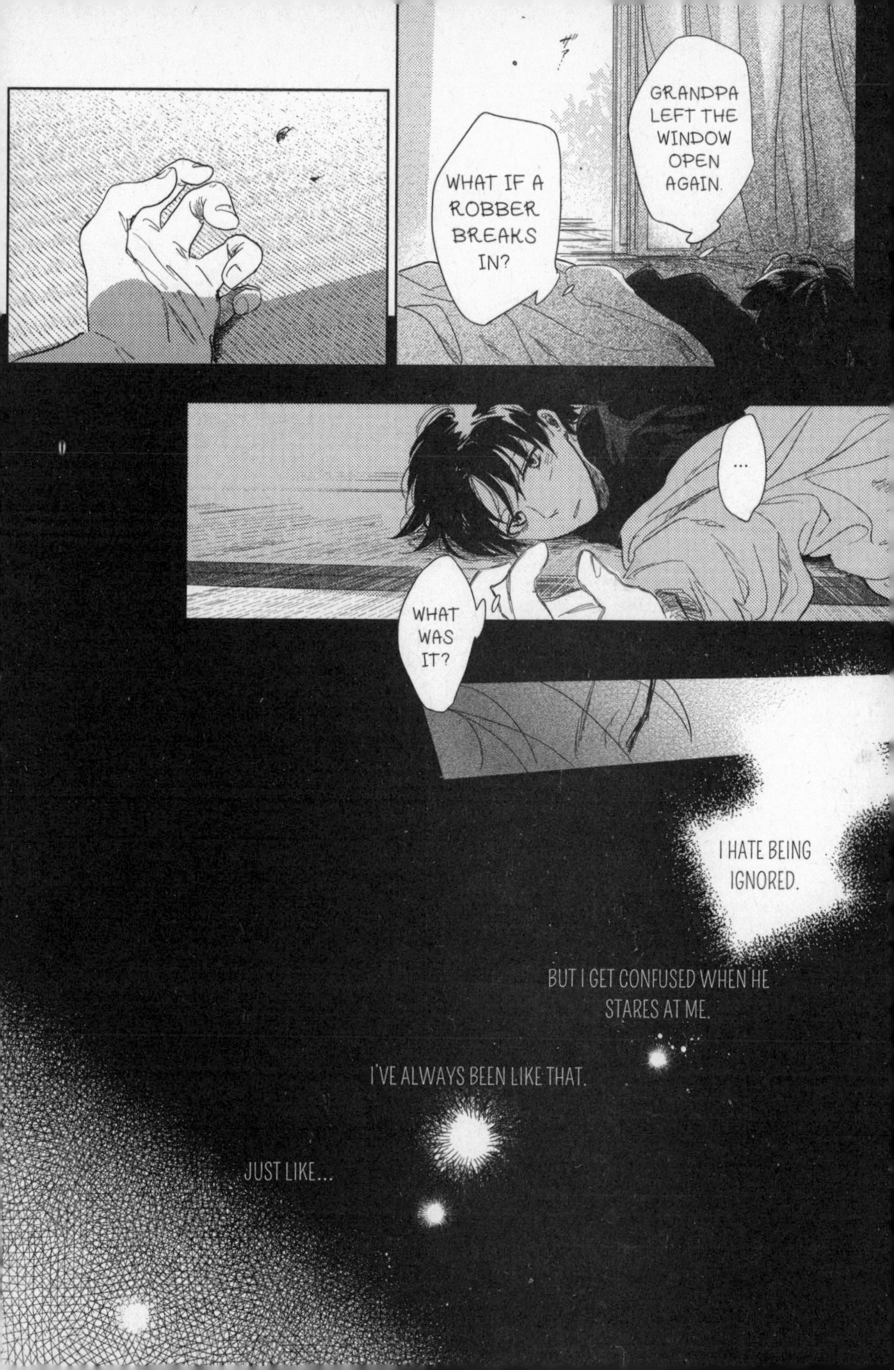
GRANDPA LEFT THE WINDOW OPEN AGAIN.
WHAT IF A ROBBER BREAKS IN?
...
WHAT WAS IT?
I HATE BEING IGNORED.
BUT I GET CONFUSED WHEN HE STARES AT ME.
I'VE ALWAYS BEEN LIKE THAT.
JUST LIKE...

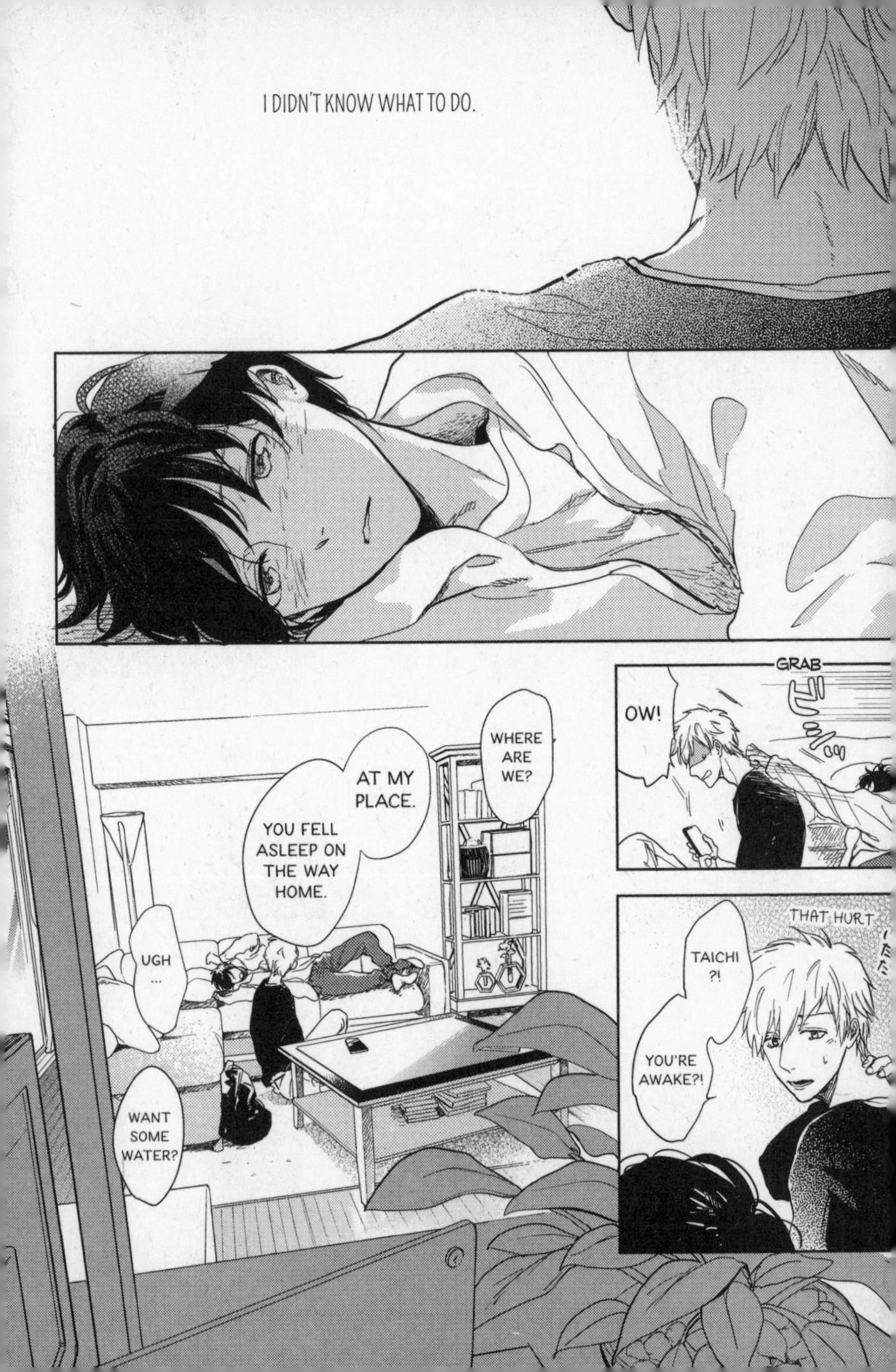
I DIDN'T KNOW WHAT TO DO.
GRAB
OW!
THAT HURT
TAICHI?!
YOU'RE AWAKE?!
WHERE ARE WE?
AT MY PLACE.
YOU FELL ASLEEP ON THE WAY HOME.
UGH...
WANT SOME WATER?

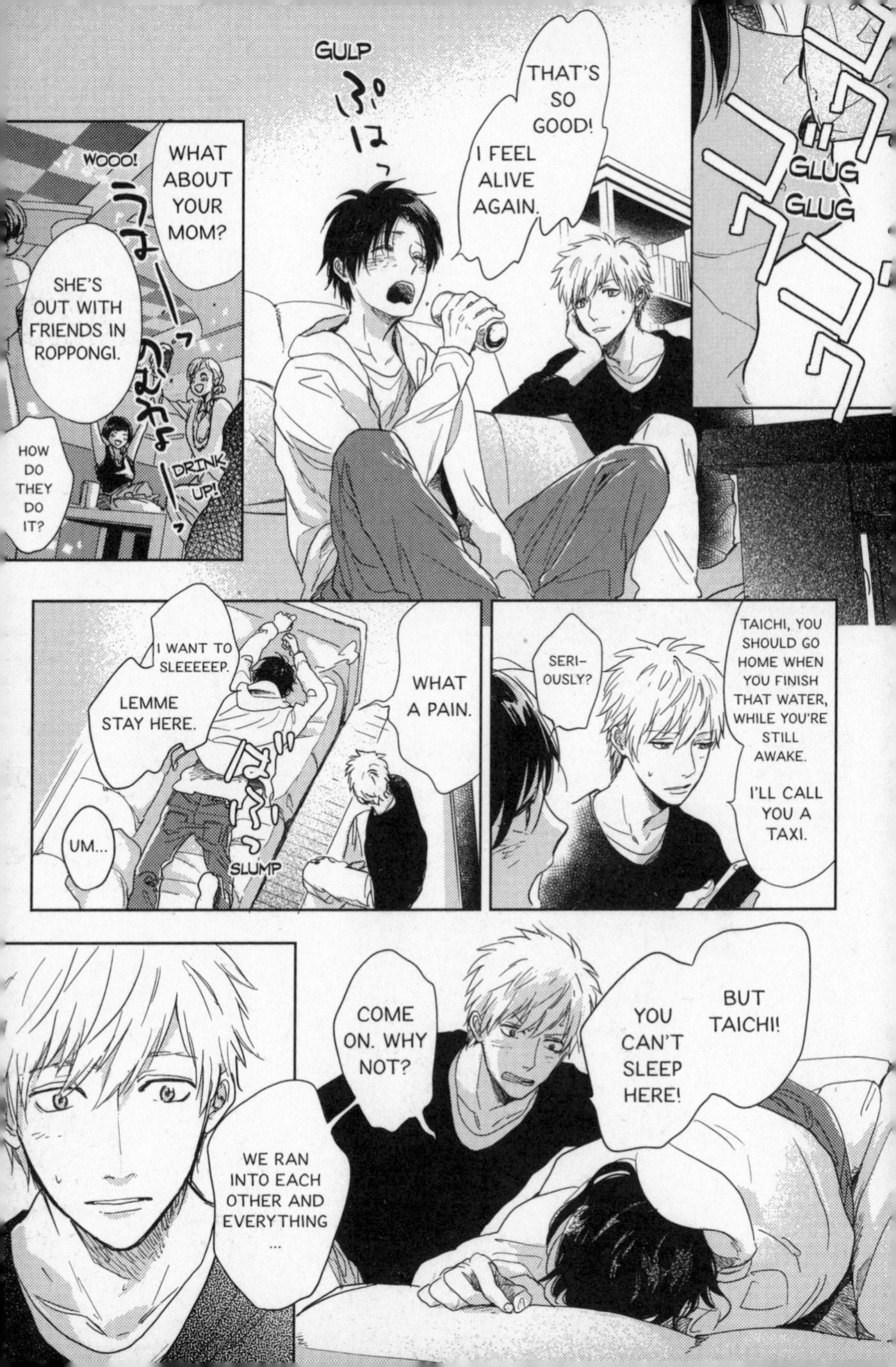
GLUG GLUG
GULP
ぷはっ
THAT'S SO GOOD! I FEEL ALIVE AGAIN.
WOOO!
WHAT ABOUT YOUR MOM?
SHE'S OUT WITH FRIENDS IN ROPPONGI.
DRINK UP!
HOW DO THEY DO IT?
SERI- OUSLY?
TAICHI, YOU SHOULD GO HOME WHEN YOU FINISH THAT WATER, WHILE YOU'RE STILL AWAKE.
I'LL CALL YOU A TAXI.
WHAT A PAIN.
I WANT TO SLEEEEEP.
LEMME STAY HERE.
SLUMP
UM...
BUT TAICHI!
YOU CAN'T SLEEP HERE!
COME ON. WHY NOT?
WE RAN INTO EACH OTHER AND EVERYTHING ...

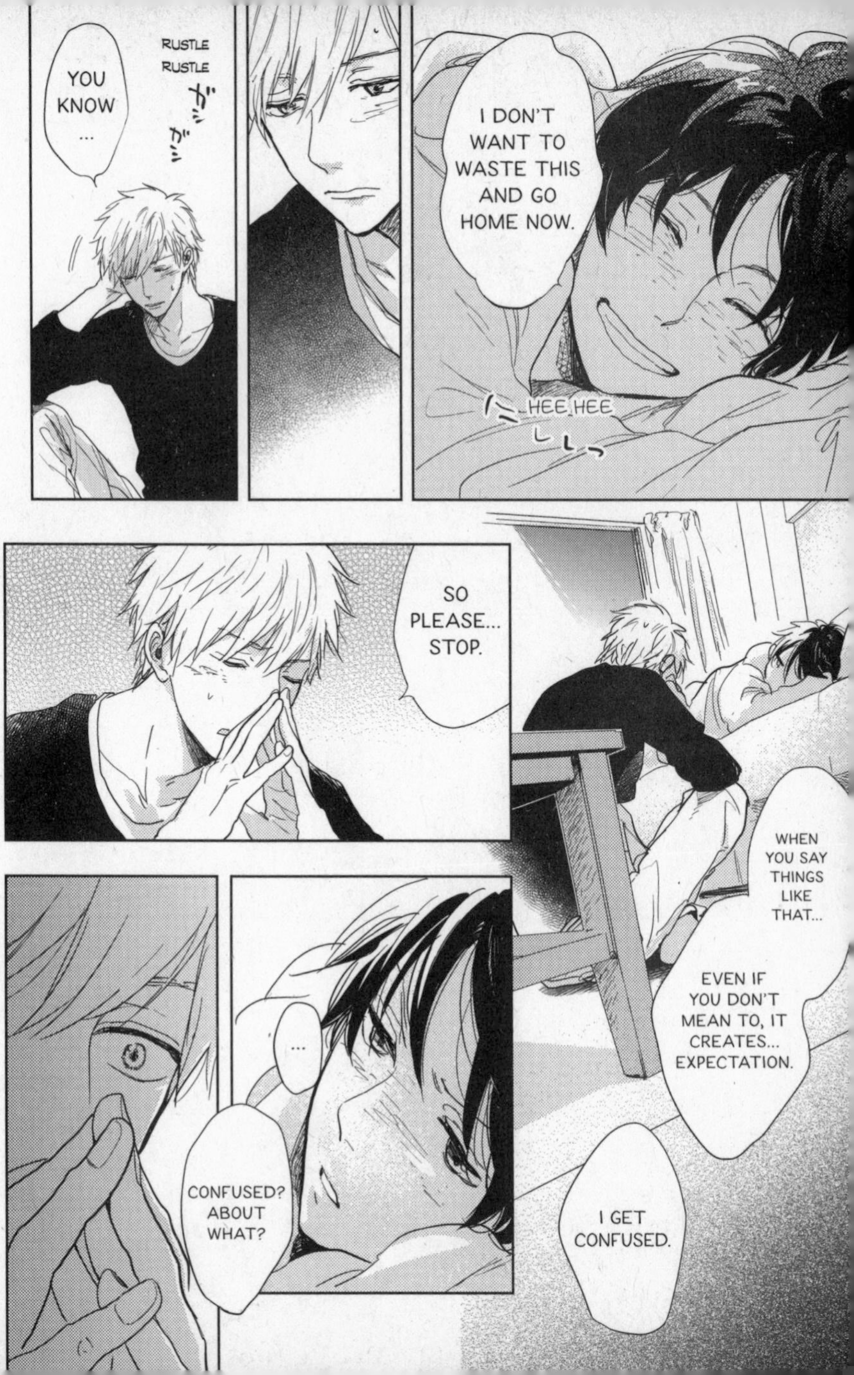
I DON'T WANT TO WASTE THIS AND GO HOME NOW.
HEE HEE
RUSTLE RUSTLE
YOU KNOW ...
WHEN YOU SAY THINGS LIKE THAT...
EVEN IF YOU DON'T MEAN TO, IT CREATES... EXPECTATION.
I GET CONFUSED.
SO PLEASE... STOP.
...
CONFUSED? ABOUT WHAT?

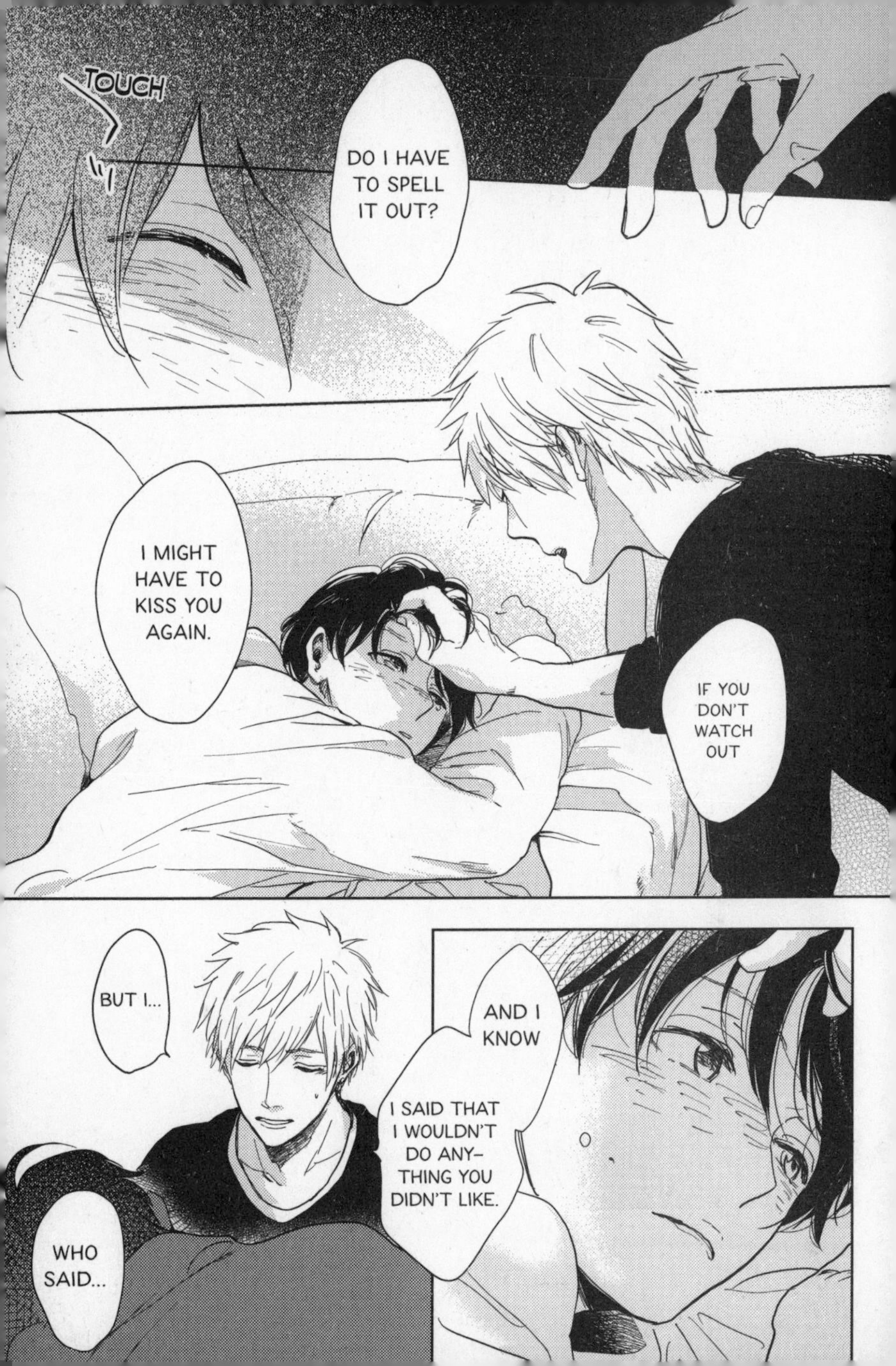
DO I HAVE TO SPELL IT OUT?
TOUCH
IF YOU DON'T WATCH OUT
I MIGHT HAVE TO KISS YOU AGAIN.
AND I KNOW
I SAID THAT I WOULDN'T DO ANY-THING YOU DIDN'T LIKE.
BUT I...
WHO SAID...

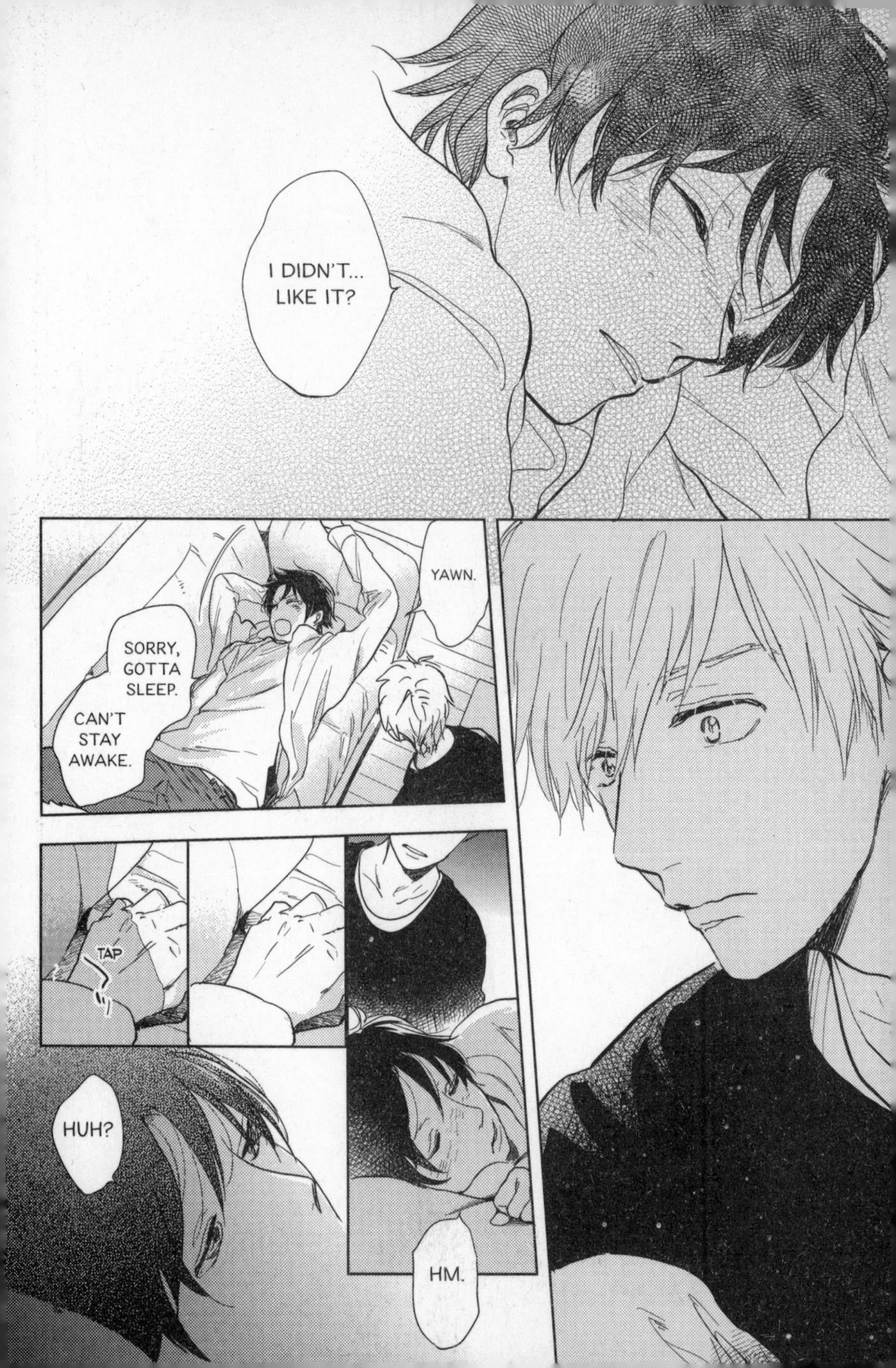
I DIDN'T... LIKE IT?
YAWN.
SORRY, GOTTA SLEEP.
CAN'T STAY AWAKE.
HM.
TAP
HUH?

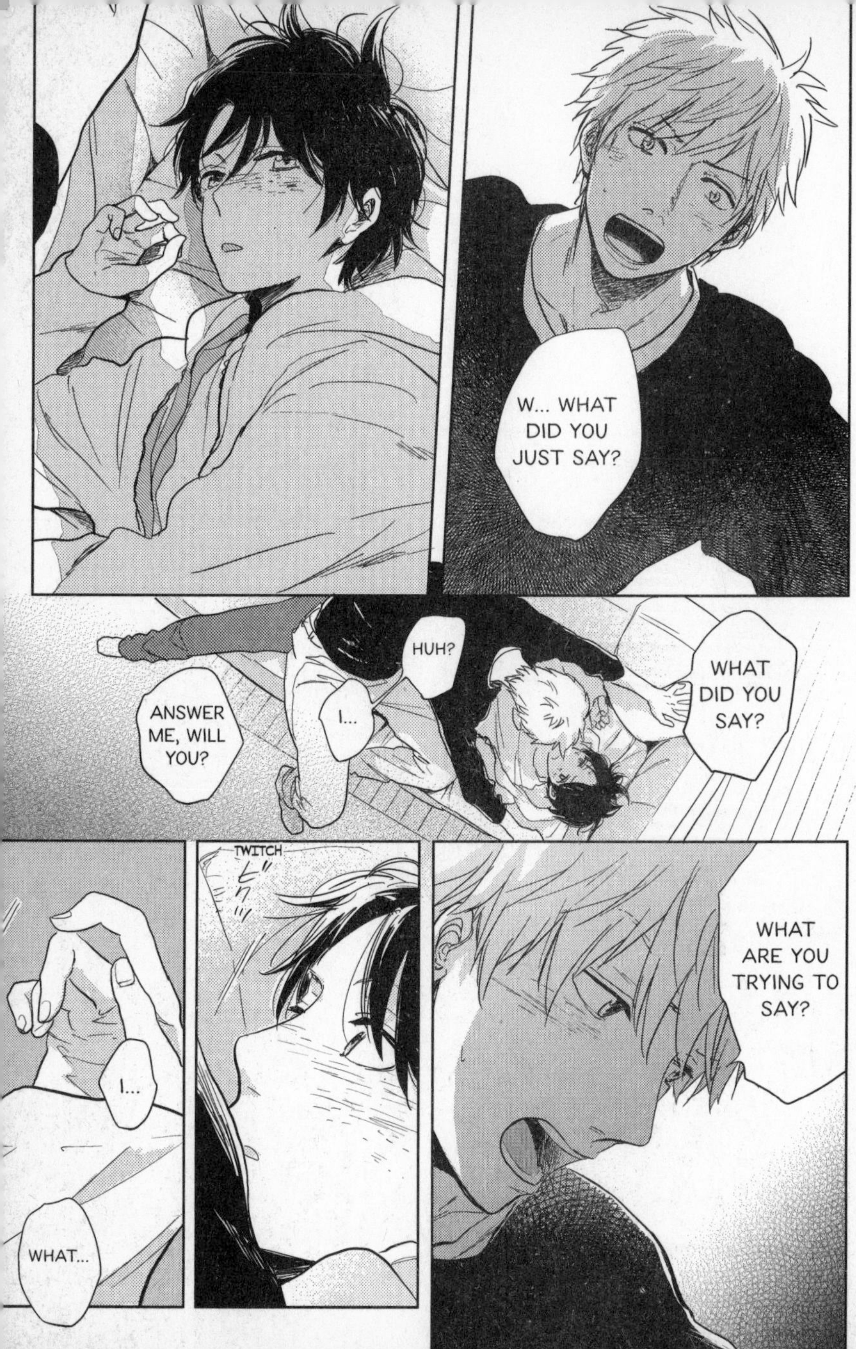
W... WHAT DID YOU JUST SAY?
WHAT DID YOU SAY?
HUH?
I...
ANSWER ME, WILL YOU?
WHAT ARE YOU TRYING TO SAY?
TWITCH
I...
WHAT...

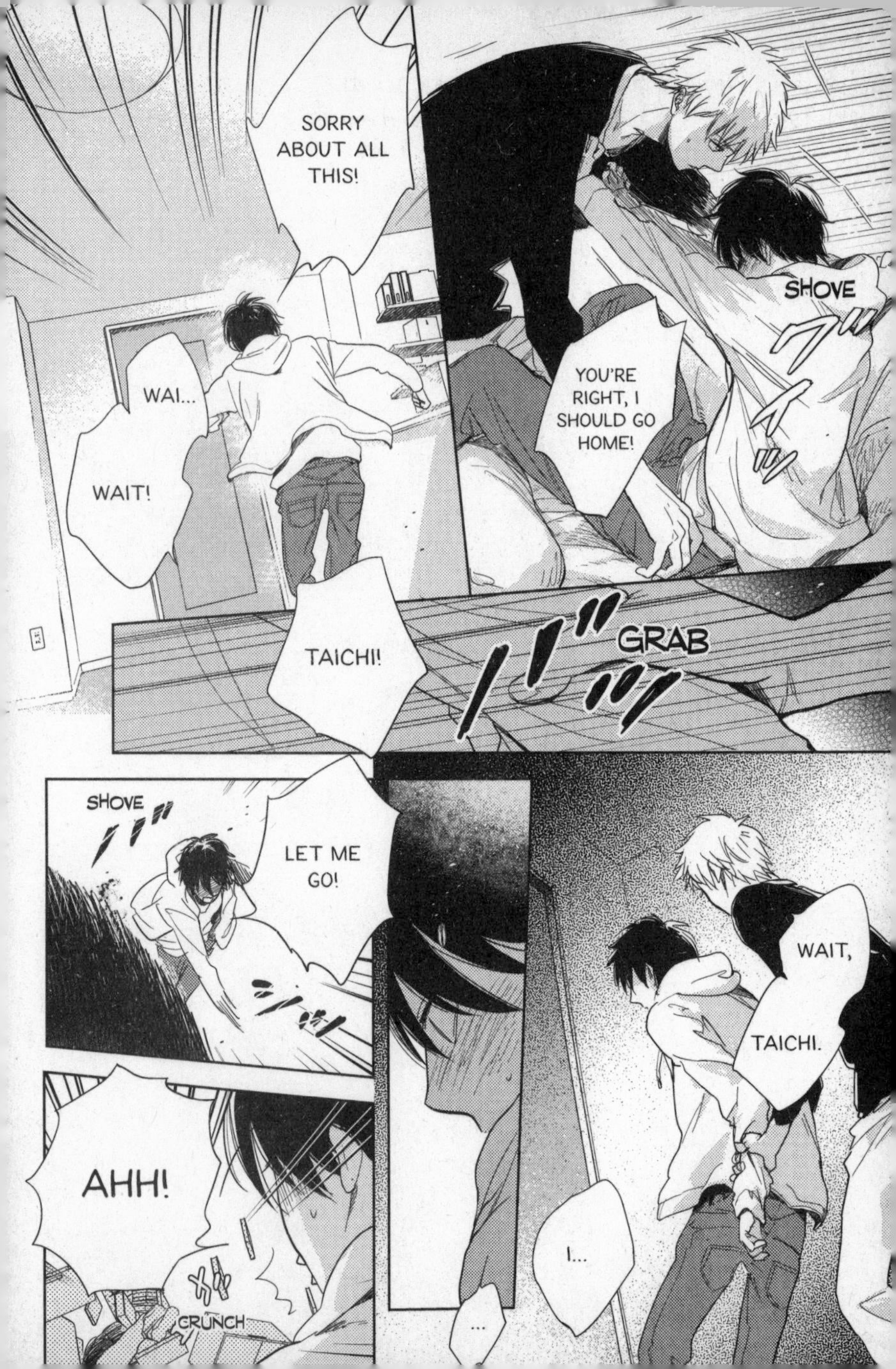
SHOVE
YOU'RE RIGHT, I SHOULD GO HOME!
SORRY ABOUT ALL THIS!
WAI...
WAIT!
TAICHI!
GRAB
WAIT, TAICHI.
I...
...
LET ME GO!
SHOVE
AHH!
CRUNCH

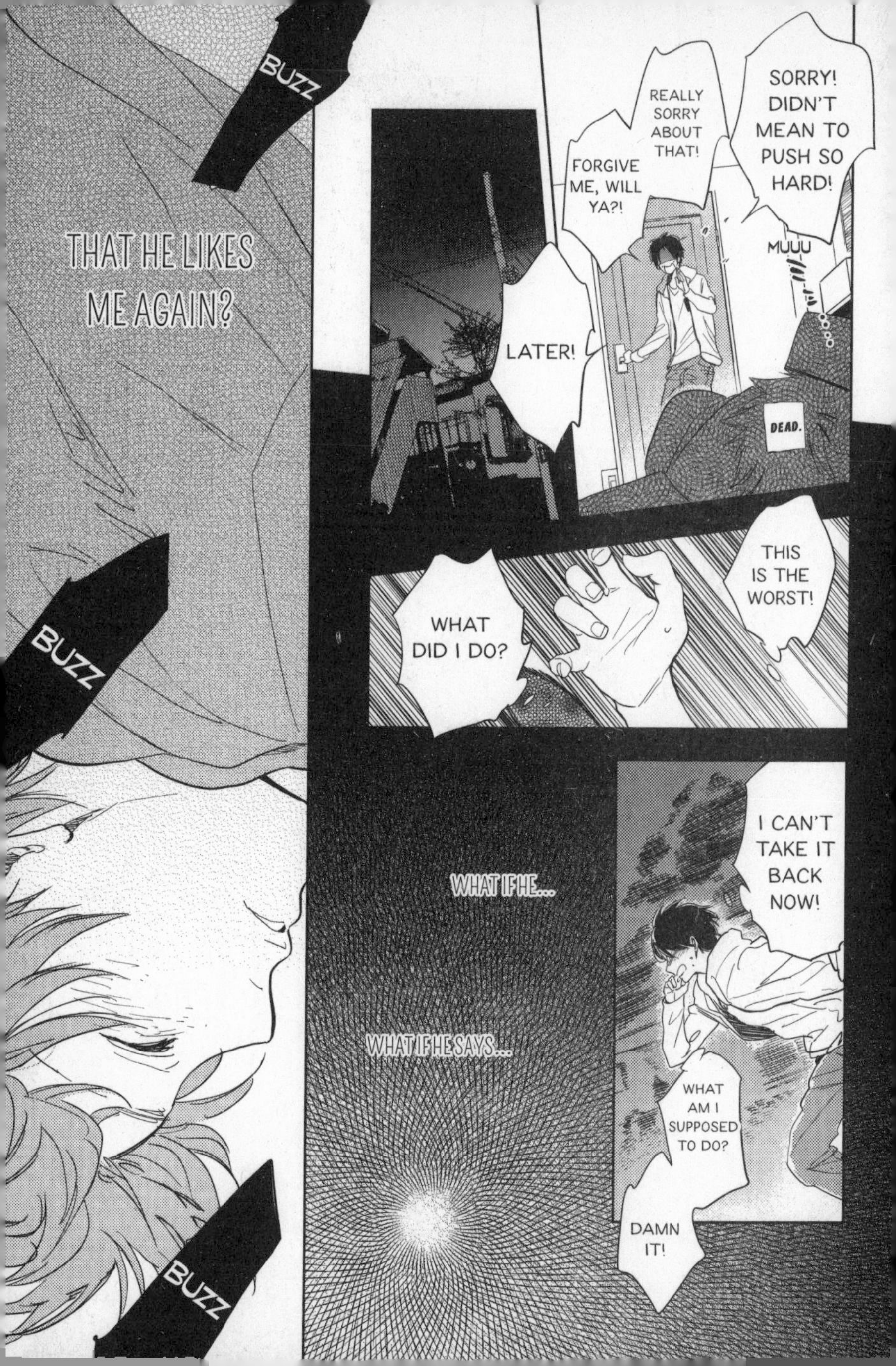
SORRY! DIDN'T MEAN TO PUSH SO HARD!
REALLY SORRY ABOUT THAT!
FORGIVE ME, WILL YA?!
MUUU
DEAD.
LATER!
THIS IS THE WORST!
WHAT DID I DO?
I CAN'T TAKE IT BACK NOW!
WHAT AM I SUPPOSED TO DO?
DAMN IT!
WHAT IF HE...
WHAT IF HE SAYS...
BUZZ
THAT HE LIKES ME AGAIN?
BUZZ
BUZZ

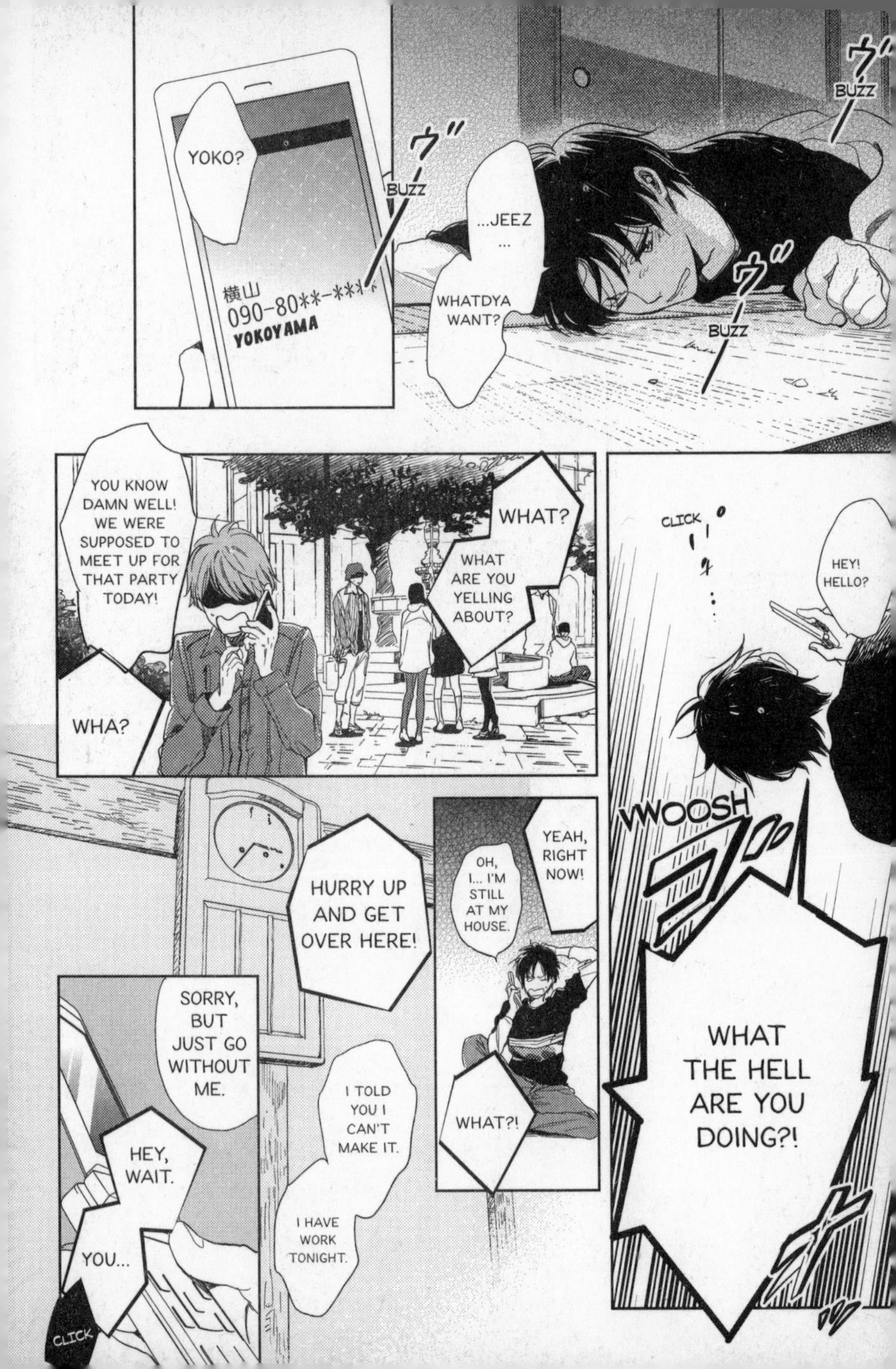
BUZZ
...JEEZ
...
BUZZ
WHATDYA WANT?
YOKO?
横山
090-80**-***
YOKOYAMA
CLICK
HEY! HELLO?
VWOOSH
WHAT THE HELL ARE YOU DOING?!
WHAT?
WHAT ARE YOU YELLING ABOUT?
YOU KNOW DAMN WELL! WE WERE SUPPOSED TO MEET UP FOR THAT PARTY TODAY!
WHA?
YEAH, RIGHT NOW!
OH, I... I'M STILL AT MY HOUSE.
WHAT?!
HURRY UP AND GET OVER HERE!
I TOLD YOU I CAN'T MAKE IT.
I HAVE WORK TONIGHT.
SORRY, BUT JUST GO WITHOUT ME.
HEY, WAIT.
YOU...
CLICK

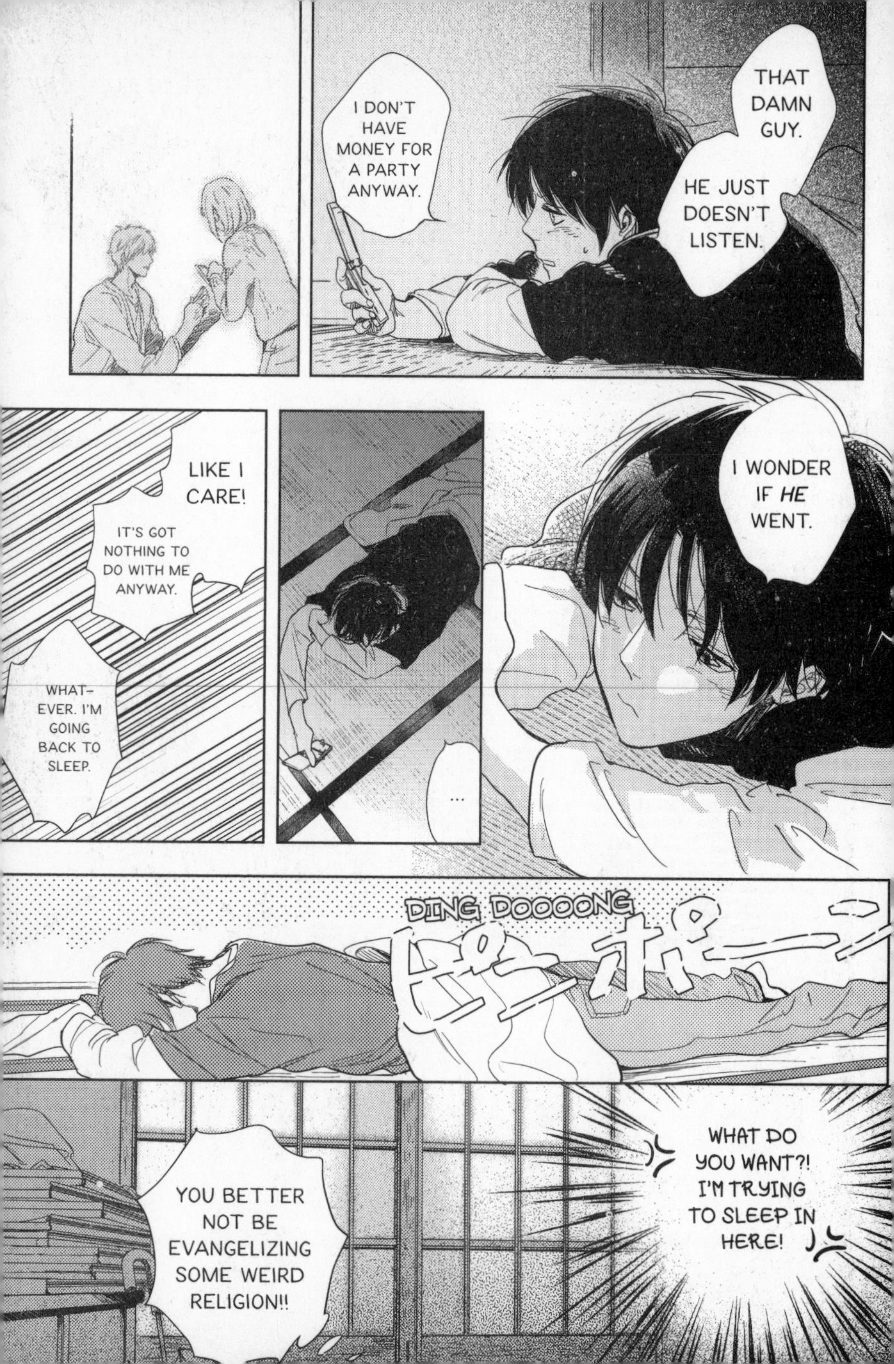
THAT DAMN GUY.
HE JUST DOESN'T LISTEN.
I DON'T HAVE MONEY FOR A PARTY ANYWAY.
I WONDER IF *HE* WENT.
...
LIKE I CARE!
IT'S GOT NOTHING TO DO WITH ME ANYWAY.
WHAT-EVER. I'M GOING BACK TO SLEEP.
DING DOOOOONG
WHAT DO YOU WANT?! I'M TRYING TO SLEEP IN HERE!
YOU BETTER NOT BE EVANGELIZING SOME WEIRD RELIGION!!

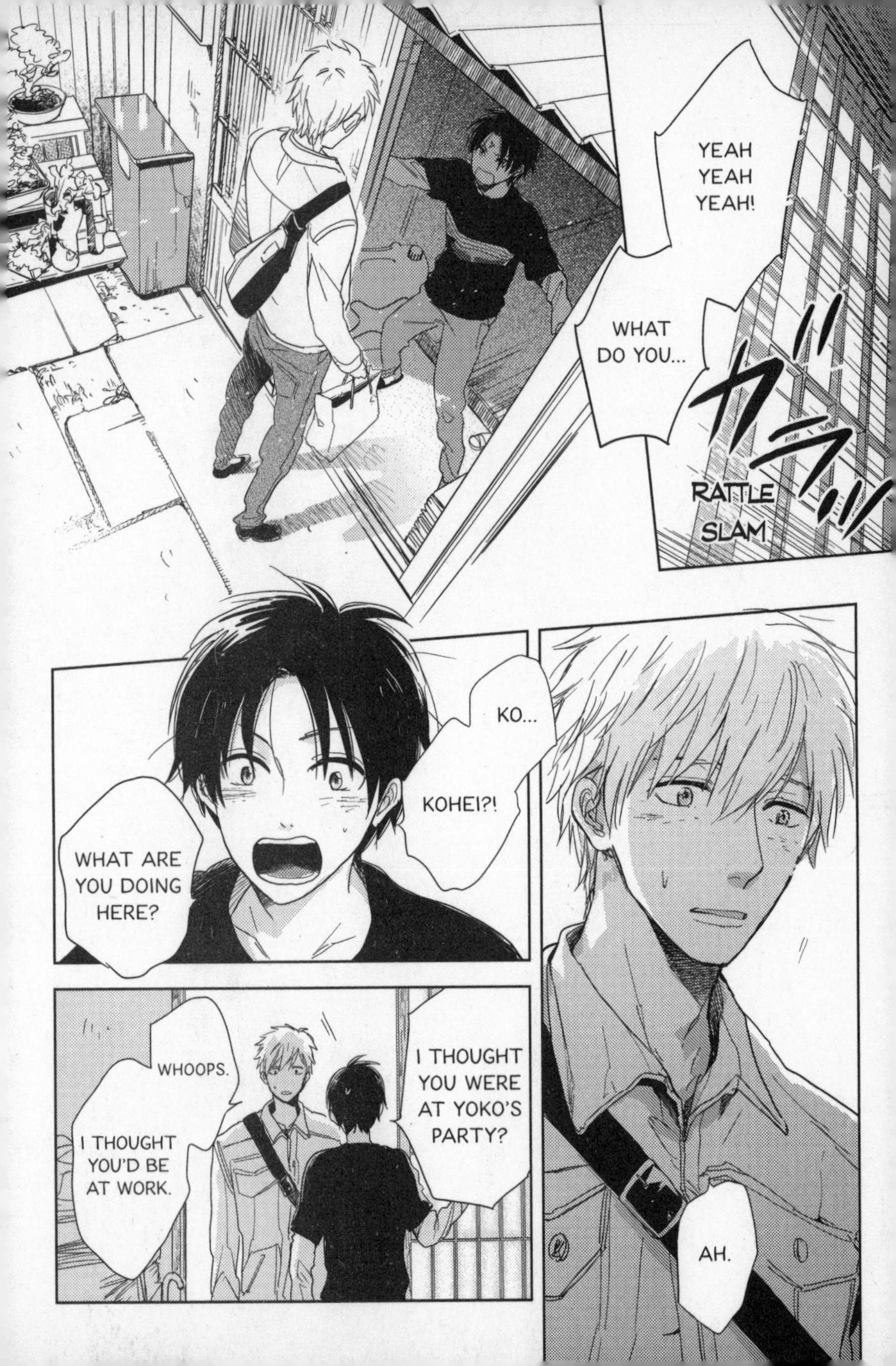
YEAH YEAH YEAH!
WHAT DO YOU...
ガラッ
RATTLE SLAM
AH.
KO...
KOHEI?!
WHAT ARE YOU DOING HERE?
I THOUGHT YOU WERE AT YOKO'S PARTY?
WHOOPS.
I THOUGHT YOU'D BE AT WORK.

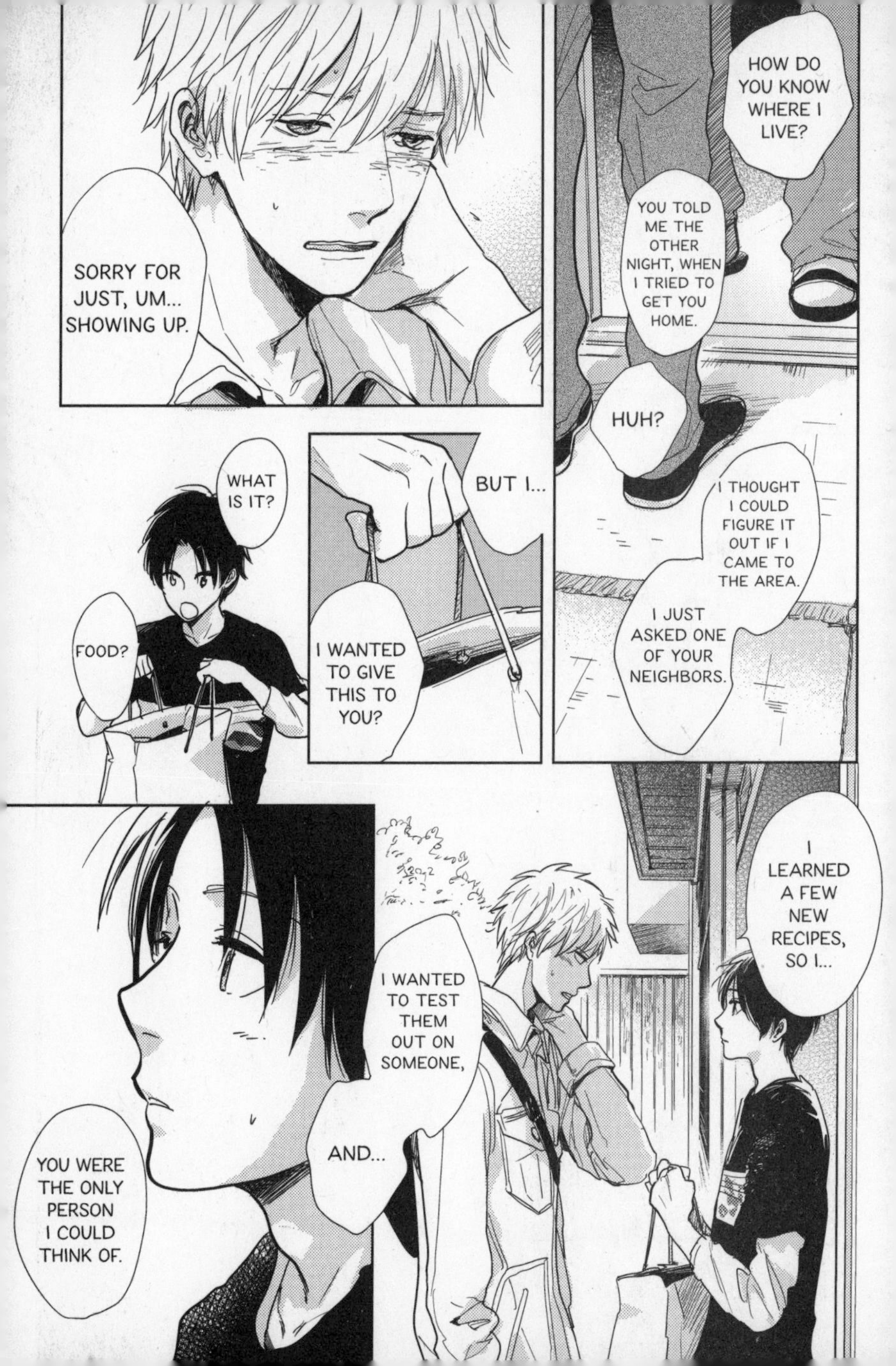
HOW DO YOU KNOW WHERE I LIVE?
YOU TOLD ME THE OTHER NIGHT, WHEN I TRIED TO GET YOU HOME.
HUH?
I THOUGHT I COULD FIGURE IT OUT IF I CAME TO THE AREA.
I JUST ASKED ONE OF YOUR NEIGHBORS.
SORRY FOR JUST, UM... SHOWING UP.
BUT I...
I WANTED TO GIVE THIS TO YOU?
WHAT IS IT?
FOOD?
I LEARNED A FEW NEW RECIPES, SO I...
I WANTED TO TEST THEM OUT ON SOMEONE,
AND...
YOU WERE THE ONLY PERSON I COULD THINK OF.

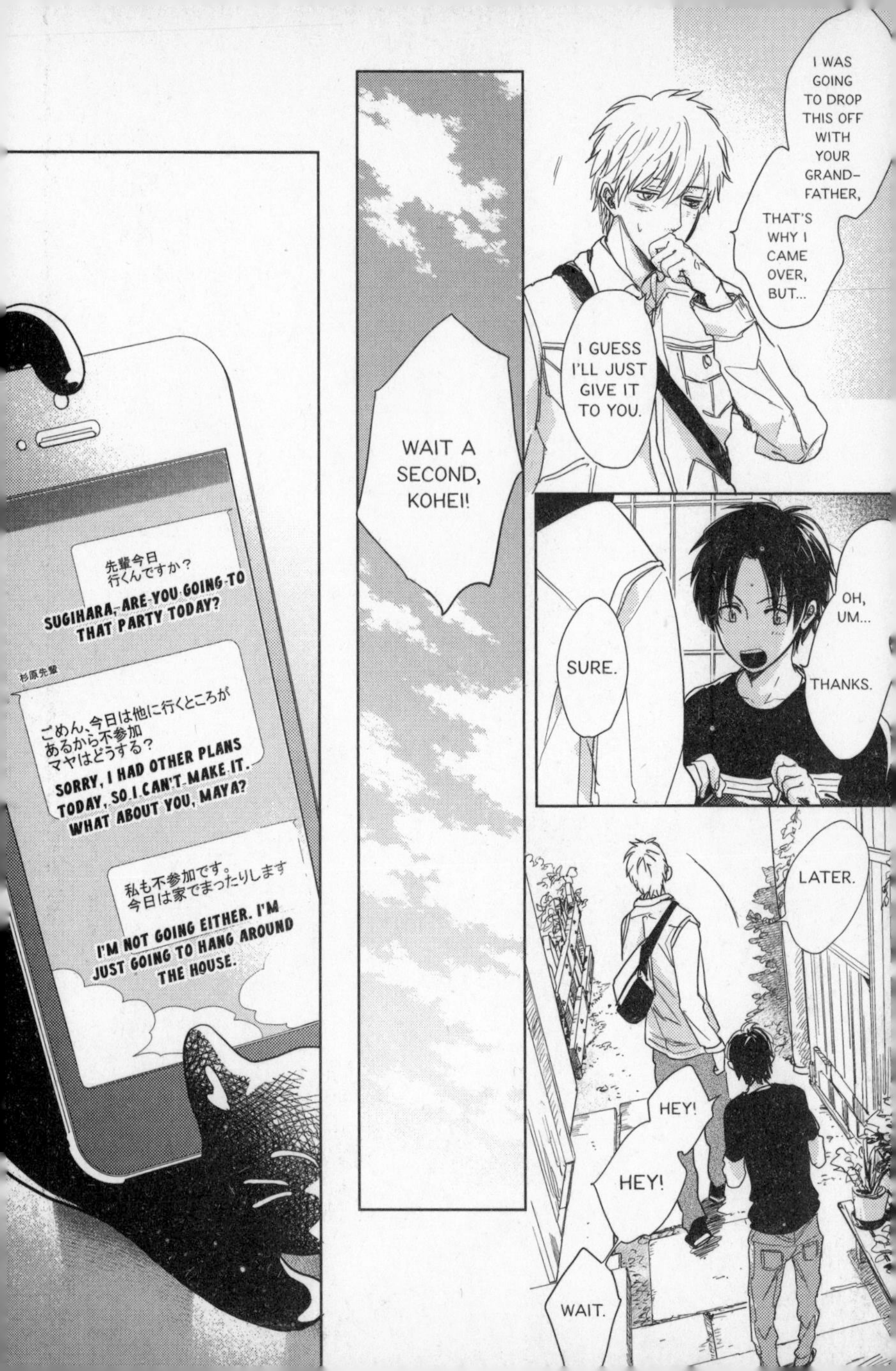
I WAS GOING TO DROP THIS OFF WITH YOUR GRAND-FATHER,
THAT'S WHY I CAME OVER, BUT...
I GUESS I'LL JUST GIVE IT TO YOU.
OH, UM...
THANKS.
SURE.
LATER.
HEY!
HEY!
WAIT.
WAIT A SECOND, KOHEI!
先輩今日行くんですか？
SUGIHARA, ARE YOU GOING TO THAT PARTY TODAY?
杉原先輩
ごめん、今日は他に行くところがあるから不参加
マヤはどうする？
SORRY, I HAD OTHER PLANS TODAY, SO I CAN'T MAKE IT. WHAT ABOUT YOU, MAYA?
私も不参加です。
今日は家でまったりします
I'M NOT GOING EITHER. I'M JUST GOING TO HANG AROUND THE HOUSE.

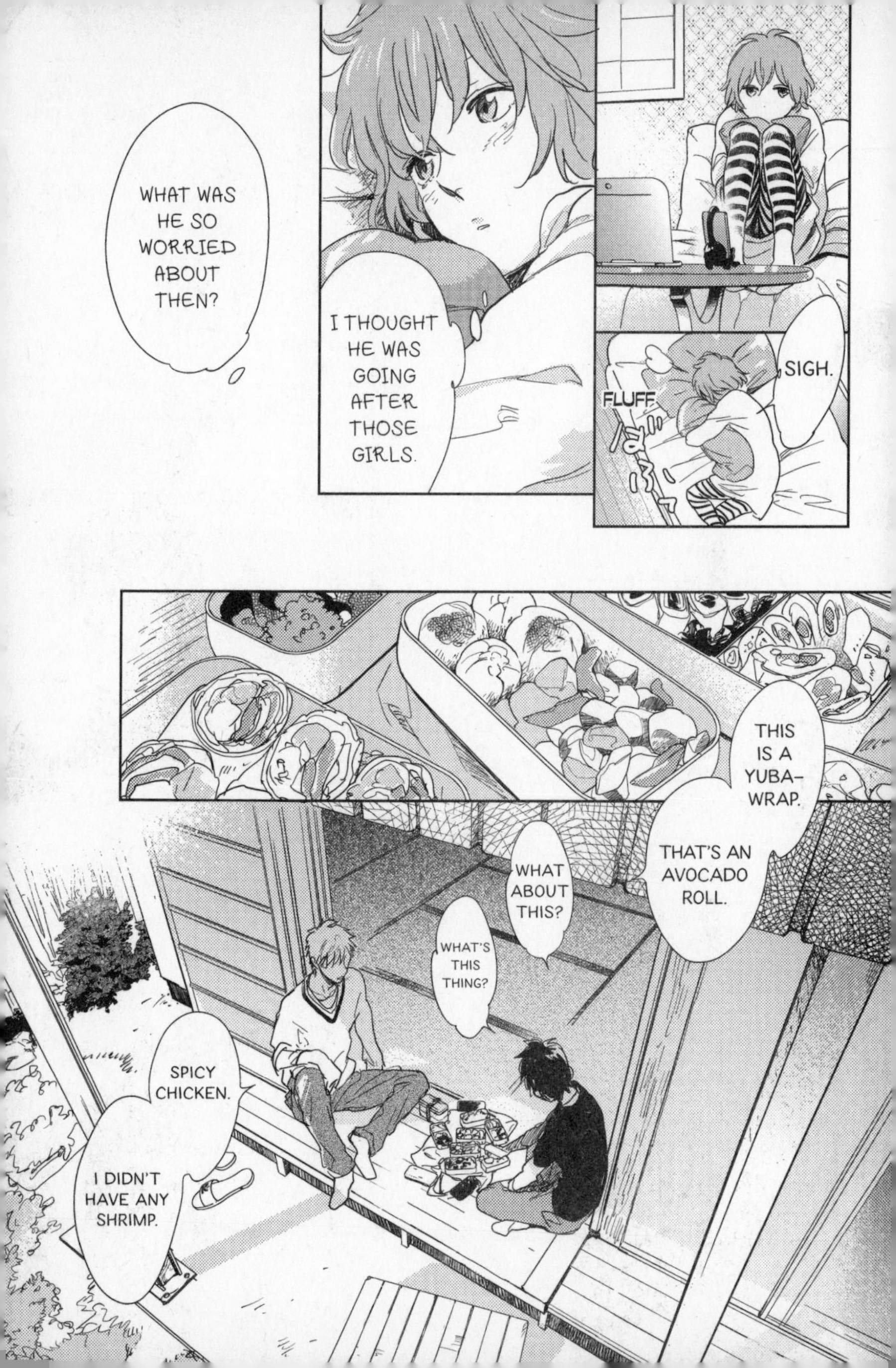
SIGH.
FLUFF
I THOUGHT HE WAS GOING AFTER THOSE GIRLS.
WHAT WAS HE SO WORRIED ABOUT THEN?
THIS IS A YUBA-WRAP.
THAT'S AN AVOCADO ROLL.
WHAT ABOUT THIS?
WHAT'S THIS THING?
SPICY CHICKEN.
I DIDN'T HAVE ANY SHRIMP.

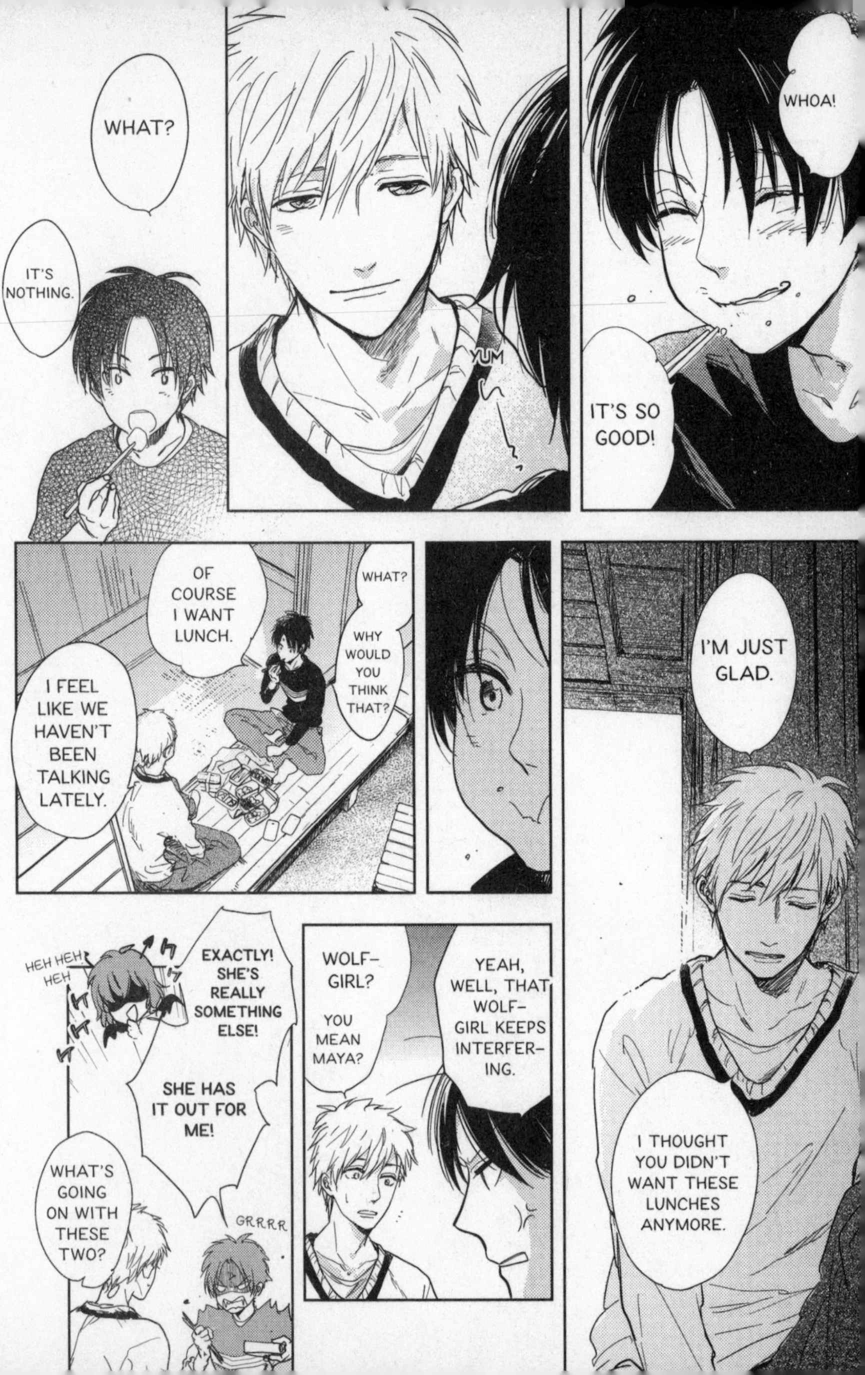
WHOA!
IT'S SO GOOD!
YUM
WHAT?
IT'S NOTHING.
I'M JUST GLAD.
I THOUGHT YOU DIDN'T WANT THESE LUNCHES ANYMORE.
WHAT?
WHY WOULD YOU THINK THAT?
OF COURSE I WANT LUNCH.
I FEEL LIKE WE HAVEN'T BEEN TALKING LATELY.
YEAH, WELL, THAT WOLF-GIRL KEEPS INTERFER-ING.
WOLF-GIRL?
YOU MEAN MAYA?
EXACTLY! SHE'S REALLY SOMETHING ELSE!
HEH HEH HEH
SHE HAS IT OUT FOR ME!
GRRRR
WHAT'S GOING ON WITH THESE TWO?

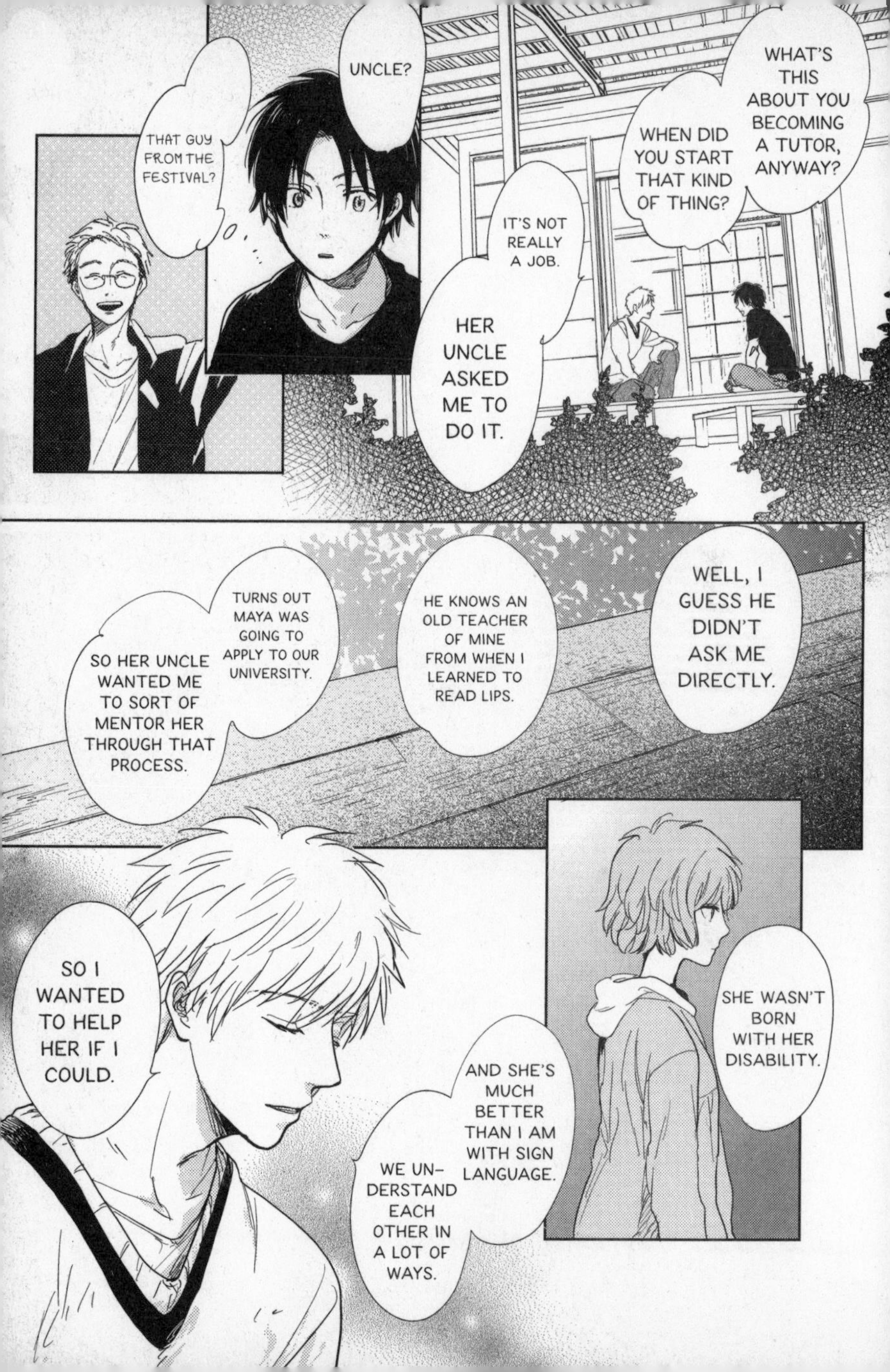
WHAT'S THIS ABOUT YOU BECOMING A TUTOR, ANYWAY?
WHEN DID YOU START THAT KIND OF THING?
IT'S NOT REALLY A JOB.
HER UNCLE ASKED ME TO DO IT.
UNCLE?
THAT GUY FROM THE FESTIVAL?
WELL, I GUESS HE DIDN'T ASK ME DIRECTLY.
HE KNOWS AN OLD TEACHER OF MINE FROM WHEN I LEARNED TO READ LIPS.
TURNS OUT MAYA WAS GOING TO APPLY TO OUR UNIVERSITY.
SO HER UNCLE WANTED ME TO SORT OF MENTOR HER THROUGH THAT PROCESS.
SHE WASN'T BORN WITH HER DISABILITY.
AND SHE'S MUCH BETTER THAN I AM WITH SIGN LANGUAGE.
WE UN-DERSTAND EACH OTHER IN A LOT OF WAYS.
SO I WANTED TO HELP HER IF I COULD.

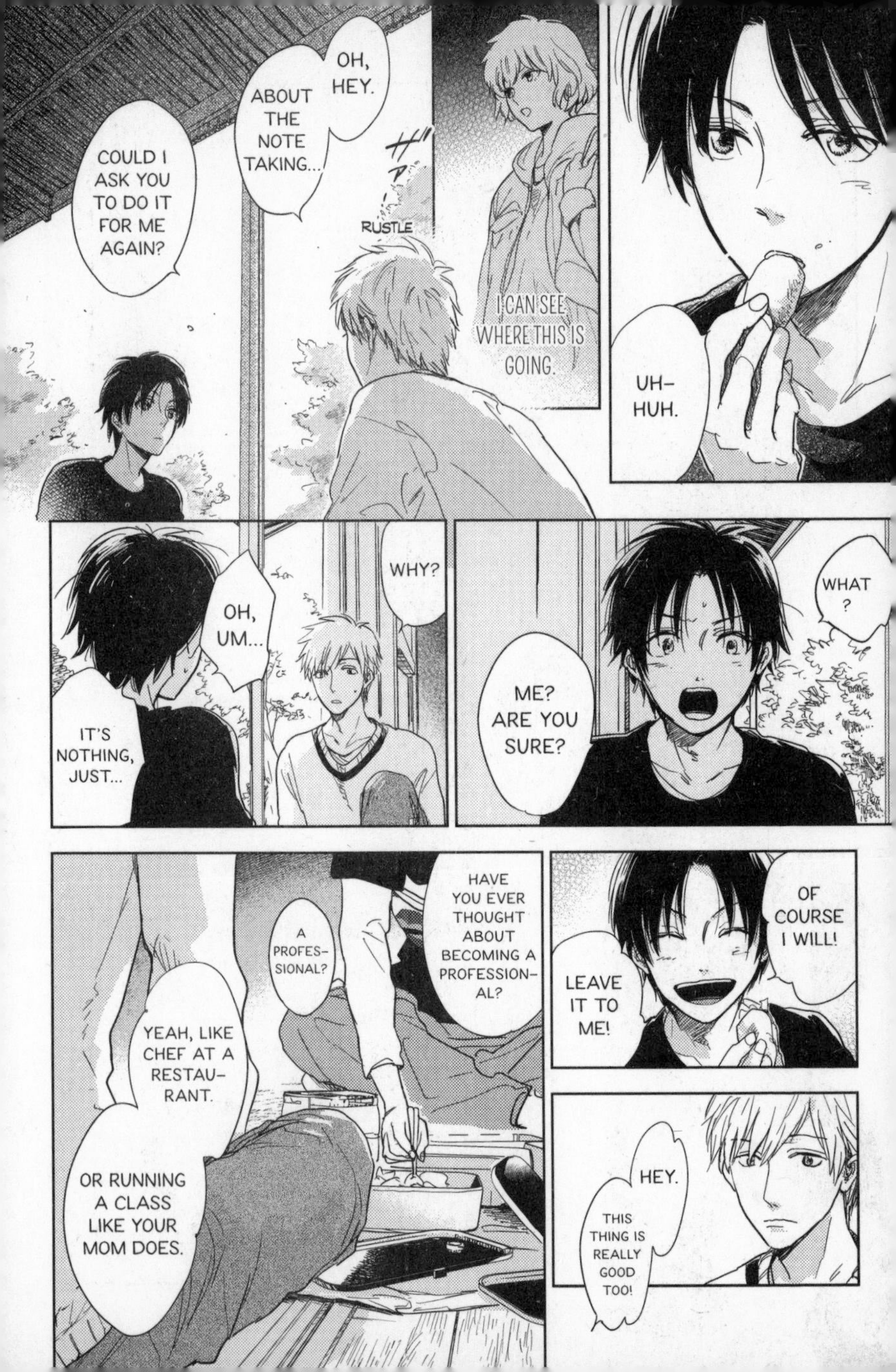
UH-HUH.
I CAN SEE WHERE THIS IS GOING.
OH, HEY.
ABOUT THE NOTE TAKING...
ザッ
RUSTLE
COULD I ASK YOU TO DO IT FOR ME AGAIN?
WHAT?
ME? ARE YOU SURE?
WHY?
OH, UM...
IT'S NOTHING, JUST...
OF COURSE I WILL!
LEAVE IT TO ME!
HEY.
THIS THING IS REALLY GOOD TOO!
HAVE YOU EVER THOUGHT ABOUT BECOMING A PROFESSIONAL?
A PROFESSIONAL?
YEAH, LIKE CHEF AT A RESTAURANT.
OR RUNNING A CLASS LIKE YOUR MOM DOES.

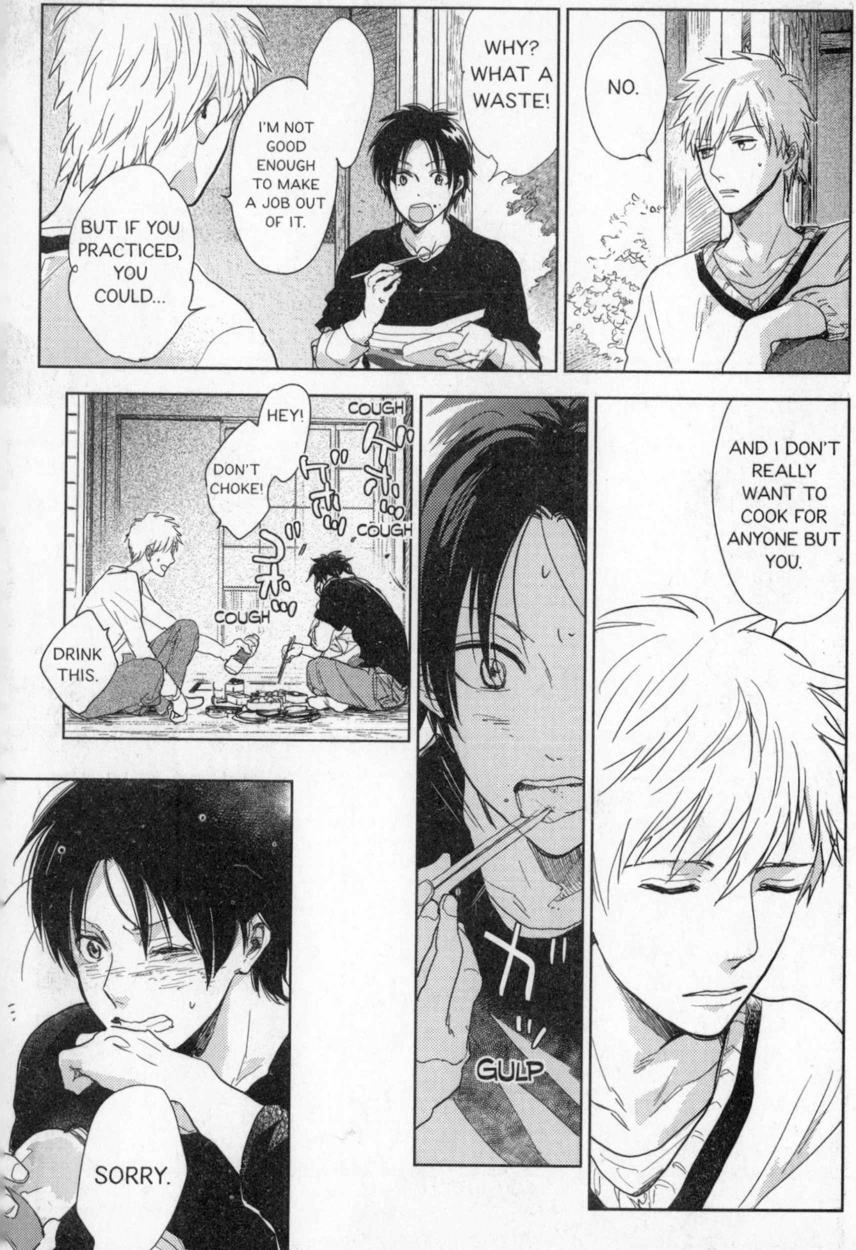
NO.
WHY? WHAT A WASTE!
I'M NOT GOOD ENOUGH TO MAKE A JOB OUT OF IT.
BUT IF YOU PRACTICED, YOU COULD...
AND I DON'T REALLY WANT TO COOK FOR ANYONE BUT YOU.
GULP
COUGH
HEY!
COUGH
DON'T CHOKE!
COUGH
DRINK THIS.
SORRY.

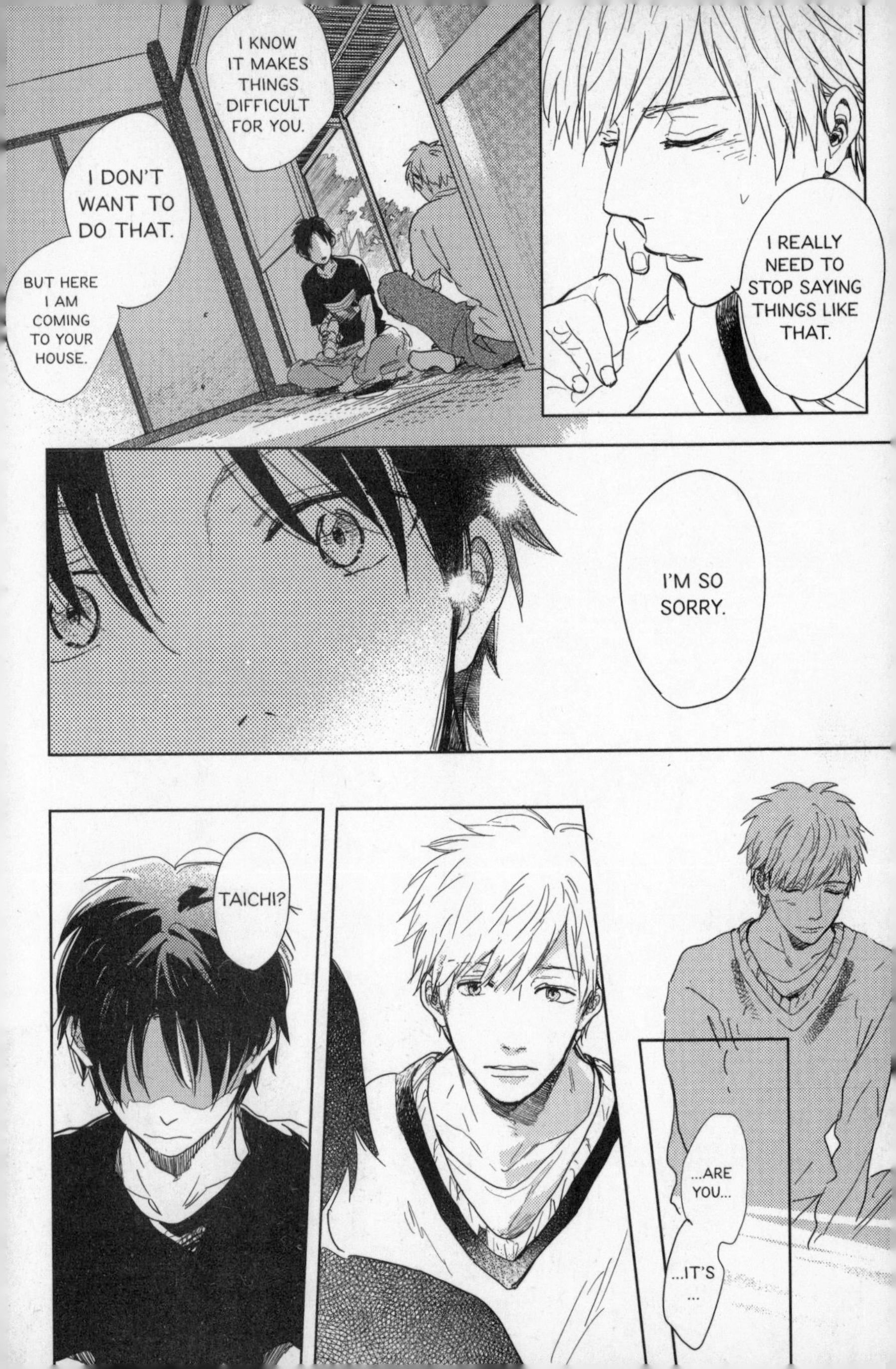
I REALLY NEED TO STOP SAYING THINGS LIKE THAT.
I KNOW IT MAKES THINGS DIFFICULT FOR YOU.
I DON'T WANT TO DO THAT.
BUT HERE I AM COMING TO YOUR HOUSE.
I'M SO SORRY.
...ARE YOU...
...IT'S ...
TAICHI?

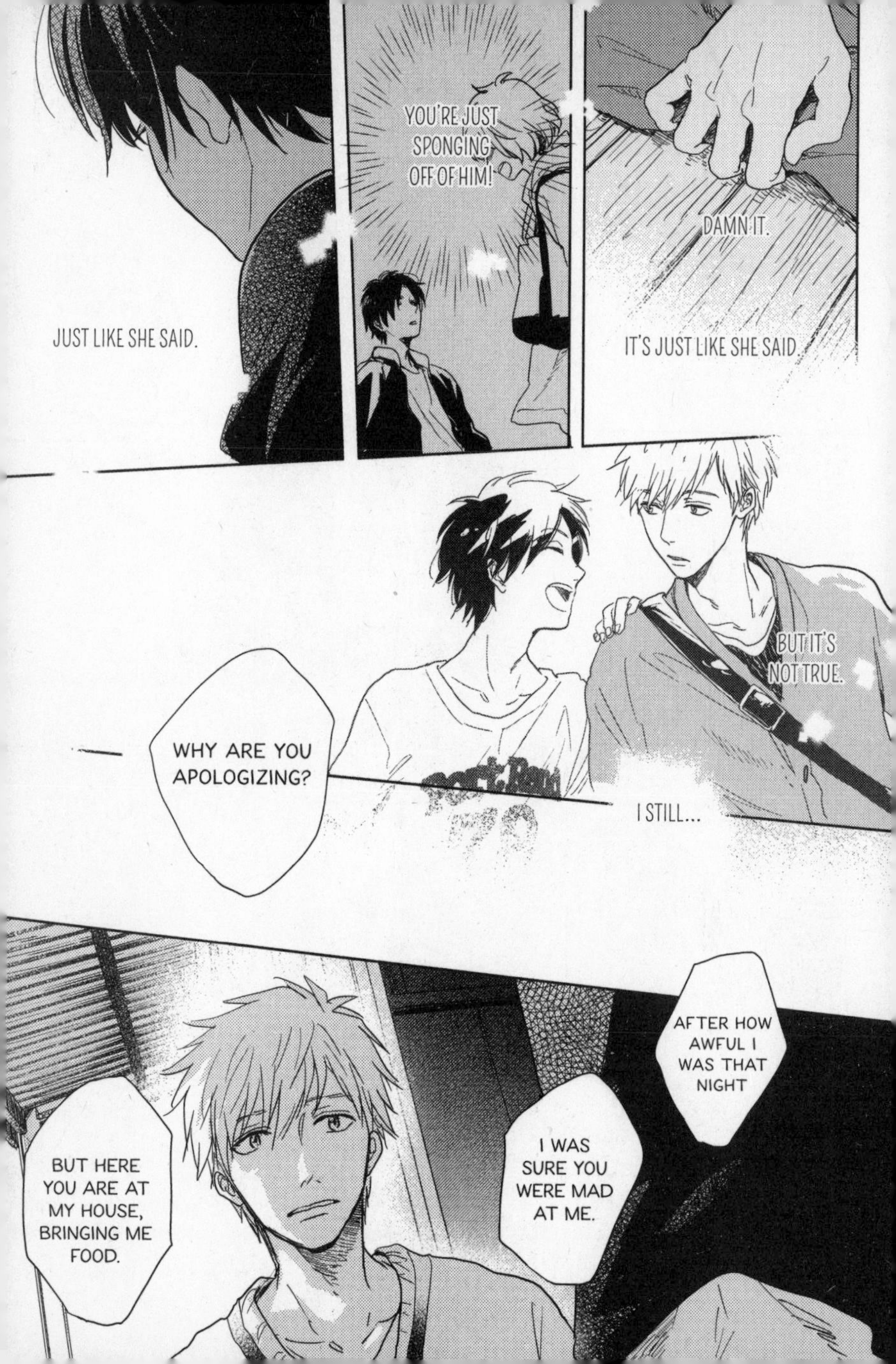
DAMN IT.
IT'S JUST LIKE SHE SAID.
YOU'RE JUST SPONGING OFF OF HIM!
JUST LIKE SHE SAID.
BUT IT'S NOT TRUE.
I STILL...
WHY ARE YOU APOLOGIZING?
AFTER HOW AWFUL I WAS THAT NIGHT
I WAS SURE YOU WERE MAD AT ME.
BUT HERE YOU ARE AT MY HOUSE, BRINGING ME FOOD.

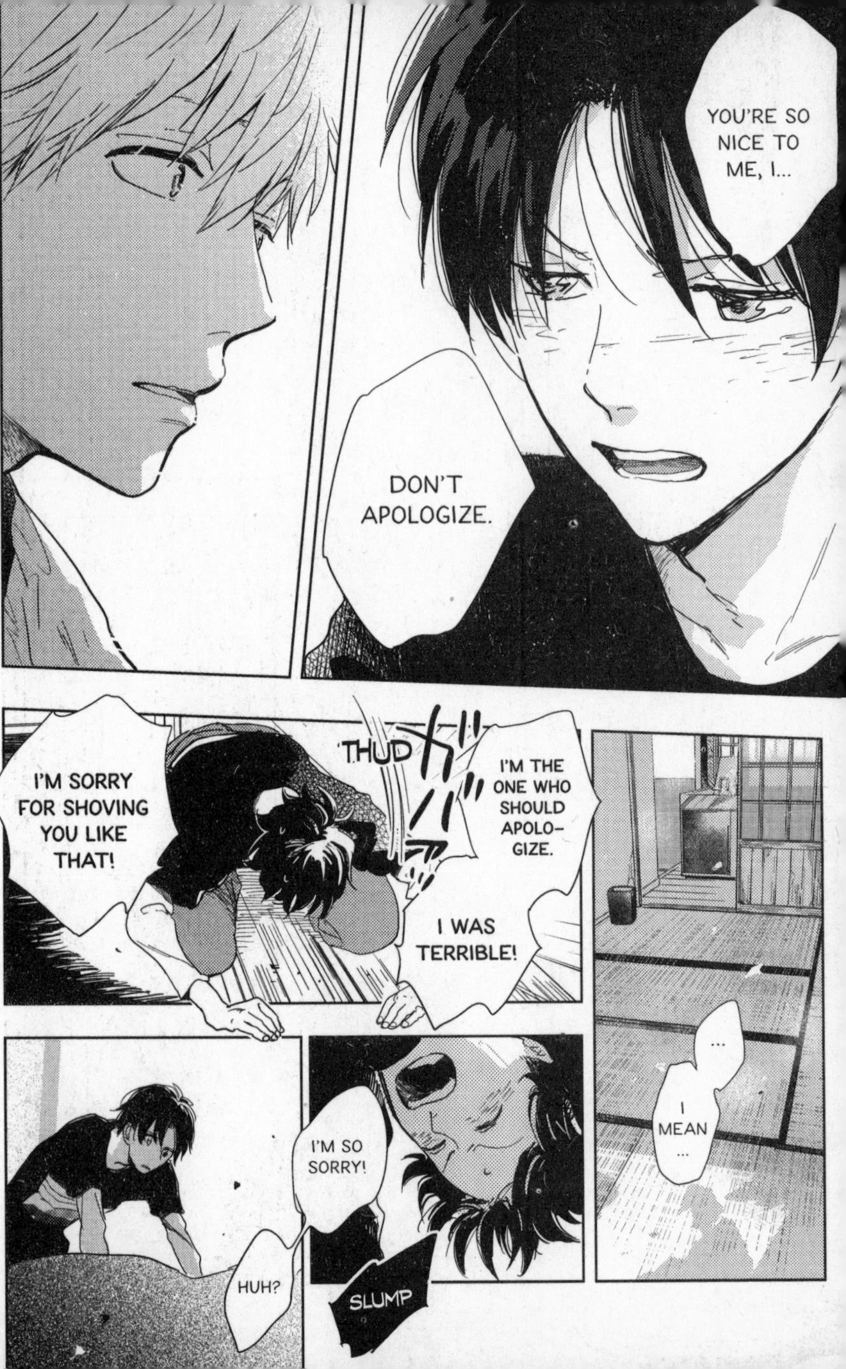
YOU'RE SO NICE TO ME, I...
DON'T APOLOGIZE.
...
I MEAN ...
THUD
I'M THE ONE WHO SHOULD APOLOGIZE.
I WAS TERRIBLE!
I'M SORRY FOR SHOVING YOU LIKE THAT!
I'M SO SORRY!
SLUMP
HUH?

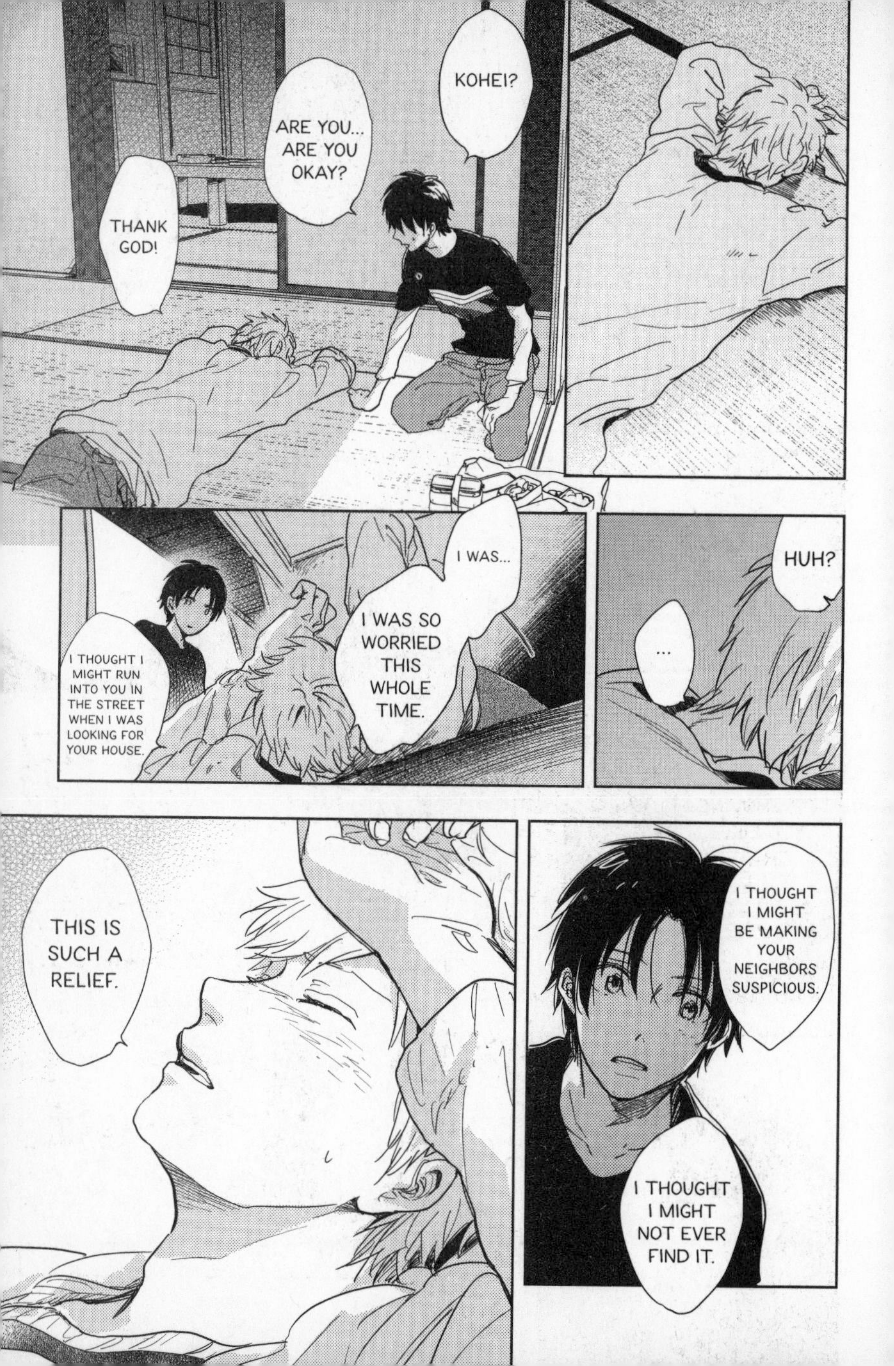
KOHEI?
ARE YOU... ARE YOU OKAY?
THANK GOD!
HUH?
...
I WAS...
I WAS SO WORRIED THIS WHOLE TIME.
I THOUGHT I MIGHT RUN INTO YOU IN THE STREET WHEN I WAS LOOKING FOR YOUR HOUSE.
I THOUGHT I MIGHT BE MAKING YOUR NEIGHBORS SUSPICIOUS.
I THOUGHT I MIGHT NOT EVER FIND IT.
THIS IS SUCH A RELIEF.

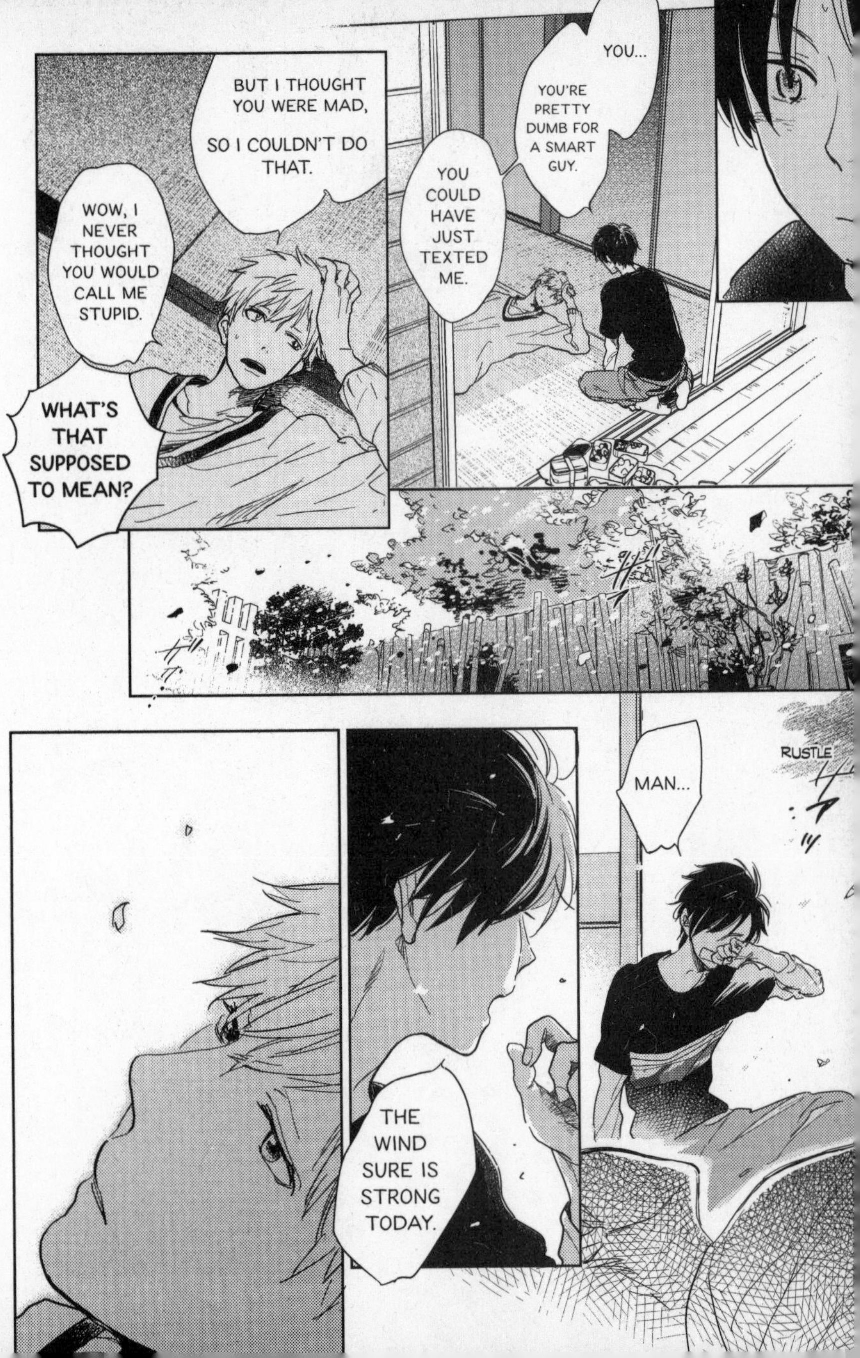
YOU...
YOU'RE PRETTY DUMB FOR A SMART GUY.
YOU COULD HAVE JUST TEXTED ME.
BUT I THOUGHT YOU WERE MAD,
SO I COULDN'T DO THAT.
WOW, I NEVER THOUGHT YOU WOULD CALL ME STUPID.
WHAT'S THAT SUPPOSED TO MEAN?
RUSTLE
MAN...
THE WIND SURE IS STRONG TODAY.

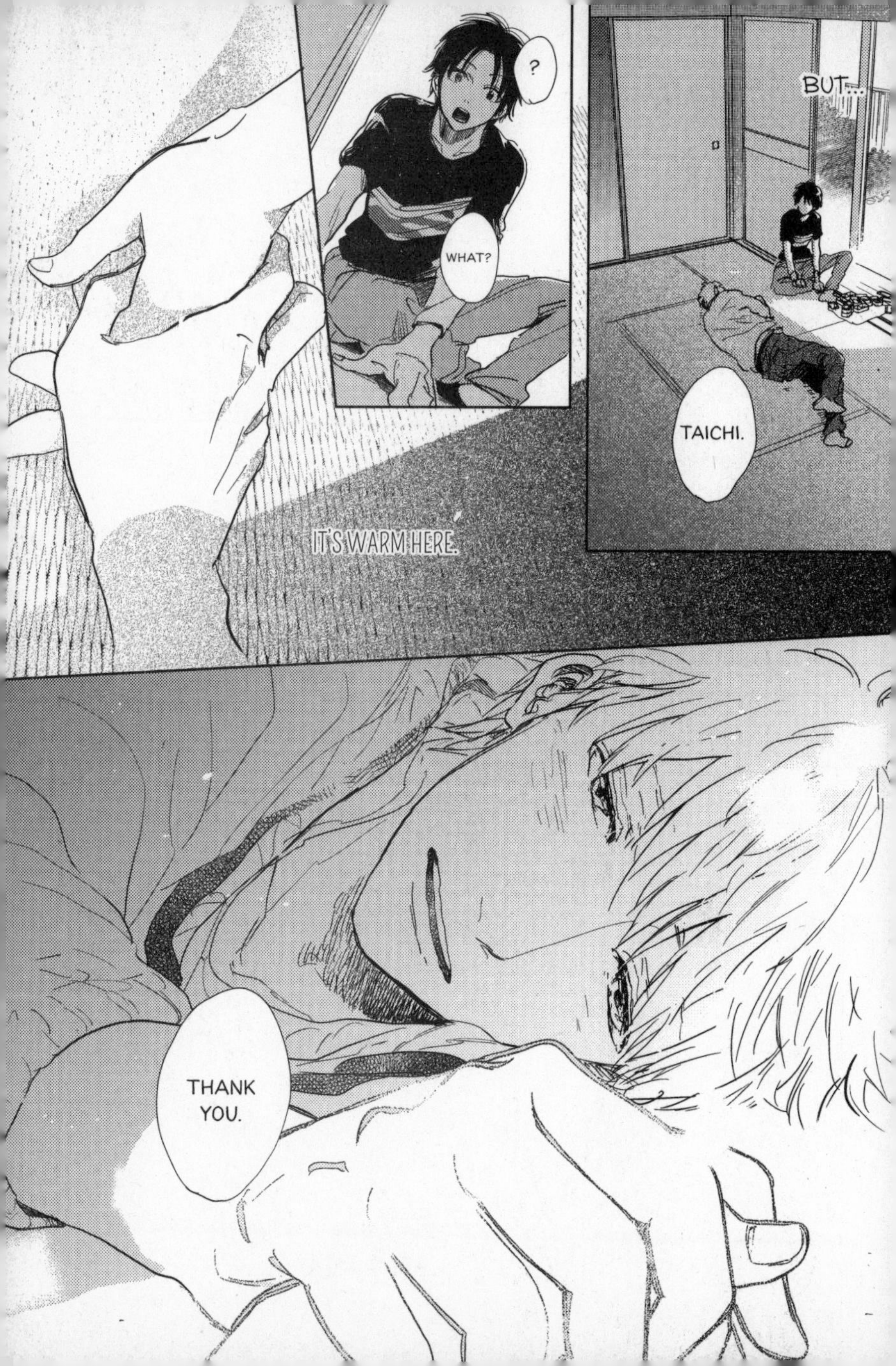
BUT...
TAICHI.
?
WHAT?
IT'S WARM HERE.
THANK YOU.

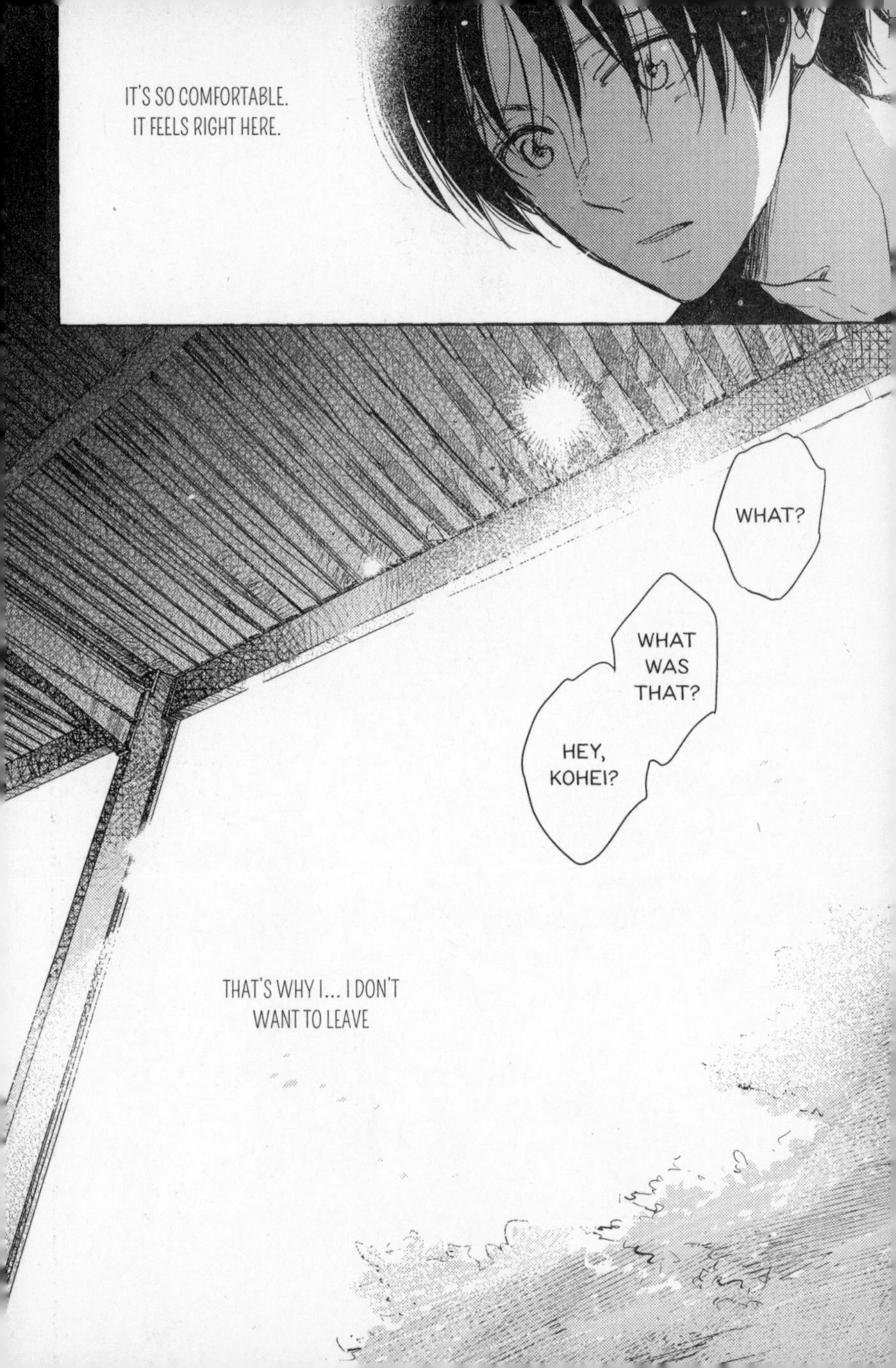
IT'S SO COMFORTABLE. IT FEELS RIGHT HERE.
WHAT?
WHAT WAS THAT?
HEY, KOHEI?
THAT'S WHY I... I DON'T WANT TO LEAVE

i hear
the
sunspot

i hear the sunspot

CHAPTER 3

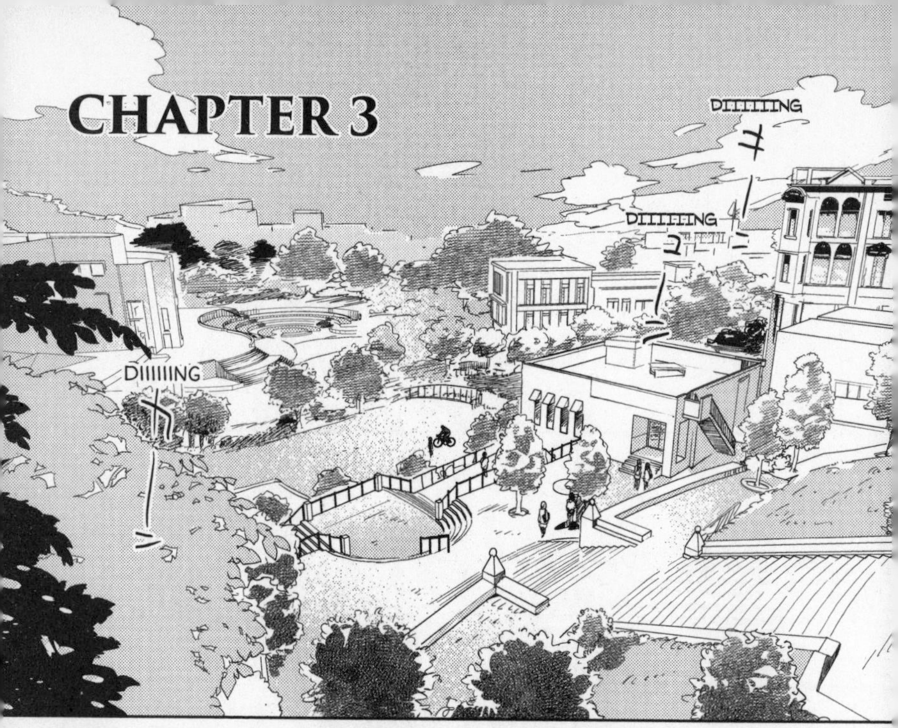
DIIIIIING
DIIIIIING
DIIIIIING

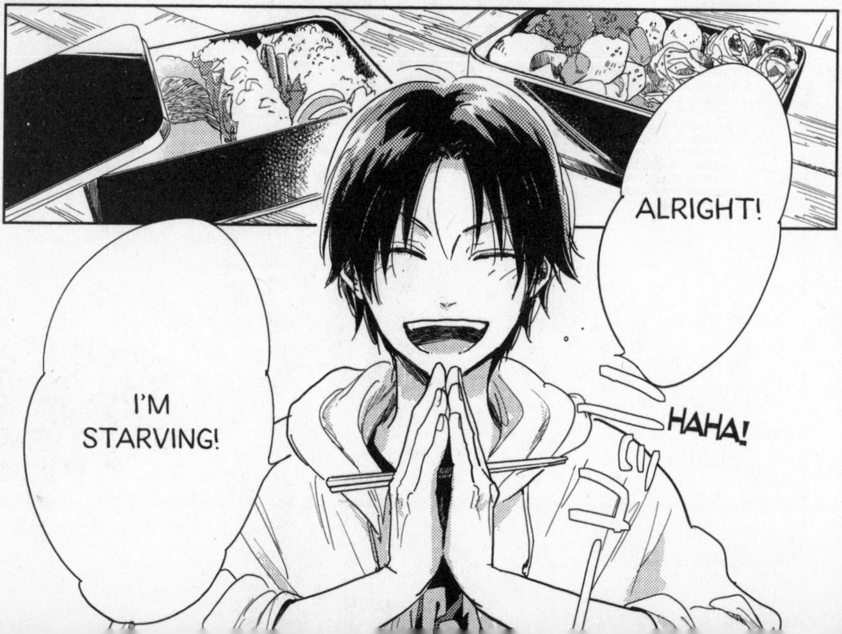
ALRIGHT!
HAHA!
I'M STARVING!

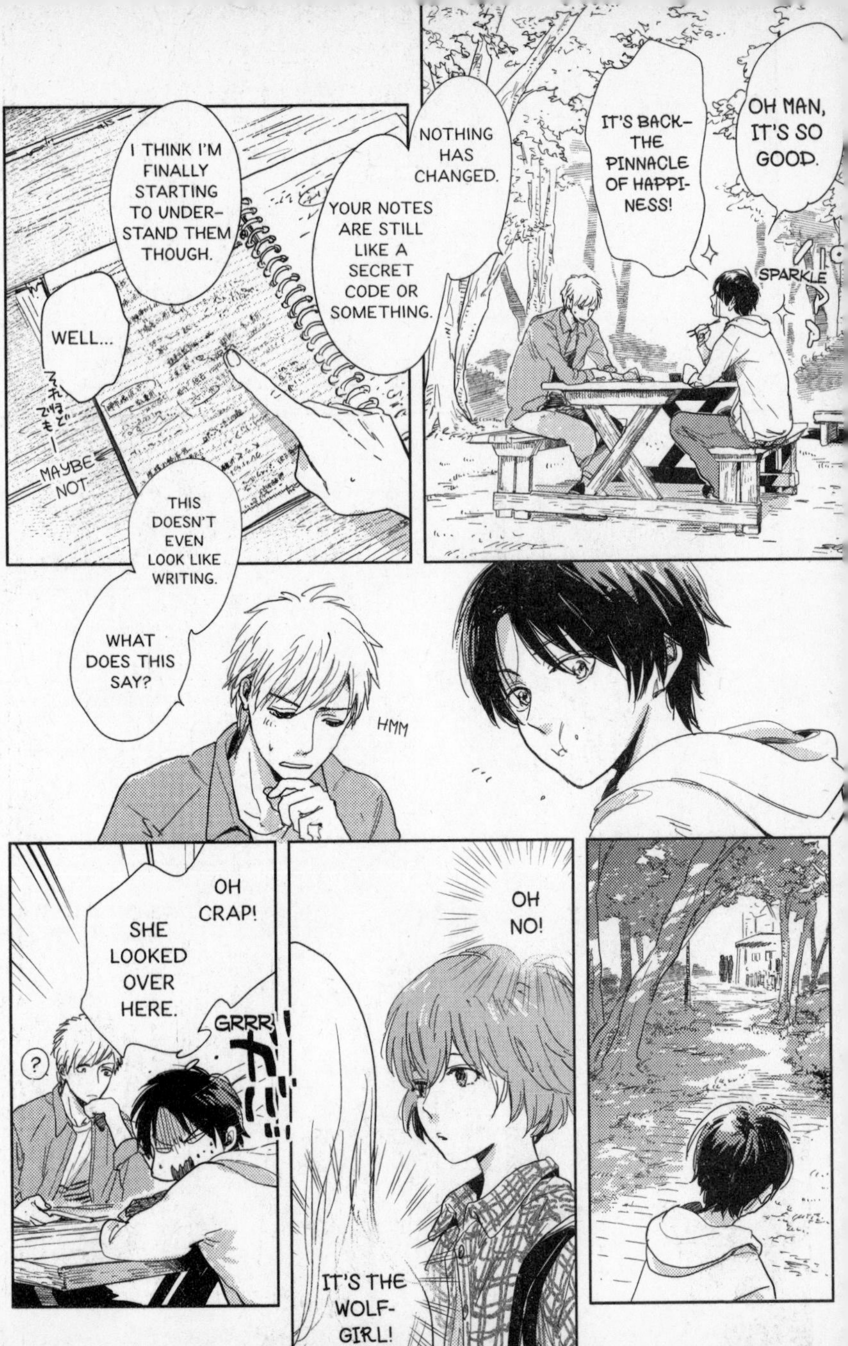
OH MAN, IT'S SO GOOD.
IT'S BACK— THE PINNACLE OF HAPPINESS!
SPARKLE
NOTHING HAS CHANGED.
YOUR NOTES ARE STILL LIKE A SECRET CODE OR SOMETHING.
I THINK I'M FINALLY STARTING TO UNDERSTAND THEM THOUGH.
WELL...
MAYBE NOT
THIS DOESN'T EVEN LOOK LIKE WRITING.
WHAT DOES THIS SAY?
HMM
...
OH NO!
IT'S THE WOLF-GIRL!
OH CRAP! SHE LOOKED OVER HERE.
GRRR
?

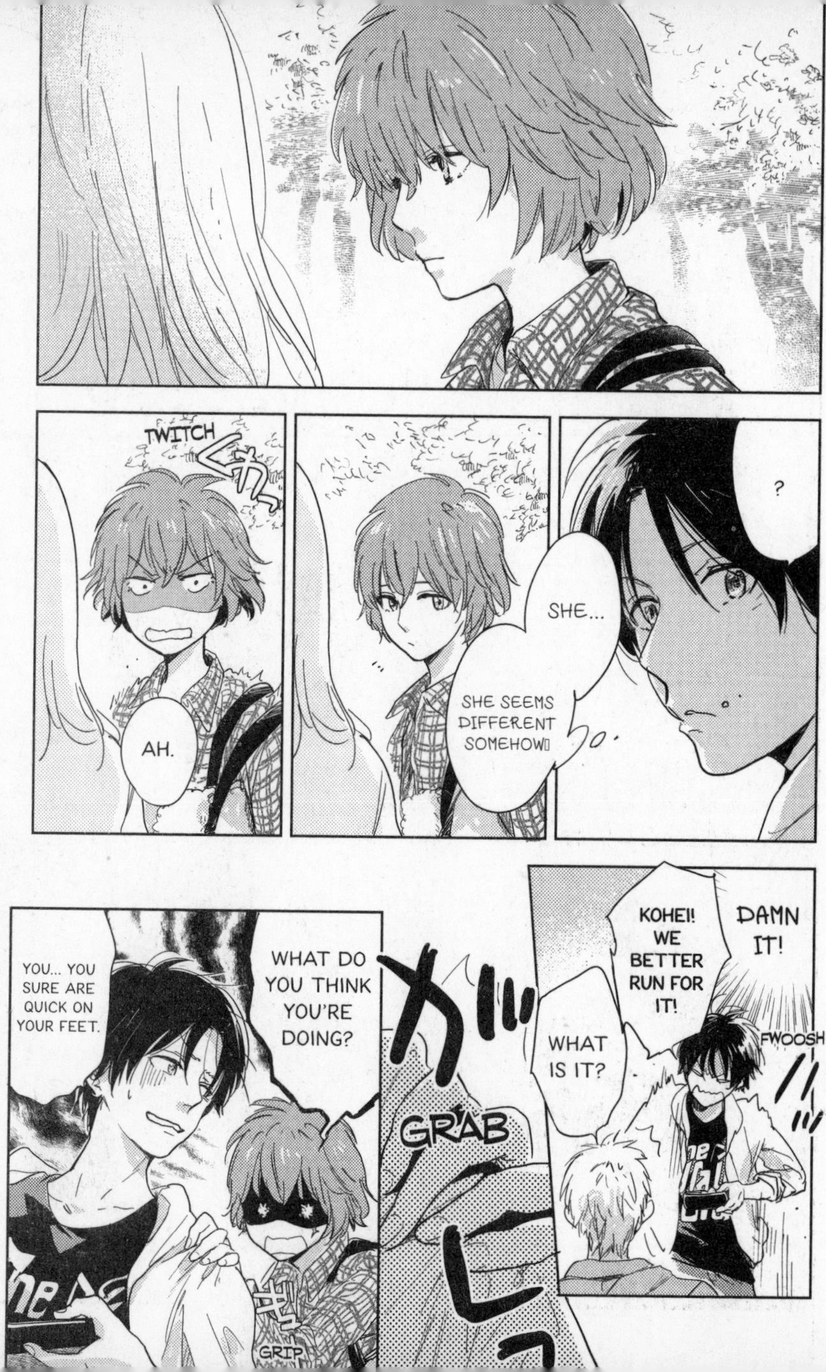
?
SHE...
SHE SEEMS DIFFERENT SOMEHOW…
TWITCH
AH.
DAMN IT!
KOHEI! WE BETTER RUN FOR IT!
FWOOSH
WHAT IS IT?
WHAT DO YOU THINK YOU'RE DOING?
GRAB
YOU... YOU SURE ARE QUICK ON YOUR FEET.
GRIP

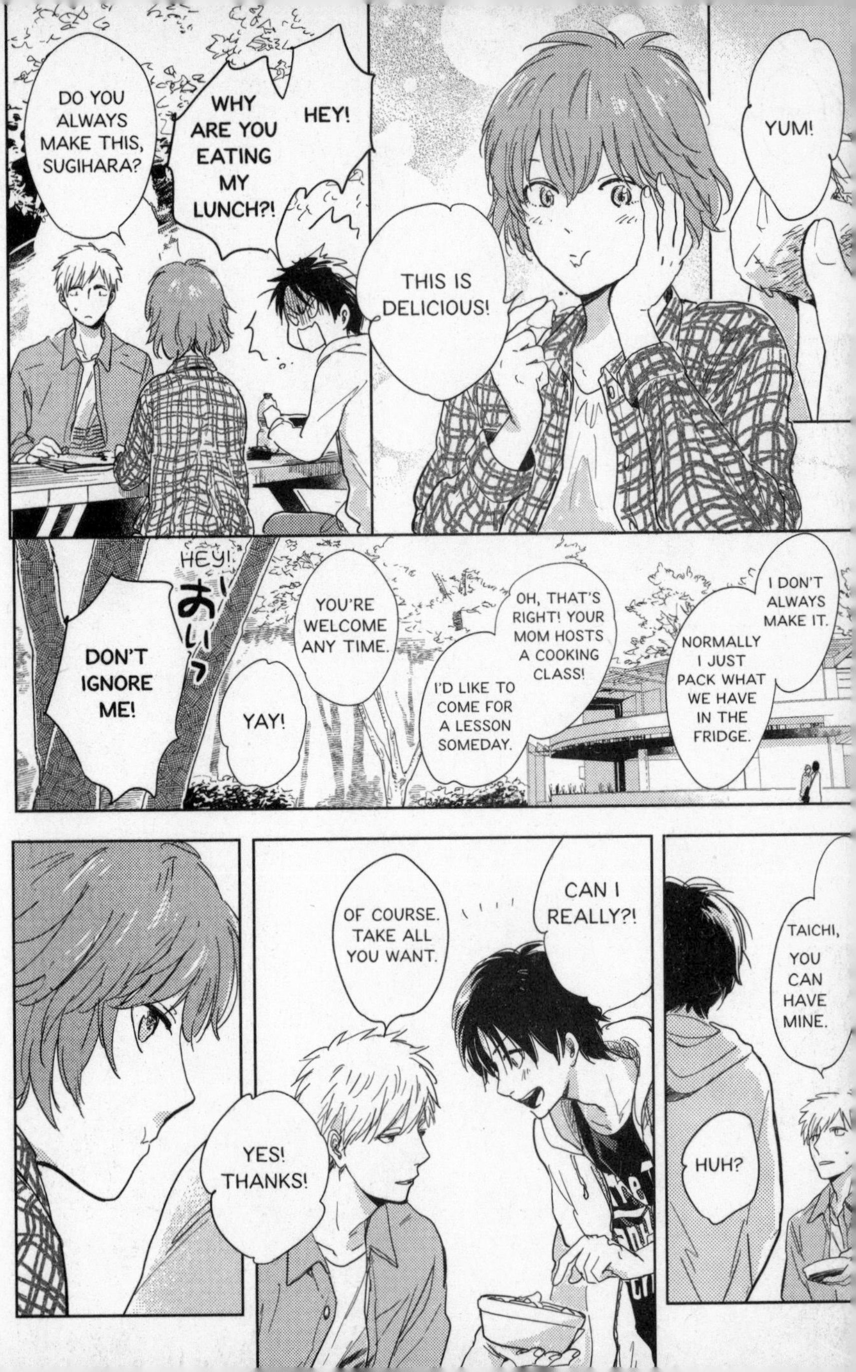
YUM!
THIS IS DELICIOUS!
HEY!
WHY ARE YOU EATING MY LUNCH?!
DO YOU ALWAYS MAKE THIS, SUGIHARA?
I DON'T ALWAYS MAKE IT.
NORMALLY I JUST PACK WHAT WE HAVE IN THE FRIDGE.
OH, THAT'S RIGHT! YOUR MOM HOSTS A COOKING CLASS!
I'D LIKE TO COME FOR A LESSON SOMEDAY.
YOU'RE WELCOME ANY TIME.
YAY!
HEY!
おいっ
DON'T IGNORE ME!
TAICHI, YOU CAN HAVE MINE.
HUH?
CAN I REALLY?!
OF COURSE. TAKE ALL YOU WANT.
YES! THANKS!

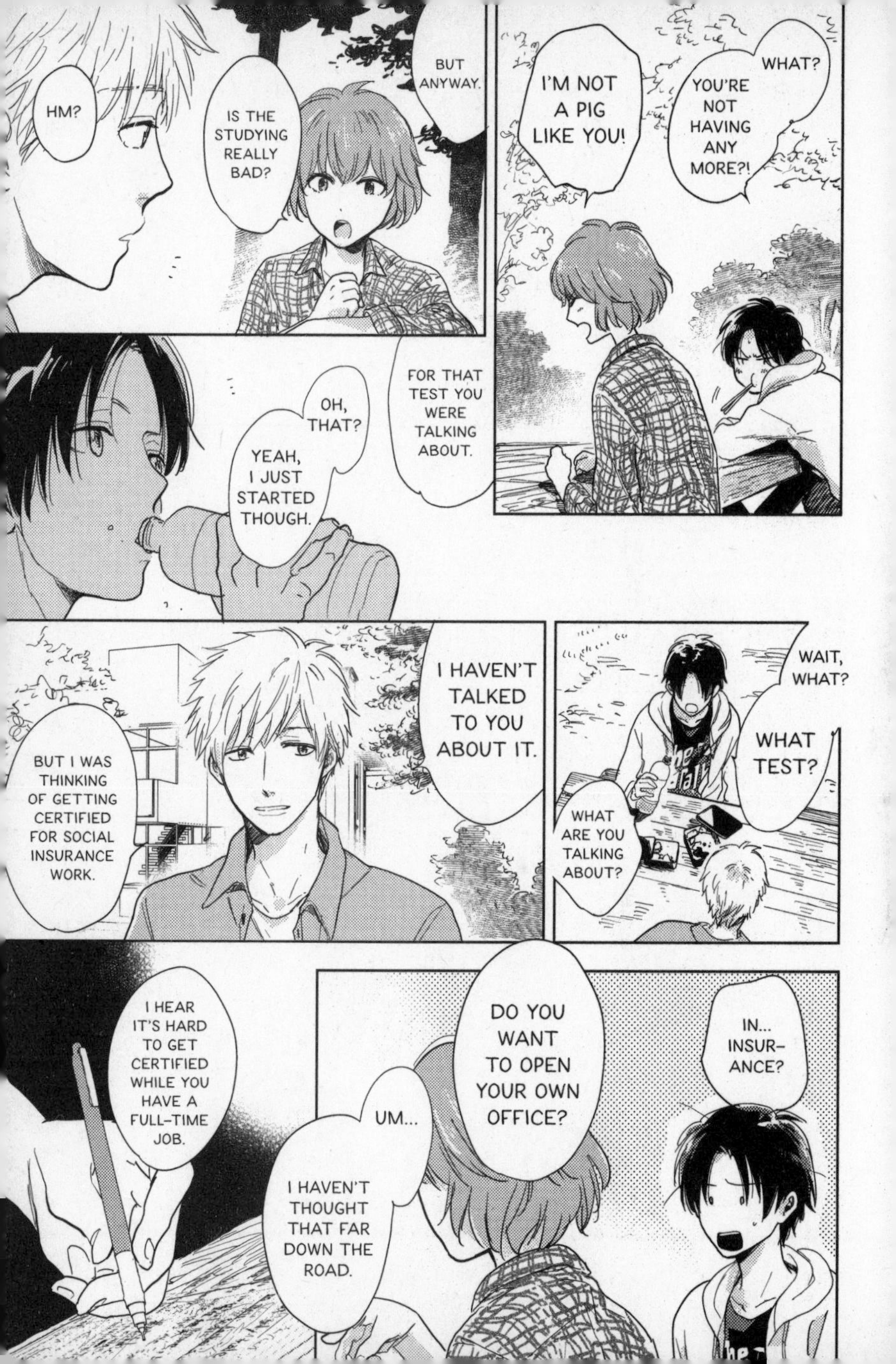
WHAT?
YOU'RE NOT HAVING ANY MORE?!
I'M NOT A PIG LIKE YOU!
BUT ANYWAY.
IS THE STUDYING REALLY BAD?
HM?
FOR THAT TEST YOU WERE TALKING ABOUT.
OH, THAT?
YEAH, I JUST STARTED THOUGH.
WAIT, WHAT?
WHAT TEST?
WHAT ARE YOU TALKING ABOUT?
I HAVEN'T TALKED TO YOU ABOUT IT.
BUT I WAS THINKING OF GETTING CERTIFIED FOR SOCIAL INSURANCE WORK.
IN... INSUR-ANCE?
DO YOU WANT TO OPEN YOUR OWN OFFICE?
UM...
I HAVEN'T THOUGHT THAT FAR DOWN THE ROAD.
I HEAR IT'S HARD TO GET CERTIFIED WHILE YOU HAVE A FULL-TIME JOB.

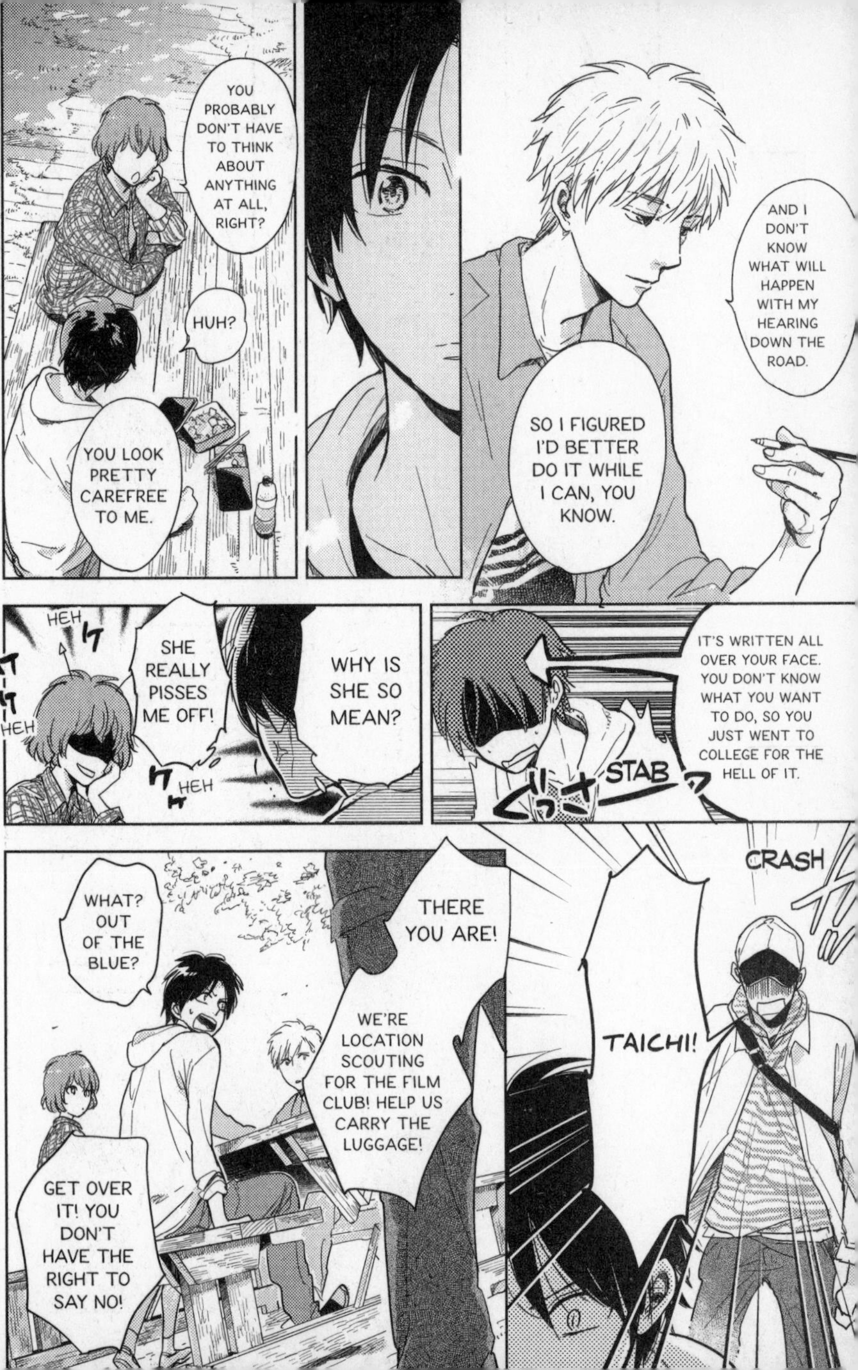
AND I DON'T KNOW WHAT WILL HAPPEN WITH MY HEARING DOWN THE ROAD.
SO I FIGURED I'D BETTER DO IT WHILE I CAN, YOU KNOW.
YOU PROBABLY DON'T HAVE TO THINK ABOUT ANYTHING AT ALL, RIGHT?
HUH?
YOU LOOK PRETTY CAREFREE TO ME.
IT'S WRITTEN ALL OVER YOUR FACE. YOU DON'T KNOW WHAT YOU WANT TO DO, SO YOU JUST WENT TO COLLEGE FOR THE HELL OF IT.
STAB
WHY IS SHE SO MEAN?
SHE REALLY PISSES ME OFF!
HEH
HEH
HEH
CRASH
TAICHI!
THERE YOU ARE!
WE'RE LOCATION SCOUTING FOR THE FILM CLUB! HELP US CARRY THE LUGGAGE!
WHAT? OUT OF THE BLUE?
GET OVER IT! YOU DON'T HAVE THE RIGHT TO SAY NO!

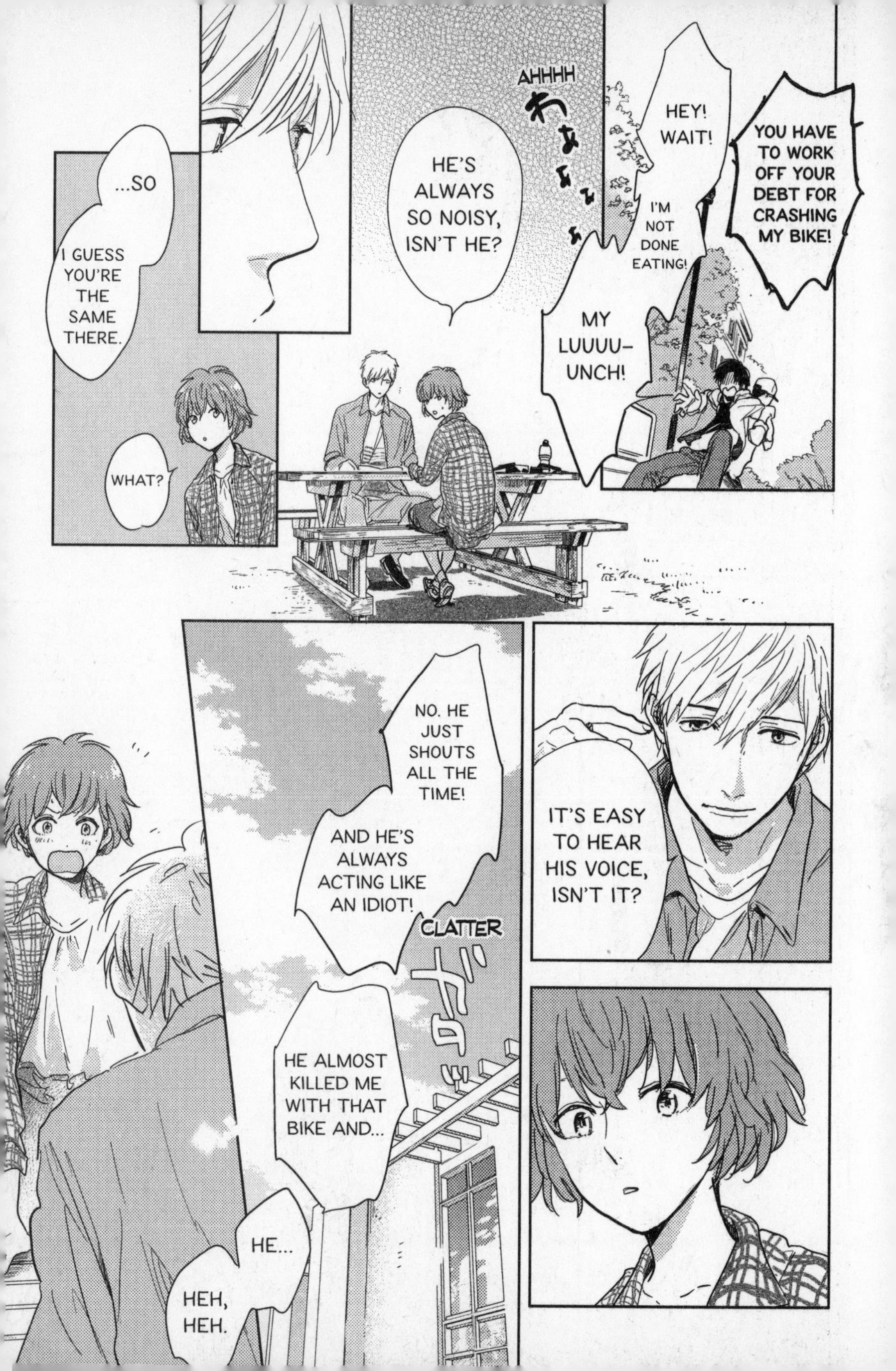
YOU HAVE TO WORK OFF YOUR DEBT FOR CRASHING MY BIKE!
HEY! WAIT!
I'M NOT DONE EATING!
AHHHH
MY LUUUU-UNCH!
HE'S ALWAYS SO NOISY, ISN'T HE?
...SO
I GUESS YOU'RE THE SAME THERE.
WHAT?
IT'S EASY TO HEAR HIS VOICE, ISN'T IT?
NO. HE JUST SHOUTS ALL THE TIME!
AND HE'S ALWAYS ACTING LIKE AN IDIOT!
CLATTER
HE ALMOST KILLED ME WITH THAT BIKE AND...
HE...
HEH, HEH.

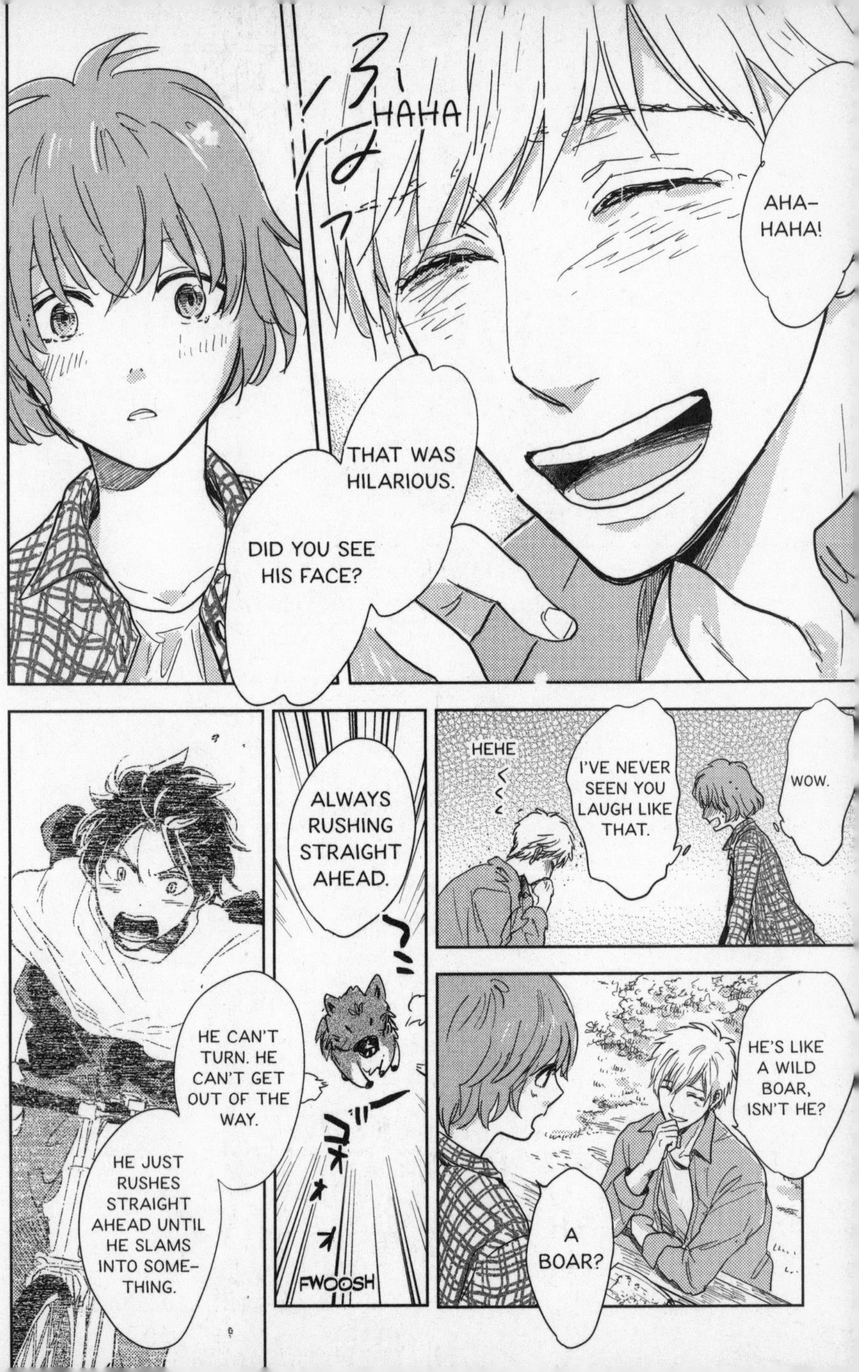
HAHA
AHA-HAHA!
THAT WAS HILARIOUS.
DID YOU SEE HIS FACE?
WOW.
I'VE NEVER SEEN YOU LAUGH LIKE THAT.
HEHE
HE'S LIKE A WILD BOAR, ISN'T HE?
A BOAR?
ALWAYS RUSHING STRAIGHT AHEAD.
FWOOSH
HE CAN'T TURN. HE CAN'T GET OUT OF THE WAY.
HE JUST RUSHES STRAIGHT AHEAD UNTIL HE SLAMS INTO SOME-THING.

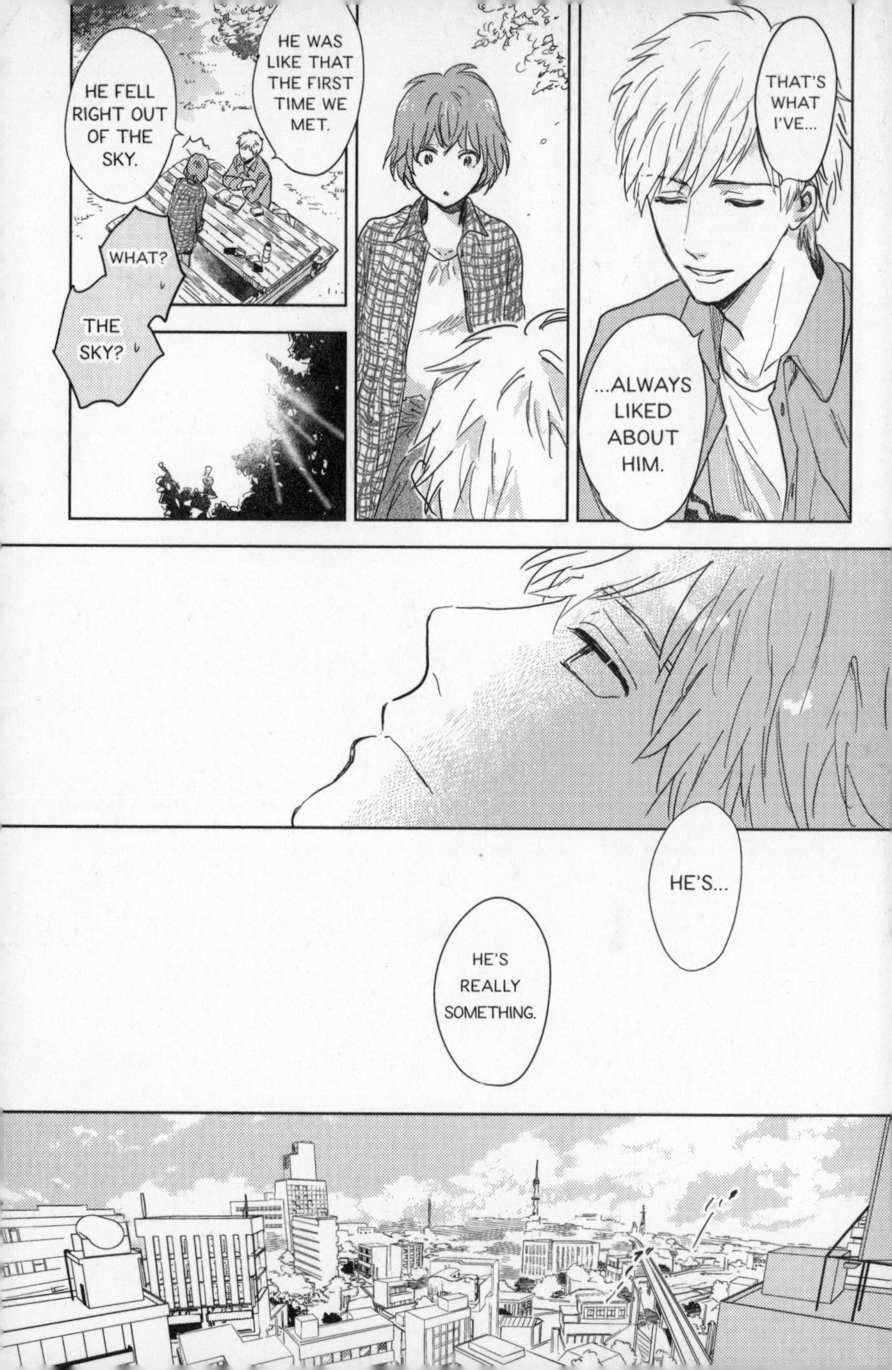
THAT'S WHAT I'VE...
...ALWAYS LIKED ABOUT HIM.
HE WAS LIKE THAT THE FIRST TIME WE MET.
HE FELL RIGHT OUT OF THE SKY.
WHAT?
THE SKY?
HE'S...
HE'S REALLY SOMETHING.

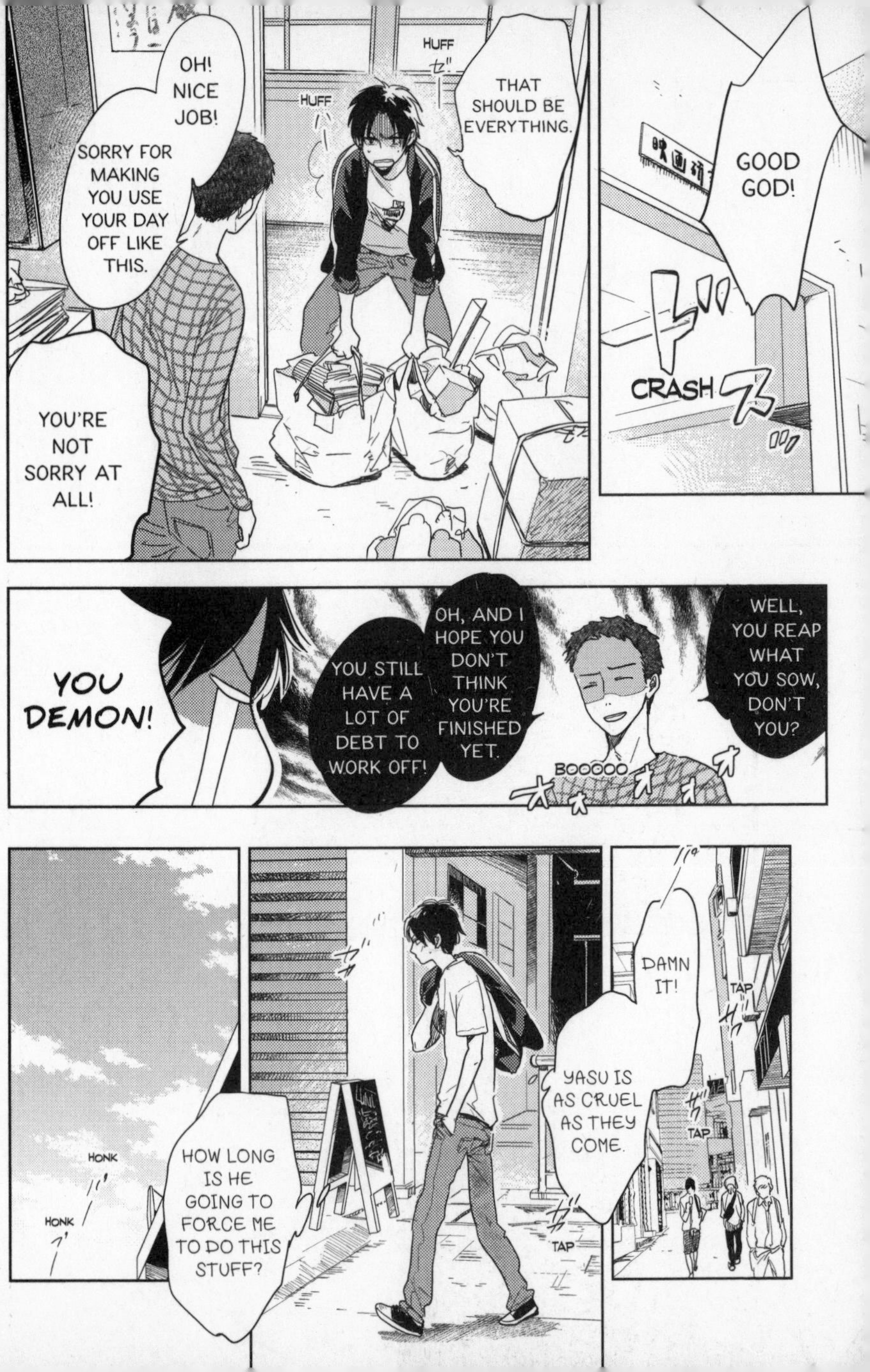
GOOD GOD!
CRASH
HUFF
THAT SHOULD BE EVERYTHING.
HUFF
OH! NICE JOB!
SORRY FOR MAKING YOU USE YOUR DAY OFF LIKE THIS.
YOU'RE NOT SORRY AT ALL!
WELL, YOU REAP WHAT YOU SOW, DON'T YOU?
BOOOOO
OH, AND I HOPE YOU DON'T THINK YOU'RE FINISHED YET.
YOU STILL HAVE A LOT OF DEBT TO WORK OFF!
YOU DEMON!
DAMN IT!
TAP
TAP
YASU IS AS CRUEL AS THEY COME.
TAP
HOW LONG IS HE GOING TO FORCE ME TO DO THIS STUFF?
HONK
HONK

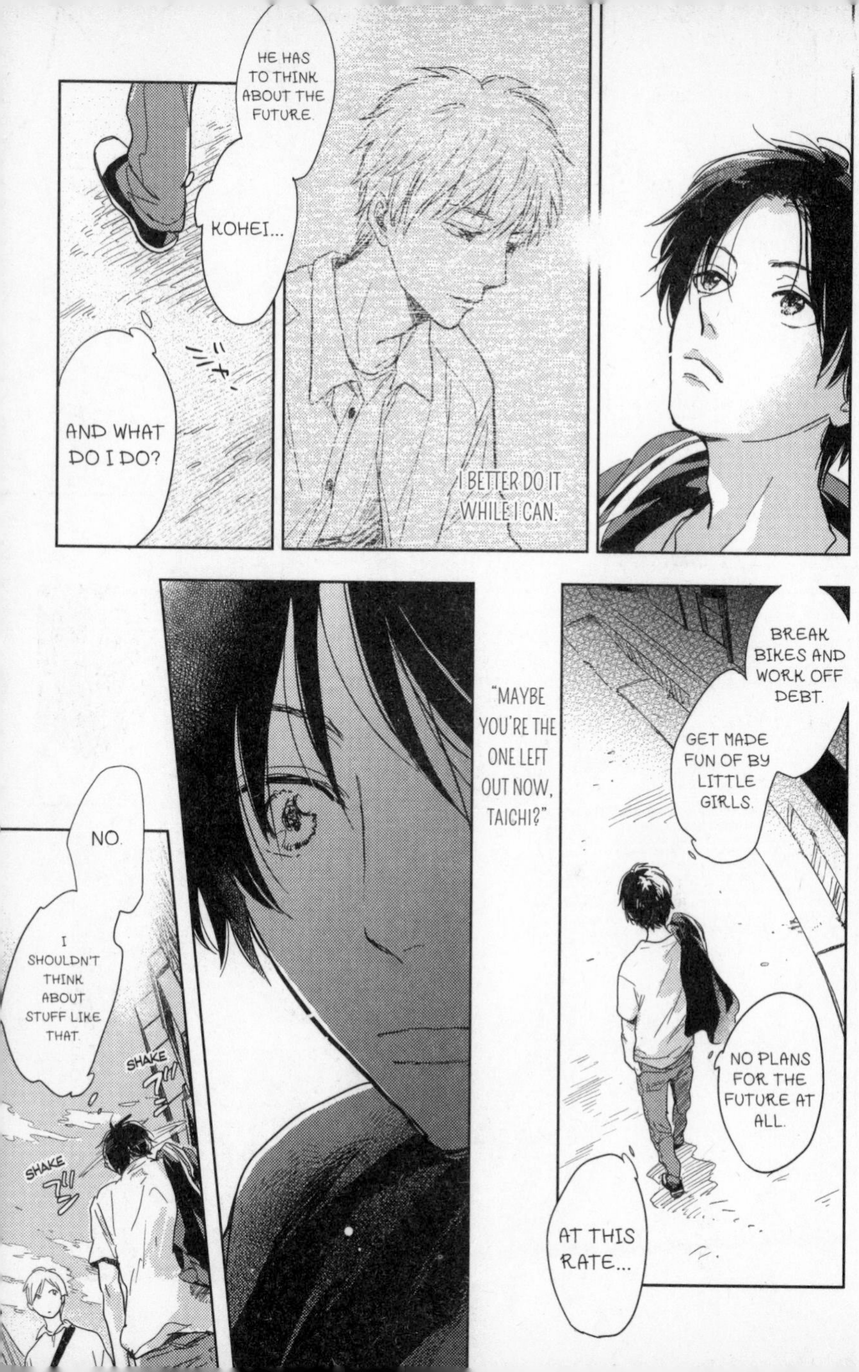
I BETTER DO IT WHILE I CAN.
HE HAS TO THINK ABOUT THE FUTURE.
KOHEI...
AND WHAT DO I DO?
BREAK BIKES AND WORK OFF DEBT.
GET MADE FUN OF BY LITTLE GIRLS.
NO PLANS FOR THE FUTURE AT ALL.
AT THIS RATE...
"MAYBE YOU'RE THE ONE LEFT OUT NOW, TAICHI?"
NO.
I SHOULDN'T THINK ABOUT STUFF LIKE THAT.
SHAKE
SHAKE

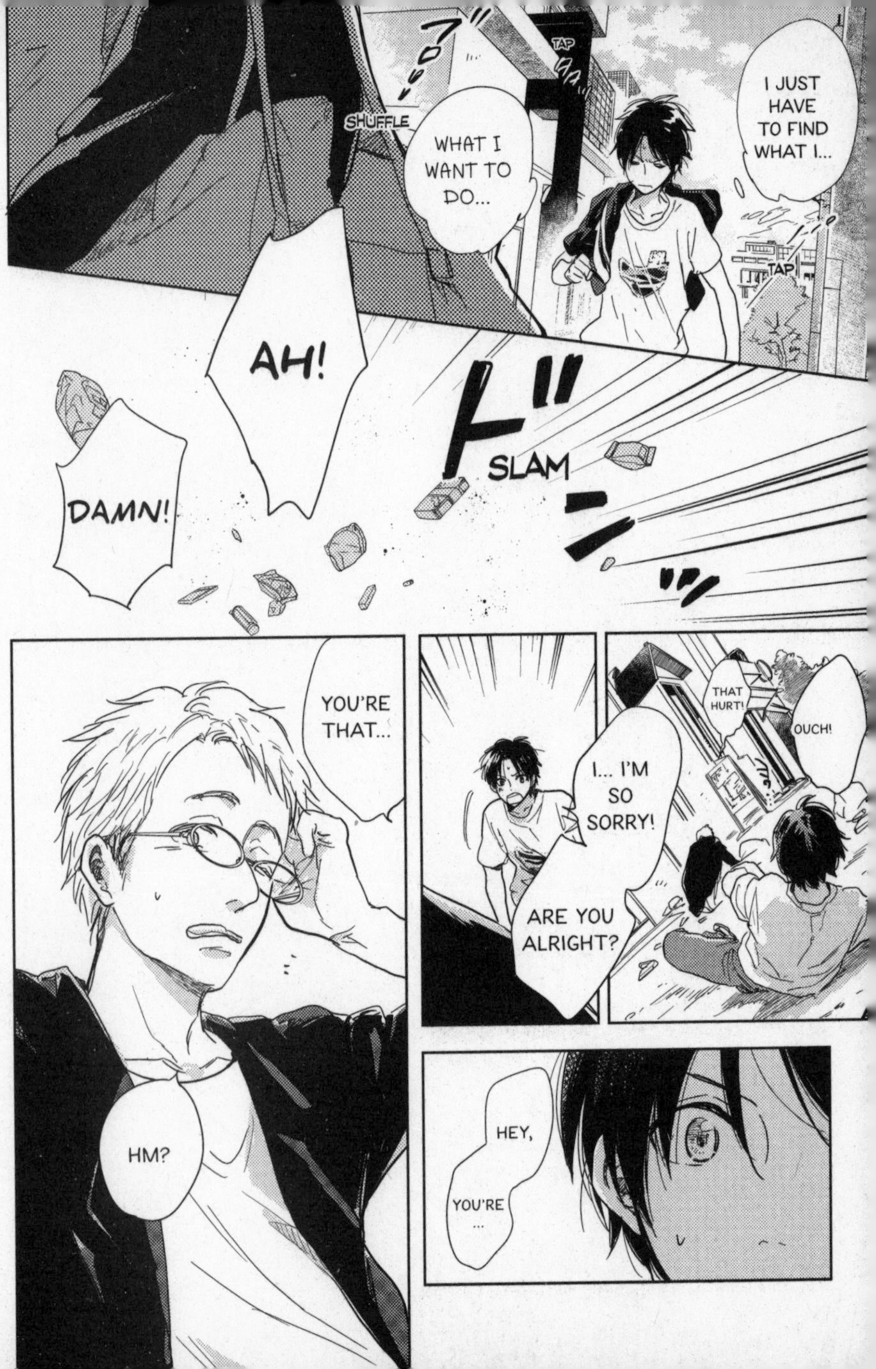

I JUST HAVE TO FIND WHAT I...
TAP
TAP
WHAT I WANT TO DO...
SHUFFLE
SLAM
AH!
DAMN!
OUCH!
THAT HURT!
I... I'M SO SORRY!
ARE YOU ALRIGHT?
HEY,
YOU'RE ...
YOU'RE THAT...
HM?

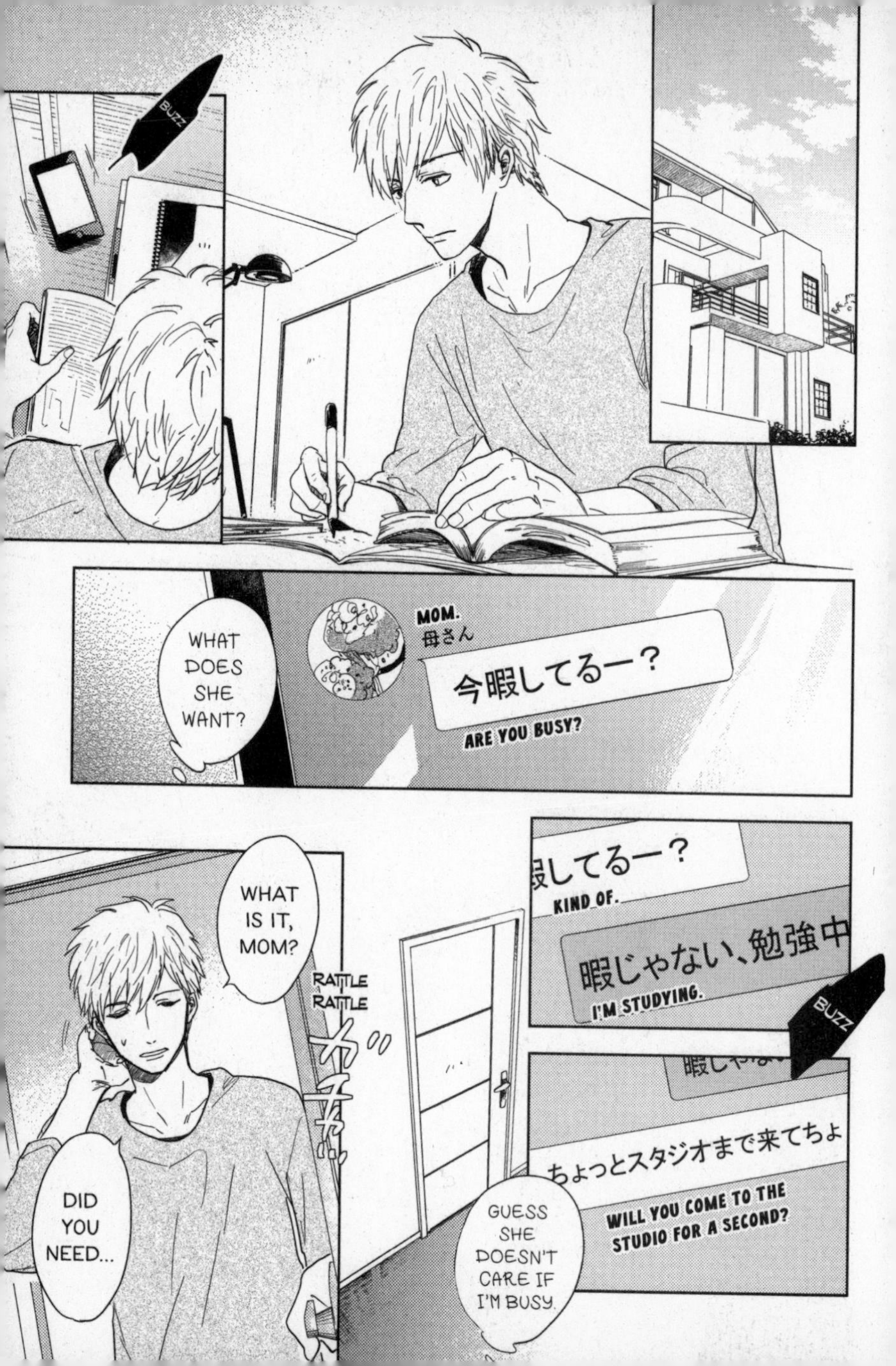

BUZZ
MOM.
母さん
今暇してるー？
ARE YOU BUSY?
WHAT DOES SHE WANT?
暇してるー？
KIND OF.
暇じゃない、勉強中
I'M STUDYING.
BUZZ
ちょっとスタジオまで来てちょ
WILL YOU COME TO THE STUDIO FOR A SECOND?
GUESS SHE DOESN'T CARE IF I'M BUSY.
WHAT IS IT, MOM?
RATTLE RATTLE
DID YOU NEED...

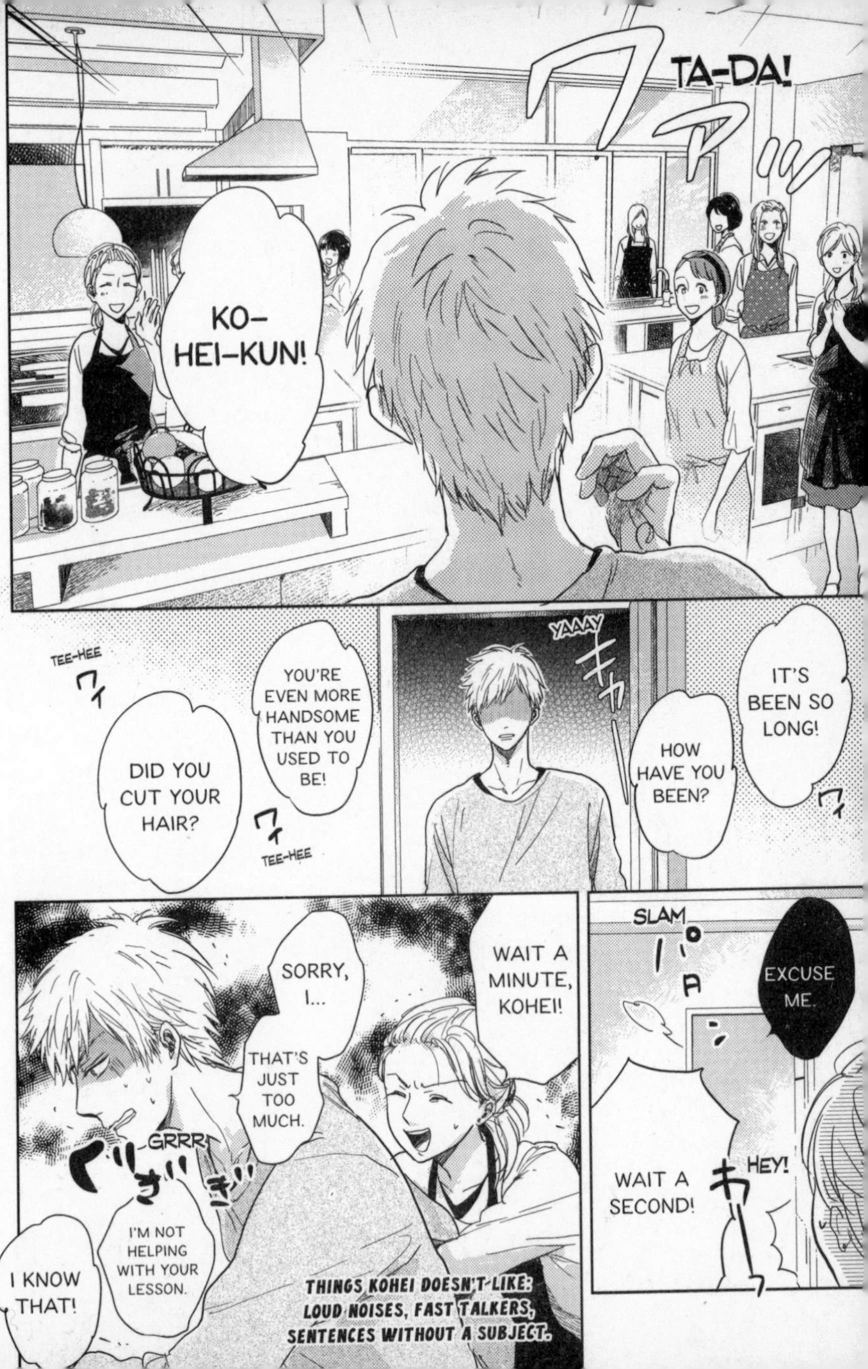
TA-DA!
KO-HEI-KUN!
IT'S BEEN SO LONG!
HOW HAVE YOU BEEN?
YAAAY
YOU'RE EVEN MORE HANDSOME THAN YOU USED TO BE!
TEE-HEE
DID YOU CUT YOUR HAIR?
TEE-HEE
SLAM
EXCUSE ME.
HEY!
WAIT A SECOND!
WAIT A MINUTE, KOHEI!
SORRY, I...
THAT'S JUST TOO MUCH.
GRRR
I'M NOT HELPING WITH YOUR LESSON.
I KNOW THAT!
THINGS KOHEI DOESN'T LIKE: LOUD NOISES, FAST TALKERS, SENTENCES WITHOUT A SUBJECT.

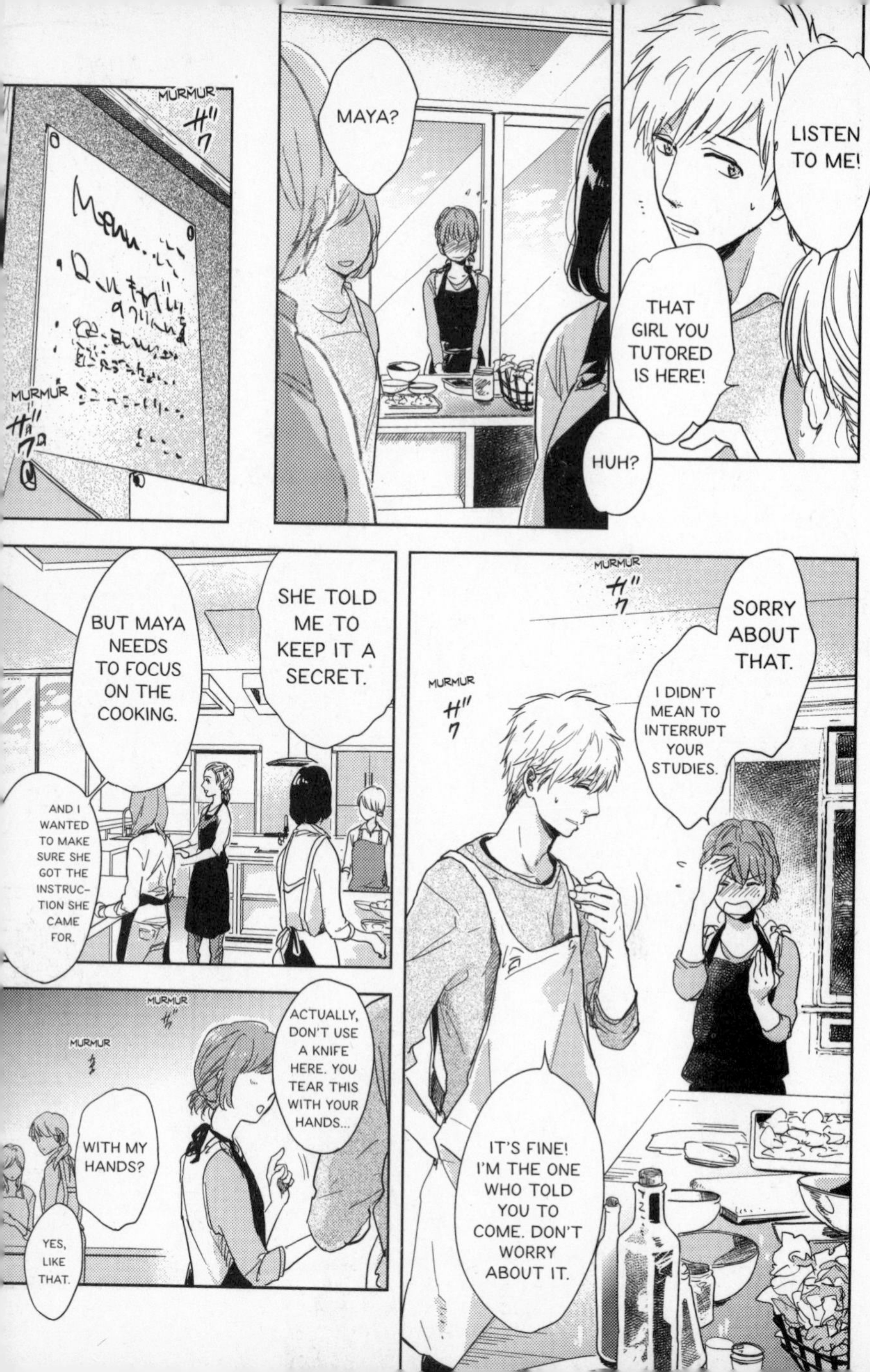
LISTEN TO ME!
THAT GIRL YOU TUTORED IS HERE!
HUH?
MAYA?
MURMUR
MURMUR
MURMUR
SORRY ABOUT THAT.
MURMUR
I DIDN'T MEAN TO INTERRUPT YOUR STUDIES.
IT'S FINE! I'M THE ONE WHO TOLD YOU TO COME. DON'T WORRY ABOUT IT.
SHE TOLD ME TO KEEP IT A SECRET.
BUT MAYA NEEDS TO FOCUS ON THE COOKING.
AND I WANTED TO MAKE SURE SHE GOT THE INSTRUCTION SHE CAME FOR.
MURMUR
ACTUALLY, DON'T USE A KNIFE HERE. YOU TEAR THIS WITH YOUR HANDS...
MURMUR
WITH MY HANDS?
YES, LIKE THAT.

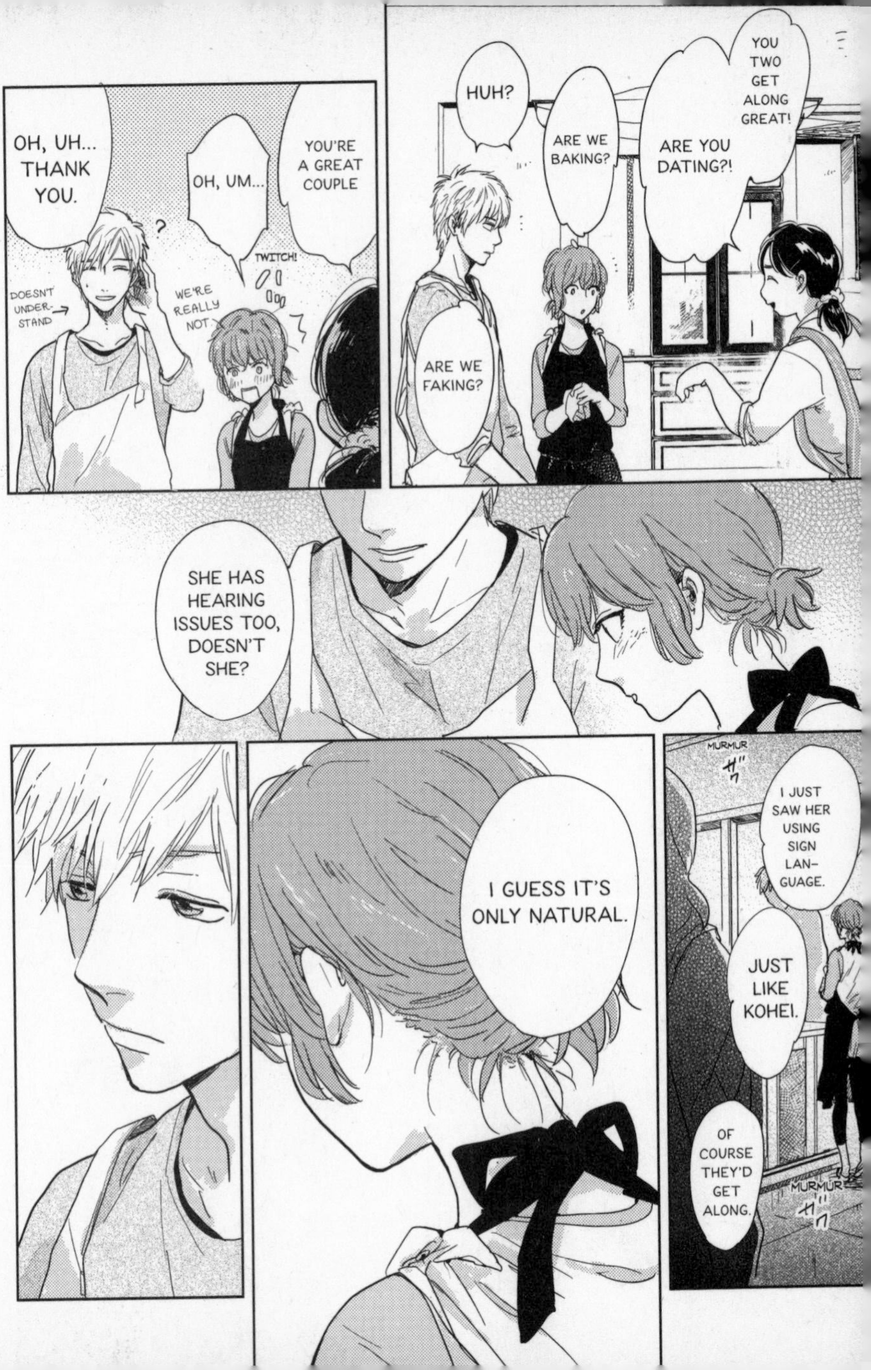
YOU TWO GET ALONG GREAT!
ARE YOU DATING?!
ARE WE BAKING?
HUH?
ARE WE FAKING?
YOU'RE A GREAT COUPLE
OH, UM...
TWITCH!
WE'RE REALLY NOT.
OH, UH... THANK YOU.
?
DOESN'T UNDER-STAND
SHE HAS HEARING ISSUES TOO, DOESN'T SHE?
MURMUR
I JUST SAW HER USING SIGN LAN-GUAGE.
JUST LIKE KOHEI.
OF COURSE THEY'D GET ALONG.
MURMUR
I GUESS IT'S ONLY NATURAL.

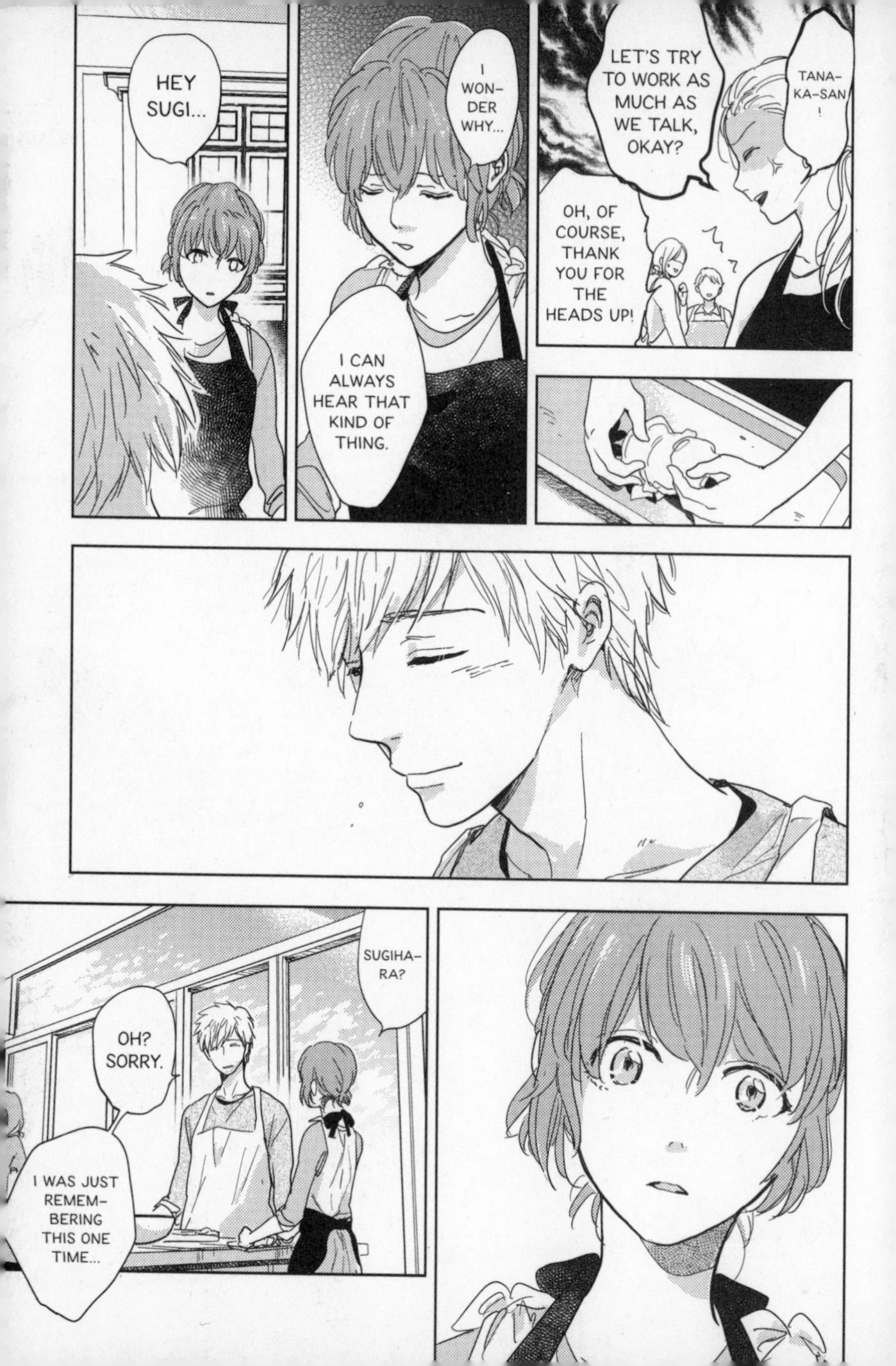
TANA-KA-SAN!
LET'S TRY TO WORK AS MUCH AS WE TALK, OKAY?
OH, OF COURSE, THANK YOU FOR THE HEADS UP!
I WONDER WHY...
I CAN ALWAYS HEAR THAT KIND OF THING.
HEY SUGI...
SUGIHA-RA?
OH? SORRY.
I WAS JUST REMEMBERING THIS ONE TIME...

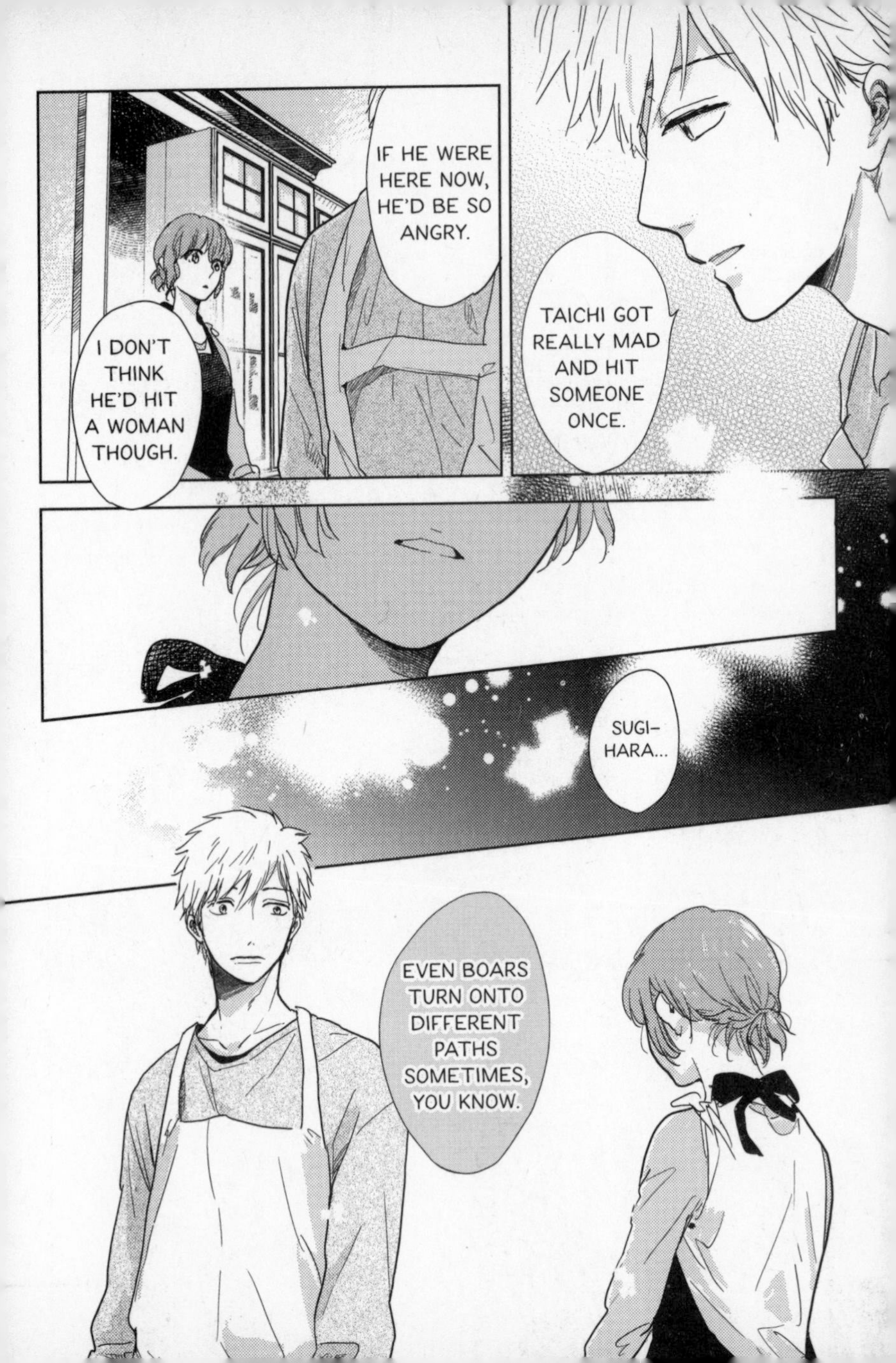
TAICHI GOT REALLY MAD AND HIT SOMEONE ONCE.
IF HE WERE HERE NOW, HE'D BE SO ANGRY.
I DON'T THINK HE'D HIT A WOMAN THOUGH.
SUGI-HARA...
EVEN BOARS TURN ONTO DIFFERENT PATHS SOMETIMES, YOU KNOW.

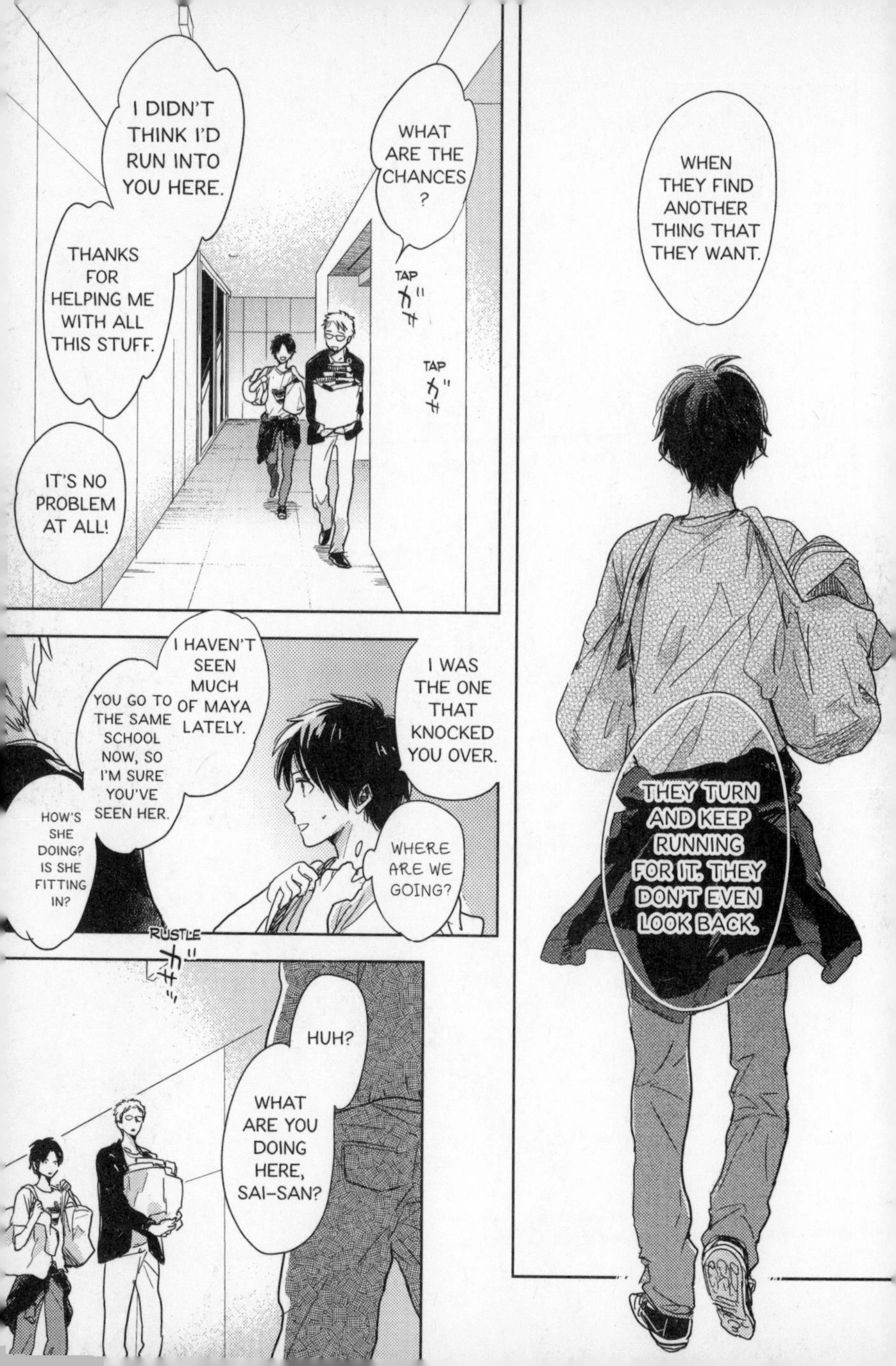
WHEN THEY FIND ANOTHER THING THAT THEY WANT.
THEY TURN AND KEEP RUNNING FOR IT. THEY DON'T EVEN LOOK BACK.
WHAT ARE THE CHANCES?
TAP
TAP
I DIDN'T THINK I'D RUN INTO YOU HERE.
THANKS FOR HELPING ME WITH ALL THIS STUFF.
IT'S NO PROBLEM AT ALL!
I WAS THE ONE THAT KNOCKED YOU OVER.
WHERE ARE WE GOING?
I HAVEN'T SEEN MUCH OF MAYA LATELY.
YOU GO TO THE SAME SCHOOL NOW, SO I'M SURE YOU'VE SEEN HER.
HOW'S SHE DOING? IS SHE FITTING IN?
RUSTLE
HUH?
WHAT ARE YOU DOING HERE, SAI-SAN?

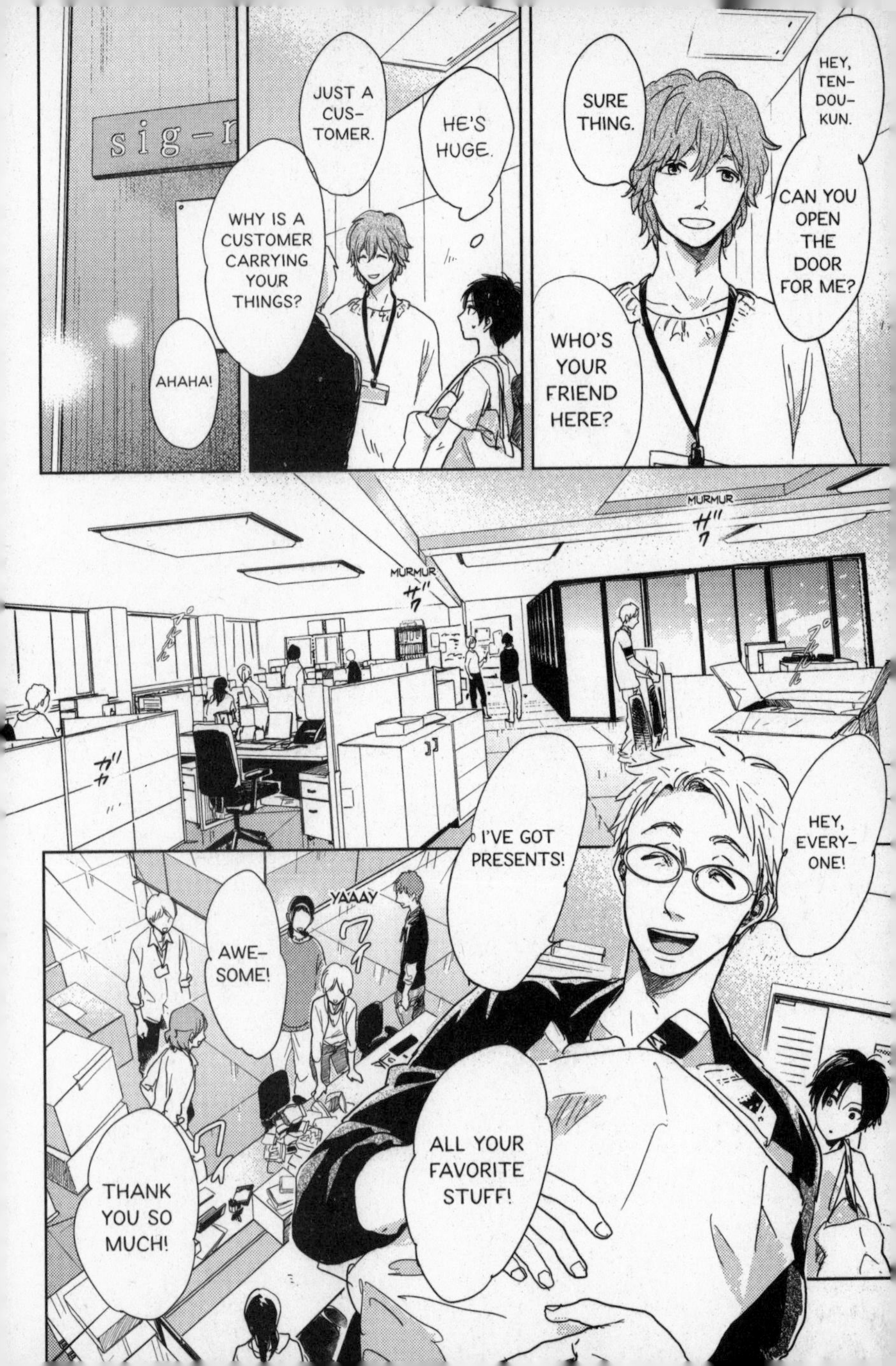
HEY, TEN-DOU-KUN.
CAN YOU OPEN THE DOOR FOR ME?
SURE THING.
WHO'S YOUR FRIEND HERE?
HE'S HUGE.
JUST A CUS-TOMER.
WHY IS A CUSTOMER CARRYING YOUR THINGS?
AHAHA!
sig-r
MURMUR
MURMUR
HEY, EVERY-ONE!
I'VE GOT PRESENTS!
ALL YOUR FAVORITE STUFF!
YAAAY
AWE-SOME!
THANK YOU SO MUCH!

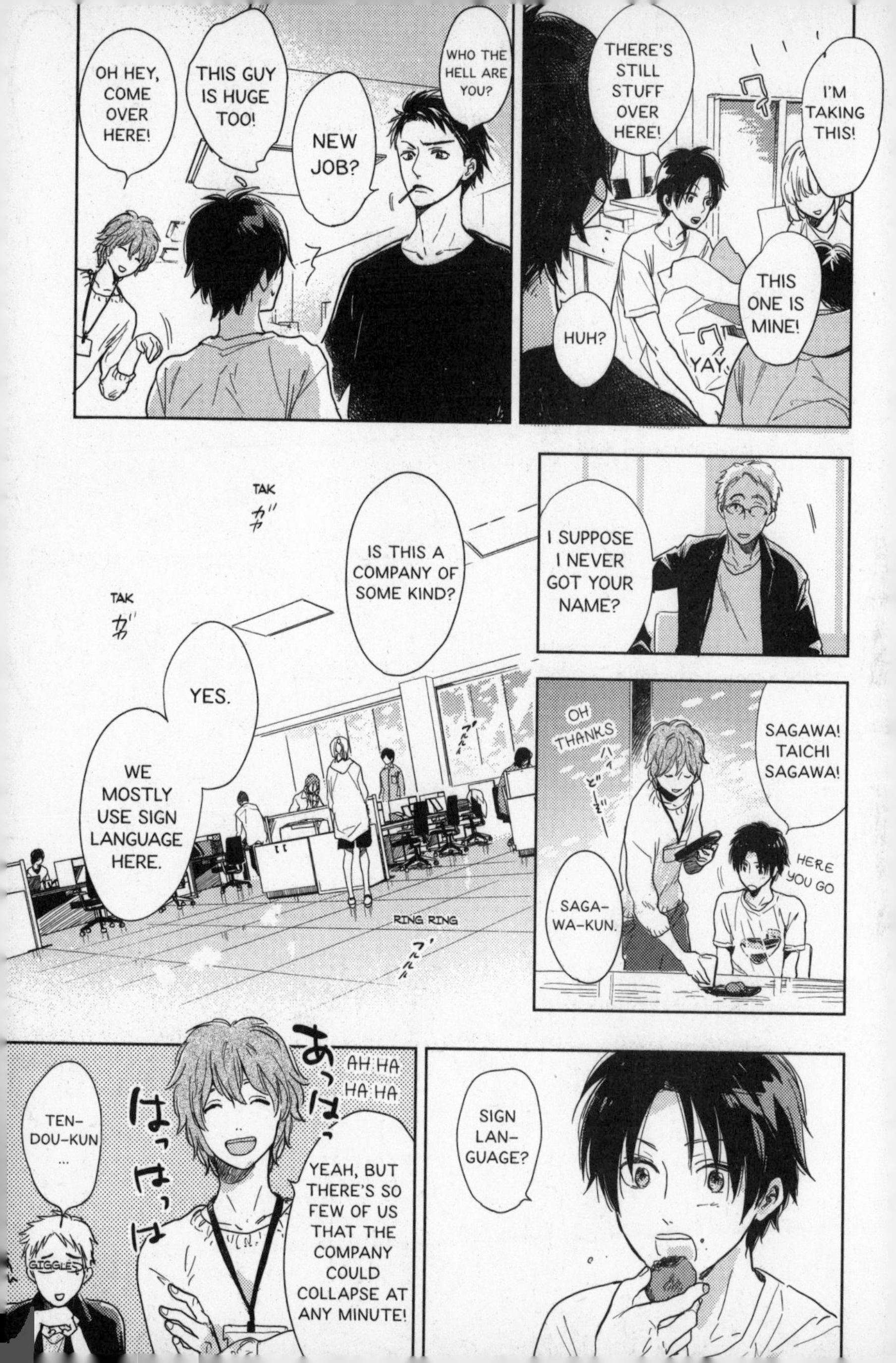
I'M TAKING THIS!
THERE'S STILL STUFF OVER HERE!
THIS ONE IS MINE!
YAY
HUH?
WHO THE HELL ARE YOU?
NEW JOB?
THIS GUY IS HUGE TOO!
OH HEY, COME OVER HERE!
I SUPPOSE I NEVER GOT YOUR NAME?
SAGAWA! TAICHI SAGAWA!
HERE YOU GO
OH THANKS
SAGA-WA-KUN.
IS THIS A COMPANY OF SOME KIND?
TAK
TAK
YES.
WE MOSTLY USE SIGN LANGUAGE HERE.
RING RING
SIGN LAN-GUAGE?
AH HA HA HA
あっはっはっは
YEAH, BUT THERE'S SO FEW OF US THAT THE COMPANY COULD COLLAPSE AT ANY MINUTE!
TEN-DOU-KUN ...
GIGGLES

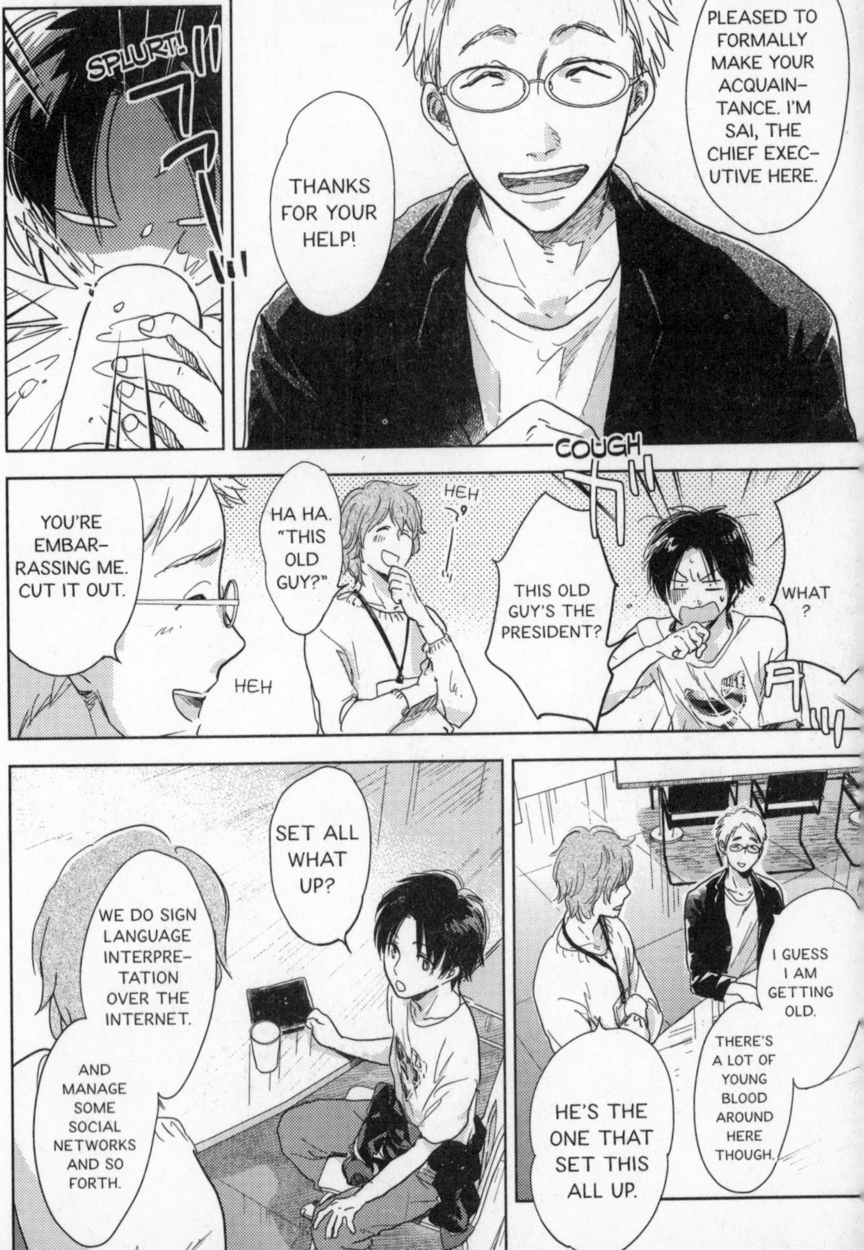
PLEASED TO FORMALLY MAKE YOUR ACQUAIN-TANCE. I'M SAI, THE CHIEF EXEC-UTIVE HERE.
THANKS FOR YOUR HELP!
SPLURT!
COUGH
WHAT?
THIS OLD GUY'S THE PRESIDENT?
HEH
HA HA. "THIS OLD GUY?"
YOU'RE EMBAR-RASSING ME. CUT IT OUT.
HEH
I GUESS I AM GETTING OLD.
THERE'S A LOT OF YOUNG BLOOD AROUND HERE THOUGH.
HE'S THE ONE THAT SET THIS ALL UP.
SET ALL WHAT UP?
WE DO SIGN LANGUAGE INTERPRE-TATION OVER THE INTERNET.
AND MANAGE SOME SOCIAL NETWORKS AND SO FORTH.

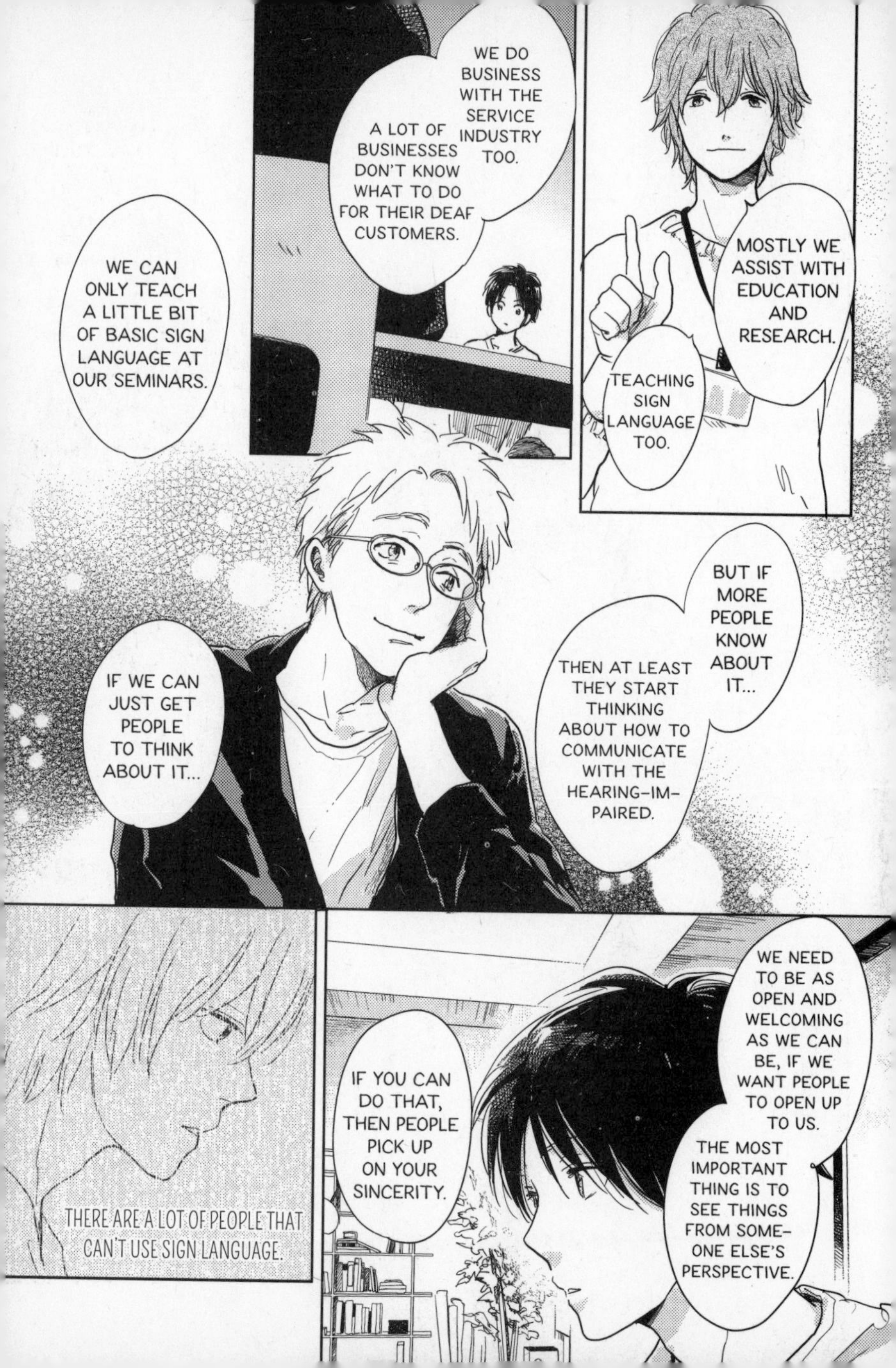
MOSTLY WE ASSIST WITH EDUCATION AND RESEARCH.
TEACHING SIGN LANGUAGE TOO.
WE DO BUSINESS WITH THE SERVICE INDUSTRY TOO.
A LOT OF BUSINESSES DON'T KNOW WHAT TO DO FOR THEIR DEAF CUSTOMERS.
WE CAN ONLY TEACH A LITTLE BIT OF BASIC SIGN LANGUAGE AT OUR SEMINARS.
BUT IF MORE PEOPLE KNOW ABOUT IT...
THEN AT LEAST THEY START THINKING ABOUT HOW TO COMMUNICATE WITH THE HEARING-IMPAIRED.
IF WE CAN JUST GET PEOPLE TO THINK ABOUT IT...
WE NEED TO BE AS OPEN AND WELCOMING AS WE CAN BE, IF WE WANT PEOPLE TO OPEN UP TO US.
THE MOST IMPORTANT THING IS TO SEE THINGS FROM SOME-ONE ELSE'S PERSPECTIVE.
IF YOU CAN DO THAT, THEN PEOPLE PICK UP ON YOUR SINCERITY.
THERE ARE A LOT OF PEOPLE THAT CAN'T USE SIGN LANGUAGE.

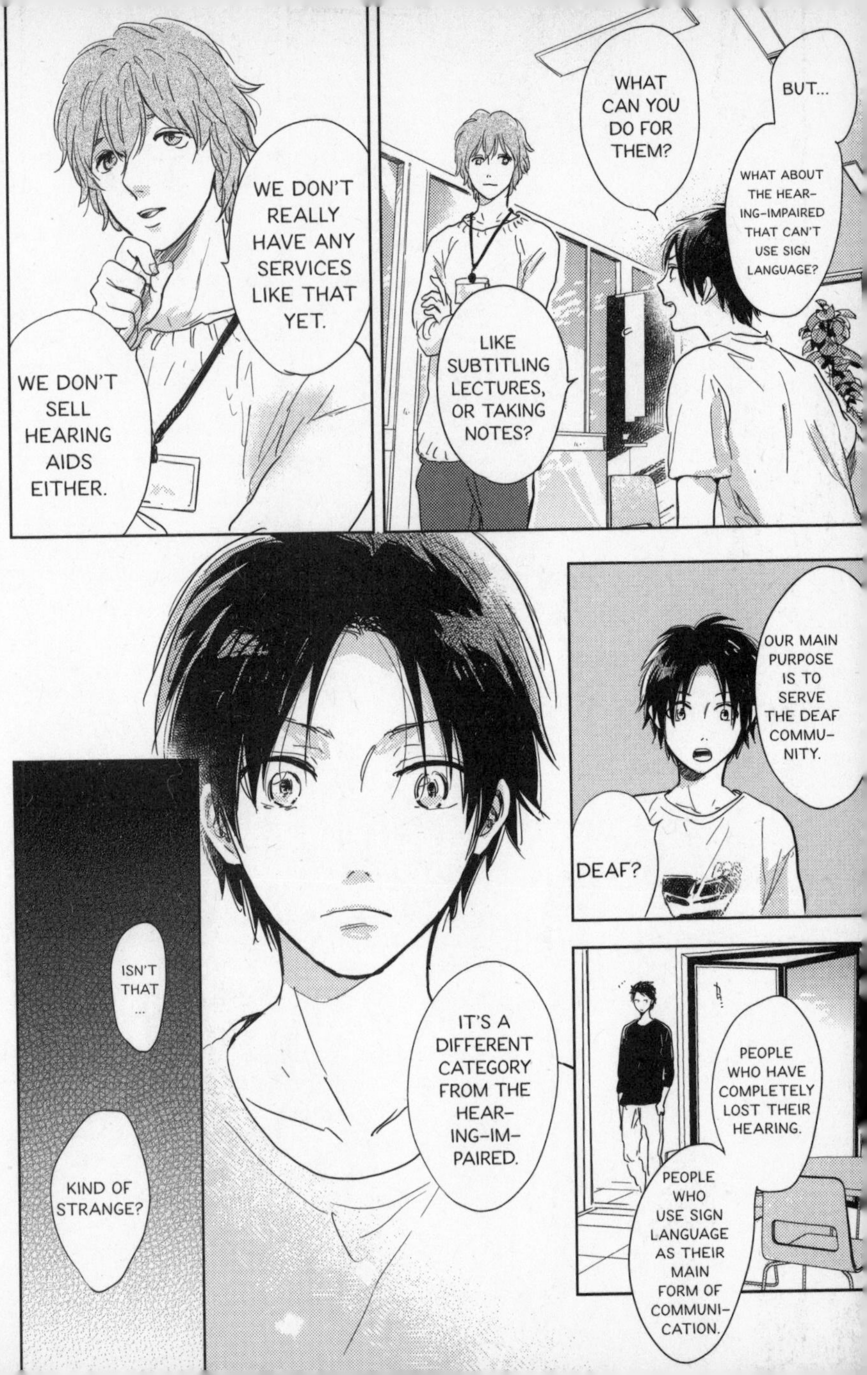
BUT...
WHAT ABOUT THE HEARING-IMPAIRED THAT CAN'T USE SIGN LANGUAGE?
WHAT CAN YOU DO FOR THEM?
LIKE SUBTITLING LECTURES, OR TAKING NOTES?
WE DON'T REALLY HAVE ANY SERVICES LIKE THAT YET.
WE DON'T SELL HEARING AIDS EITHER.
OUR MAIN PURPOSE IS TO SERVE THE DEAF COMMUNITY.
DEAF?
PEOPLE WHO HAVE COMPLETELY LOST THEIR HEARING.
PEOPLE WHO USE SIGN LANGUAGE AS THEIR MAIN FORM OF COMMUNICATION.
IT'S A DIFFERENT CATEGORY FROM THE HEARING-IMPAIRED.
ISN'T THAT ...
KIND OF STRANGE?

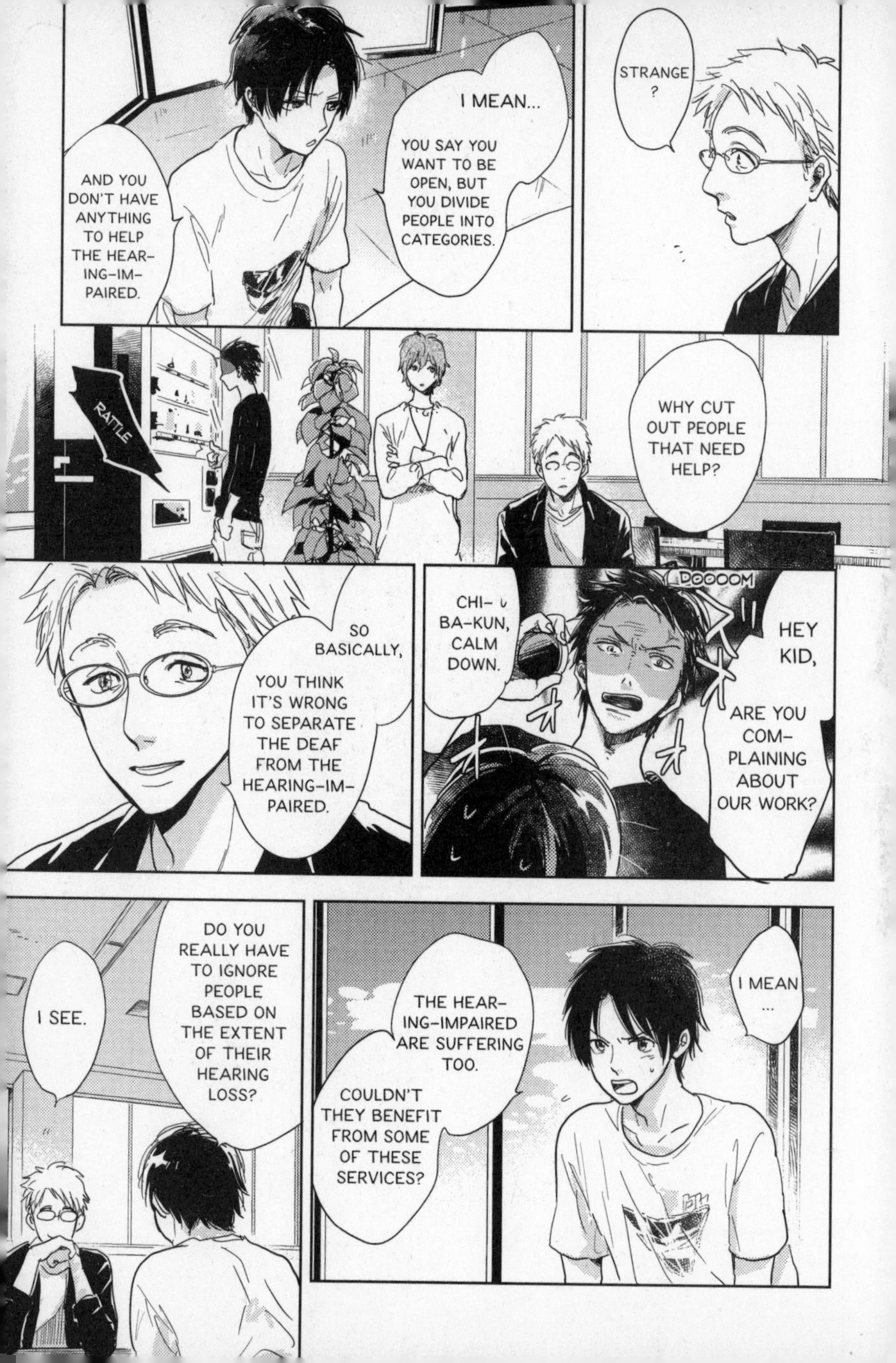
STRANGE?
I MEAN...
YOU SAY YOU WANT TO BE OPEN, BUT YOU DIVIDE PEOPLE INTO CATEGORIES.
AND YOU DON'T HAVE ANYTHING TO HELP THE HEAR-ING-IM-PAIRED.
WHY CUT OUT PEOPLE THAT NEED HELP?
RATTLE
DOOOOM
HEY KID,
ARE YOU COM-PLAINING ABOUT OUR WORK?
CHI-BA-KUN, CALM DOWN.
SO BASICALLY,
YOU THINK IT'S WRONG TO SEPARATE THE DEAF FROM THE HEARING-IM-PAIRED.
I MEAN...
THE HEAR-ING-IMPAIRED ARE SUFFERING TOO.
COULDN'T THEY BENEFIT FROM SOME OF THESE SERVICES?
DO YOU REALLY HAVE TO IGNORE PEOPLE BASED ON THE EXTENT OF THEIR HEARING LOSS?
I SEE.

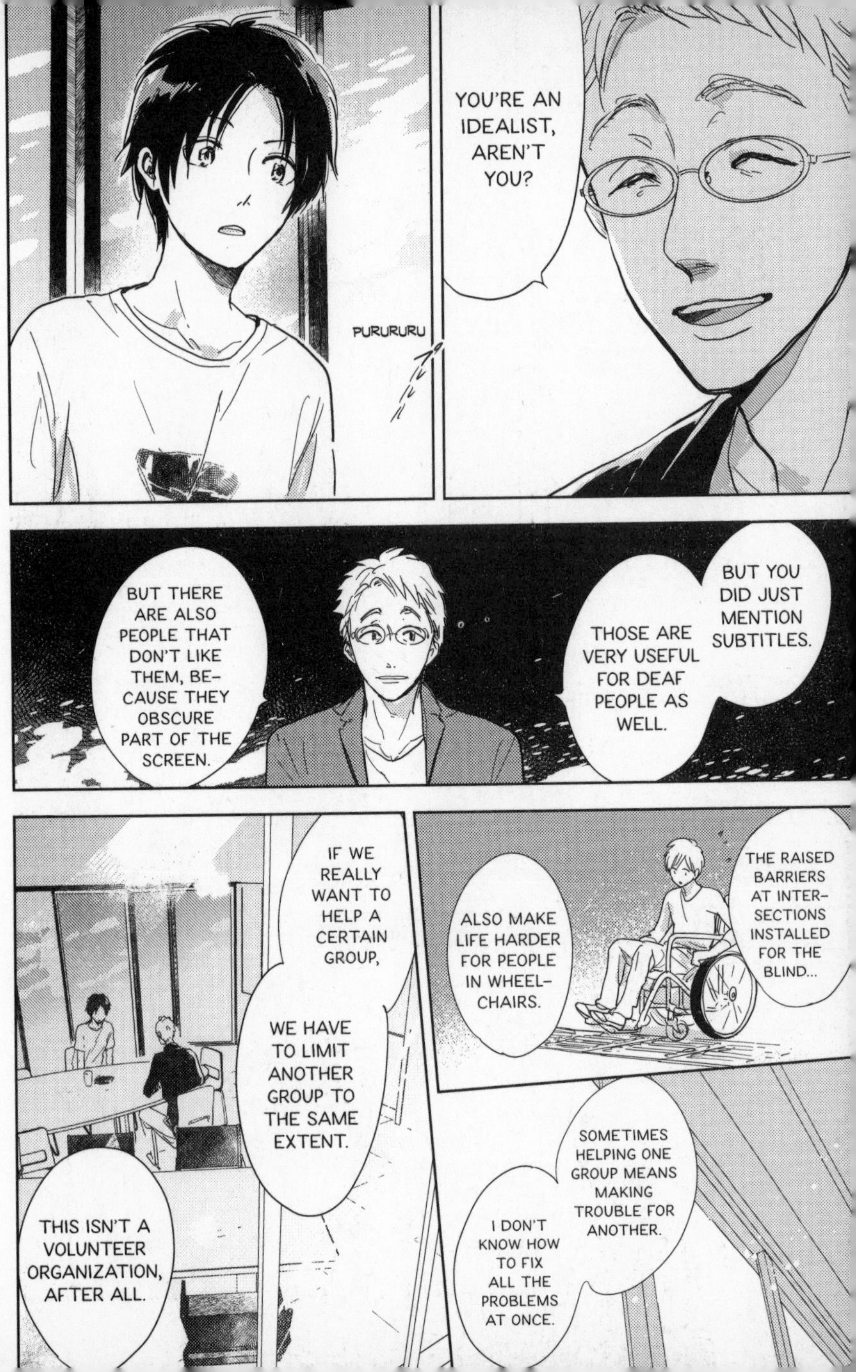
YOU'RE AN IDEALIST, AREN'T YOU?
PURURURU
BUT YOU DID JUST MENTION SUBTITLES.
THOSE ARE VERY USEFUL FOR DEAF PEOPLE AS WELL.
BUT THERE ARE ALSO PEOPLE THAT DON'T LIKE THEM, BECAUSE THEY OBSCURE PART OF THE SCREEN.
THE RAISED BARRIERS AT INTERSECTIONS INSTALLED FOR THE BLIND...
ALSO MAKE LIFE HARDER FOR PEOPLE IN WHEELCHAIRS.
SOMETIMES HELPING ONE GROUP MEANS MAKING TROUBLE FOR ANOTHER.
I DON'T KNOW HOW TO FIX ALL THE PROBLEMS AT ONCE.
IF WE REALLY WANT TO HELP A CERTAIN GROUP,
WE HAVE TO LIMIT ANOTHER GROUP TO THE SAME EXTENT.
THIS ISN'T A VOLUNTEER ORGANIZATION, AFTER ALL.

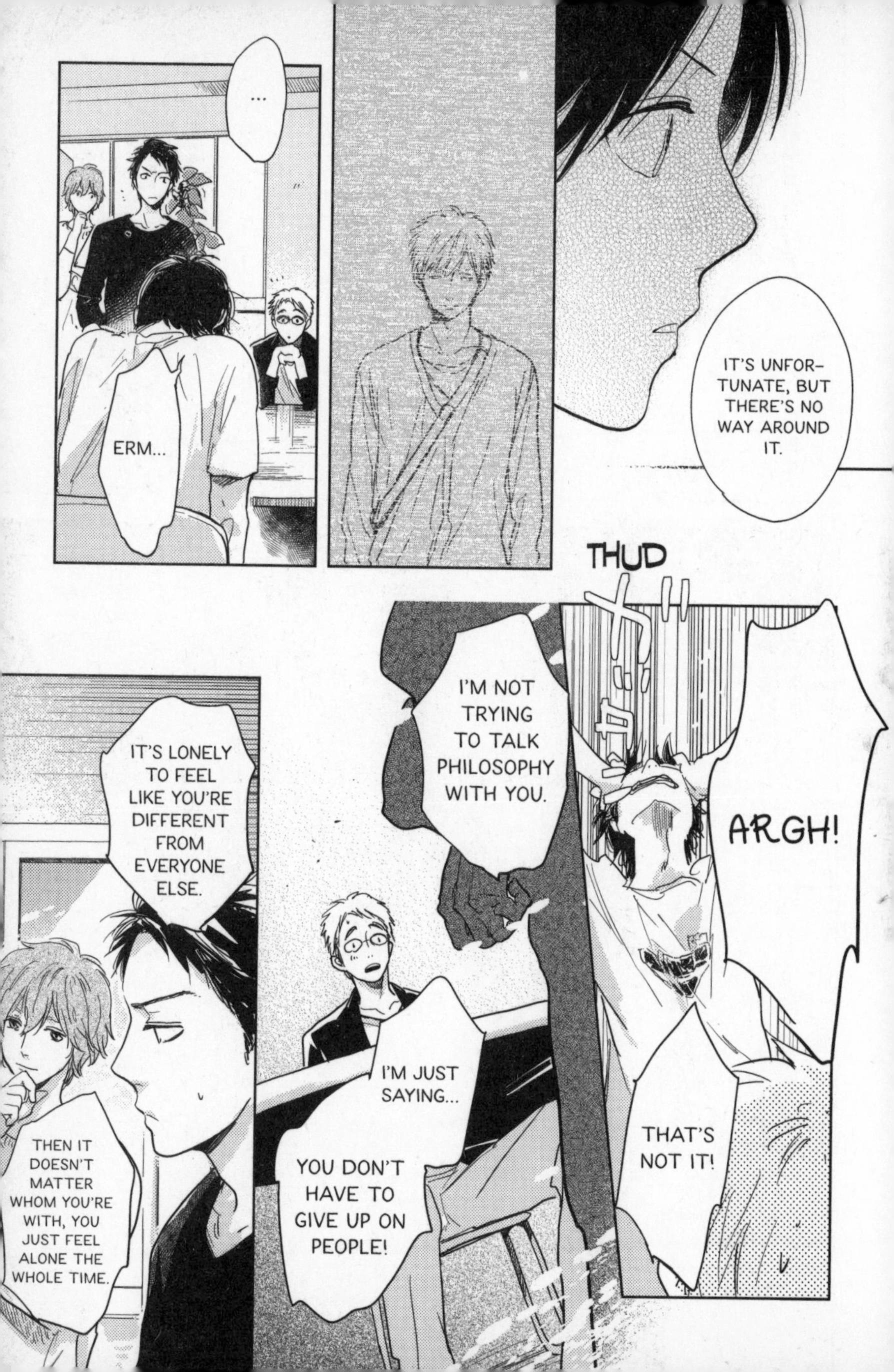
IT'S UNFOR-TUNATE, BUT THERE'S NO WAY AROUND IT.
...
ERM...
THUD
ARGH!
THAT'S NOT IT!
I'M NOT TRYING TO TALK PHILOSOPHY WITH YOU.
I'M JUST SAYING...
YOU DON'T HAVE TO GIVE UP ON PEOPLE!
IT'S LONELY TO FEEL LIKE YOU'RE DIFFERENT FROM EVERYONE ELSE.
THEN IT DOESN'T MATTER WHOM YOU'RE WITH, YOU JUST FEEL ALONE THE WHOLE TIME.

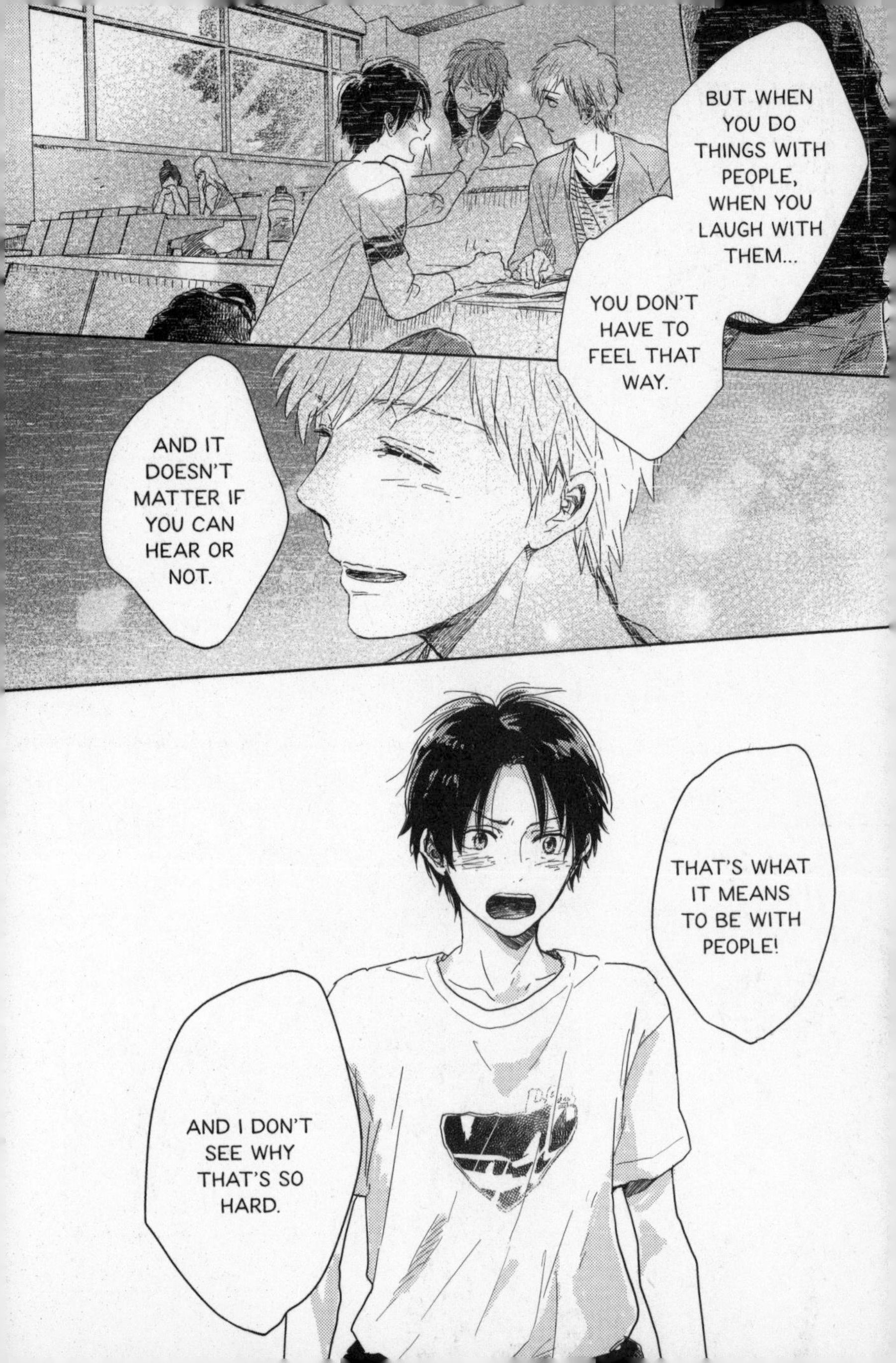
BUT WHEN YOU DO THINGS WITH PEOPLE, WHEN YOU LAUGH WITH THEM...
YOU DON'T HAVE TO FEEL THAT WAY.
AND IT DOESN'T MATTER IF YOU CAN HEAR OR NOT.
THAT'S WHAT IT MEANS TO BE WITH PEOPLE!
AND I DON'T SEE WHY THAT'S SO HARD.

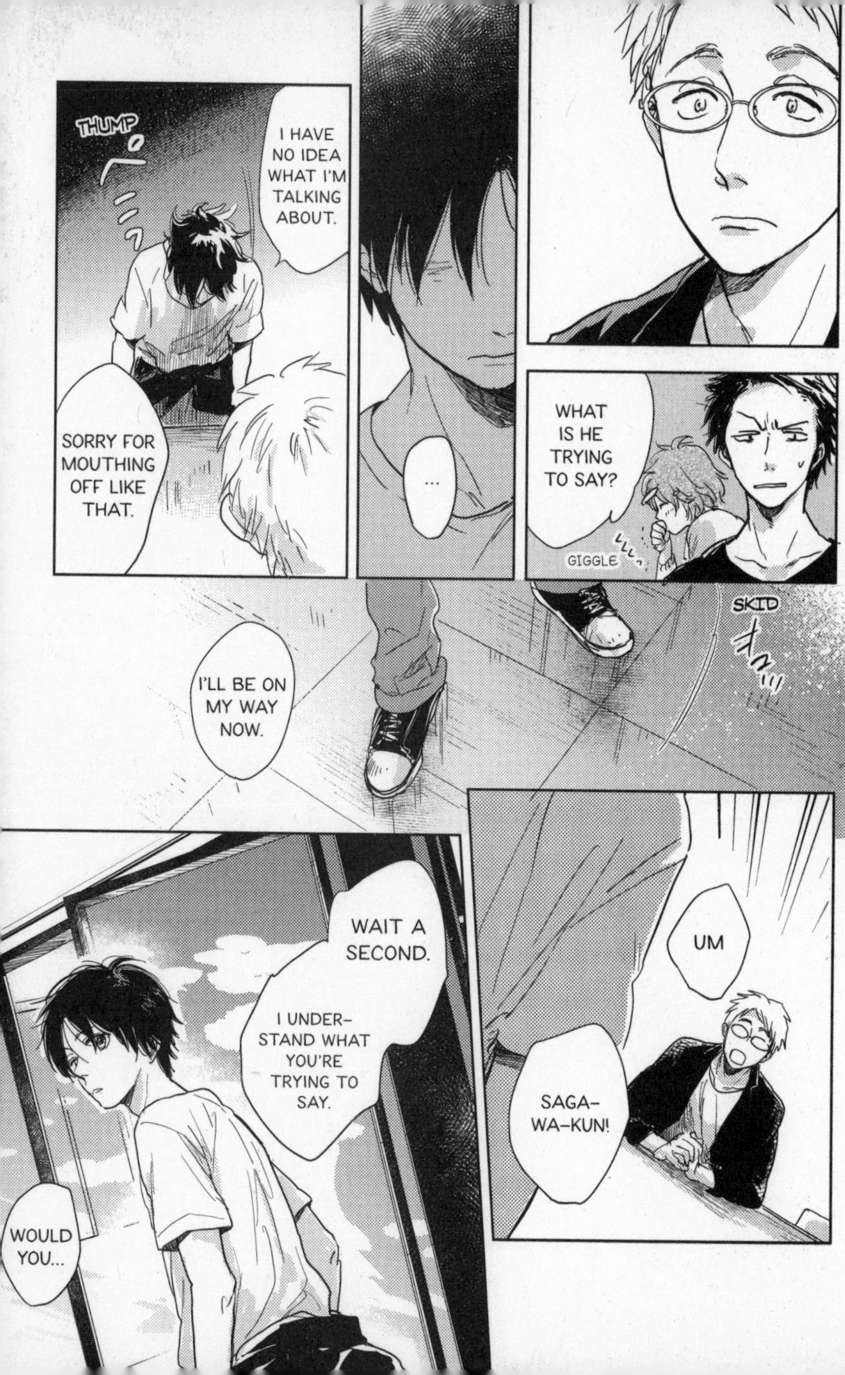
WHAT IS HE TRYING TO SAY?
GIGGLE
...
I HAVE NO IDEA WHAT I'M TALKING ABOUT.
THUMP
SORRY FOR MOUTHING OFF LIKE THAT.
SKID
I'LL BE ON MY WAY NOW.
UM
SAGA-WA-KUN!
WAIT A SECOND.
I UNDER-STAND WHAT YOU'RE TRYING TO SAY.
WOULD YOU...

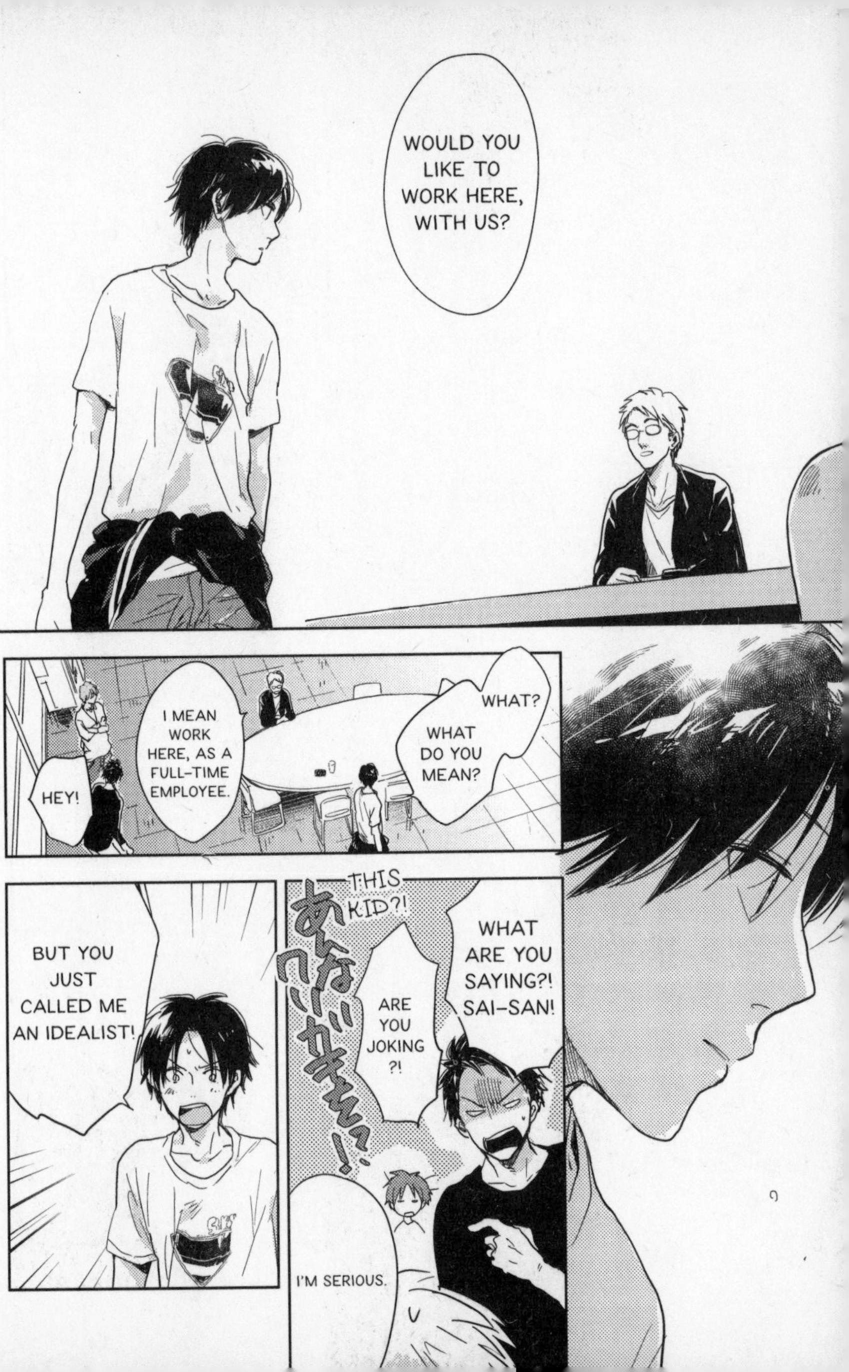
WOULD YOU LIKE TO WORK HERE, WITH US?
WHAT?
WHAT DO YOU MEAN?
I MEAN WORK HERE, AS A FULL-TIME EMPLOYEE.
HEY!
WHAT ARE YOU SAYING?! SAI-SAN!
THIS KID?!
ARE YOU JOKING?!
I'M SERIOUS.
BUT YOU JUST CALLED ME AN IDEALIST!

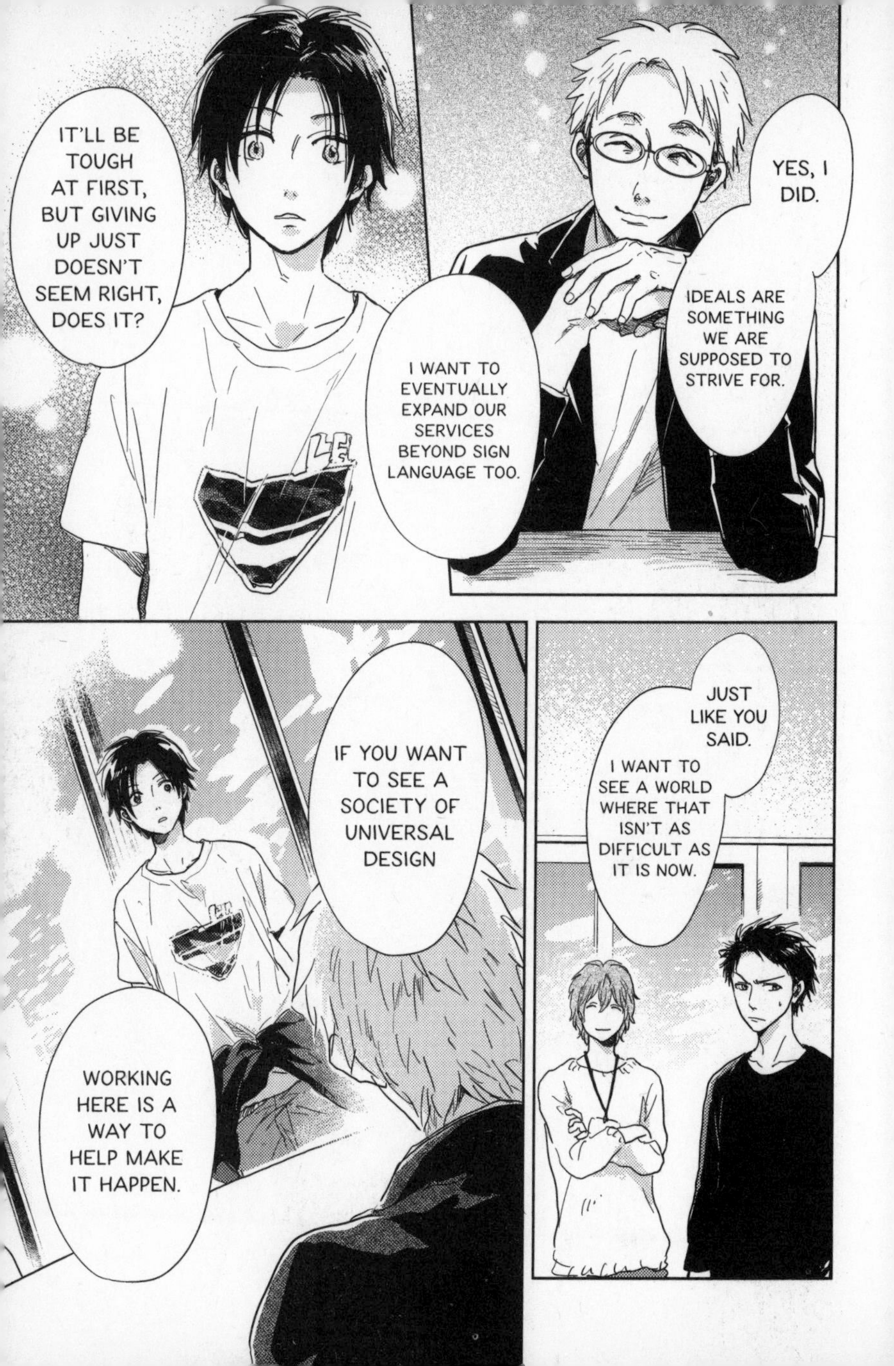
YES, I DID.
IDEALS ARE SOMETHING WE ARE SUPPOSED TO STRIVE FOR.
I WANT TO EVENTUALLY EXPAND OUR SERVICES BEYOND SIGN LANGUAGE TOO.
IT'LL BE TOUGH AT FIRST, BUT GIVING UP JUST DOESN'T SEEM RIGHT, DOES IT?
JUST LIKE YOU SAID.
I WANT TO SEE A WORLD WHERE THAT ISN'T AS DIFFICULT AS IT IS NOW.
IF YOU WANT TO SEE A SOCIETY OF UNIVERSAL DESIGN
WORKING HERE IS A WAY TO HELP MAKE IT HAPPEN.

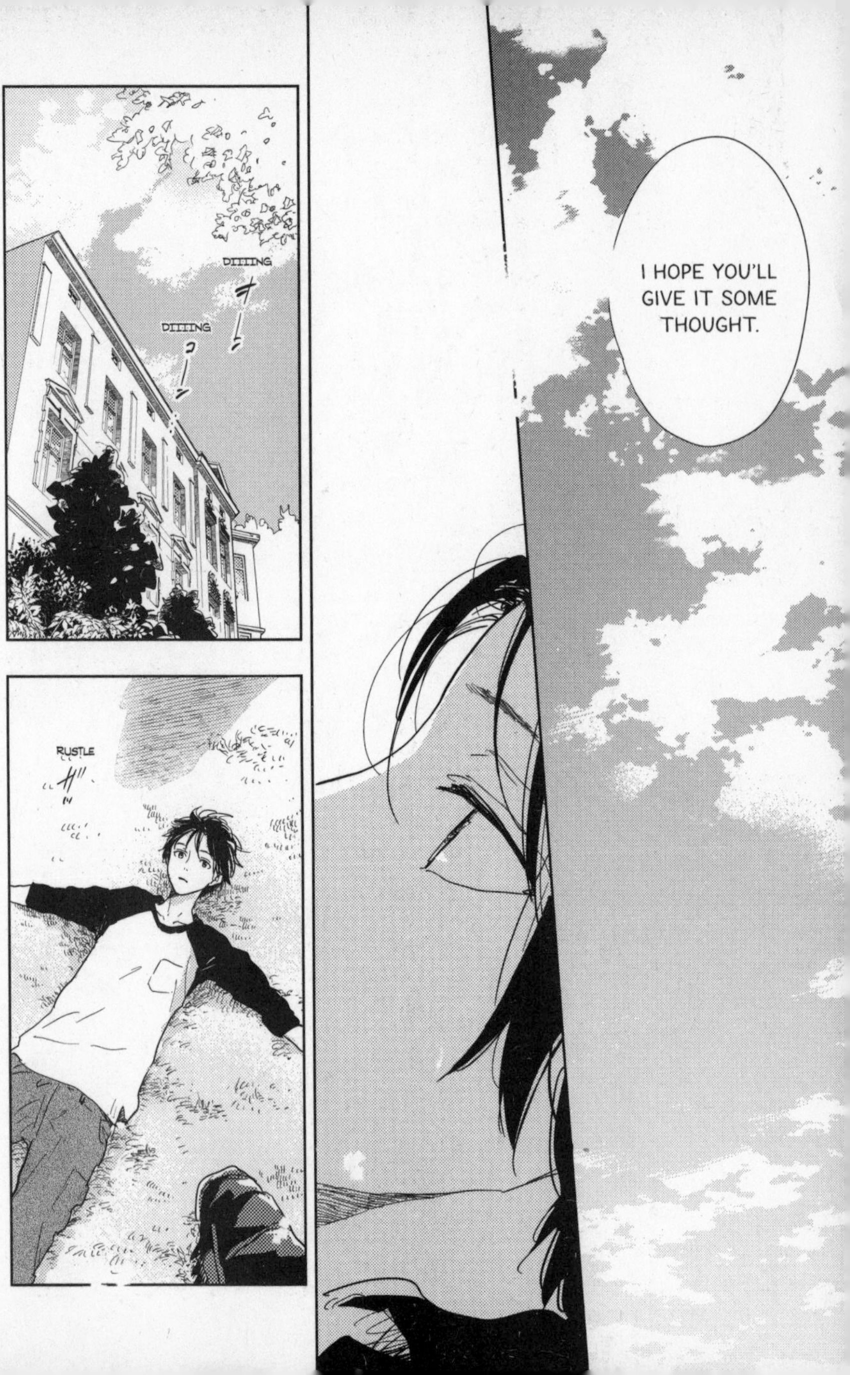
I HOPE YOU'LL GIVE IT SOME THOUGHT.
DIIIING
DIIIING
RUSTLE

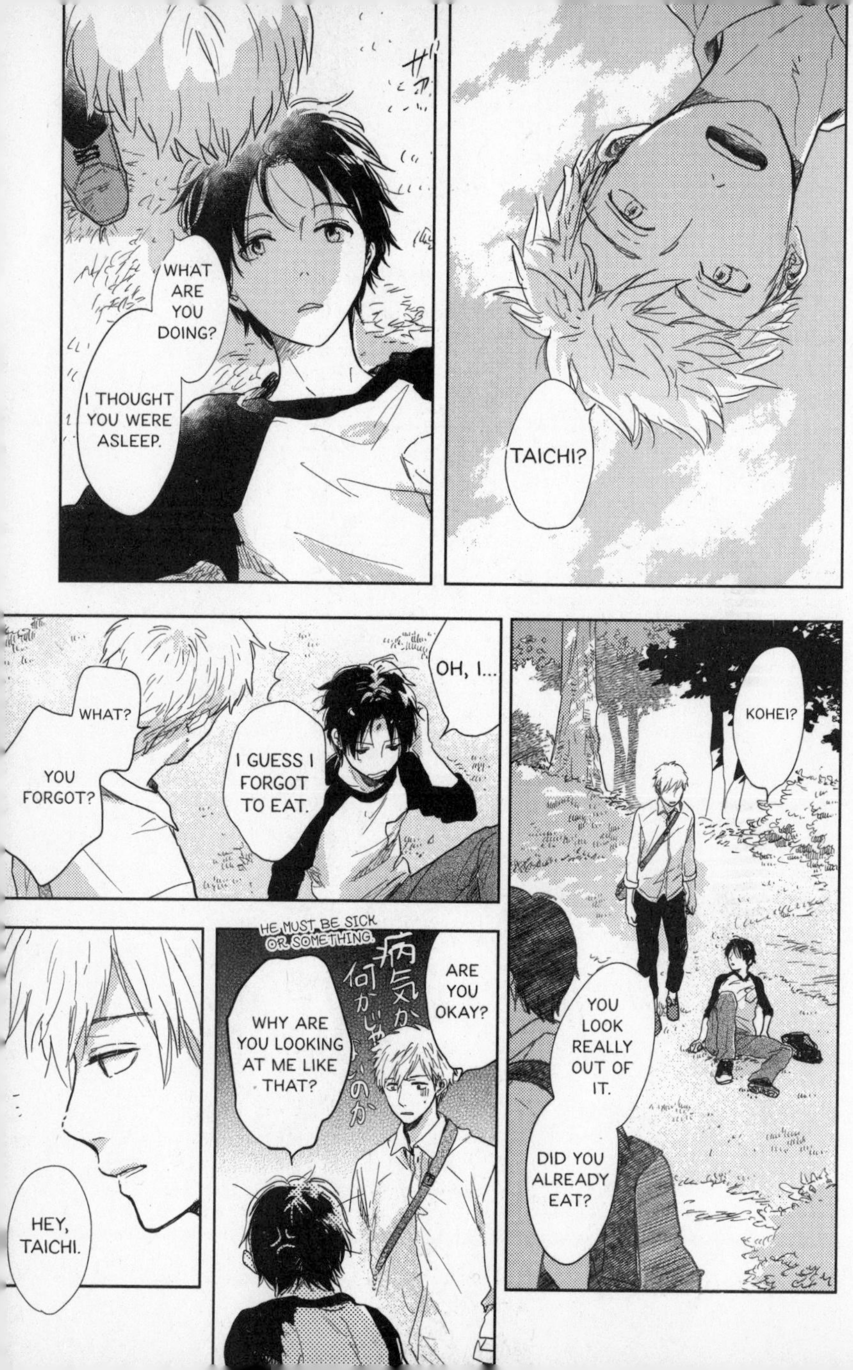
TAICHI?
WHAT ARE YOU DOING?
I THOUGHT YOU WERE ASLEEP.
KOHEI?
YOU LOOK REALLY OUT OF IT.
DID YOU ALREADY EAT?
OH, I...
I GUESS I FORGOT TO EAT.
WHAT?
YOU FORGOT?
HE MUST BE SICK OR SOMETHING.
ARE YOU OKAY?
WHY ARE YOU LOOKING AT ME LIKE THAT?
HEY, TAICHI.

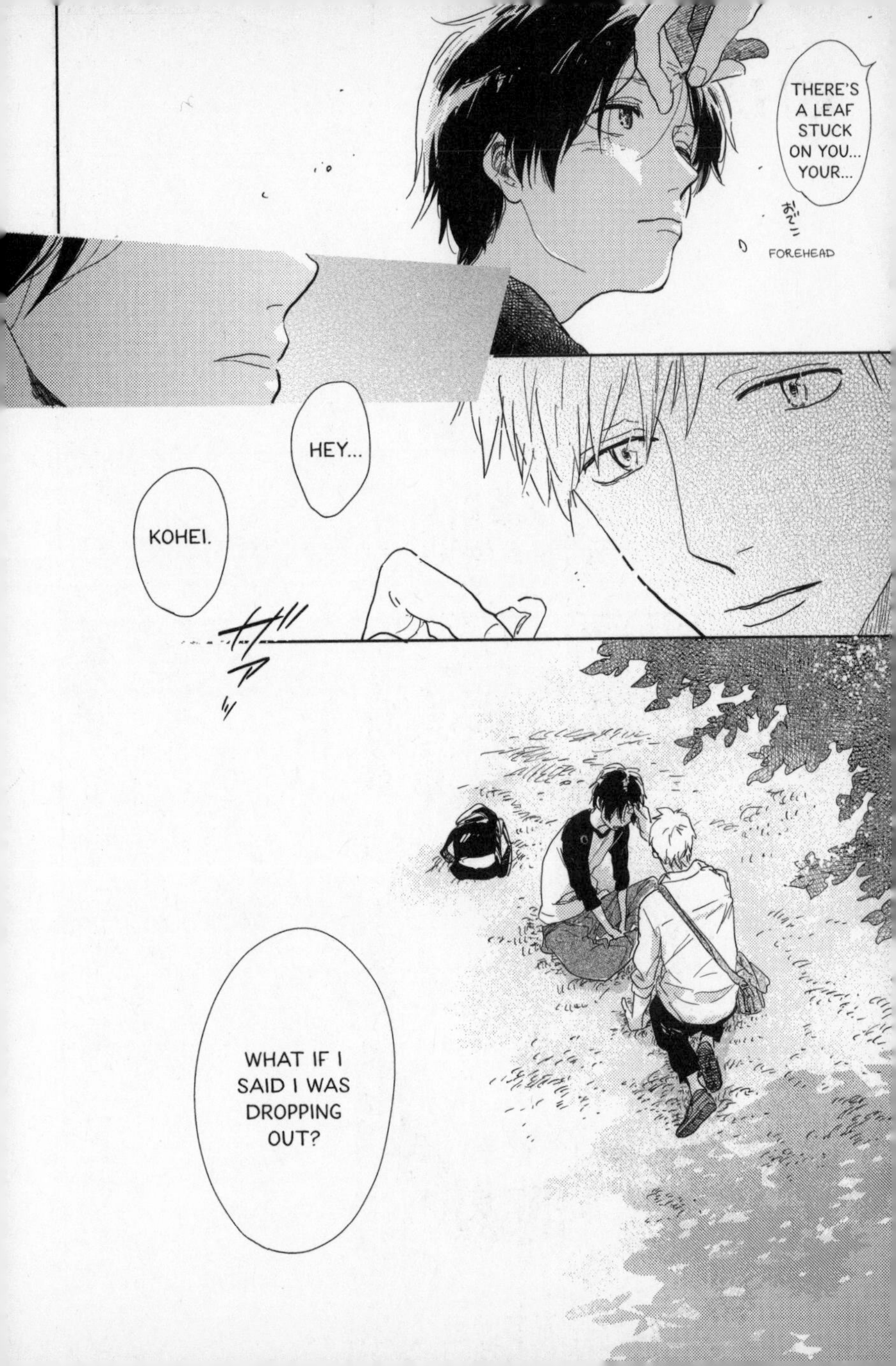
THERE'S A LEAF STUCK ON YOU... YOUR...
おでこ
FOREHEAD
HEY...
KOHEI.
ザァッ
WHAT IF I SAID I WAS DROPPING OUT?

CHAPTER 4

WHAT IF I SAID I WAS DROPPING OUT?

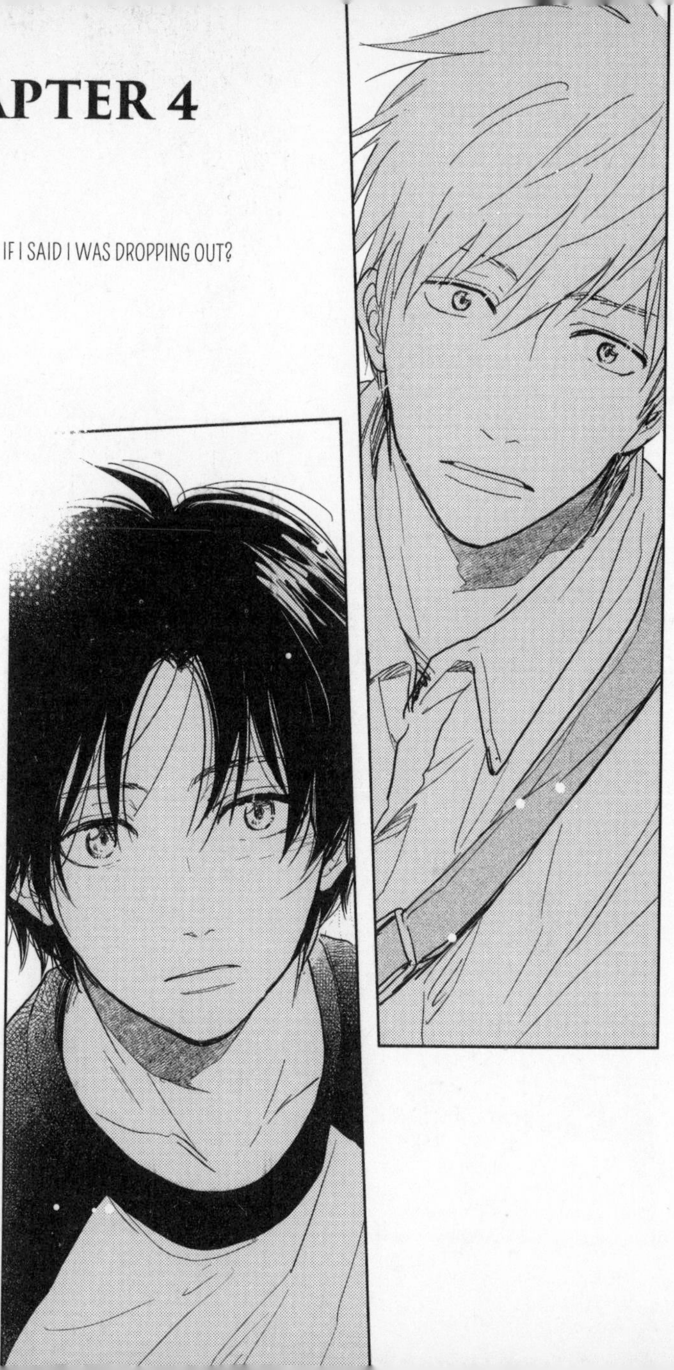

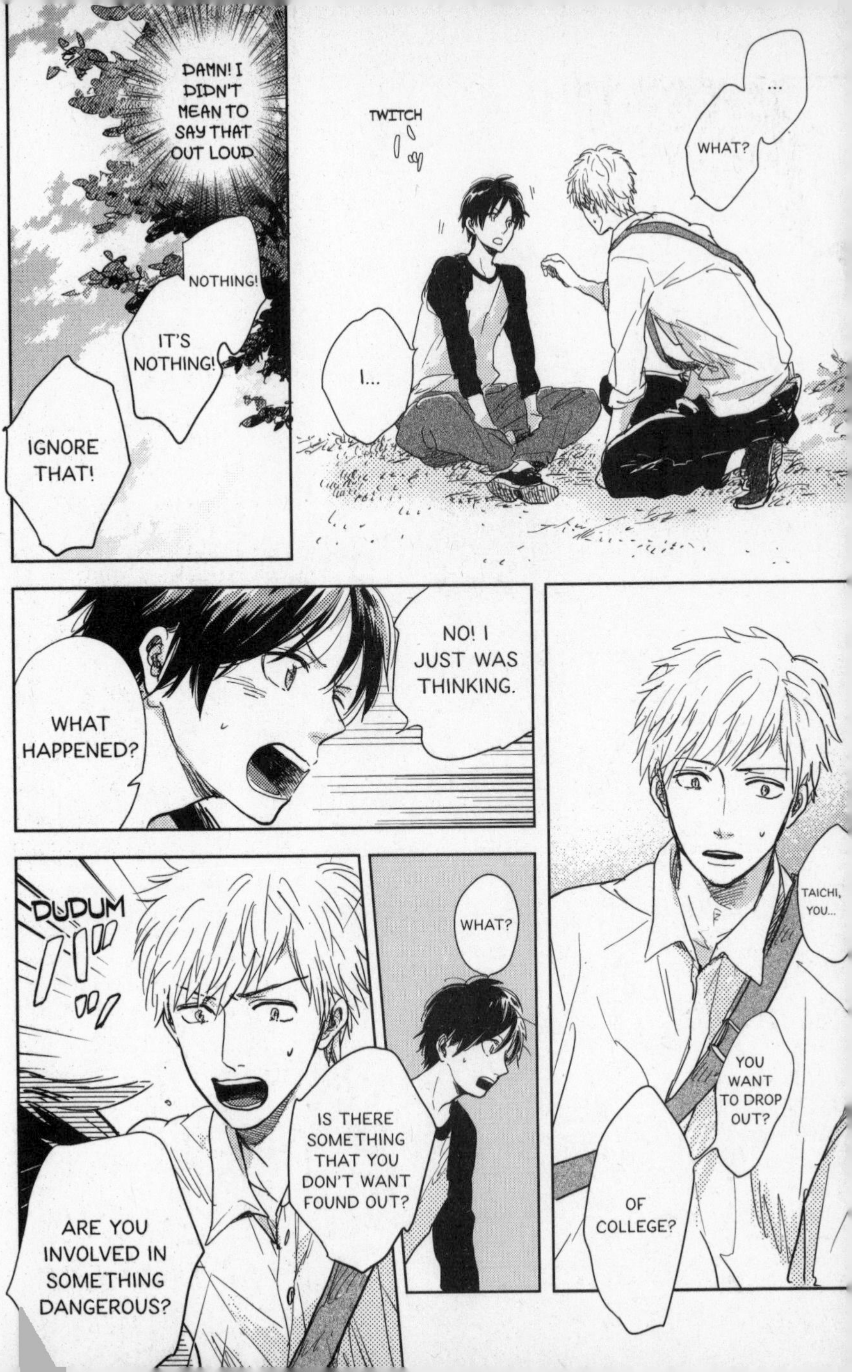
...
WHAT?
TWITCH
I...
DAMN! I DIDN'T MEAN TO SAY THAT OUT LOUD
NOTHING!
IT'S NOTHING!
IGNORE THAT!
TAICHI, YOU...
YOU WANT TO DROP OUT?
OF COLLEGE?
NO! I JUST WAS THINKING.
WHAT HAPPENED?
WHAT?
DUDUM
IS THERE SOMETHING THAT YOU DON'T WANT FOUND OUT?
ARE YOU INVOLVED IN SOMETHING DANGEROUS?

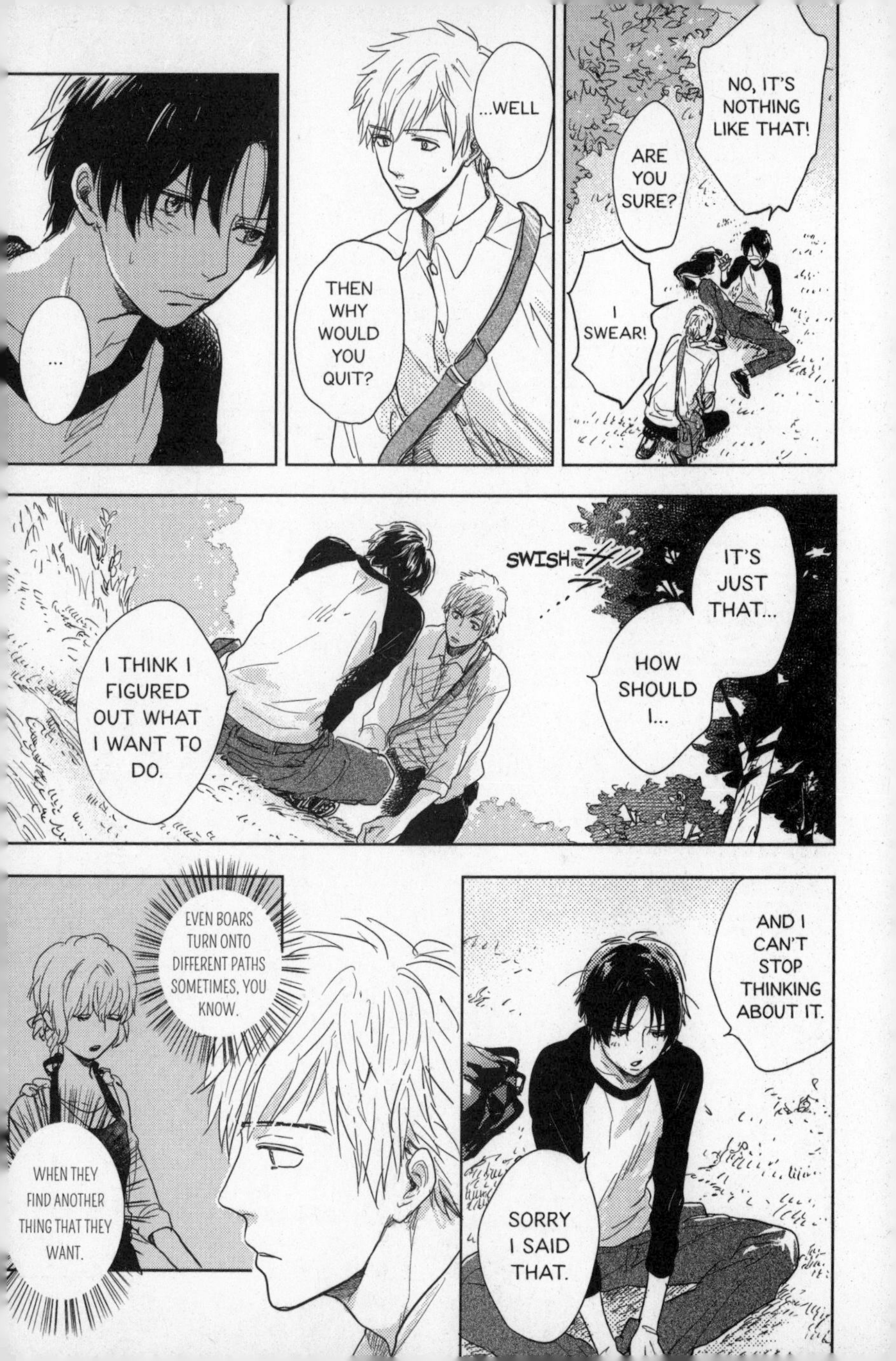
NO, IT'S NOTHING LIKE THAT!
ARE YOU SURE?
I SWEAR!
...WELL
THEN WHY WOULD YOU QUIT?
...
SWISH
IT'S JUST THAT...
HOW SHOULD I...
I THINK I FIGURED OUT WHAT I WANT TO DO.
AND I CAN'T STOP THINKING ABOUT IT.
SORRY I SAID THAT.
EVEN BOARS TURN ONTO DIFFERENT PATHS SOMETIMES, YOU KNOW.
WHEN THEY FIND ANOTHER THING THAT THEY WANT.

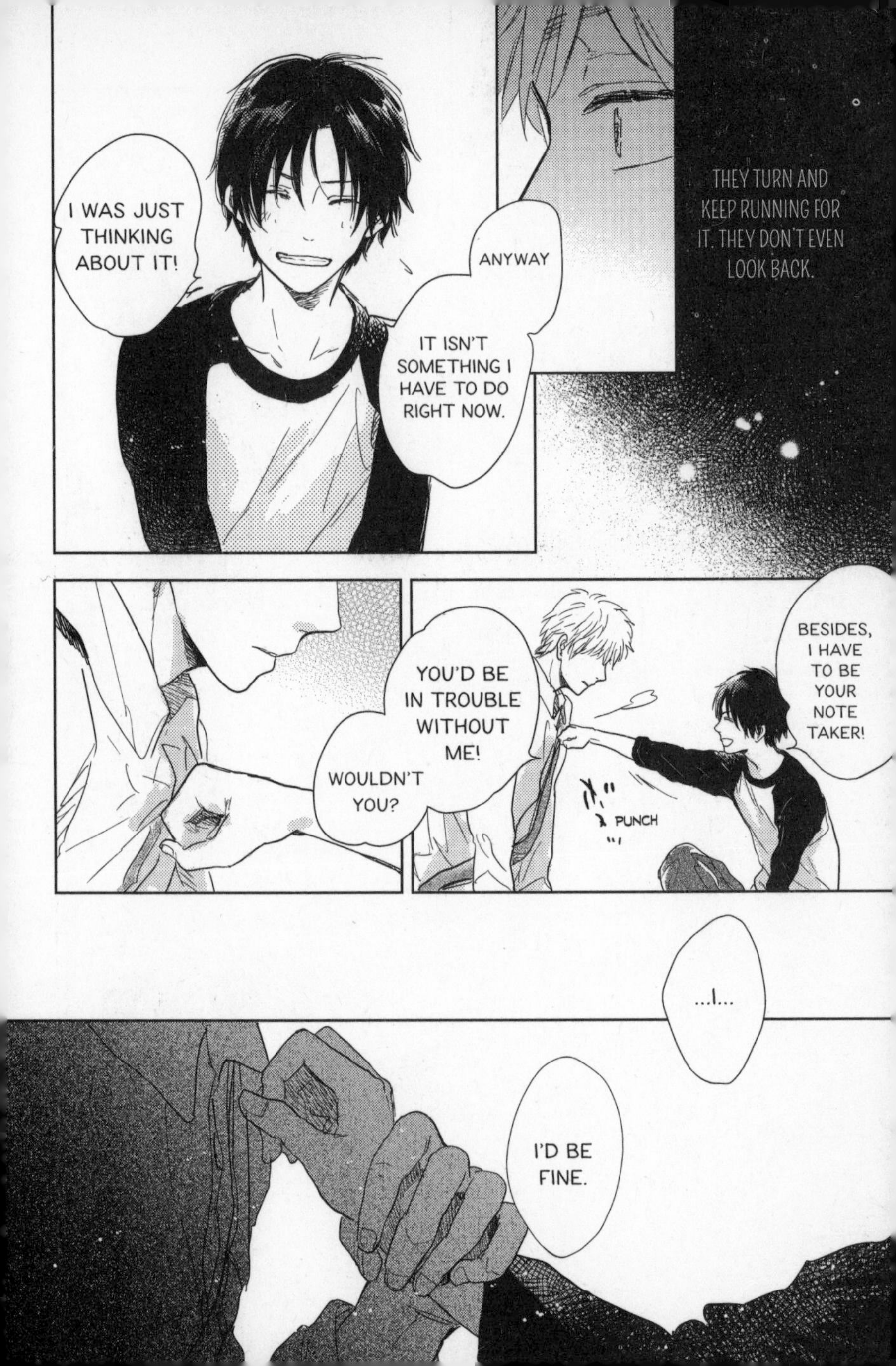
THEY TURN AND KEEP RUNNING FOR IT. THEY DON'T EVEN LOOK BACK.
I WAS JUST THINKING ABOUT IT!
ANYWAY
IT ISN'T SOMETHING I HAVE TO DO RIGHT NOW.
BESIDES, I HAVE TO BE YOUR NOTE TAKER!
PUNCH
YOU'D BE IN TROUBLE WITHOUT ME!
WOULDN'T YOU?
...I...
I'D BE FINE.

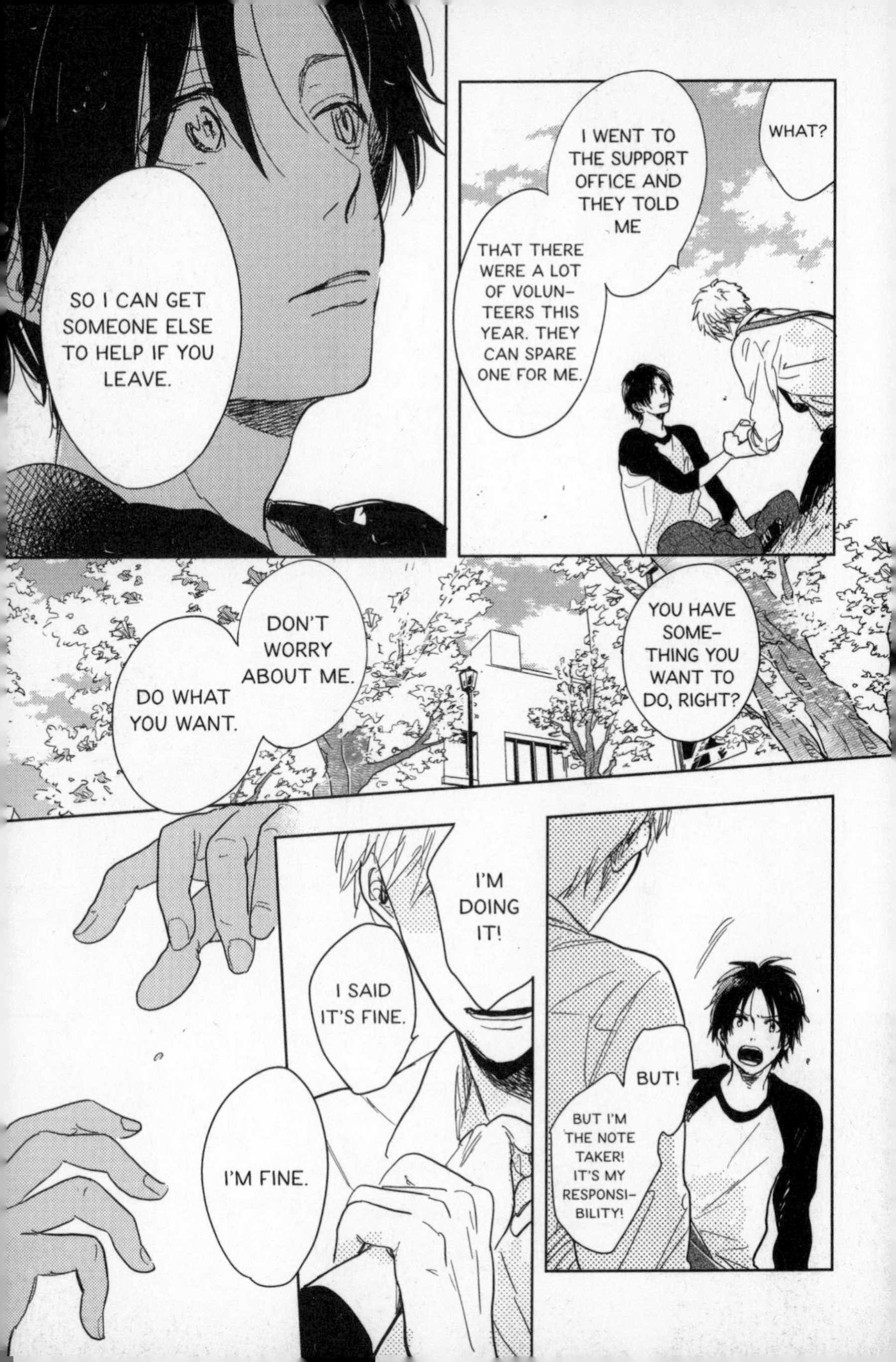
WHAT?
I WENT TO THE SUPPORT OFFICE AND THEY TOLD ME
THAT THERE WERE A LOT OF VOLUNTEERS THIS YEAR. THEY CAN SPARE ONE FOR ME.
SO I CAN GET SOMEONE ELSE TO HELP IF YOU LEAVE.
YOU HAVE SOMETHING YOU WANT TO DO, RIGHT?
DON'T WORRY ABOUT ME.
DO WHAT YOU WANT.
BUT!
BUT I'M THE NOTE TAKER! IT'S MY RESPONSIBILITY!
I'M DOING IT!
I SAID IT'S FINE.
I'M FINE.

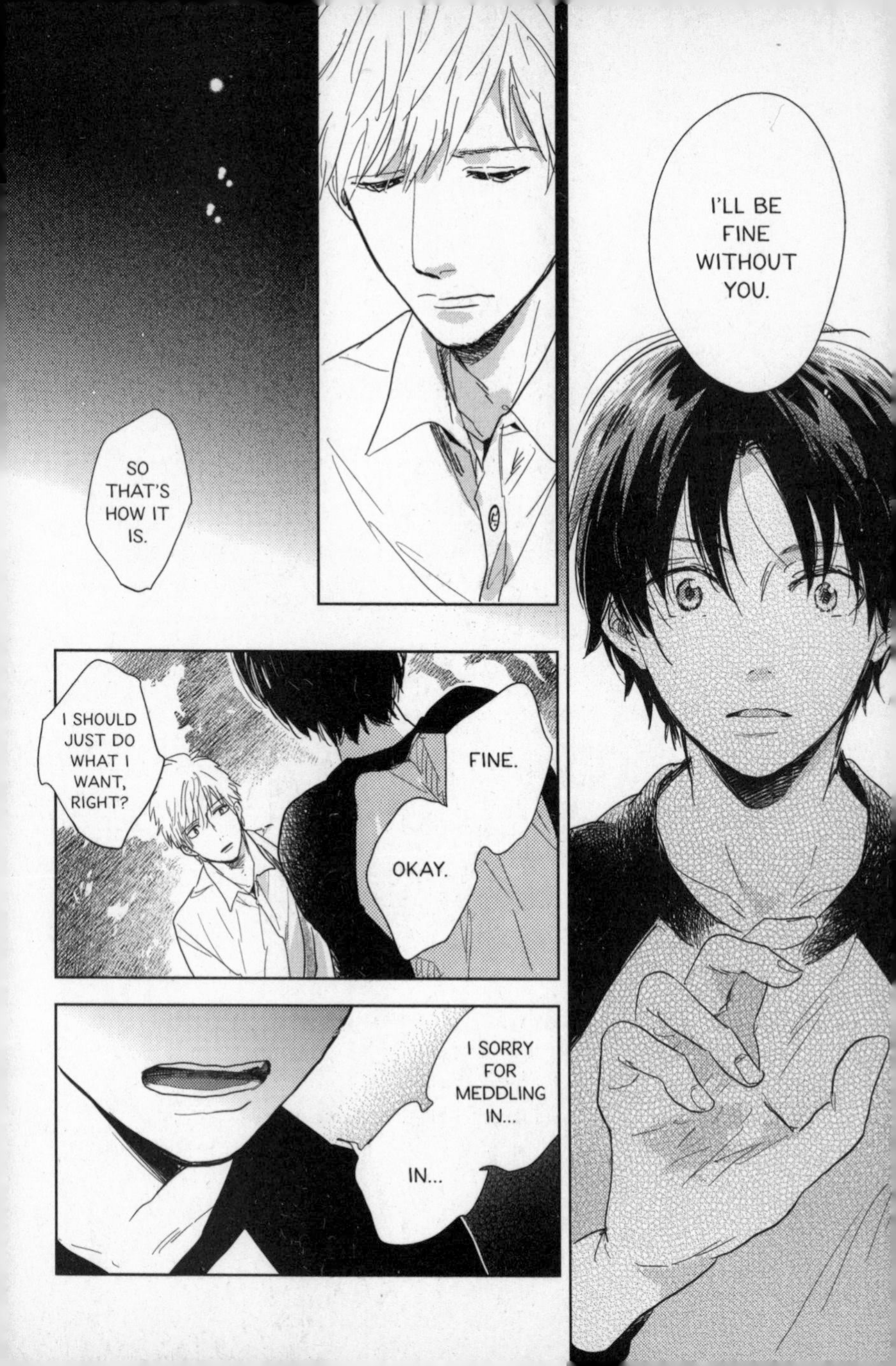
I'LL BE FINE WITHOUT YOU.
SO THAT'S HOW IT IS.
FINE.
OKAY.
I SHOULD JUST DO WHAT I WANT, RIGHT?
I SORRY FOR MEDDLING IN...
IN...

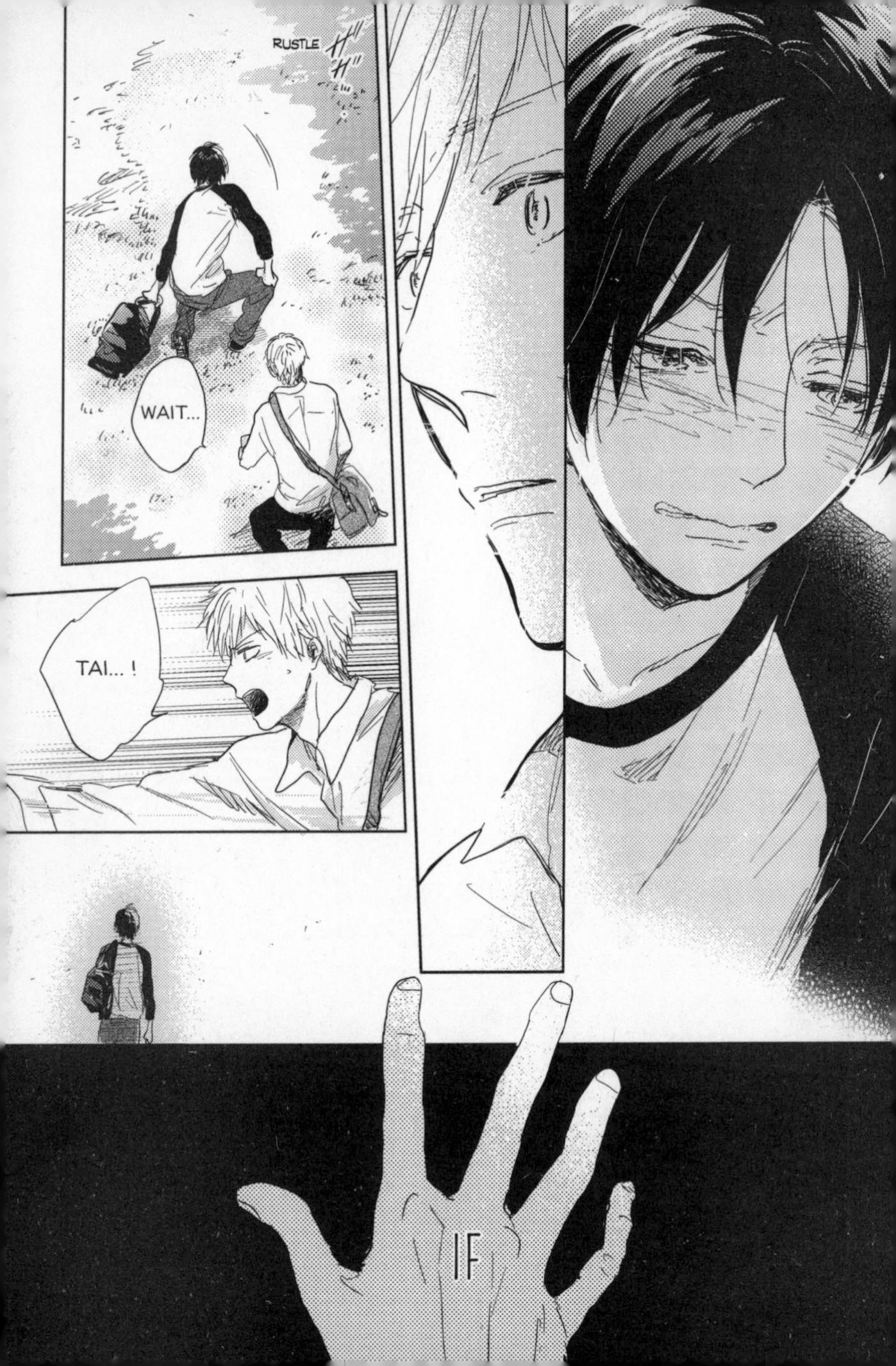
RUSTLE
WAIT...
TAI... !
IF

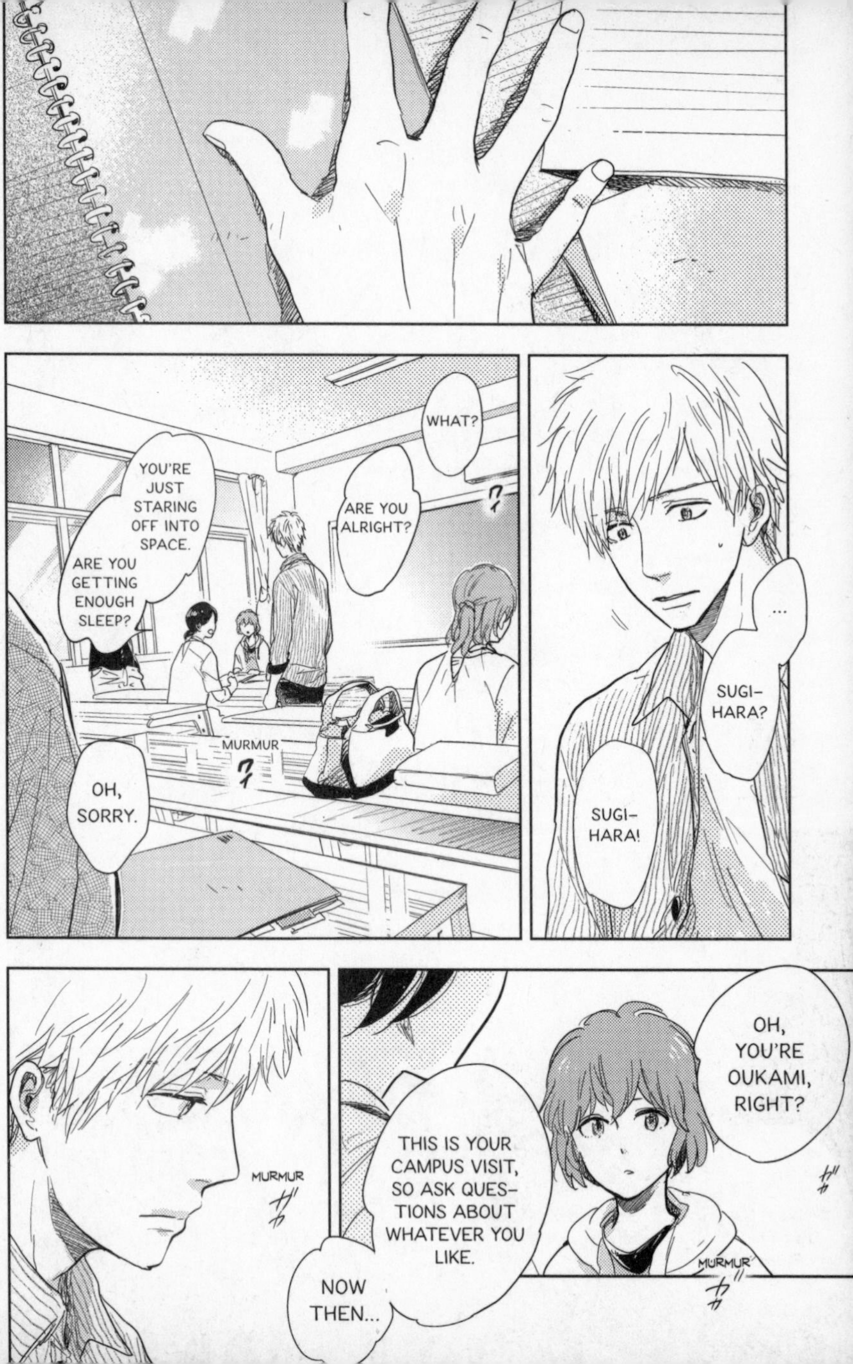
...
SUGI-HARA?
SUGI-HARA!
WHAT?
ARE YOU ALRIGHT?
YOU'RE JUST STARING OFF INTO SPACE.
ARE YOU GETTING ENOUGH SLEEP?
MURMUR
OH, SORRY.
OH, YOU'RE OUKAMI, RIGHT?
THIS IS YOUR CAMPUS VISIT, SO ASK QUESTIONS ABOUT WHATEVER YOU LIKE.
MURMUR
NOW THEN...
MURMUR

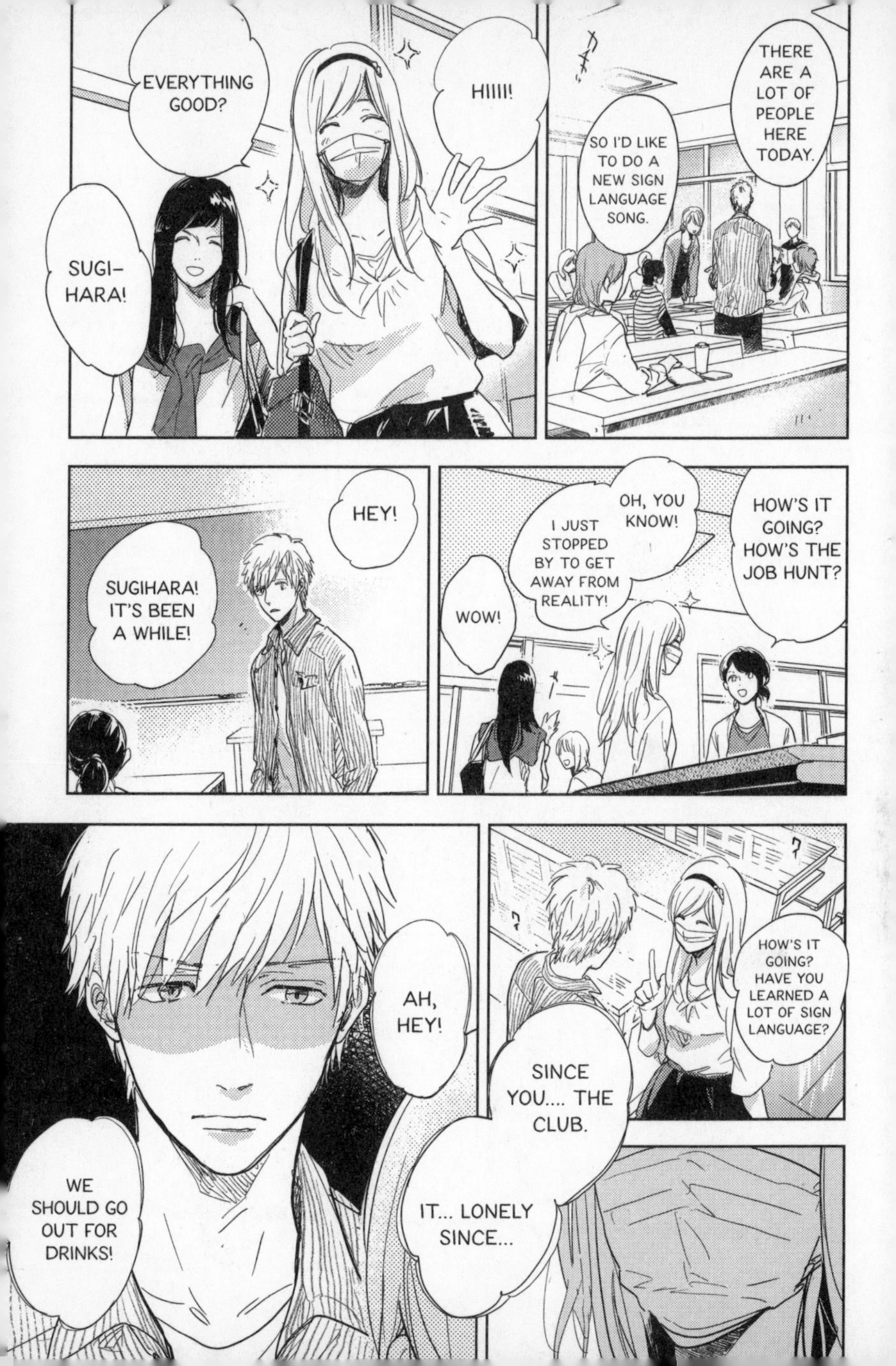
THERE ARE A LOT OF PEOPLE HERE TODAY.
SO I'D LIKE TO DO A NEW SIGN LANGUAGE SONG.
HIIII!
EVERYTHING GOOD?
SUGI-HARA!
HOW'S IT GOING? HOW'S THE JOB HUNT?
OH, YOU KNOW!
I JUST STOPPED BY TO GET AWAY FROM REALITY!
WOW!
HEY!
SUGIHARA! IT'S BEEN A WHILE!
HOW'S IT GOING? HAVE YOU LEARNED A LOT OF SIGN LANGUAGE?
SINCE YOU.... THE CLUB.
IT... LONELY SINCE...
AH, HEY!
WE SHOULD GO OUT FOR DRINKS!

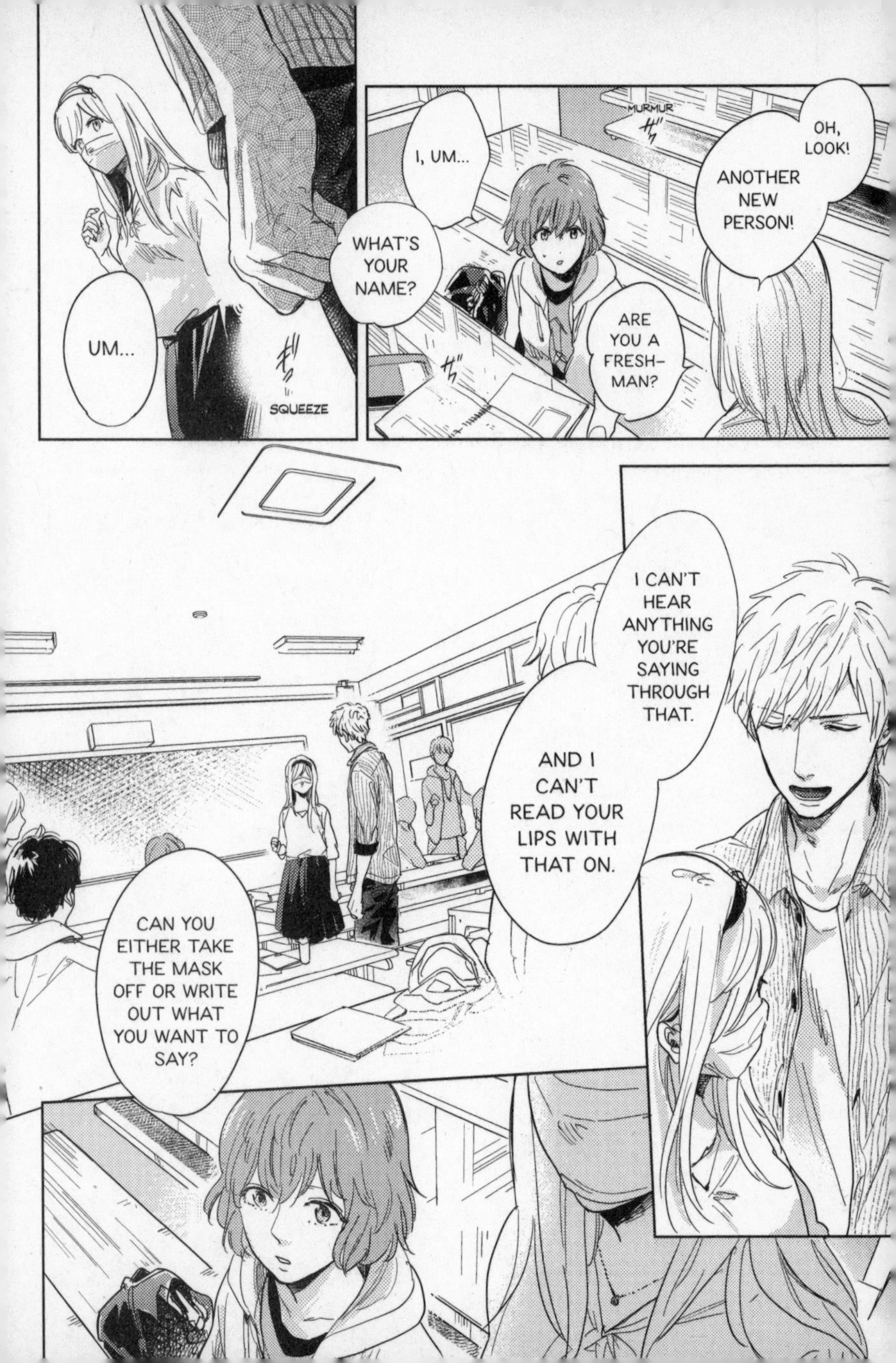
OH, LOOK!
ANOTHER NEW PERSON!
MURMUR
I, UM...
WHAT'S YOUR NAME?
ARE YOU A FRESHMAN?
UM...
SQUEEZE
I CAN'T HEAR ANYTHING YOU'RE SAYING THROUGH THAT.
AND I CAN'T READ YOUR LIPS WITH THAT ON.
CAN YOU EITHER TAKE THE MASK OFF OR WRITE OUT WHAT YOU WANT TO SAY?

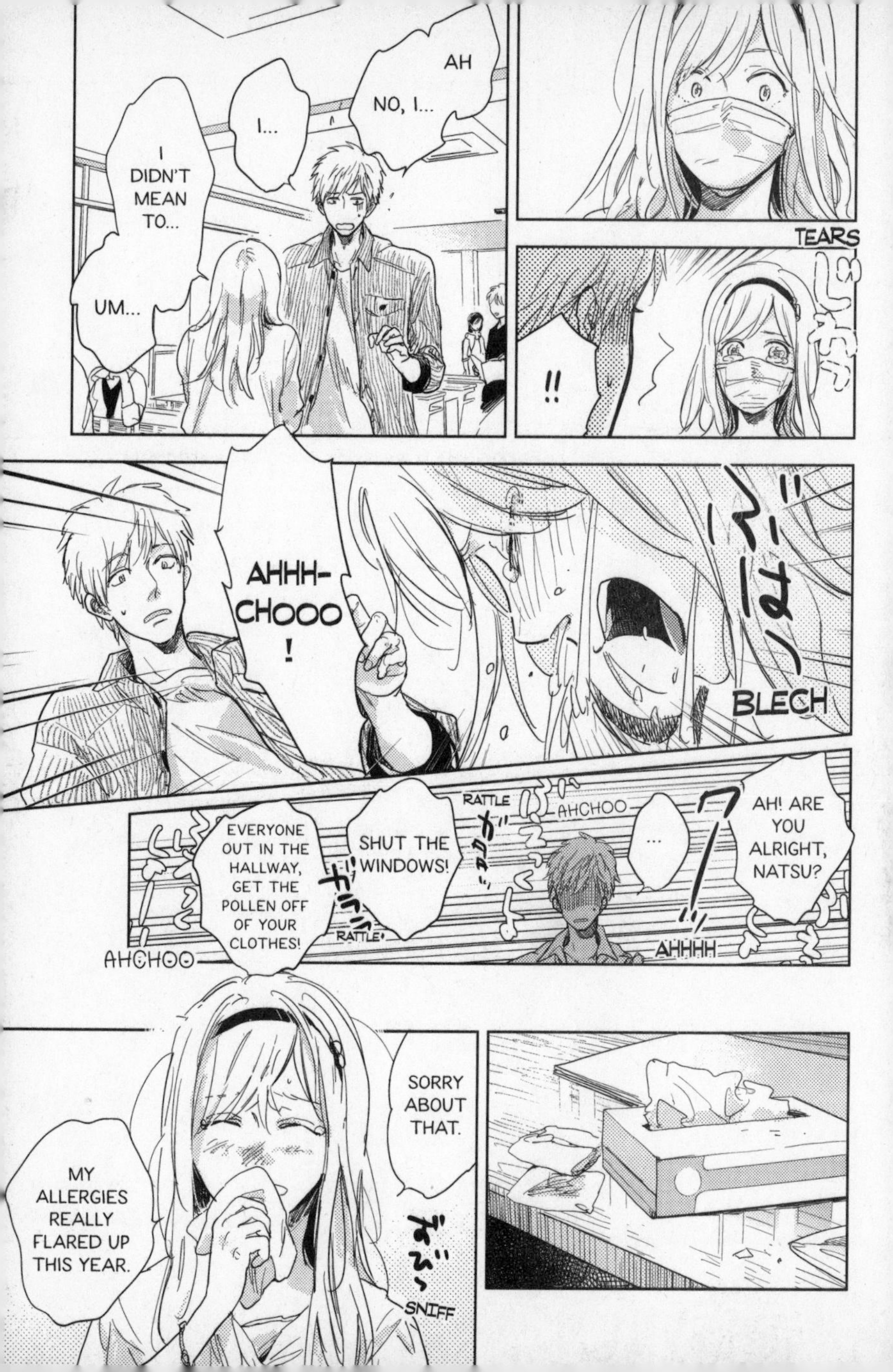
TEARS
!!
AH
NO, I...
I...
I DIDN'T MEAN TO...
UM...
AHHH-CHOOO!
BLECH
AH! ARE YOU ALRIGHT, NATSU?
AHHHH
...
AHCHOO
RATTLE
SHUT THE WINDOWS!
RATTLE
EVERYONE OUT IN THE HALLWAY, GET THE POLLEN OFF OF YOUR CLOTHES!
AHCHOO
SORRY ABOUT THAT.
MY ALLERGIES REALLY FLARED UP THIS YEAR.
SNIFF

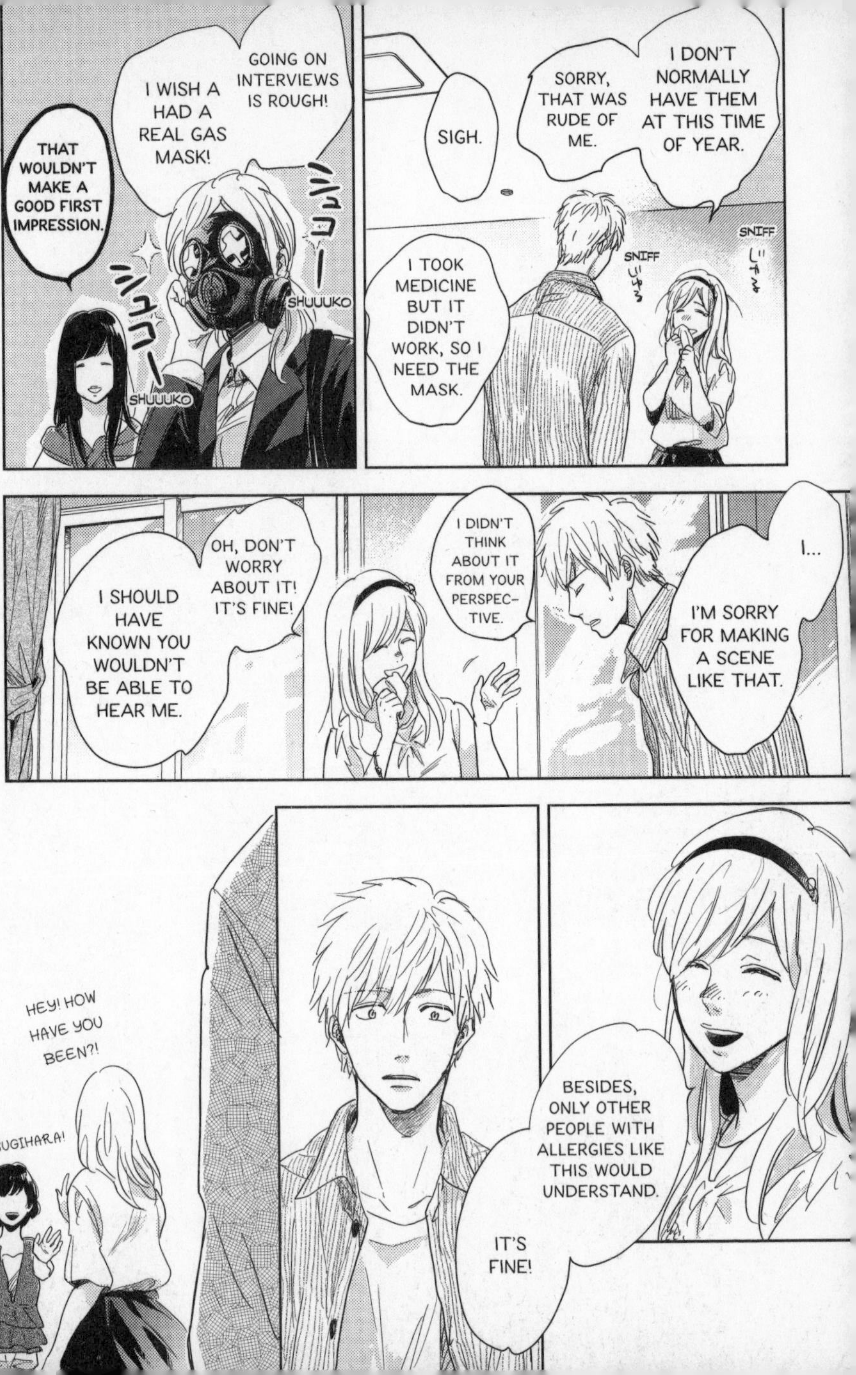
I DON'T NORMALLY HAVE THEM AT THIS TIME OF YEAR.
SORRY, THAT WAS RUDE OF ME.
SIGH.
SNIFF
SNIFF
I TOOK MEDICINE BUT IT DIDN'T WORK, SO I NEED THE MASK.
GOING ON INTERVIEWS IS ROUGH!
I WISH A HAD A REAL GAS MASK!
SHUUUKO
SHUUUKO
THAT WOULDN'T MAKE A GOOD FIRST IMPRESSION.
I...
I'M SORRY FOR MAKING A SCENE LIKE THAT.
I DIDN'T THINK ABOUT IT FROM YOUR PERSPEC-TIVE.
OH, DON'T WORRY ABOUT IT! IT'S FINE!
I SHOULD HAVE KNOWN YOU WOULDN'T BE ABLE TO HEAR ME.
BESIDES, ONLY OTHER PEOPLE WITH ALLERGIES LIKE THIS WOULD UNDERSTAND.
IT'S FINE!
HEY! HOW HAVE YOU BEEN?!
SUGIHARA!

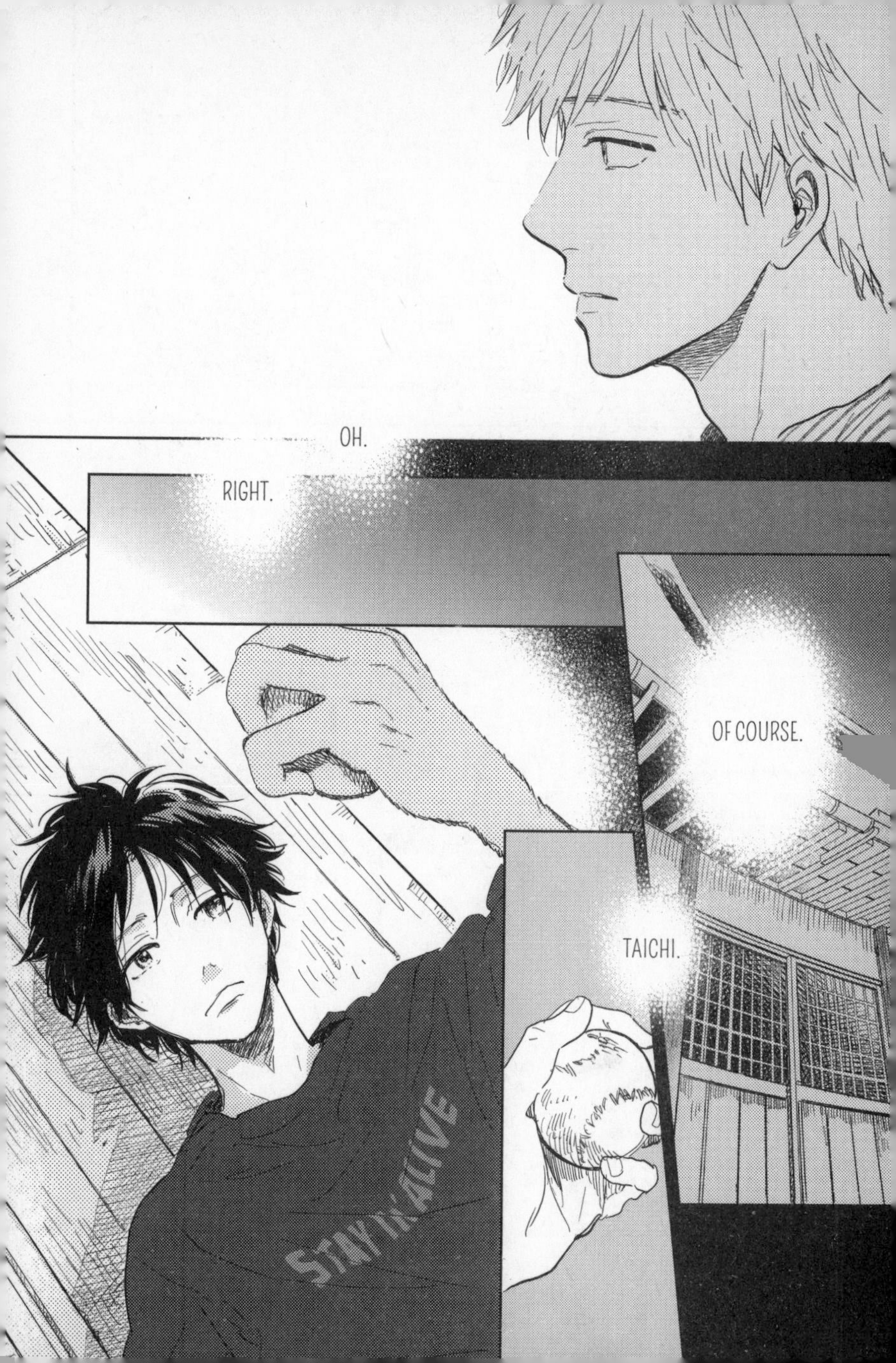
OH.
RIGHT.
OF COURSE.
TAICHI.

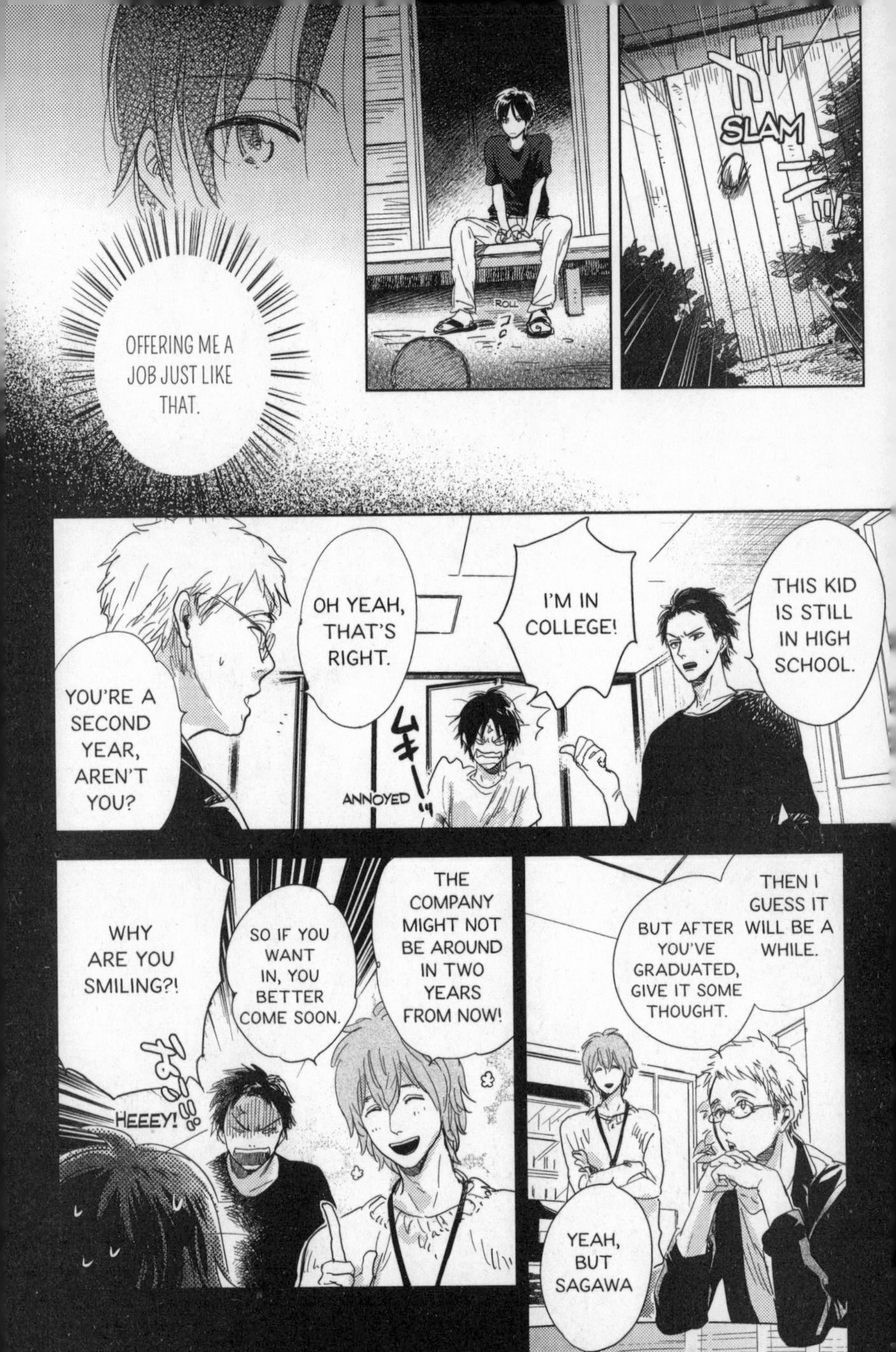
SLAM
ROLL
OFFERING ME A JOB JUST LIKE THAT.
THIS KID IS STILL IN HIGH SCHOOL.
I'M IN COLLEGE!
OH YEAH, THAT'S RIGHT.
YOU'RE A SECOND YEAR, AREN'T YOU?
ANNOYED
THEN I GUESS IT WILL BE A WHILE.
BUT AFTER YOU'VE GRADUATED, GIVE IT SOME THOUGHT.
YEAH, BUT SAGAWA
THE COMPANY MIGHT NOT BE AROUND IN TWO YEARS FROM NOW!
SO IF YOU WANT IN, YOU BETTER COME SOON.
WHY ARE YOU SMILING?!
HEEEY!

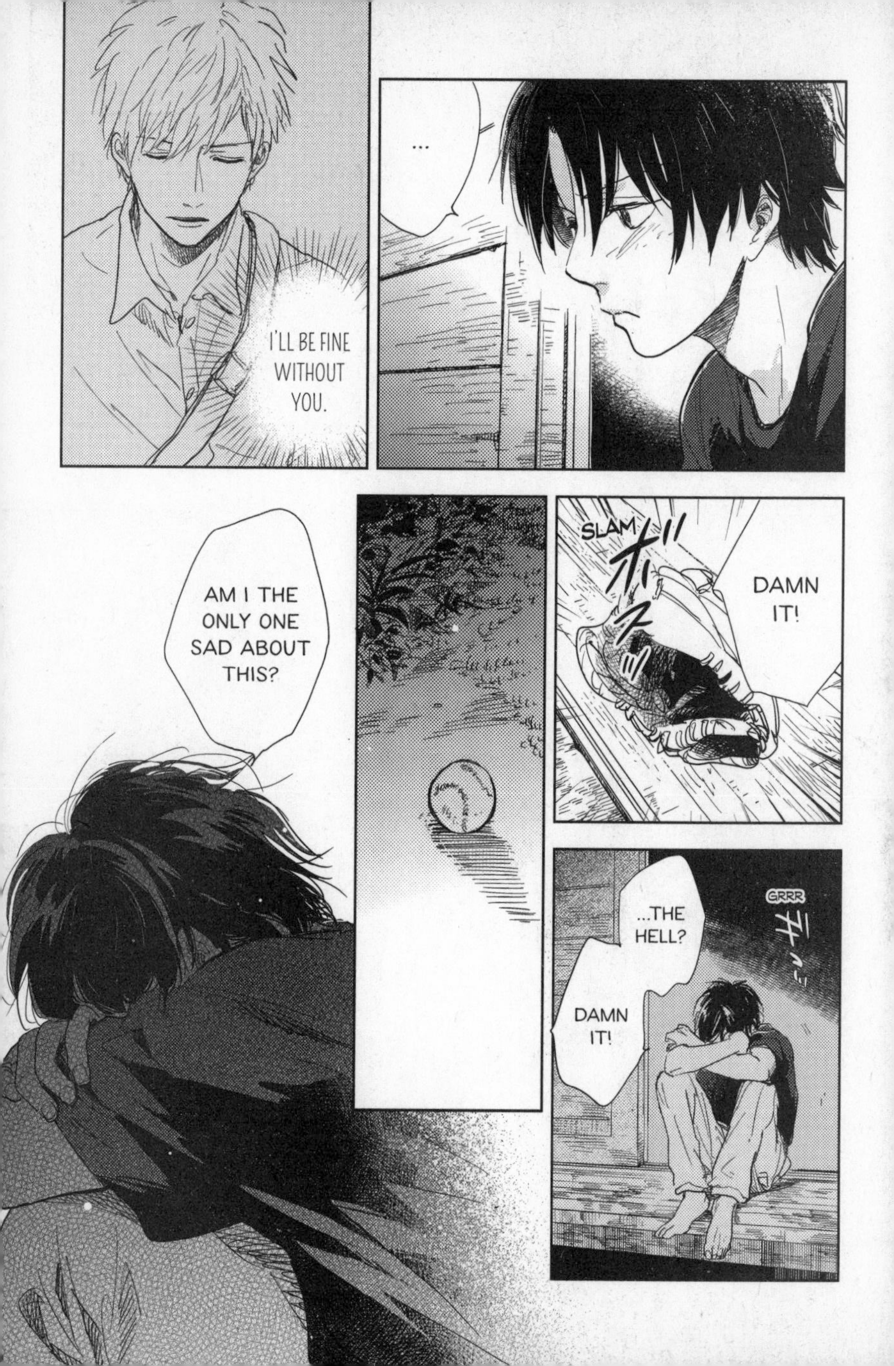
...
I'LL BE FINE WITHOUT YOU.
SLAM
DAMN IT!
GRRR
...THE HELL?
DAMN IT!
AM I THE ONLY ONE SAD ABOUT THIS?

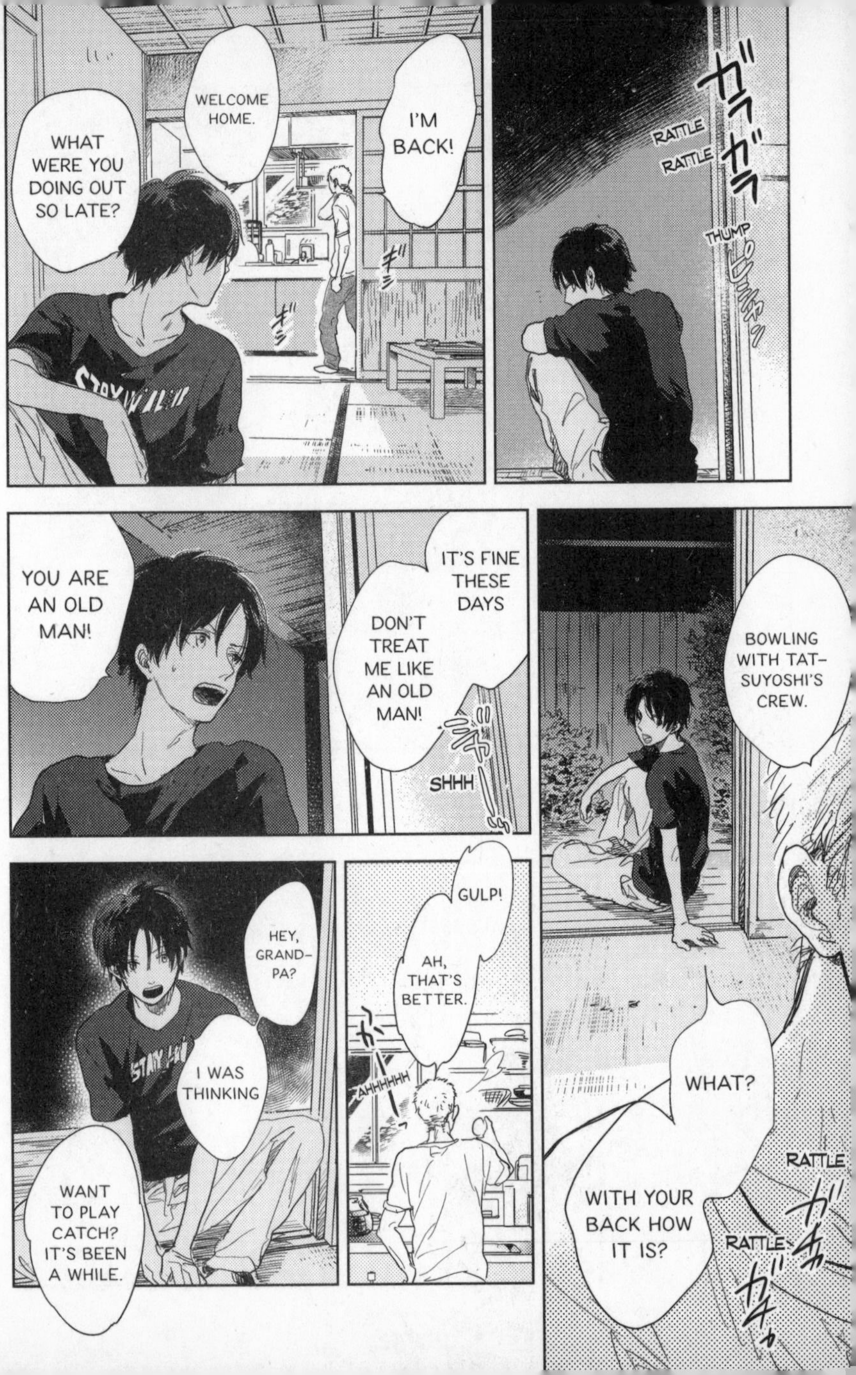
RATTLE
RATTLE
THUMP
I'M BACK!
WELCOME HOME.
WHAT WERE YOU DOING OUT SO LATE?
BOWLING WITH TAT-SUYOSHI'S CREW.
WHAT?
WITH YOUR BACK HOW IT IS?
RATTLE
RATTLE
IT'S FINE THESE DAYS
DON'T TREAT ME LIKE AN OLD MAN!
SHHH
YOU ARE AN OLD MAN!
GULP!
AH, THAT'S BETTER.
AHHHHHH
HEY, GRAND-PA?
I WAS THINKING
WANT TO PLAY CATCH? IT'S BEEN A WHILE.

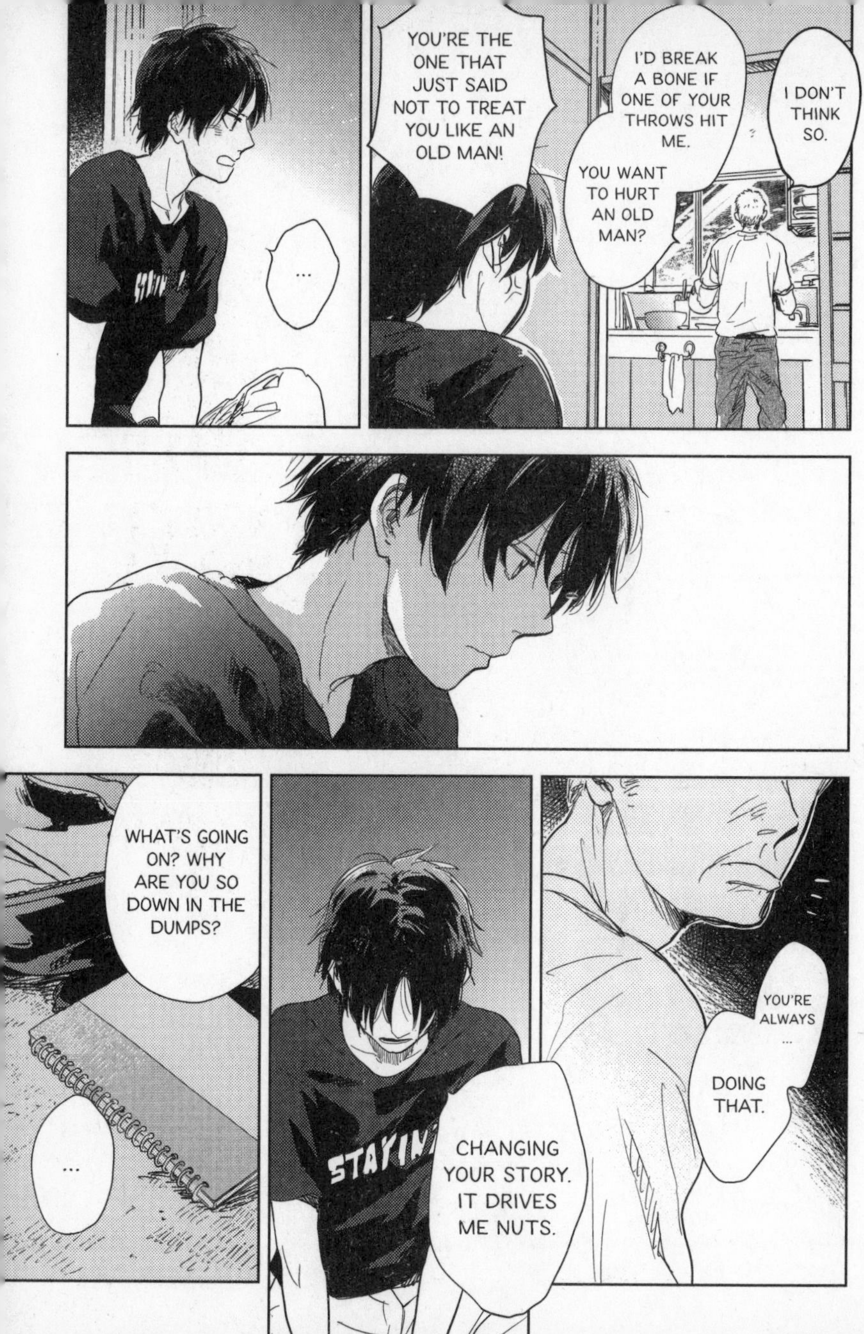
I DON'T THINK SO.
I'D BREAK A BONE IF ONE OF YOUR THROWS HIT ME.
YOU WANT TO HURT AN OLD MAN?
YOU'RE THE ONE THAT JUST SAID NOT TO TREAT YOU LIKE AN OLD MAN!
...
YOU'RE ALWAYS ... DOING THAT.
CHANGING YOUR STORY. IT DRIVES ME NUTS.
WHAT'S GOING ON? WHY ARE YOU SO DOWN IN THE DUMPS?
...

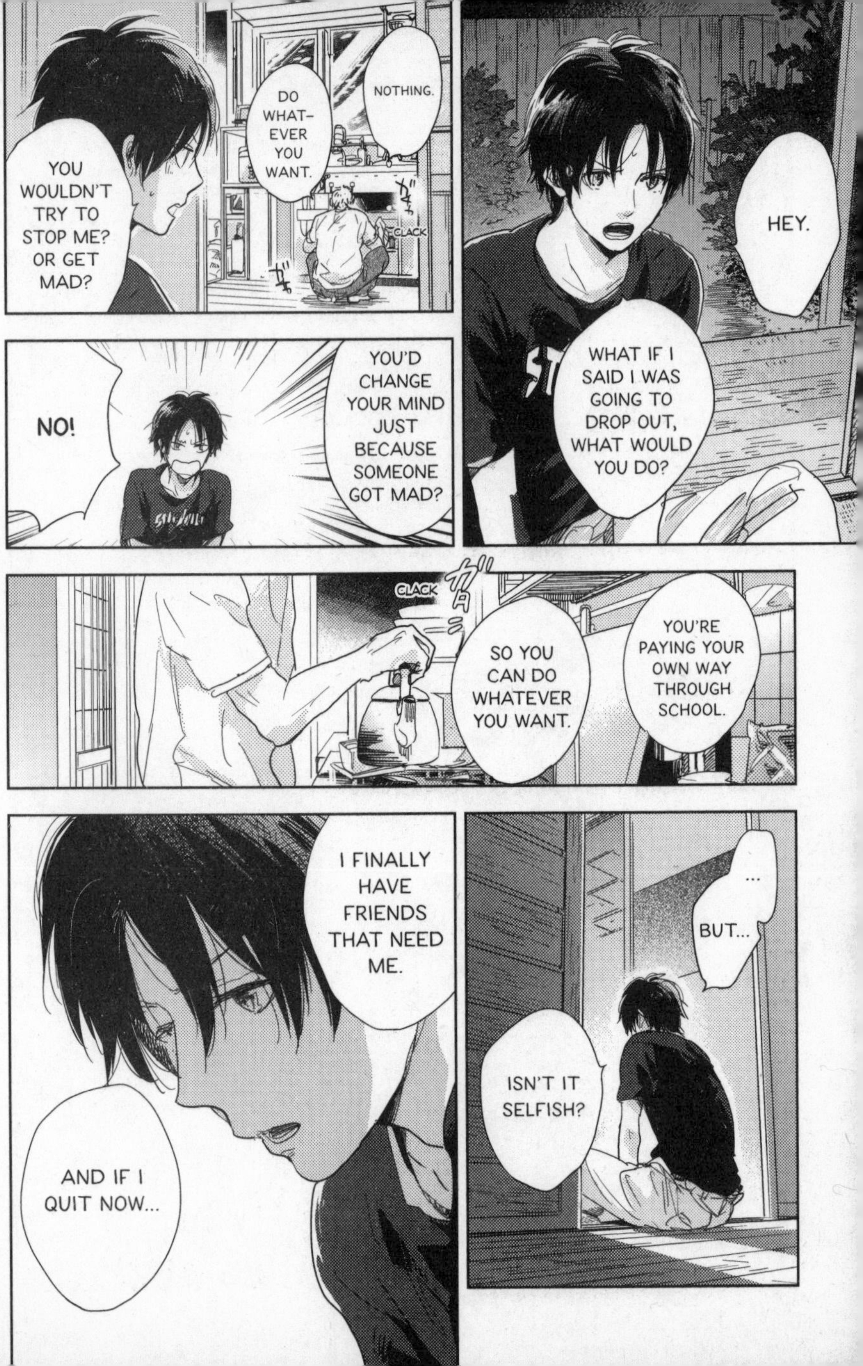
HEY.
WHAT IF I SAID I WAS GOING TO DROP OUT, WHAT WOULD YOU DO?
NOTHING.
DO WHATEVER YOU WANT.
CLACK
YOU WOULDN'T TRY TO STOP ME? OR GET MAD?
YOU'D CHANGE YOUR MIND JUST BECAUSE SOMEONE GOT MAD?
NO!
CLACK
YOU'RE PAYING YOUR OWN WAY THROUGH SCHOOL.
SO YOU CAN DO WHATEVER YOU WANT.
...
BUT...
ISN'T IT SELFISH?
I FINALLY HAVE FRIENDS THAT NEED ME.
AND IF I QUIT NOW...

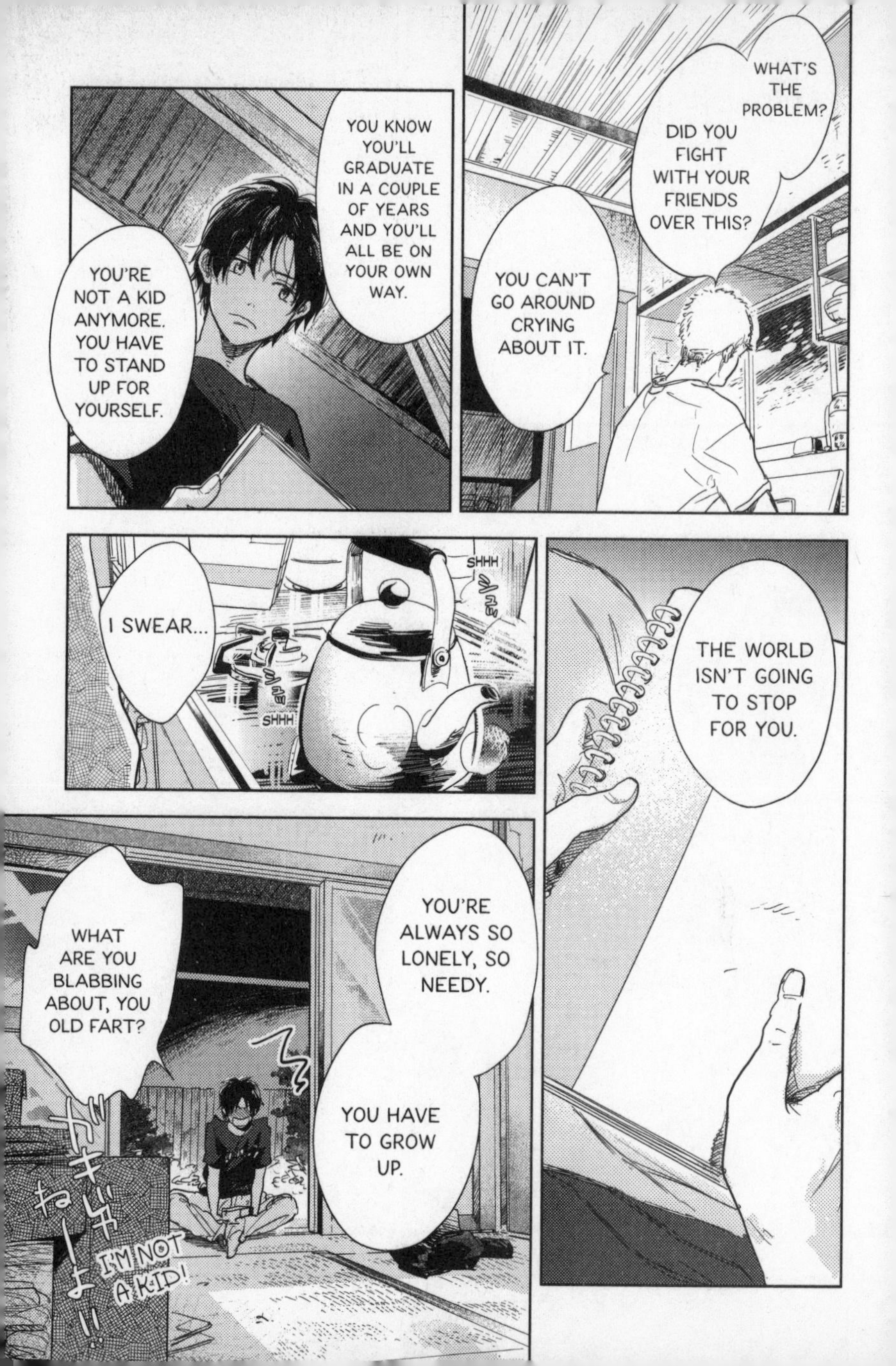
WHAT'S THE PROBLEM?
DID YOU FIGHT WITH YOUR FRIENDS OVER THIS?
YOU CAN'T GO AROUND CRYING ABOUT IT.
YOU KNOW YOU'LL GRADUATE IN A COUPLE OF YEARS AND YOU'LL ALL BE ON YOUR OWN WAY.
YOU'RE NOT A KID ANYMORE. YOU HAVE TO STAND UP FOR YOURSELF.
THE WORLD ISN'T GOING TO STOP FOR YOU.
SHHH
SHHH
I SWEAR...
YOU'RE ALWAYS SO LONELY, SO NEEDY.
YOU HAVE TO GROW UP.
WHAT ARE YOU BLABBING ABOUT, YOU OLD FART?
I'M NOT A KID!

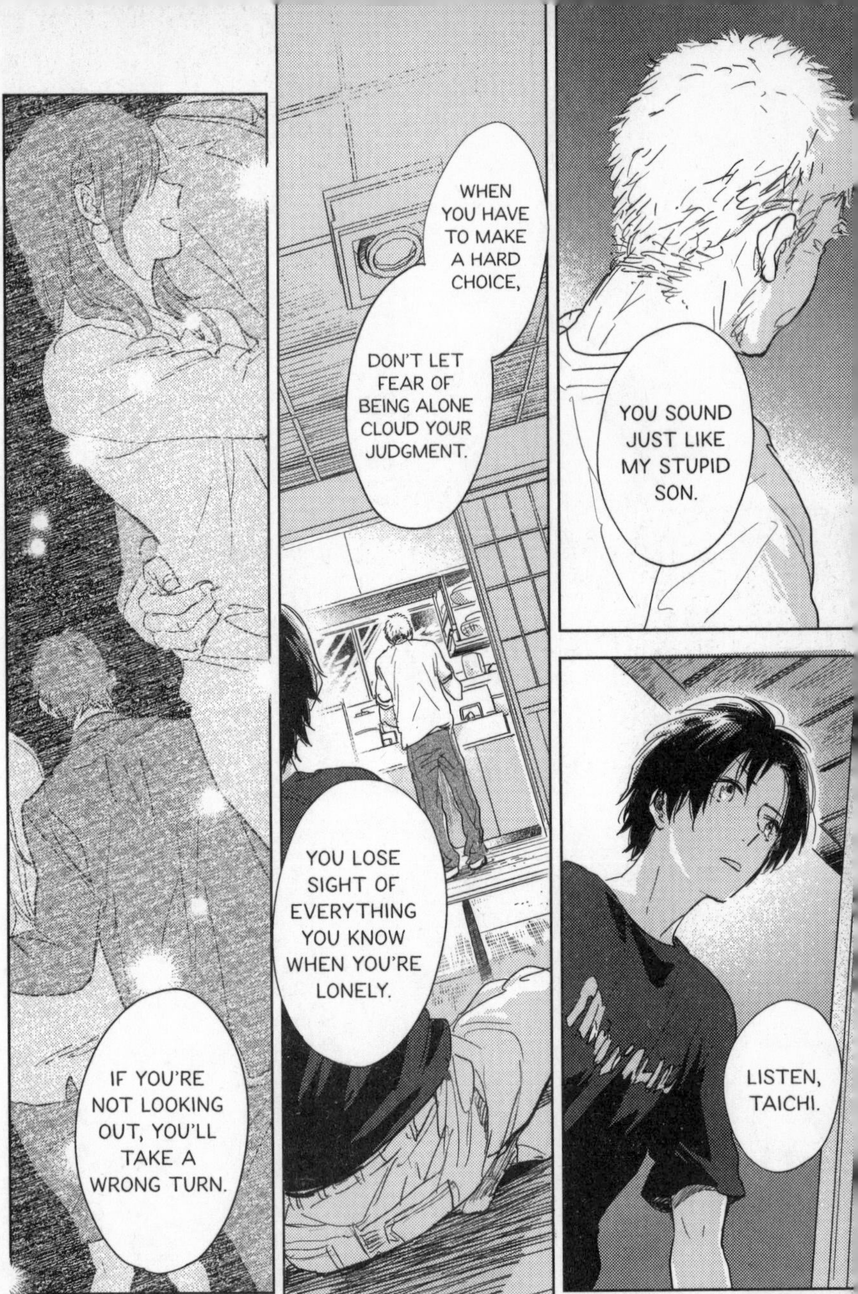
YOU SOUND JUST LIKE MY STUPID SON.
LISTEN, TAICHI.
WHEN YOU HAVE TO MAKE A HARD CHOICE,
DON'T LET FEAR OF BEING ALONE CLOUD YOUR JUDGMENT.
YOU LOSE SIGHT OF EVERYTHING YOU KNOW WHEN YOU'RE LONELY.
IF YOU'RE NOT LOOKING OUT, YOU'LL TAKE A WRONG TURN.

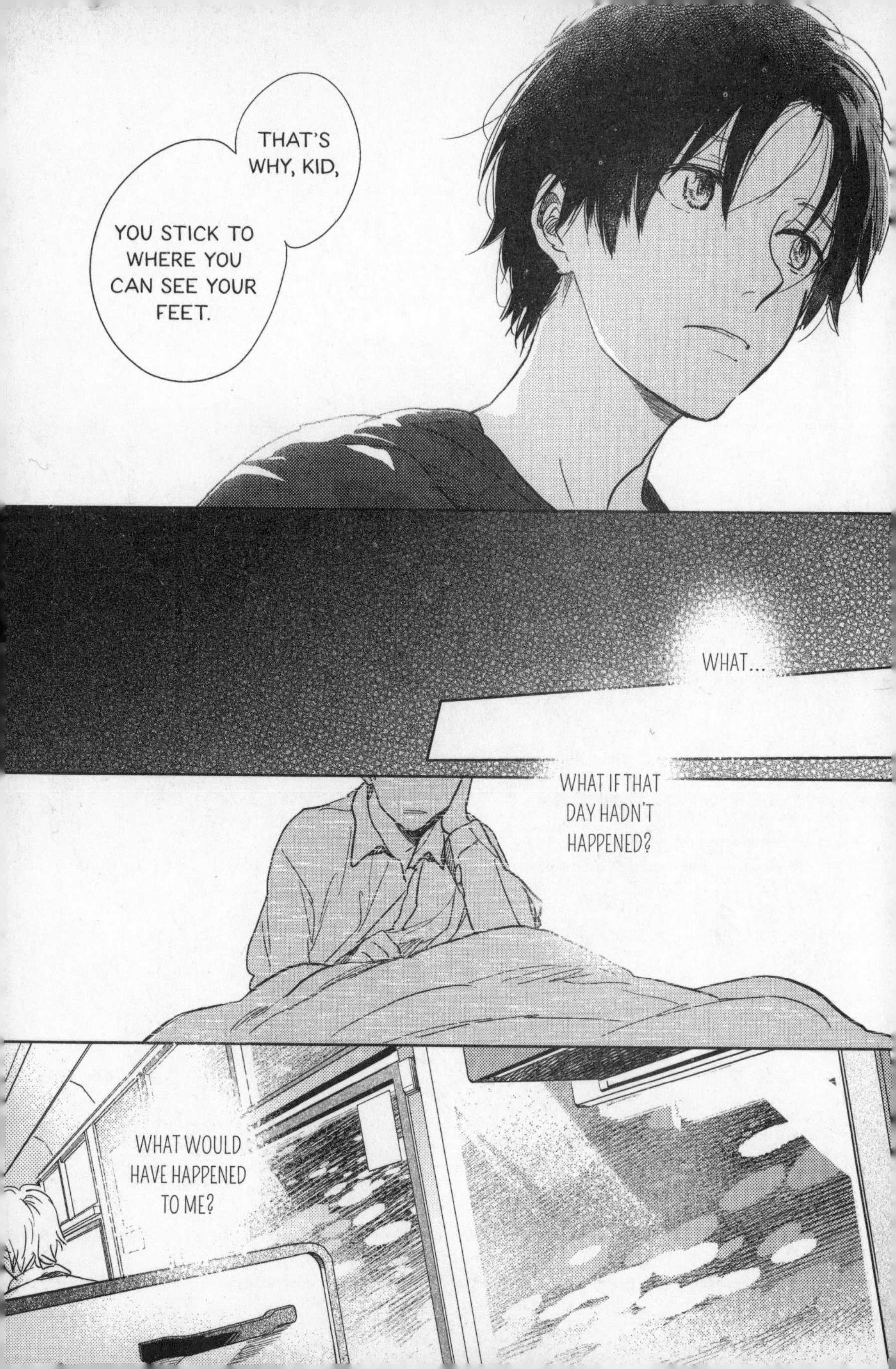
THAT'S WHY, KID,
YOU STICK TO WHERE YOU CAN SEE YOUR FEET.
WHAT...
WHAT IF THAT DAY HADN'T HAPPENED?
WHAT WOULD HAVE HAPPENED TO ME?

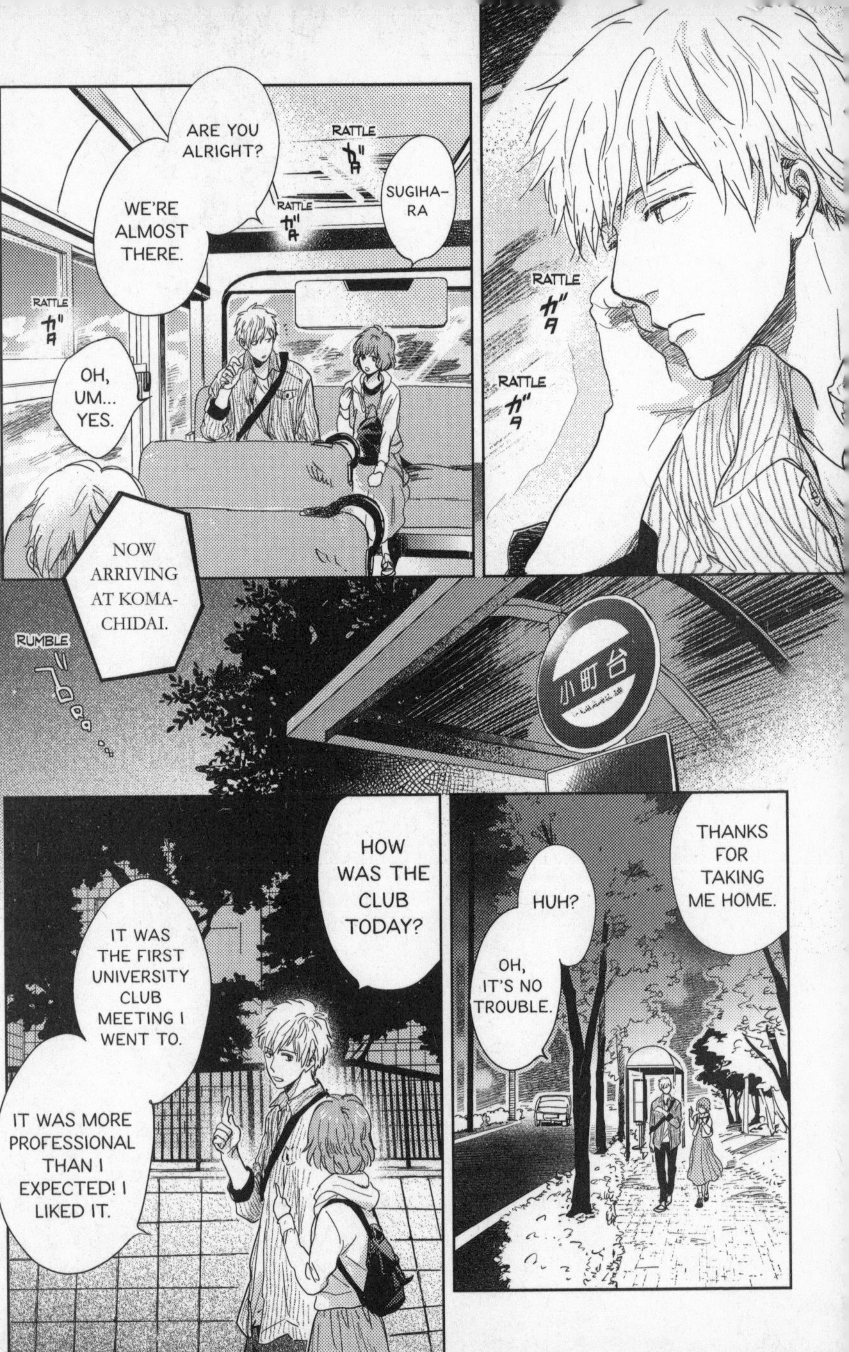
RATTLE
RATTLE
RATTLE
SUGIHARA-RA
RATTLE
ARE YOU ALRIGHT?
WE'RE ALMOST THERE.
RATTLE
OH, UM... YES.
NOW ARRIVING AT KOMACHIDAI.
RUMBLE
小町台
THANKS FOR TAKING ME HOME.
HUH?
OH, IT'S NO TROUBLE.
HOW WAS THE CLUB TODAY?
IT WAS THE FIRST UNIVERSITY CLUB MEETING I WENT TO.
IT WAS MORE PROFESSIONAL THAN I EXPECTED! I LIKED IT.

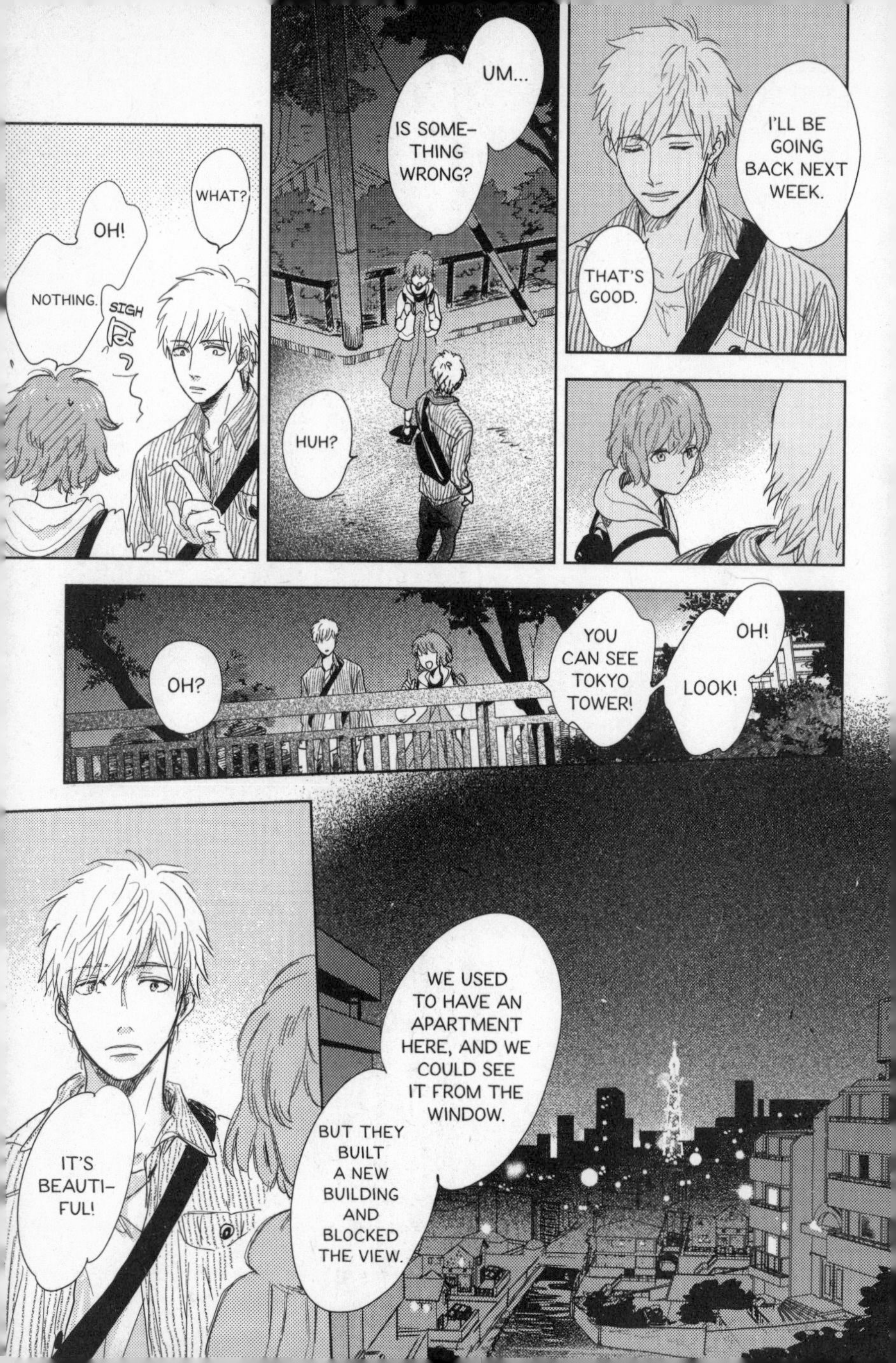
I'LL BE GOING BACK NEXT WEEK.
THAT'S GOOD.
UM...
IS SOMETHING WRONG?
HUH?
WHAT?
OH!
NOTHING.
SIGH
はっ
OH!
LOOK!
YOU CAN SEE TOKYO TOWER!
OH?
WE USED TO HAVE AN APARTMENT HERE, AND WE COULD SEE IT FROM THE WINDOW.
BUT THEY BUILT A NEW BUILDING AND BLOCKED THE VIEW.
IT'S BEAUTIFUL!

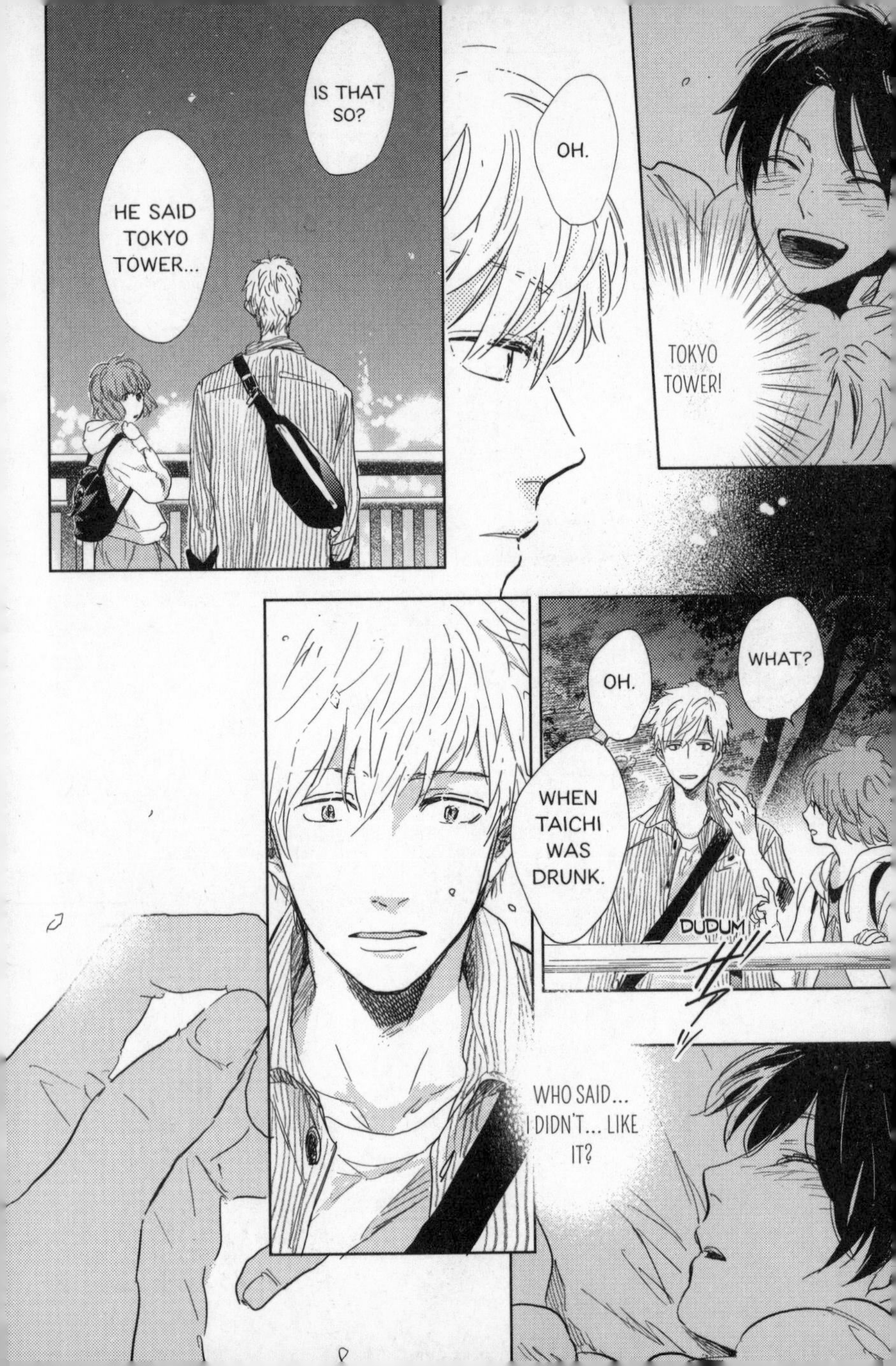
TOKYO TOWER!
OH.
IS THAT SO?
HE SAID TOKYO TOWER...
WHAT?
OH.
WHEN TAICHI WAS DRUNK.
DUDUM
WHO SAID... I DIDN'T... LIKE IT?

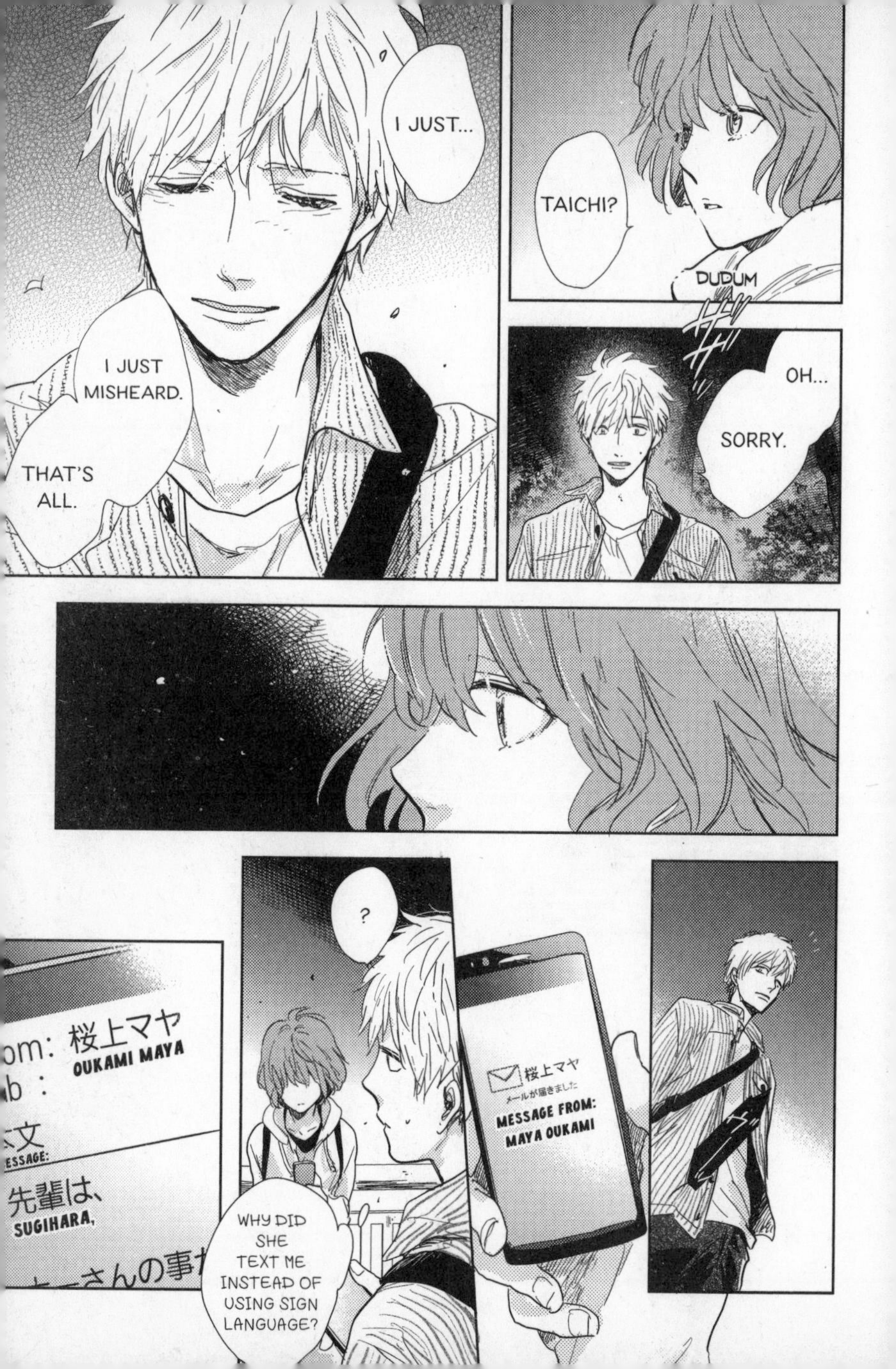
TAICHI?
DUDUM
OH...
SORRY.
I JUST...
I JUST MISHEARD.
THAT'S ALL.
?
桜上マヤ
メールが届きました
MESSAGE FROM: MAYA OUKAMI
WHY DID SHE TEXT ME INSTEAD OF USING SIGN LANGUAGE?
om: 桜上マヤ
OUKAMI MAYA
b :
文
ESSAGE:
先輩は、
SUGIHARA,
さんの事

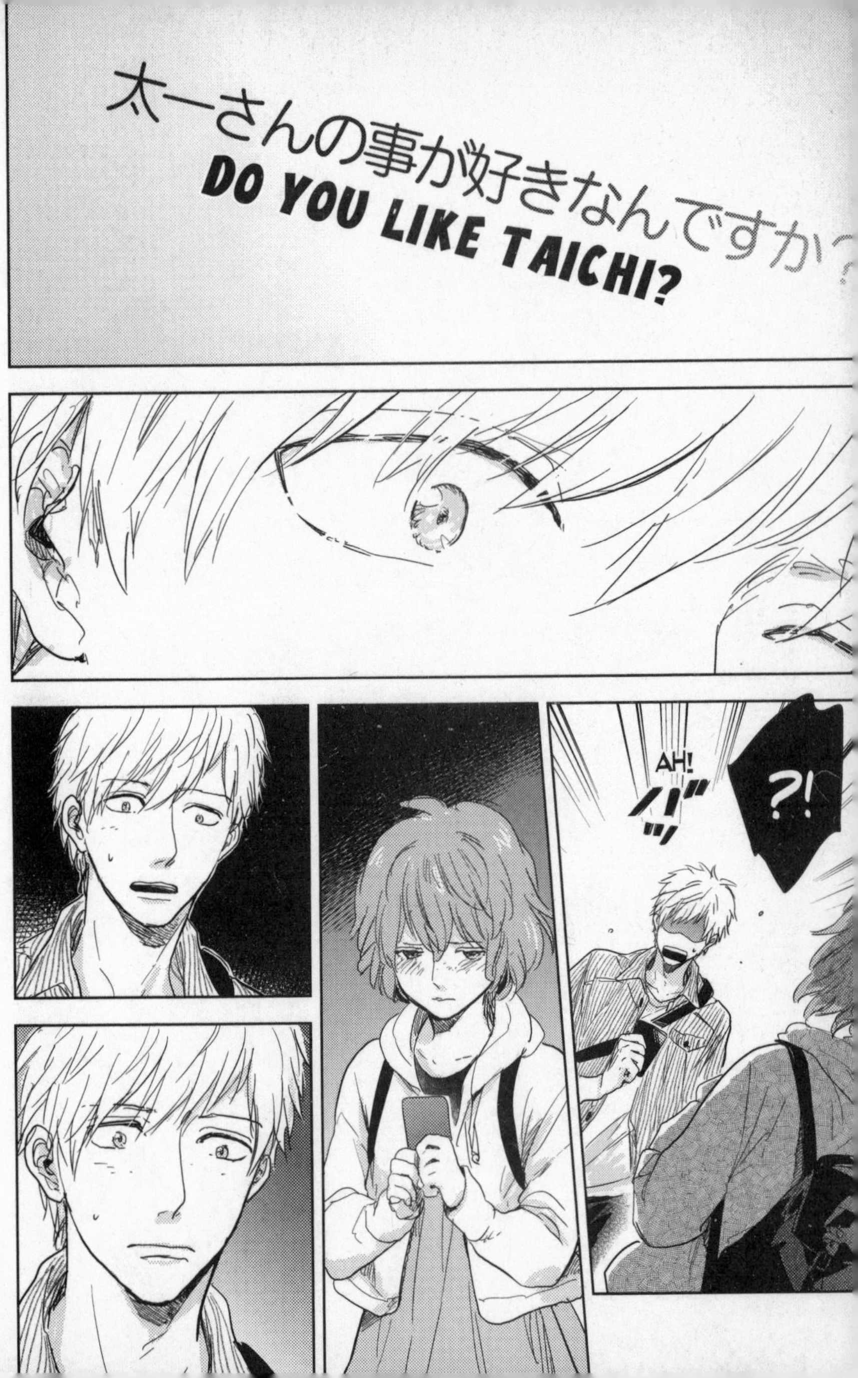
太一さんの事が好きなんですか?
DO YOU LIKE TAICHI?
?!
AH!
バッ

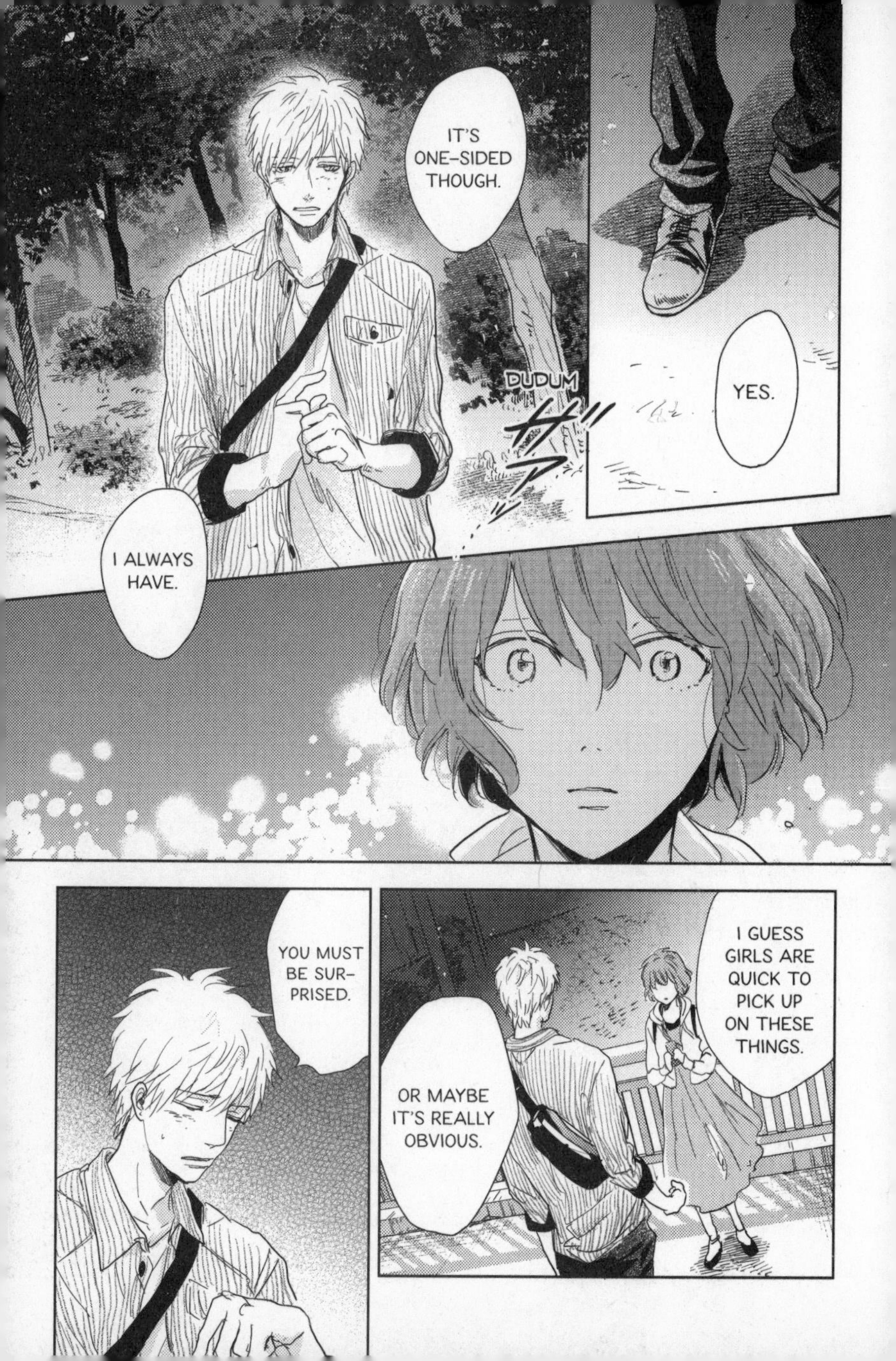
YES.
IT'S ONE-SIDED THOUGH.
DUDUM
I ALWAYS HAVE.
I GUESS GIRLS ARE QUICK TO PICK UP ON THESE THINGS.
OR MAYBE IT'S REALLY OBVIOUS.
YOU MUST BE SURPRISED.

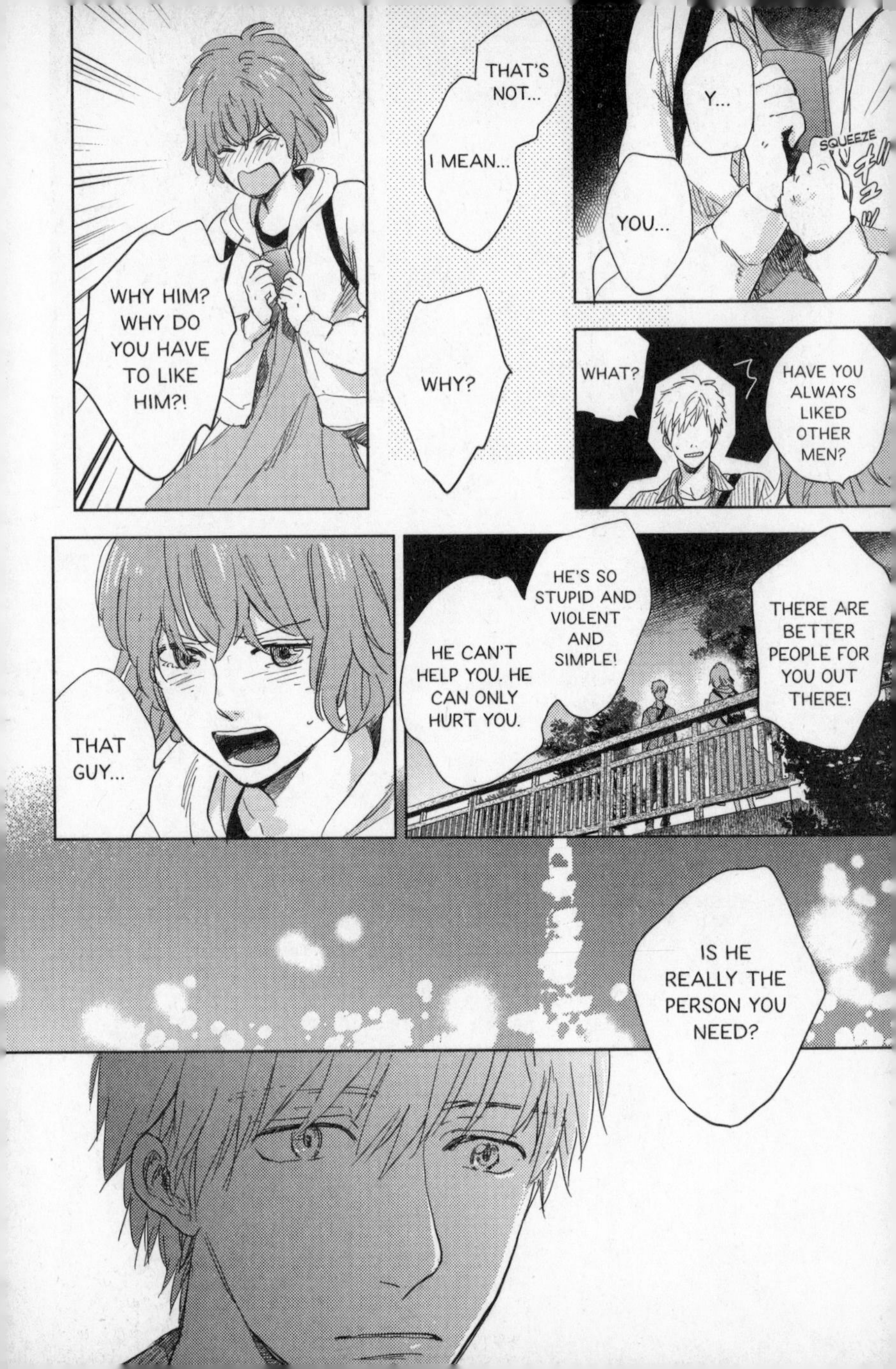
Y...
SQUEEZE
YOU...
HAVE YOU ALWAYS LIKED OTHER MEN?
WHAT?
THAT'S NOT...
I MEAN...
WHY?
WHY HIM? WHY DO YOU HAVE TO LIKE HIM?!
THERE ARE BETTER PEOPLE FOR YOU OUT THERE!
HE'S SO STUPID AND VIOLENT AND SIMPLE!
HE CAN'T HELP YOU. HE CAN ONLY HURT YOU.
THAT GUY...
IS HE REALLY THE PERSON YOU NEED?

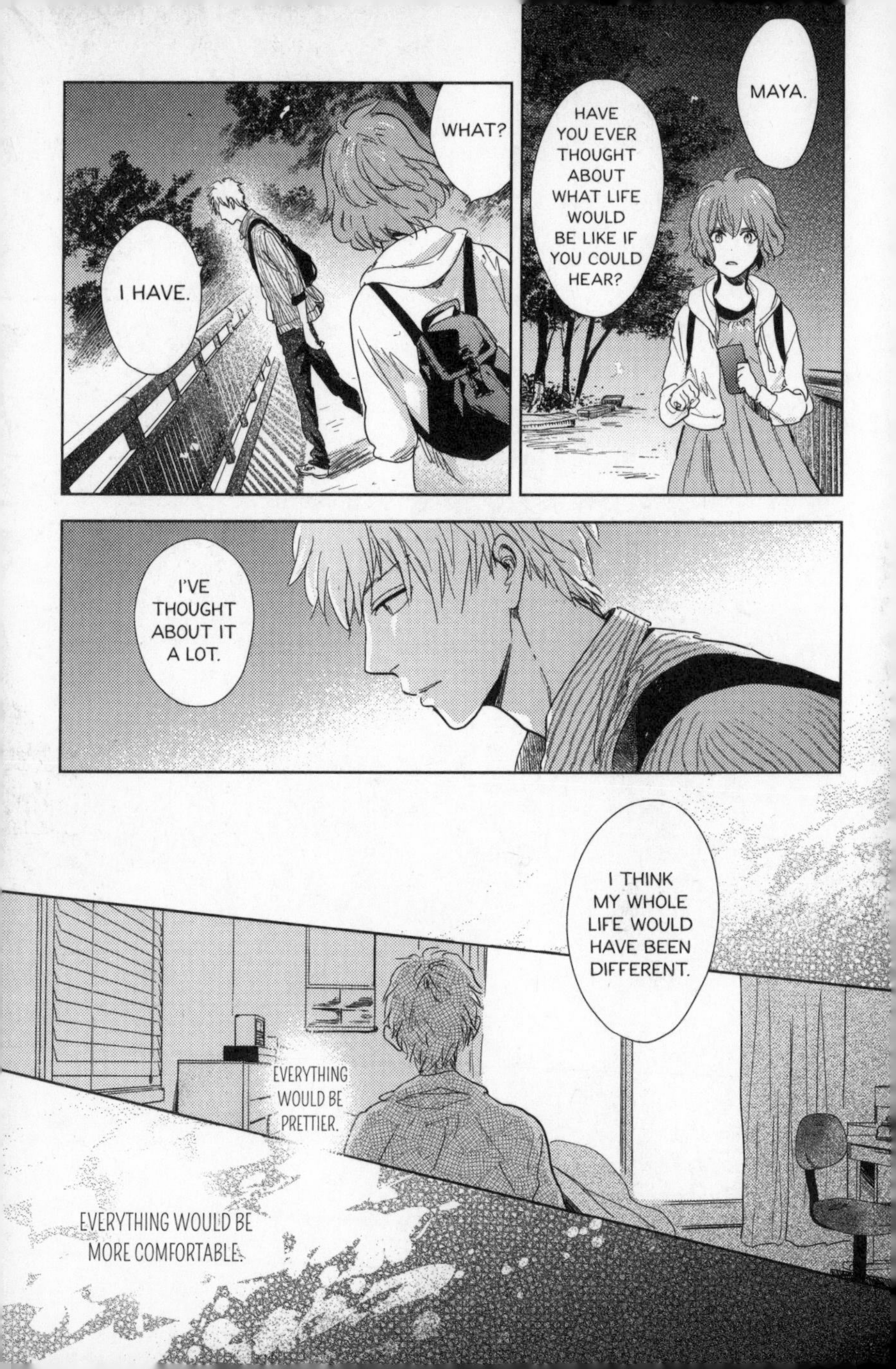
MAYA.
HAVE YOU EVER THOUGHT ABOUT WHAT LIFE WOULD BE LIKE IF YOU COULD HEAR?
WHAT?
I HAVE.
I'VE THOUGHT ABOUT IT A LOT.
I THINK MY WHOLE LIFE WOULD HAVE BEEN DIFFERENT.
EVERYTHING WOULD BE PRETTIER.
EVERYTHING WOULD BE MORE COMFORTABLE.

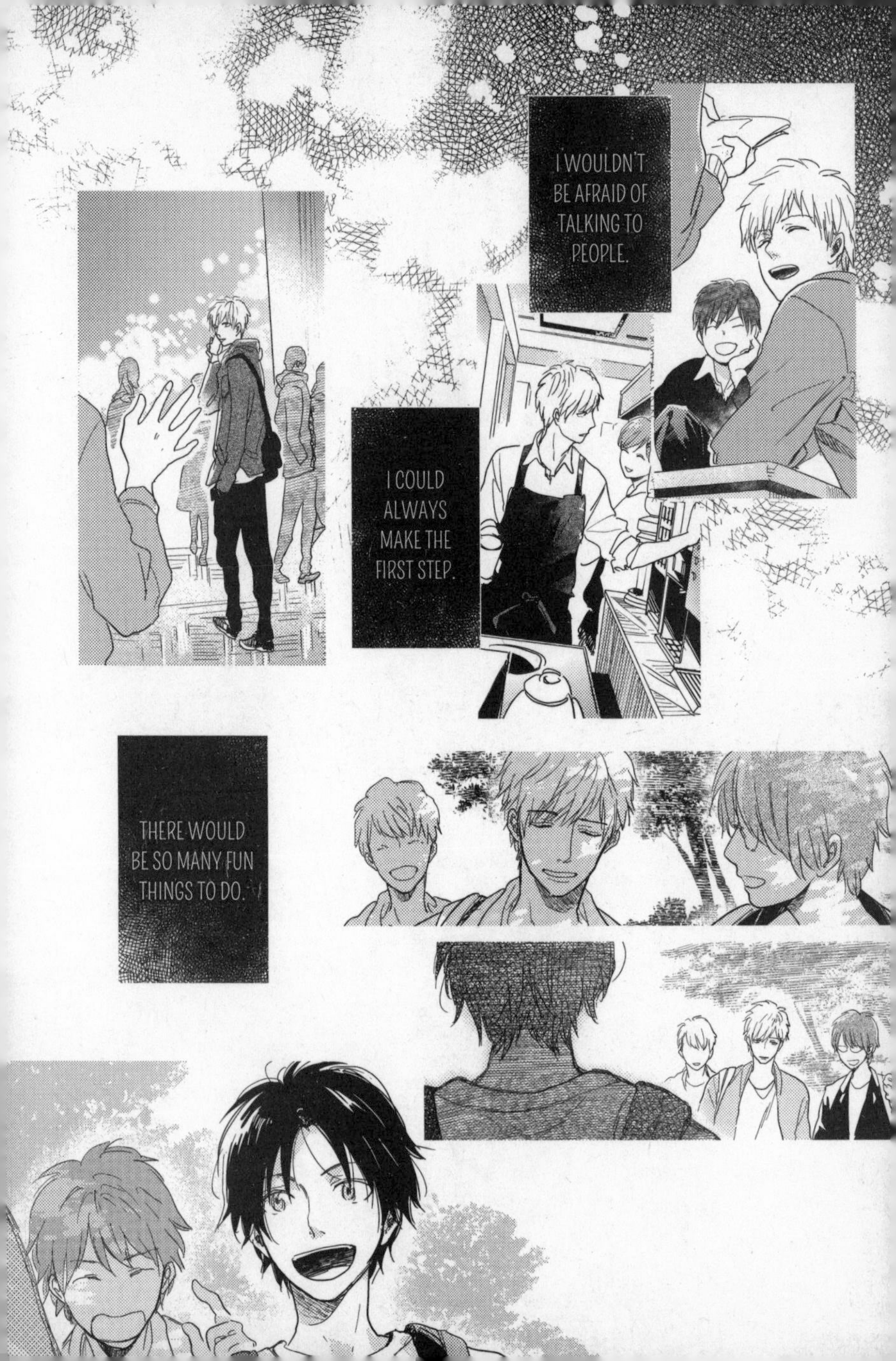
I WOULDN'T BE AFRAID OF TALKING TO PEOPLE.
I COULD ALWAYS MAKE THE FIRST STEP.
THERE WOULD BE SO MANY FUN THINGS TO DO.

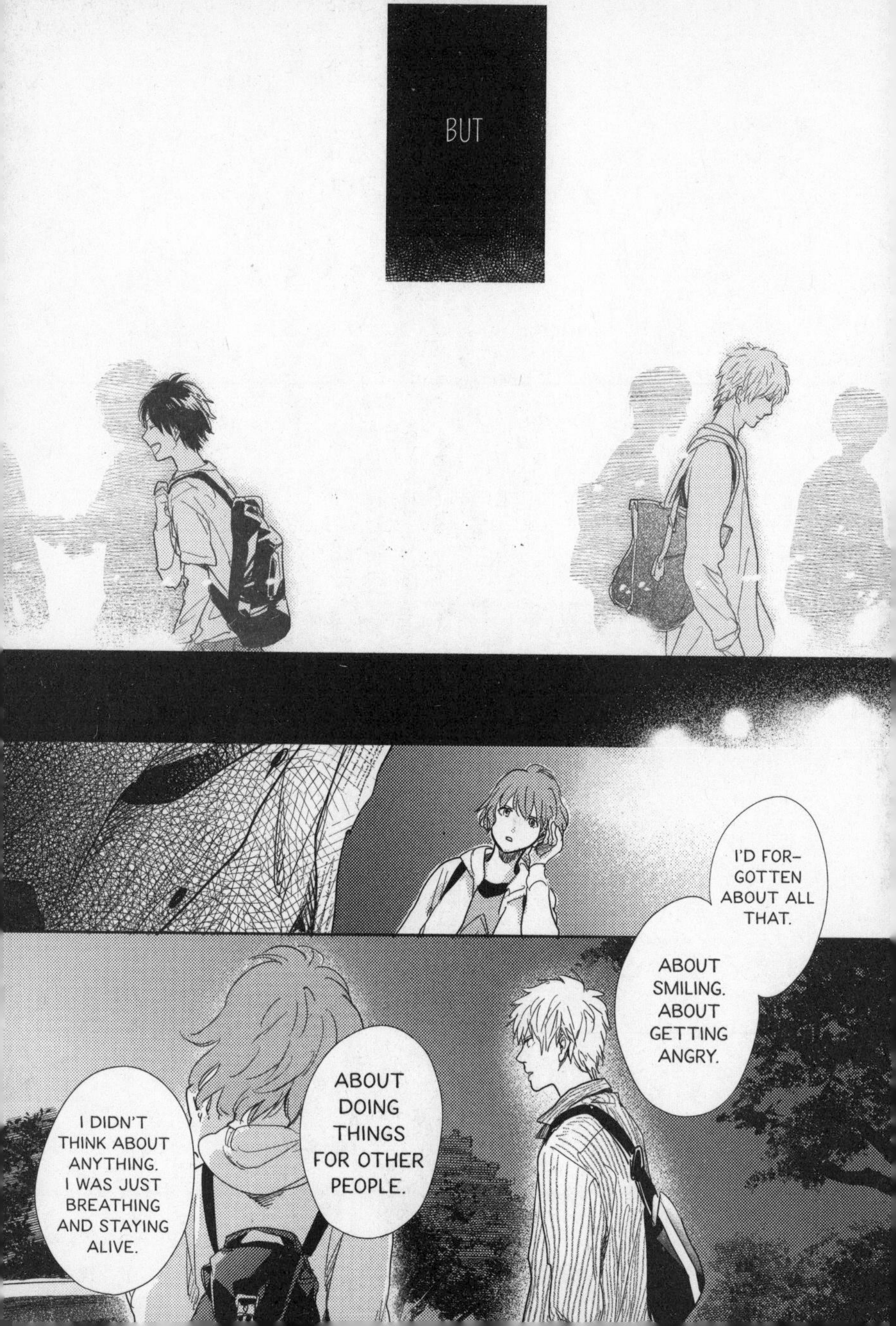
BUT
I'D FOR-GOTTEN ABOUT ALL THAT.
ABOUT SMILING. ABOUT GETTING ANGRY.
ABOUT DOING THINGS FOR OTHER PEOPLE.
I DIDN'T THINK ABOUT ANYTHING. I WAS JUST BREATHING AND STAYING ALIVE.

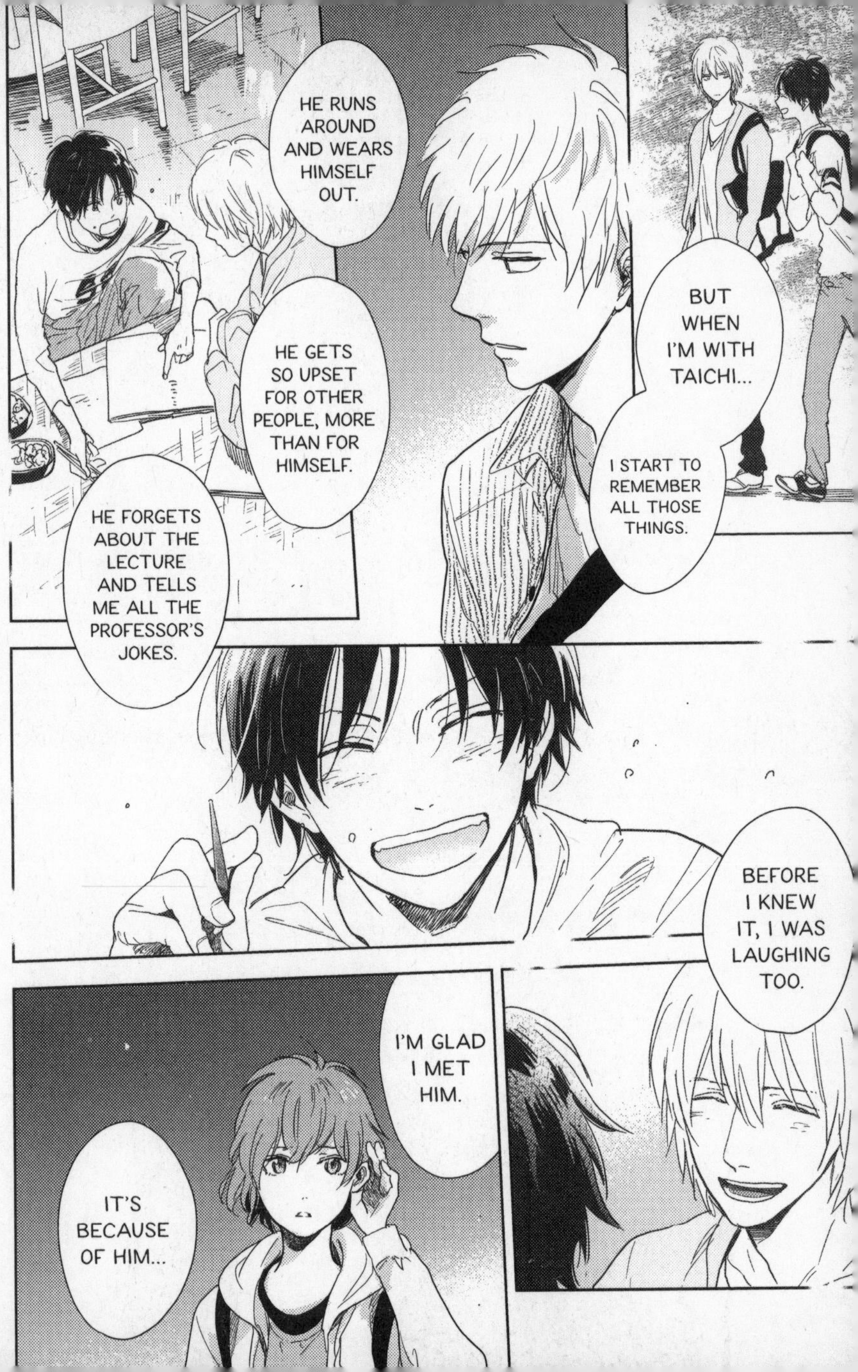
BUT WHEN I'M WITH TAICHI...
I START TO REMEMBER ALL THOSE THINGS.
HE RUNS AROUND AND WEARS HIMSELF OUT.
HE GETS SO UPSET FOR OTHER PEOPLE, MORE THAN FOR HIMSELF.
HE FORGETS ABOUT THE LECTURE AND TELLS ME ALL THE PROFESSOR'S JOKES.
BEFORE I KNEW IT, I WAS LAUGHING TOO.
I'M GLAD I MET HIM.
IT'S BECAUSE OF HIM...

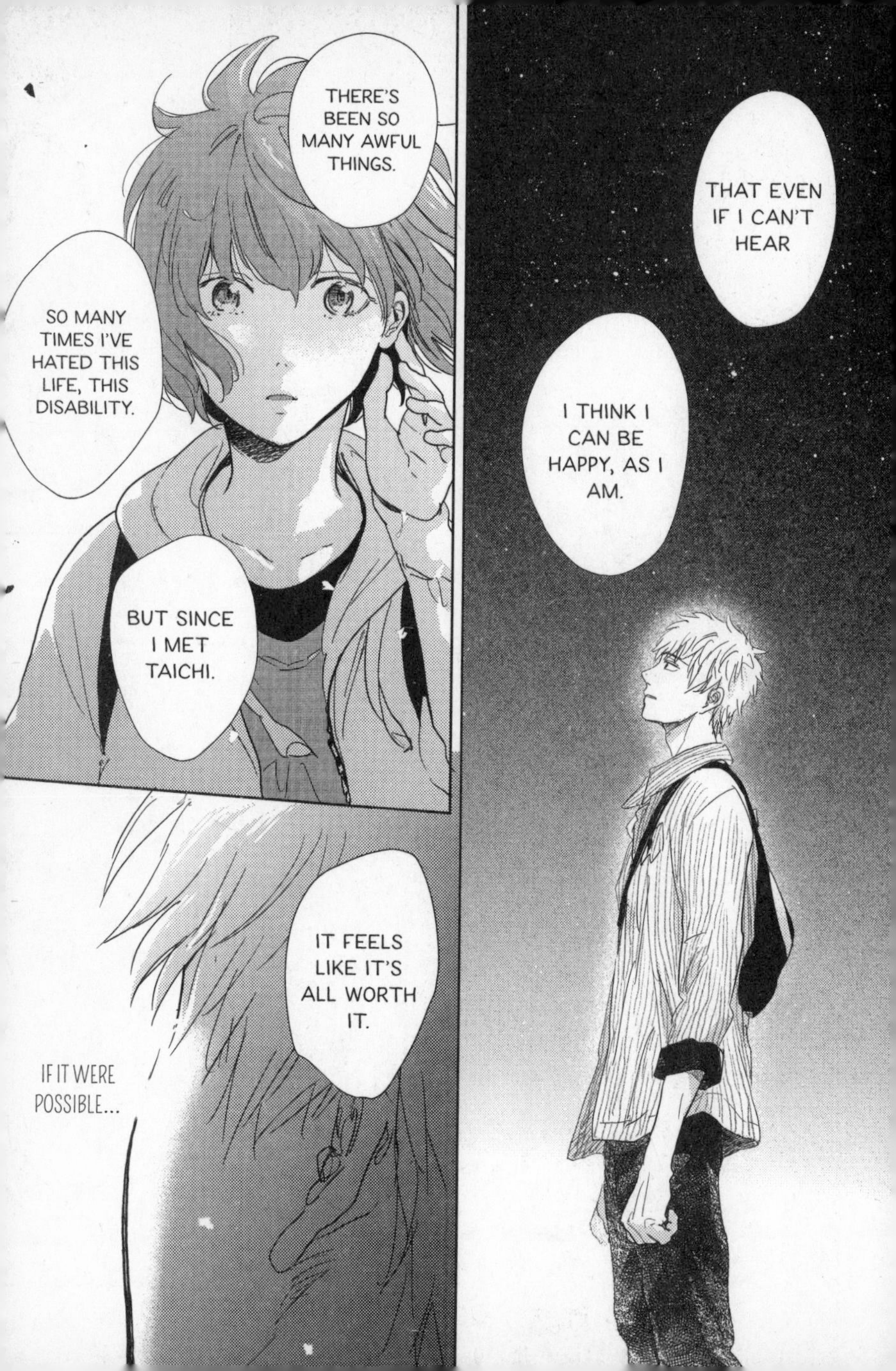
THERE'S BEEN SO MANY AWFUL THINGS.
SO MANY TIMES I'VE HATED THIS LIFE, THIS DISABILITY.
BUT SINCE I MET TAICHI.
IT FEELS LIKE IT'S ALL WORTH IT.
IF IT WERE POSSIBLE...
THAT EVEN IF I CAN'T HEAR
I THINK I CAN BE HAPPY, AS I AM.

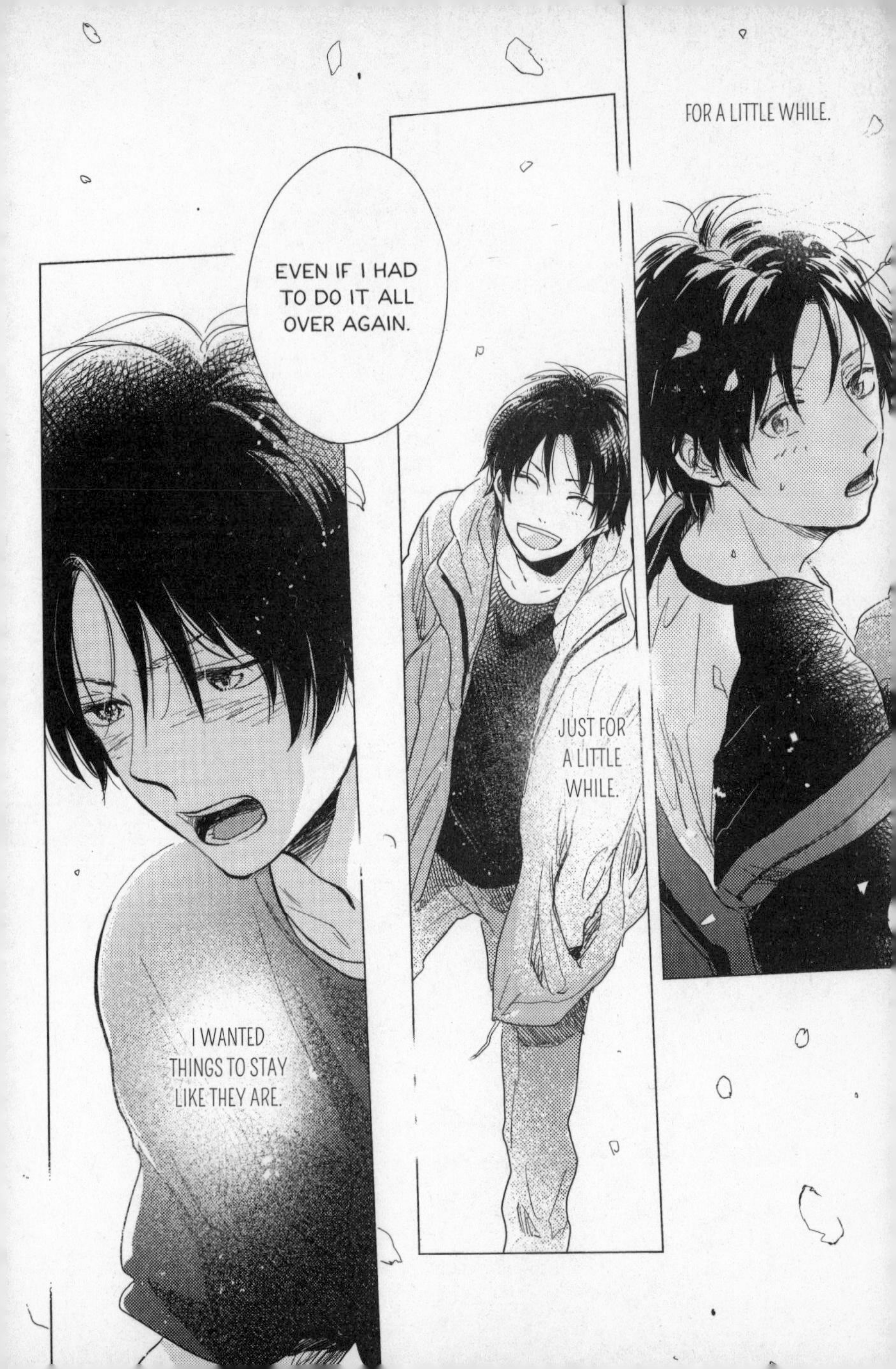
FOR A LITTLE WHILE.
JUST FOR A LITTLE WHILE.
EVEN IF I HAD TO DO IT ALL OVER AGAIN.
I WANTED THINGS TO STAY LIKE THEY ARE.

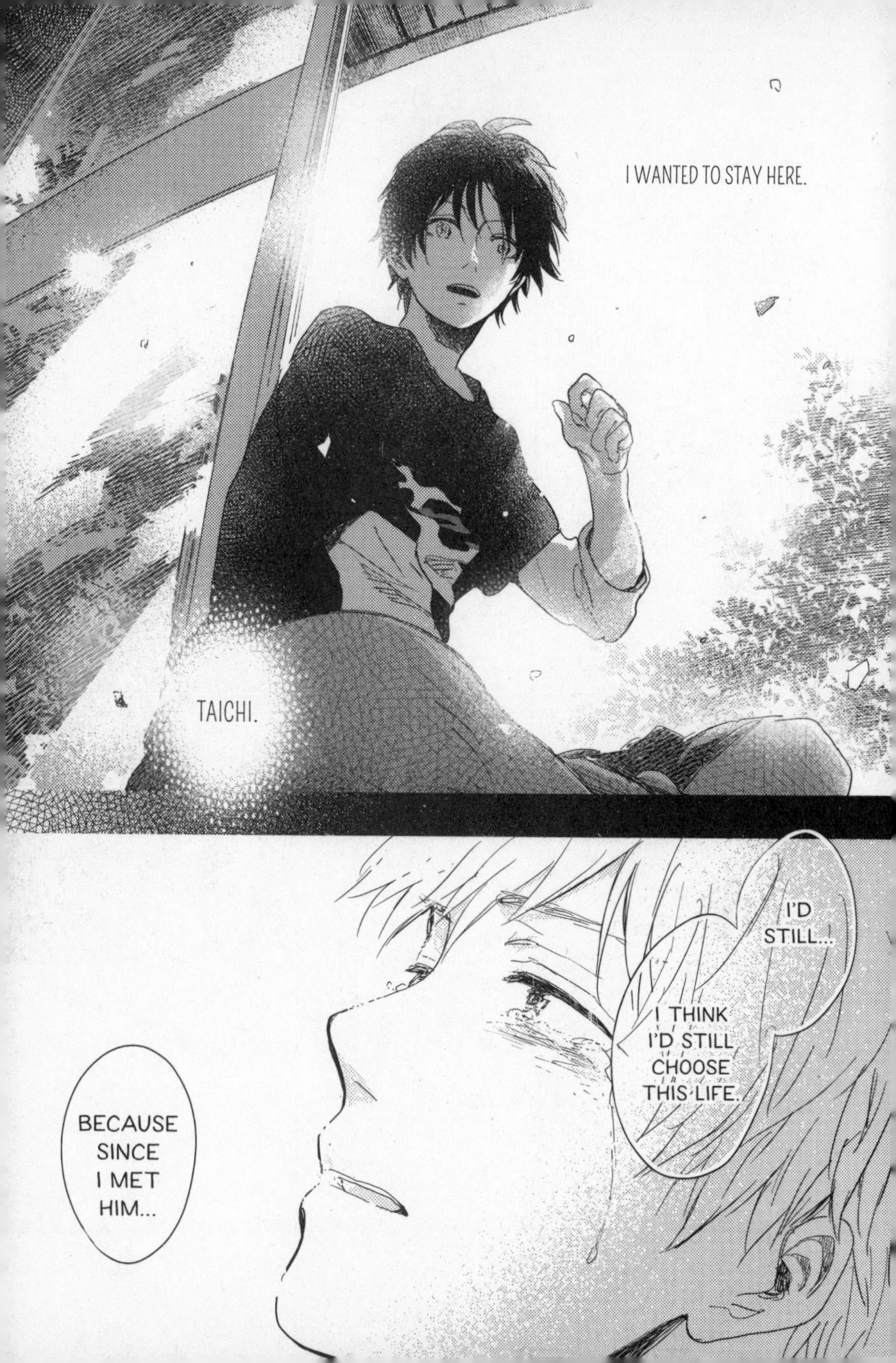
I WANTED TO STAY HERE.
TAICHI.
I'D STILL...
I THINK I'D STILL CHOOSE THIS LIFE.
BECAUSE SINCE I MET HIM...

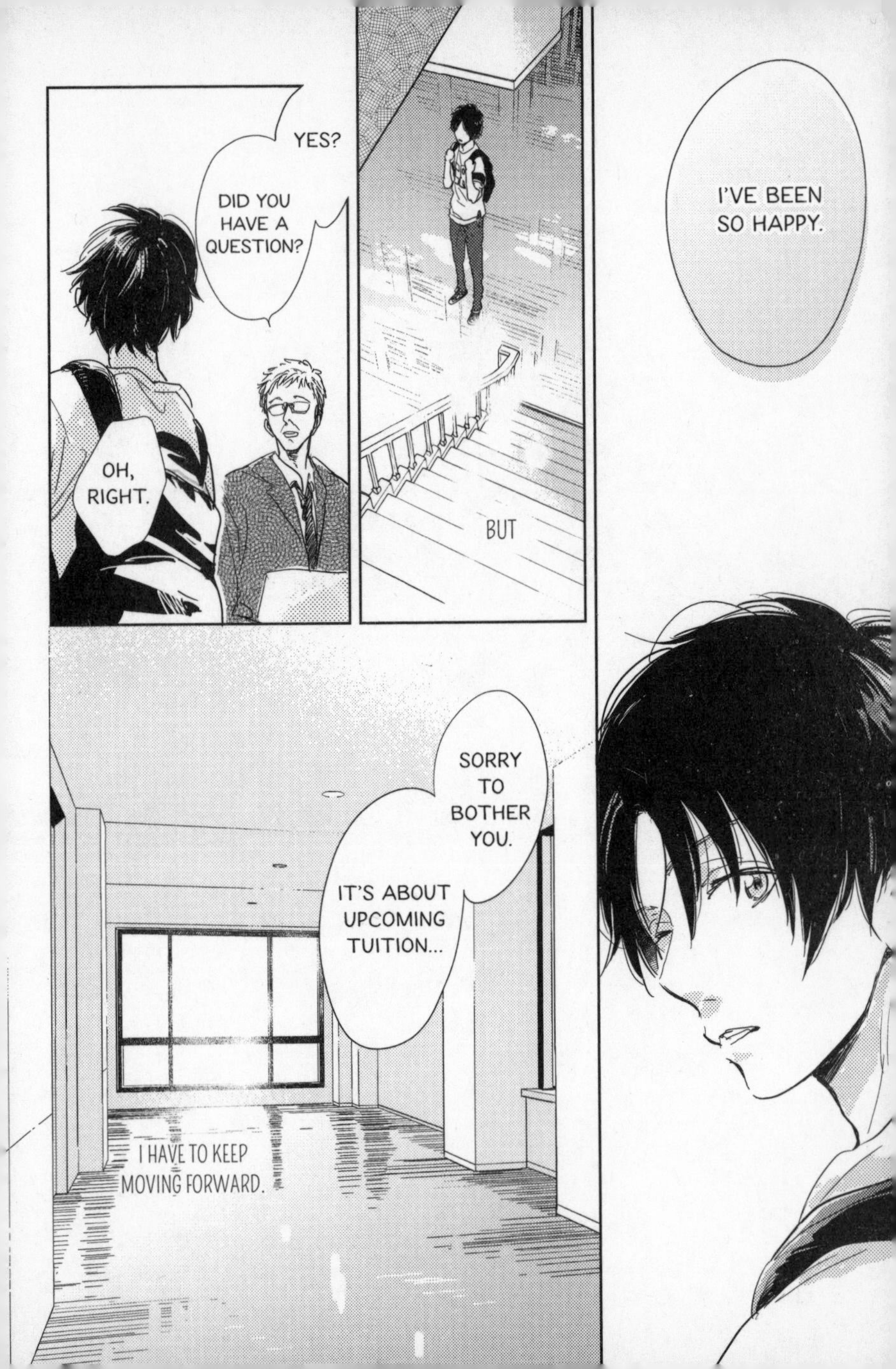
I'VE BEEN SO HAPPY.
BUT
YES?
DID YOU HAVE A QUESTION?
OH, RIGHT.
SORRY TO BOTHER YOU.
IT'S ABOUT UPCOMING TUITION...
I HAVE TO KEEP MOVING FORWARD.

i hear
the
sunspot

i hear the sunspot

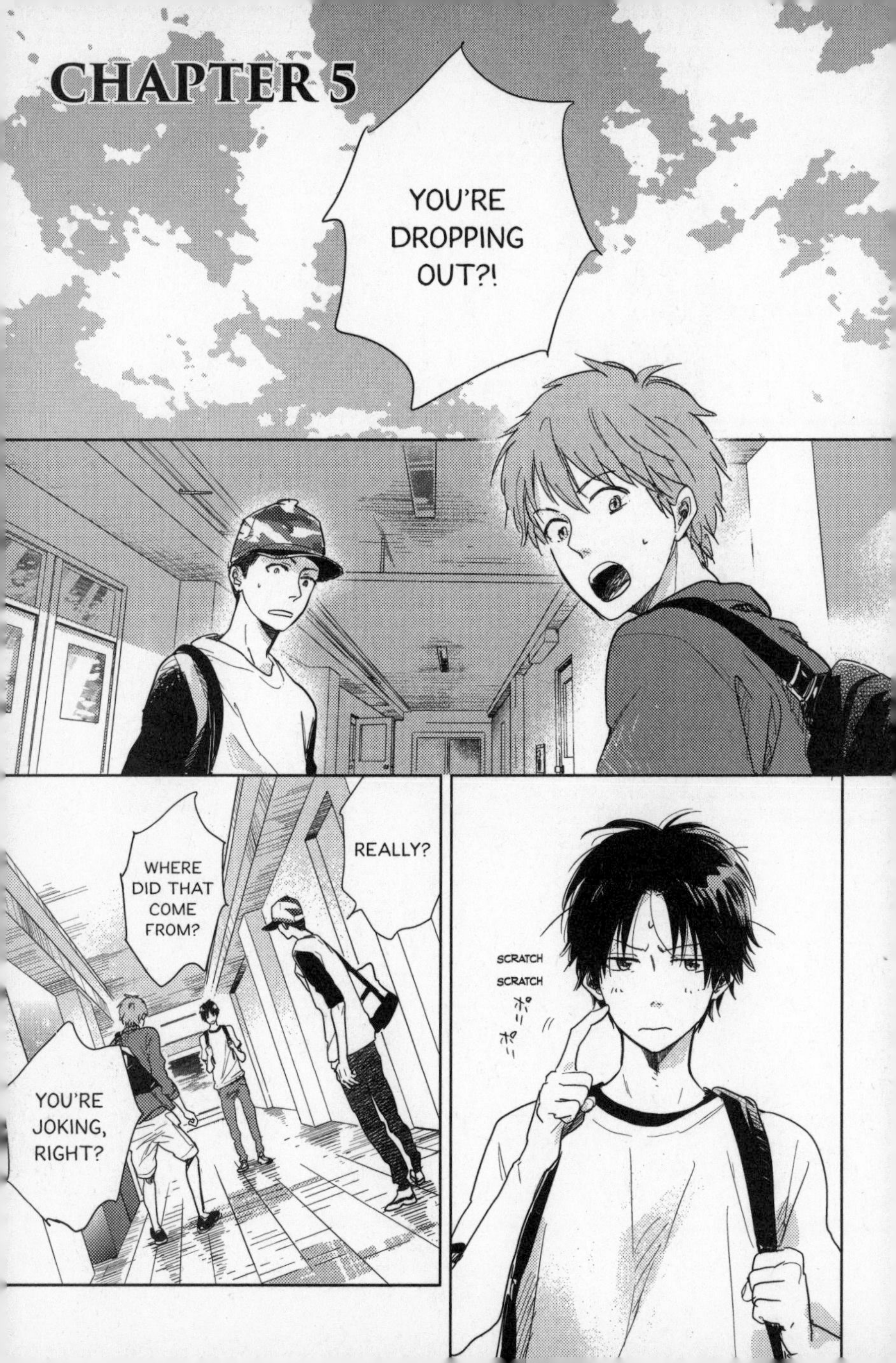
CHAPTER 5
YOU'RE DROPPING OUT?!
SCRATCH SCRATCH
ポリ ポリ
REALLY?
WHERE DID THAT COME FROM?
YOU'RE JOKING, RIGHT?

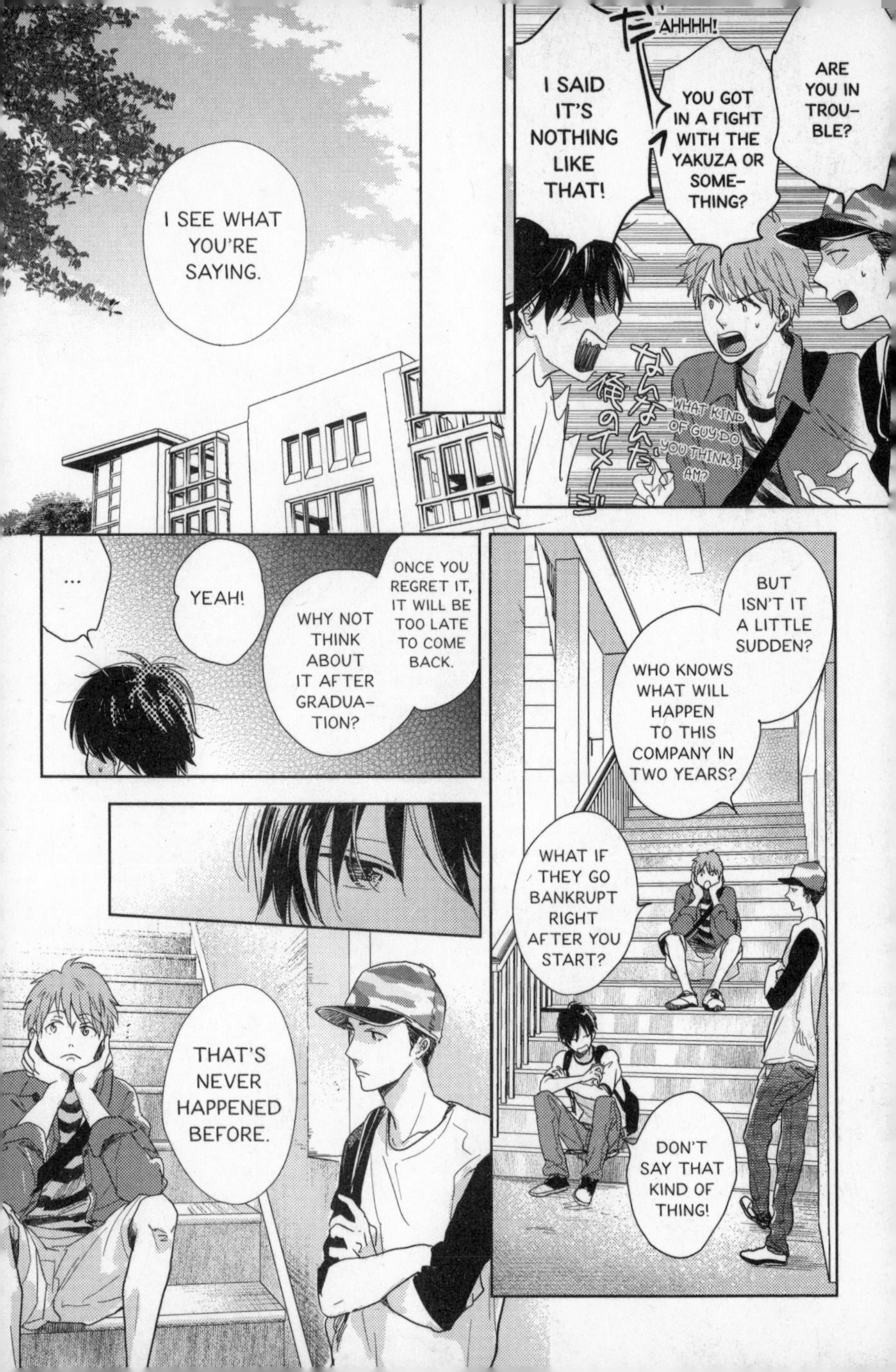

ARE YOU IN TROU-BLE?
だ
AHHHH!
YOU GOT IN A FIGHT WITH THE YAKUZA OR SOME-THING?
I SAID IT'S NOTHING LIKE THAT!
なんなんだ俺のイメージ
WHAT KIND OF GUY DO YOU THINK I AM?
I SEE WHAT YOU'RE SAYING.
BUT ISN'T IT A LITTLE SUDDEN?
WHO KNOWS WHAT WILL HAPPEN TO THIS COMPANY IN TWO YEARS?
WHAT IF THEY GO BANKRUPT RIGHT AFTER YOU START?
DON'T SAY THAT KIND OF THING!
ONCE YOU REGRET IT, IT WILL BE TOO LATE TO COME BACK.
WHY NOT THINK ABOUT IT AFTER GRADUA-TION?
YEAH!
...
THAT'S NEVER HAPPENED BEFORE.

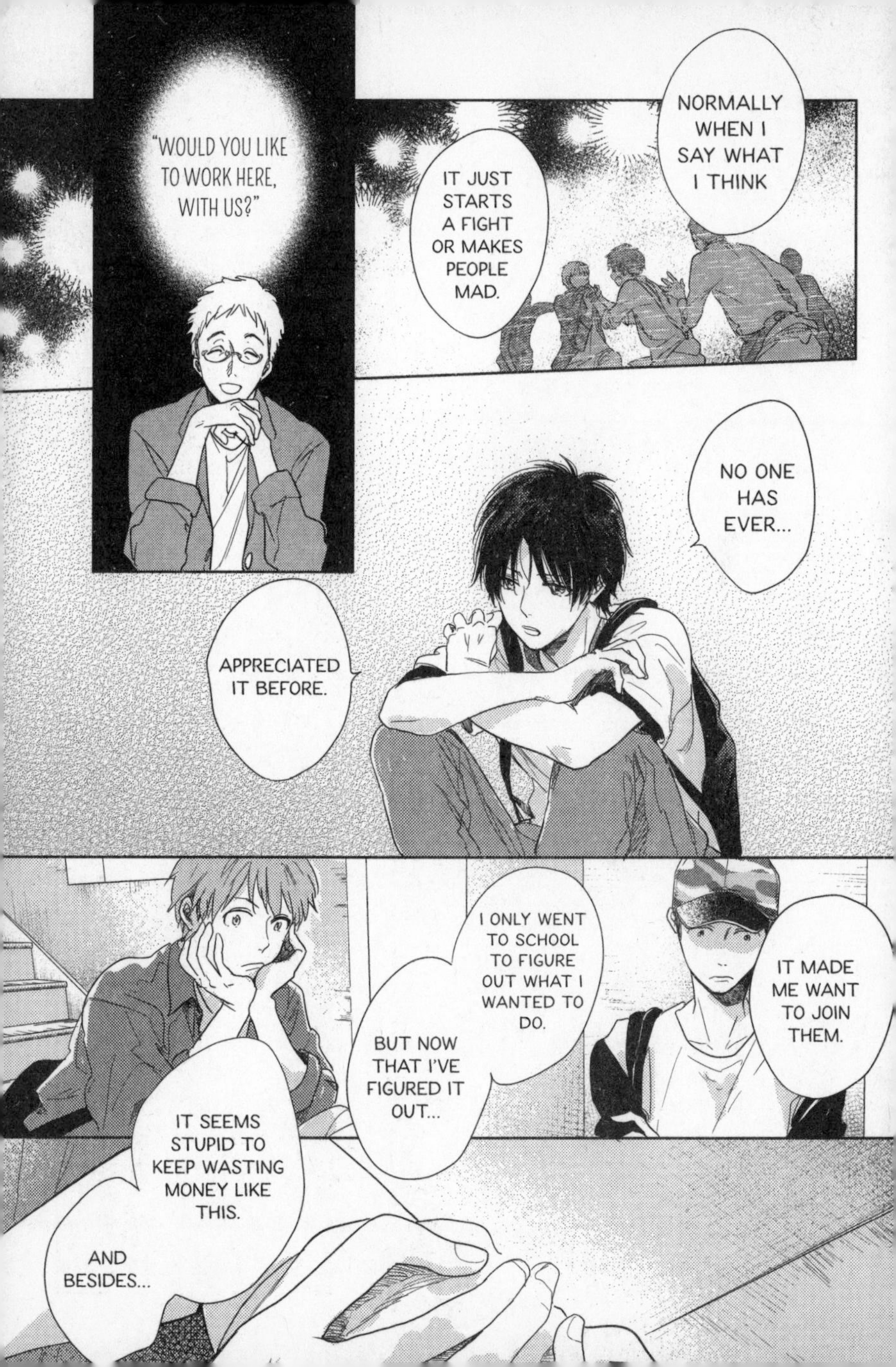
NORMALLY WHEN I SAY WHAT I THINK
IT JUST STARTS A FIGHT OR MAKES PEOPLE MAD.
"WOULD YOU LIKE TO WORK HERE, WITH US?"
NO ONE HAS EVER...
APPRECIATED IT BEFORE.
IT MADE ME WANT TO JOIN THEM.
I ONLY WENT TO SCHOOL TO FIGURE OUT WHAT I WANTED TO DO.
BUT NOW THAT I'VE FIGURED IT OUT...
IT SEEMS STUPID TO KEEP WASTING MONEY LIKE THIS.
AND BESIDES...

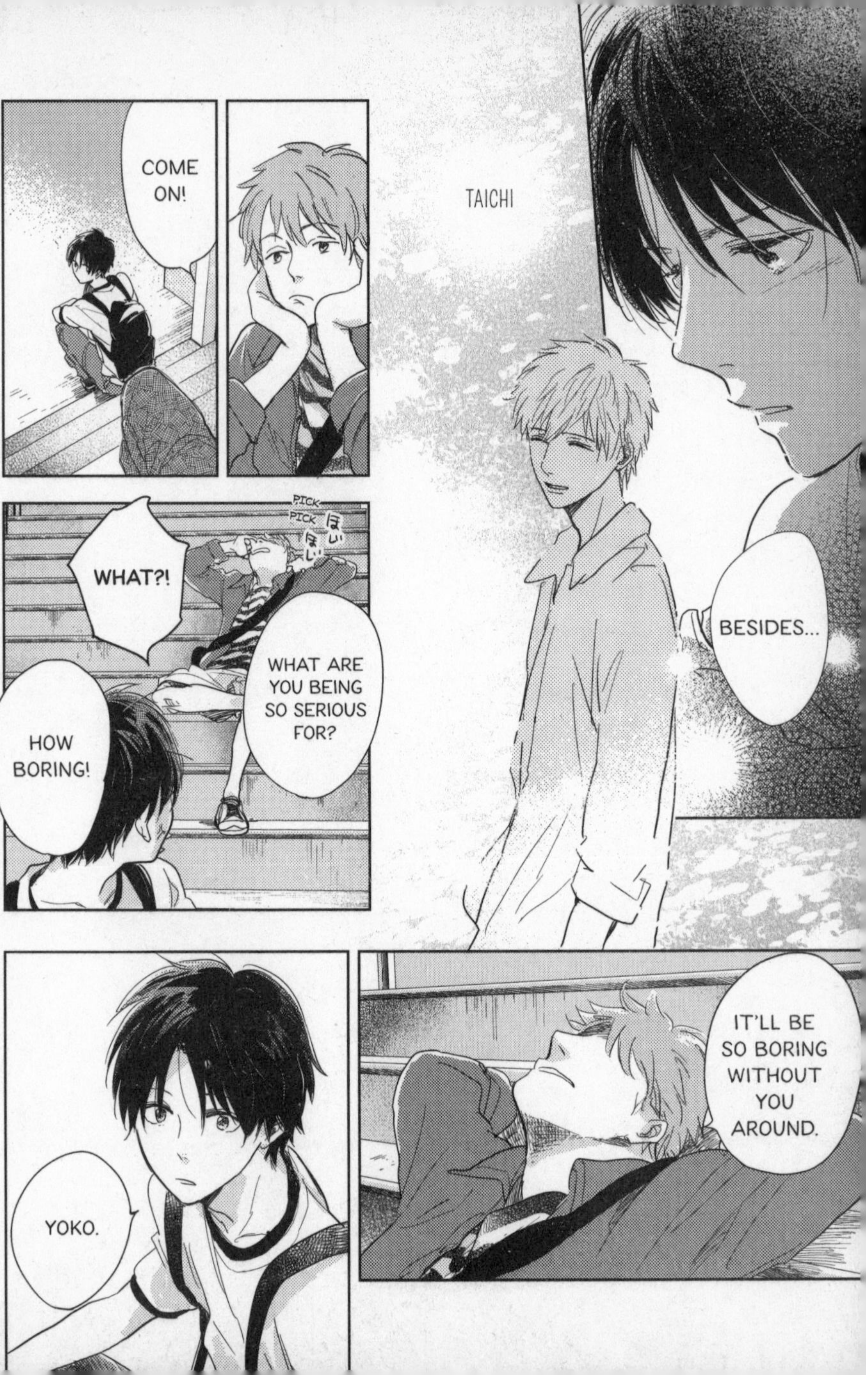

TAICHI
BESIDES...
COME ON!
PICK PICK
ほじほじ
WHAT?!
WHAT ARE YOU BEING SO SERIOUS FOR?
HOW BORING!
IT'LL BE SO BORING WITHOUT YOU AROUND.
YOKO.

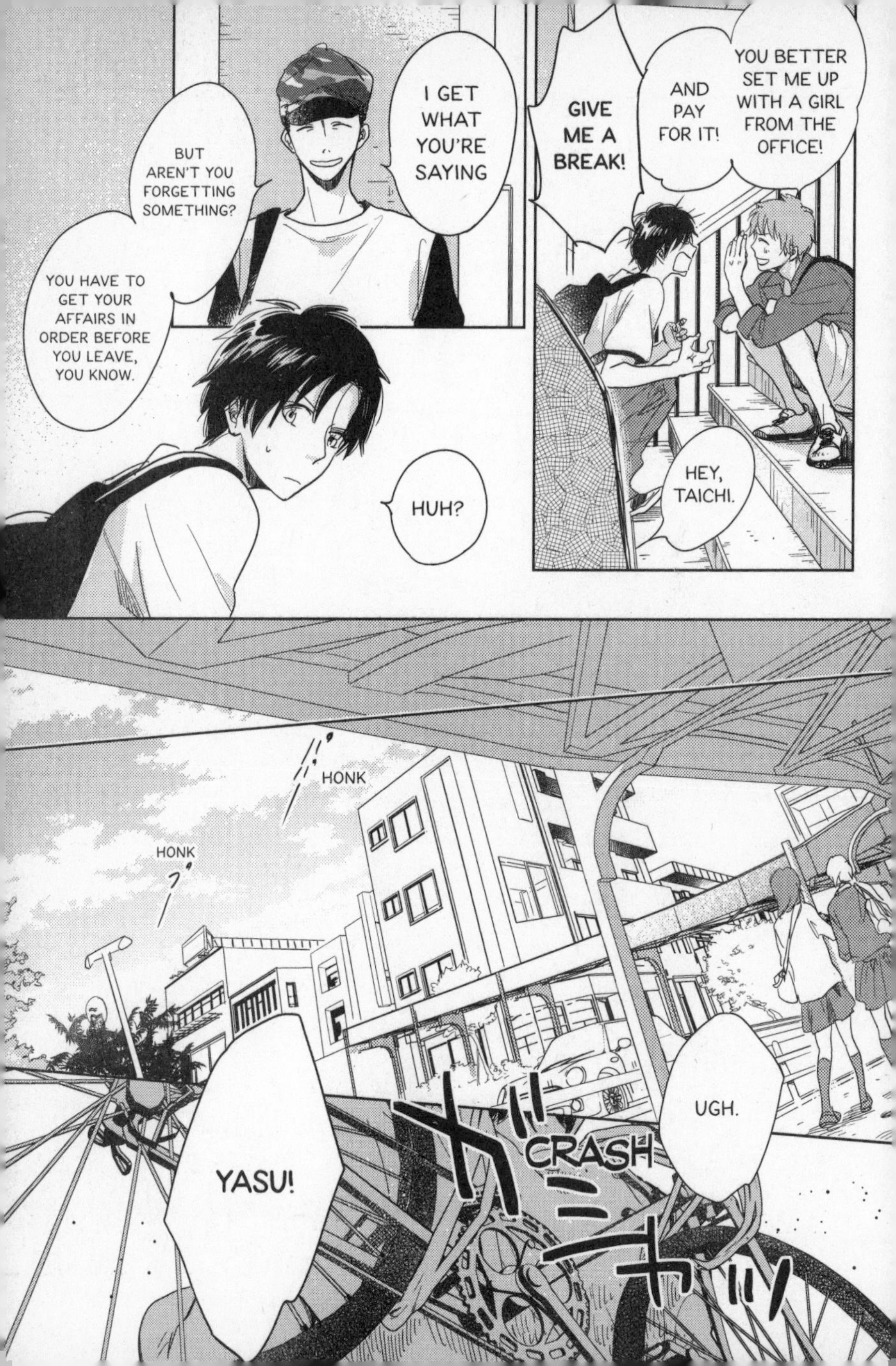
YOU BETTER SET ME UP WITH A GIRL FROM THE OFFICE!
AND PAY FOR IT!
GIVE ME A BREAK!
HEY, TAICHI.
I GET WHAT YOU'RE SAYING
BUT AREN'T YOU FORGETTING SOMETHING?
YOU HAVE TO GET YOUR AFFAIRS IN ORDER BEFORE YOU LEAVE, YOU KNOW.
HUH?
HONK
HONK
UGH.
CRASH
YASU!

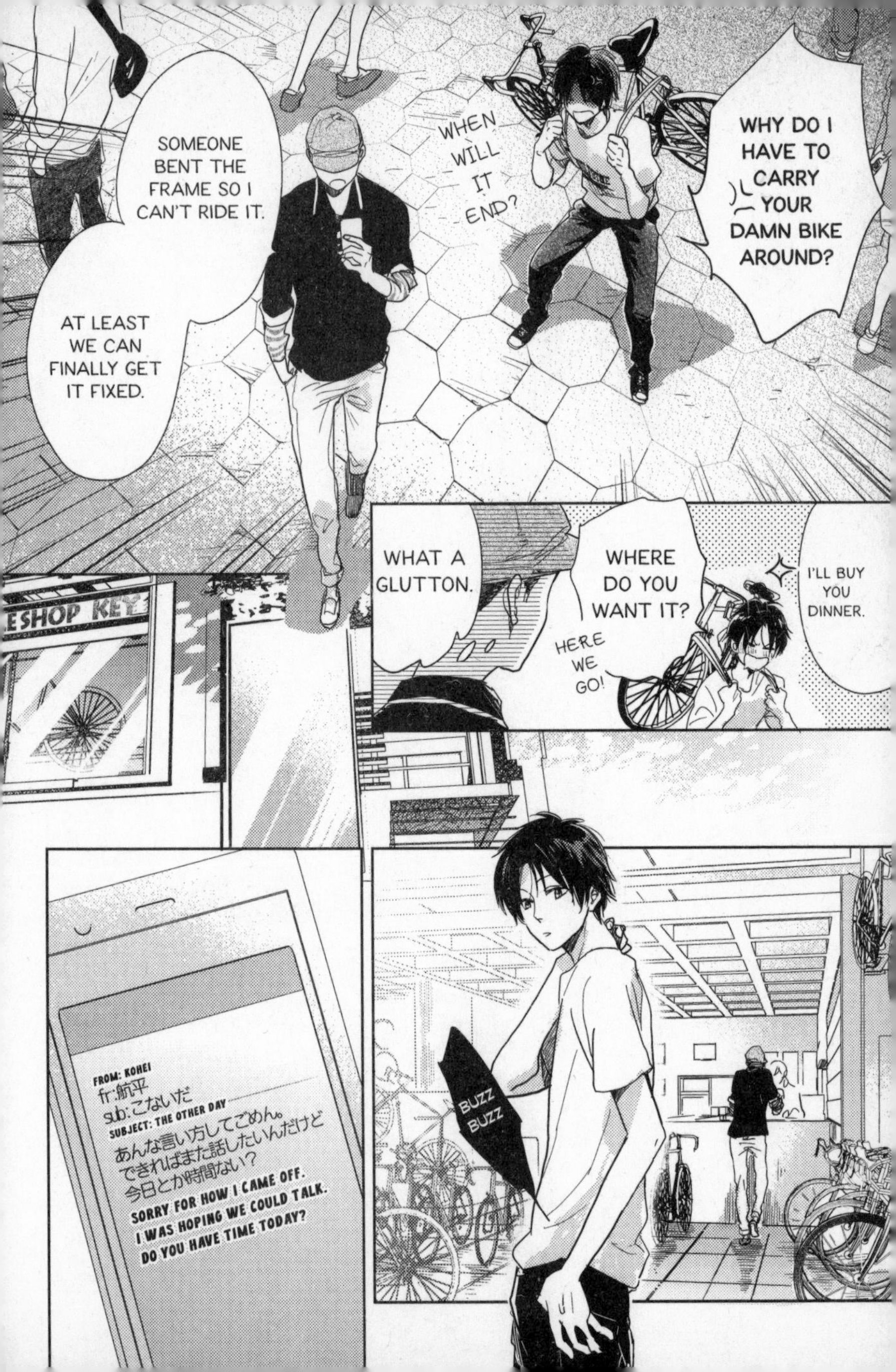
WHY DO I HAVE TO CARRY YOUR DAMN BIKE AROUND?
WHEN WILL IT END?
SOMEONE BENT THE FRAME SO I CAN'T RIDE IT.
AT LEAST WE CAN FINALLY GET IT FIXED.
I'LL BUY YOU DINNER.
WHERE DO YOU WANT IT?
HERE WE GO!
WHAT A GLUTTON.
ESHOP KEY
BUZZ BUZZ
FROM: KOHEI
fr:航平
sub:こないだ
SUBJECT: THE OTHER DAY
あんな言い方してごめん。
できればまた話したいんだけど
今日とか時間ない？
SORRY FOR HOW I CAME OFF.
I WAS HOPING WE COULD TALK.
DO YOU HAVE TIME TODAY?

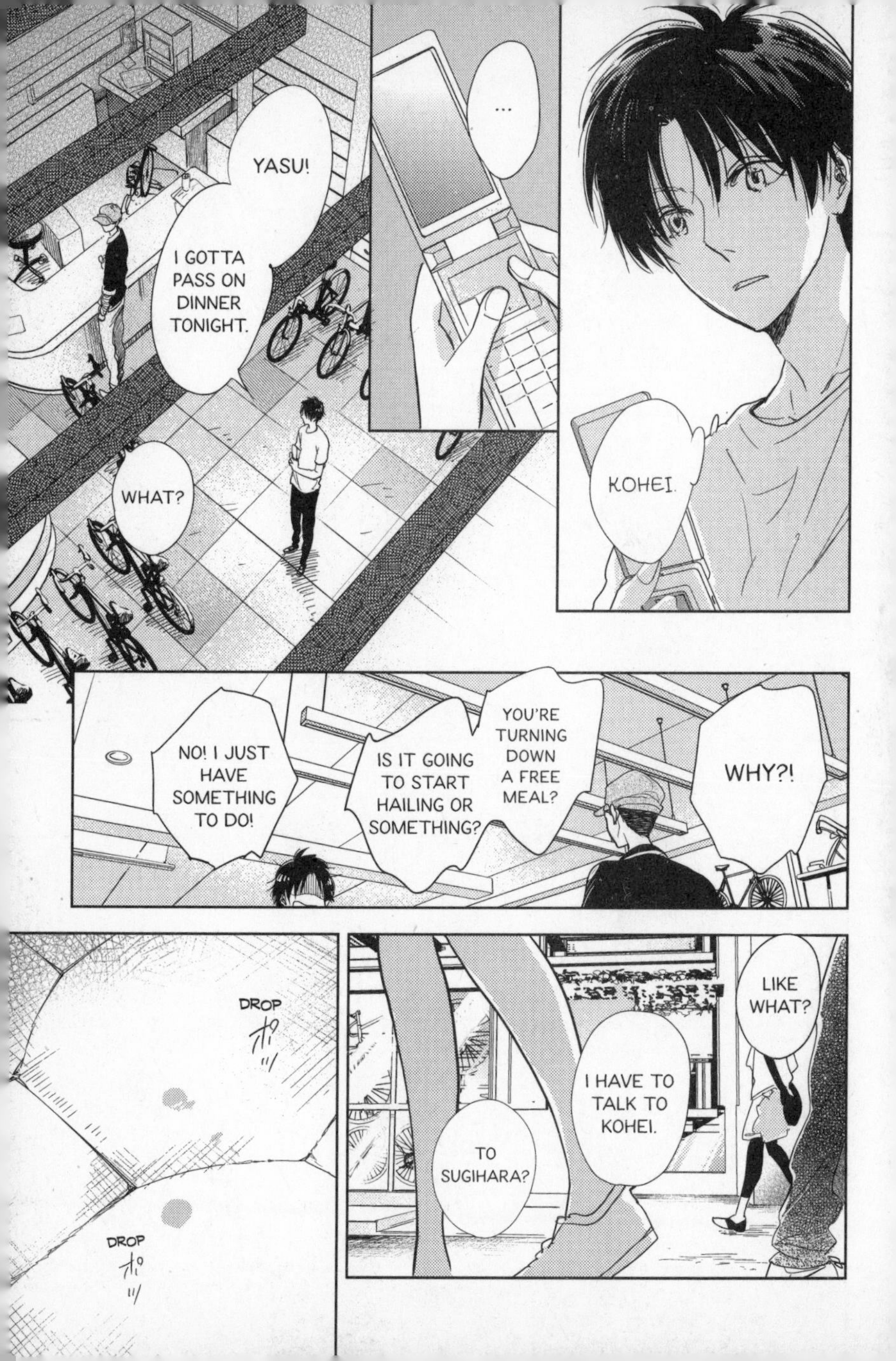
KOHEI.
...
YASU!
I GOTTA PASS ON DINNER TONIGHT.
WHAT?
WHY?!
YOU'RE TURNING DOWN A FREE MEAL?
IS IT GOING TO START HAILING OR SOMETHING?
NO! I JUST HAVE SOMETHING TO DO!
LIKE WHAT?
I HAVE TO TALK TO KOHEI.
TO SUGIHARA?
DROP
ポツ
DROP
ポツ

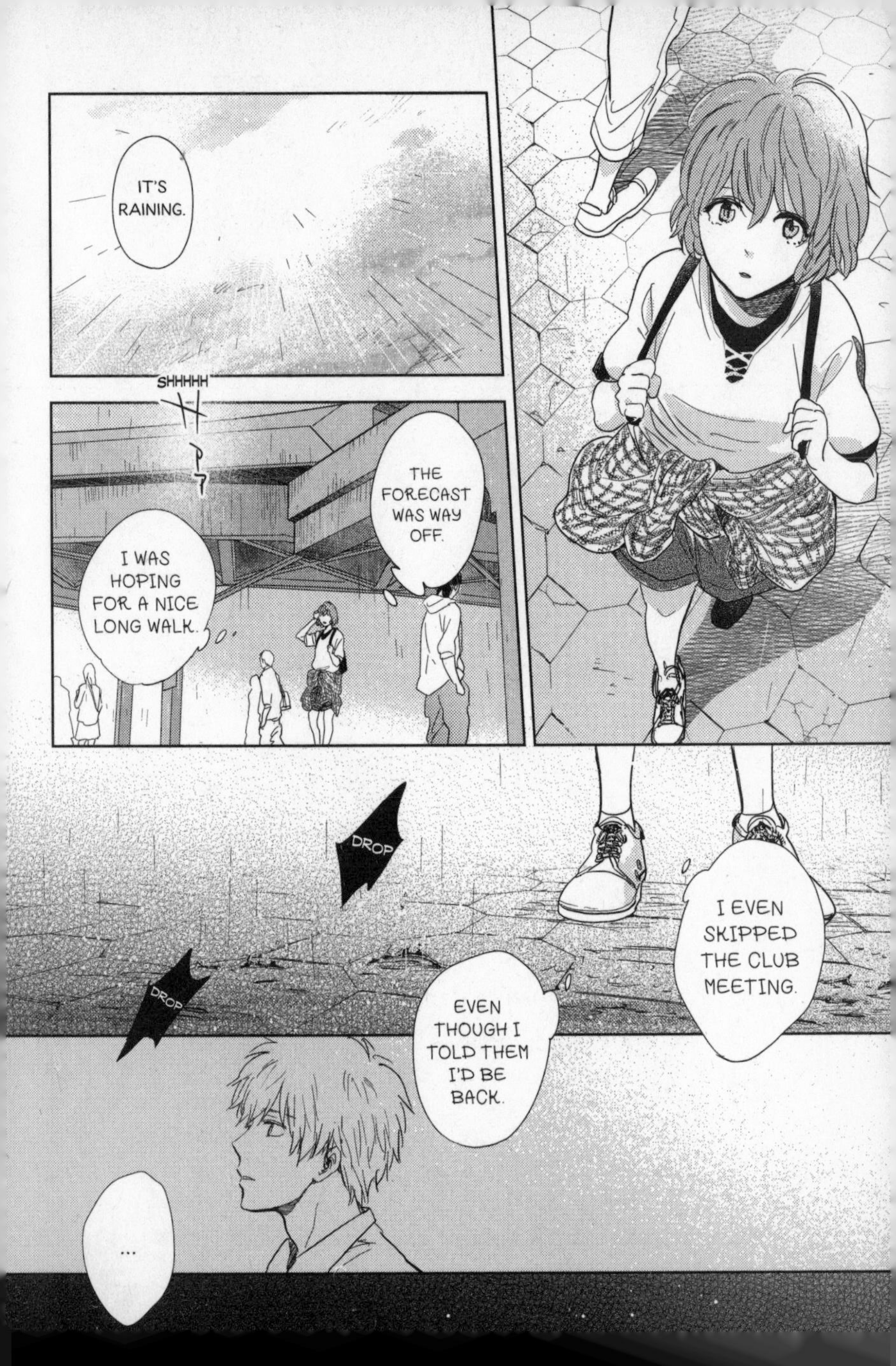
IT'S RAINING.
SHHHHH
THE FORECAST WAS WAY OFF.
I WAS HOPING FOR A NICE LONG WALK.
DROP
I EVEN SKIPPED THE CLUB MEETING.
DROP
EVEN THOUGH I TOLD THEM I'D BE BACK.
...

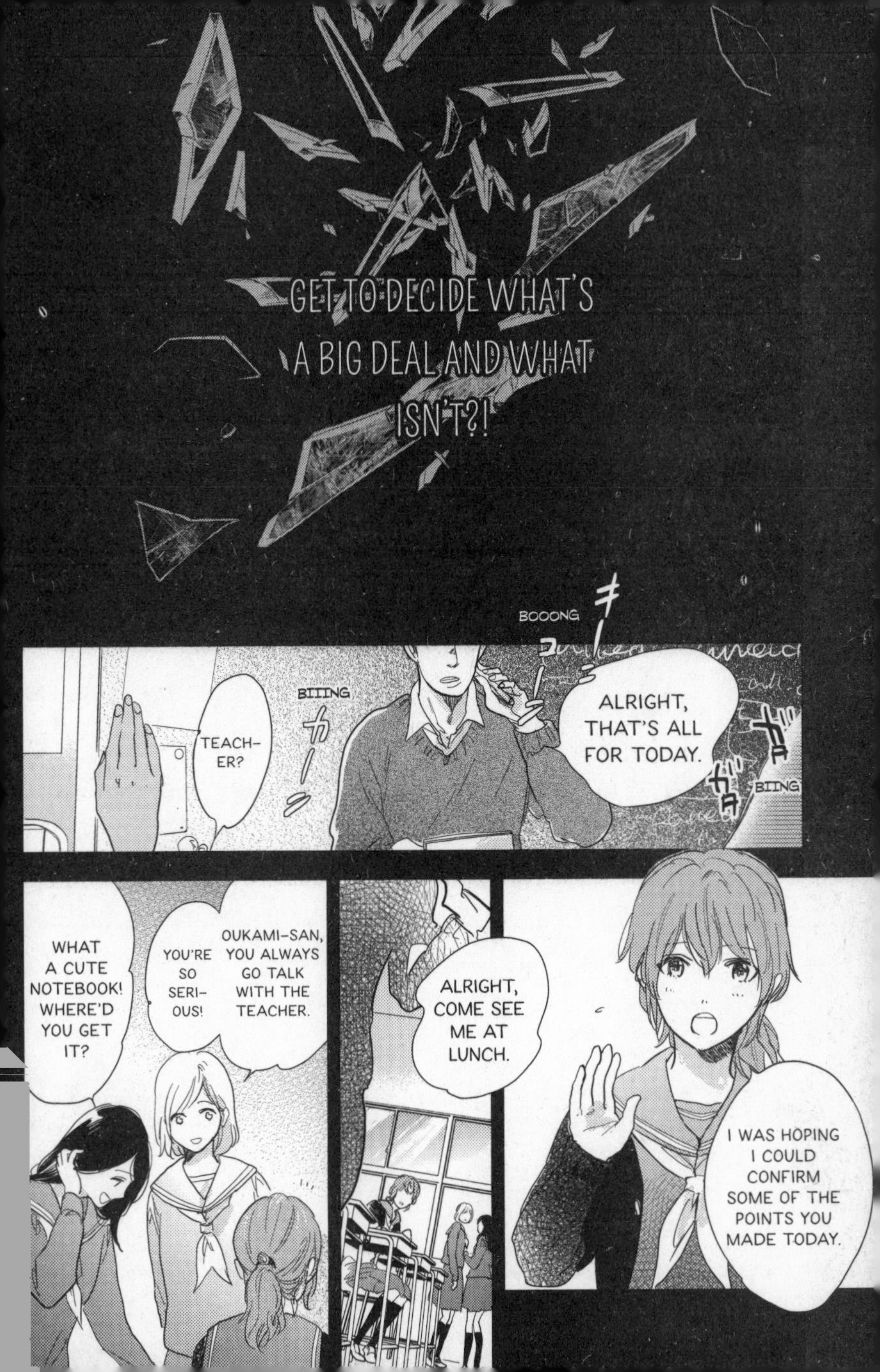
GET TO DECIDE WHAT'S A BIG DEAL AND WHAT ISN'T?!
BOOONG
ALRIGHT, THAT'S ALL FOR TODAY.
BIING
BIING
TEACHER-ER?
I WAS HOPING I COULD CONFIRM SOME OF THE POINTS YOU MADE TODAY.
ALRIGHT, COME SEE ME AT LUNCH.
OUKAMI-SAN, YOU ALWAYS GO TALK WITH THE TEACHER.
YOU'RE SO SERI-OUS!
WHAT A CUTE NOTEBOOK! WHERE'D YOU GET IT?

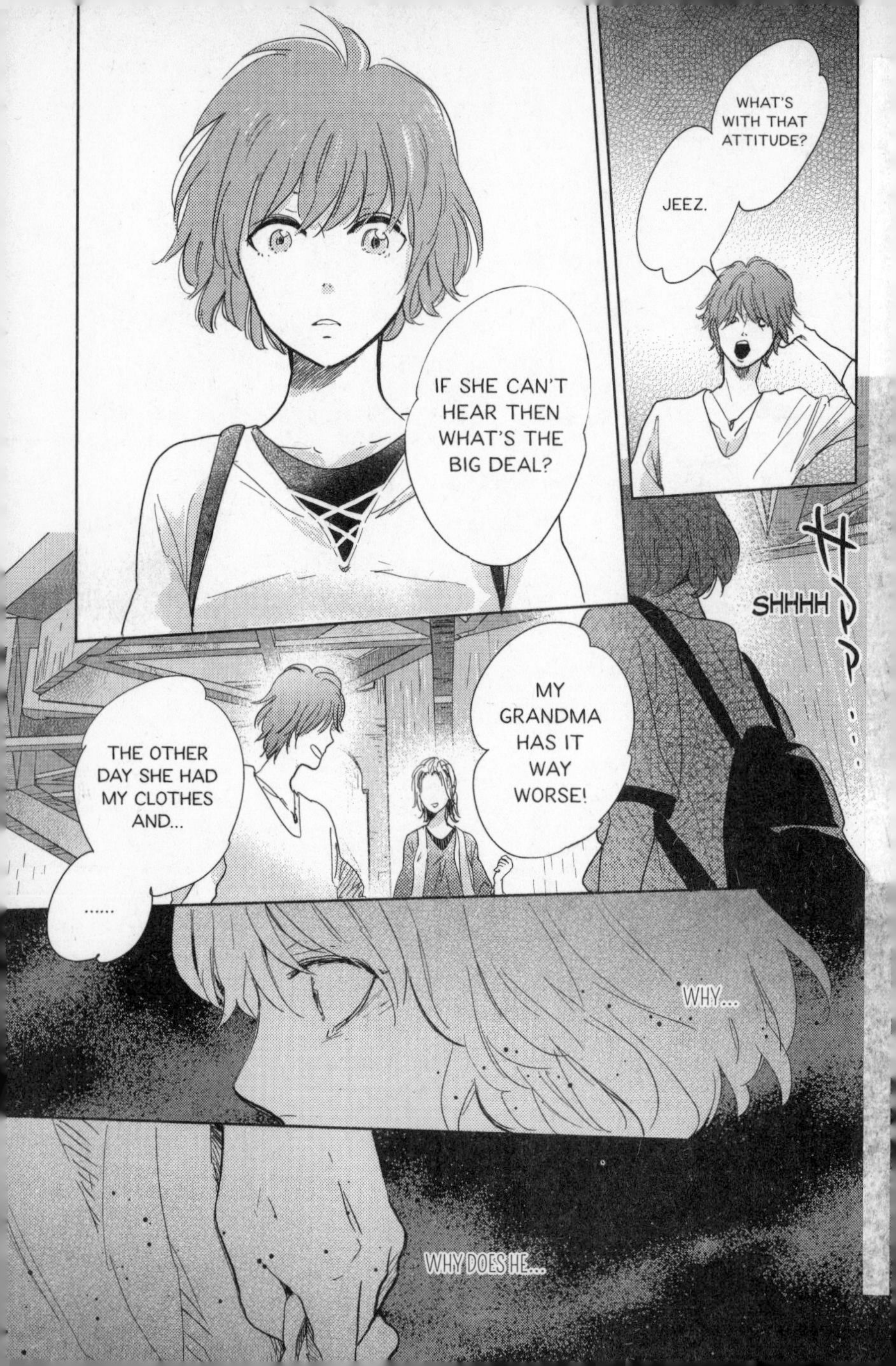
WHAT'S WITH THAT ATTITUDE?
JEEZ.
IF SHE CAN'T HEAR THEN WHAT'S THE BIG DEAL?
SHHHH
MY GRANDMA HAS IT WAY WORSE!
THE OTHER DAY SHE HAD MY CLOTHES AND...
......
WHY...
WHY DOES HE...

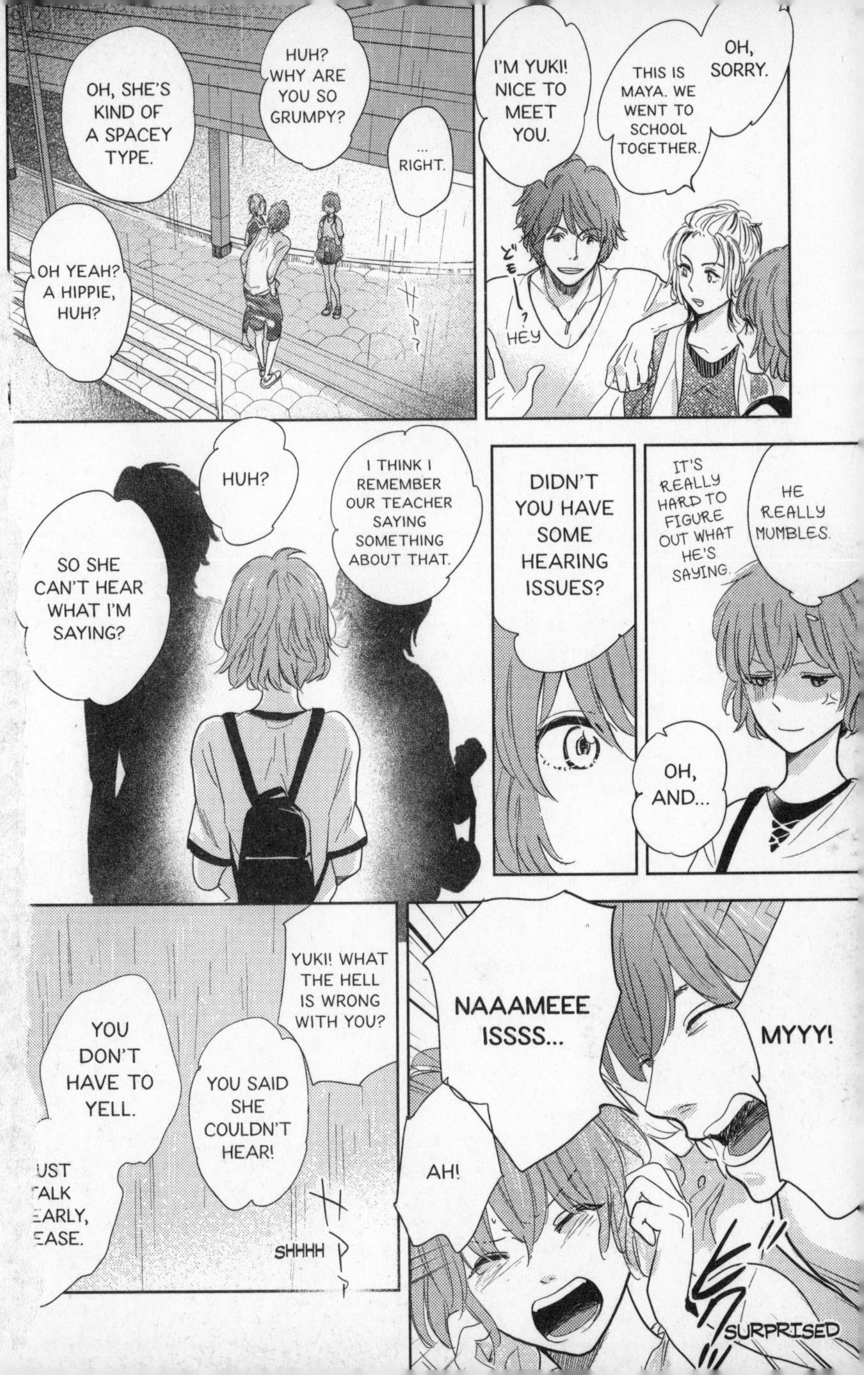
OH, SORRY.
THIS IS MAYA. WE WENT TO SCHOOL TOGETHER.
I'M YUKI! NICE TO MEET YOU.
HEY
... RIGHT.
HUH? WHY ARE YOU SO GRUMPY?
OH, SHE'S KIND OF A SPACEY TYPE.
OH YEAH? A HIPPIE, HUH?
HE REALLY MUMBLES.
IT'S REALLY HARD TO FIGURE OUT WHAT HE'S SAYING.
OH, AND...
DIDN'T YOU HAVE SOME HEARING ISSUES?
I THINK I REMEMBER OUR TEACHER SAYING SOMETHING ABOUT THAT.
HUH?
SO SHE CAN'T HEAR WHAT I'M SAYING?
MYYY!
NAAAMEEE ISSSS...
AH!
SURPRISED
YUKI! WHAT THE HELL IS WRONG WITH YOU?
YOU SAID SHE COULDN'T HEAR!
YOU DON'T HAVE TO YELL.
UST TALK EARLY, EASE.
SHHHH

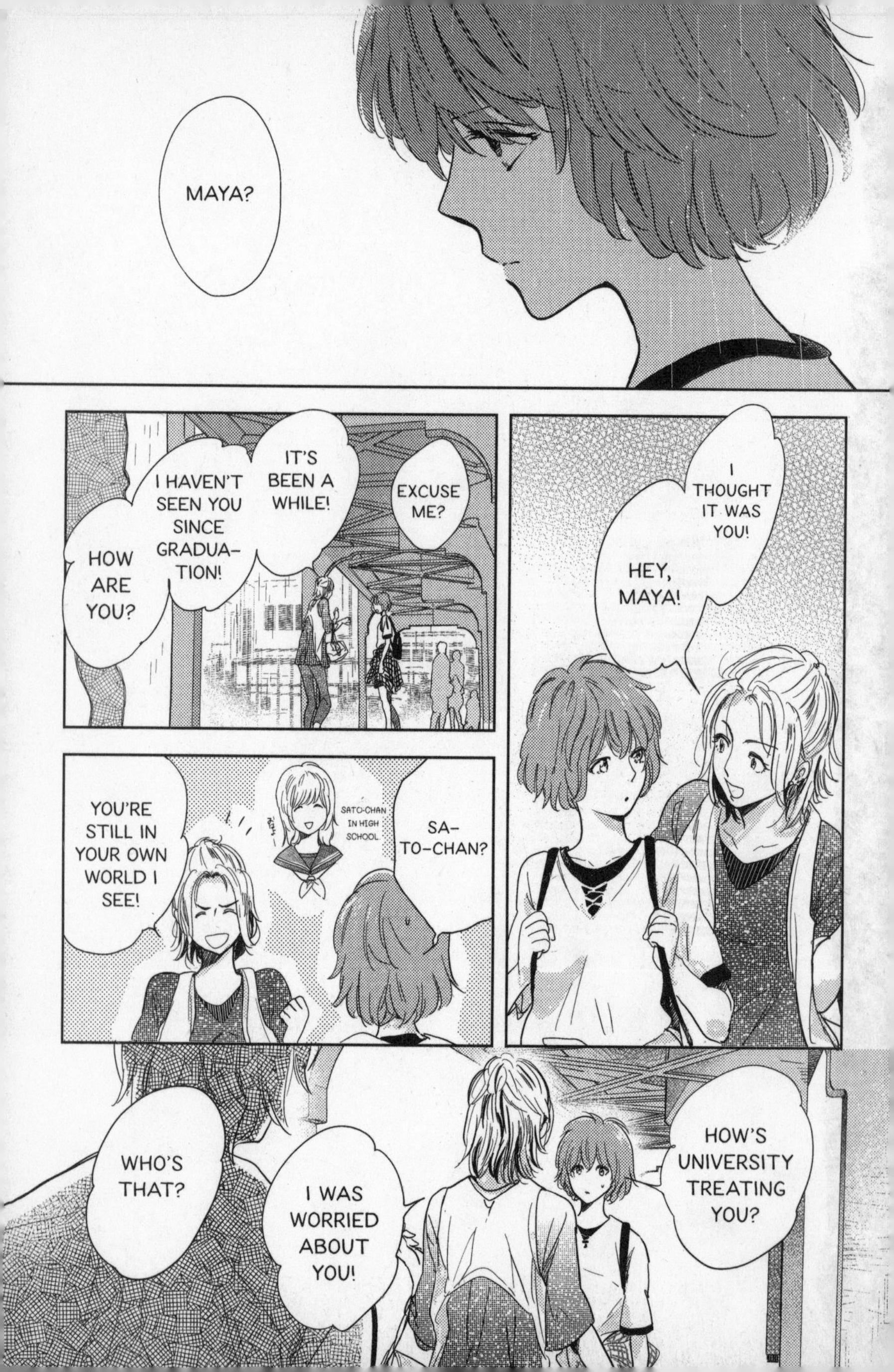
MAYA?
I THOUGHT IT WAS YOU!
HEY, MAYA!
EXCUSE ME?
IT'S BEEN A WHILE!
I HAVEN'T SEEN YOU SINCE GRADUA-TION!
HOW ARE YOU?
SA-TO-CHAN?
SATO-CHAN IN HIGH SCHOOL.
YOU'RE STILL IN YOUR OWN WORLD I SEE!
HOW'S UNIVERSITY TREATING YOU?
I WAS WORRIED ABOUT YOU!
WHO'S THAT?

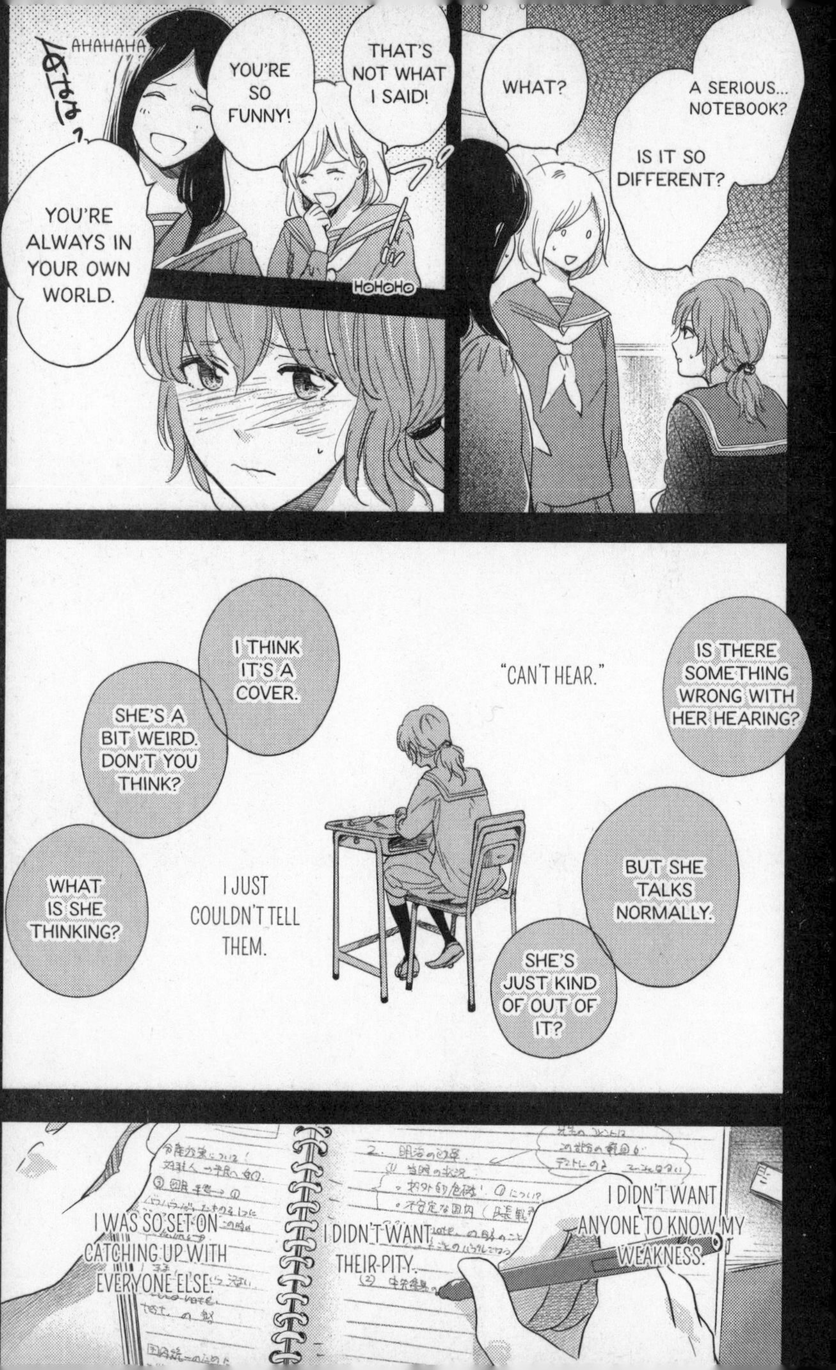
A SERIOUS... NOTEBOOK?
WHAT?
IS IT SO DIFFERENT?
THAT'S NOT WHAT I SAID!
YOU'RE SO FUNNY!
AHAHAHA
あはは
YOU'RE ALWAYS IN YOUR OWN WORLD.
HOHOHO
IS THERE SOMETHING WRONG WITH HER HEARING?
"CAN'T HEAR."
I THINK IT'S A COVER.
SHE'S A BIT WEIRD. DON'T YOU THINK?
BUT SHE TALKS NORMALLY.
SHE'S JUST KIND OF OUT OF IT?
I JUST COULDN'T TELL THEM.
WHAT IS SHE THINKING?
I DIDN'T WANT ANYONE TO KNOW MY WEAKNESS.
I DIDN'T WANT THEIR PITY.
I WAS SO SET ON CATCHING UP WITH EVERYONE ELSE.

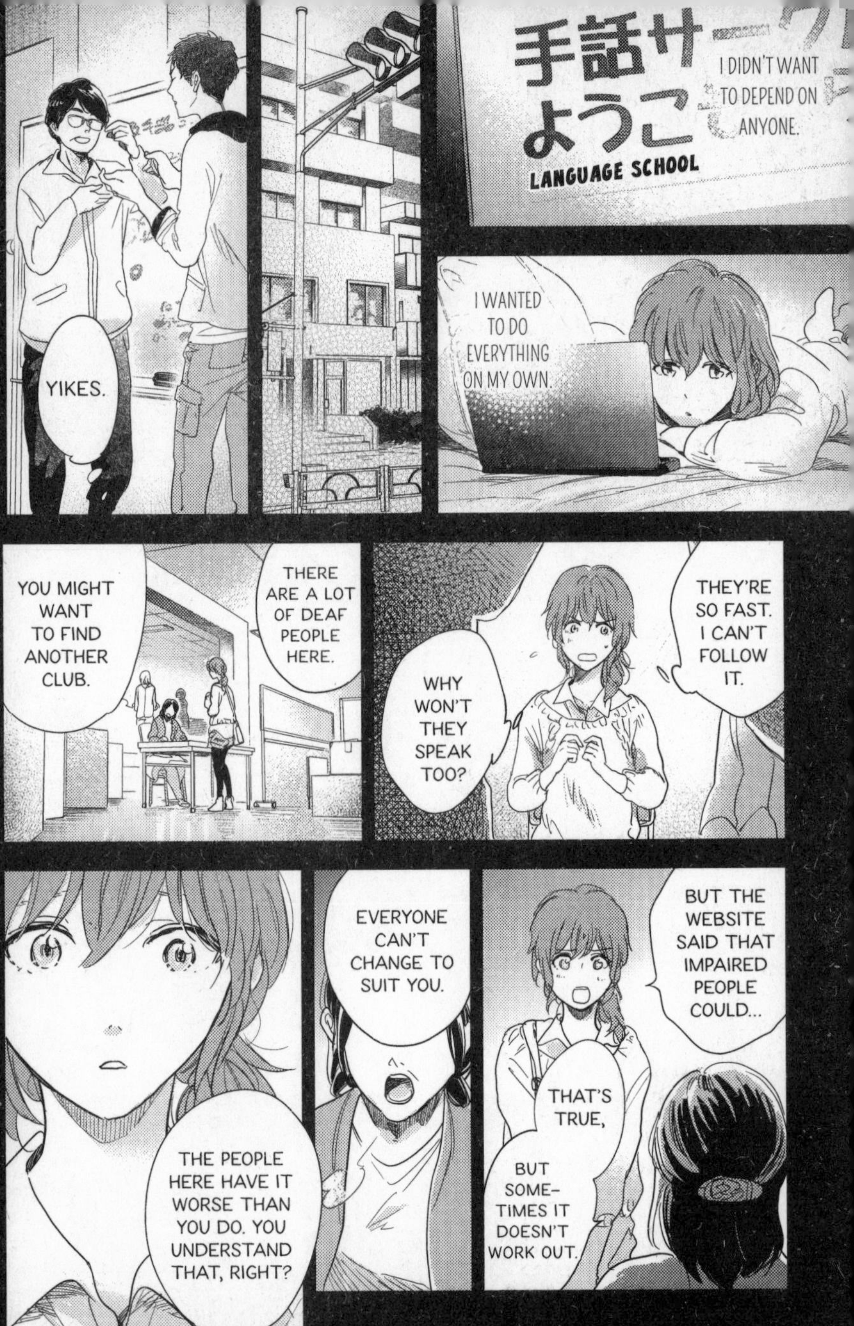
手話サーク
ようこ
LANGUAGE SCHOOL
I DIDN'T WANT TO DEPEND ON ANYONE.
I WANTED TO DO EVERYTHING ON MY OWN.
YIKES.
THEY'RE SO FAST. I CAN'T FOLLOW IT.
WHY WON'T THEY SPEAK TOO?
THERE ARE A LOT OF DEAF PEOPLE HERE.
YOU MIGHT WANT TO FIND ANOTHER CLUB.
BUT THE WEBSITE SAID THAT IMPAIRED PEOPLE COULD...
THAT'S TRUE,
BUT SOME-TIMES IT DOESN'T WORK OUT.
EVERYONE CAN'T CHANGE TO SUIT YOU.
THE PEOPLE HERE HAVE IT WORSE THAN YOU DO. YOU UNDERSTAND THAT, RIGHT?

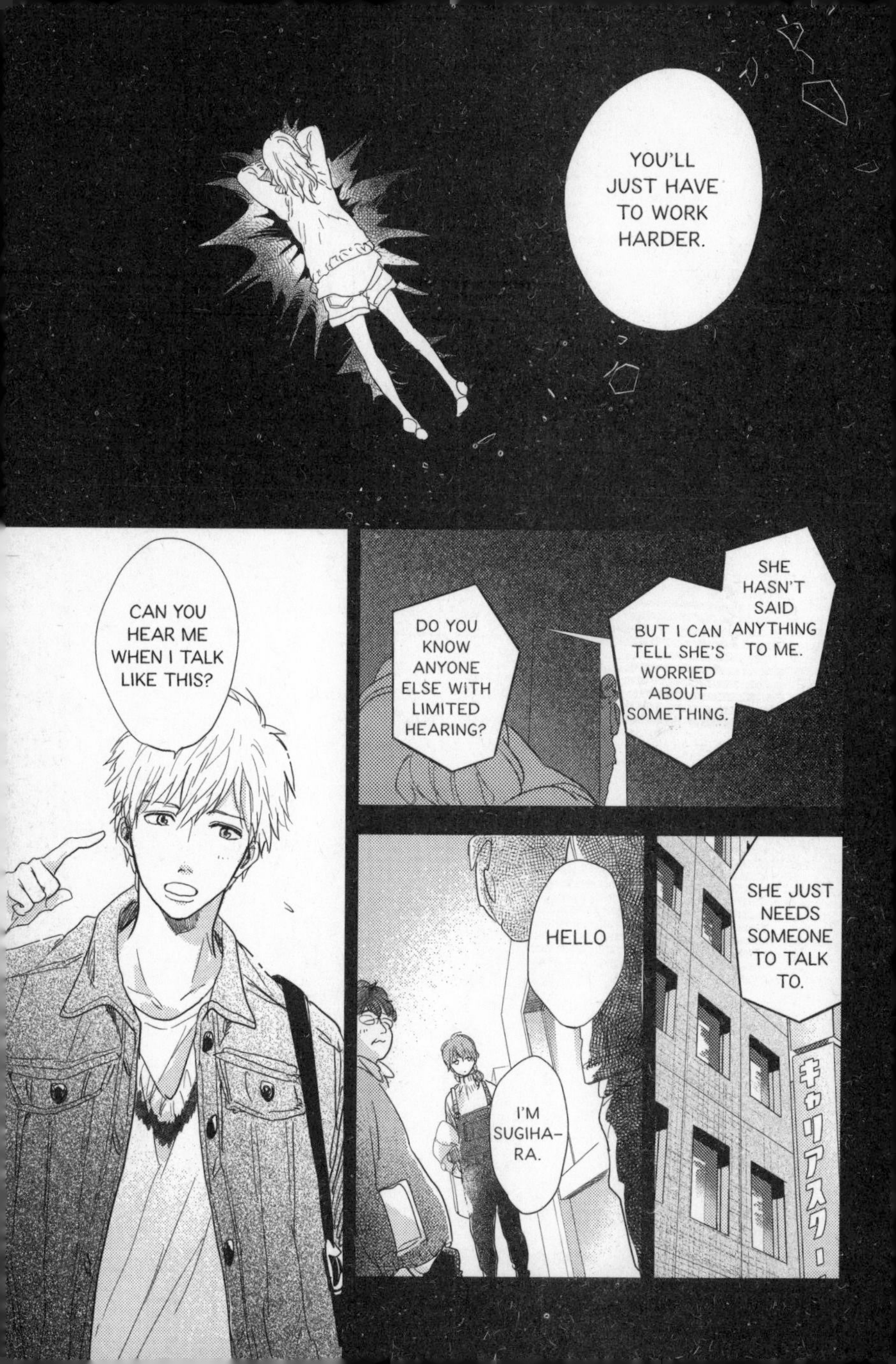
YOU'LL JUST HAVE TO WORK HARDER.
SHE HASN'T SAID ANYTHING TO ME.
BUT I CAN TELL SHE'S WORRIED ABOUT SOMETHING.
DO YOU KNOW ANYONE ELSE WITH LIMITED HEARING?
SHE JUST NEEDS SOMEONE TO TALK TO.
キャリアスクー
HELLO
I'M SUGIHA-RA.
CAN YOU HEAR ME WHEN I TALK LIKE THIS?

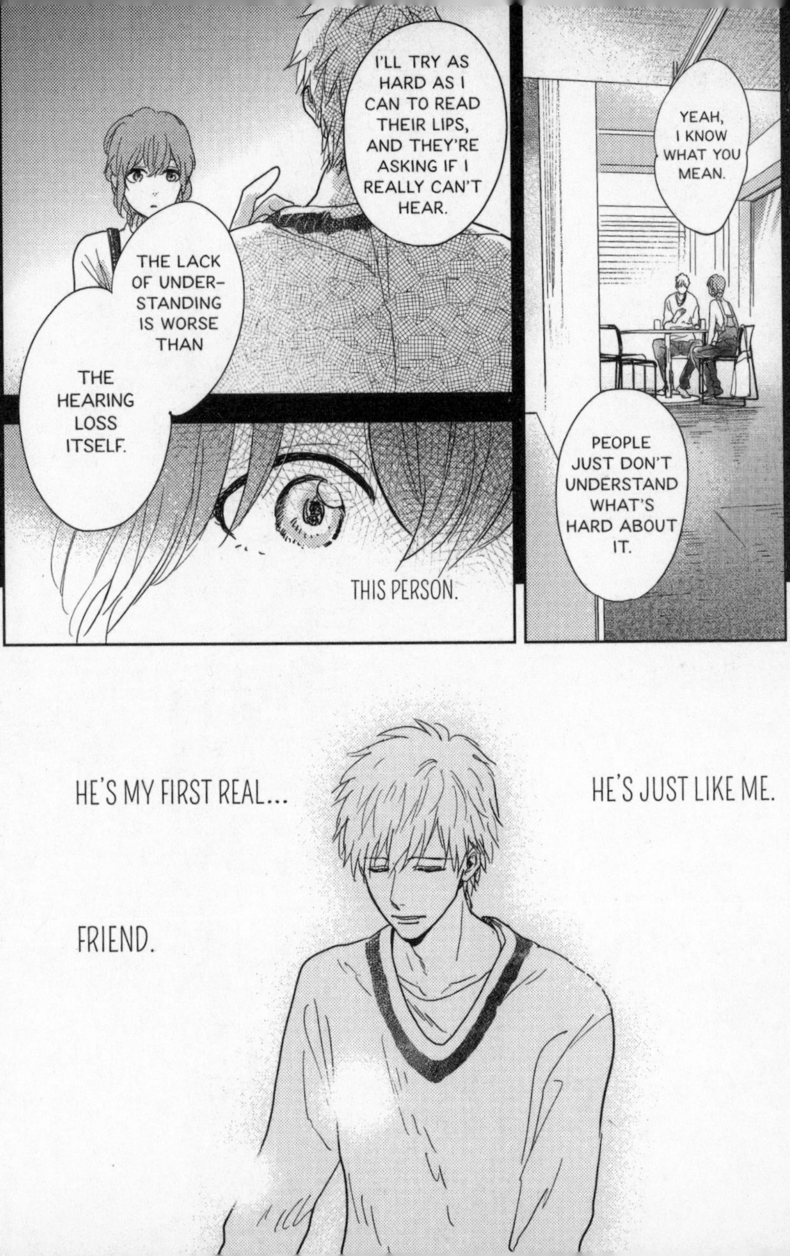
YEAH, I KNOW WHAT YOU MEAN.
PEOPLE JUST DON'T UNDERSTAND WHAT'S HARD ABOUT IT.
I'LL TRY AS HARD AS I CAN TO READ THEIR LIPS, AND THEY'RE ASKING IF I REALLY CAN'T HEAR.
THE LACK OF UNDER-STANDING IS WORSE THAN
THE HEARING LOSS ITSELF.
THIS PERSON.
HE'S JUST LIKE ME.
HE'S MY FIRST REAL...
FRIEND.

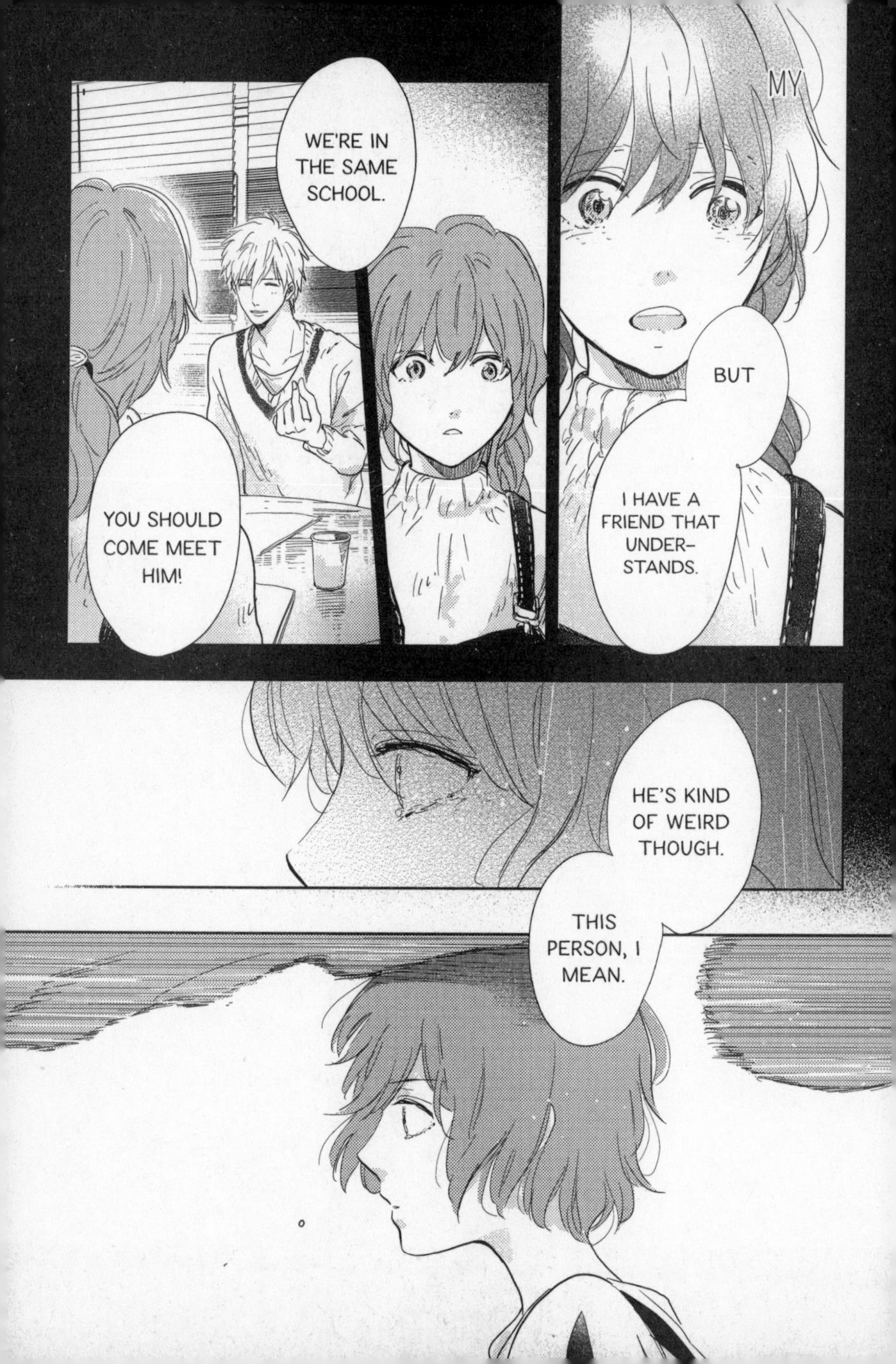
MY
BUT
I HAVE A FRIEND THAT UNDER-STANDS.
WE'RE IN THE SAME SCHOOL.
YOU SHOULD COME MEET HIM!
HE'S KIND OF WEIRD THOUGH.
THIS PERSON, I MEAN.

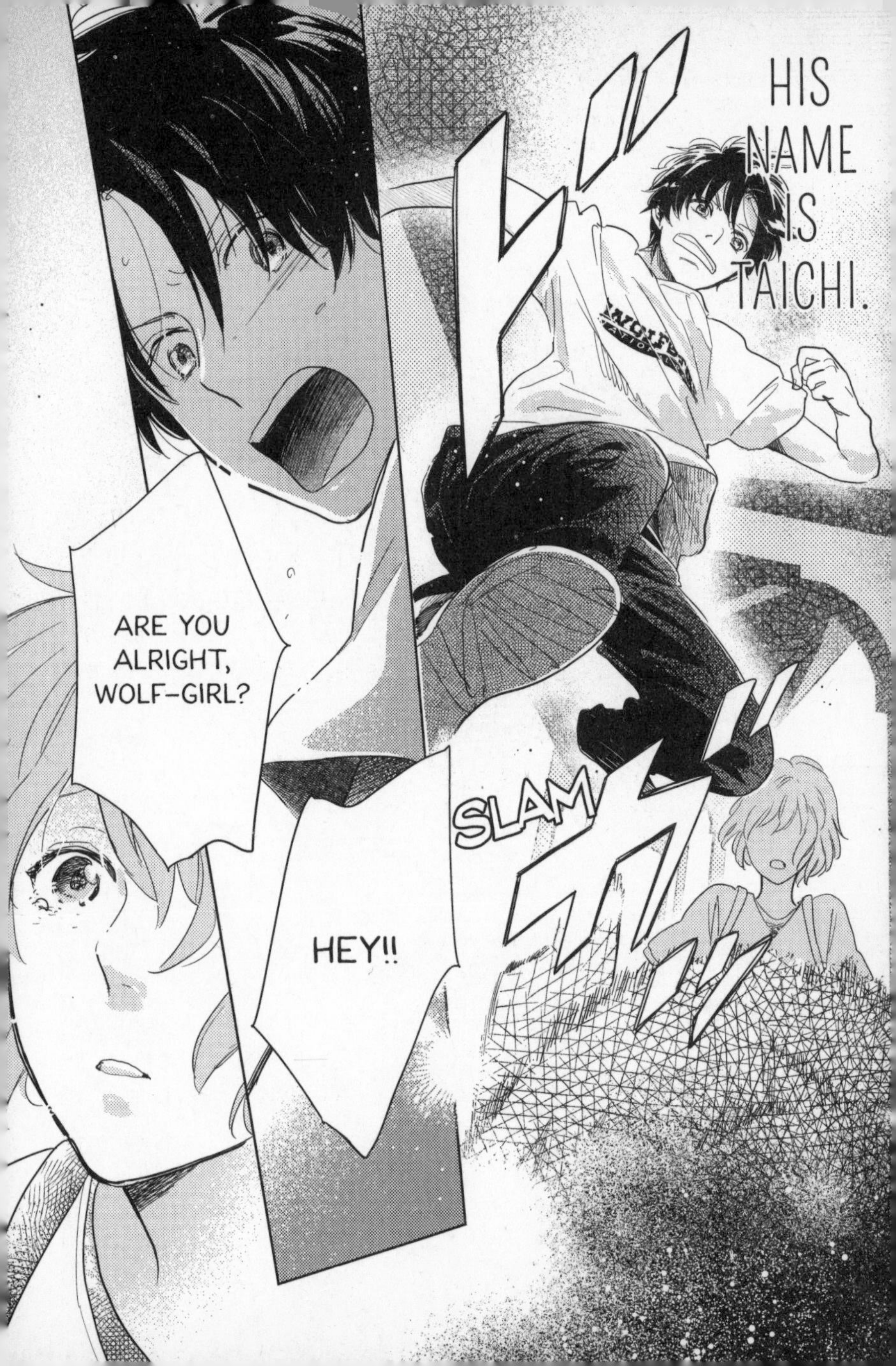
HIS NAME IS TAICHI.
SLAM
ARE YOU ALRIGHT, WOLF-GIRL?
HEY!!

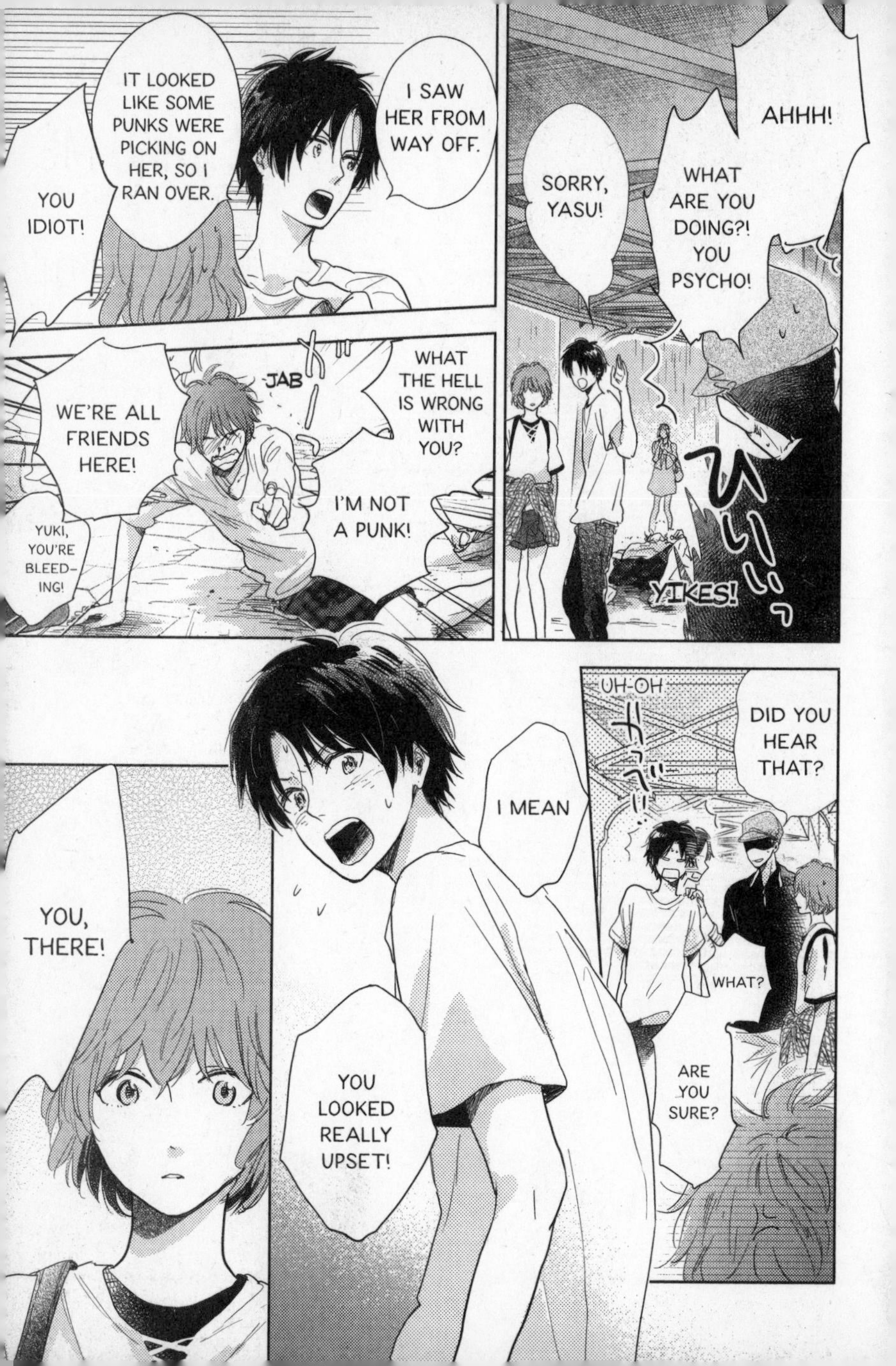
AHHH!
WHAT ARE YOU DOING?! YOU PSYCHO!
SORRY, YASU!
YIKES!
I SAW HER FROM WAY OFF.
IT LOOKED LIKE SOME PUNKS WERE PICKING ON HER, SO I RAN OVER.
YOU IDIOT!
JAB
WHAT THE HELL IS WRONG WITH YOU?
I'M NOT A PUNK!
WE'RE ALL FRIENDS HERE!
YUKI, YOU'RE BLEED-ING!
DID YOU HEAR THAT?
UH-OH
WHAT?
ARE YOU SURE?
I MEAN
YOU LOOKED REALLY UPSET!
YOU, THERE!

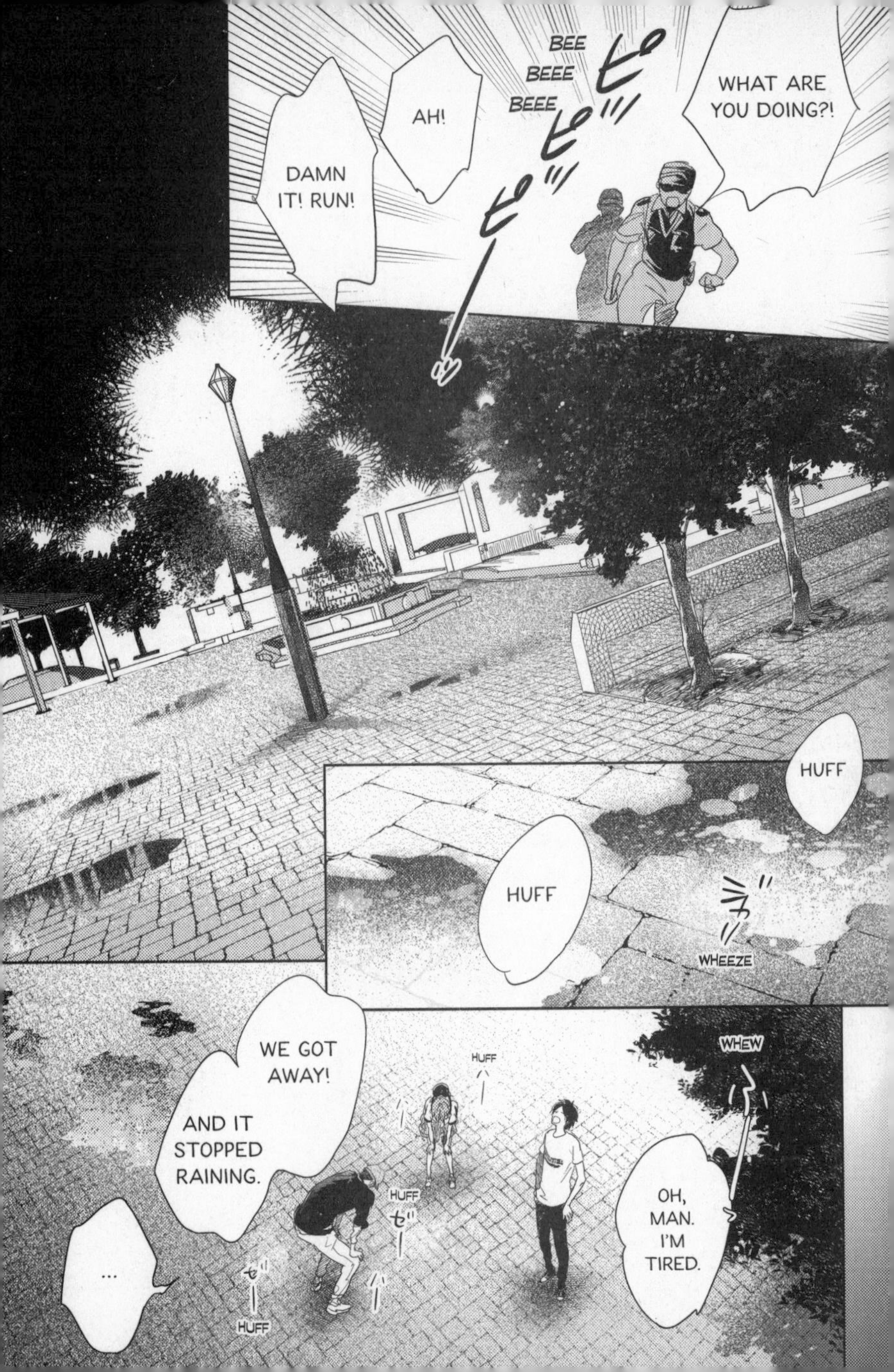

WHAT ARE YOU DOING?!
BEE
BEEE
BEEE
AH!
DAMN IT! RUN!
HUFF
WHEEZE
HUFF
WHEW
OH, MAN. I'M TIRED.
HUFF
WE GOT AWAY!
AND IT STOPPED RAINING.
HUFF
...
HUFF

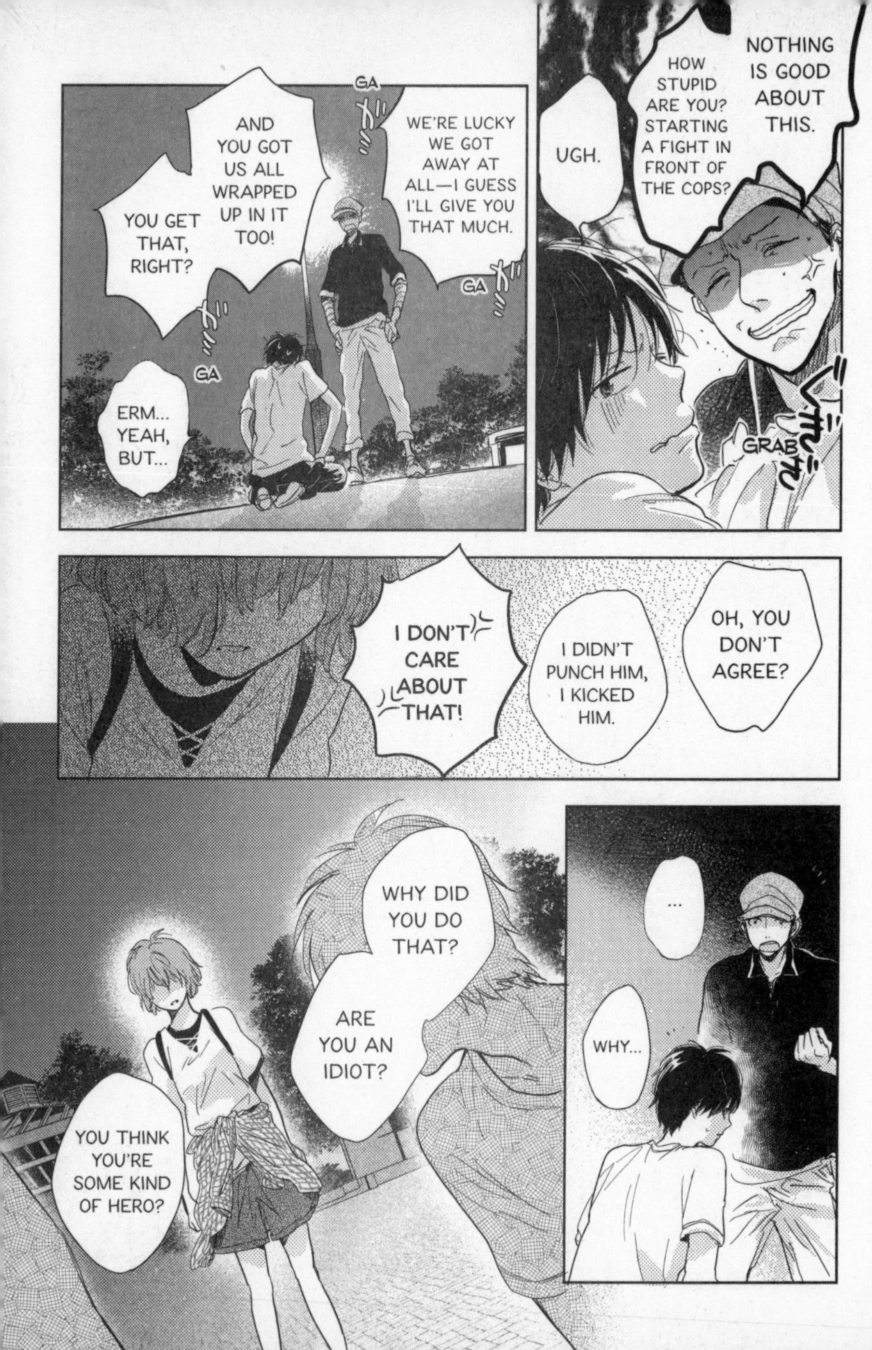
NOTHING IS GOOD ABOUT THIS.
HOW STUPID ARE YOU? STARTING A FIGHT IN FRONT OF THE COPS?
UGH.
GRAB
WE'RE LUCKY WE GOT AWAY AT ALL—I GUESS I'LL GIVE YOU THAT MUCH.
GA
GA
AND YOU GOT US ALL WRAPPED UP IN IT TOO!
YOU GET THAT, RIGHT?
GA
ERM... YEAH, BUT...
OH, YOU DON'T AGREE?
I DIDN'T PUNCH HIM, I KICKED HIM.
I DON'T CARE ABOUT THAT!
...
WHY...
WHY DID YOU DO THAT?
ARE YOU AN IDIOT?
YOU THINK YOU'RE SOME KIND OF HERO?

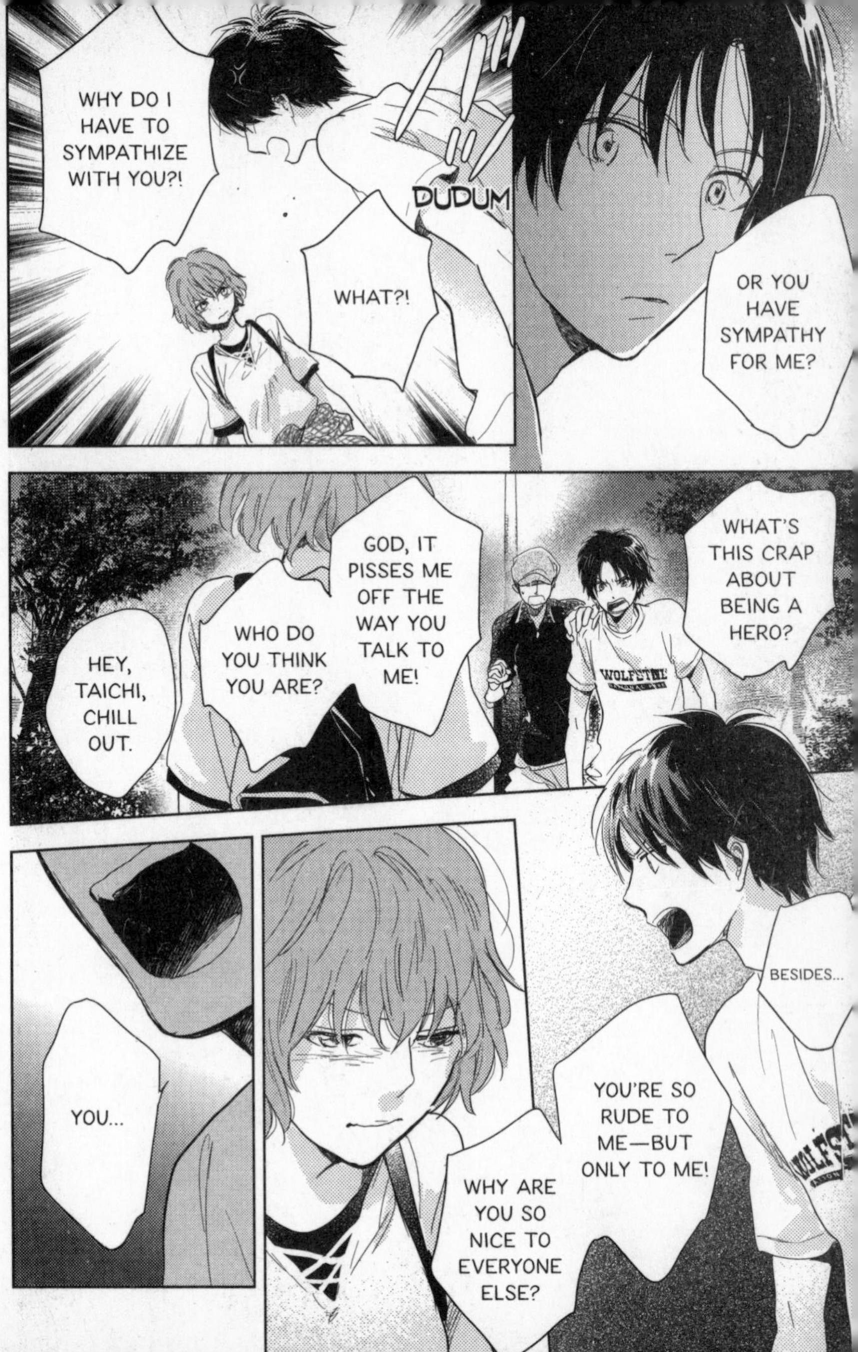
OR YOU HAVE SYMPATHY FOR ME?
DUDUM
WHAT?!
WHY DO I HAVE TO SYMPATHIZE WITH YOU?!
WHAT'S THIS CRAP ABOUT BEING A HERO?
GOD, IT PISSES ME OFF THE WAY YOU TALK TO ME!
WHO DO YOU THINK YOU ARE?
HEY, TAICHI, CHILL OUT.
BESIDES...
YOU'RE SO RUDE TO ME—BUT ONLY TO ME!
WHY ARE YOU SO NICE TO EVERYONE ELSE?
YOU...

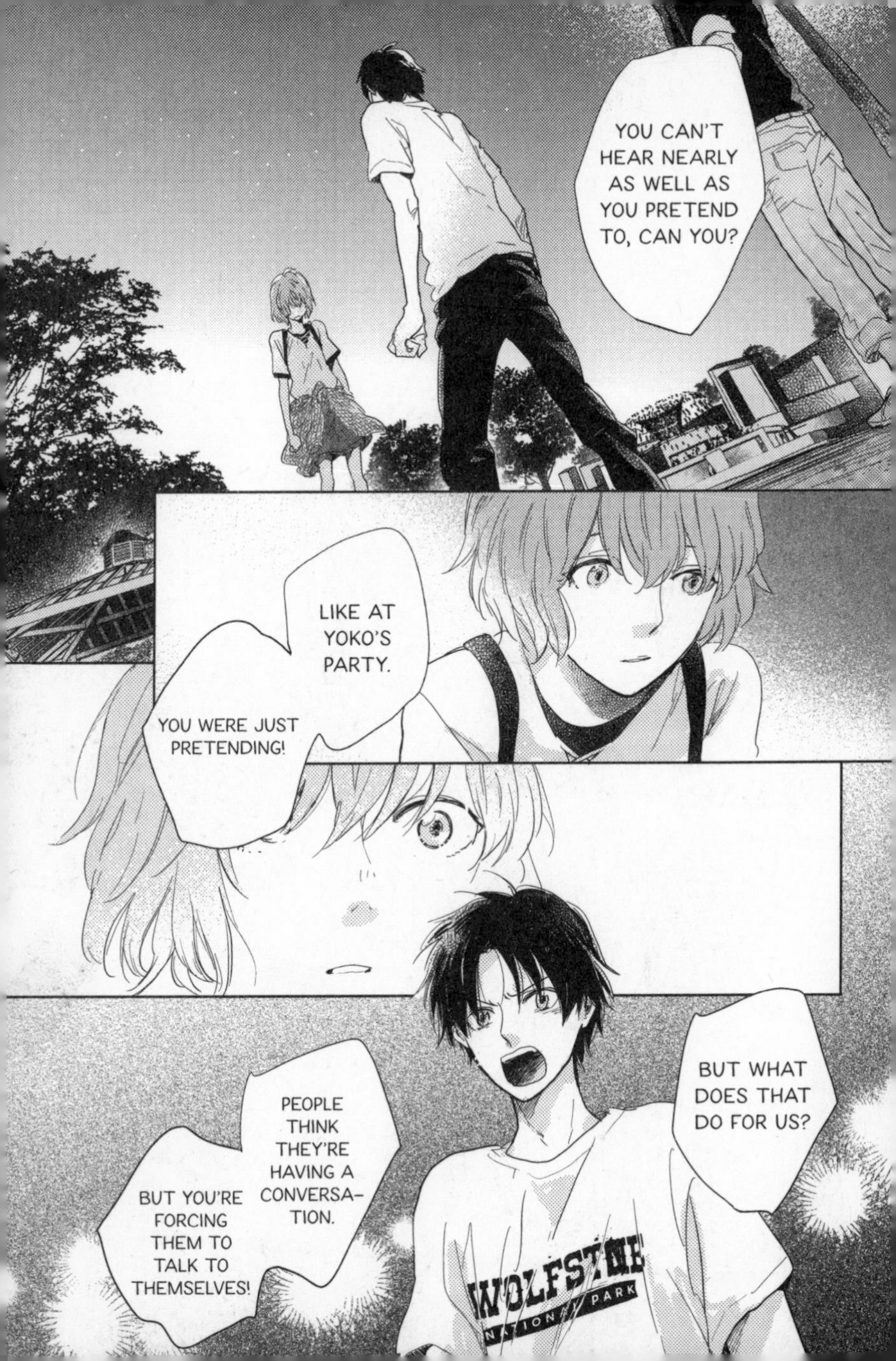
YOU CAN'T HEAR NEARLY AS WELL AS YOU PRETEND TO, CAN YOU?
LIKE AT YOKO'S PARTY.
YOU WERE JUST PRETENDING!
BUT WHAT DOES THAT DO FOR US?
PEOPLE THINK THEY'RE HAVING A CONVERSA-TION.
BUT YOU'RE FORCING THEM TO TALK TO THEMSELVES!

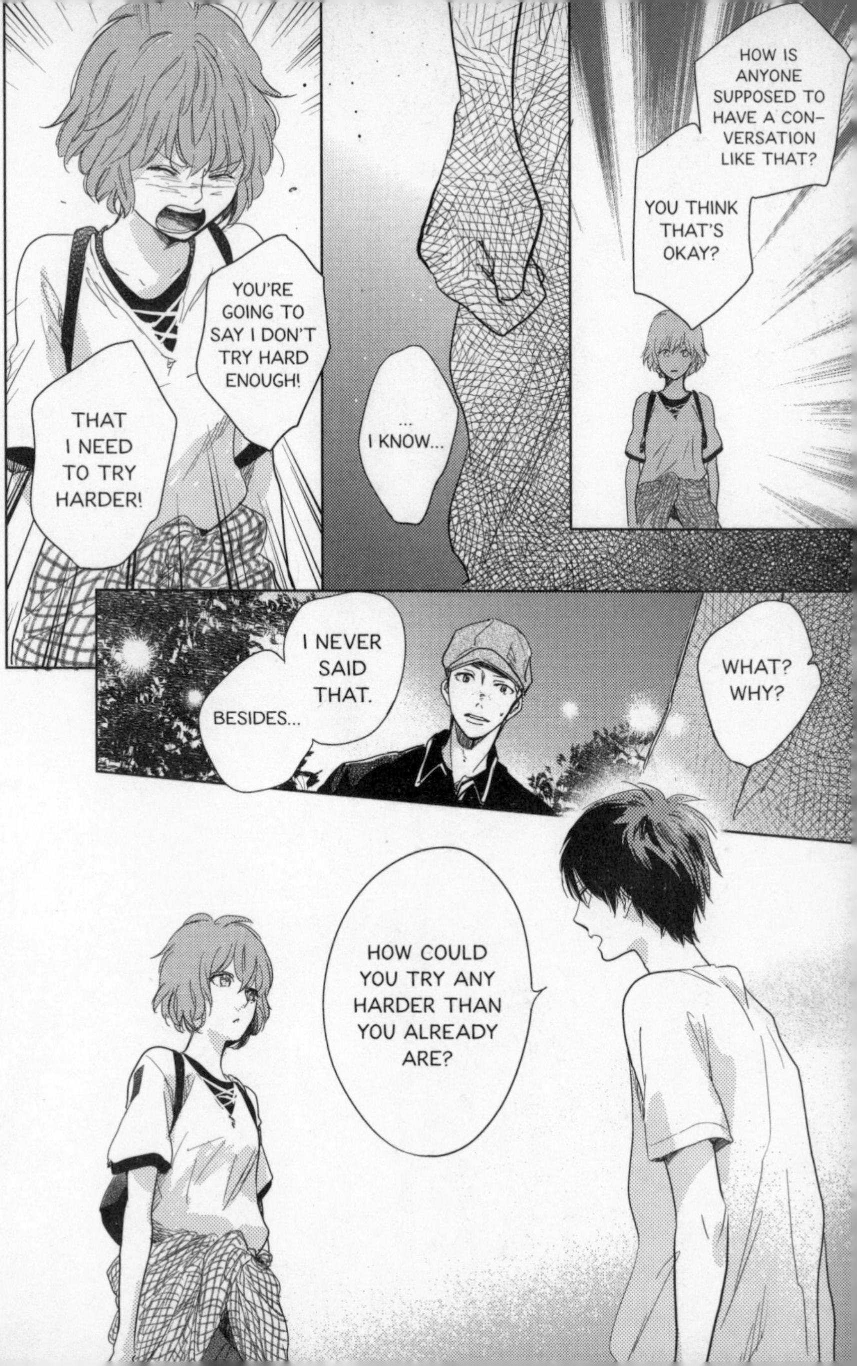
HOW IS ANYONE SUPPOSED TO HAVE A CON-VERSATION LIKE THAT?
YOU THINK THAT'S OKAY?
... I KNOW...
YOU'RE GOING TO SAY I DON'T TRY HARD ENOUGH!
THAT I NEED TO TRY HARDER!
WHAT? WHY?
I NEVER SAID THAT.
BESIDES...
HOW COULD YOU TRY ANY HARDER THAN YOU ALREADY ARE?

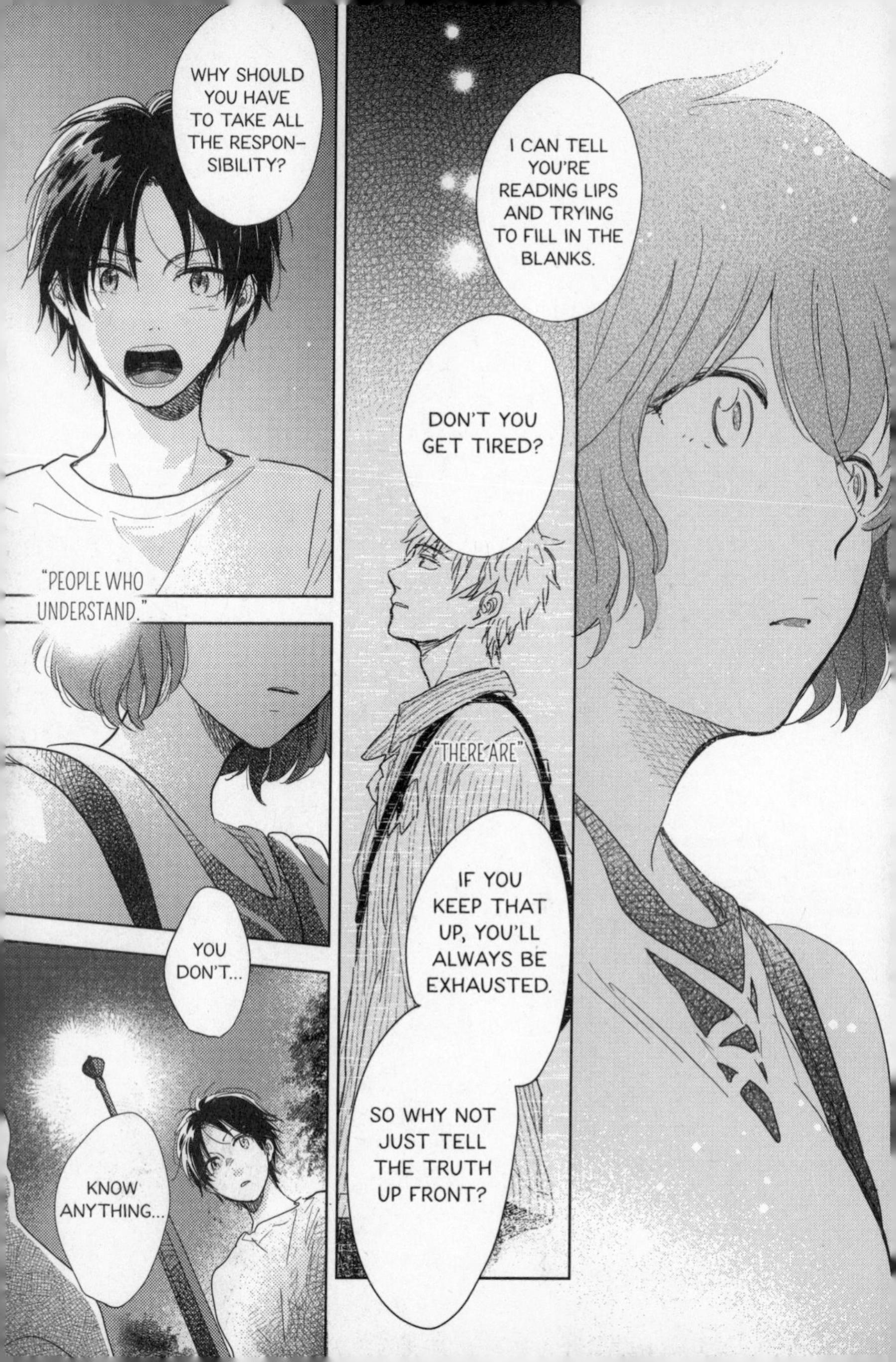

I CAN TELL YOU'RE READING LIPS AND TRYING TO FILL IN THE BLANKS.
DON'T YOU GET TIRED?
"THERE ARE"
IF YOU KEEP THAT UP, YOU'LL ALWAYS BE EXHAUSTED.
SO WHY NOT JUST TELL THE TRUTH UP FRONT?
WHY SHOULD YOU HAVE TO TAKE ALL THE RESPON-SIBILITY?
"PEOPLE WHO UNDERSTAND."
YOU DON'T...
KNOW ANYTHING...

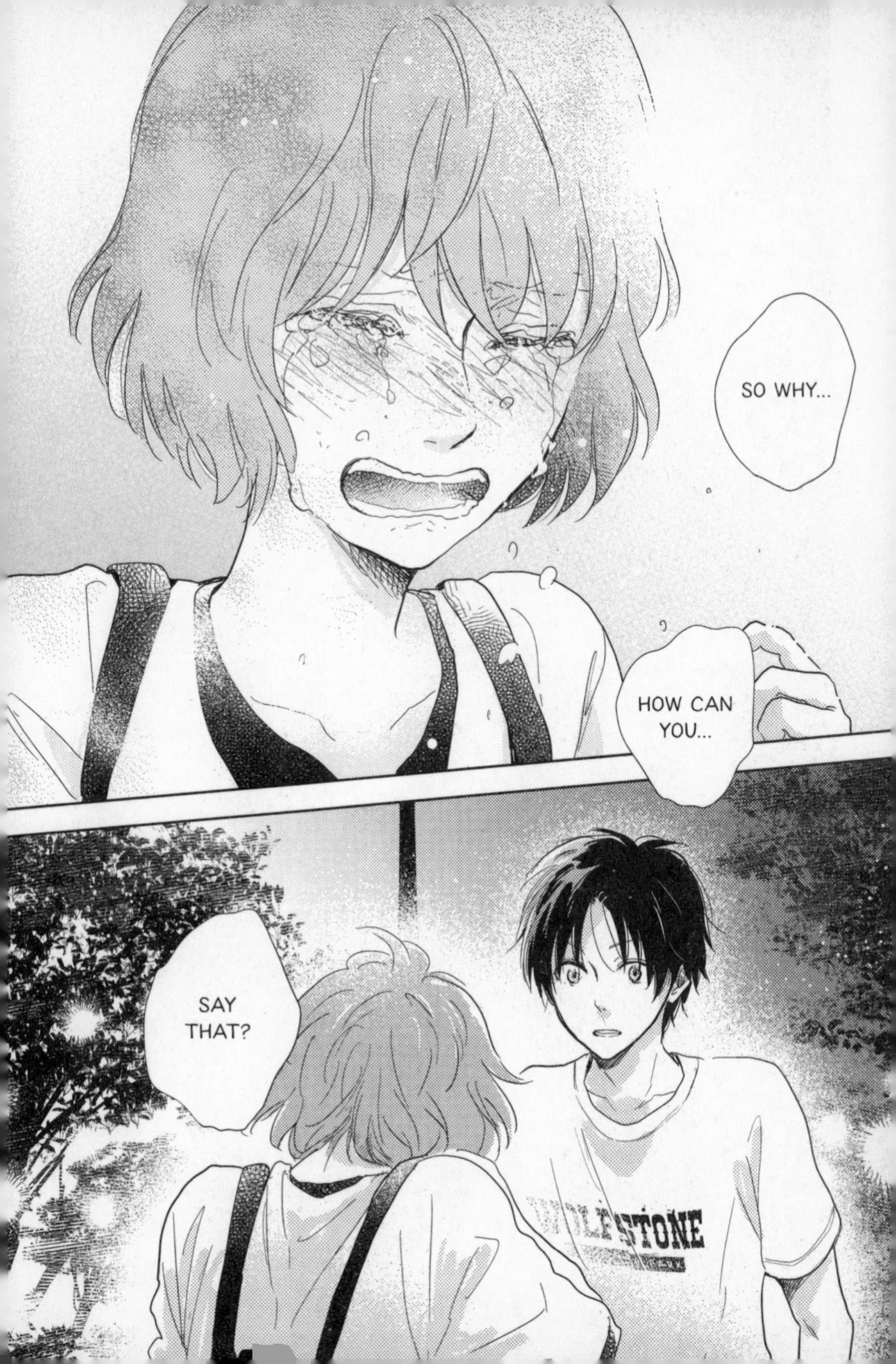
SO WHY...
HOW CAN YOU...
SAY THAT?

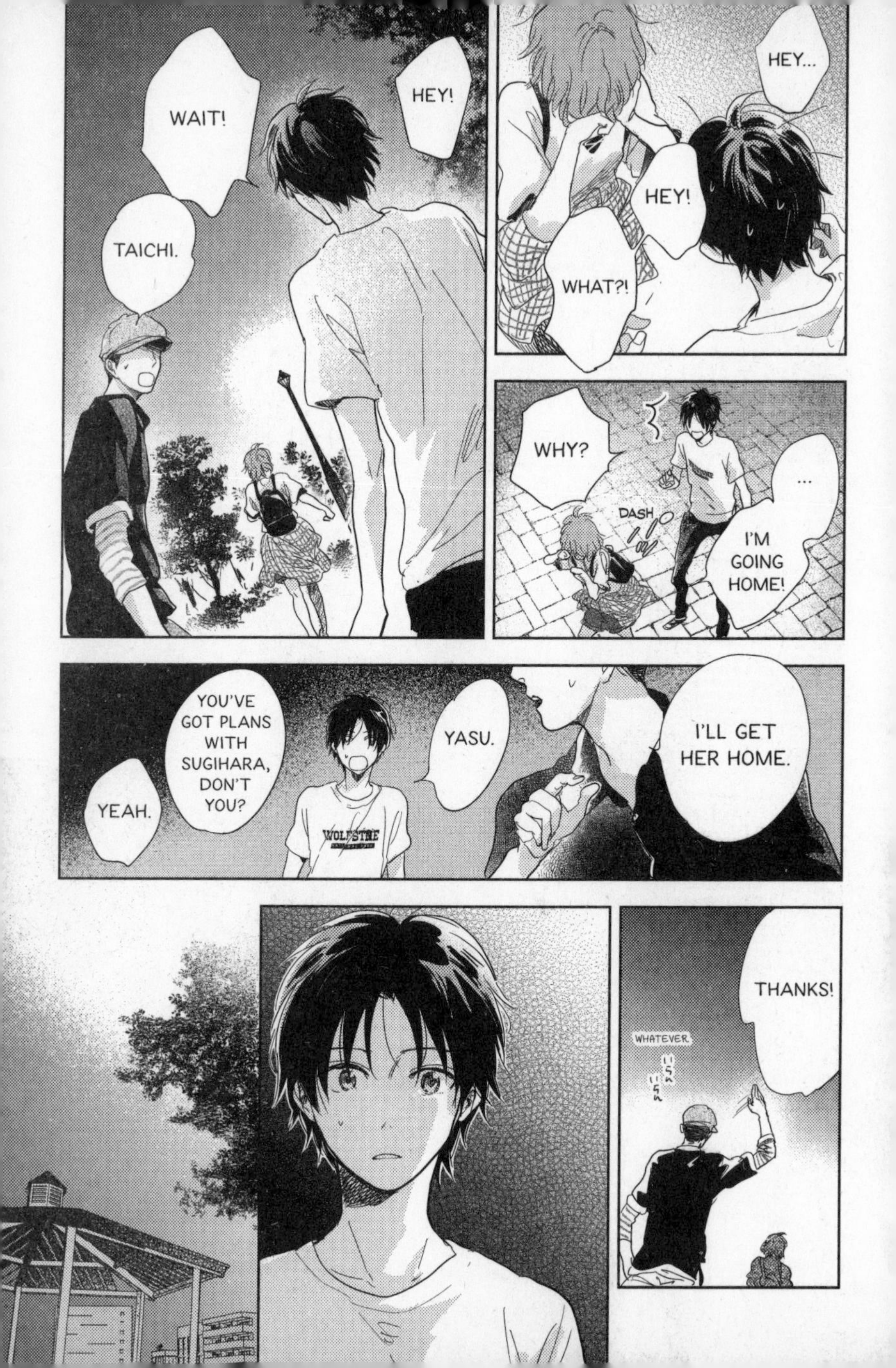
HEY...
HEY!
WHAT?!
...
I'M GOING HOME!
WHY?
DASH
HEY!
WAIT!
TAICHI.
I'LL GET HER HOME.
YASU.
YOU'VE GOT PLANS WITH SUGIHARA, DON'T YOU?
YEAH.
THANKS!
WHATEVER

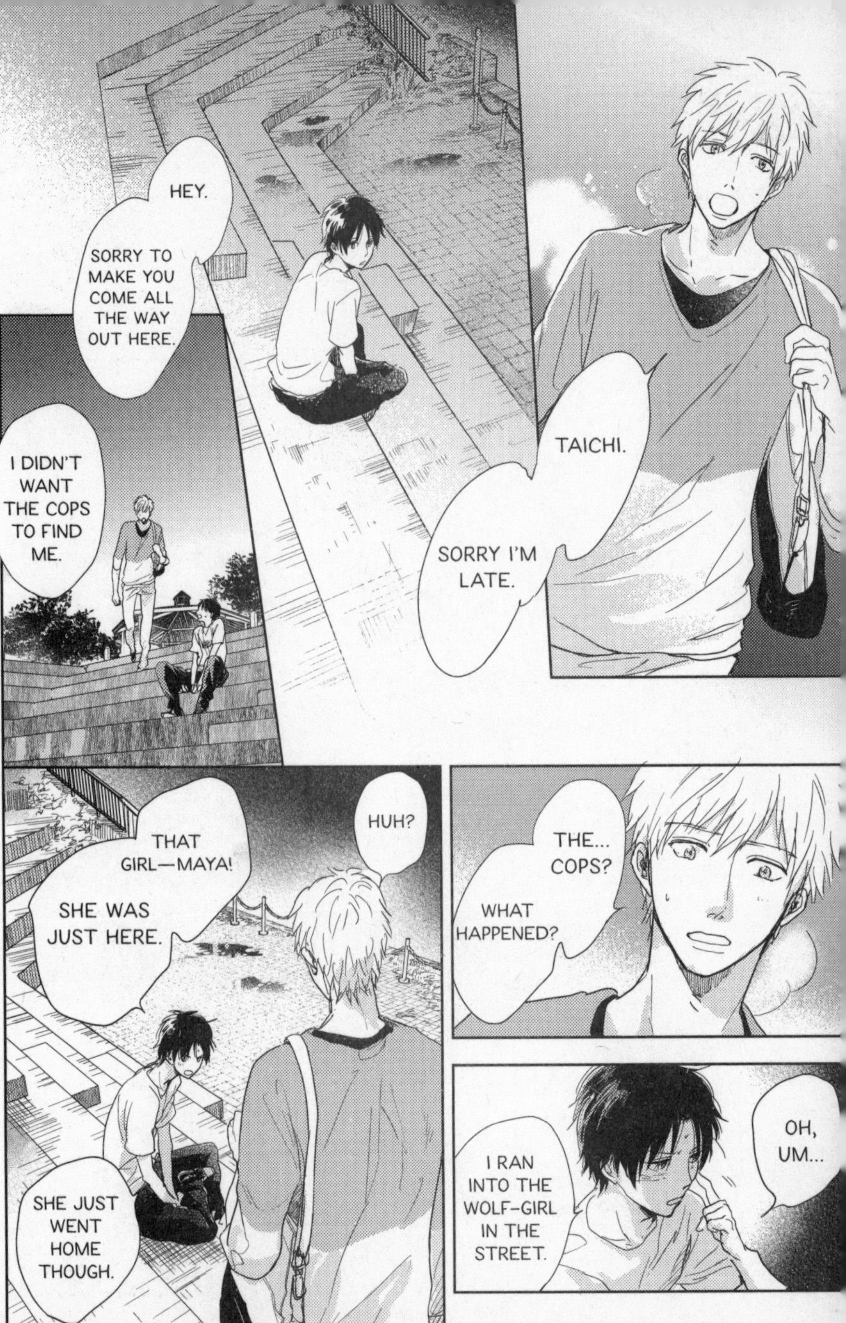
TAICHI.
SORRY I'M LATE.
HEY.
SORRY TO MAKE YOU COME ALL THE WAY OUT HERE.
I DIDN'T WANT THE COPS TO FIND ME.
THE... COPS?
WHAT HAPPENED?
OH, UM...
I RAN INTO THE WOLF-GIRL IN THE STREET.
HUH?
THAT GIRL—MAYA!
SHE WAS JUST HERE.
SHE JUST WENT HOME THOUGH.

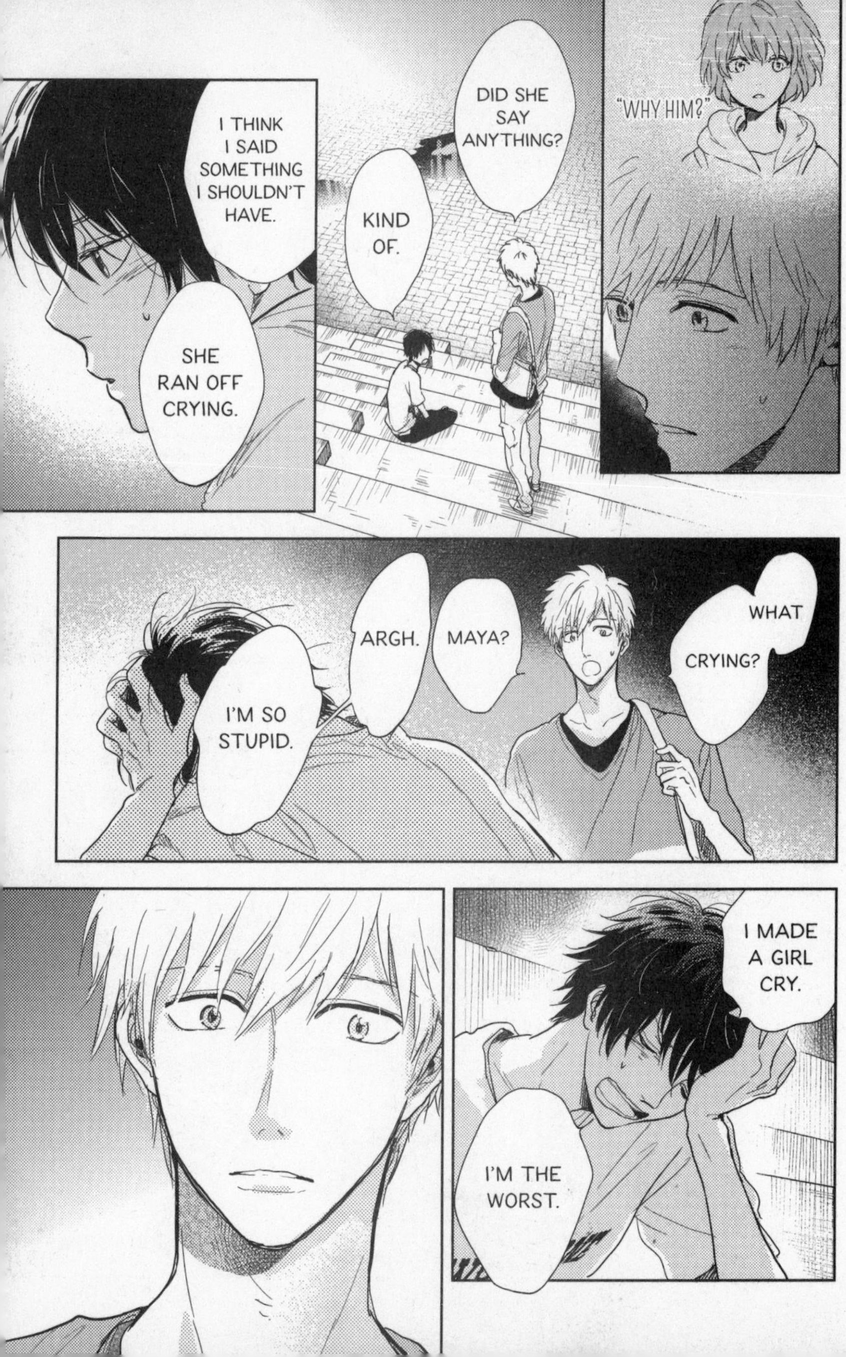
"WHY HIM?"
DID SHE SAY ANYTHING?
KIND OF.
I THINK I SAID SOMETHING I SHOULDN'T HAVE.
SHE RAN OFF CRYING.
WHAT CRYING?
MAYA?
ARGH.
I'M SO STUPID.
I MADE A GIRL CRY.
I'M THE WORST.

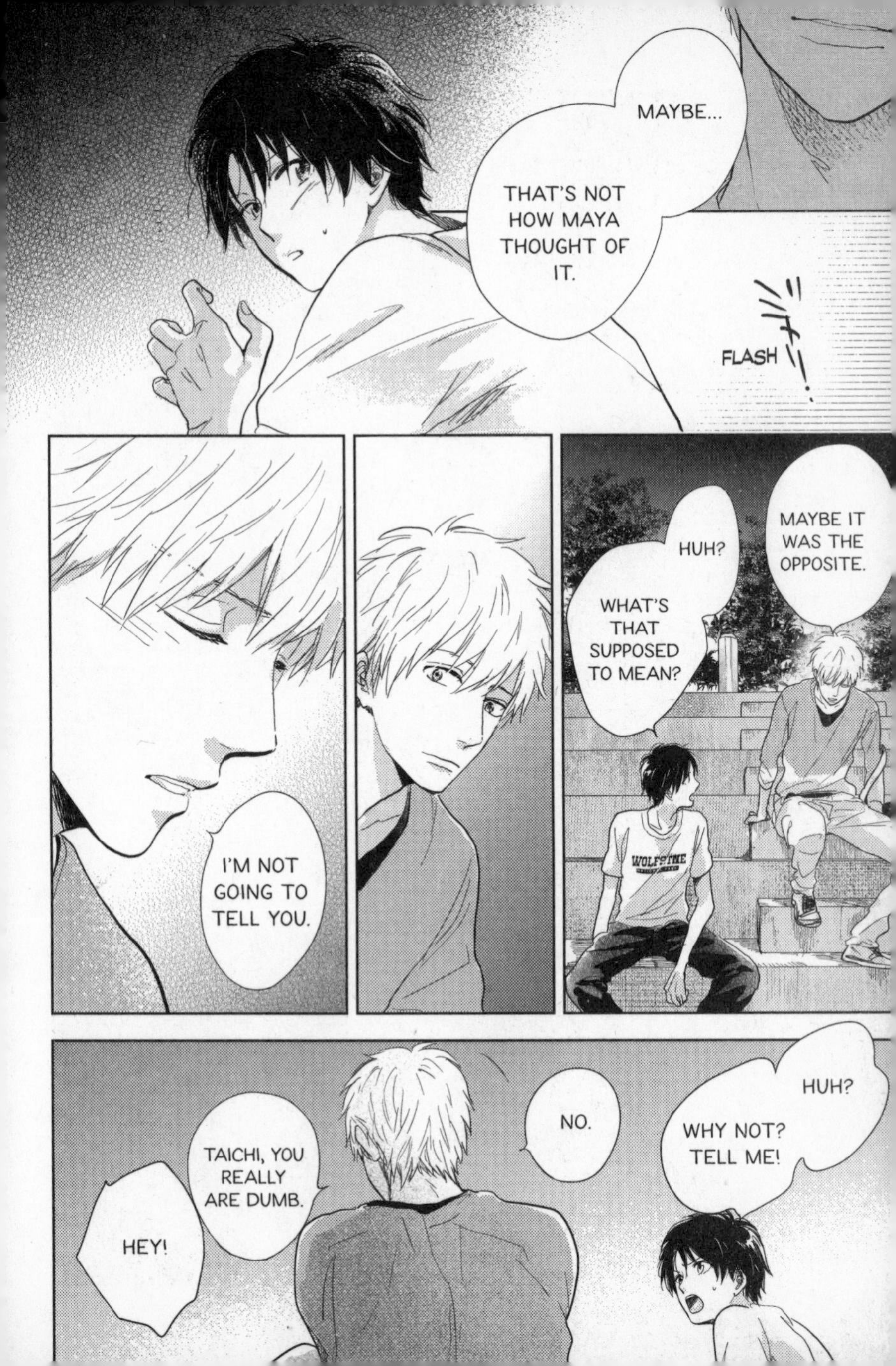
MAYBE...
THAT'S NOT HOW MAYA THOUGHT OF IT.
FLASH
MAYBE IT WAS THE OPPOSITE.
HUH?
WHAT'S THAT SUPPOSED TO MEAN?
I'M NOT GOING TO TELL YOU.
HUH?
WHY NOT? TELL ME!
NO.
TAICHI, YOU REALLY ARE DUMB.
HEY!

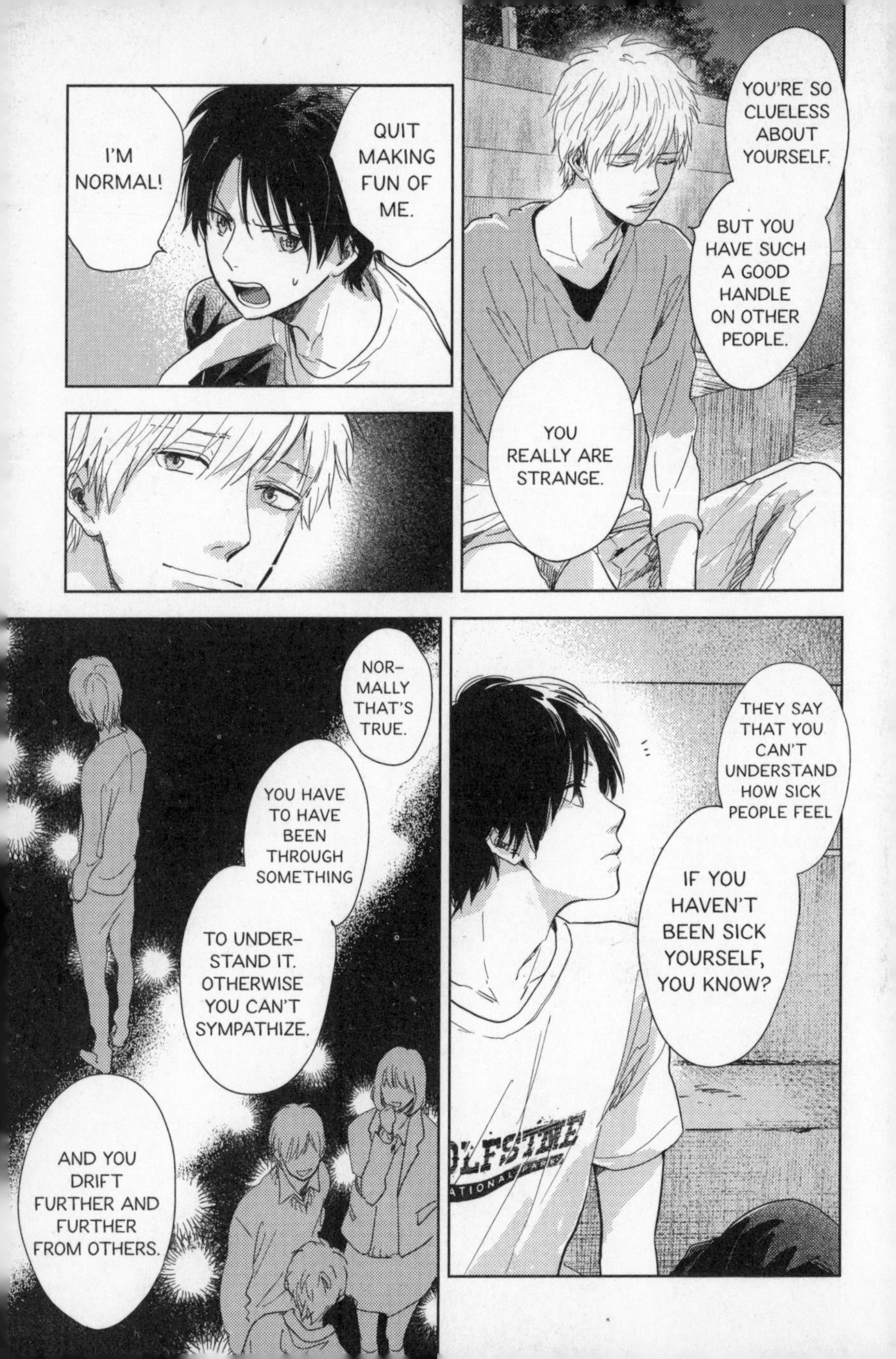
YOU'RE SO CLUELESS ABOUT YOURSELF.
BUT YOU HAVE SUCH A GOOD HANDLE ON OTHER PEOPLE.
YOU REALLY ARE STRANGE.
QUIT MAKING FUN OF ME.
I'M NORMAL!
THEY SAY THAT YOU CAN'T UNDERSTAND HOW SICK PEOPLE FEEL
IF YOU HAVEN'T BEEN SICK YOURSELF, YOU KNOW?
NOR-MALLY THAT'S TRUE.
YOU HAVE TO HAVE BEEN THROUGH SOMETHING
TO UNDER-STAND IT. OTHERWISE YOU CAN'T SYMPATHIZE.
AND YOU DRIFT FURTHER AND FURTHER FROM OTHERS.

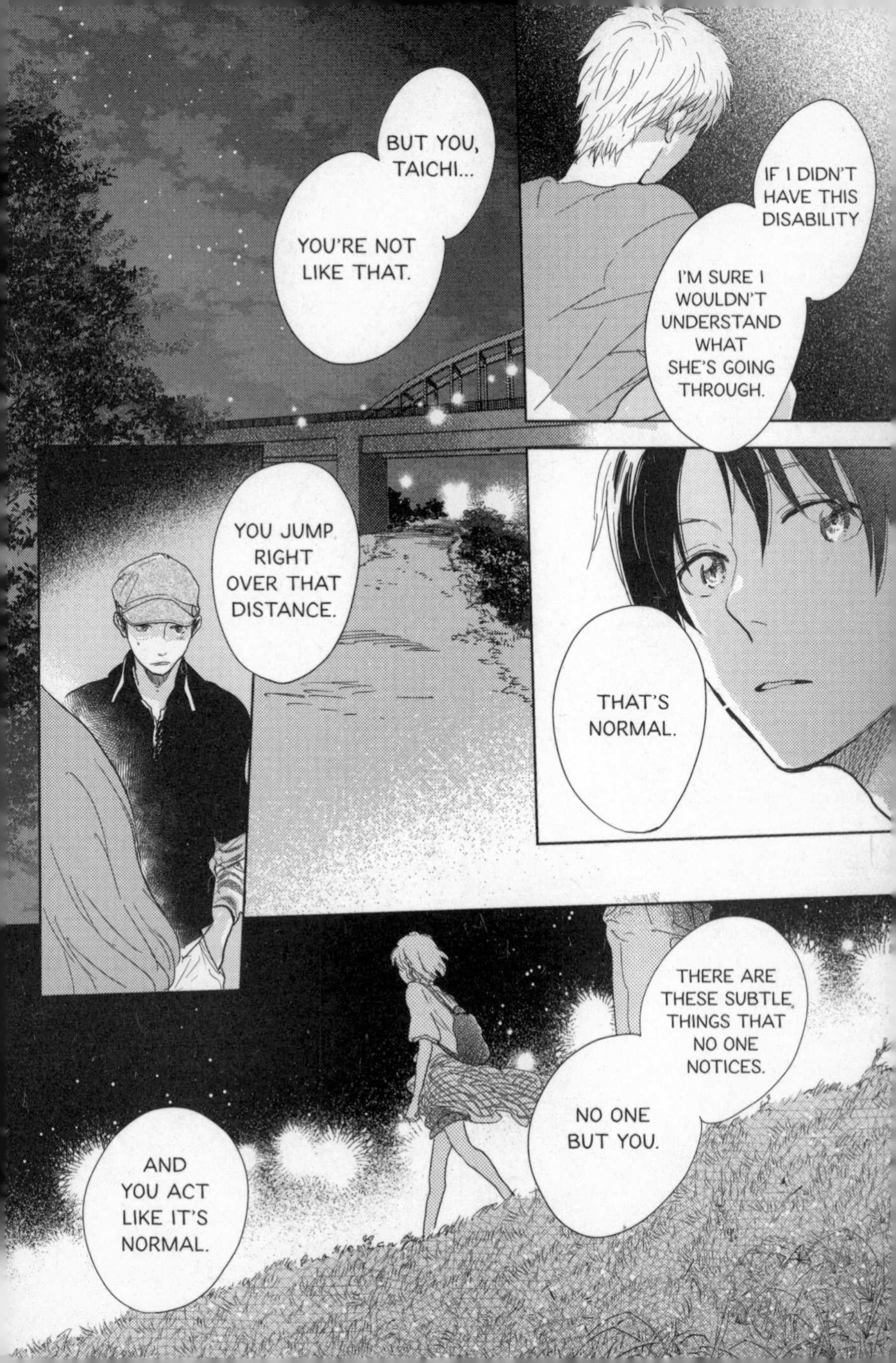
IF I DIDN'T HAVE THIS DISABILITY
I'M SURE I WOULDN'T UNDERSTAND WHAT SHE'S GOING THROUGH.
THAT'S NORMAL.
BUT YOU, TAICHI...
YOU'RE NOT LIKE THAT.
YOU JUMP RIGHT OVER THAT DISTANCE.
THERE ARE THESE SUBTLE THINGS THAT NO ONE NOTICES.
NO ONE BUT YOU.
AND YOU ACT LIKE IT'S NORMAL.

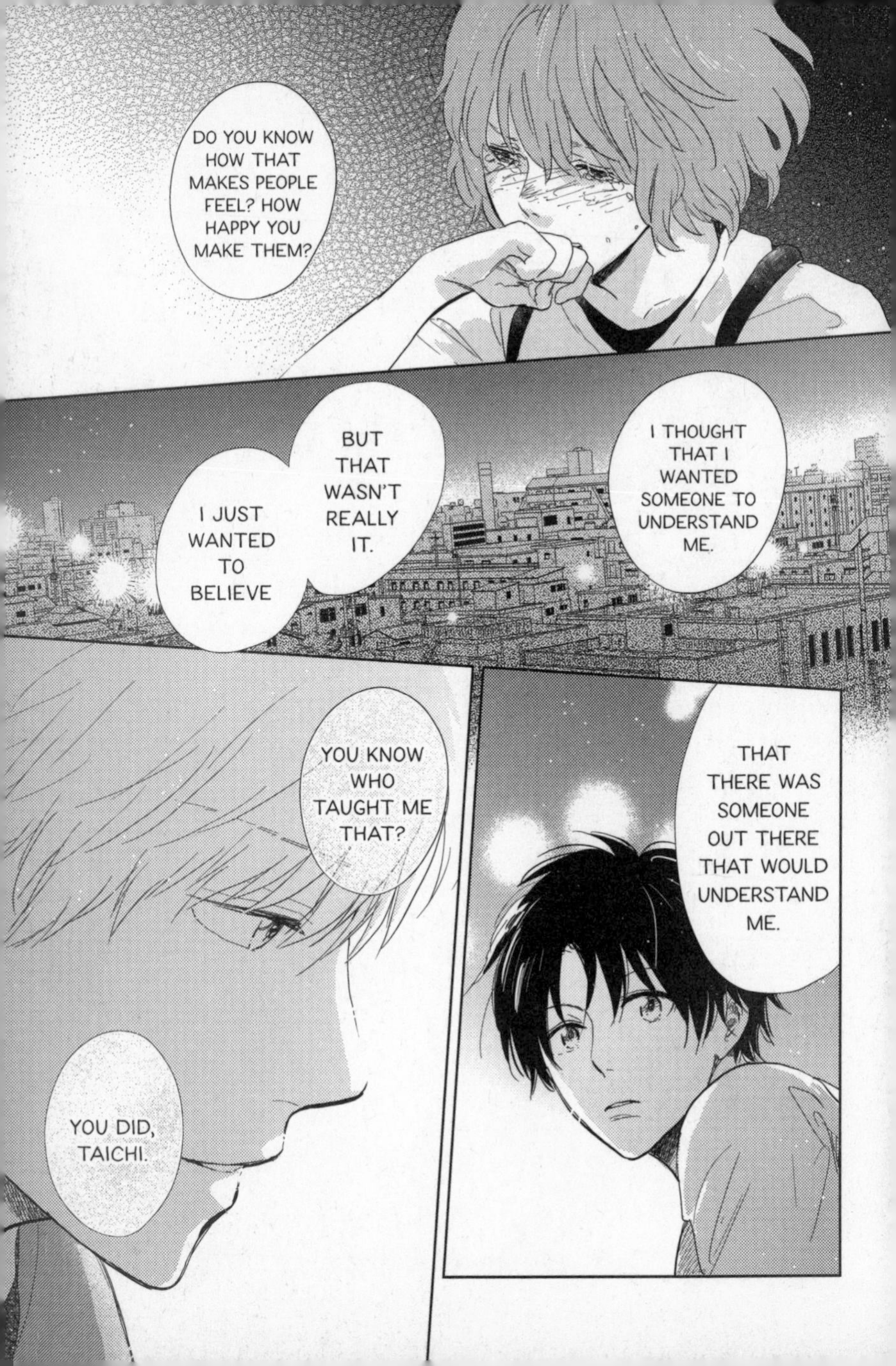
DO YOU KNOW HOW THAT MAKES PEOPLE FEEL? HOW HAPPY YOU MAKE THEM?
I THOUGHT THAT I WANTED SOMEONE TO UNDERSTAND ME.
BUT THAT WASN'T REALLY IT.
I JUST WANTED TO BELIEVE
THAT THERE WAS SOMEONE OUT THERE THAT WOULD UNDERSTAND ME.
YOU KNOW WHO TAUGHT ME THAT?
YOU DID, TAICHI.

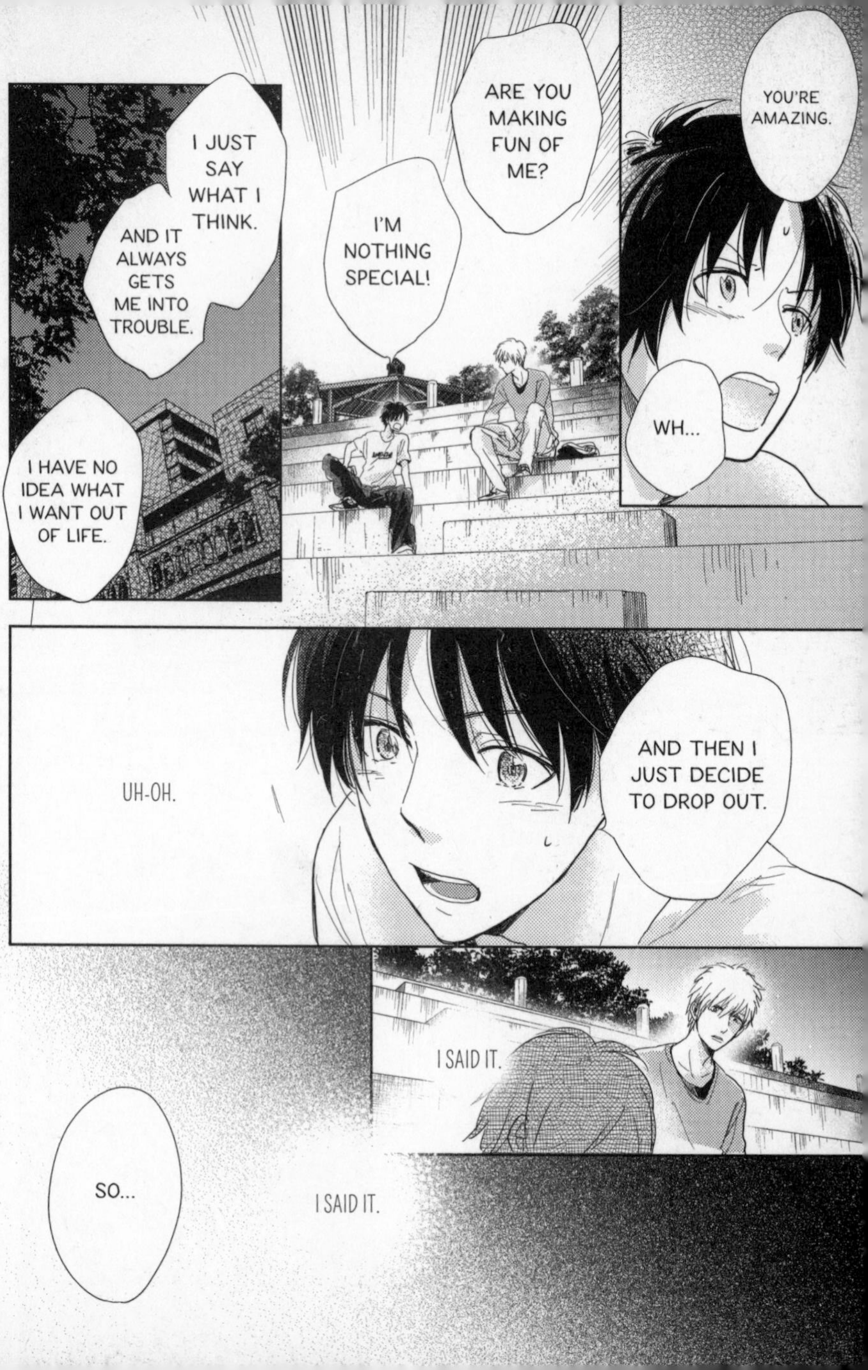
YOU'RE AMAZING.
WH...
ARE YOU MAKING FUN OF ME?
I'M NOTHING SPECIAL!
I JUST SAY WHAT I THINK.
AND IT ALWAYS GETS ME INTO TROUBLE.
I HAVE NO IDEA WHAT I WANT OUT OF LIFE.
AND THEN I JUST DECIDE TO DROP OUT.
UH-OH.
I SAID IT.
I SAID IT.
SO...

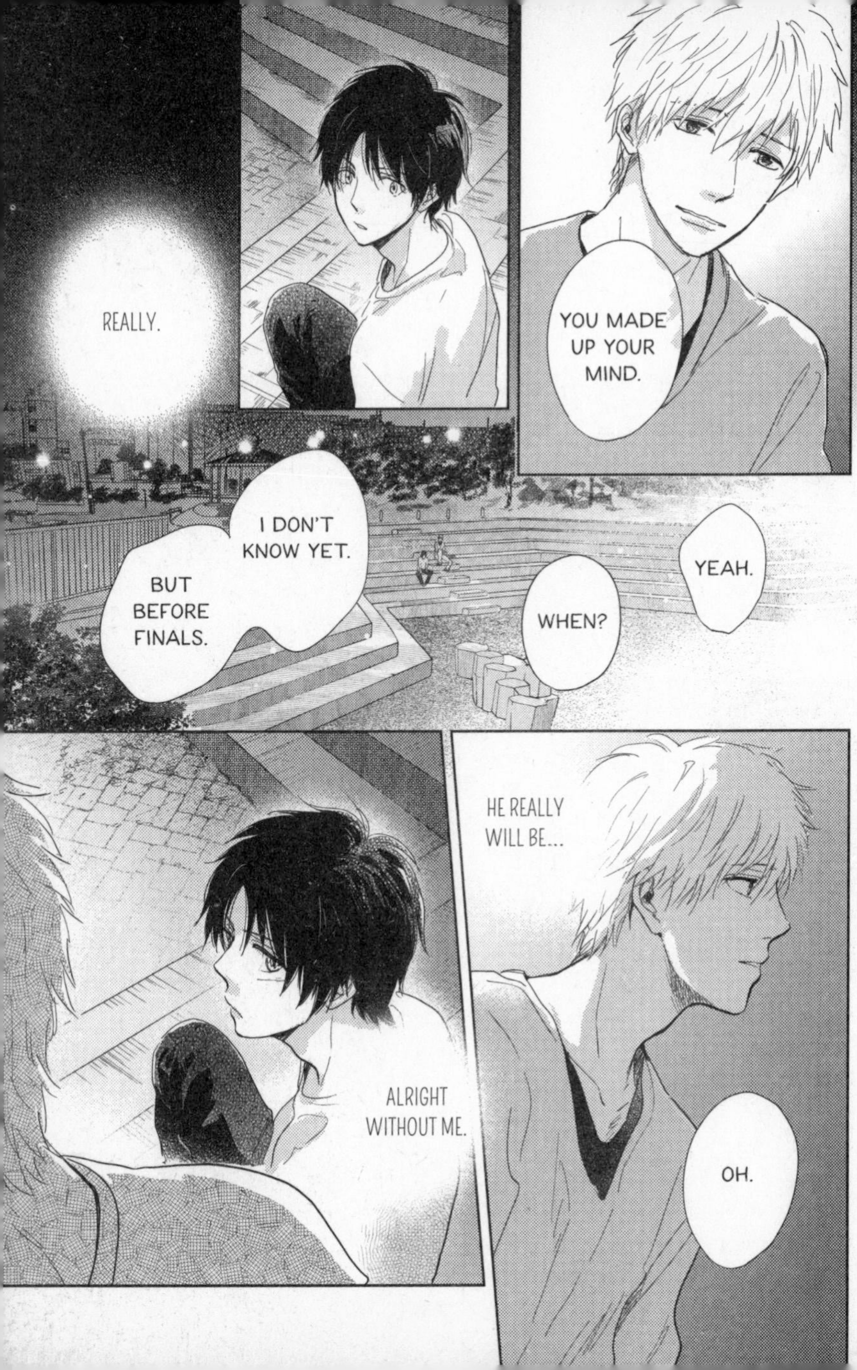
YOU MADE UP YOUR MIND.
REALLY.
YEAH.
WHEN?
I DON'T KNOW YET.
BUT BEFORE FINALS.
HE REALLY WILL BE...
OH.
ALRIGHT WITHOUT ME.

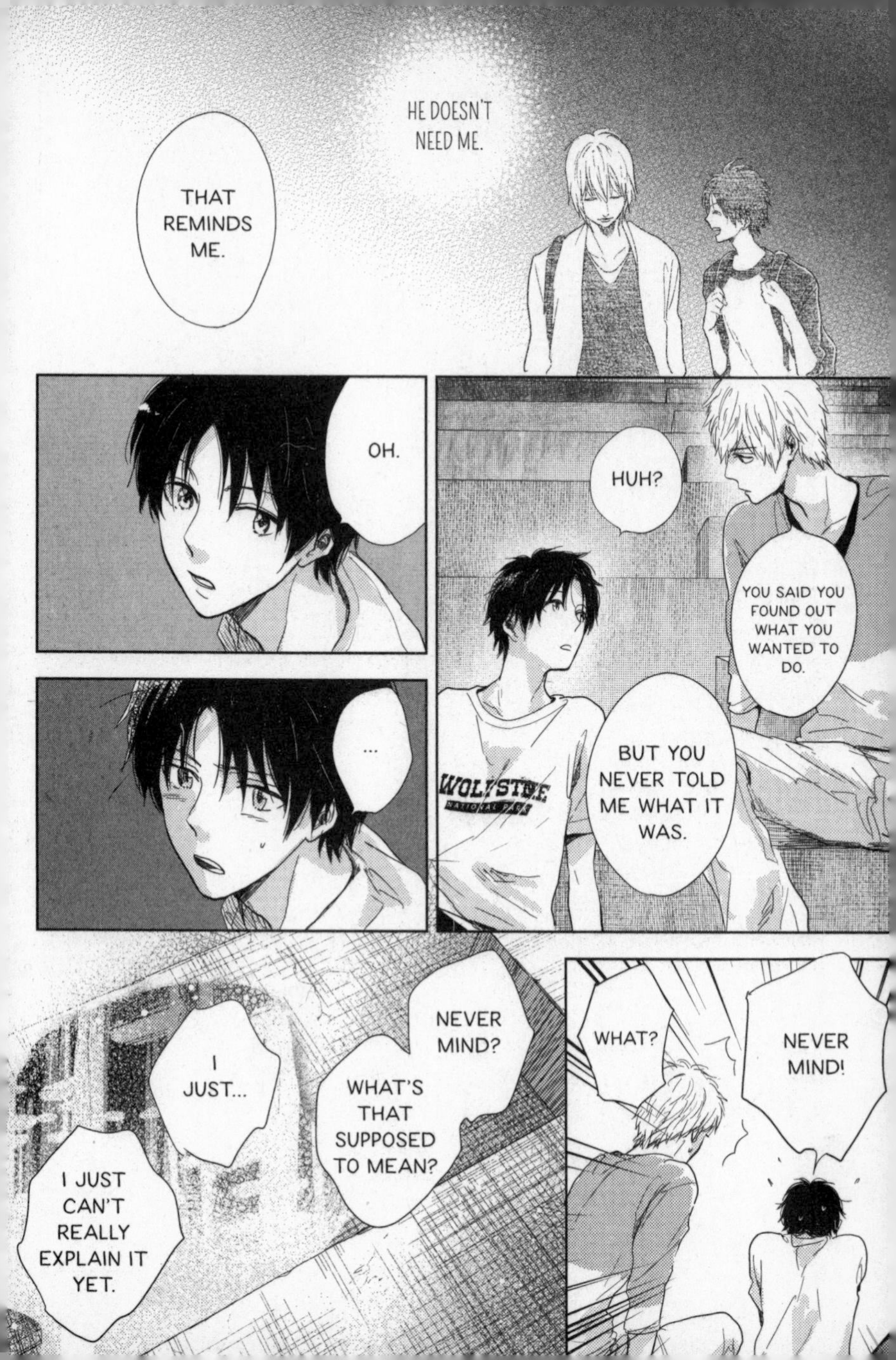
HE DOESN'T NEED ME.
THAT REMINDS ME.
HUH?
YOU SAID YOU FOUND OUT WHAT YOU WANTED TO DO.
BUT YOU NEVER TOLD ME WHAT IT WAS.
OH.
...
WHAT?
NEVER MIND!
NEVER MIND?
WHAT'S THAT SUPPOSED TO MEAN?
I JUST...
I JUST CAN'T REALLY EXPLAIN IT YET.

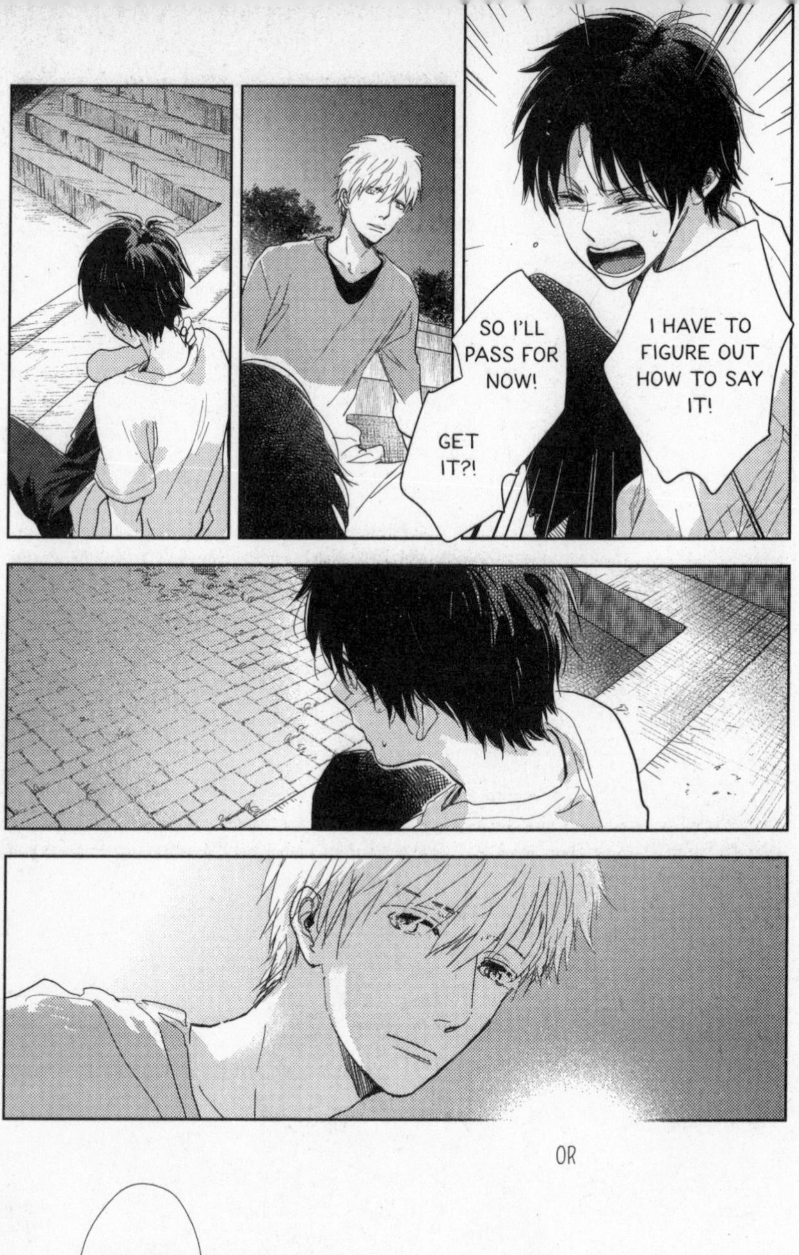
I HAVE TO FIGURE OUT HOW TO SAY IT!
SO I'LL PASS FOR NOW!
GET IT?!
OR
TAICHI.

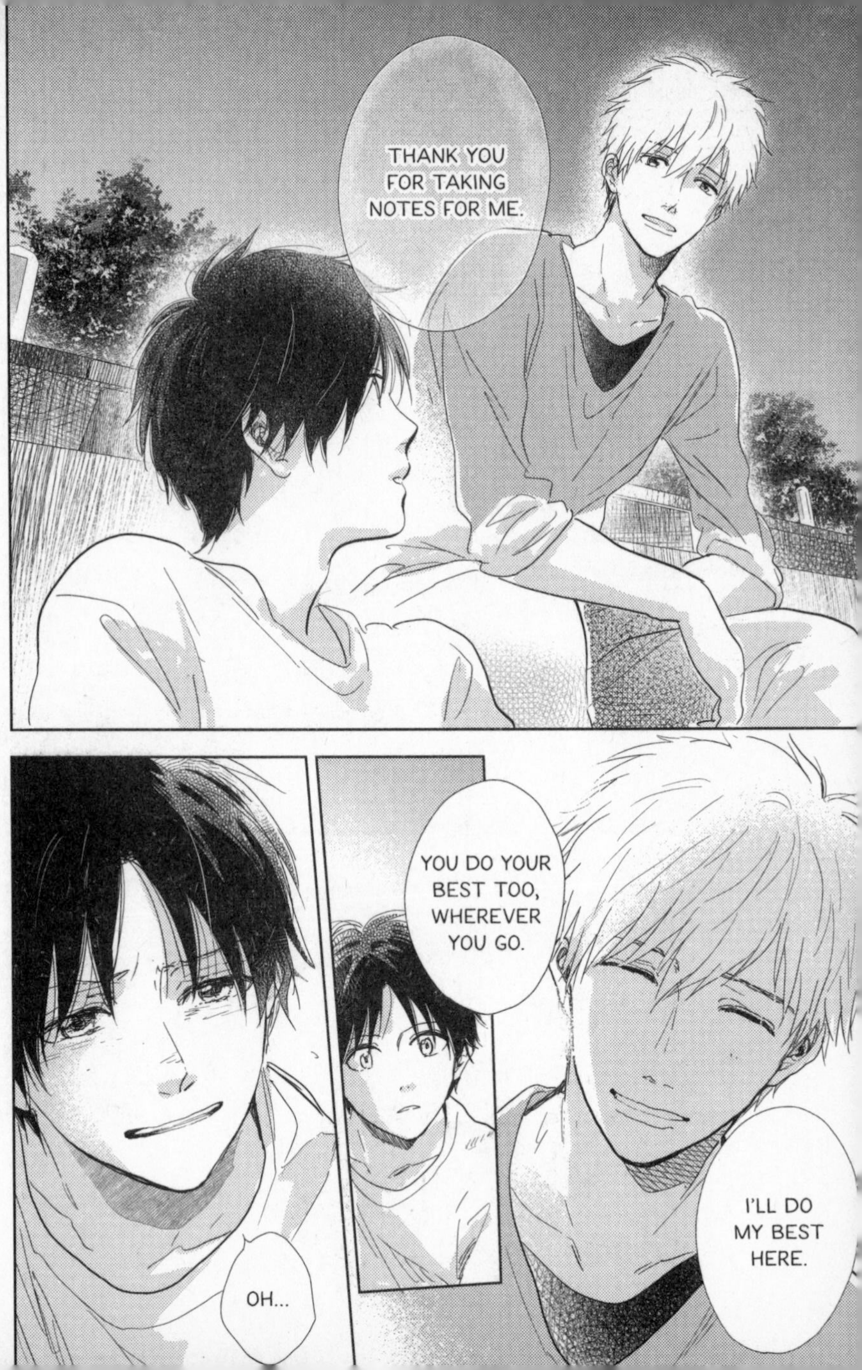
THANK YOU FOR TAKING NOTES FOR ME.
YOU DO YOUR BEST TOO, WHEREVER YOU GO.
I'LL DO MY BEST HERE.
OH...

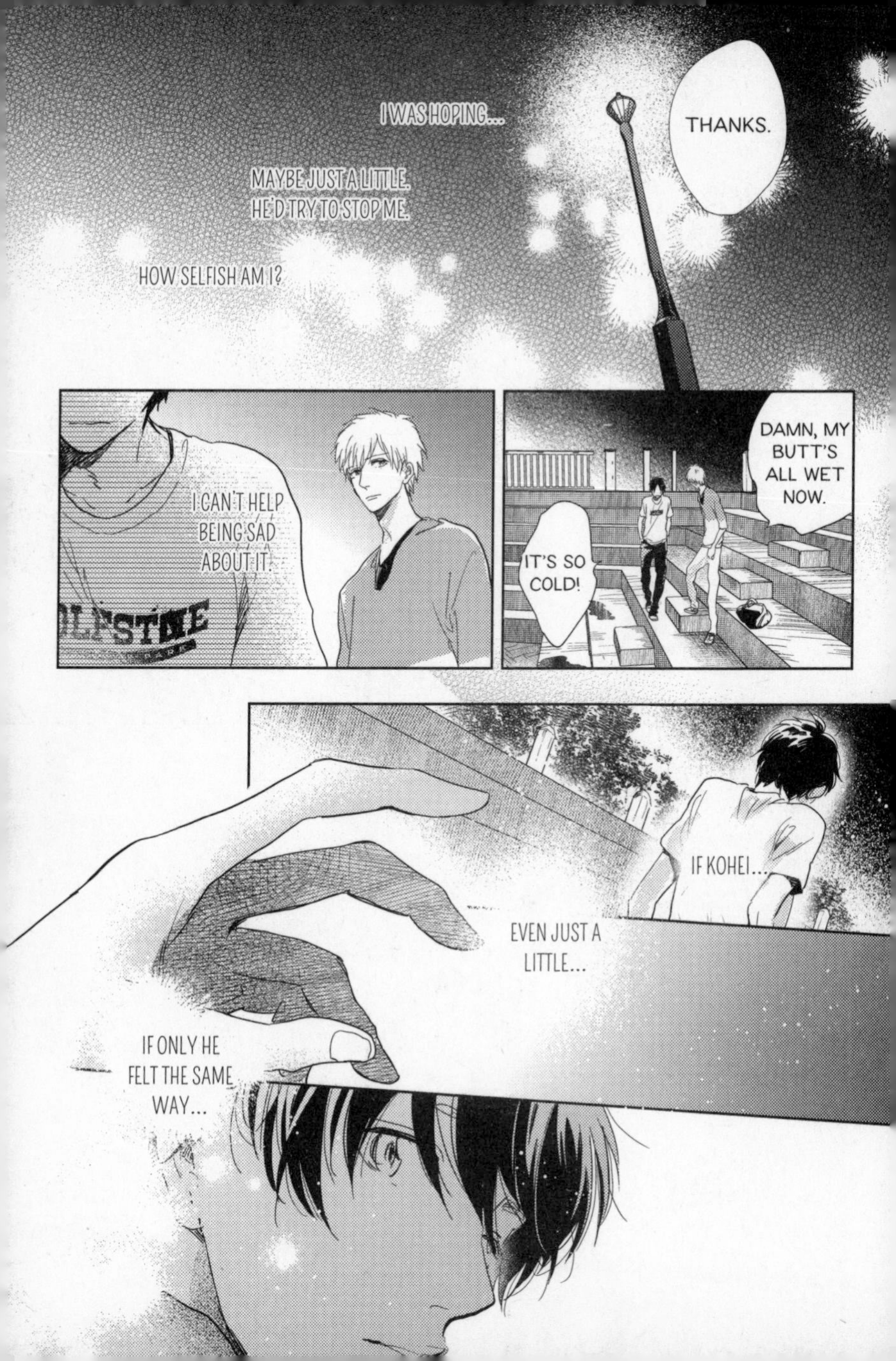
THANKS.
I WAS HOPING...
MAYBE JUST A LITTLE. HE'D TRY TO STOP ME.
HOW SELFISH AM I?
DAMN, MY BUTT'S ALL WET NOW.
IT'S SO COLD!
I CAN'T HELP BEING SAD ABOUT IT.
IF KOHEI...
EVEN JUST A LITTLE...
IF ONLY HE FELT THE SAME WAY...

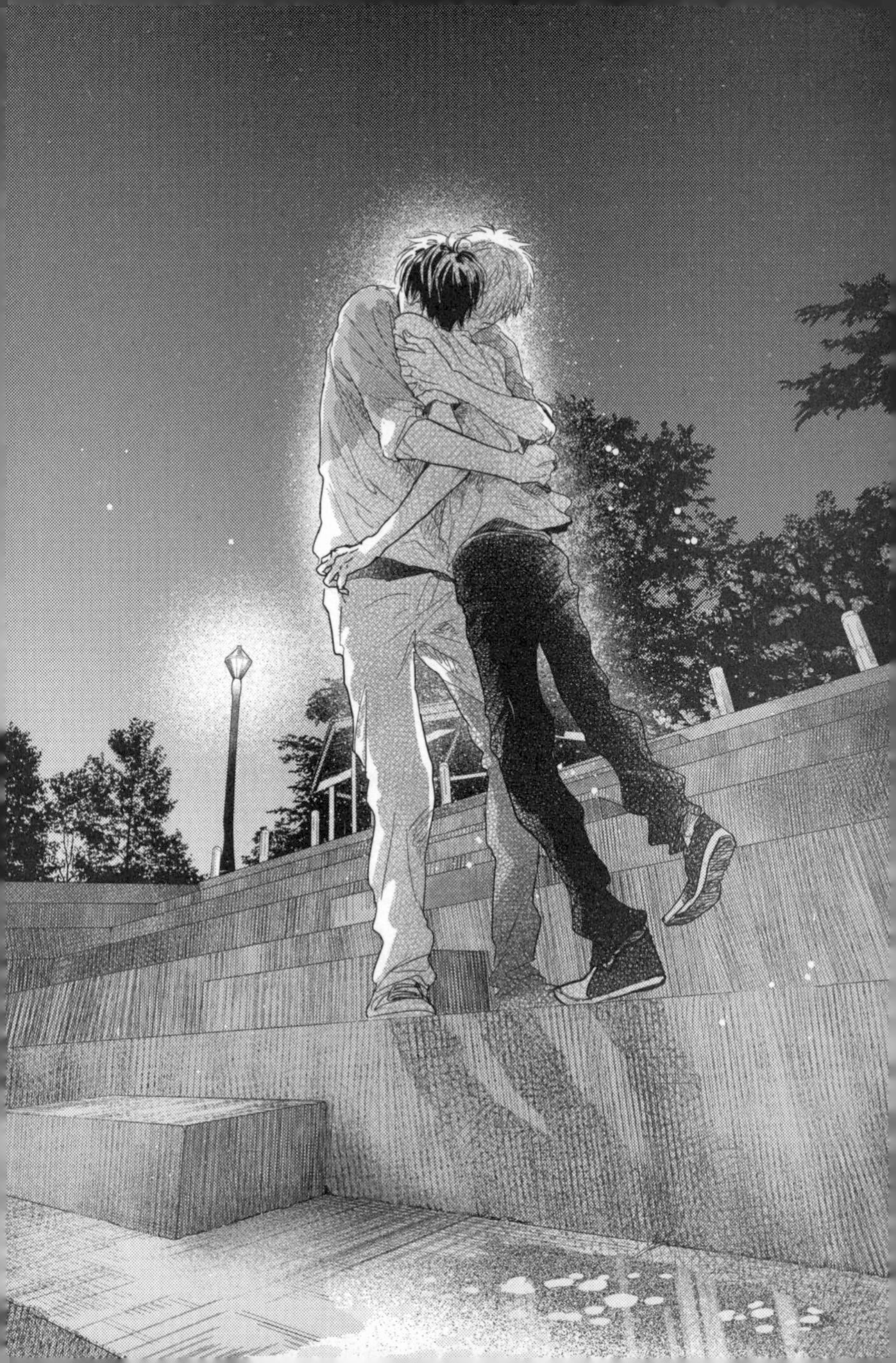

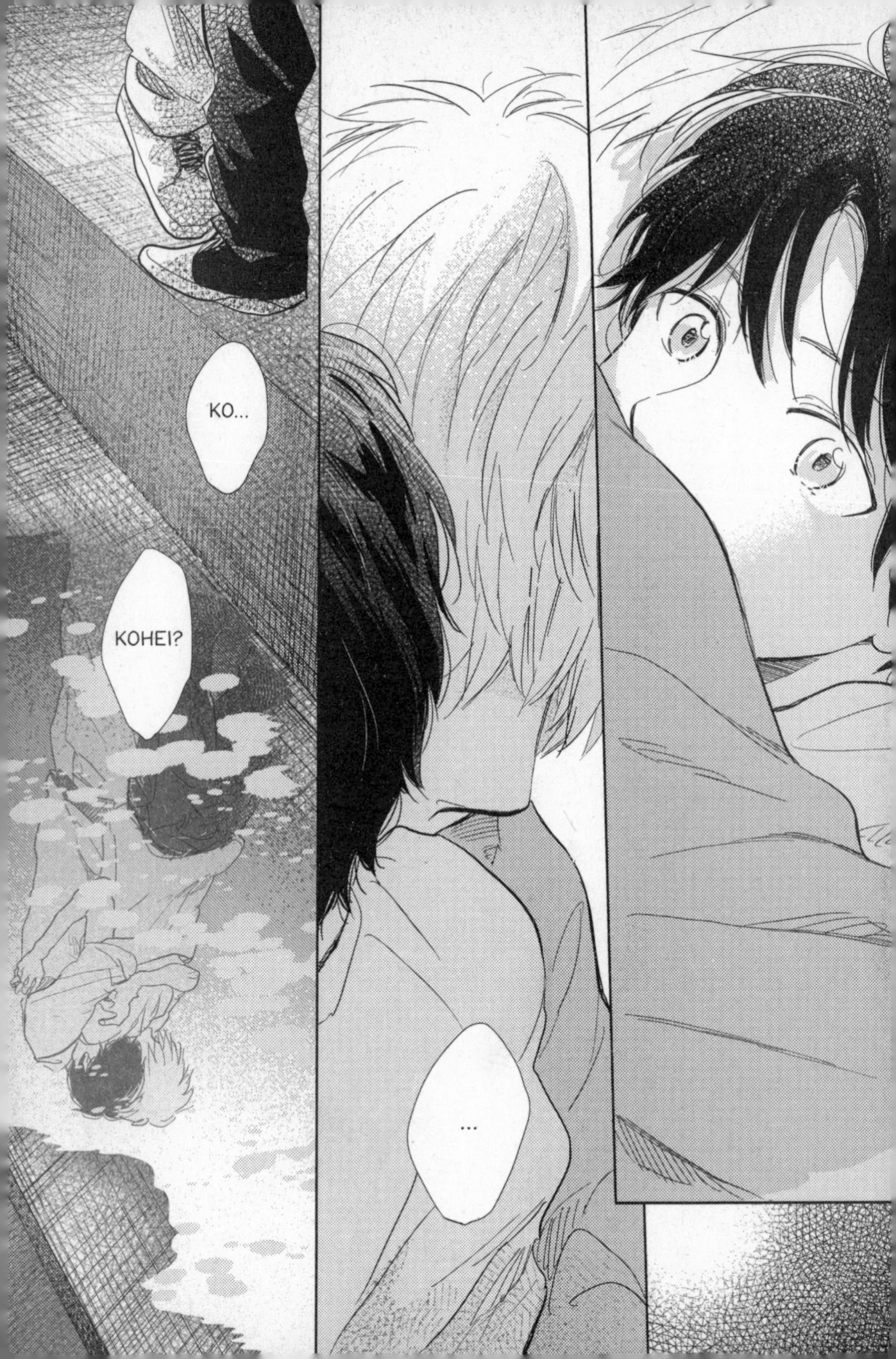
...
KO...
KOHEI?

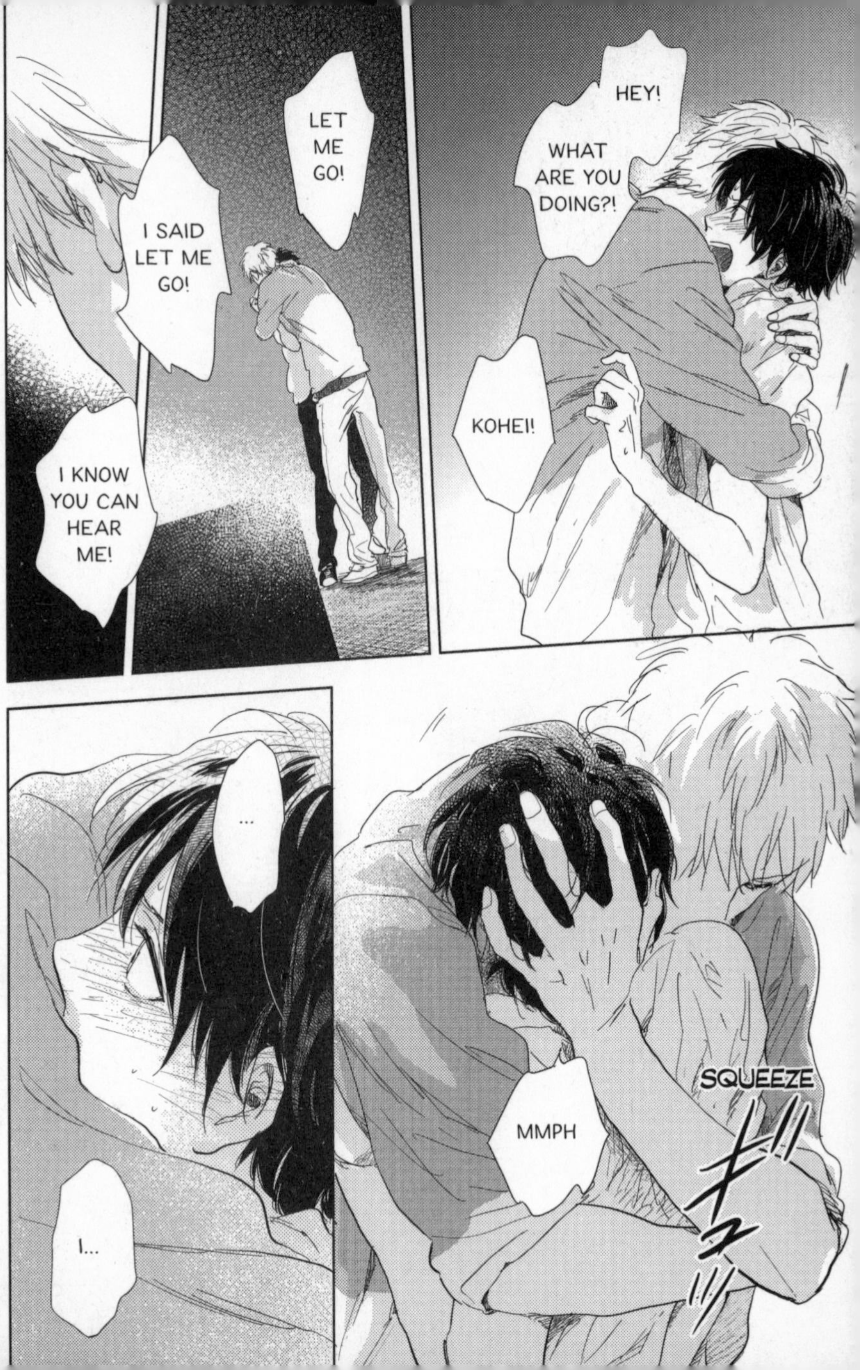
HEY!
WHAT ARE YOU DOING?!
KOHEI!
LET ME GO!
I SAID LET ME GO!
I KNOW YOU CAN HEAR ME!
SQUEEZE
MMPH
...
I...

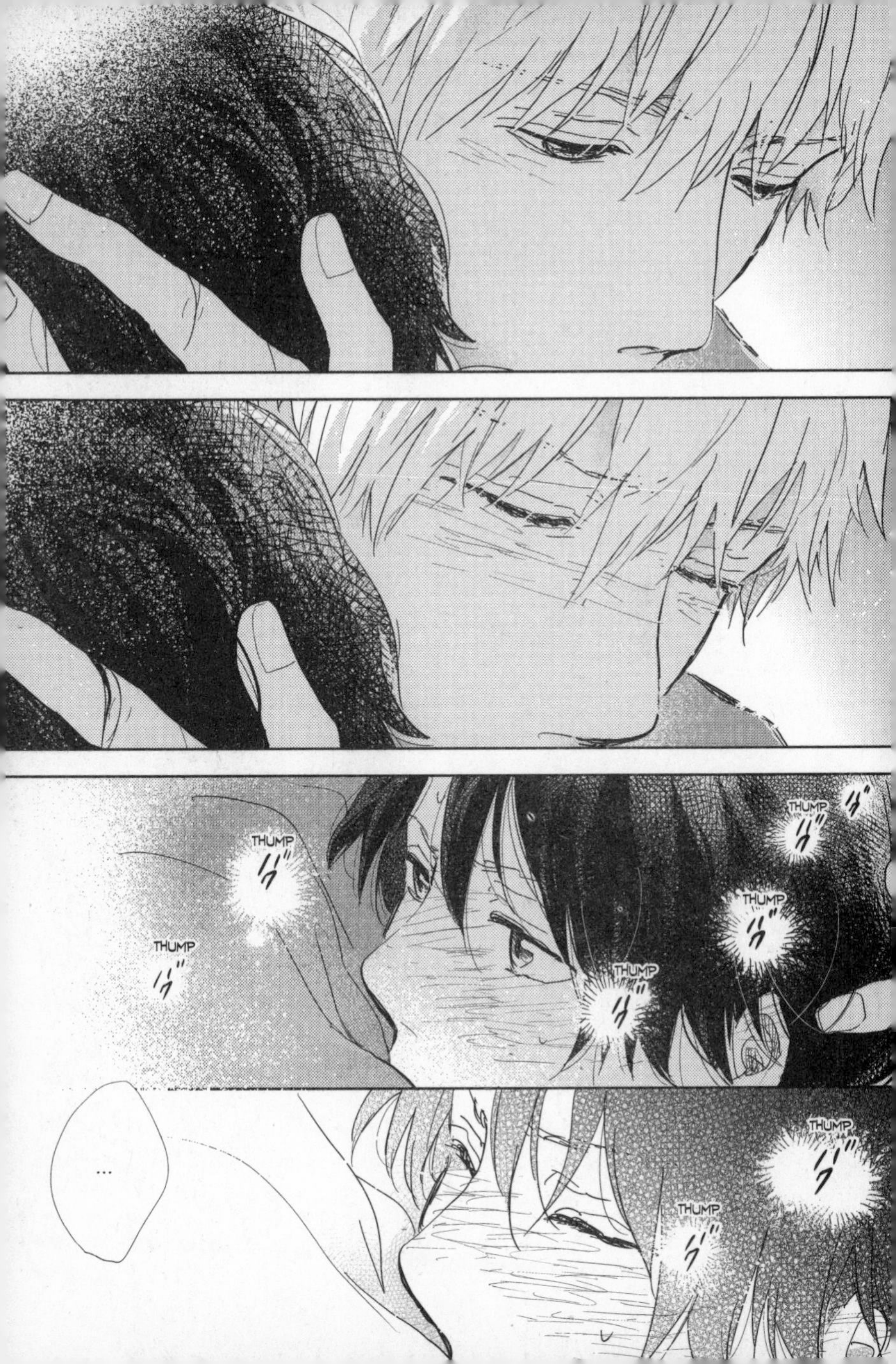
THUMP
THUMP
THUMP
THUMP
THUMP
THUMP
THUMP
...

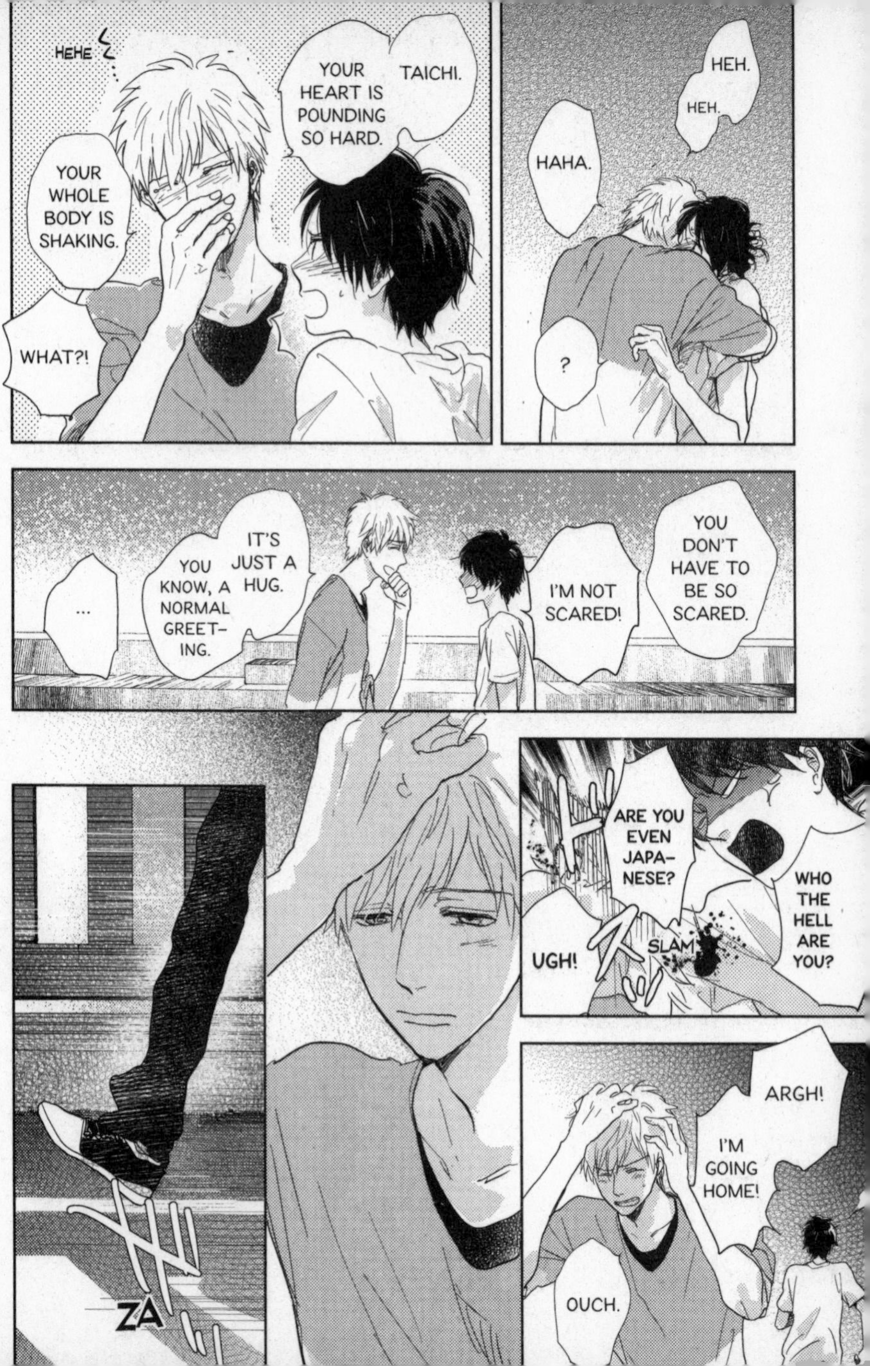
HEH.
HEH.
HAHA.
?
TAICHI.
YOUR HEART IS POUNDING SO HARD.
HEHE
YOUR WHOLE BODY IS SHAKING.
WHAT?!
YOU DON'T HAVE TO BE SO SCARED.
I'M NOT SCARED!
IT'S JUST A HUG.
YOU KNOW, A NORMAL GREET-ING.
...
WHO THE HELL ARE YOU?
ARE YOU EVEN JAPA-NESE?
SLAM
UGH!
ARGH!
I'M GOING HOME!
OUCH.
ZA

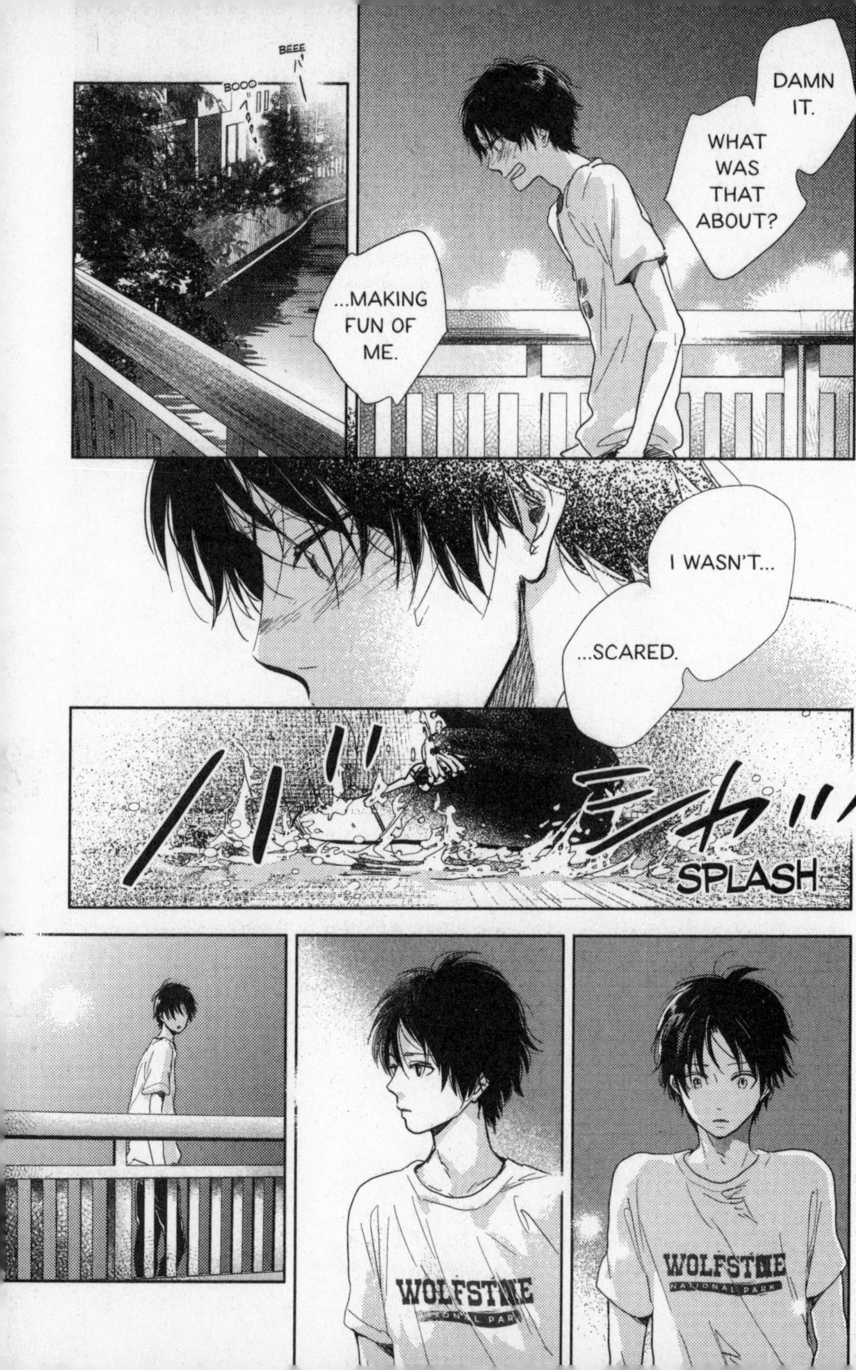
DAMN IT.
WHAT WAS THAT ABOUT?
...MAKING FUN OF ME.
BEEE
BOOO
I WASN'T...
...SCARED.
SPLASH

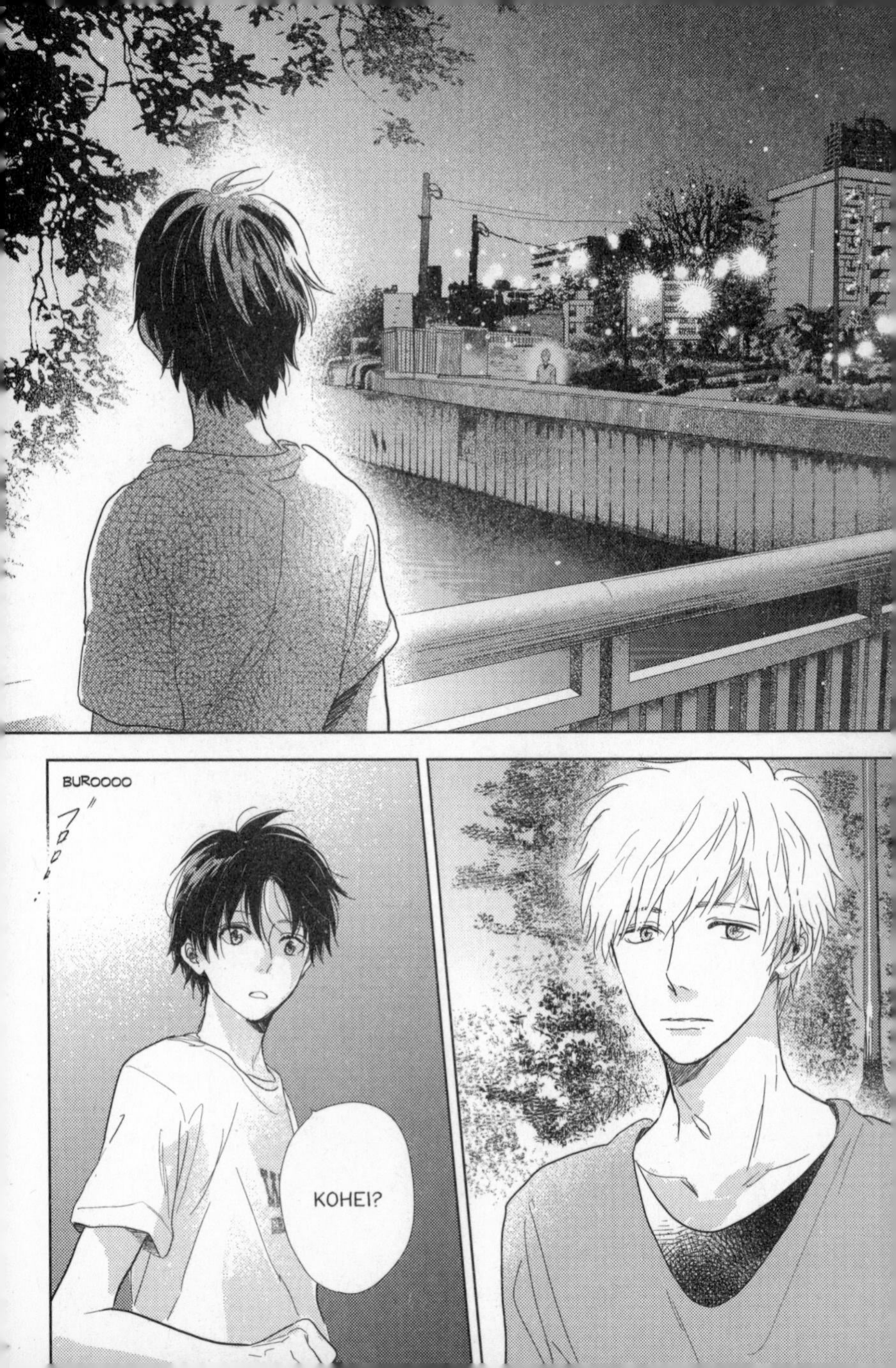
BUROOOO
KOHEI?

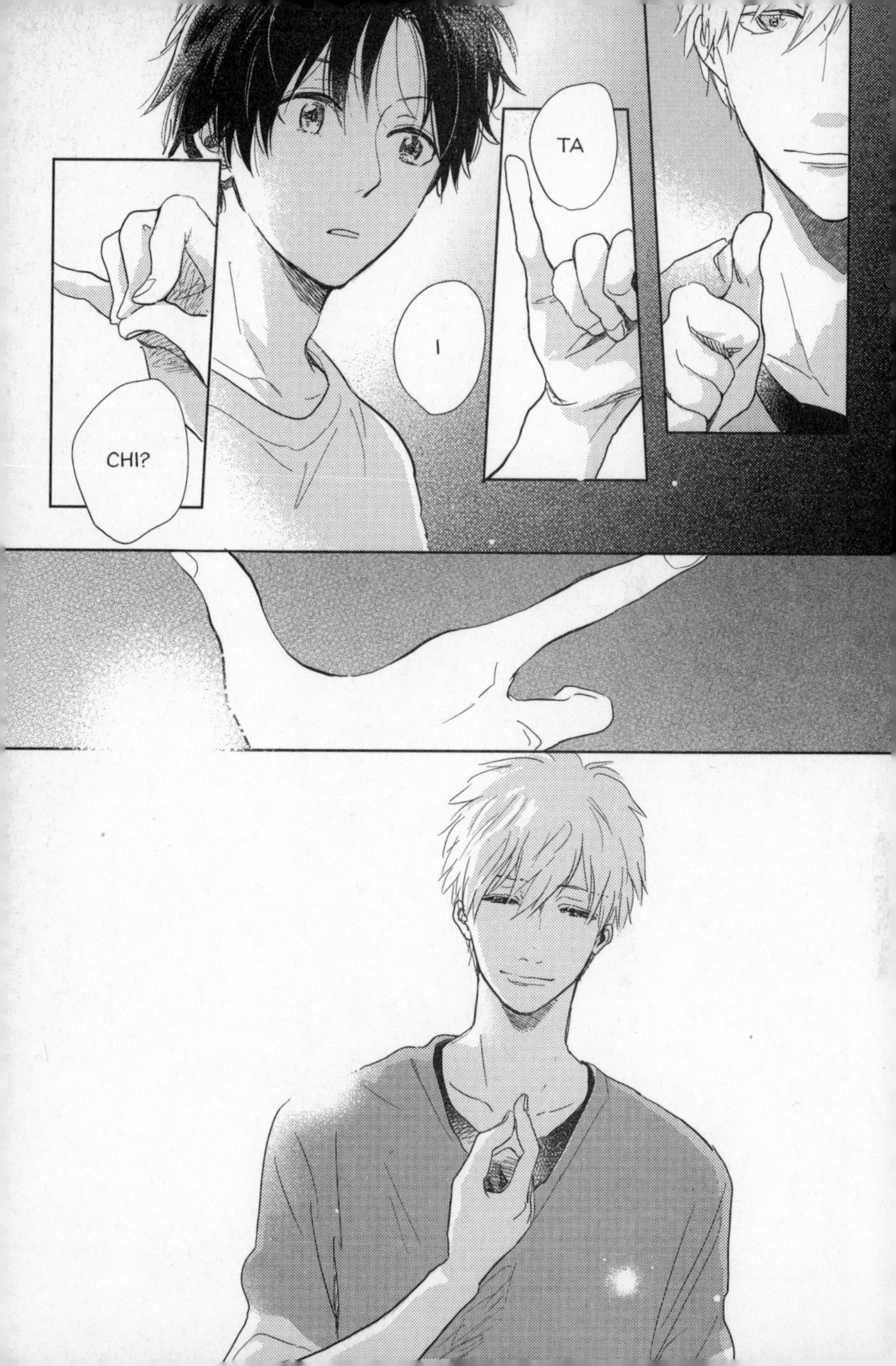
TA
I
CHI?

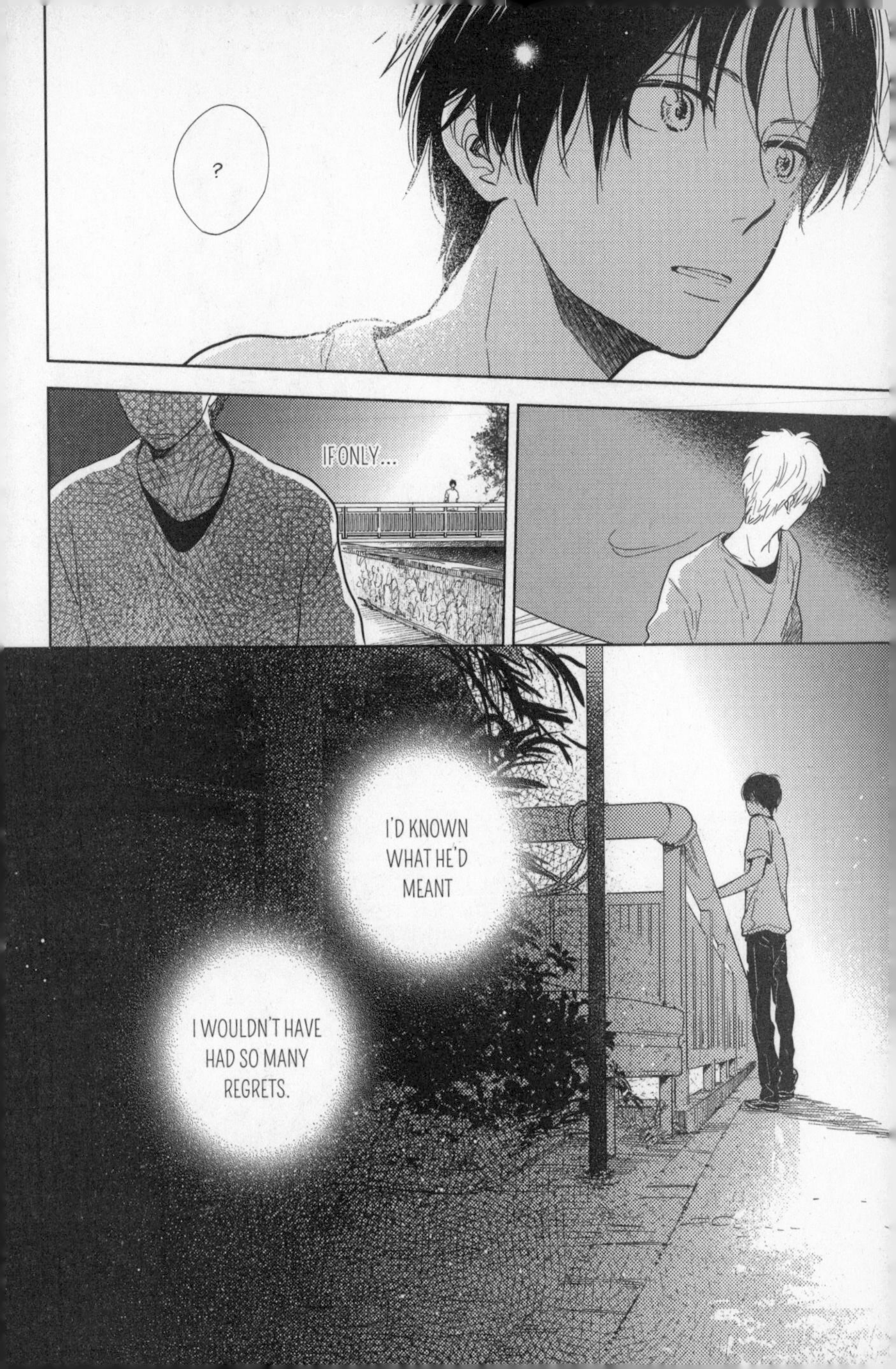
?
IF ONLY...
I'D KNOWN WHAT HE'D MEANT
I WOULDN'T HAVE HAD SO MANY REGRETS.

i hear
the
sunspot

i hear the sunspot

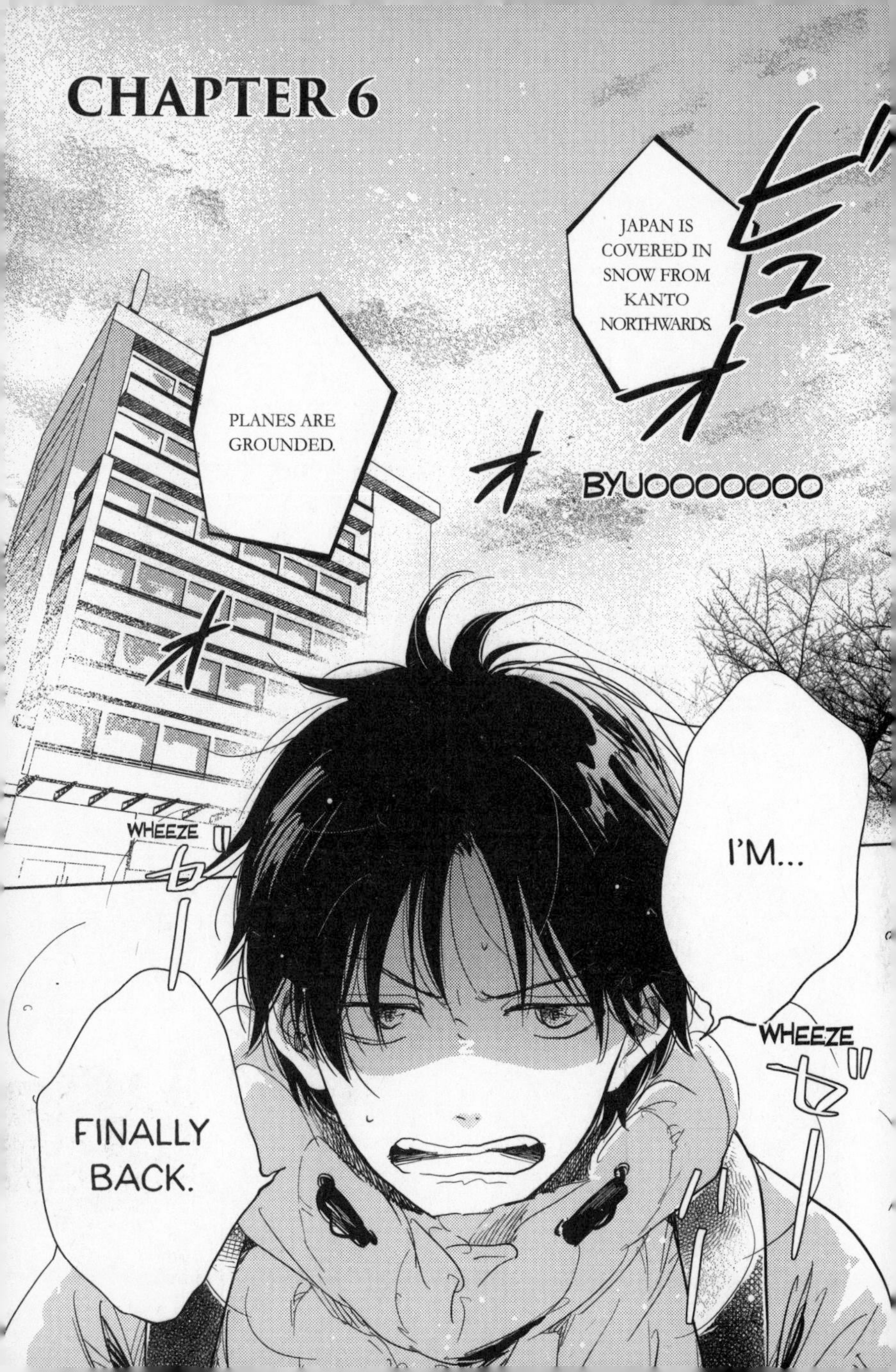
CHAPTER 6
JAPAN IS COVERED IN SNOW FROM KANTO NORTHWARDS.
BYUOOOOOOO
PLANES ARE GROUNDED.
I'M...
WHEEZE
WHEEZE
FINALLY BACK.

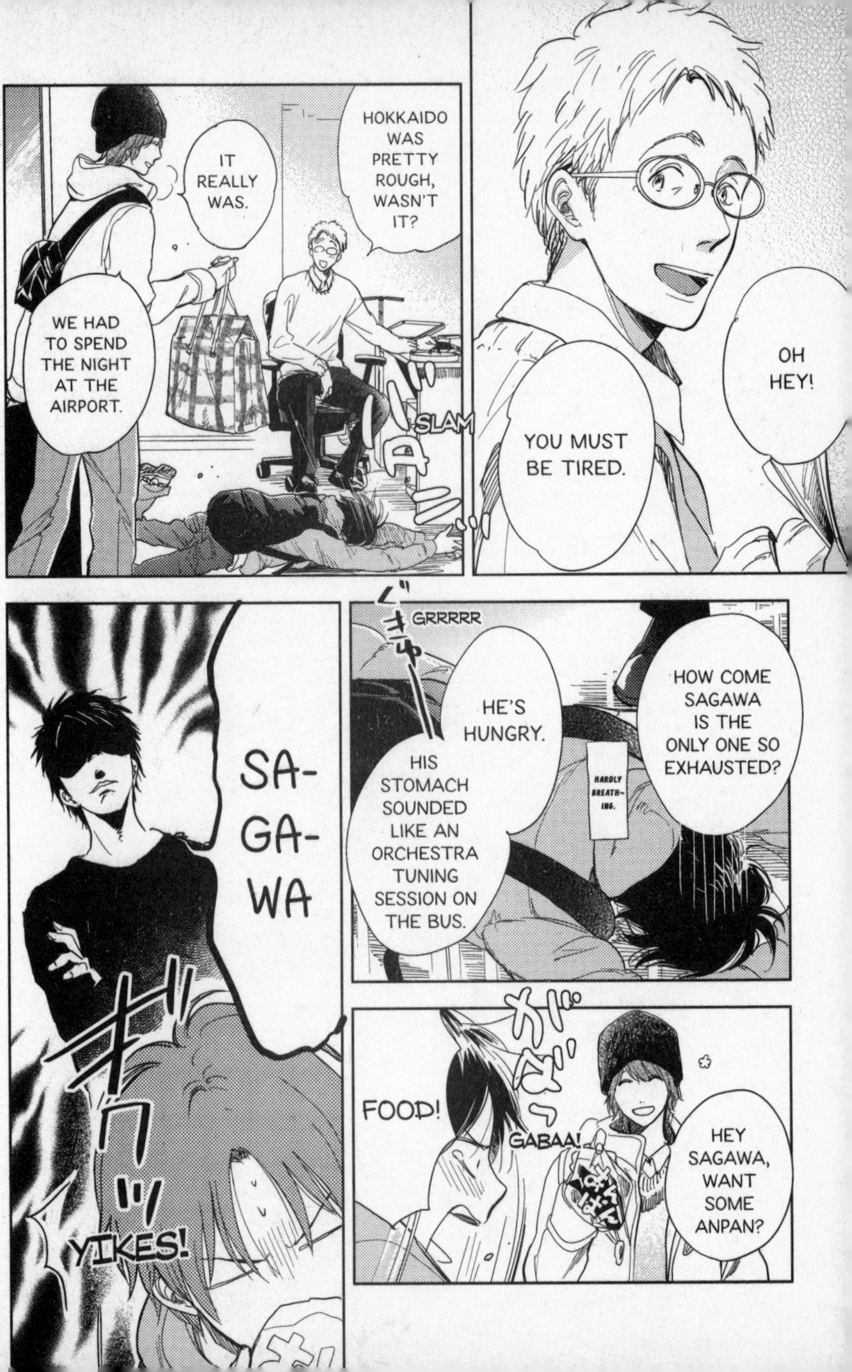
OH HEY!
YOU MUST BE TIRED.
HOKKAIDO WAS PRETTY ROUGH, WASN'T IT?
IT REALLY WAS.
WE HAD TO SPEND THE NIGHT AT THE AIRPORT.
SLAM
HOW COME SAGAWA IS THE ONLY ONE SO EXHAUSTED?
HARDLY BREATHING.
HE'S HUNGRY.
HIS STOMACH SOUNDED LIKE AN ORCHESTRA TUNING SESSION ON THE BUS.
GRRRRR
HEY SAGAWA, WANT SOME ANPAN?
GABAA!
FOOD!
SA-GA-WA
YIKES!

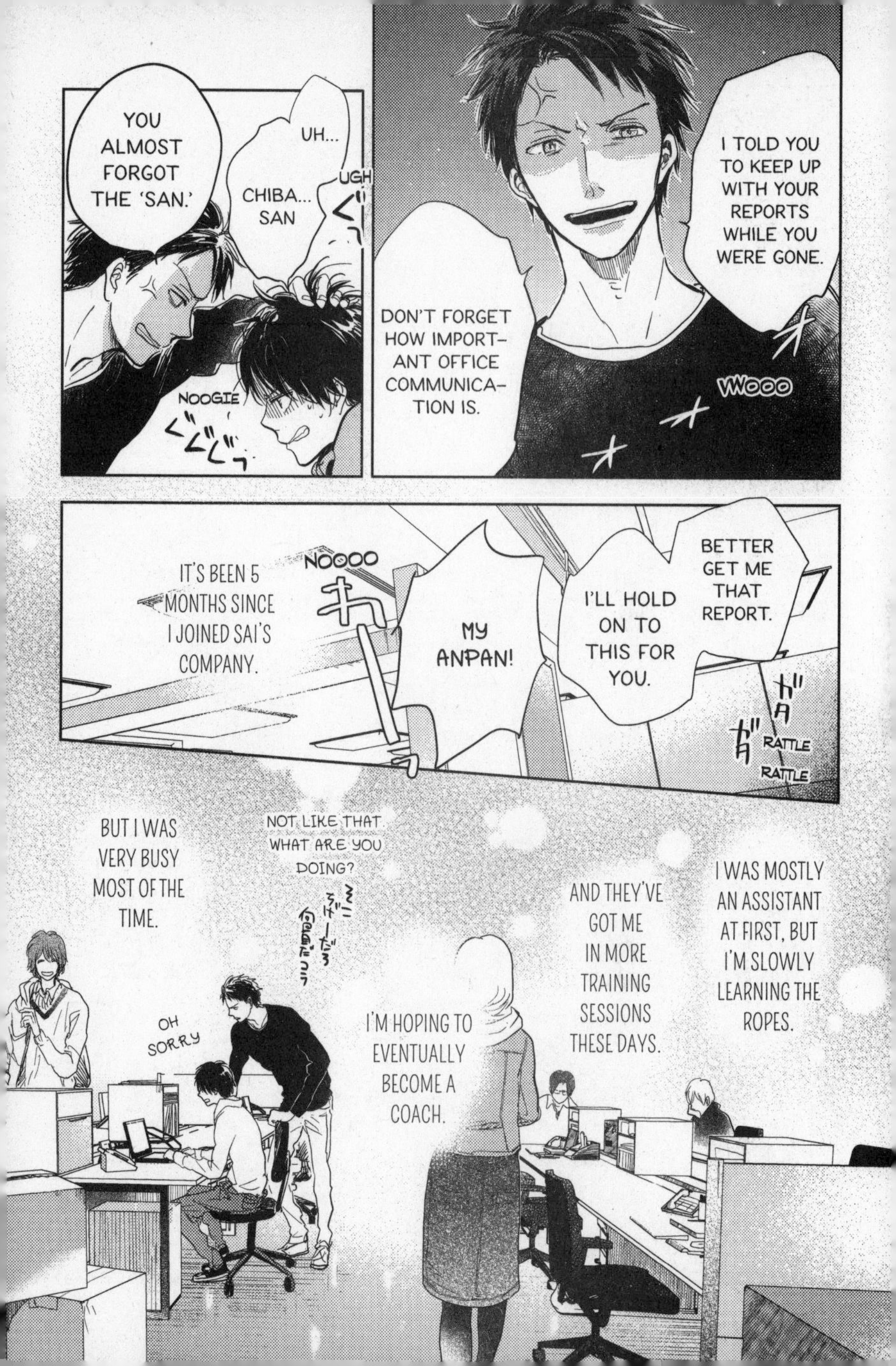
I TOLD YOU TO KEEP UP WITH YOUR REPORTS WHILE YOU WERE GONE.
DON'T FORGET HOW IMPORTANT OFFICE COMMUNICATION IS.
VWOOO
UH...
CHIBA... SAN
UGH
YOU ALMOST FORGOT THE 'SAN.'
NOOGIE
BETTER GET ME THAT REPORT.
I'LL HOLD ON TO THIS FOR YOU.
RATTLE
RATTLE
MY ANPAN!
NOOOO
IT'S BEEN 5 MONTHS SINCE I JOINED SAI'S COMPANY.
I WAS MOSTLY AN ASSISTANT AT FIRST, BUT I'M SLOWLY LEARNING THE ROPES.
AND THEY'VE GOT ME IN MORE TRAINING SESSIONS THESE DAYS.
I'M HOPING TO EVENTUALLY BECOME A COACH.
NOT LIKE THAT. WHAT ARE YOU DOING?
BUT I WAS VERY BUSY MOST OF THE TIME.
OH SORRY

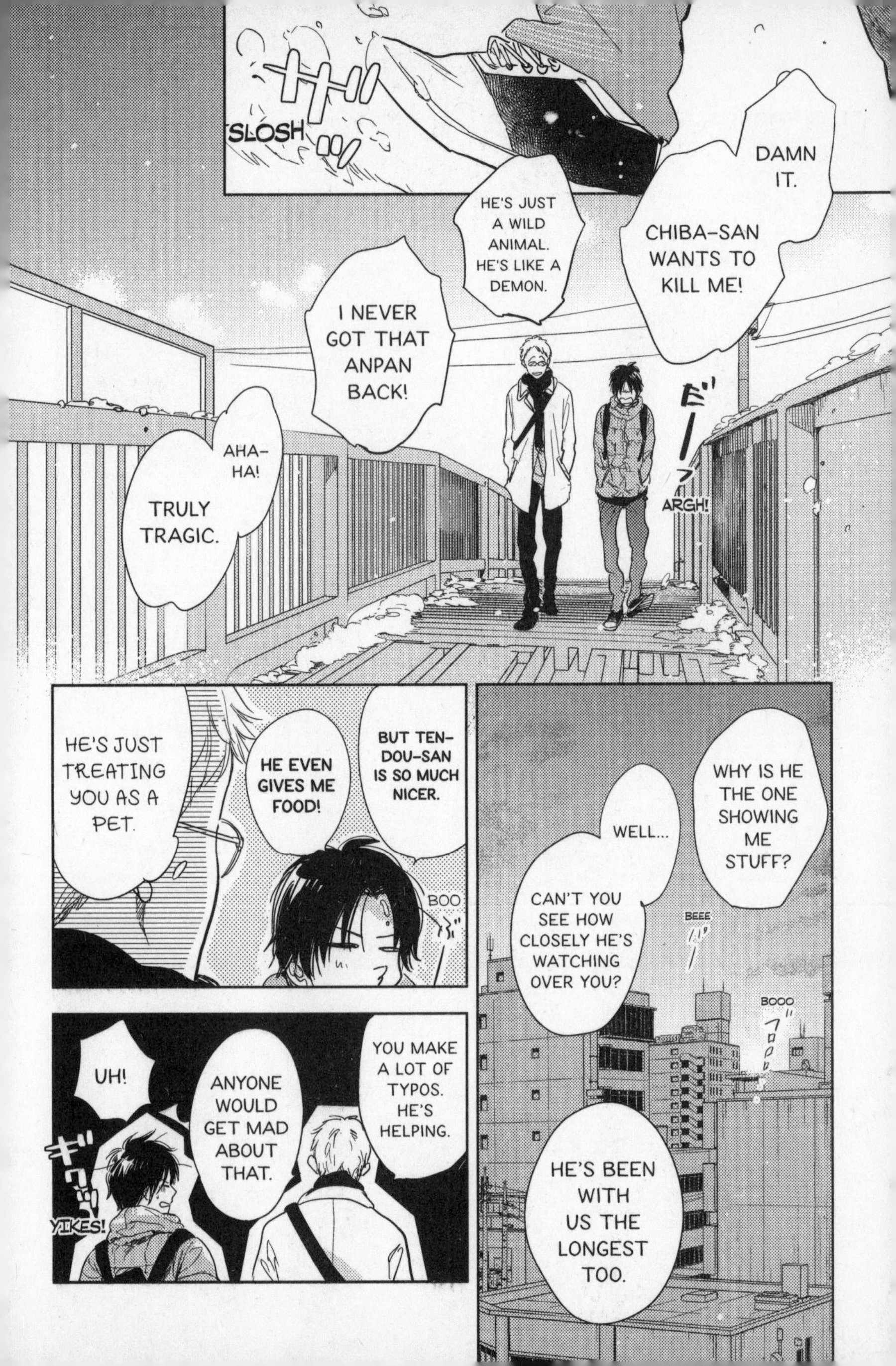
SLOSH
DAMN IT.
CHIBA-SAN WANTS TO KILL ME!
HE'S JUST A WILD ANIMAL. HE'S LIKE A DEMON.
I NEVER GOT THAT ANPAN BACK!
ARGH!
AHA-HA!
TRULY TRAGIC.
WHY IS HE THE ONE SHOWING ME STUFF?
BEEE
WELL...
CAN'T YOU SEE HOW CLOSELY HE'S WATCHING OVER YOU?
BOOO
HE'S BEEN WITH US THE LONGEST TOO.
BUT TEN-DOU-SAN IS SO MUCH NICER.
HE EVEN GIVES ME FOOD!
BOO
HE'S JUST TREATING YOU AS A PET.
YOU MAKE A LOT OF TYPOS. HE'S HELPING.
ANYONE WOULD GET MAD ABOUT THAT.
UH!
YIKES!

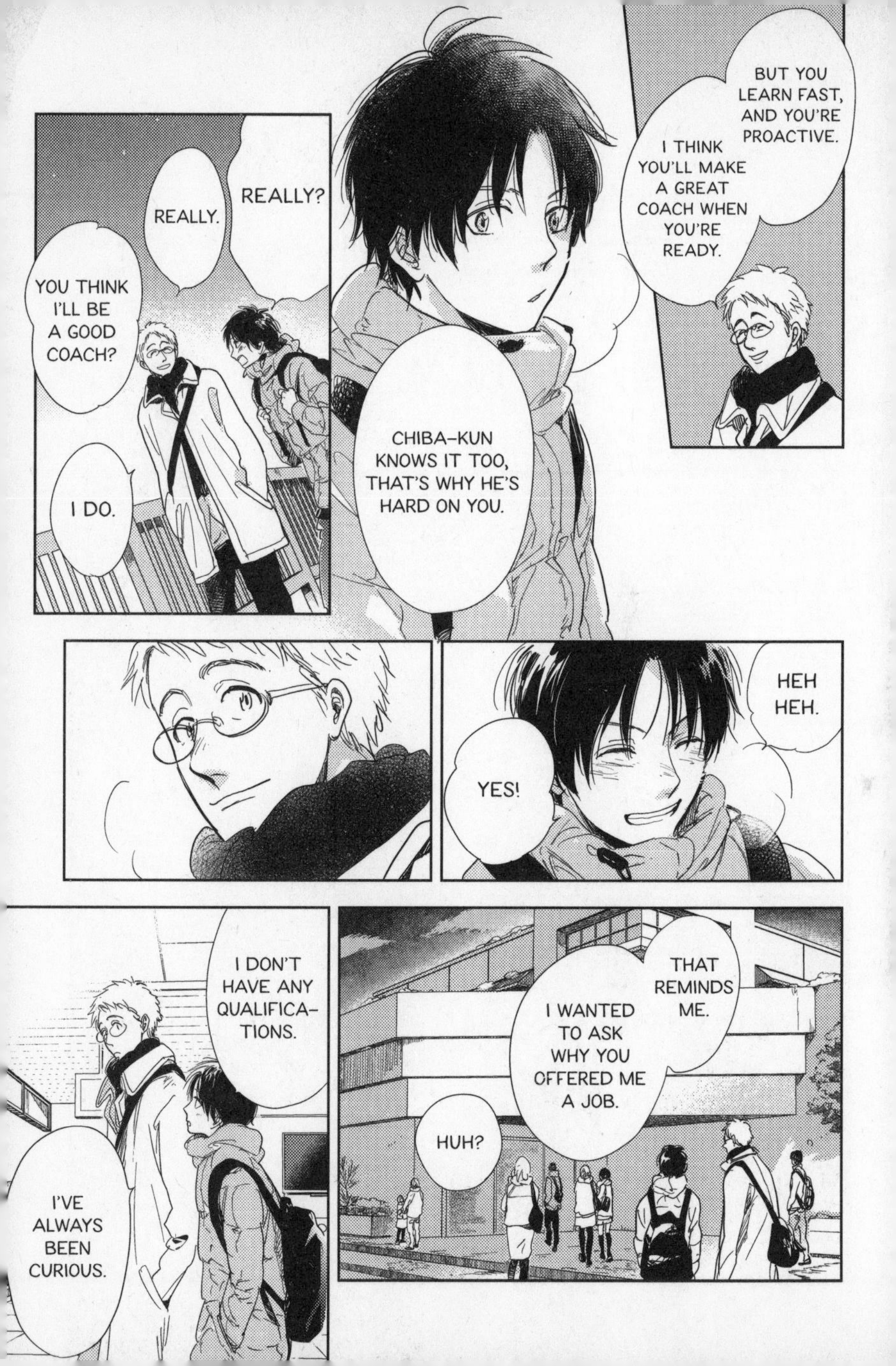
BUT YOU LEARN FAST, AND YOU'RE PROACTIVE.
I THINK YOU'LL MAKE A GREAT COACH WHEN YOU'RE READY.
CHIBA-KUN KNOWS IT TOO, THAT'S WHY HE'S HARD ON YOU.
REALLY?
REALLY.
YOU THINK I'LL BE A GOOD COACH?
I DO.
HEH HEH.
YES!
THAT REMINDS ME.
I WANTED TO ASK WHY YOU OFFERED ME A JOB.
HUH?
I DON'T HAVE ANY QUALIFICA-TIONS.
I'VE ALWAYS BEEN CURIOUS.

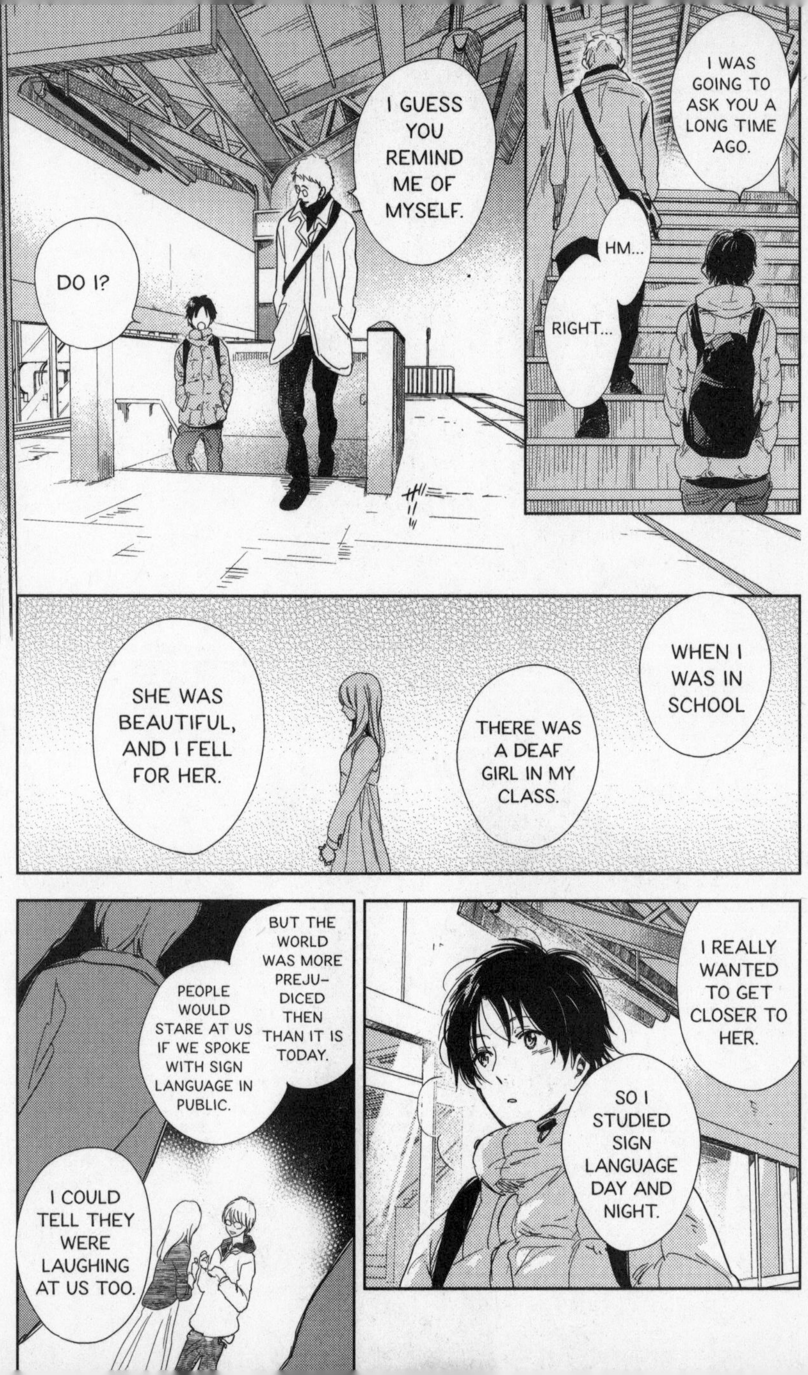
I WAS GOING TO ASK YOU A LONG TIME AGO.
HM...
RIGHT...
I GUESS YOU REMIND ME OF MYSELF.
DO I?
WHEN I WAS IN SCHOOL
THERE WAS A DEAF GIRL IN MY CLASS.
SHE WAS BEAUTIFUL, AND I FELL FOR HER.
I REALLY WANTED TO GET CLOSER TO HER.
SO I STUDIED SIGN LANGUAGE DAY AND NIGHT.
BUT THE WORLD WAS MORE PREJUDICED THEN THAN IT IS TODAY.
PEOPLE WOULD STARE AT US IF WE SPOKE WITH SIGN LANGUAGE IN PUBLIC.
I COULD TELL THEY WERE LAUGHING AT US TOO.

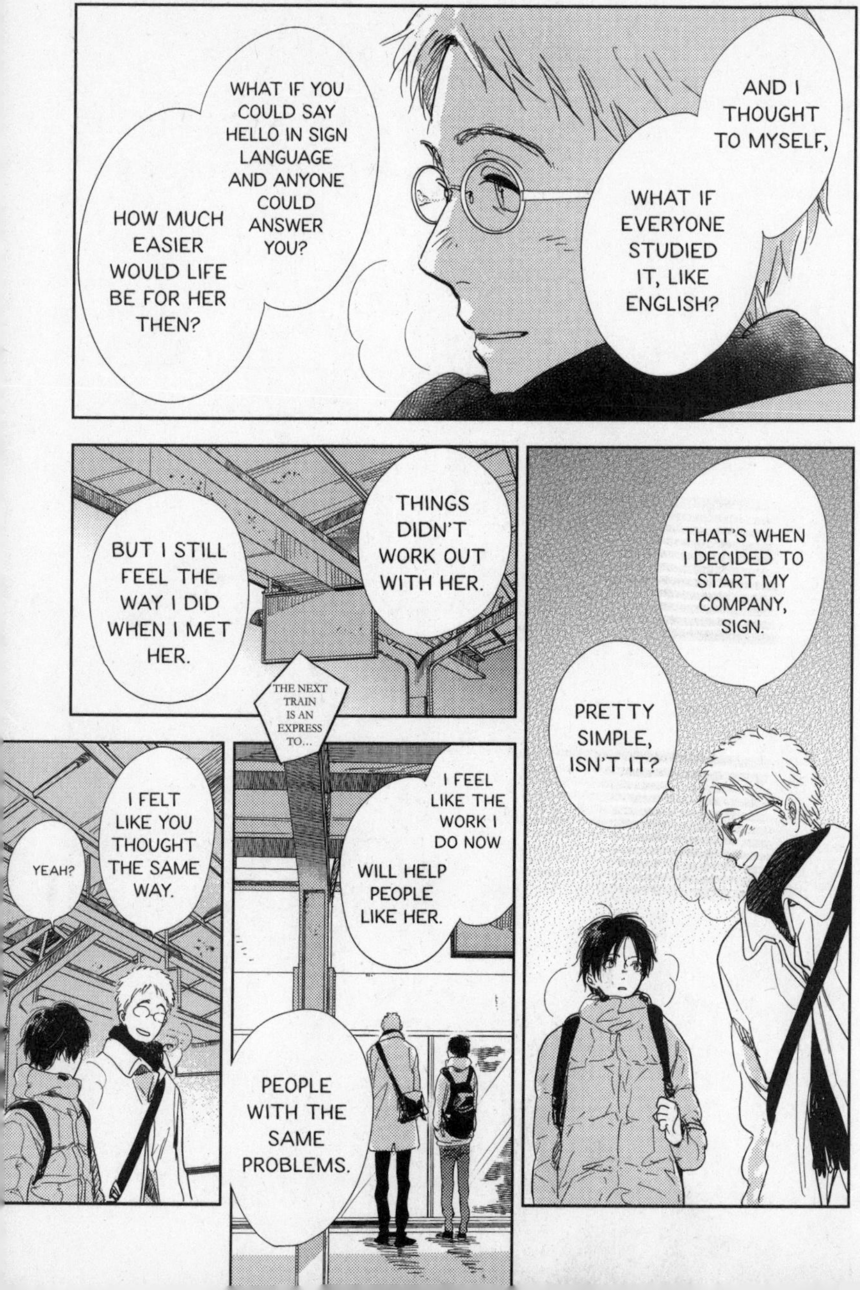
AND I THOUGHT TO MYSELF,
WHAT IF EVERYONE STUDIED IT, LIKE ENGLISH?
WHAT IF YOU COULD SAY HELLO IN SIGN LANGUAGE AND ANYONE COULD ANSWER YOU?
HOW MUCH EASIER WOULD LIFE BE FOR HER THEN?
THAT'S WHEN I DECIDED TO START MY COMPANY, SIGN.
PRETTY SIMPLE, ISN'T IT?
THINGS DIDN'T WORK OUT WITH HER.
BUT I STILL FEEL THE WAY I DID WHEN I MET HER.
THE NEXT TRAIN IS AN EXPRESS TO…
I FEEL LIKE THE WORK I DO NOW
WILL HELP PEOPLE LIKE HER.
PEOPLE WITH THE SAME PROBLEMS.
I FELT LIKE YOU THOUGHT THE SAME WAY.
YEAH?

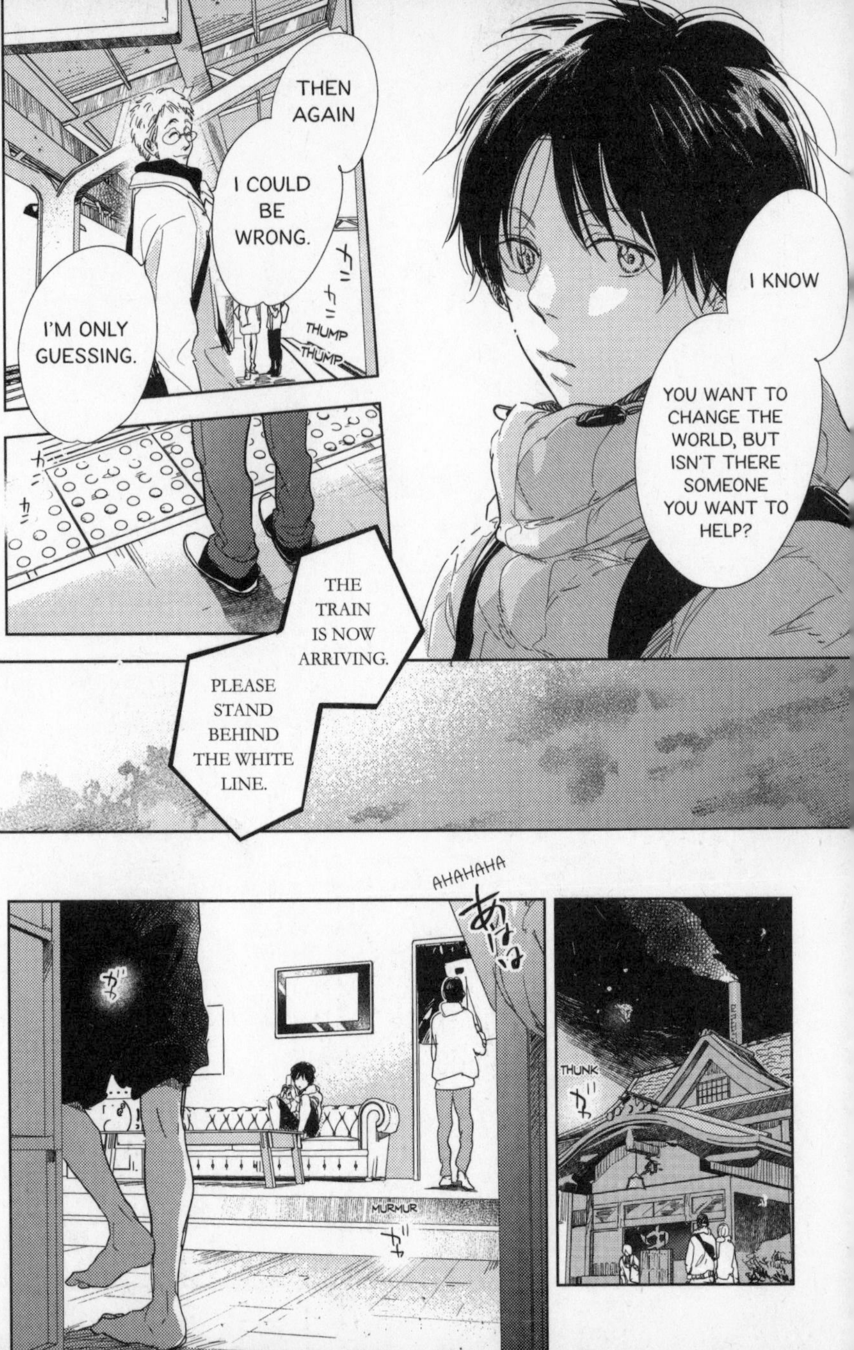
I KNOW
YOU WANT TO CHANGE THE WORLD, BUT ISN'T THERE SOMEONE YOU WANT TO HELP?
THEN AGAIN
I COULD BE WRONG.
THUMP THUMP
I'M ONLY GUESSING.
THE TRAIN IS NOW ARRIVING.
PLEASE STAND BEHIND THE WHITE LINE.
THUNK
AHAHAHA
MURMUR

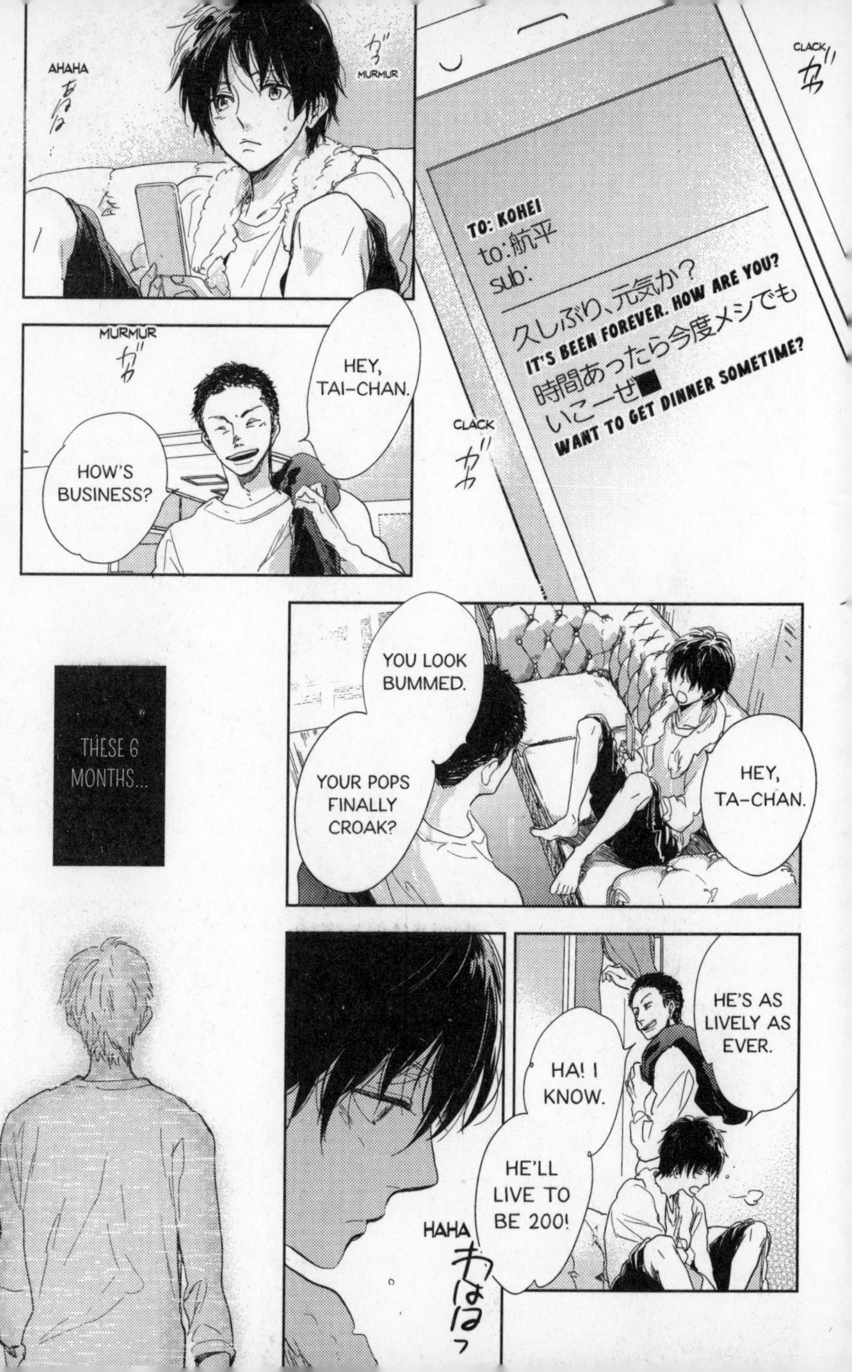
CLACK
TO: KOHEI
to:航平
sub:
久しぶり、元気か？
IT'S BEEN FOREVER. HOW ARE YOU?
時間あったら今度メシでも
いこーぜ
WANT TO GET DINNER SOMETIME?
CLACK
MURMUR
AHAHA
MURMUR
HEY, TAI-CHAN.
HOW'S BUSINESS?
HEY, TA-CHAN.
YOU LOOK BUMMED.
YOUR POPS FINALLY CROAK?
THESE 6 MONTHS...
HE'S AS LIVELY AS EVER.
HA! I KNOW.
HE'LL LIVE TO BE 200!
HAHA

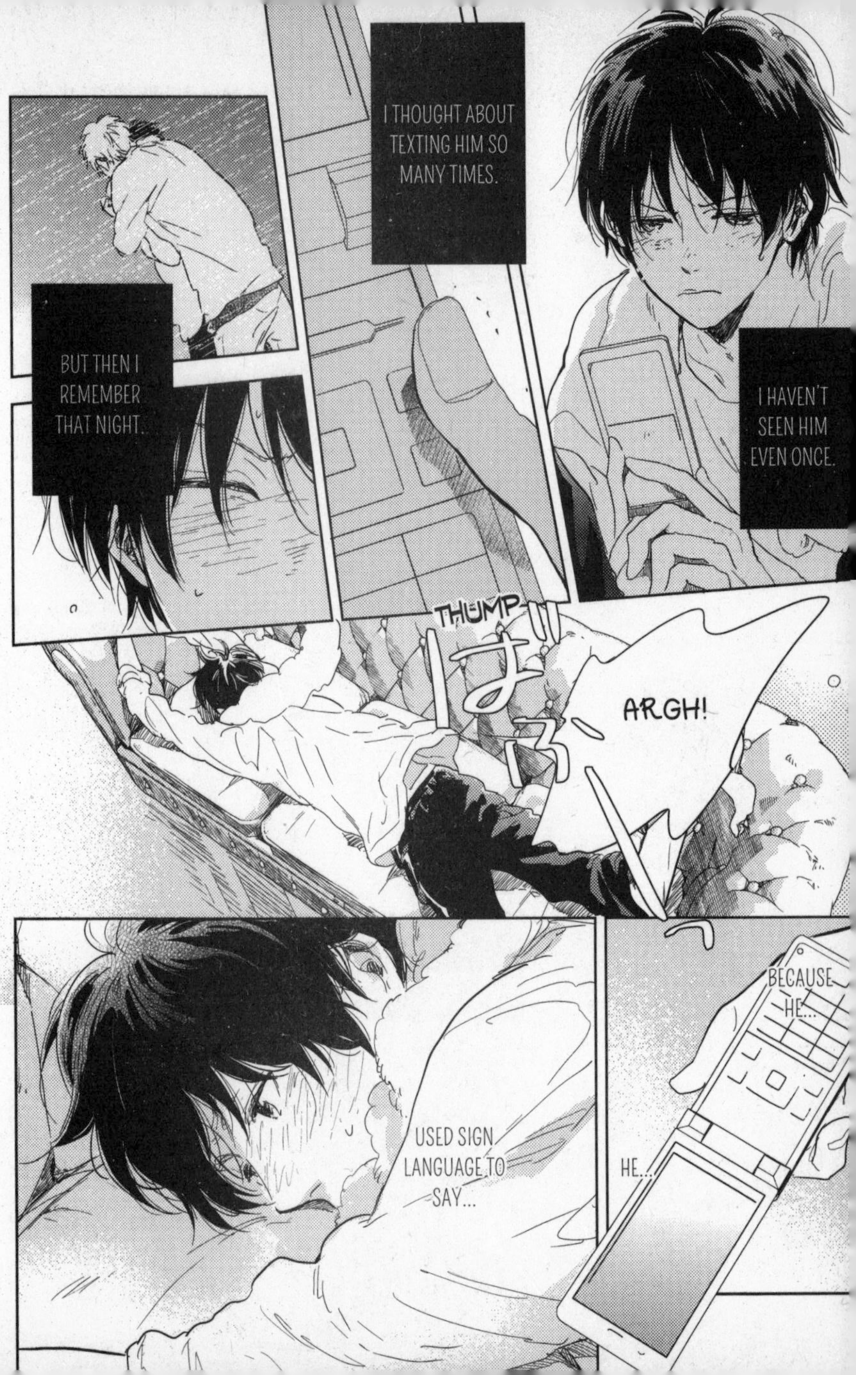
I HAVEN'T SEEN HIM EVEN ONCE.
I THOUGHT ABOUT TEXTING HIM SO MANY TIMES.
BUT THEN I REMEMBER THAT NIGHT.
THUMP
ARGH!
BECAUSE HE...
HE...
USED SIGN LANGUAGE TO SAY...

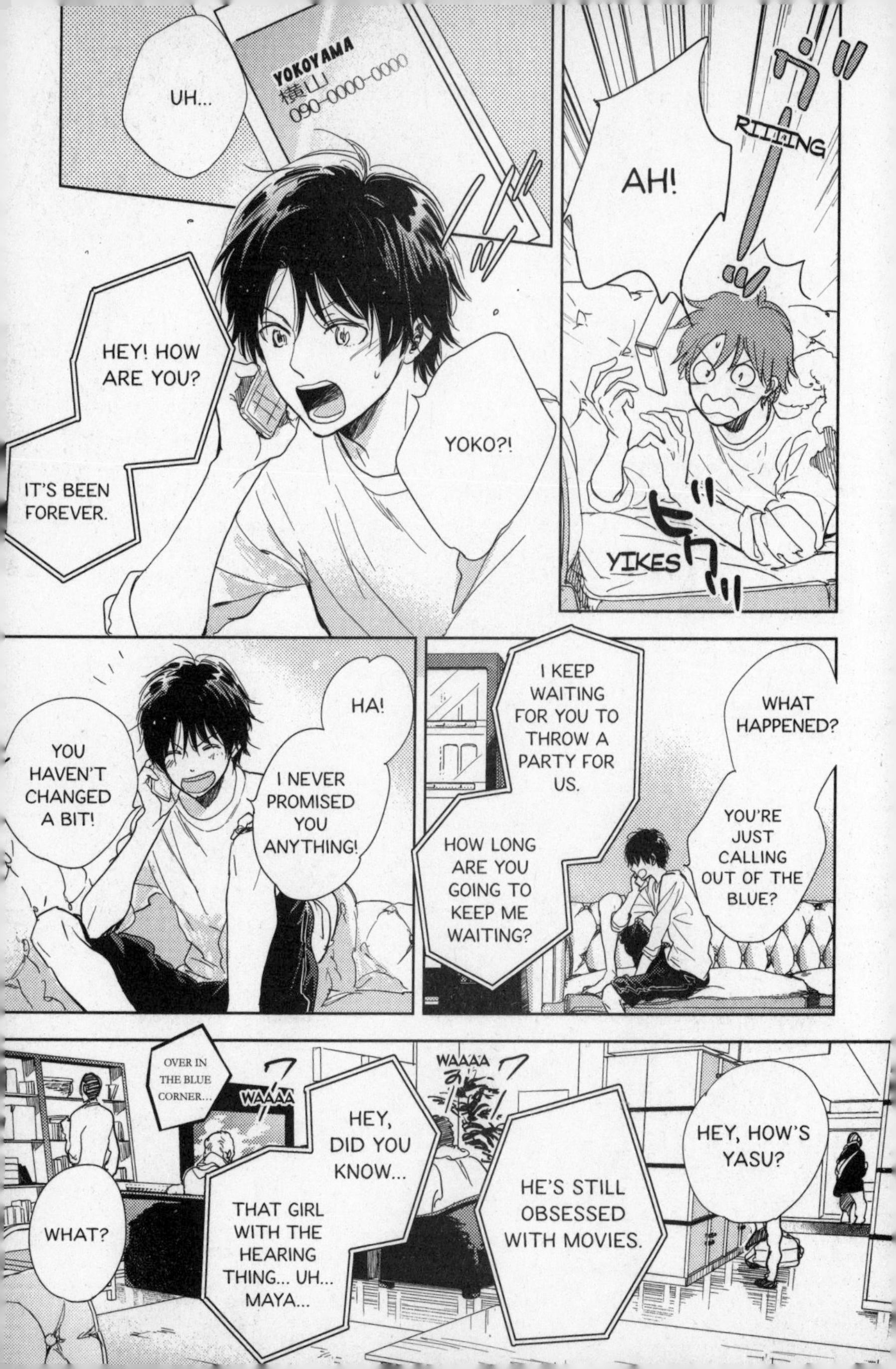
RIIIING
AH!
YIKES
UH...
YOKOYAMA
横山
090-0000-0000
YOKO?!
HEY! HOW ARE YOU?
IT'S BEEN FOREVER.
WHAT HAPPENED?
YOU'RE JUST CALLING OUT OF THE BLUE?
I KEEP WAITING FOR YOU TO THROW A PARTY FOR US.
HOW LONG ARE YOU GOING TO KEEP ME WAITING?
HA!
I NEVER PROMISED YOU ANYTHING!
YOU HAVEN'T CHANGED A BIT!
HEY, HOW'S YASU?
HE'S STILL OBSESSED WITH MOVIES.
WAAAA
HEY, DID YOU KNOW...
THAT GIRL WITH THE HEARING THING... UH... MAYA...
WAAAA
OVER IN THE BLUE CORNER...
WHAT?

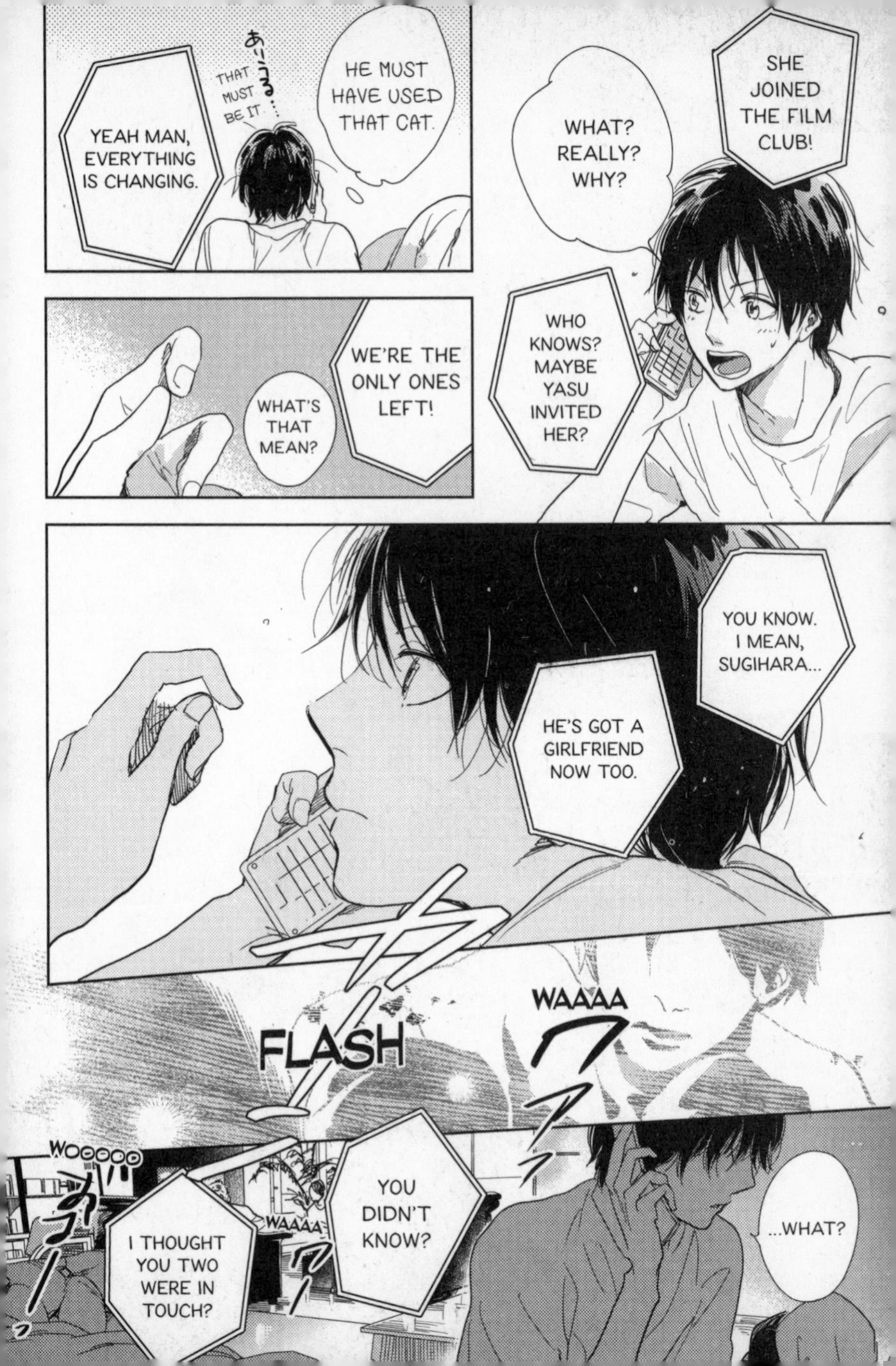
SHE JOINED THE FILM CLUB!
WHAT? REALLY? WHY?
WHO KNOWS? MAYBE YASU INVITED HER?
HE MUST HAVE USED THAT CAT.
ありうる
THAT MUST BE IT....
YEAH MAN, EVERYTHING IS CHANGING.
WE'RE THE ONLY ONES LEFT!
WHAT'S THAT MEAN?
YOU KNOW. I MEAN, SUGIHARA...
HE'S GOT A GIRLFRIEND NOW TOO.
FLASH
WAAAA
...WHAT?
YOU DIDN'T KNOW?
WAAAA
I THOUGHT YOU TWO WERE IN TOUCH?
WOOOOO

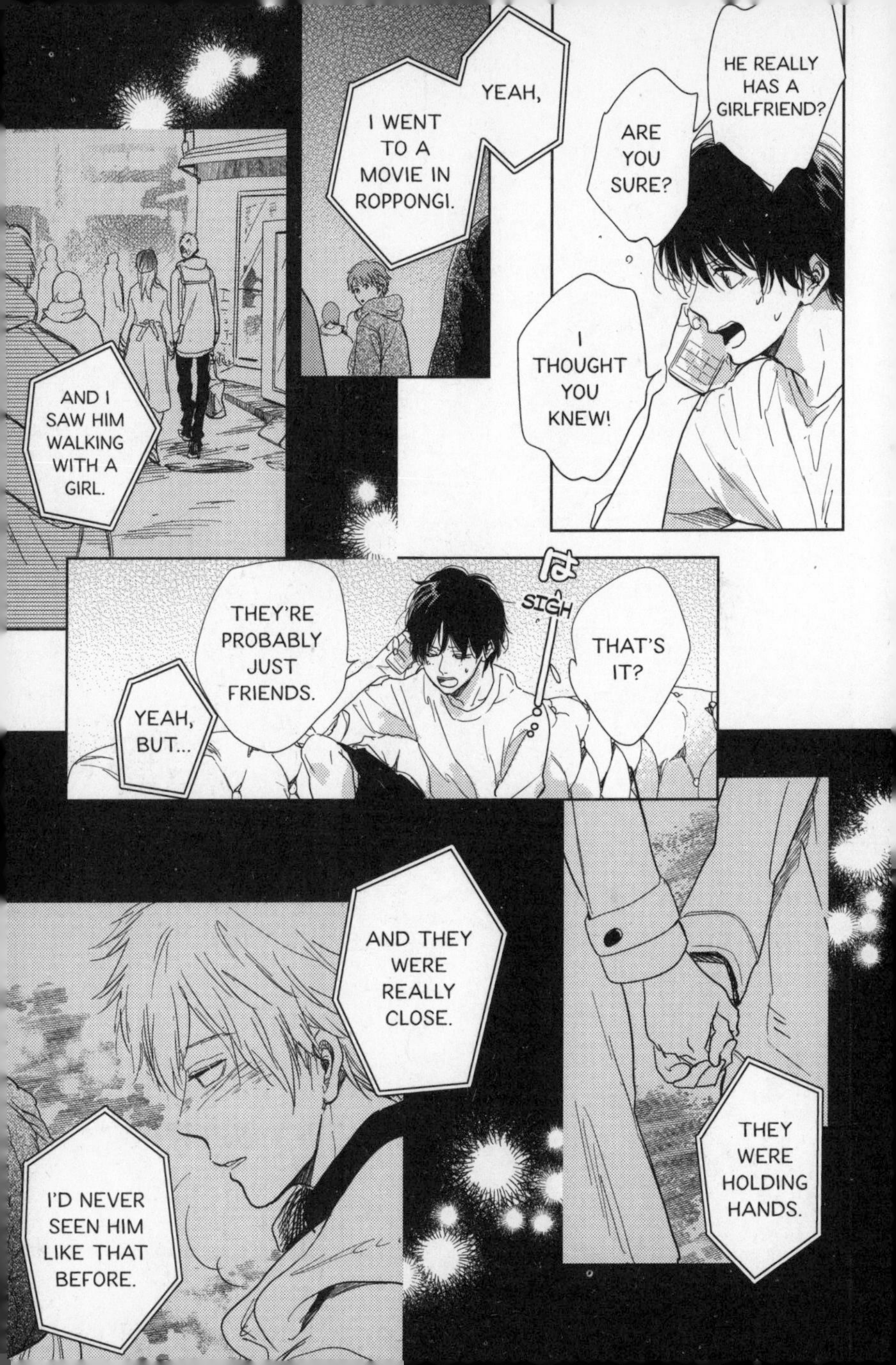
HE REALLY HAS A GIRLFRIEND?
ARE YOU SURE?
I THOUGHT YOU KNEW!
YEAH, I WENT TO A MOVIE IN ROPPONGI.
AND I SAW HIM WALKING WITH A GIRL.
は
SIGH
THAT'S IT?
THEY'RE PROBABLY JUST FRIENDS.
YEAH, BUT...
THEY WERE HOLDING HANDS.
AND THEY WERE REALLY CLOSE.
I'D NEVER SEEN HIM LIKE THAT BEFORE.

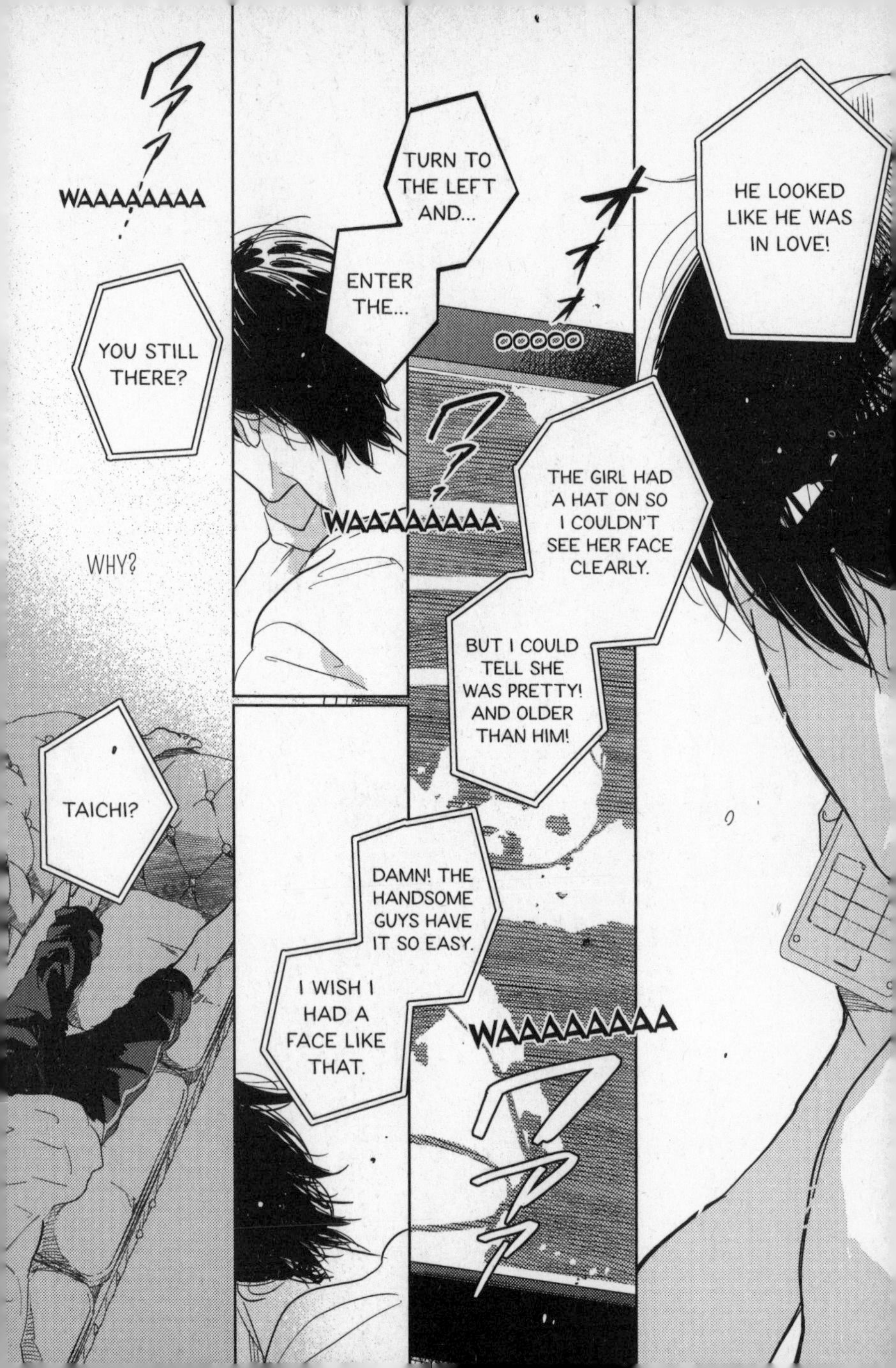
HE LOOKED LIKE HE WAS IN LOVE!
THE GIRL HAD A HAT ON SO I COULDN'T SEE HER FACE CLEARLY.
BUT I COULD TELL SHE WAS PRETTY! AND OLDER THAN HIM!
WAAAAAAAA
TURN TO THE LEFT AND...
ENTER THE...
WAAAAAAAA
DAMN! THE HANDSOME GUYS HAVE IT SO EASY.
I WISH I HAD A FACE LIKE THAT.
WAAAAAAAA
YOU STILL THERE?
WHY?
TAICHI?

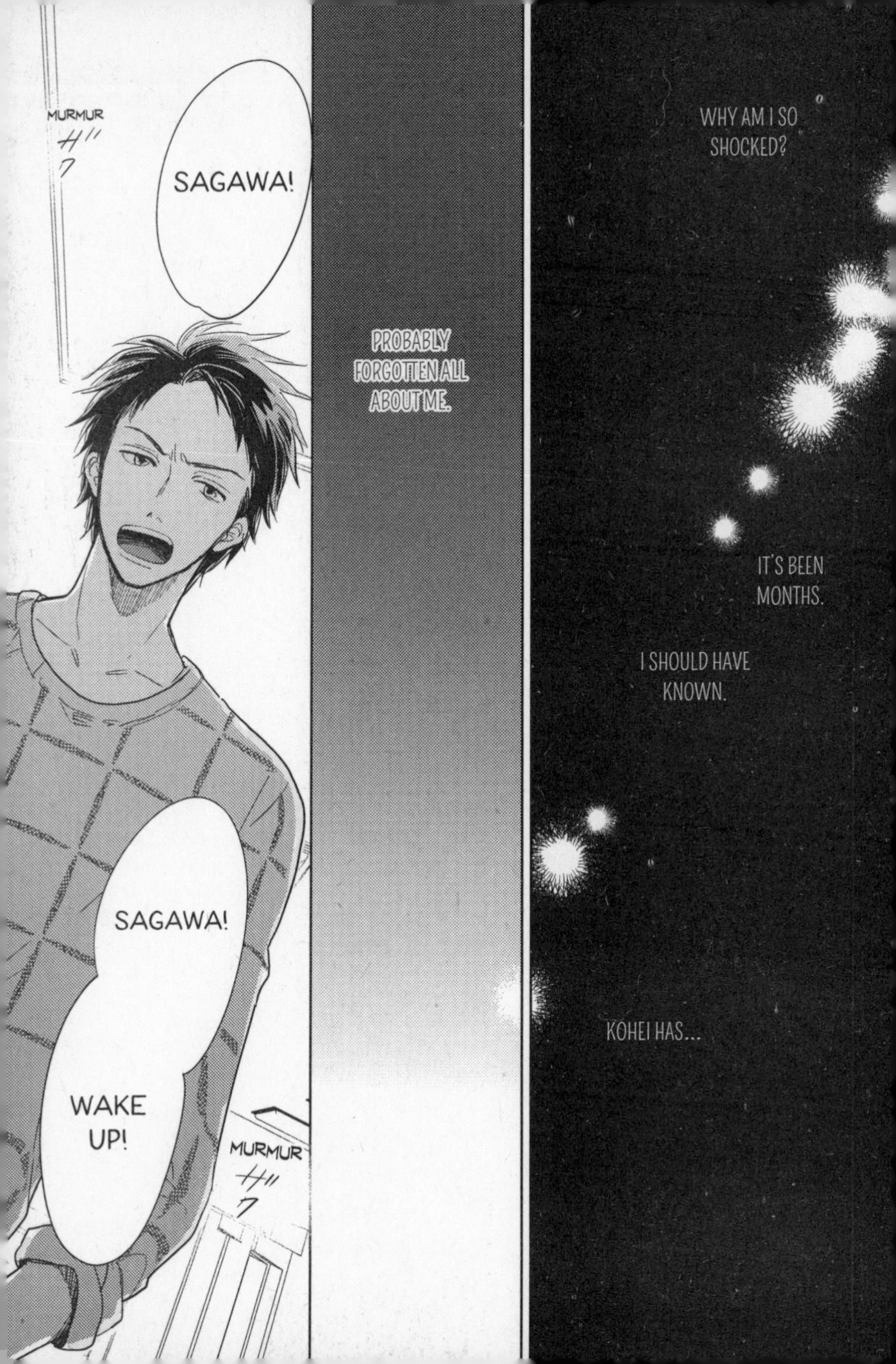
WHY AM I SO SHOCKED?
IT'S BEEN MONTHS.
I SHOULD HAVE KNOWN.
KOHEI HAS...
PROBABLY FORGOTTEN ALL ABOUT ME.
SAGAWA!
MURMUR
SAGAWA!
WAKE UP!
MURMUR

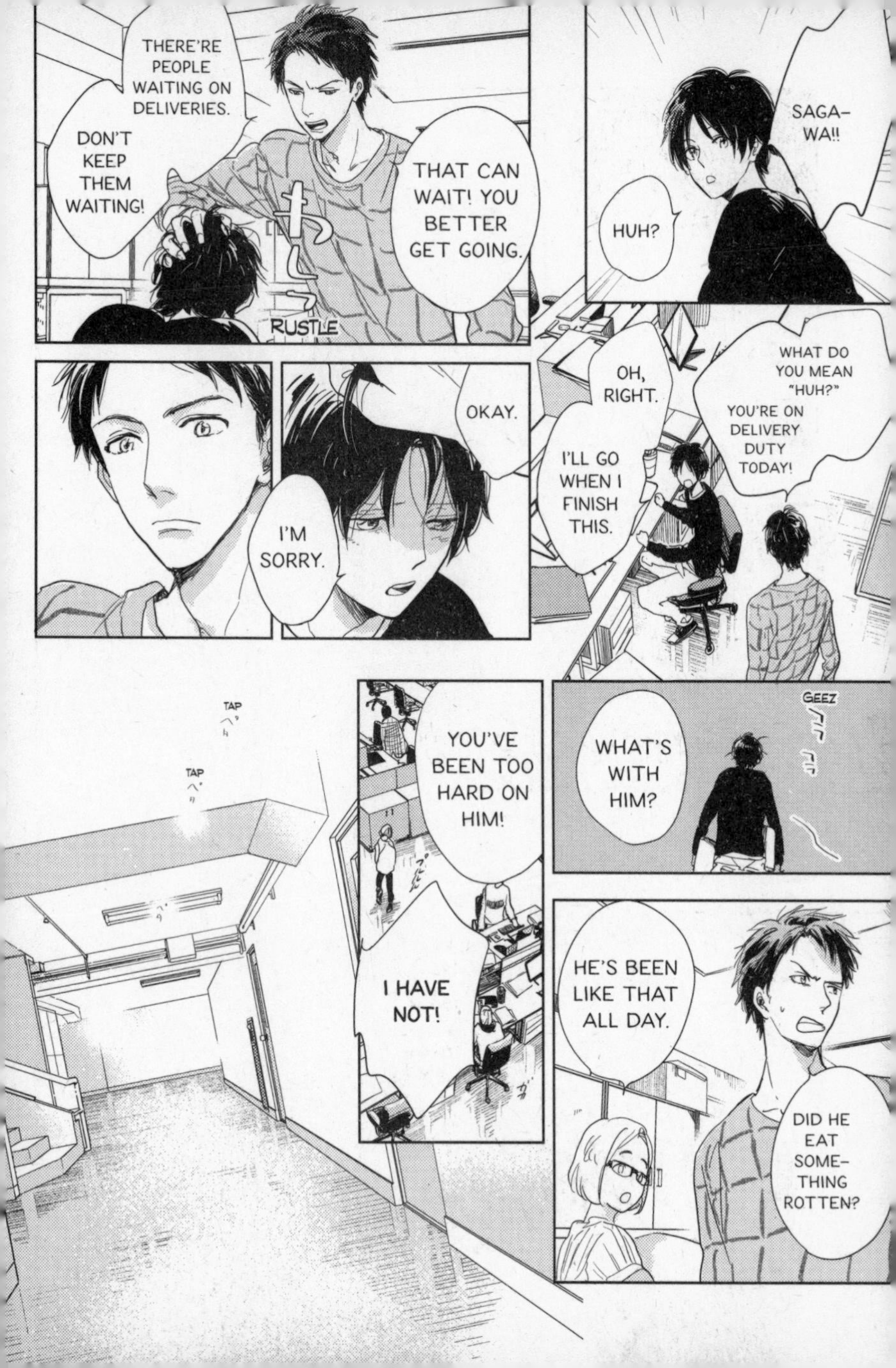
SAGA-WA!!
HUH?
WHAT DO YOU MEAN "HUH?"
YOU'RE ON DELIVERY DUTY TODAY!
OH, RIGHT.
I'LL GO WHEN I FINISH THIS.
THAT CAN WAIT! YOU BETTER GET GOING.
THERE'RE PEOPLE WAITING ON DELIVERIES.
DON'T KEEP THEM WAITING!
RUSTLE
OKAY.
I'M SORRY.
GEEZ
WHAT'S WITH HIM?
HE'S BEEN LIKE THAT ALL DAY.
DID HE EAT SOMETHING ROTTEN?
YOU'VE BEEN TOO HARD ON HIM!
I HAVE NOT!
TAP
TAP

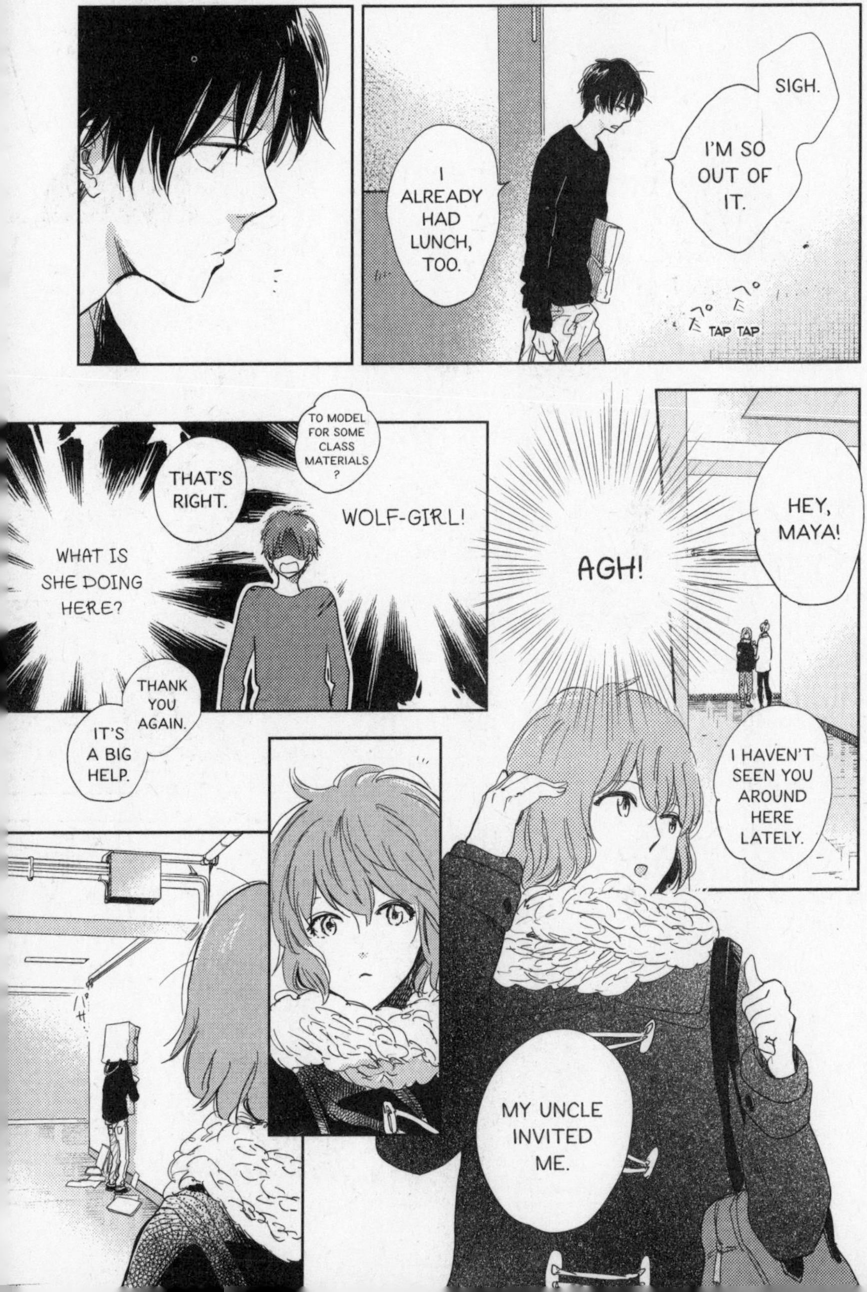
SIGH.
I'M SO OUT OF IT.
TAP TAP
I ALREADY HAD LUNCH, TOO.
HEY, MAYA!
AGH!
I HAVEN'T SEEN YOU AROUND HERE LATELY.
MY UNCLE INVITED ME.
WOLF-GIRL!
TO MODEL FOR SOME CLASS MATERIALS?
THAT'S RIGHT.
WHAT IS SHE DOING HERE?
THANK YOU AGAIN.
IT'S A BIG HELP.

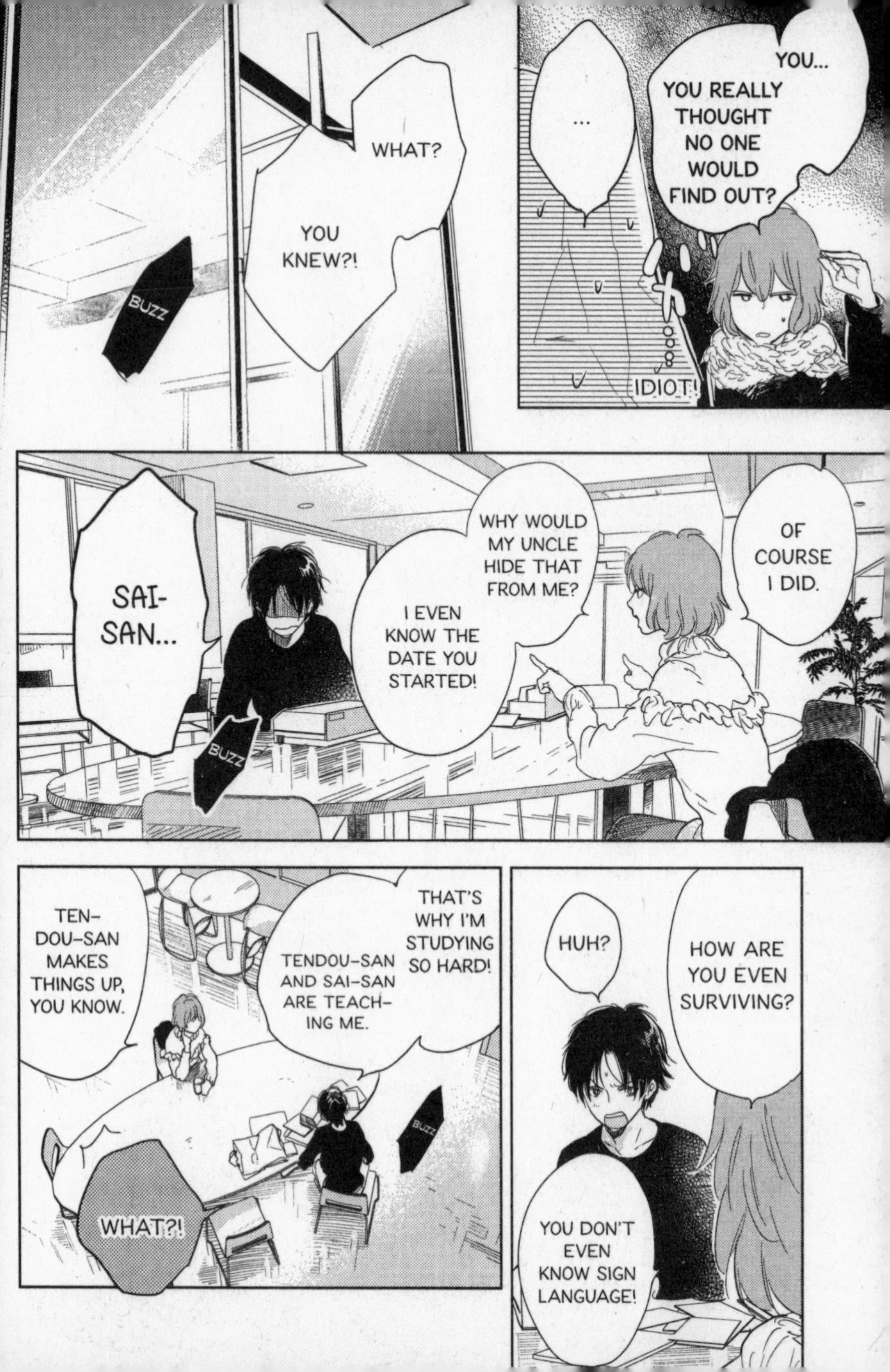
YOU... YOU REALLY THOUGHT NO ONE WOULD FIND OUT?
...
IDIOT!
WHAT?
YOU KNEW?!
BUZZ
OF COURSE I DID.
WHY WOULD MY UNCLE HIDE THAT FROM ME?
I EVEN KNOW THE DATE YOU STARTED!
SAI-SAN...
BUZZ
HOW ARE YOU EVEN SURVIVING?
HUH?
YOU DON'T EVEN KNOW SIGN LANGUAGE!
THAT'S WHY I'M STUDYING SO HARD!
TENDOU-SAN AND SAI-SAN ARE TEACH-ING ME.
TEN-DOU-SAN MAKES THINGS UP, YOU KNOW.
BUZZ
WHAT?!

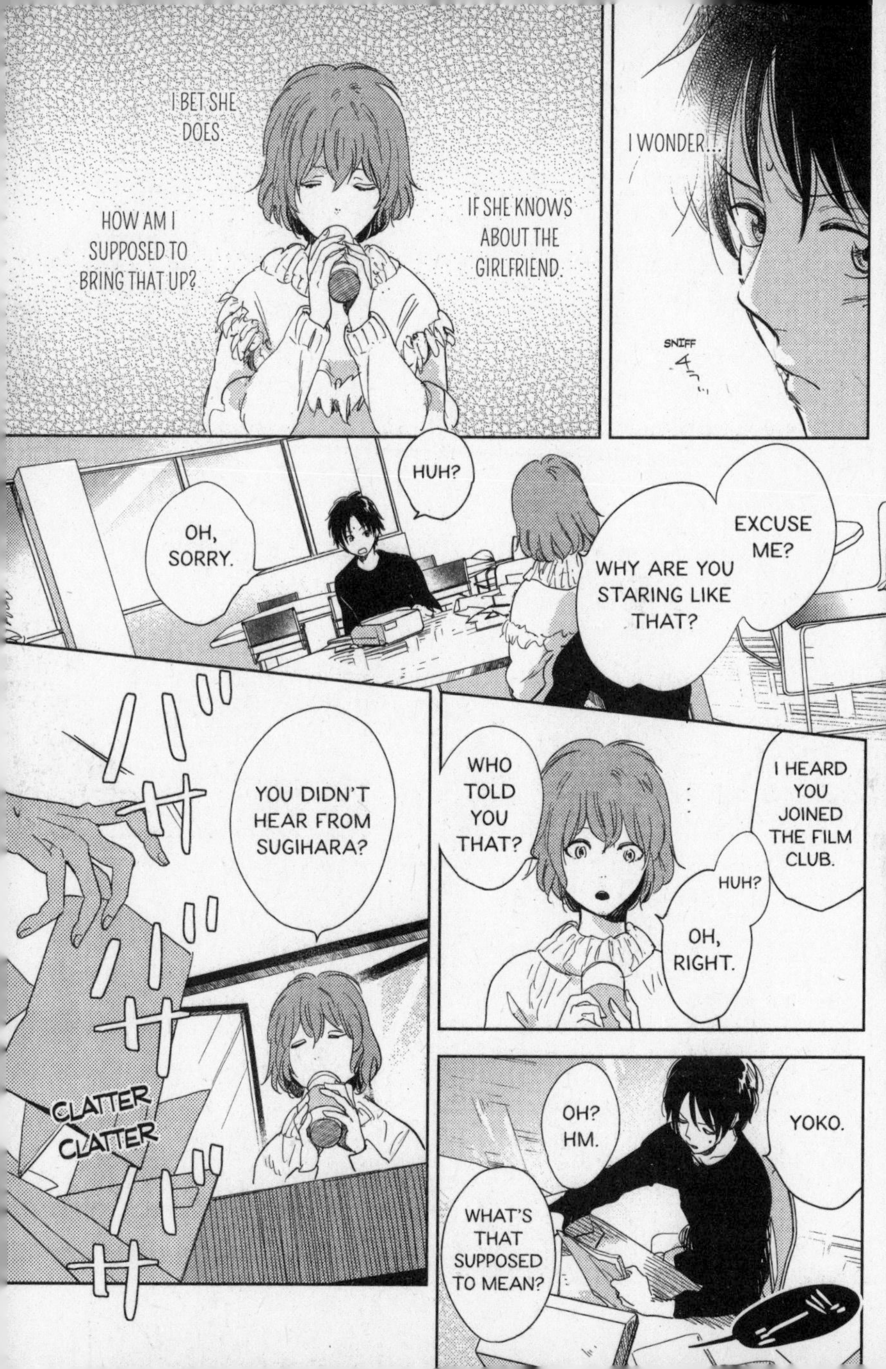

I WONDER...
SNIFF
IF SHE KNOWS ABOUT THE GIRLFRIEND.
I BET SHE DOES.
HOW AM I SUPPOSED TO BRING THAT UP?
EXCUSE ME?
WHY ARE YOU STARING LIKE THAT?
HUH?
OH, SORRY.
I HEARD YOU JOINED THE FILM CLUB.
HUH?
OH, RIGHT.
WHO TOLD YOU THAT?
YOKO.
OH? HM.
WHAT'S THAT SUPPOSED TO MEAN?
YOU DIDN'T HEAR FROM SUGIHARA?
CLATTER
CLATTER

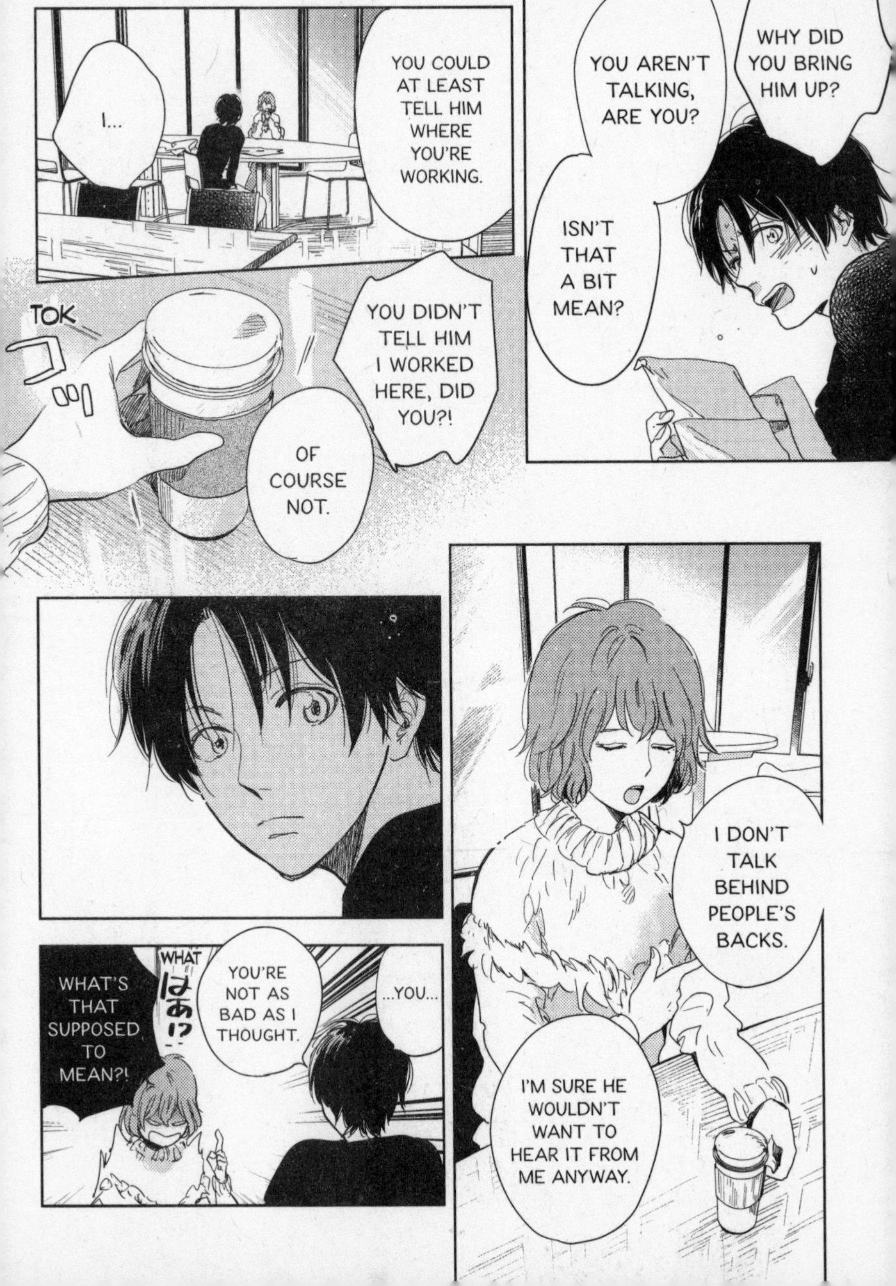
WHY DID YOU BRING HIM UP?
YOU AREN'T TALKING, ARE YOU?
ISN'T THAT A BIT MEAN?
YOU COULD AT LEAST TELL HIM WHERE YOU'RE WORKING.
I...
TOK
YOU DIDN'T TELL HIM I WORKED HERE, DID YOU?!
OF COURSE NOT.
I DON'T TALK BEHIND PEOPLE'S BACKS.
I'M SURE HE WOULDN'T WANT TO HEAR IT FROM ME ANYWAY.
...YOU...
YOU'RE NOT AS BAD AS I THOUGHT.
WHAT
はあ!?
WHAT'S THAT SUPPOSED TO MEAN?!

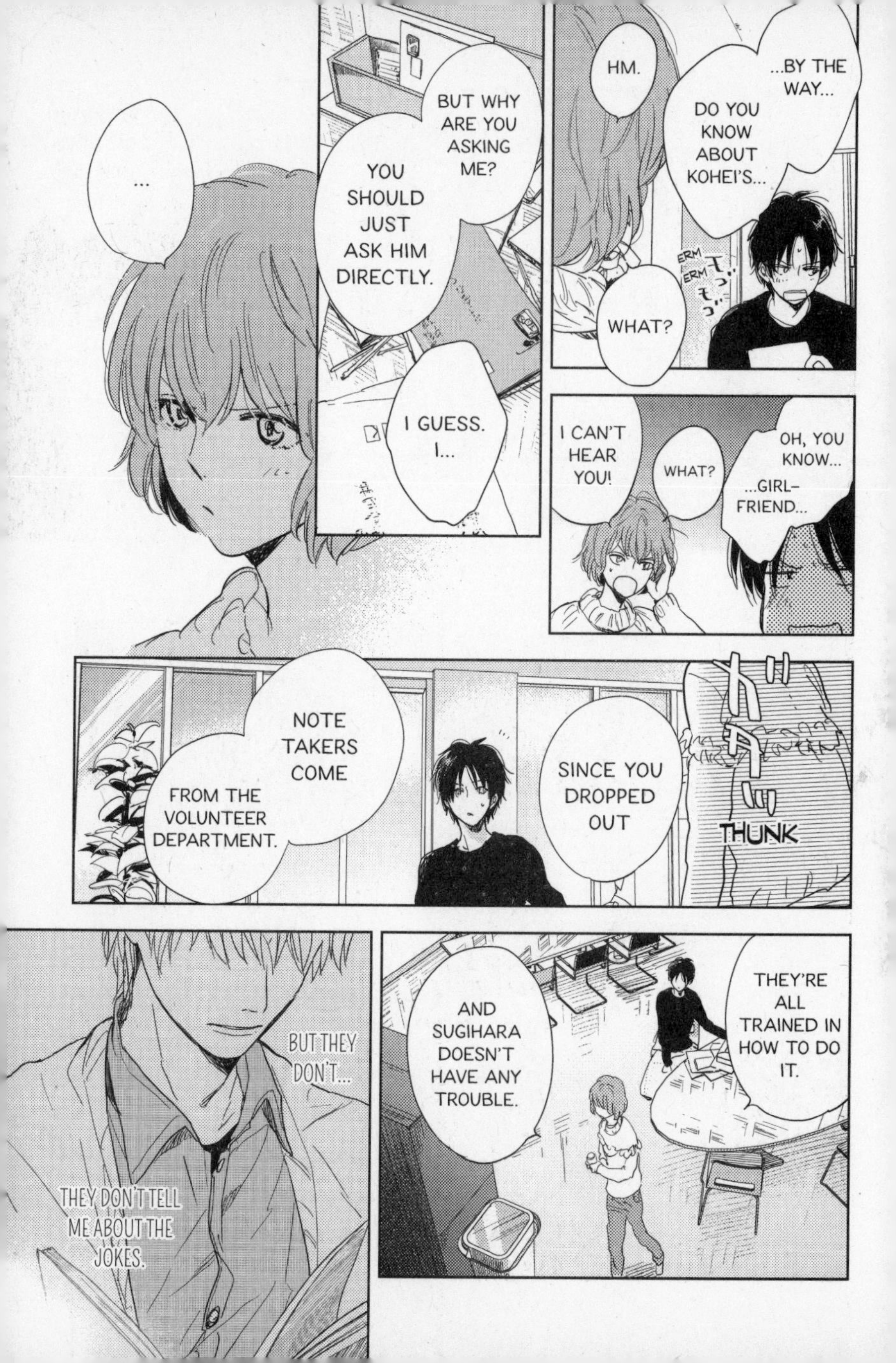
...BY THE WAY... DO YOU KNOW ABOUT KOHEI'S...
HM.
ERM ERM
WHAT?
OH, YOU KNOW... ...GIRL-FRIEND...
WHAT?
I CAN'T HEAR YOU!
BUT WHY ARE YOU ASKING ME?
YOU SHOULD JUST ASK HIM DIRECTLY.
I GUESS. I...
...
THUNK
SINCE YOU DROPPED OUT
NOTE TAKERS COME
FROM THE VOLUNTEER DEPARTMENT.
THEY'RE ALL TRAINED IN HOW TO DO IT.
AND SUGIHARA DOESN'T HAVE ANY TROUBLE.
BUT THEY DON'T...
THEY DON'T TELL ME ABOUT THE JOKES.

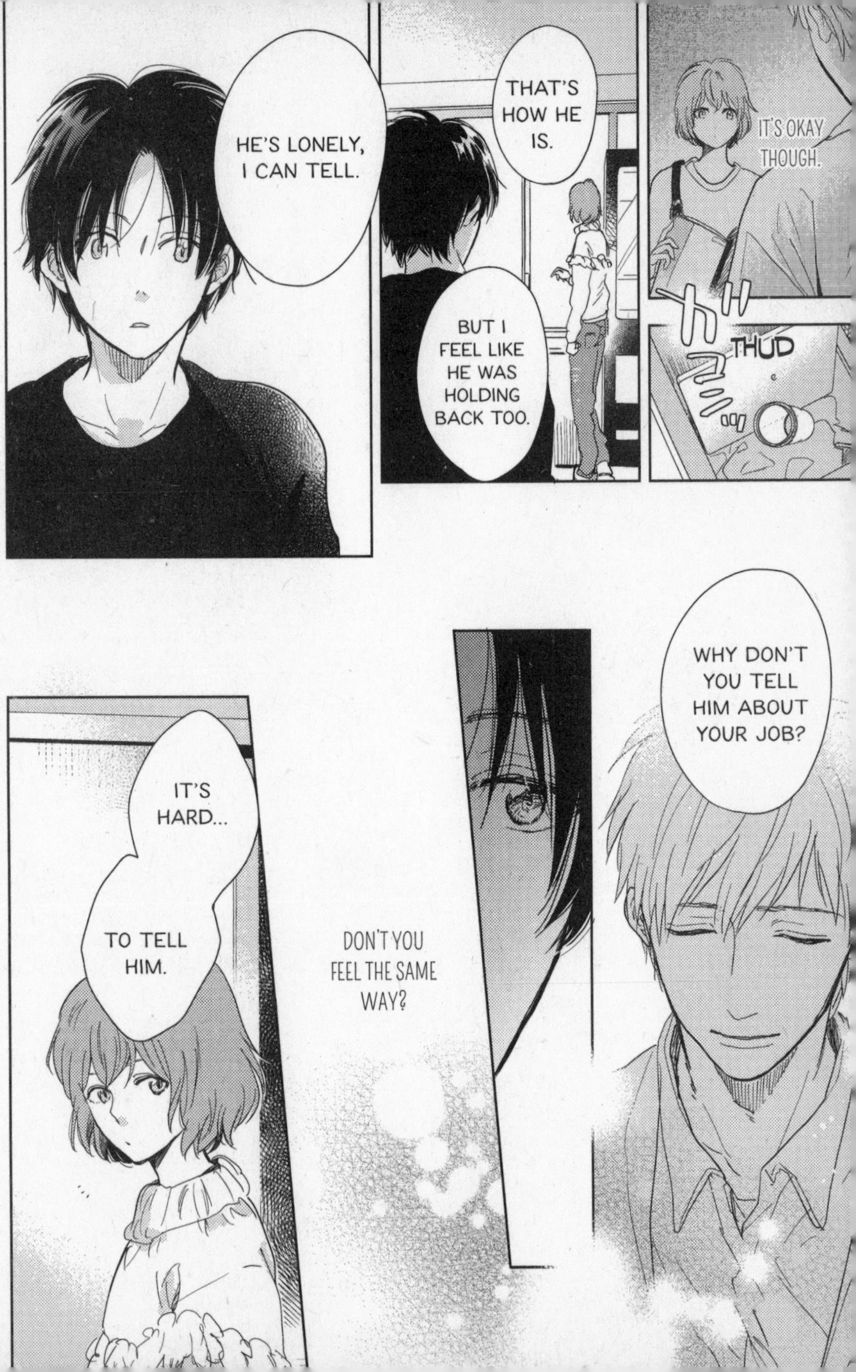
IT'S OKAY THOUGH.
THUD
THAT'S HOW HE IS.
BUT I FEEL LIKE HE WAS HOLDING BACK TOO.
HE'S LONELY, I CAN TELL.
WHY DON'T YOU TELL HIM ABOUT YOUR JOB?
DON'T YOU FEEL THE SAME WAY?
IT'S HARD...
TO TELL HIM.

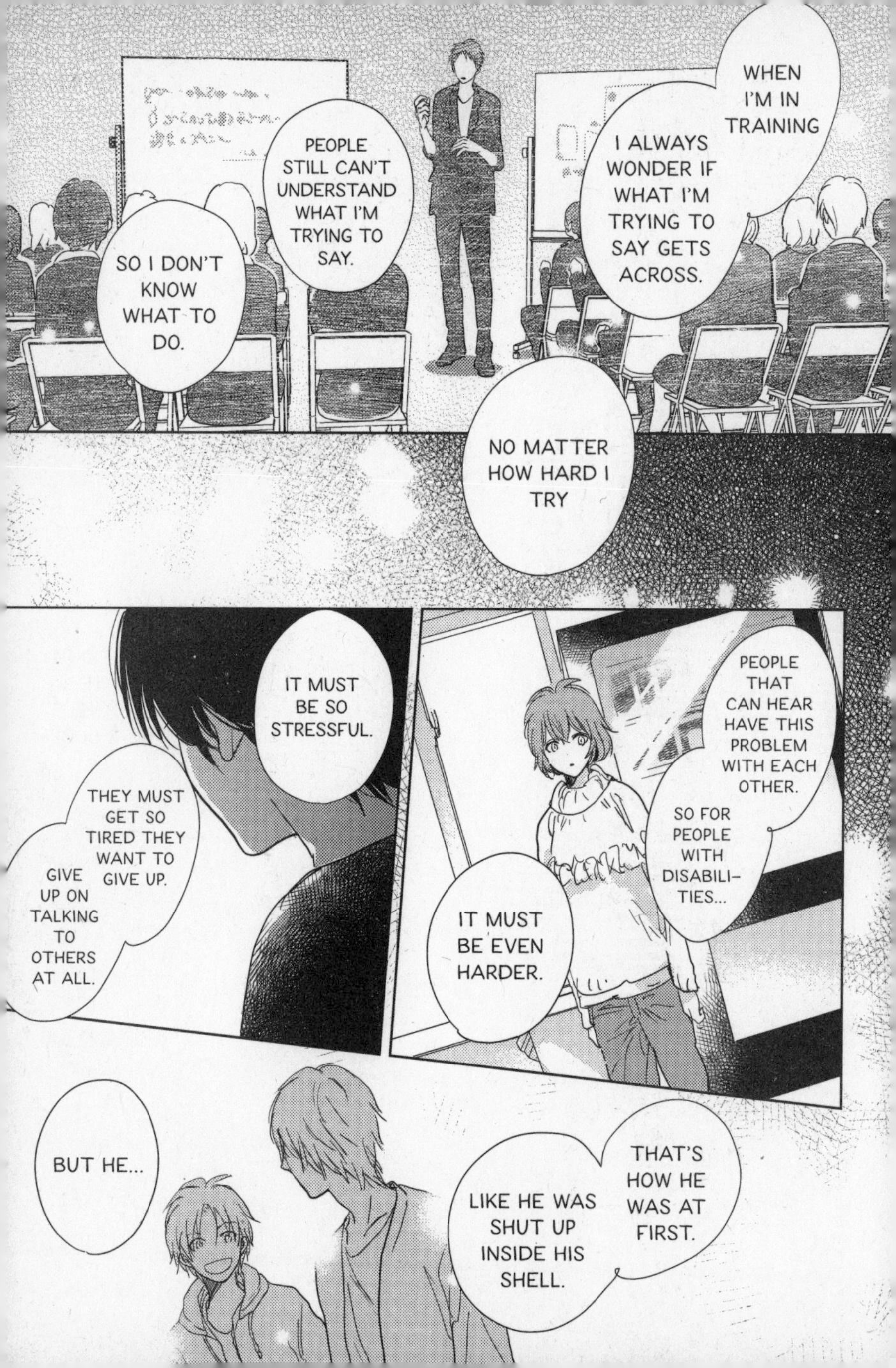
WHEN I'M IN TRAINING
I ALWAYS WONDER IF WHAT I'M TRYING TO SAY GETS ACROSS.
PEOPLE STILL CAN'T UNDERSTAND WHAT I'M TRYING TO SAY.
SO I DON'T KNOW WHAT TO DO.
NO MATTER HOW HARD I TRY
PEOPLE THAT CAN HEAR HAVE THIS PROBLEM WITH EACH OTHER.
SO FOR PEOPLE WITH DISABILI- TIES...
IT MUST BE EVEN HARDER.
IT MUST BE SO STRESSFUL.
THEY MUST GET SO TIRED THEY WANT TO GIVE UP.
GIVE UP ON TALKING TO OTHERS AT ALL.
THAT'S HOW HE WAS AT FIRST.
LIKE HE WAS SHUT UP INSIDE HIS SHELL.
BUT HE...

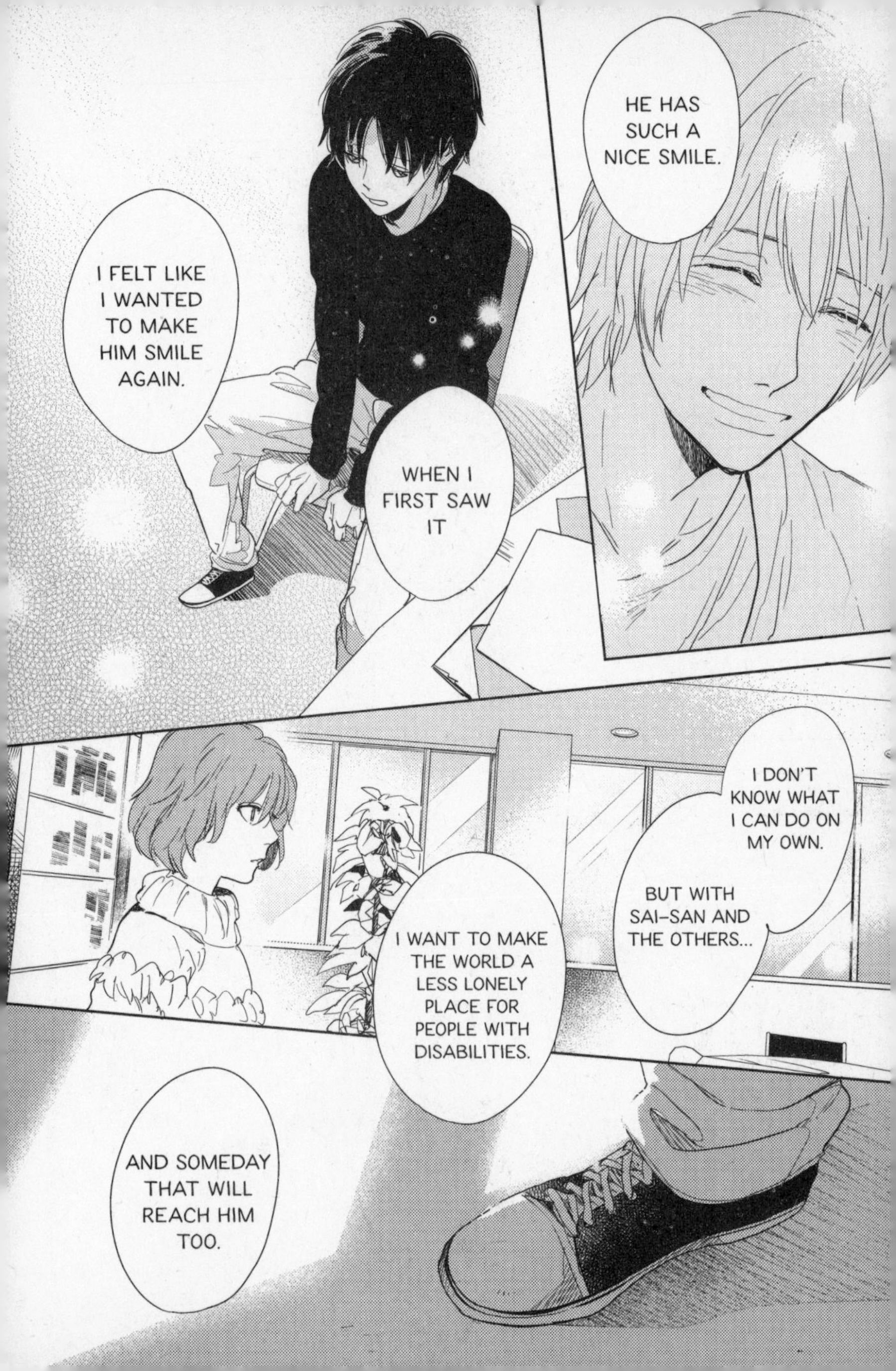
HE HAS SUCH A NICE SMILE.
WHEN I FIRST SAW IT
I FELT LIKE I WANTED TO MAKE HIM SMILE AGAIN.
I DON'T KNOW WHAT I CAN DO ON MY OWN.
BUT WITH SAI-SAN AND THE OTHERS...
I WANT TO MAKE THE WORLD A LESS LONELY PLACE FOR PEOPLE WITH DISABILITIES.
AND SOMEDAY THAT WILL REACH HIM TOO.

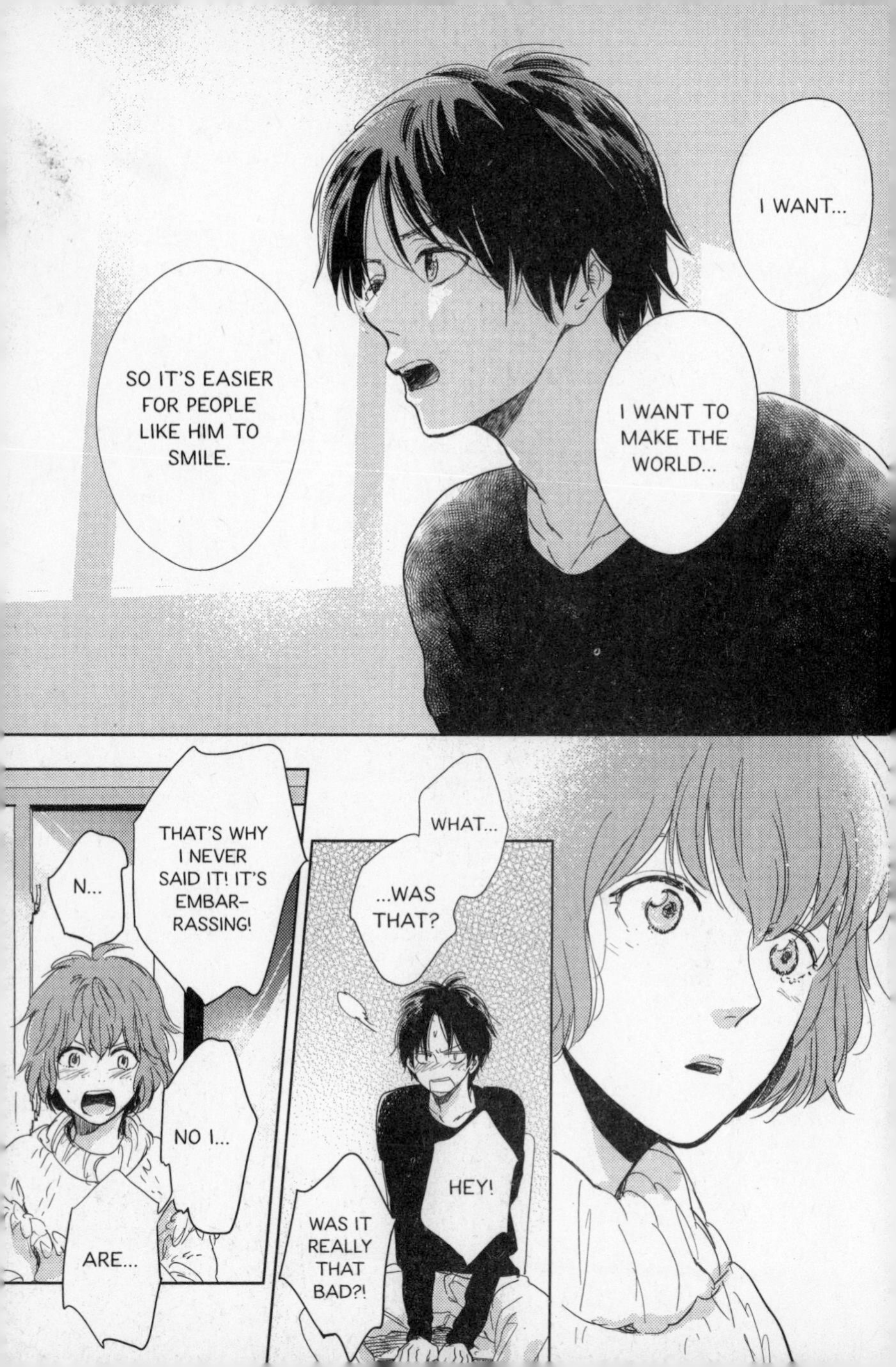
I WANT...
I WANT TO MAKE THE WORLD...
SO IT'S EASIER FOR PEOPLE LIKE HIM TO SMILE.
WHAT...
...WAS THAT?
HEY!
WAS IT REALLY THAT BAD?!
THAT'S WHY I NEVER SAID IT! IT'S EMBAR-RASSING!
N...
NO I...
ARE...

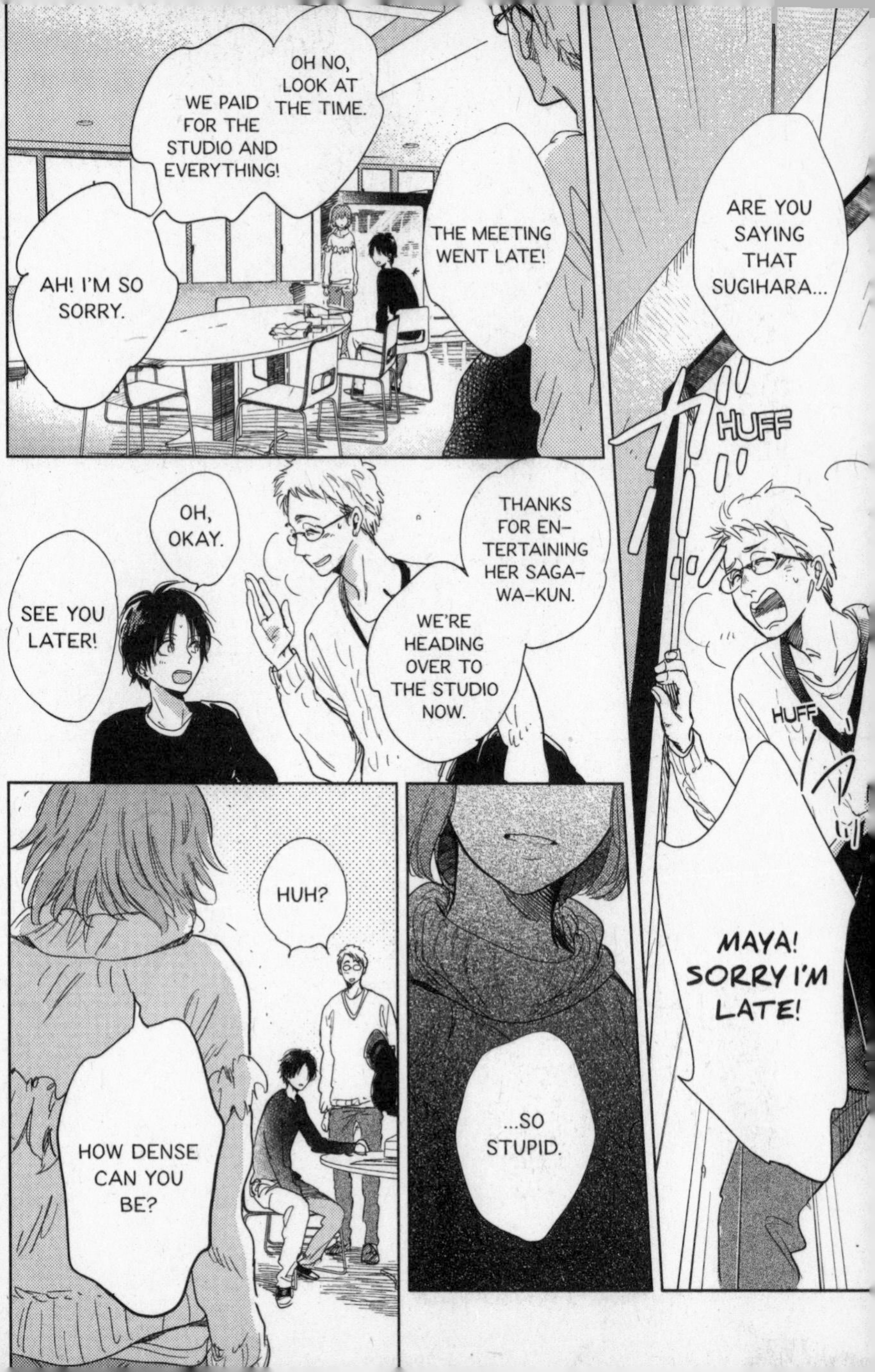
ARE YOU SAYING THAT SUGIHARA...
HUFF
HUFF
MAYA! SORRY I'M LATE!
THE MEETING WENT LATE!
OH NO, LOOK AT THE TIME.
WE PAID FOR THE STUDIO AND EVERYTHING!
AH! I'M SO SORRY.
THANKS FOR EN-TERTAINING HER SAGA-WA-KUN.
WE'RE HEADING OVER TO THE STUDIO NOW.
OH, OKAY.
SEE YOU LATER!
...SO STUPID.
HUH?
HOW DENSE CAN YOU BE?

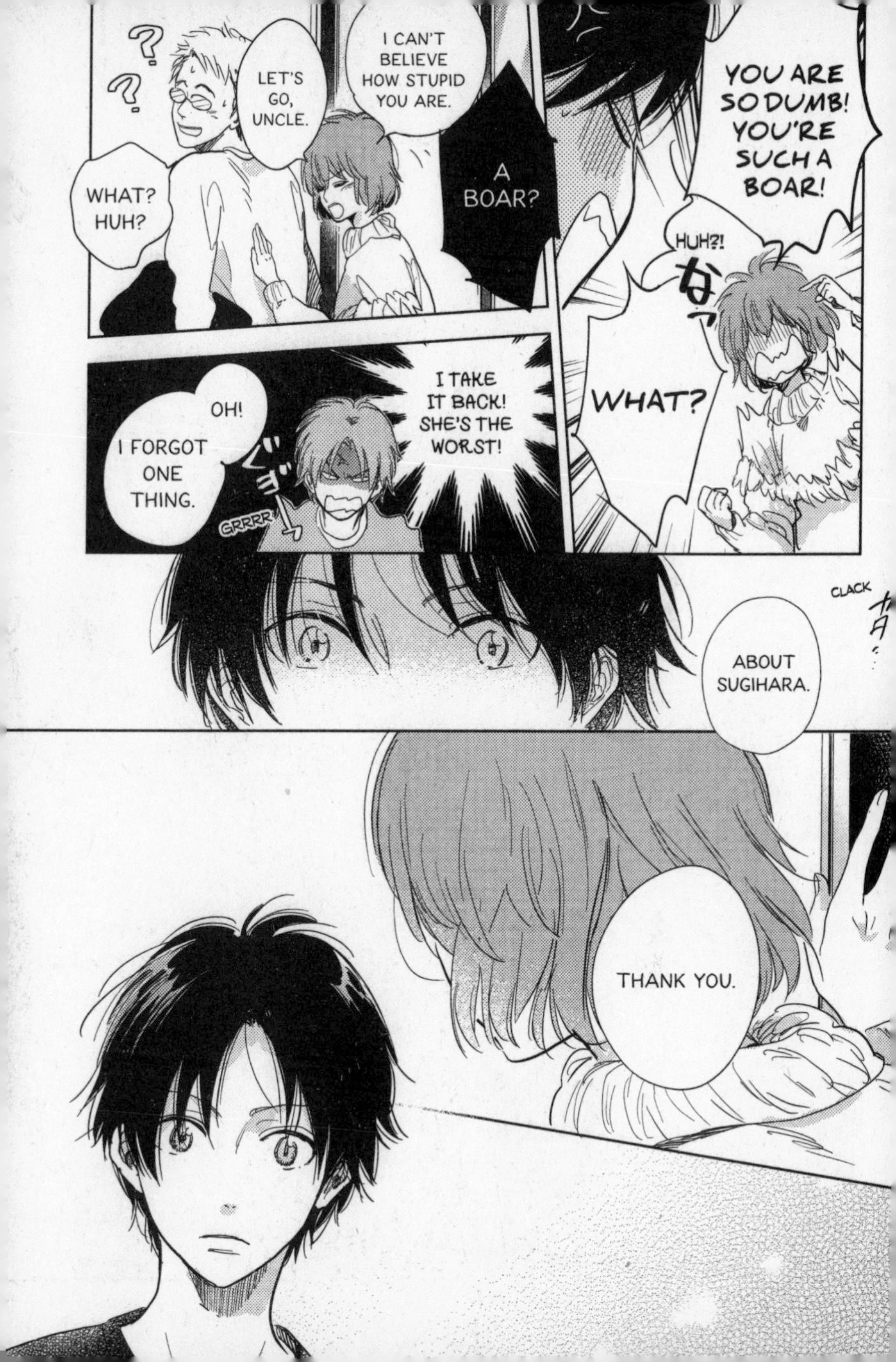
YOU ARE SO DUMB! YOU'RE SUCH A BOAR!
HUH?!
な
WHAT?
A BOAR?
I CAN'T BELIEVE HOW STUPID YOU ARE.
LET'S GO, UNCLE.
WHAT? HUH?
I TAKE IT BACK! SHE'S THE WORST!
GRRRR
OH!
I FORGOT ONE THING.
CLACK
ABOUT SUGIHARA.
THANK YOU.

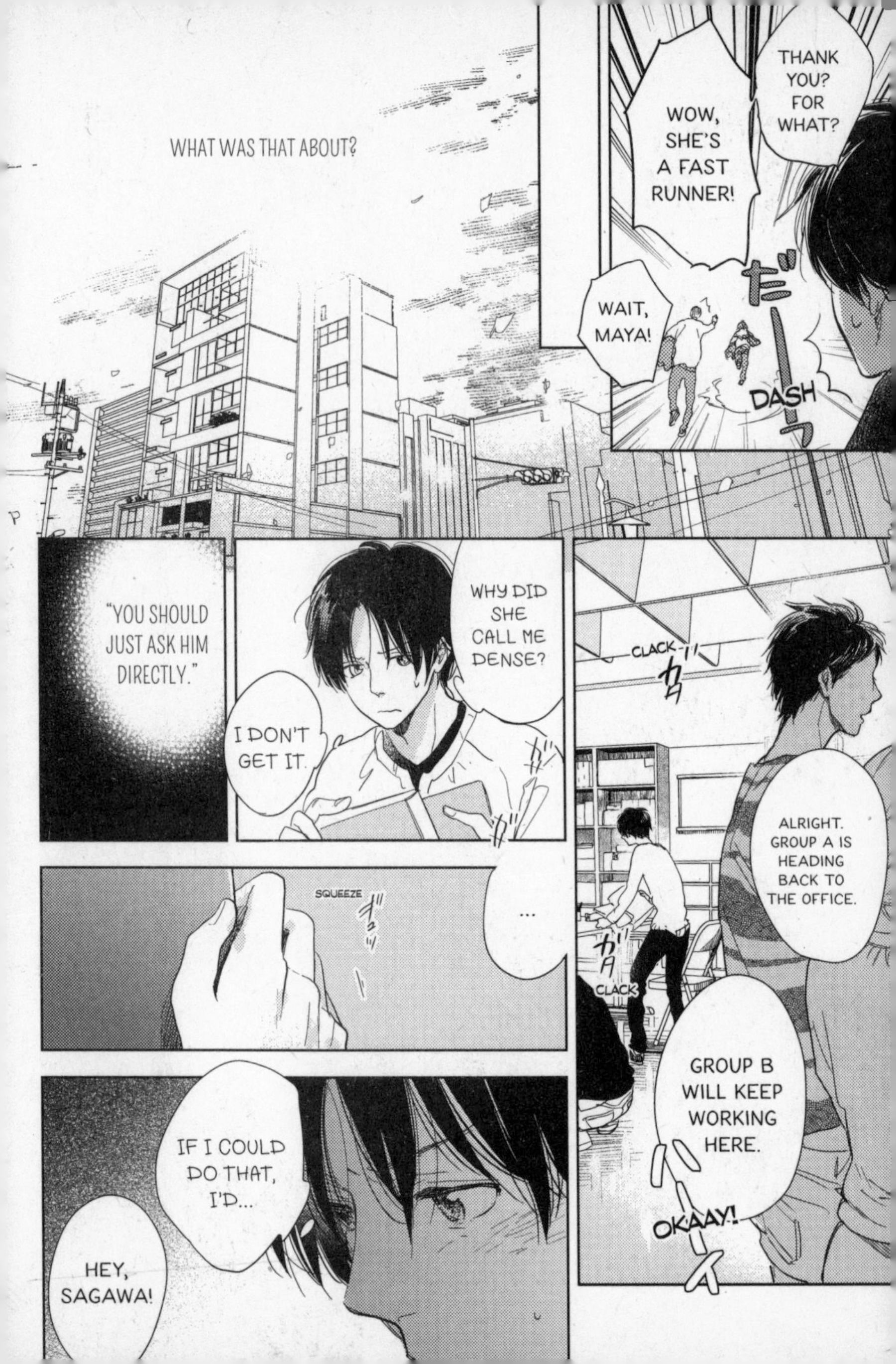
THANK YOU? FOR WHAT?
WOW, SHE'S A FAST RUNNER!
WAIT, MAYA!
DASH
WHAT WAS THAT ABOUT?
CLACK
ALRIGHT. GROUP A IS HEADING BACK TO THE OFFICE.
CLACK
GROUP B WILL KEEP WORKING HERE.
OKAAY!
WHY DID SHE CALL ME DENSE?
I DON'T GET IT.
"YOU SHOULD JUST ASK HIM DIRECTLY."
SQUEEZE
...
IF I COULD DO THAT, I'D...
HEY, SAGAWA!

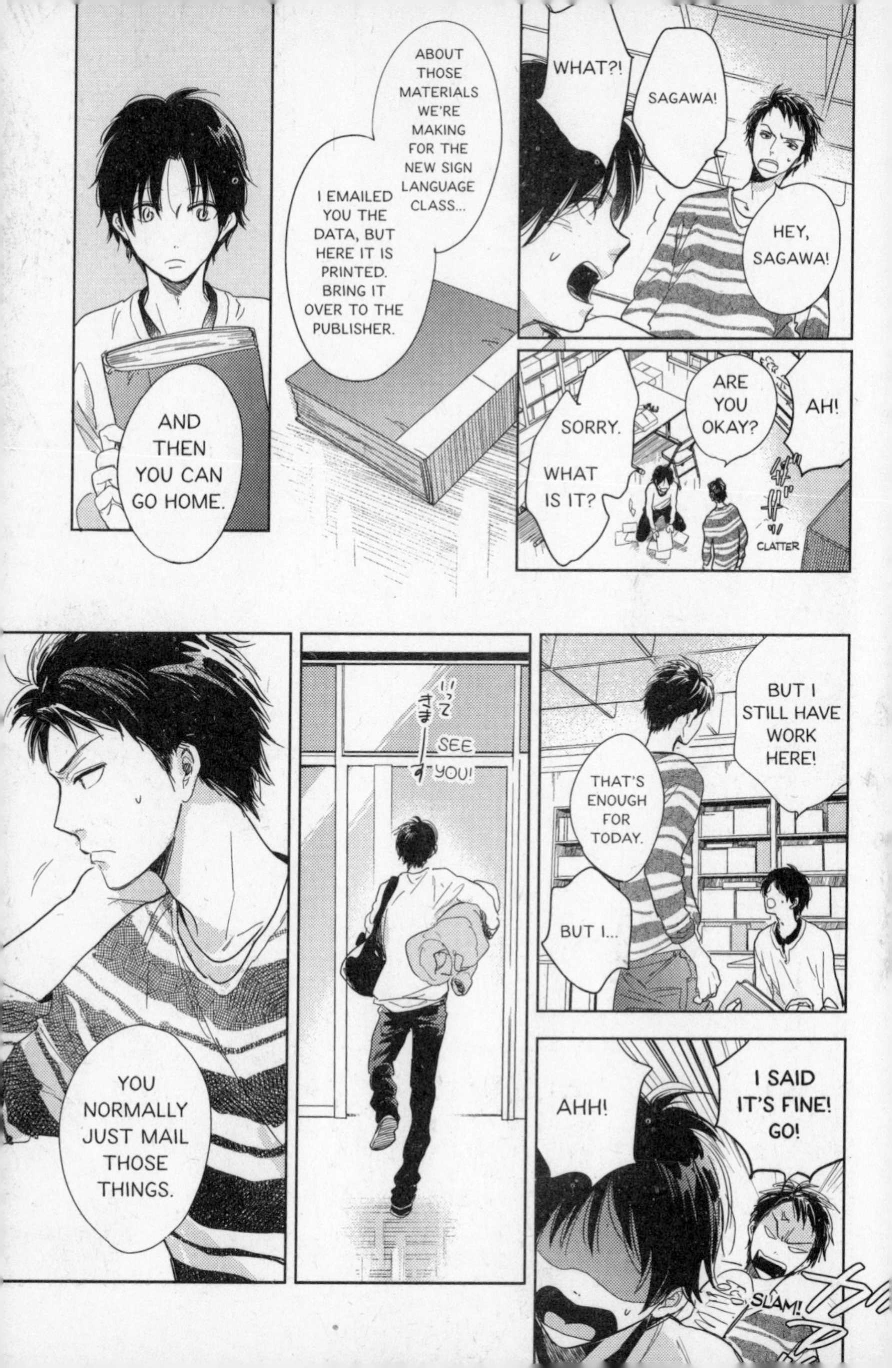
SAGAWA!
WHAT?!
HEY, SAGAWA!
AH!
CLATTER
ARE YOU OKAY?
SORRY.
WHAT IS IT?
ABOUT THOSE MATERIALS WE'RE MAKING FOR THE NEW SIGN LANGUAGE CLASS...
I EMAILED YOU THE DATA, BUT HERE IT IS PRINTED. BRING IT OVER TO THE PUBLISHER.
AND THEN YOU CAN GO HOME.
BUT I STILL HAVE WORK HERE!
THAT'S ENOUGH FOR TODAY.
BUT I...
I SAID IT'S FINE! GO!
AHH!
SLAM!
いってきまーす
SEE YOU!
YOU NORMALLY JUST MAIL THOSE THINGS.

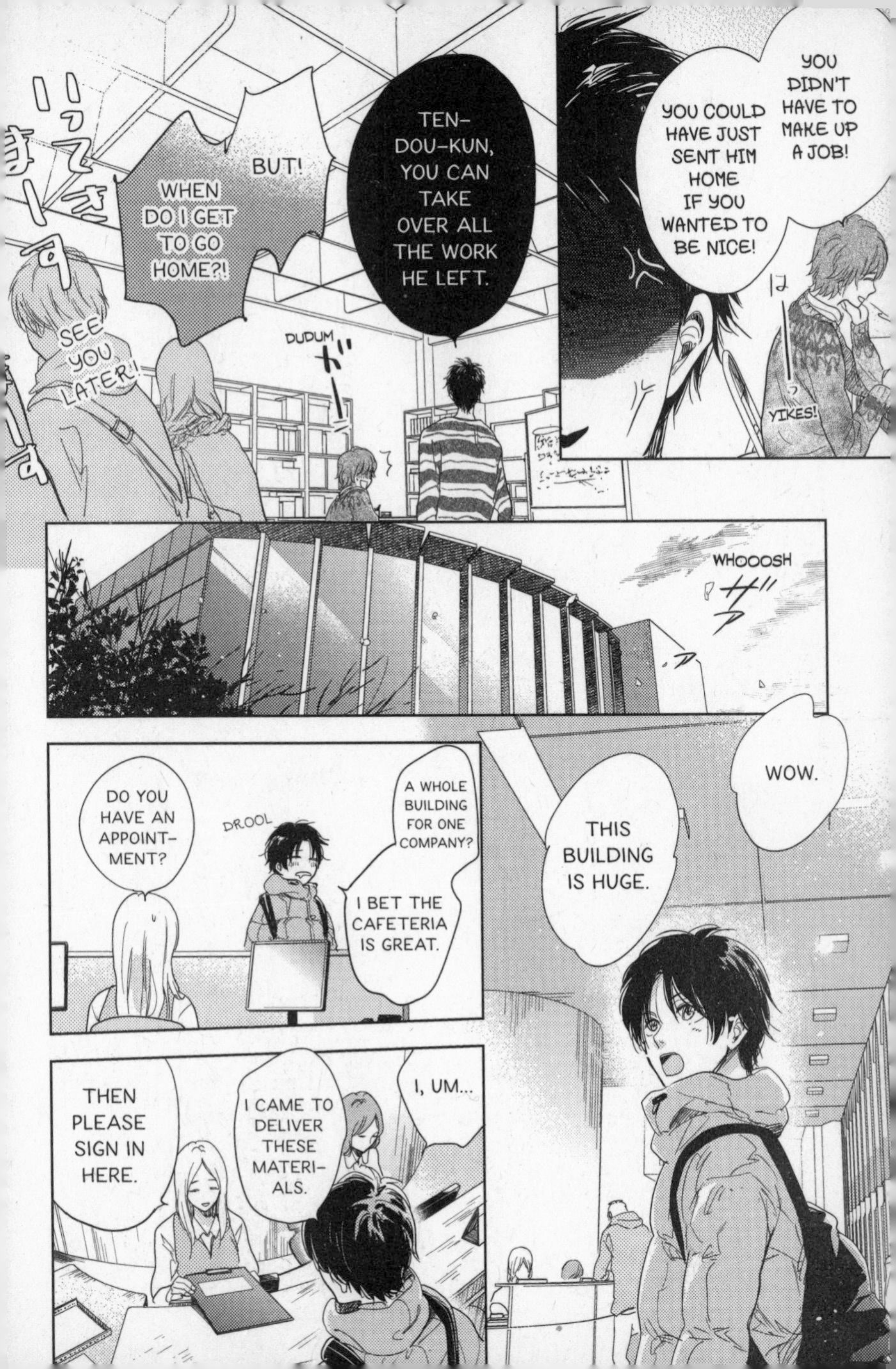
YOU DIDN'T HAVE TO MAKE UP A JOB!
YOU COULD HAVE JUST SENT HIM HOME IF YOU WANTED TO BE NICE!
YIKES!
TEN-DOU-KUN, YOU CAN TAKE OVER ALL THE WORK HE LEFT.
DUDUM
BUT!
WHEN DO I GET TO GO HOME?!
SEE YOU LATER!
WHOOOSH
WOW.
THIS BUILDING IS HUGE.
A WHOLE BUILDING FOR ONE COMPANY?
DROOL
I BET THE CAFETERIA IS GREAT.
DO YOU HAVE AN APPOINTMENT?
I, UM...
I CAME TO DELIVER THESE MATERIALS.
THEN PLEASE SIGN IN HERE.

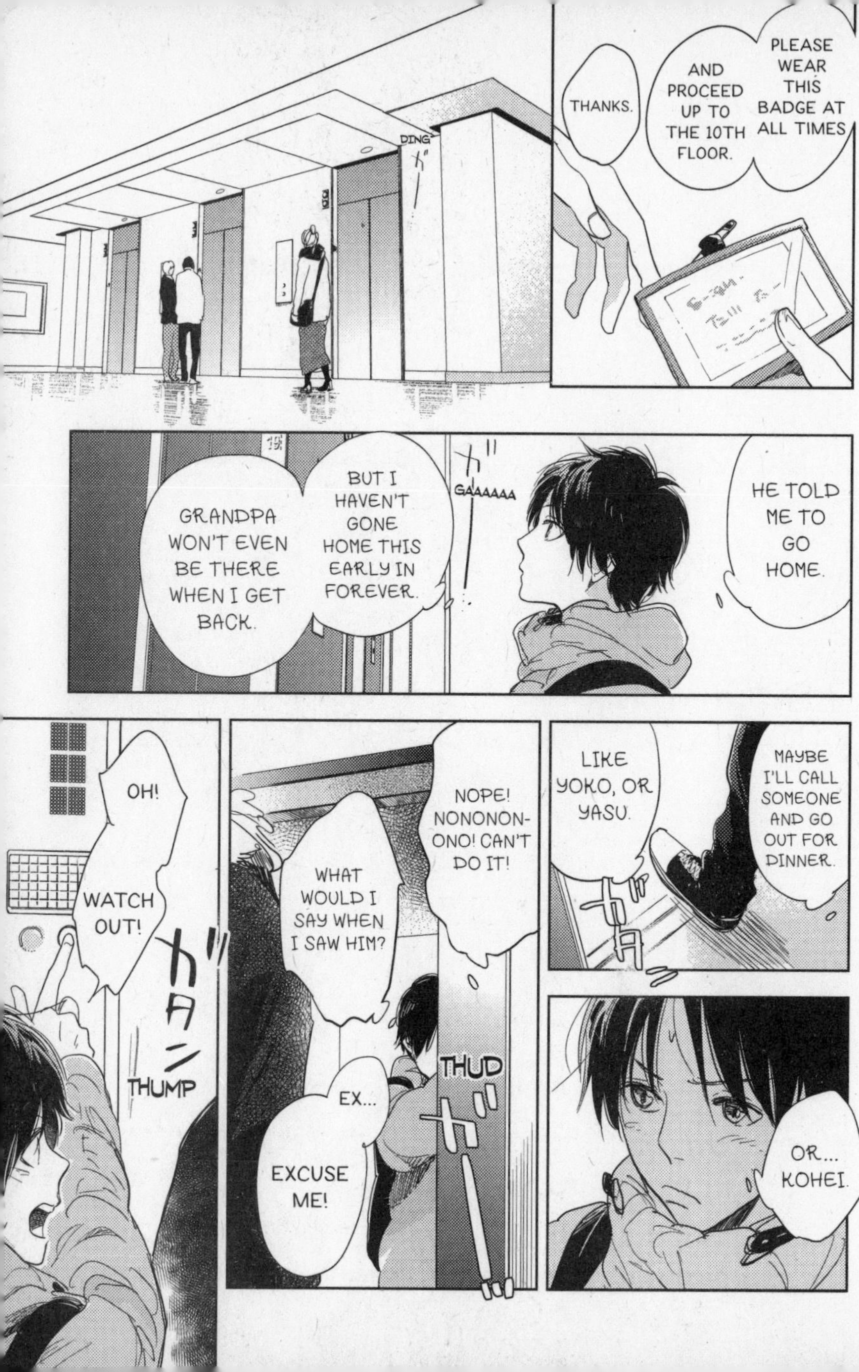
PLEASE WEAR THIS BADGE AT ALL TIMES
AND PROCEED UP TO THE 10TH FLOOR.
THANKS.
DING
HE TOLD ME TO GO HOME.
GAAAAAA
BUT I HAVEN'T GONE HOME THIS EARLY IN FOREVER.
GRANDPA WON'T EVEN BE THERE WHEN I GET BACK.
MAYBE I'LL CALL SOMEONE AND GO OUT FOR DINNER.
LIKE YOKO, OR YASU.
OR... KOHEI.
NOPE! NONONON-ONO! CAN'T DO IT!
WHAT WOULD I SAY WHEN I SAW HIM?
THUD
EX...
EXCUSE ME!
OH!
WATCH OUT!
THUMP

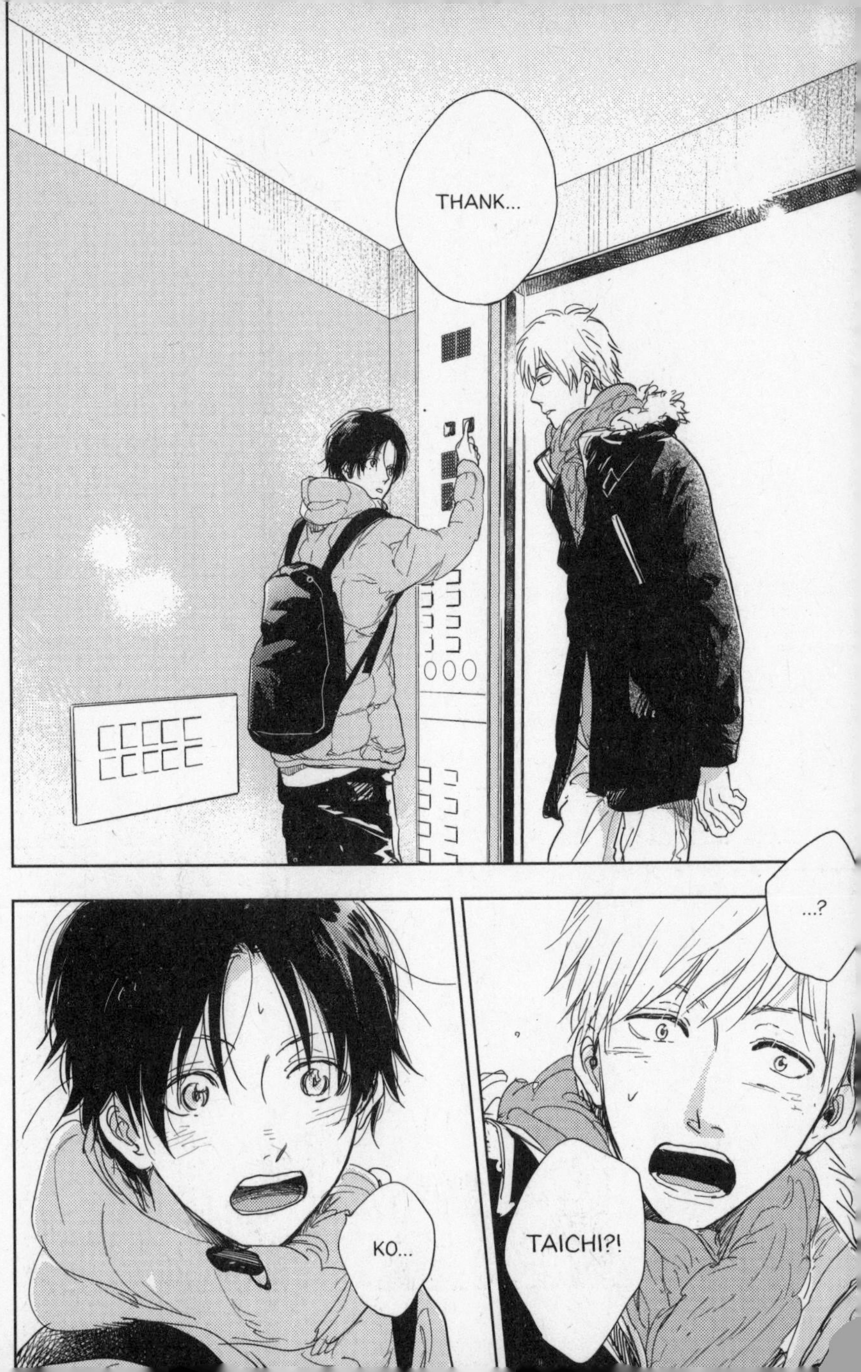
THANK...
...?
TAICHI?!
KO...

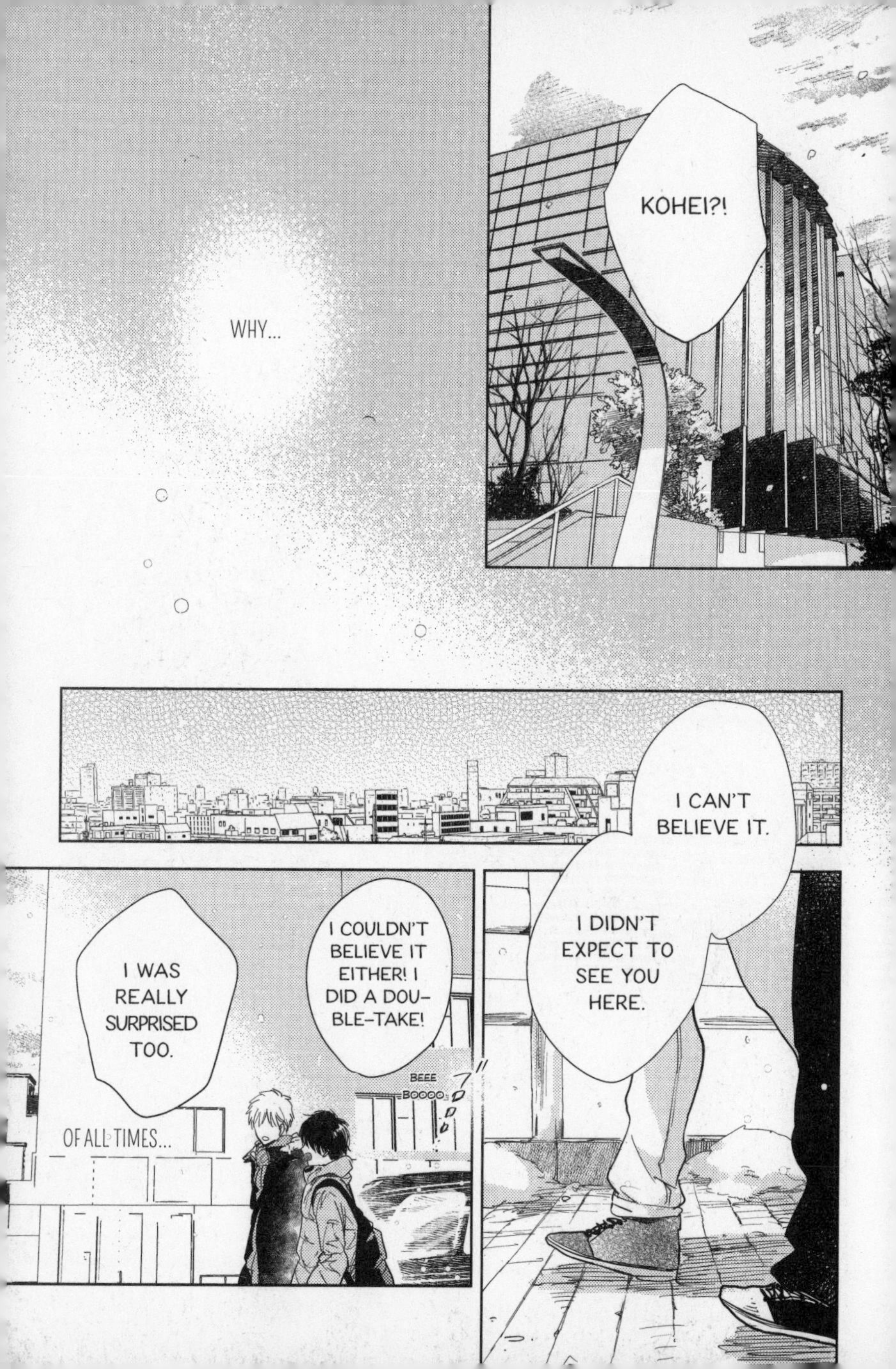
KOHEI?!
WHY...
I CAN'T BELIEVE IT.
I DIDN'T EXPECT TO SEE YOU HERE.
I COULDN'T BELIEVE IT EITHER! I DID A DOU-BLE-TAKE!
I WAS REALLY SURPRISED TOO.
BEEE BOOOO
OF ALL TIMES...

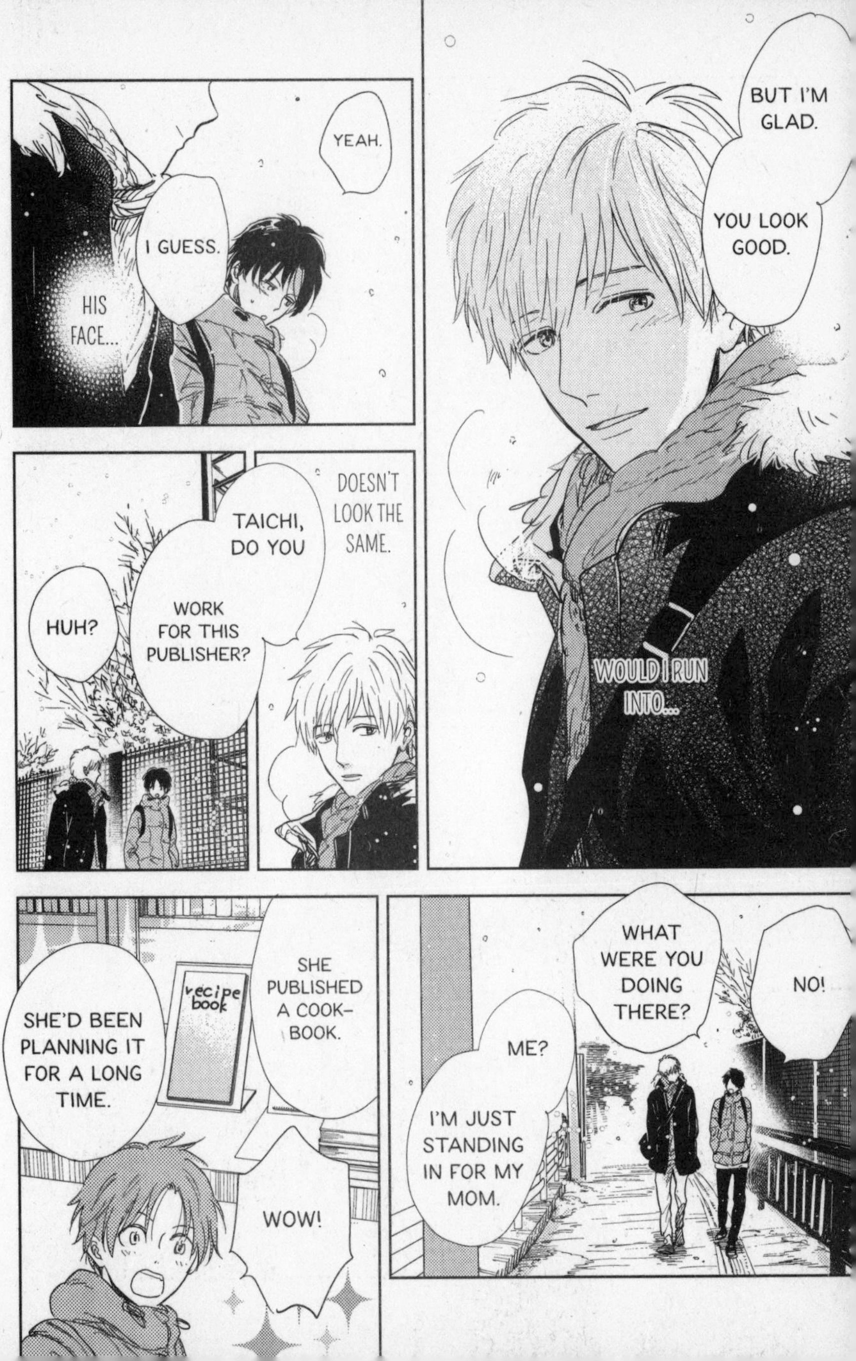
BUT I'M GLAD.
YOU LOOK GOOD.
WOULD I RUN INTO...
YEAH.
I GUESS.
HIS FACE...
DOESN'T LOOK THE SAME.
TAICHI, DO YOU
WORK FOR THIS PUBLISHER?
HUH?
NO!
WHAT WERE YOU DOING THERE?
ME?
I'M JUST STANDING IN FOR MY MOM.
SHE PUBLISHED A COOK-BOOK.
SHE'D BEEN PLANNING IT FOR A LONG TIME.
recipe book
WOW!

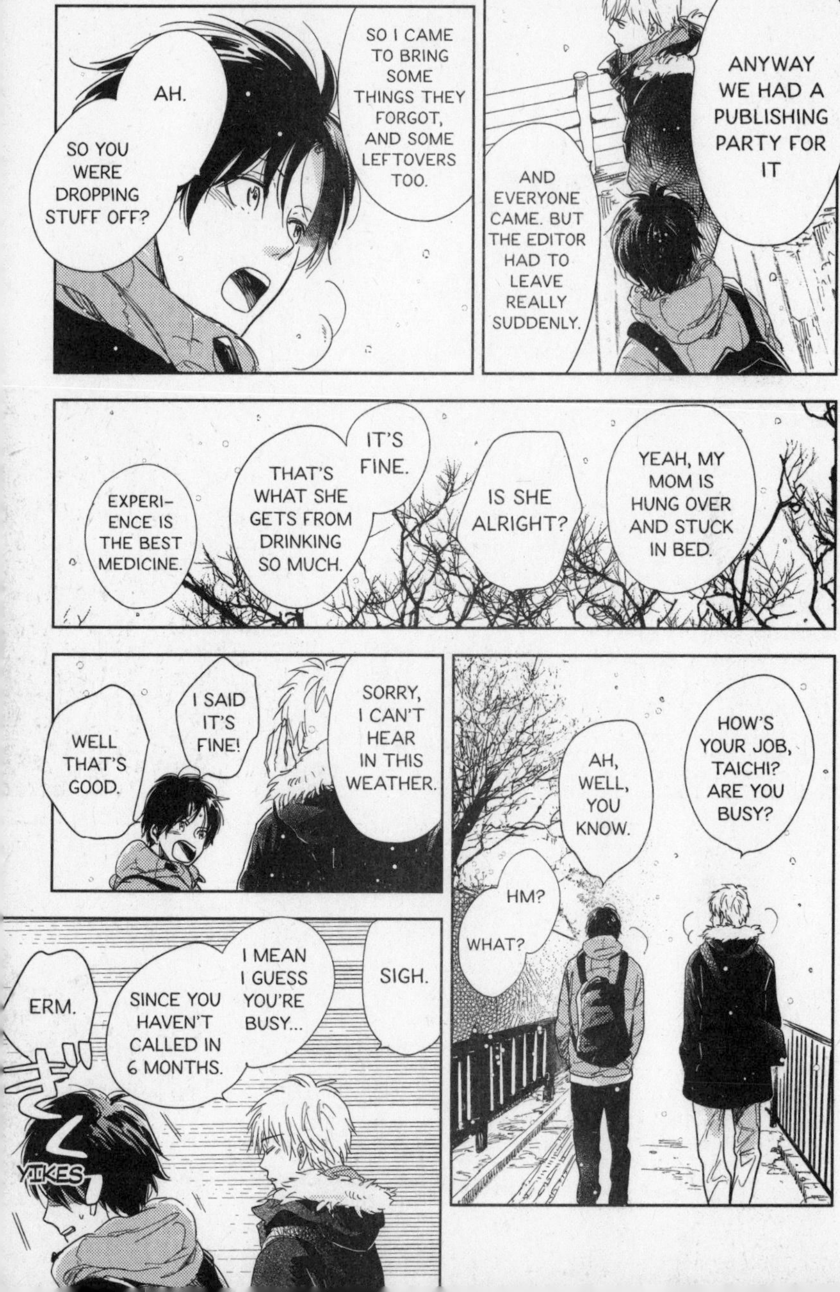
ANYWAY WE HAD A PUBLISHING PARTY FOR IT
AND EVERYONE CAME. BUT THE EDITOR HAD TO LEAVE REALLY SUDDENLY.
SO I CAME TO BRING SOME THINGS THEY FORGOT, AND SOME LEFTOVERS TOO.
AH.
SO YOU WERE DROPPING STUFF OFF?
YEAH, MY MOM IS HUNG OVER AND STUCK IN BED.
IS SHE ALRIGHT?
IT'S FINE.
THAT'S WHAT SHE GETS FROM DRINKING SO MUCH.
EXPERI-ENCE IS THE BEST MEDICINE.
HOW'S YOUR JOB, TAICHI? ARE YOU BUSY?
AH, WELL, YOU KNOW.
HM?
WHAT?
SORRY, I CAN'T HEAR IN THIS WEATHER.
I SAID IT'S FINE!
WELL THAT'S GOOD.
SIGH.
I MEAN I GUESS YOU'RE BUSY...
SINCE YOU HAVEN'T CALLED IN 6 MONTHS.
ERM.
YIKES

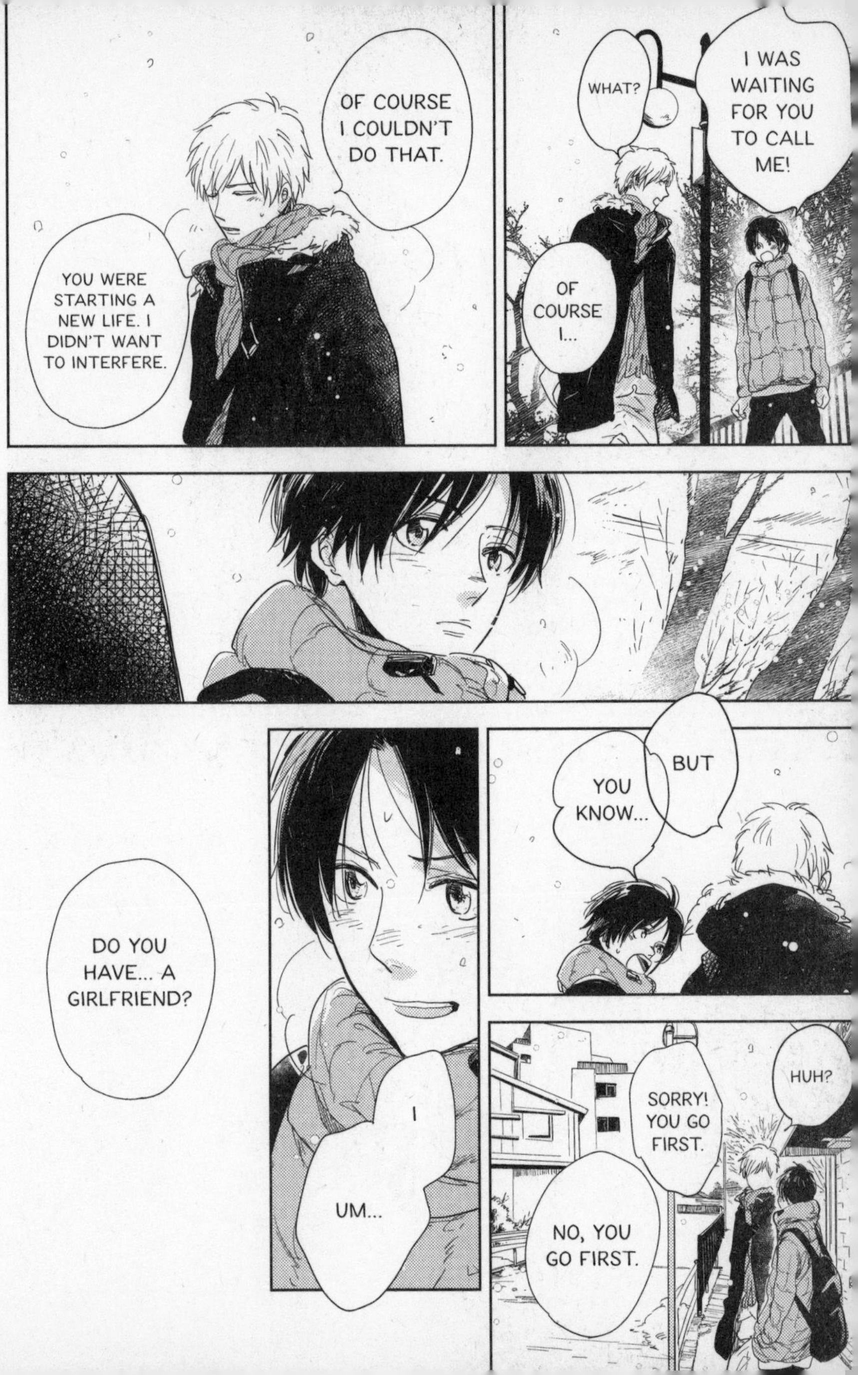
I WAS WAITING FOR YOU TO CALL ME!
WHAT?
OF COURSE I...
OF COURSE I COULDN'T DO THAT.
YOU WERE STARTING A NEW LIFE. I DIDN'T WANT TO INTERFERE.
BUT
YOU KNOW...
HUH?
SORRY! YOU GO FIRST.
NO, YOU GO FIRST.
I
UM...
DO YOU HAVE... A GIRLFRIEND?

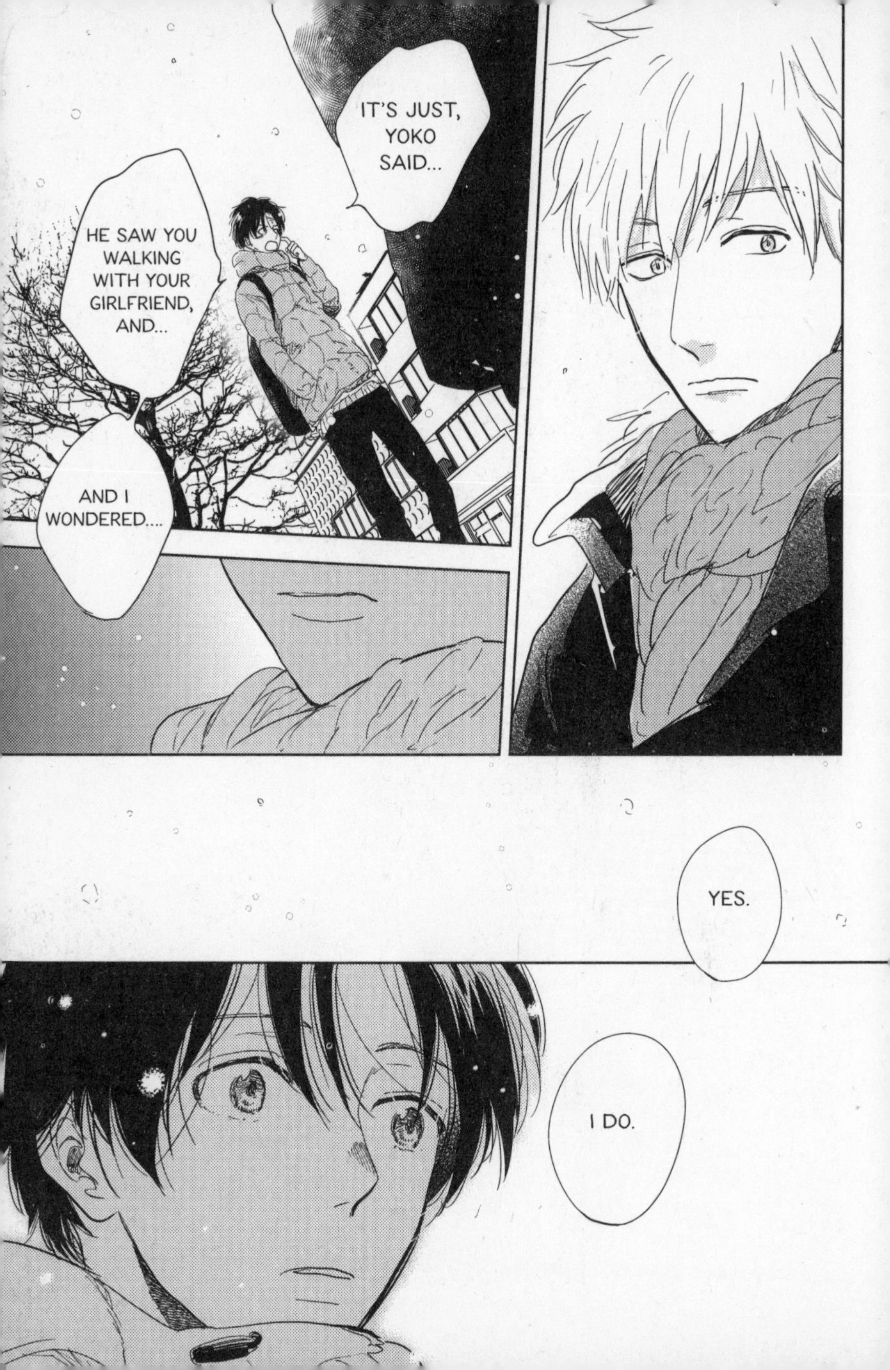
IT'S JUST, YOKO SAID...
HE SAW YOU WALKING WITH YOUR GIRLFRIEND, AND...
AND I WONDERED....
YES.
I DO.

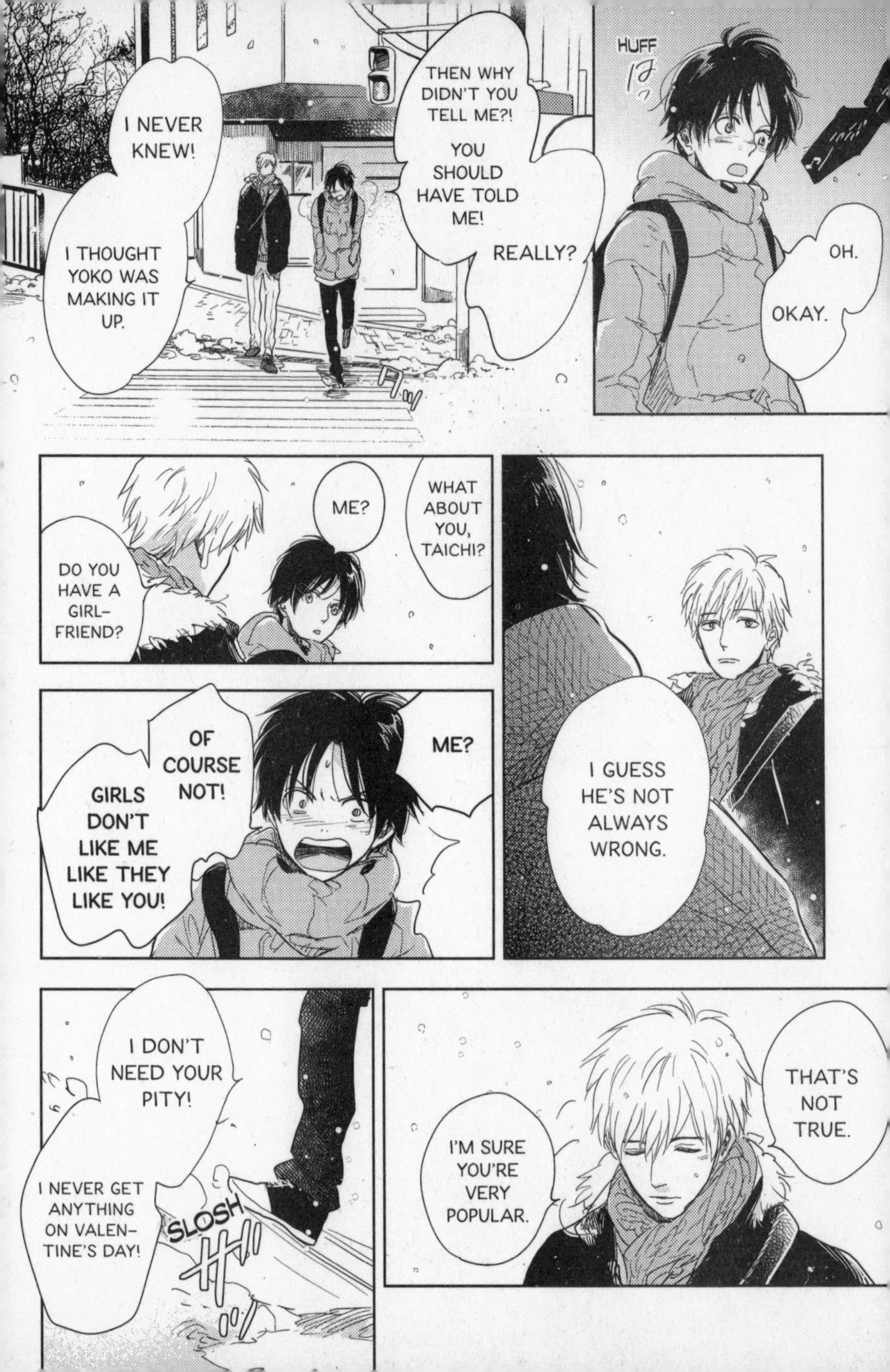
HUFF
OH.
OKAY.
THEN WHY DIDN'T YOU TELL ME?!
YOU SHOULD HAVE TOLD ME!
REALLY?
I NEVER KNEW!
I THOUGHT YOKO WAS MAKING IT UP.
I GUESS HE'S NOT ALWAYS WRONG.
WHAT ABOUT YOU, TAICHI?
ME?
DO YOU HAVE A GIRL-FRIEND?
ME?
OF COURSE NOT!
GIRLS DON'T LIKE ME LIKE THEY LIKE YOU!
THAT'S NOT TRUE.
I'M SURE YOU'RE VERY POPULAR.
I DON'T NEED YOUR PITY!
I NEVER GET ANYTHING ON VALEN-TINE'S DAY!
SLOSH

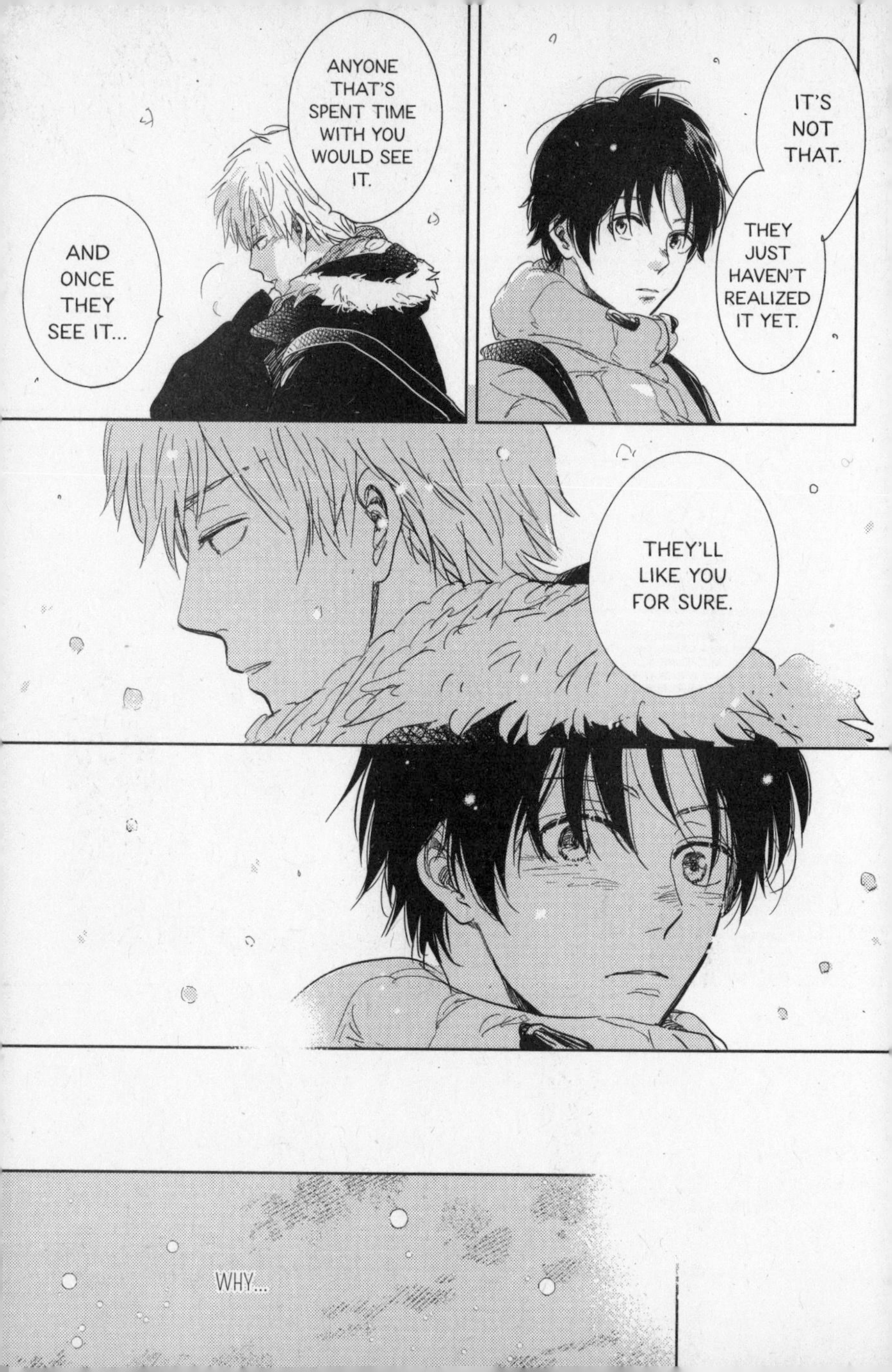
IT'S NOT THAT.
THEY JUST HAVEN'T REALIZED IT YET.
ANYONE THAT'S SPENT TIME WITH YOU WOULD SEE IT.
AND ONCE THEY SEE IT...
THEY'LL LIKE YOU FOR SURE.
WHY...

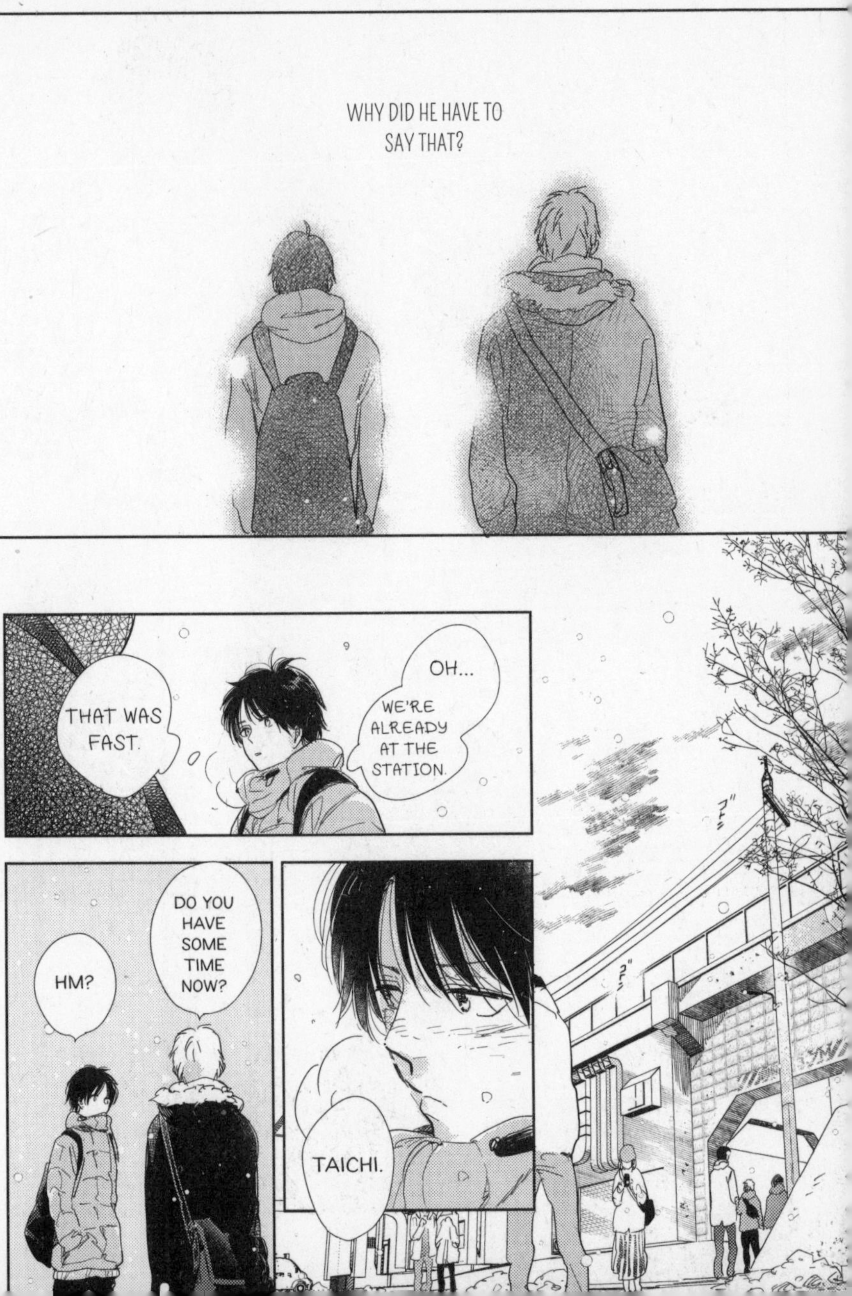
WHY DID HE HAVE TO SAY THAT?
OH...
WE'RE ALREADY AT THE STATION.
THAT WAS FAST.
TAICHI.
DO YOU HAVE SOME TIME NOW?
HM?

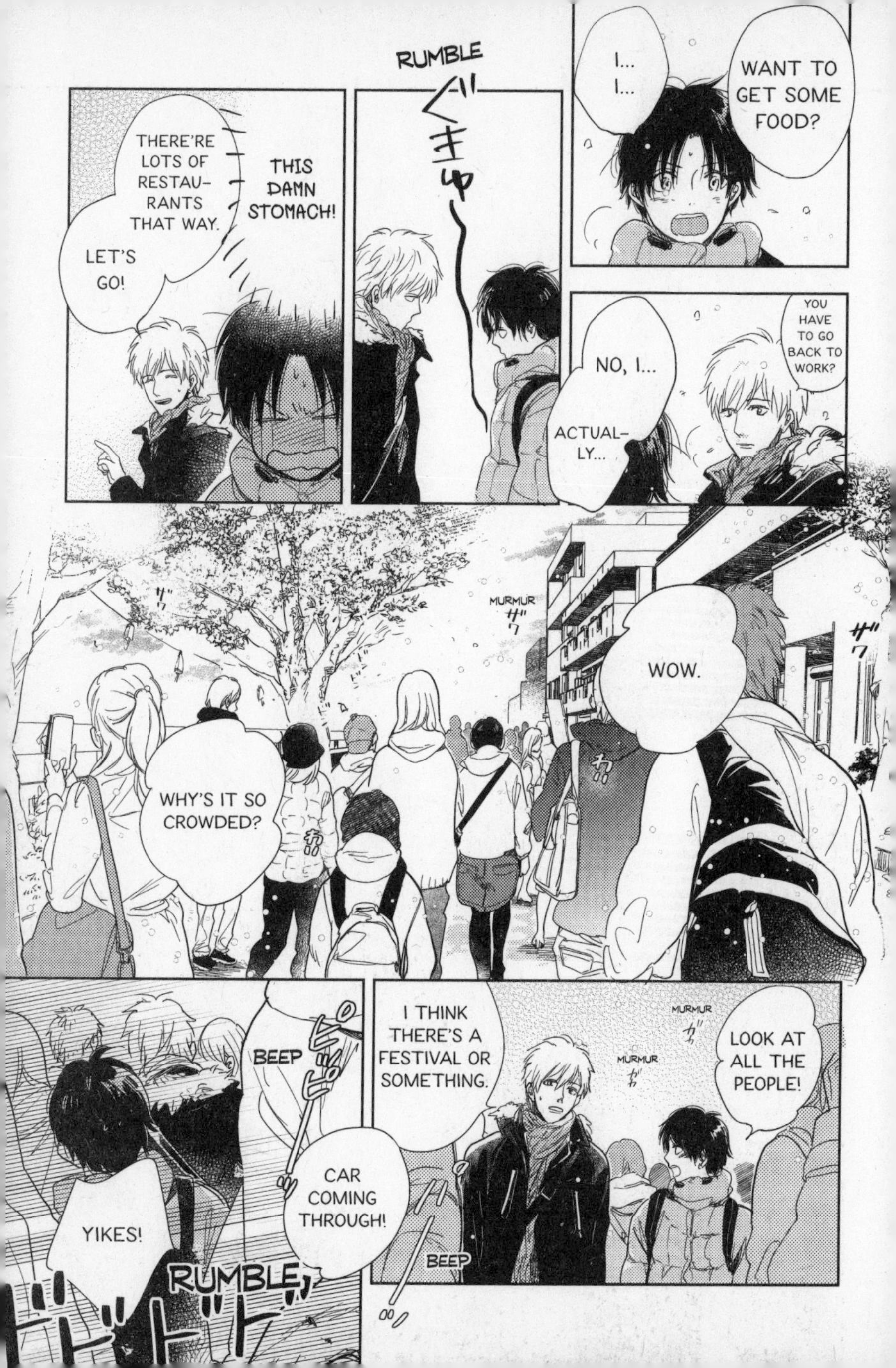
WANT TO GET SOME FOOD?
I... I...
YOU HAVE TO GO BACK TO WORK?
NO, I...
ACTUAL-LY...
RUMBLE
THIS DAMN STOMACH!
THERE'RE LOTS OF RESTAU-RANTS THAT WAY.
LET'S GO!
WOW.
MURMUR
WHY'S IT SO CROWDED?
LOOK AT ALL THE PEOPLE!
MURMUR
MURMUR
I THINK THERE'S A FESTIVAL OR SOMETHING.
BEEP
CAR COMING THROUGH!
BEEP
YIKES!
RUMBLE

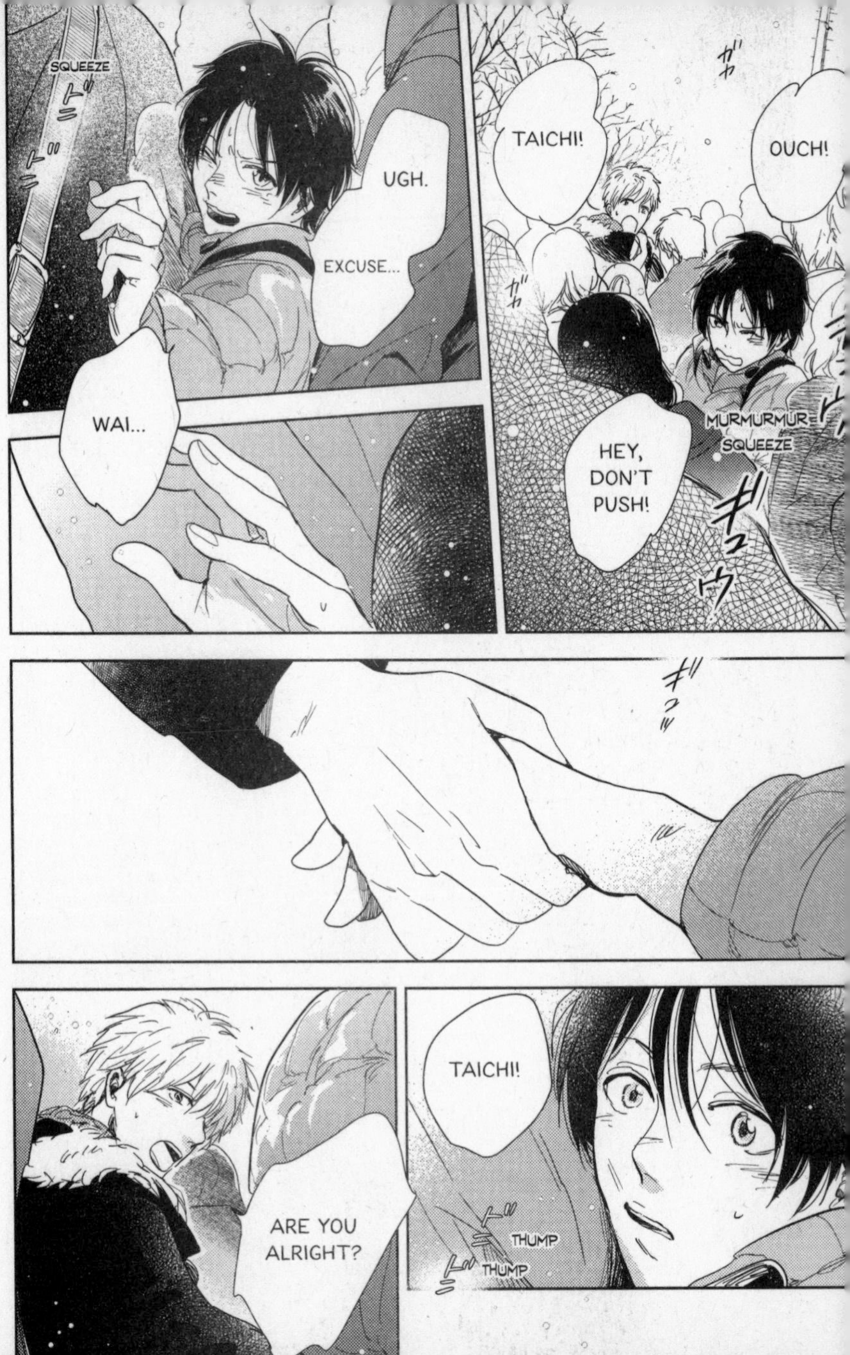

OUCH!
TAICHI!
MURMURMUR
SQUEEZE
HEY, DON'T PUSH!
SQUEEZE
UGH.
EXCUSE...
WAI...
TAICHI!
THUMP
THUMP
ARE YOU ALRIGHT?

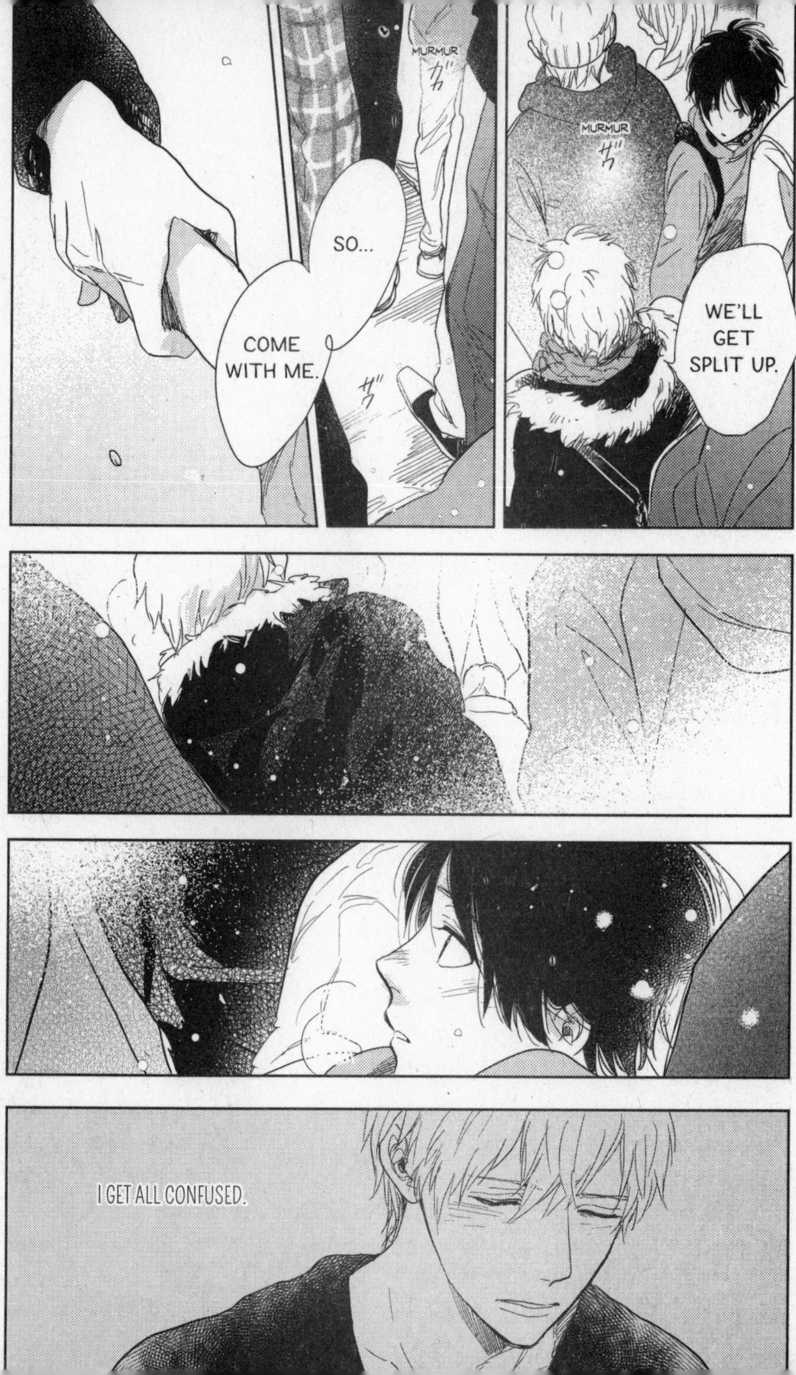
MURMUR
WE'LL GET SPLIT UP.
MURMUR
SO...
COME WITH ME.
I GET ALL CONFUSED.

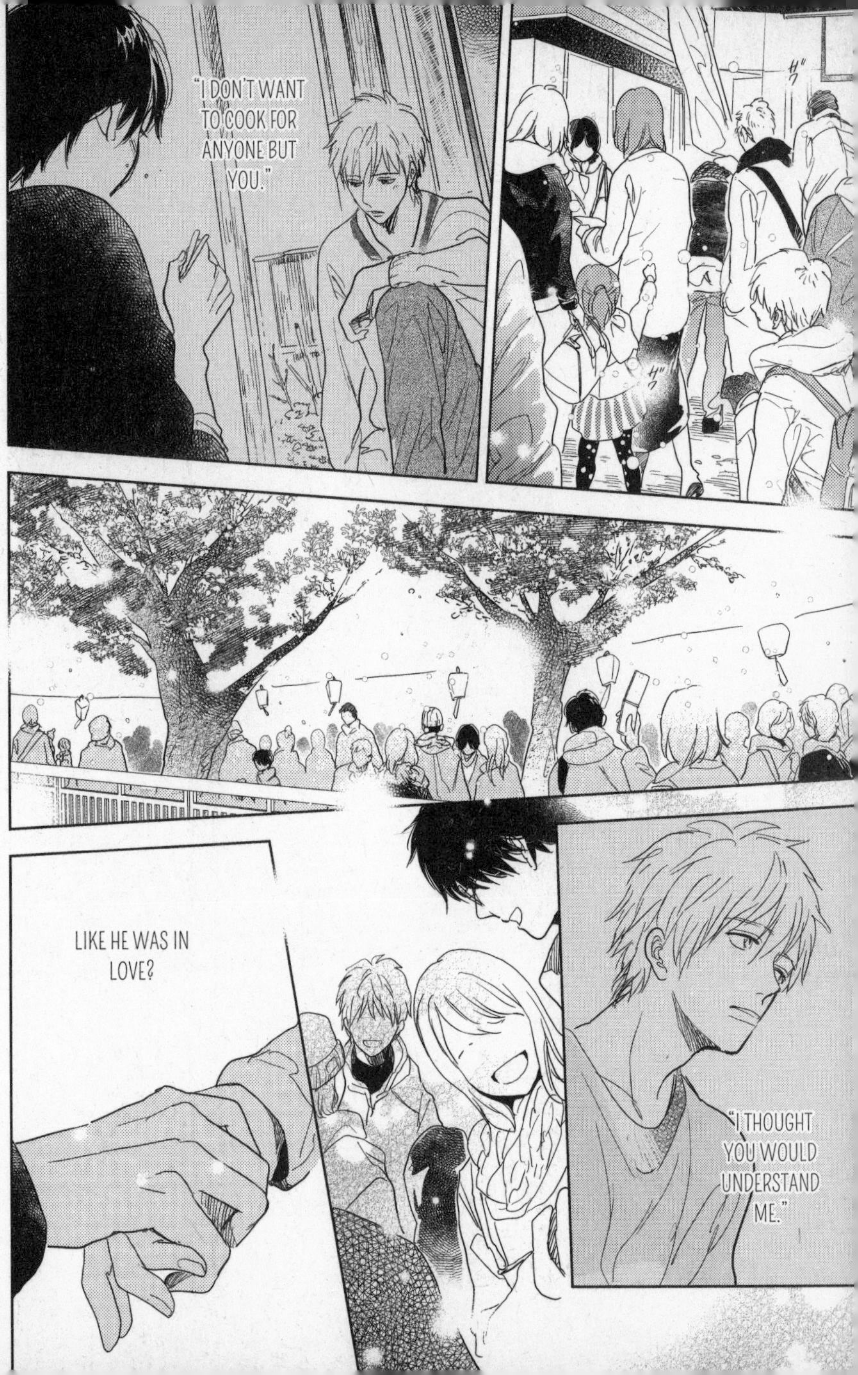
"I DON'T WANT TO COOK FOR ANYONE BUT YOU."
"I THOUGHT YOU WOULD UNDERSTAND ME."
LIKE HE WAS IN LOVE?

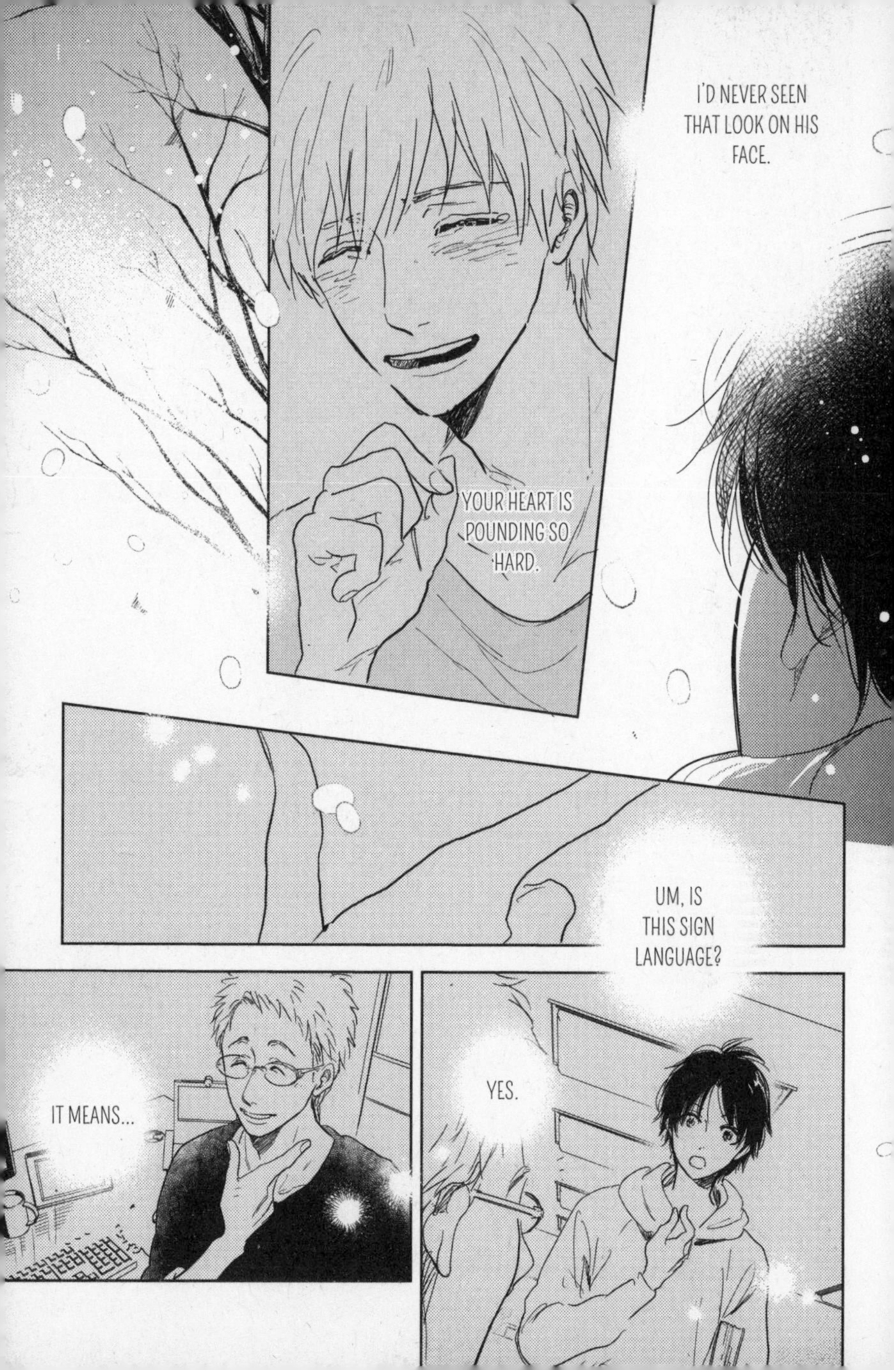
I'D NEVER SEEN THAT LOOK ON HIS FACE.
YOUR HEART IS POUNDING SO HARD.
UM, IS THIS SIGN LANGUAGE?
YES.
IT MEANS...

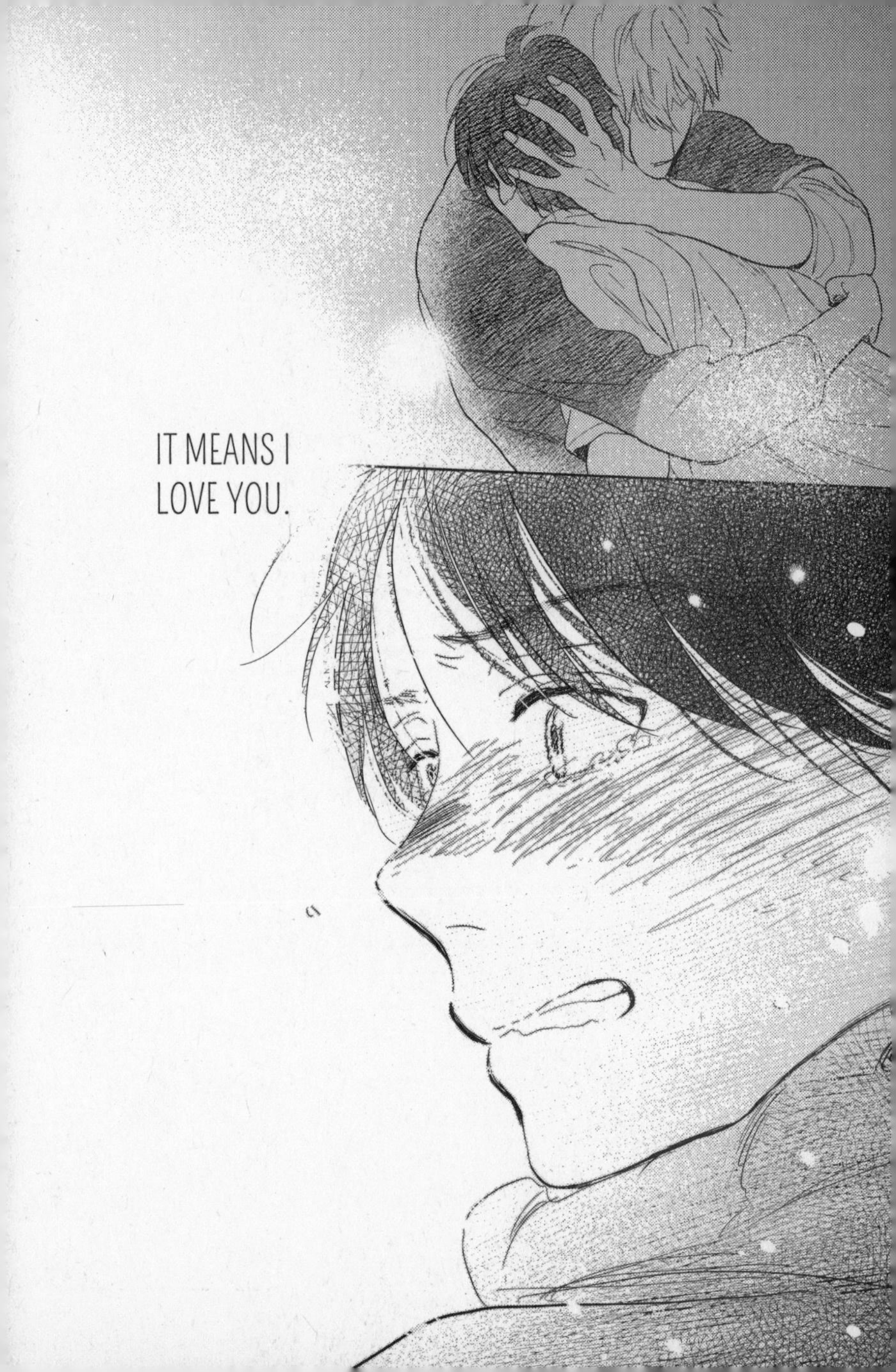
IT MEANS I LOVE YOU.

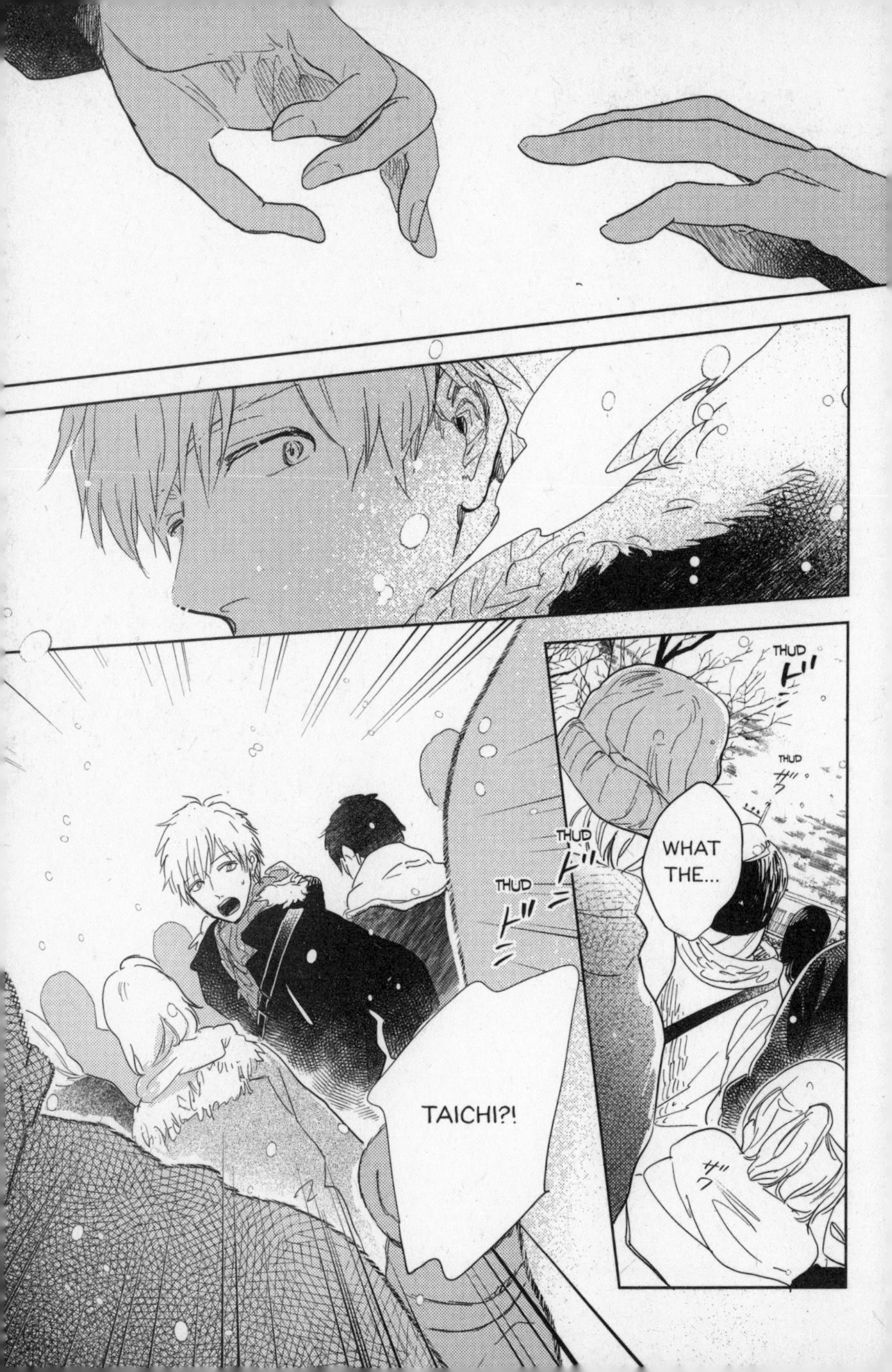
THUD
THUD
WHAT THE...
THUD
THUD
TAICHI?!

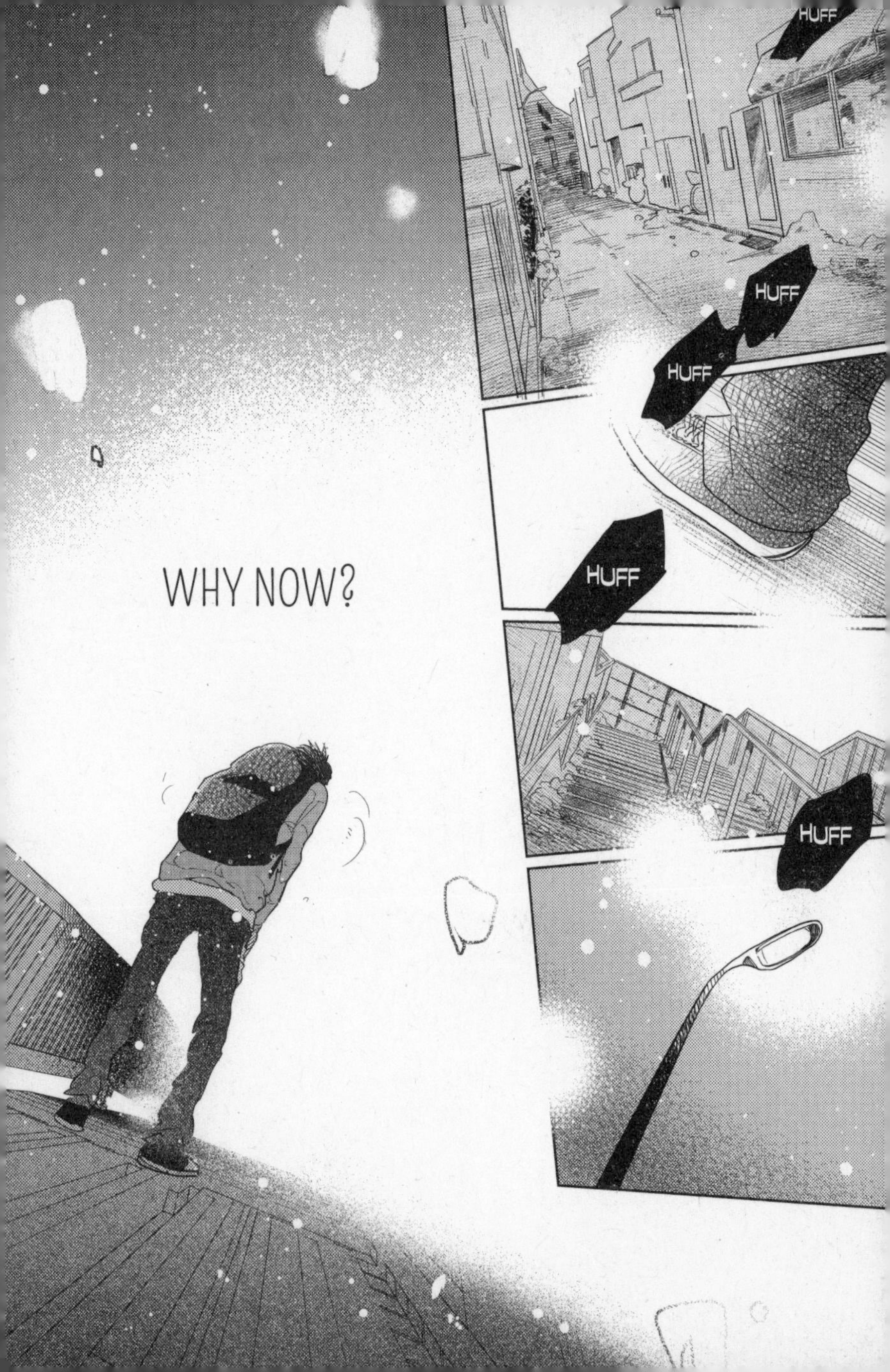
HUFF
HUFF
HUFF
HUFF
HUFF
WHY NOW?

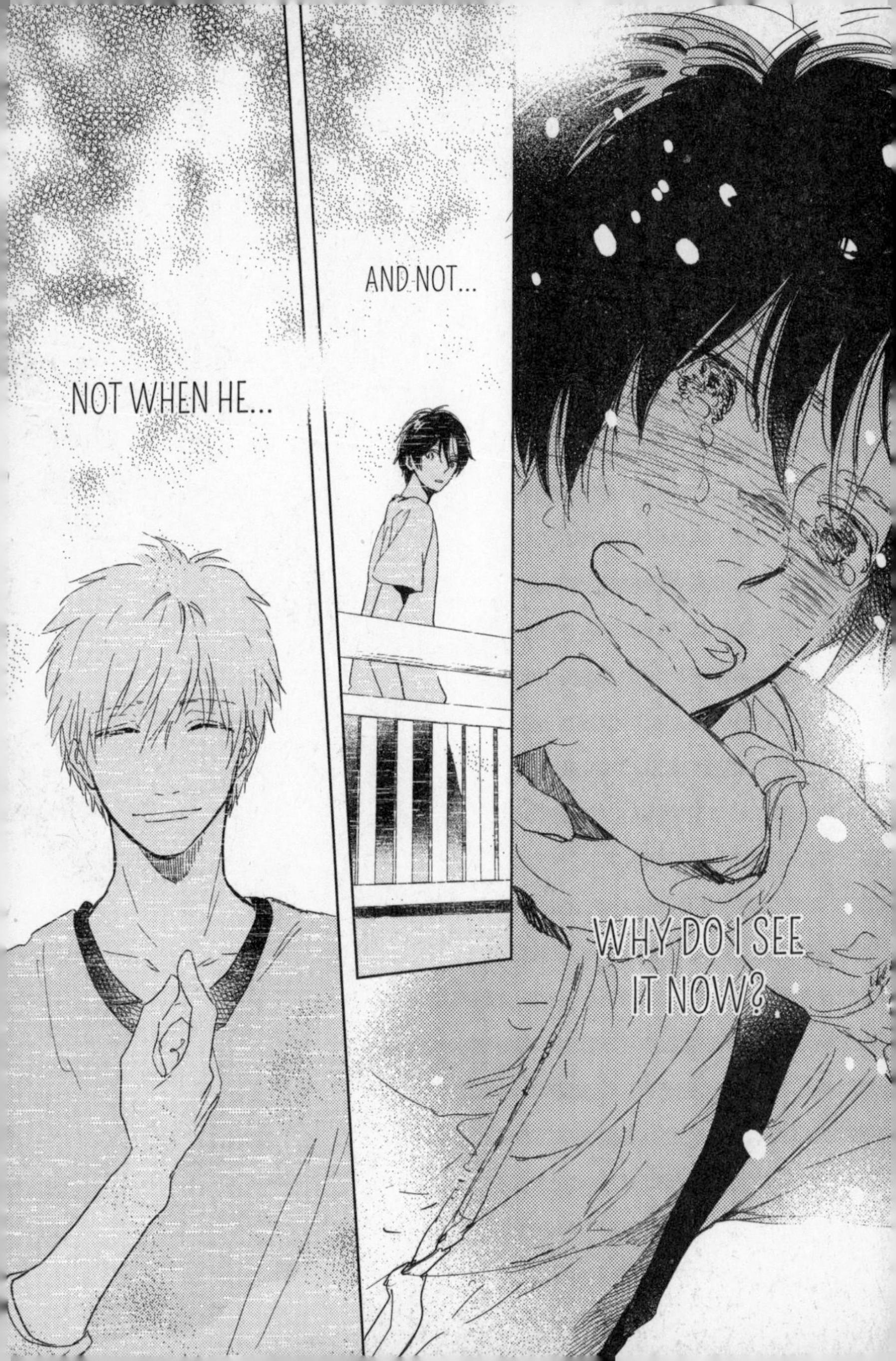
NOT WHEN HE...
AND NOT...
WHY DO I SEE IT NOW?

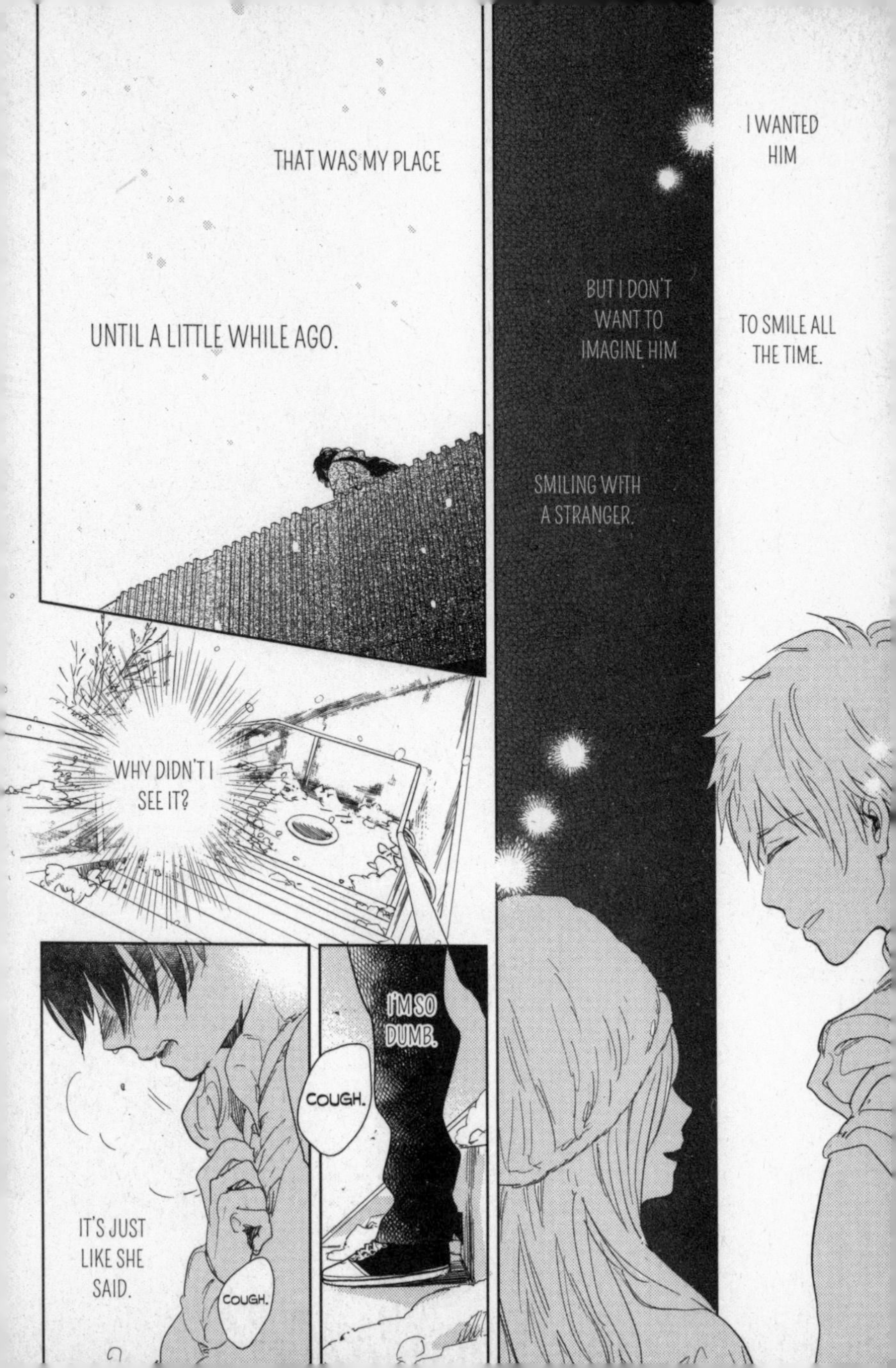
I WANTED HIM
TO SMILE ALL THE TIME.
BUT I DON'T WANT TO IMAGINE HIM
SMILING WITH A STRANGER.
THAT WAS MY PLACE
UNTIL A LITTLE WHILE AGO.
WHY DIDN'T I SEE IT?
I'M SO DUMB.
COUGH.
COUGH.
IT'S JUST LIKE SHE SAID.

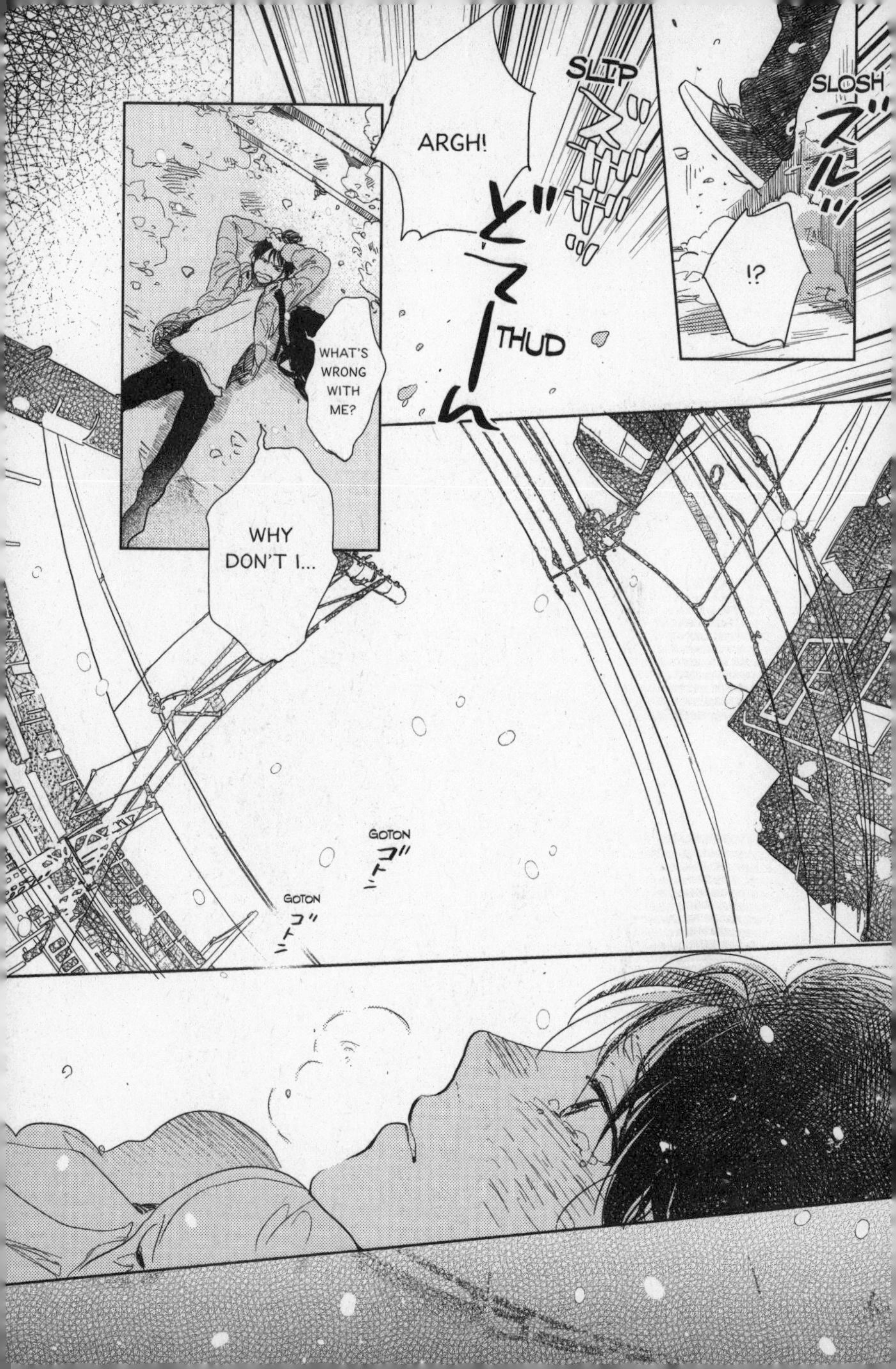
SLOSH
ズルッ
!?
SLIP
ズザザッ
ARGH!
どてーん
THUD
WHAT'S WRONG WITH ME?
WHY DON'T I...
GOTON
ゴトン
GOTON
ゴトン

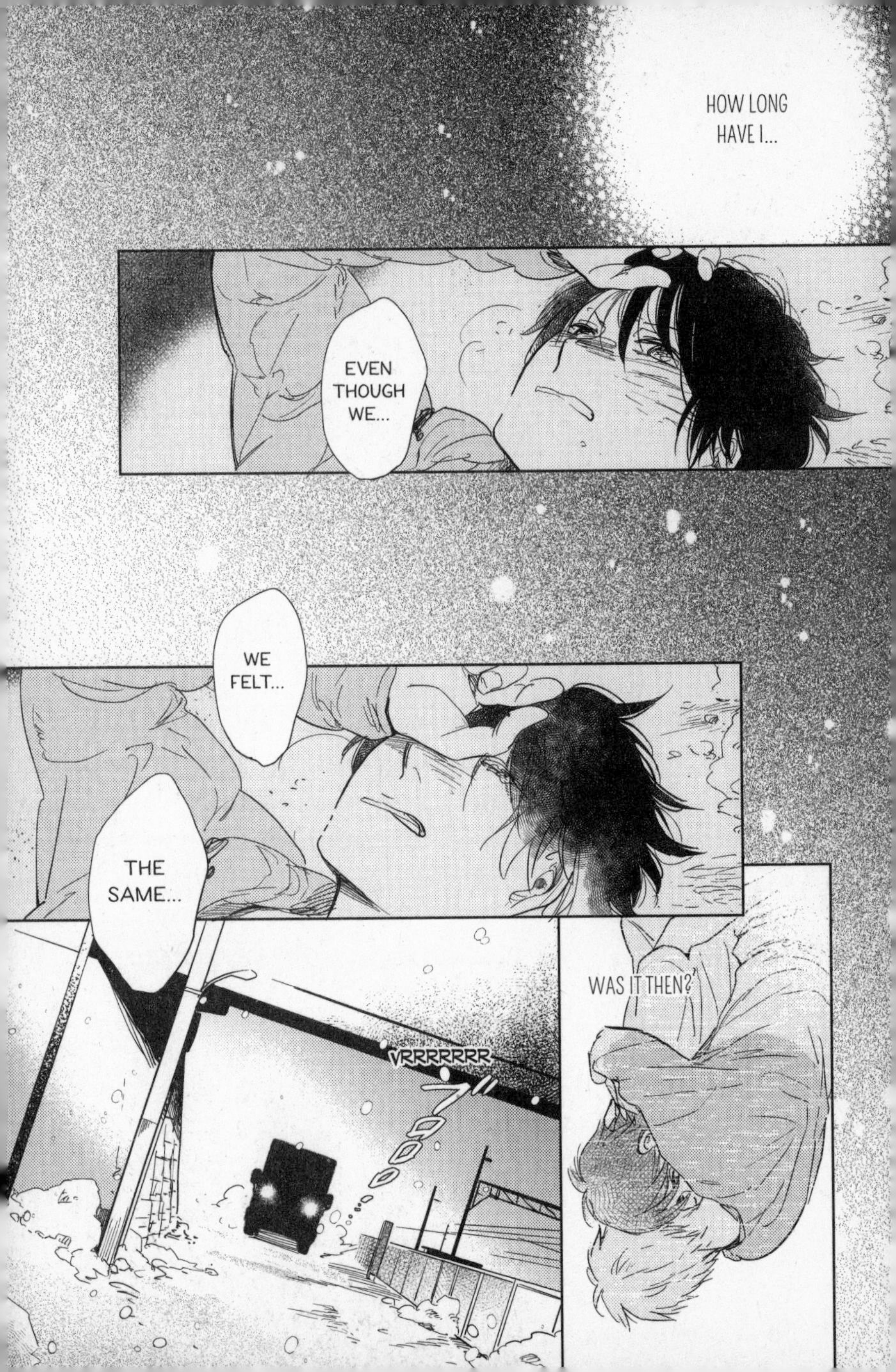
HOW LONG
HAVE I...
EVEN THOUGH WE...
WE FELT...
THE SAME...
WAS IT THEN?
VRRRRRRR

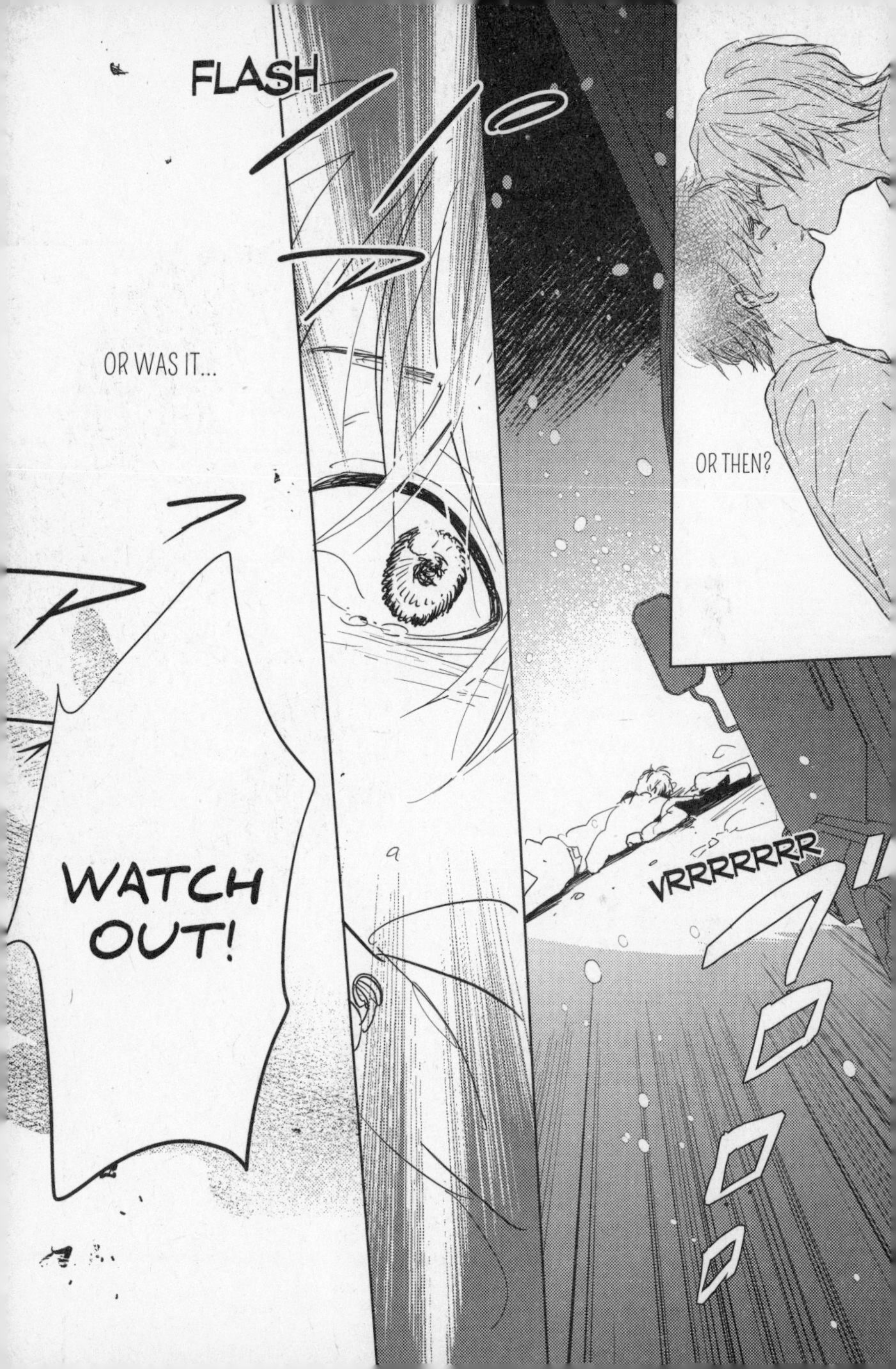
OR THEN?
VRRRRRRR
FLASH
OR WAS IT...
WATCH OUT!

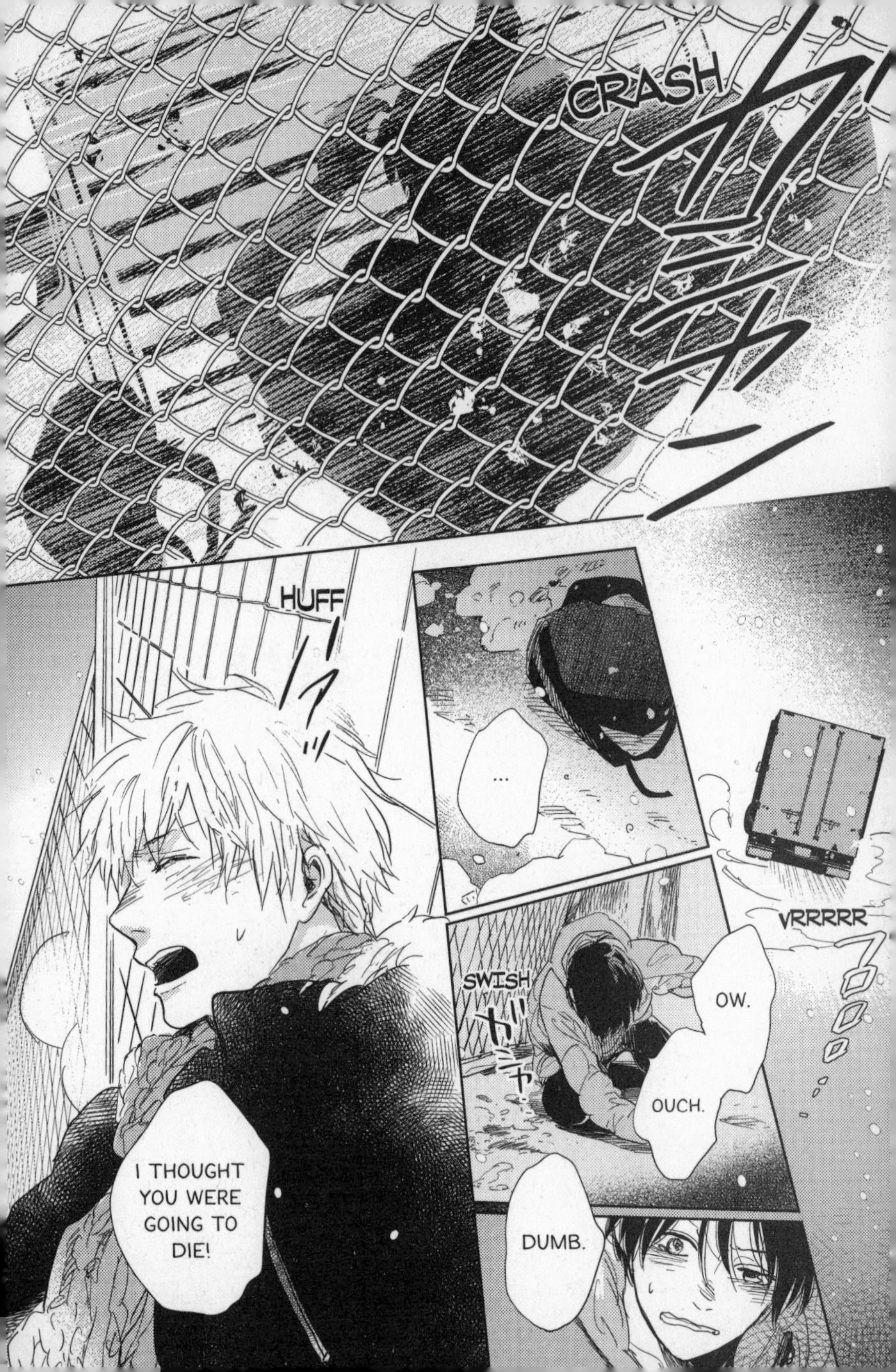
CRASH
...
VRRRRR
SWISH
OW.
OUCH.
DUMB.
HUFF
I THOUGHT YOU WERE GOING TO DIE!

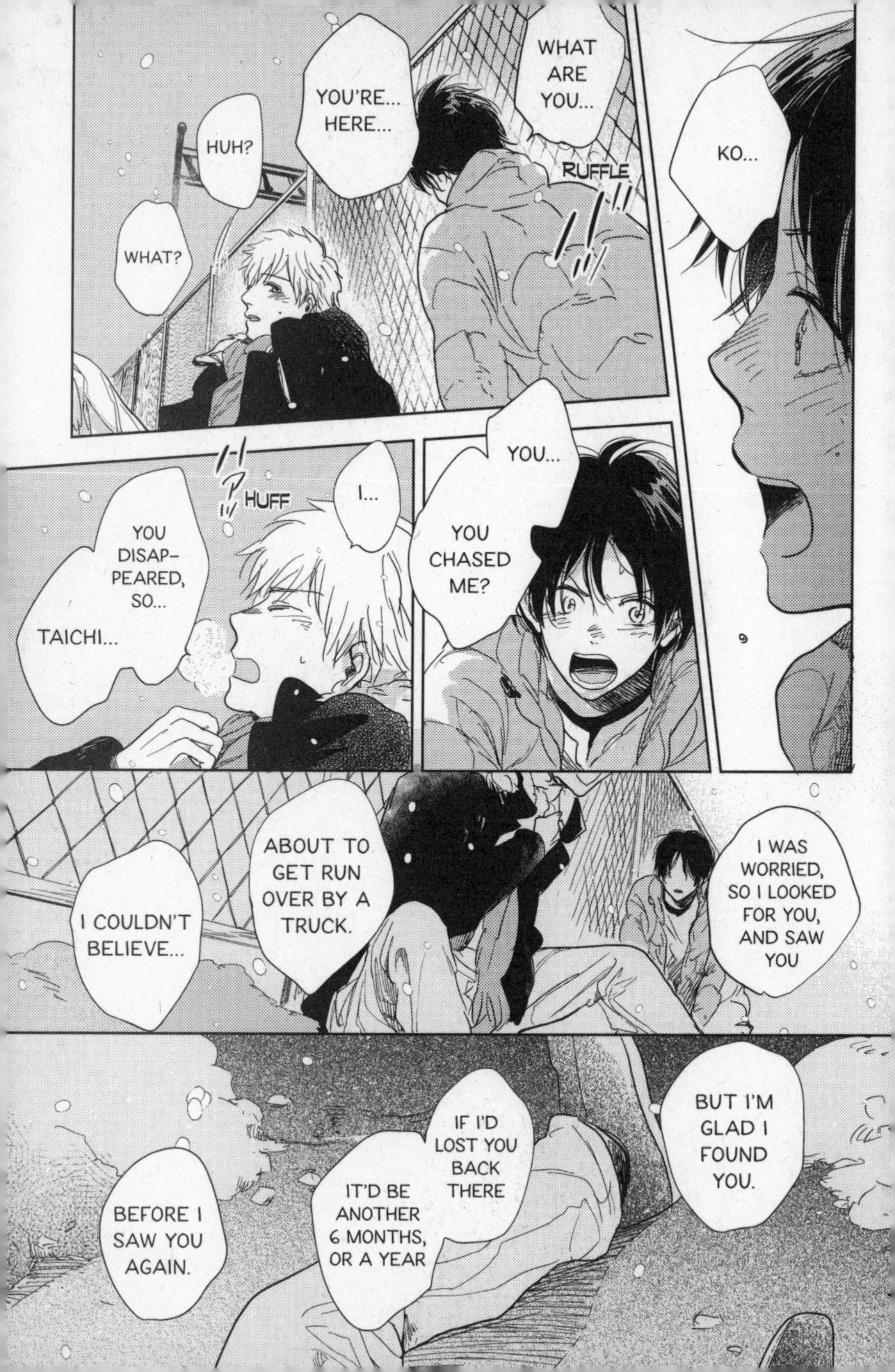
KO...
WHAT ARE YOU...
YOU'RE... HERE...
HUH?
RUFFLE
WHAT?
YOU...
YOU CHASED ME?
I...
HUFF
YOU DISAP-PEARED, SO...
TAICHI...
I WAS WORRIED, SO I LOOKED FOR YOU, AND SAW YOU
ABOUT TO GET RUN OVER BY A TRUCK.
I COULDN'T BELIEVE...
BUT I'M GLAD I FOUND YOU.
IF I'D LOST YOU BACK THERE
IT'D BE ANOTHER 6 MONTHS, OR A YEAR
BEFORE I SAW YOU AGAIN.

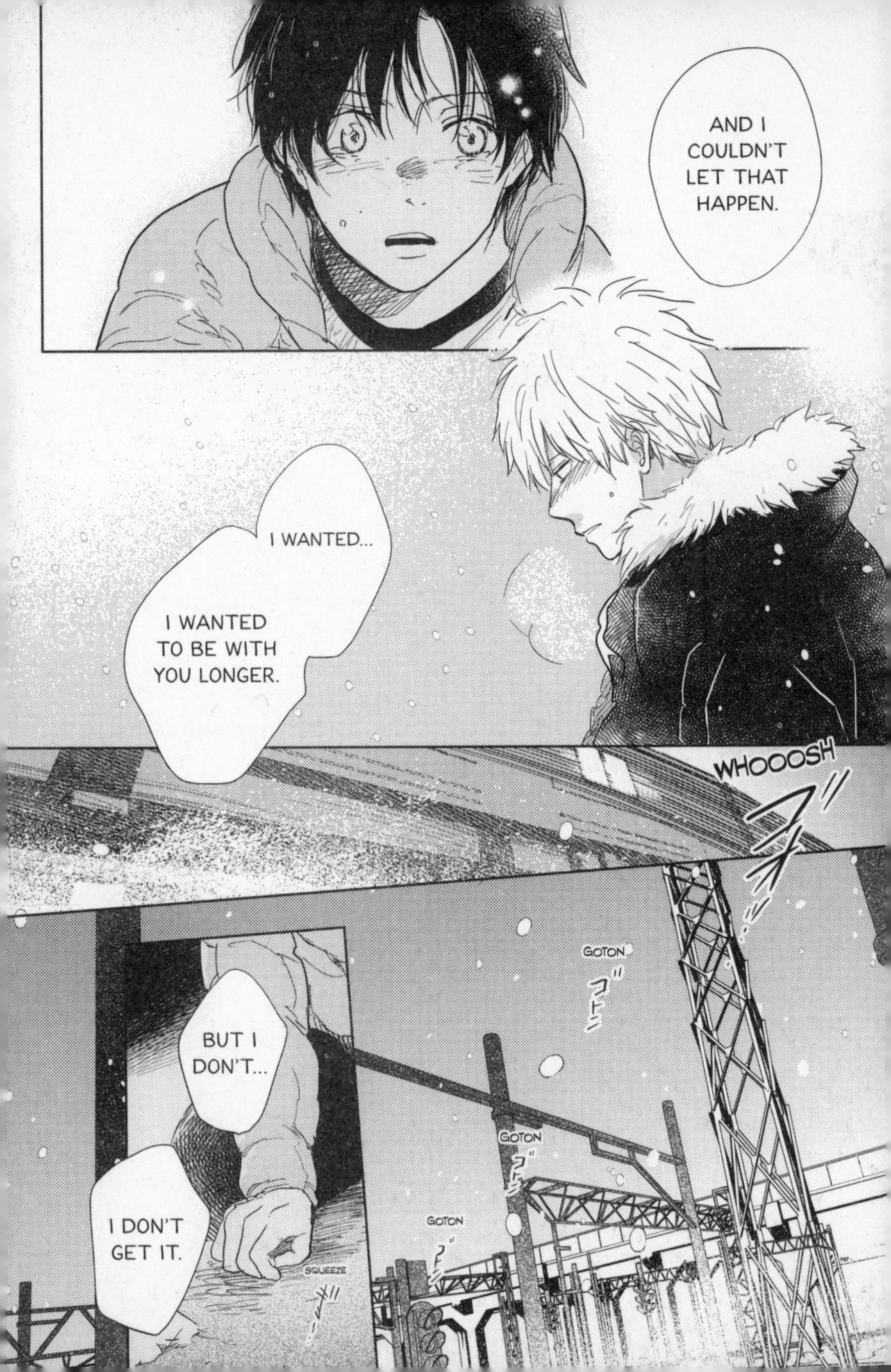
AND I COULDN'T LET THAT HAPPEN.
I WANTED...
I WANTED TO BE WITH YOU LONGER.
WHOOOSH
GOTON
GOTON
GOTON
BUT I DON'T...
I DON'T GET IT.
SQUEEZE

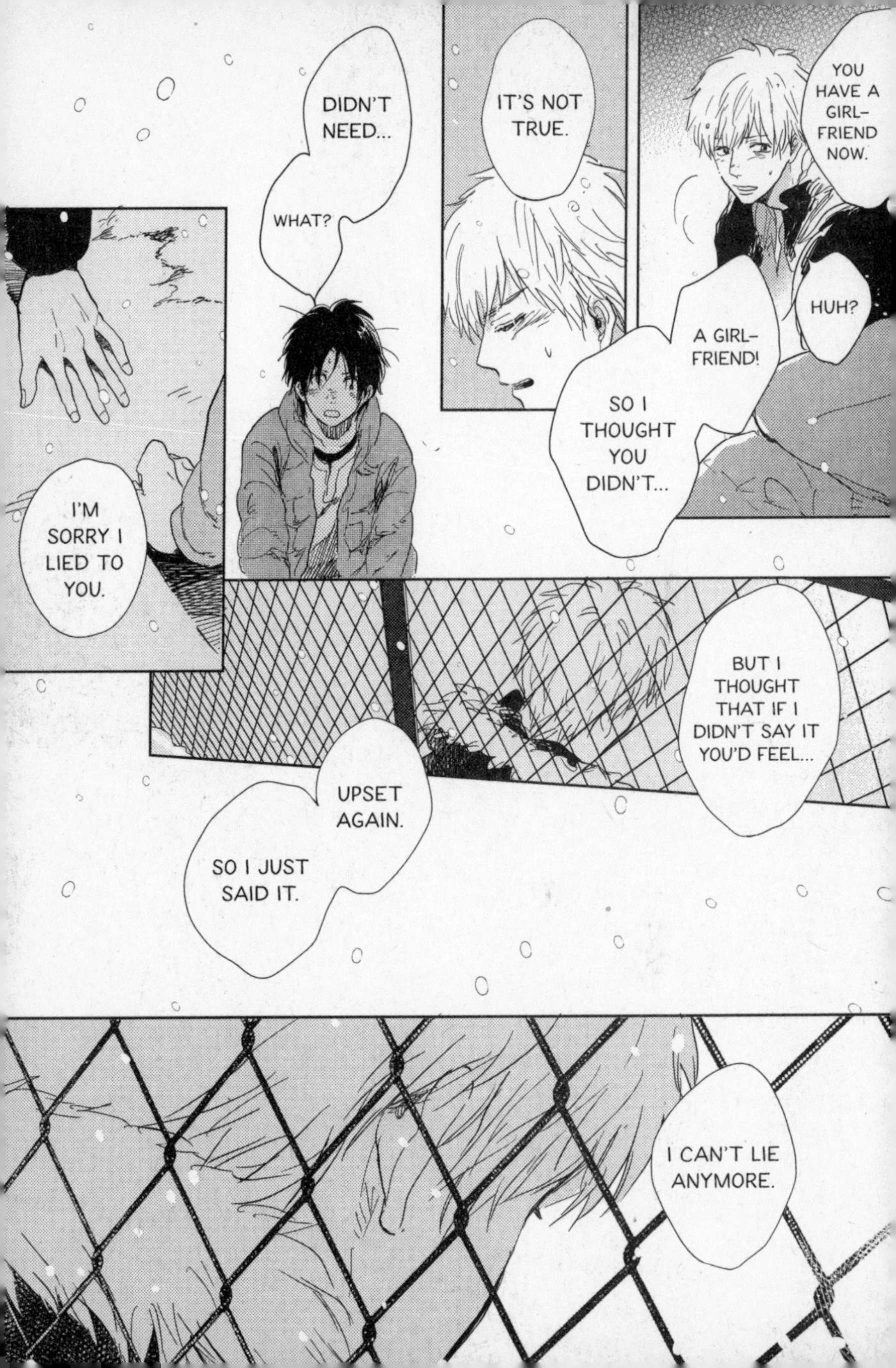
YOU HAVE A GIRL-FRIEND NOW.
HUH?
A GIRL-FRIEND!
SO I THOUGHT YOU DIDN'T...
IT'S NOT TRUE.
DIDN'T NEED...
WHAT?
I'M SORRY I LIED TO YOU.
BUT I THOUGHT THAT IF I DIDN'T SAY IT YOU'D FEEL...
UPSET AGAIN.
SO I JUST SAID IT.
I CAN'T LIE ANYMORE.

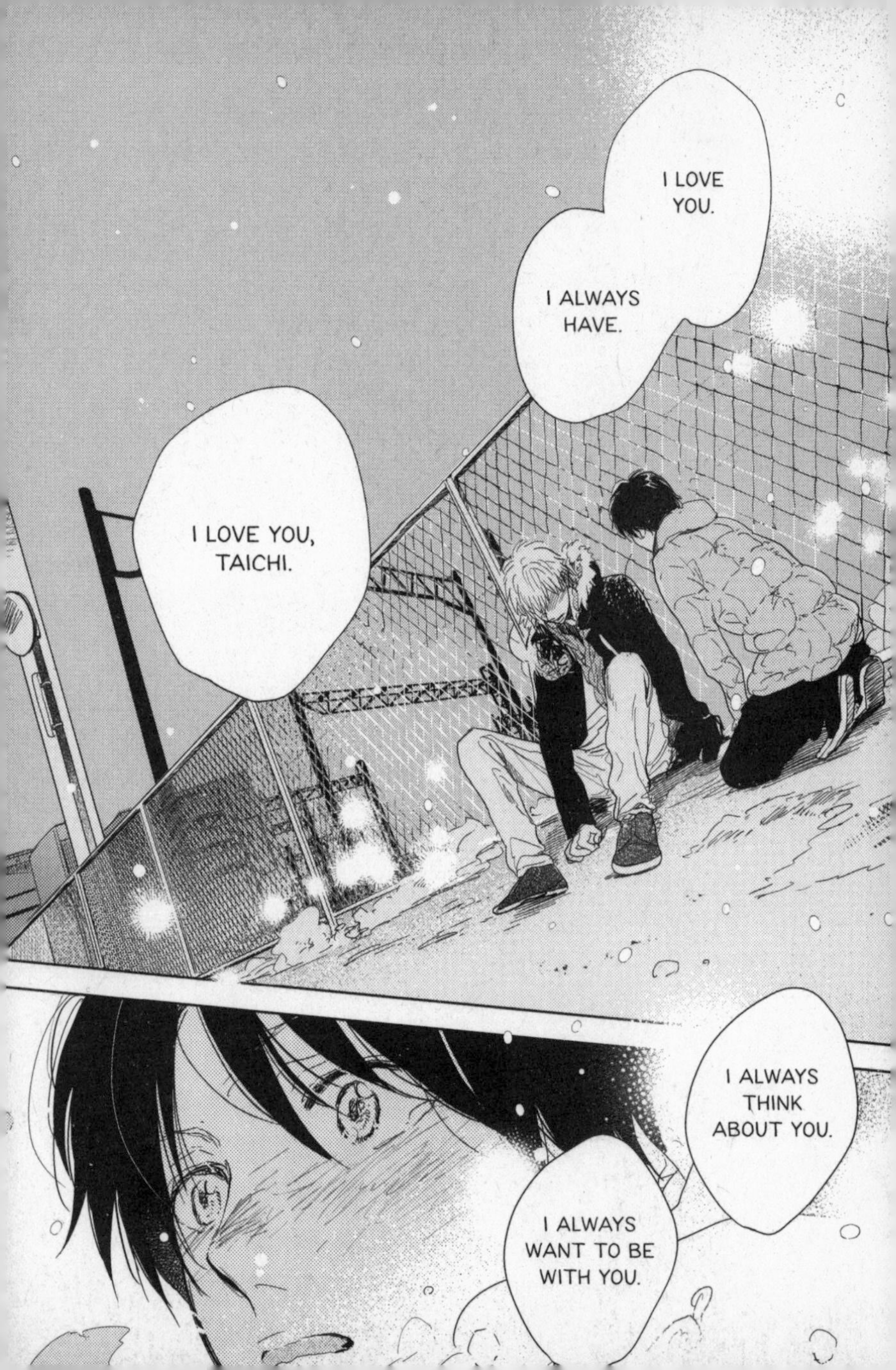
I LOVE YOU.
I ALWAYS HAVE.
I LOVE YOU, TAICHI.
I ALWAYS THINK ABOUT YOU.
I ALWAYS WANT TO BE WITH YOU.

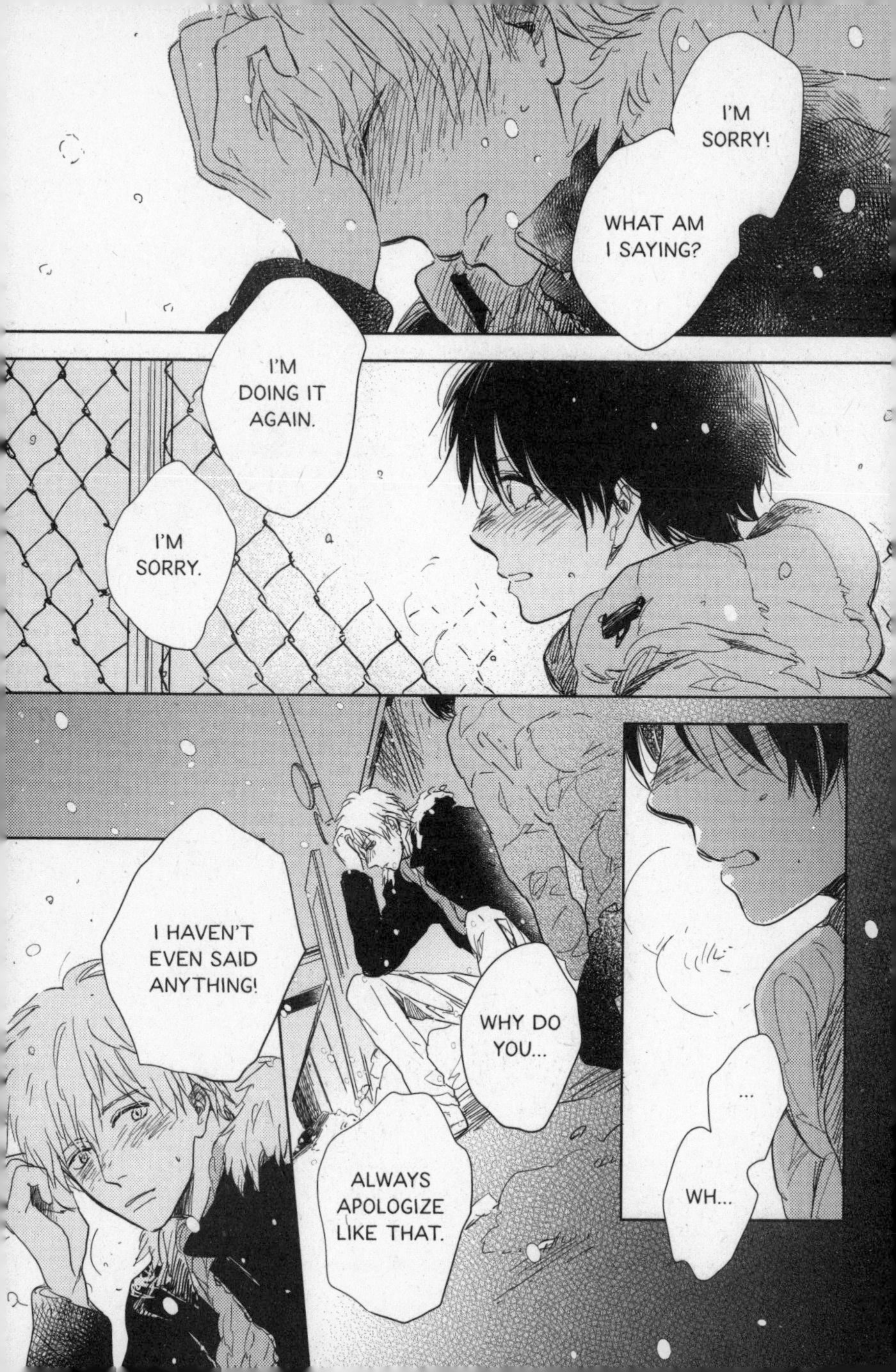
I'M SORRY!
WHAT AM I SAYING?
I'M DOING IT AGAIN.
I'M SORRY.
...
WH...
WHY DO YOU...
ALWAYS APOLOGIZE LIKE THAT.
I HAVEN'T EVEN SAID ANYTHING!

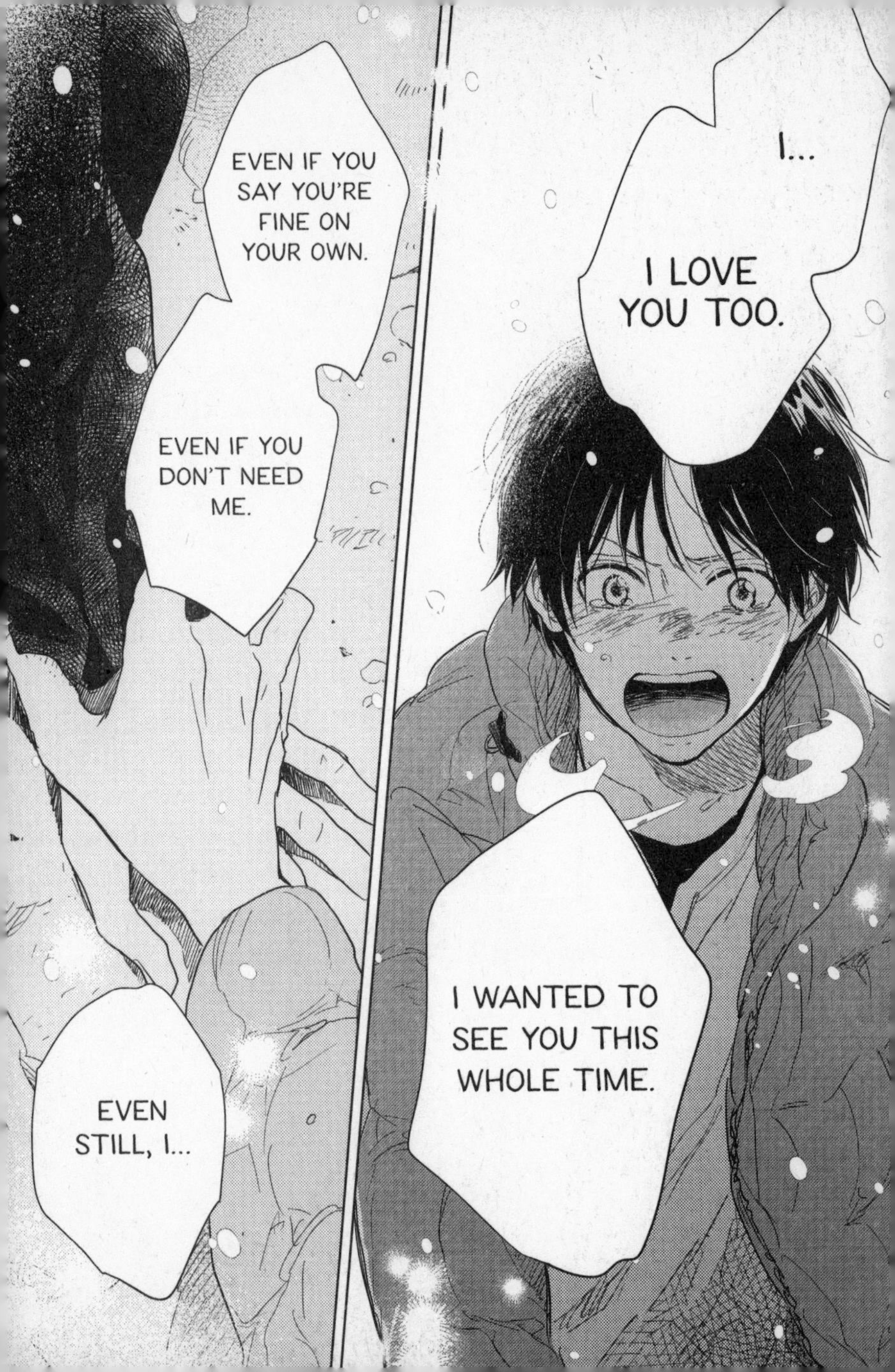
I...
I LOVE YOU TOO.
I WANTED TO SEE YOU THIS WHOLE TIME.
EVEN IF YOU SAY YOU'RE FINE ON YOUR OWN.
EVEN IF YOU DON'T NEED ME.
EVEN STILL, I...

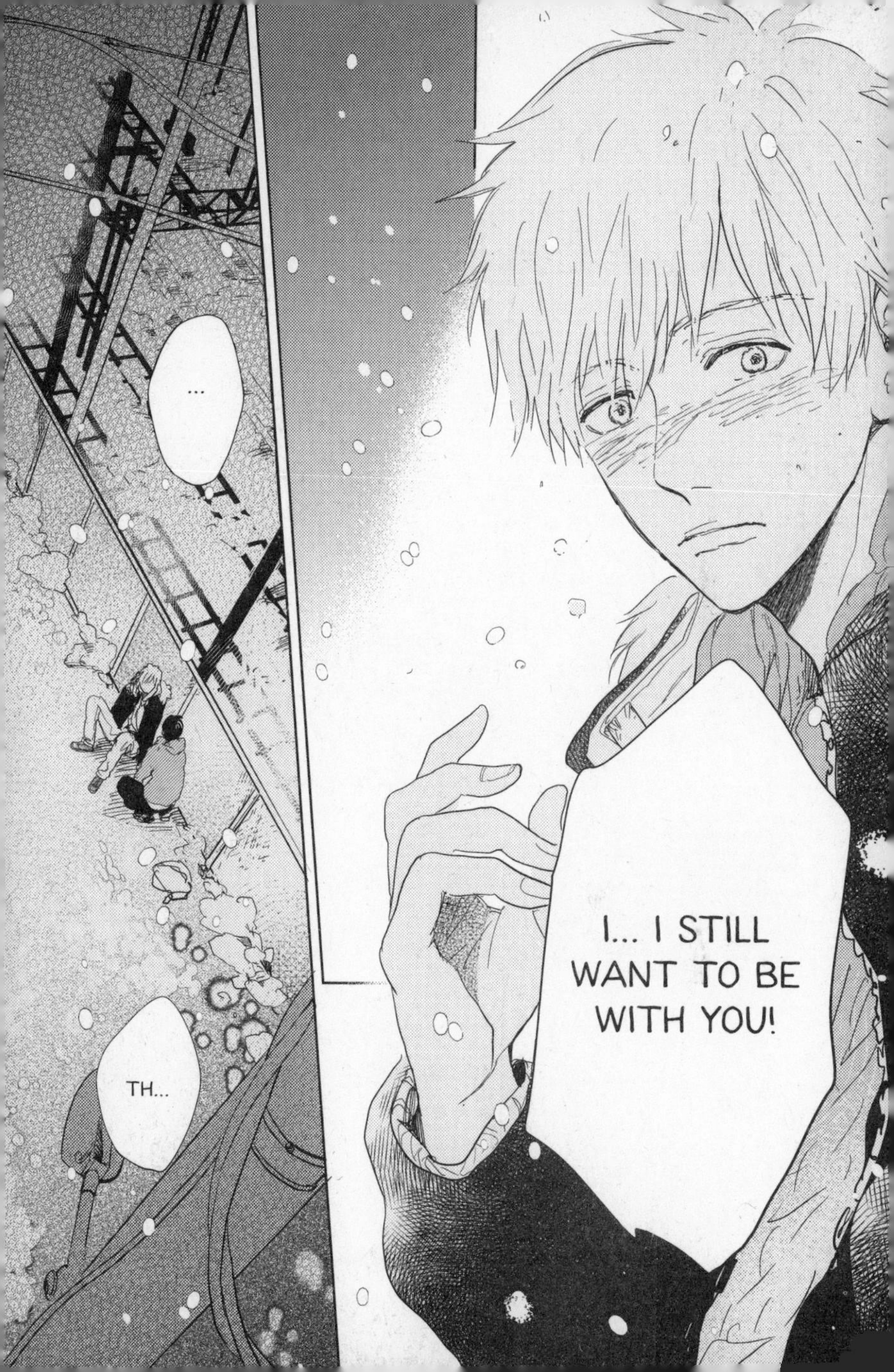
I... I STILL WANT TO BE WITH YOU!
...
TH...

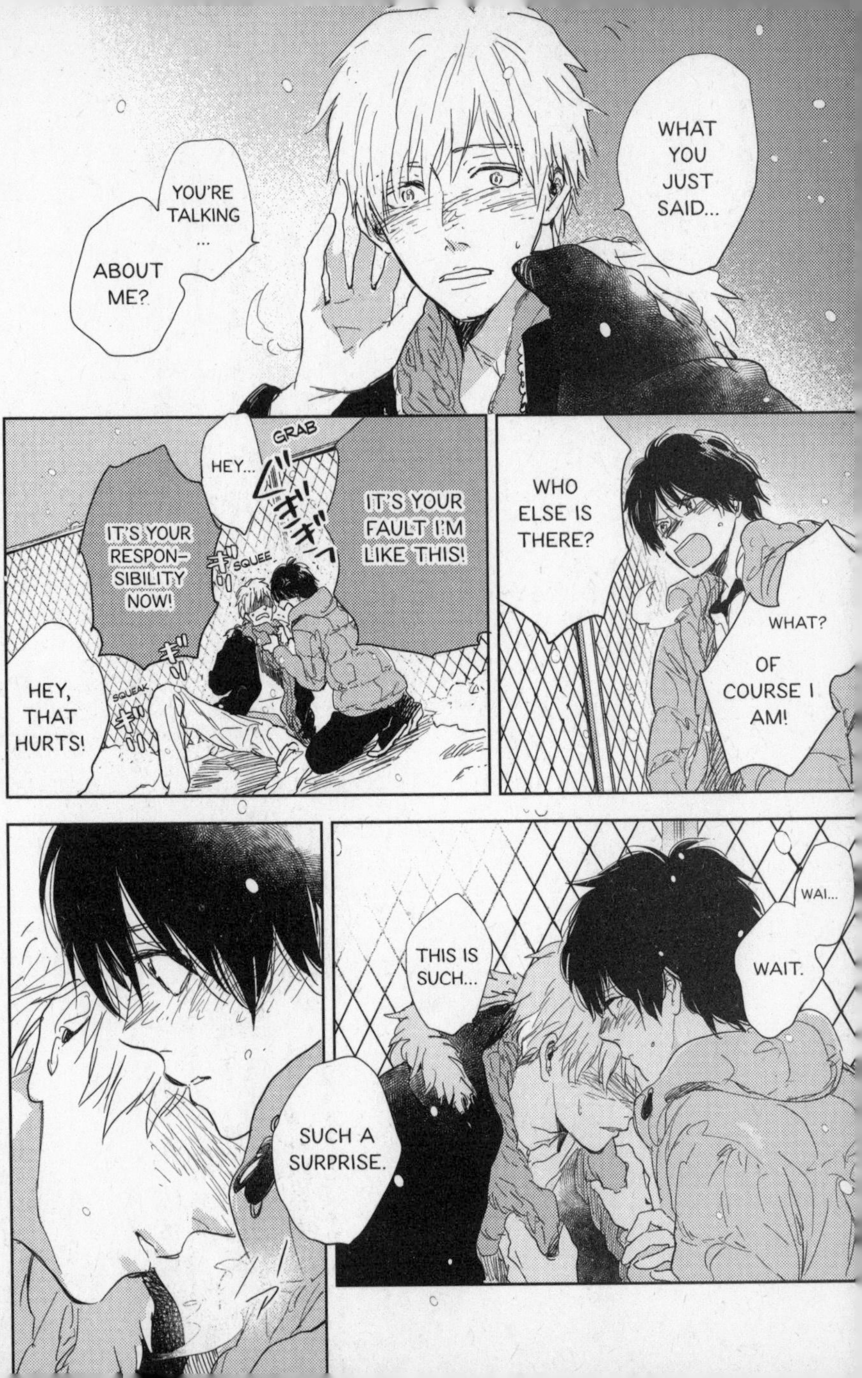
WHAT YOU JUST SAID...
YOU'RE TALKING ... ABOUT ME?
WHAT?
OF COURSE I AM!
WHO ELSE IS THERE?
IT'S YOUR FAULT I'M LIKE THIS!
GRAB
HEY...
IT'S YOUR RESPON-SIBILITY NOW!
SQUEE
SQUEAK
HEY, THAT HURTS!
WAI...
WAIT.
THIS IS SUCH...
SUCH A SURPRISE.

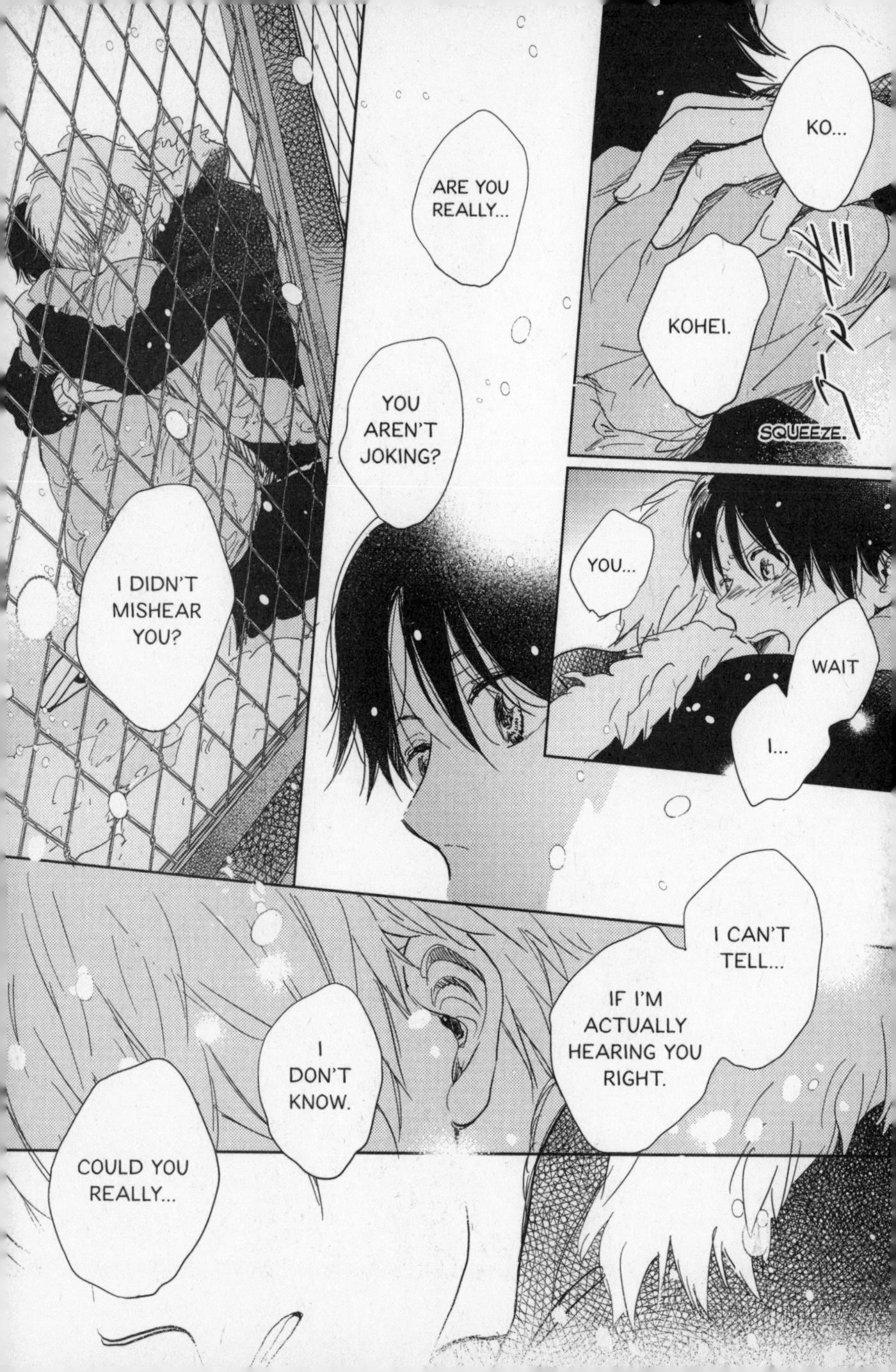
KO...
KOHEI.
SQUEEZE.
YOU...
WAIT
I...
ARE YOU REALLY...
YOU AREN'T JOKING?
I DIDN'T MISHEAR YOU?
I CAN'T TELL...
IF I'M ACTUALLY HEARING YOU RIGHT.
I DON'T KNOW.
COULD YOU REALLY...

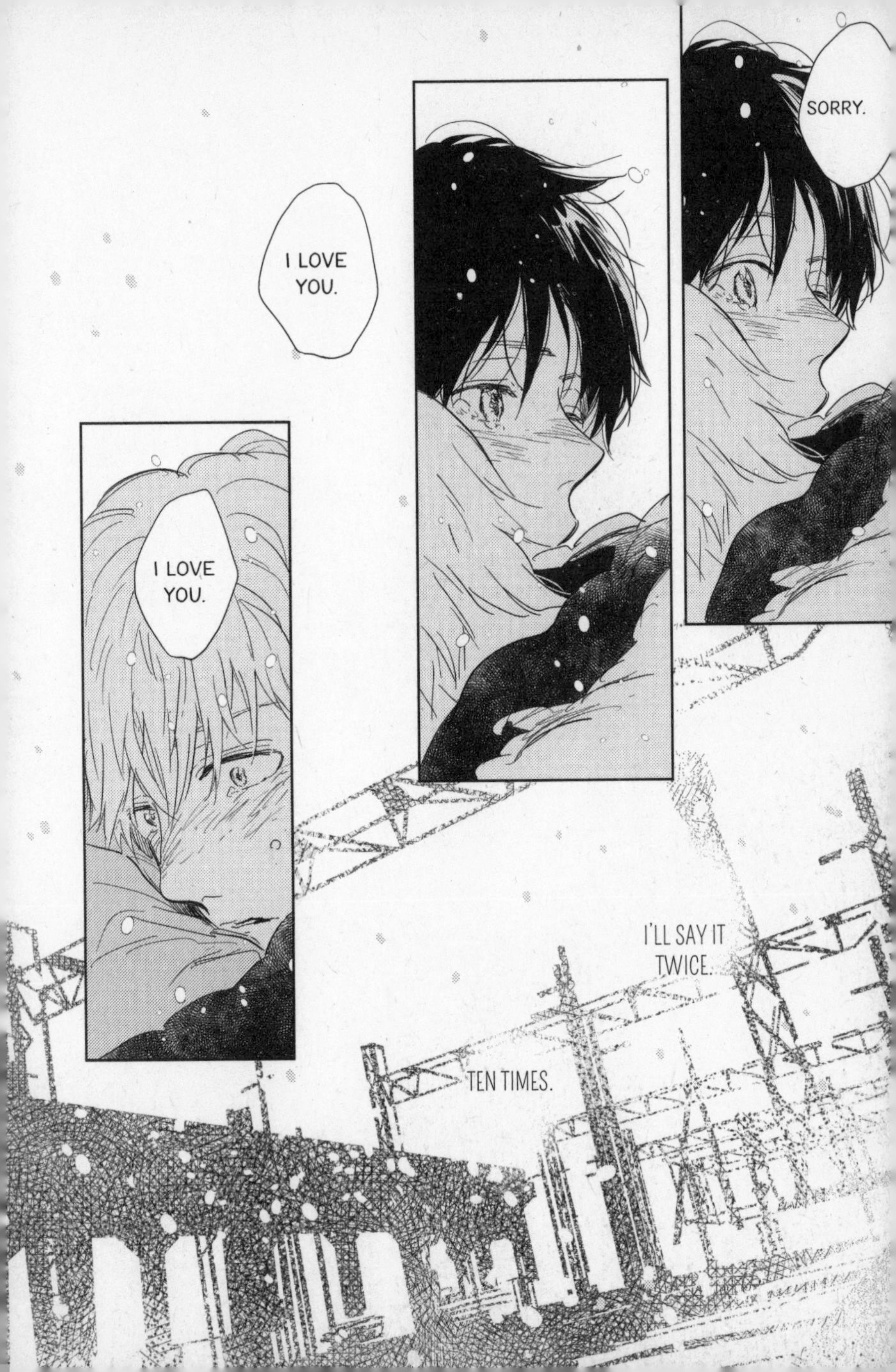
SORRY.
I LOVE YOU.
I LOVE YOU.
I'LL SAY IT TWICE.
TEN TIMES.

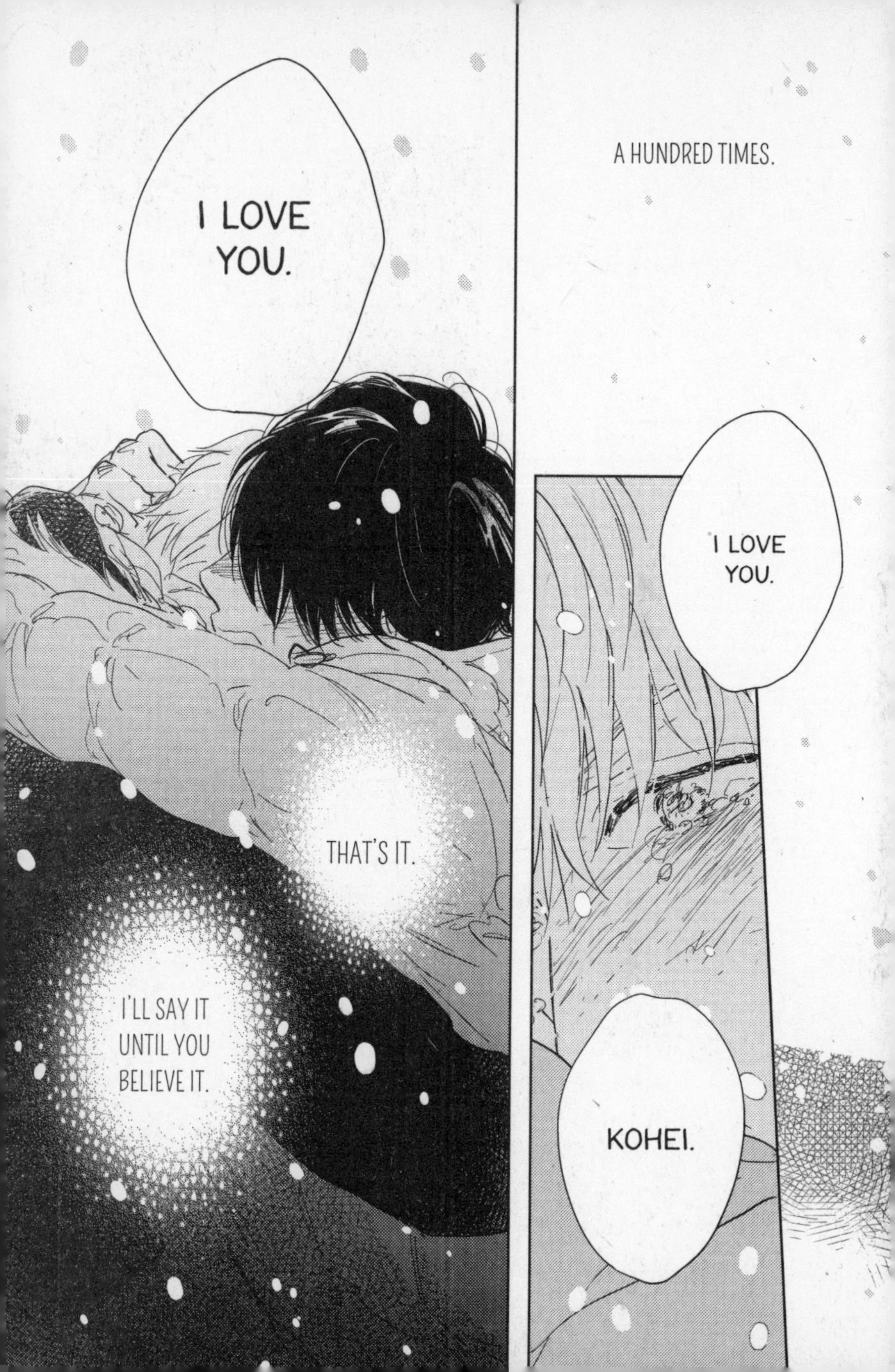
A HUNDRED TIMES.
I LOVE YOU.
KOHEI.
I LOVE YOU.
THAT'S IT.
I'LL SAY IT UNTIL YOU BELIEVE IT.

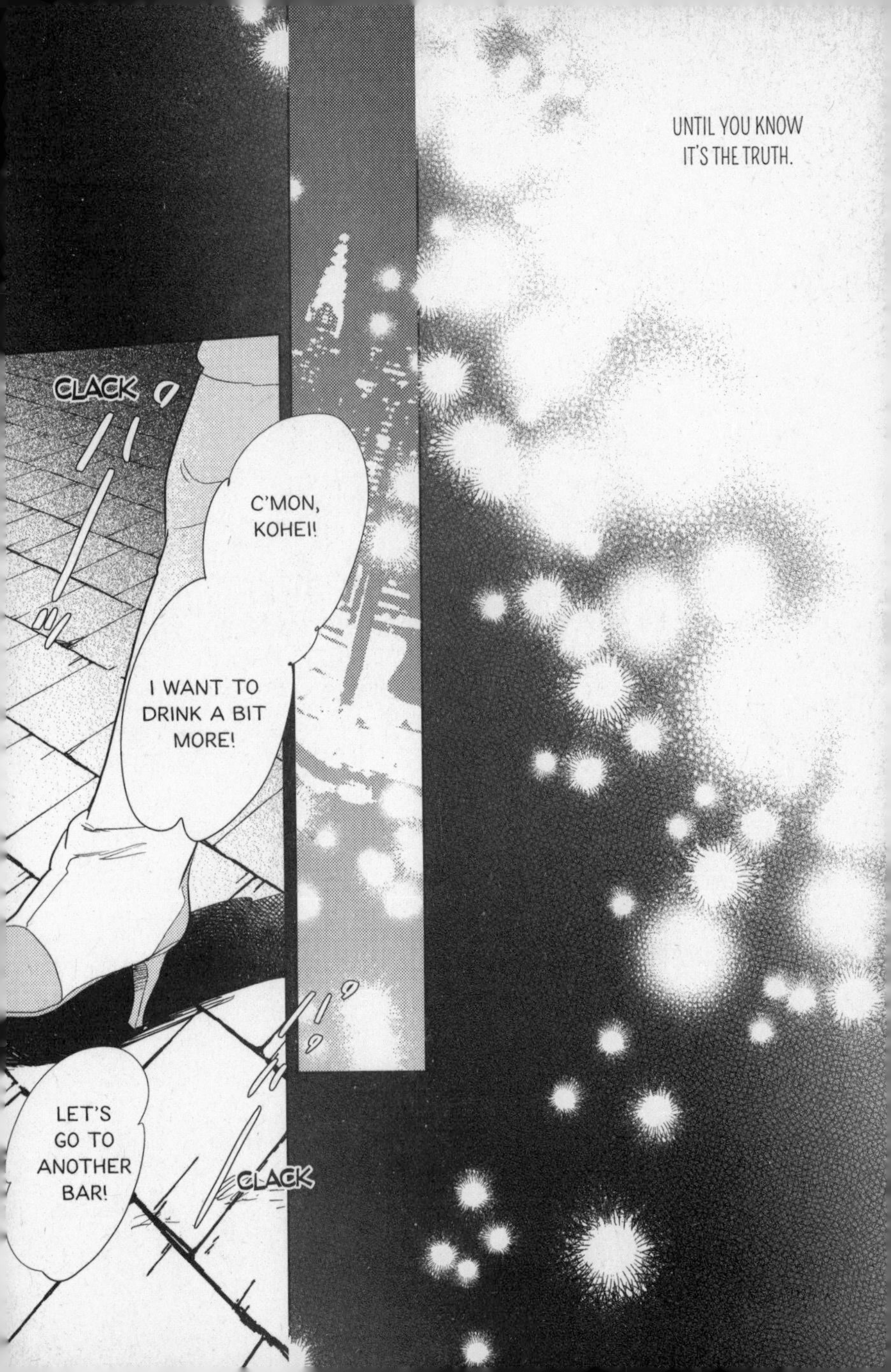
UNTIL YOU KNOW IT'S THE TRUTH.
CLACK
C'MON, KOHEI!
I WANT TO DRINK A BIT MORE!
LET'S GO TO ANOTHER BAR!
CLACK

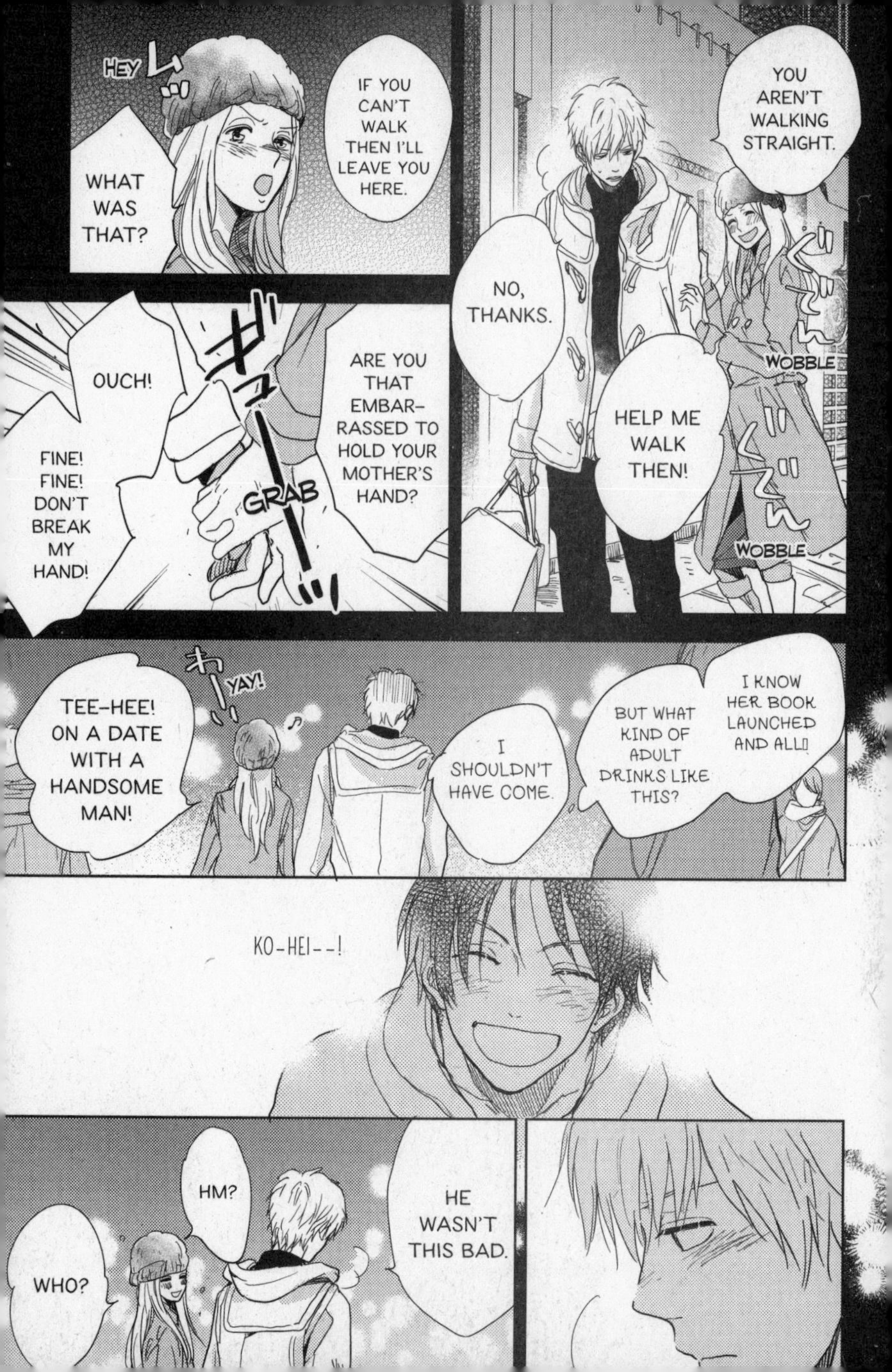
YOU AREN'T WALKING STRAIGHT.
WOBBLE
HELP ME WALK THEN!
WOBBLE
NO, THANKS.
HEY
IF YOU CAN'T WALK THEN I'LL LEAVE YOU HERE.
WHAT WAS THAT?
ARE YOU THAT EMBARRASSED TO HOLD YOUR MOTHER'S HAND?
GRAB
OUCH!
FINE! FINE! DON'T BREAK MY HAND!
I KNOW HER BOOK LAUNCHED AND ALL…
BUT WHAT KIND OF ADULT DRINKS LIKE THIS?
I SHOULDN'T HAVE COME.
YAY!
TEE-HEE! ON A DATE WITH A HANDSOME MAN!
KO-HEI--!
HE WASN'T THIS BAD.
HM?
WHO?

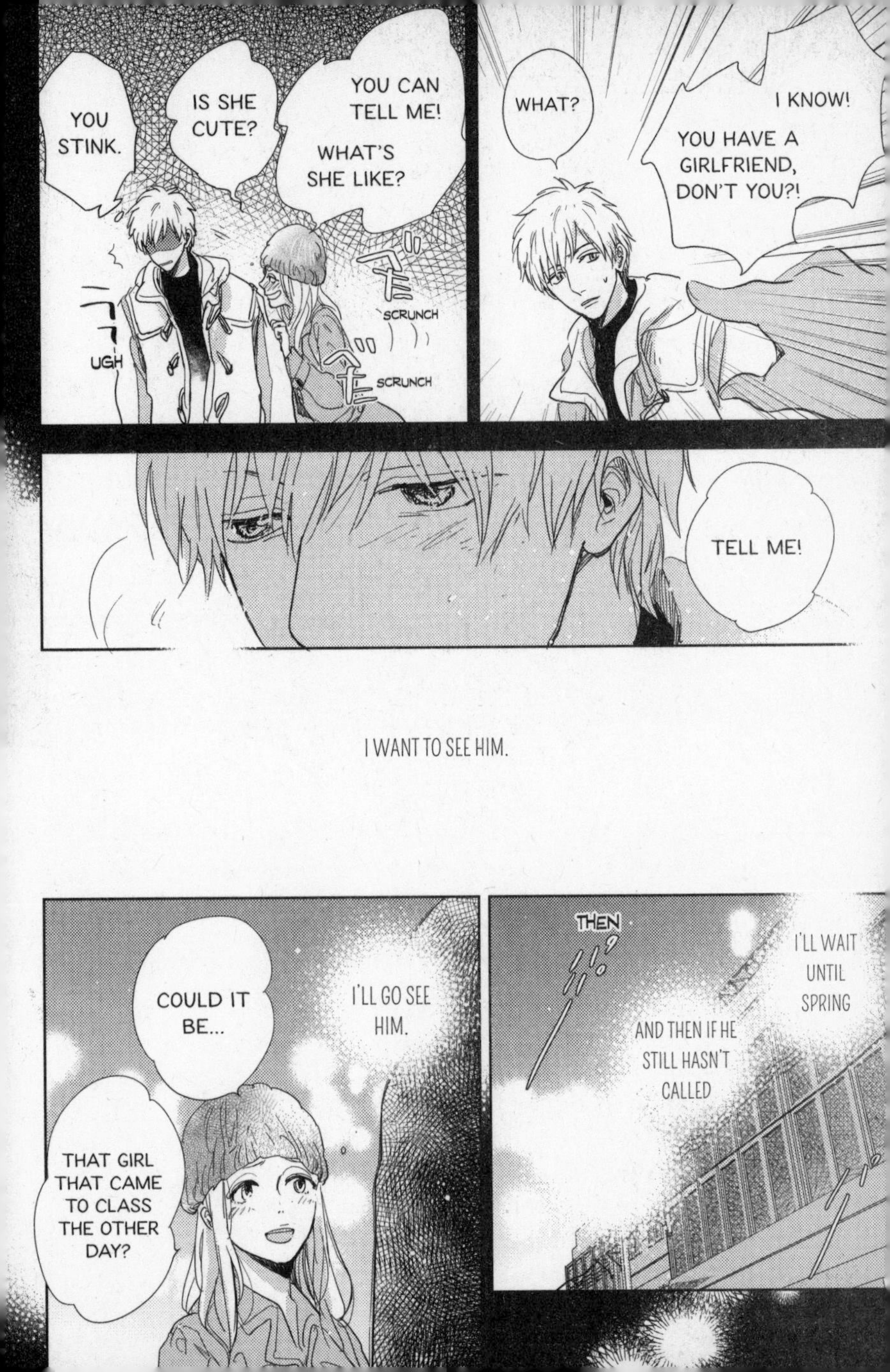

I KNOW!
YOU HAVE A GIRLFRIEND, DON'T YOU?!
WHAT?
YOU CAN TELL ME!
WHAT'S SHE LIKE?
IS SHE CUTE?
SCRUNCH
SCRUNCH
YOU STINK.
UGH
TELL ME!
I WANT TO SEE HIM.
I'LL WAIT UNTIL SPRING
AND THEN IF HE STILL HASN'T CALLED
THEN
I'LL GO SEE HIM.
COULD IT BE...
THAT GIRL THAT CAME TO CLASS THE OTHER DAY?

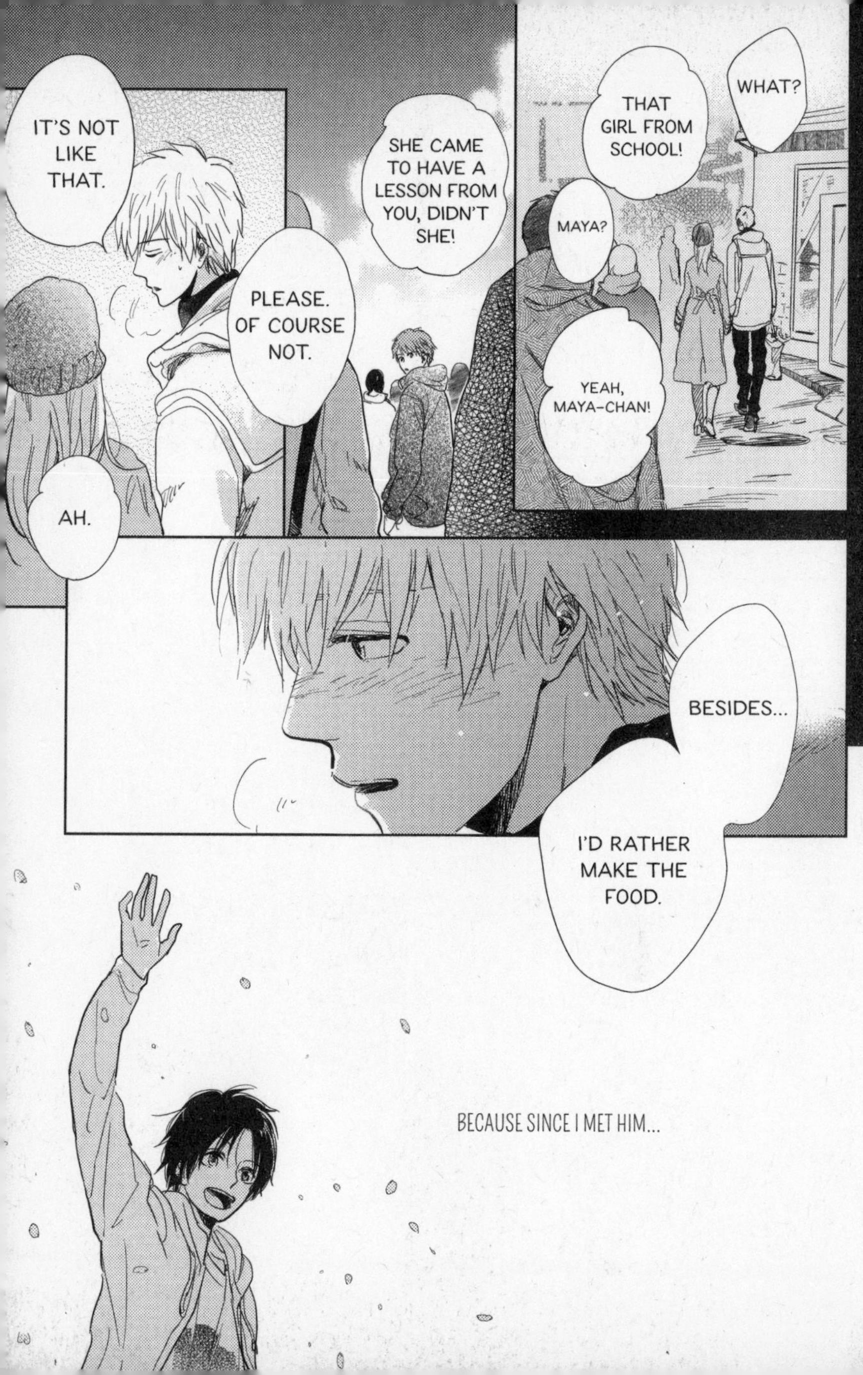
WHAT?
THAT GIRL FROM SCHOOL!
MAYA?
YEAH, MAYA-CHAN!
SHE CAME TO HAVE A LESSON FROM YOU, DIDN'T SHE!
PLEASE. OF COURSE NOT.
IT'S NOT LIKE THAT.
AH.
BESIDES...
I'D RATHER MAKE THE FOOD.
BECAUSE SINCE I MET HIM...

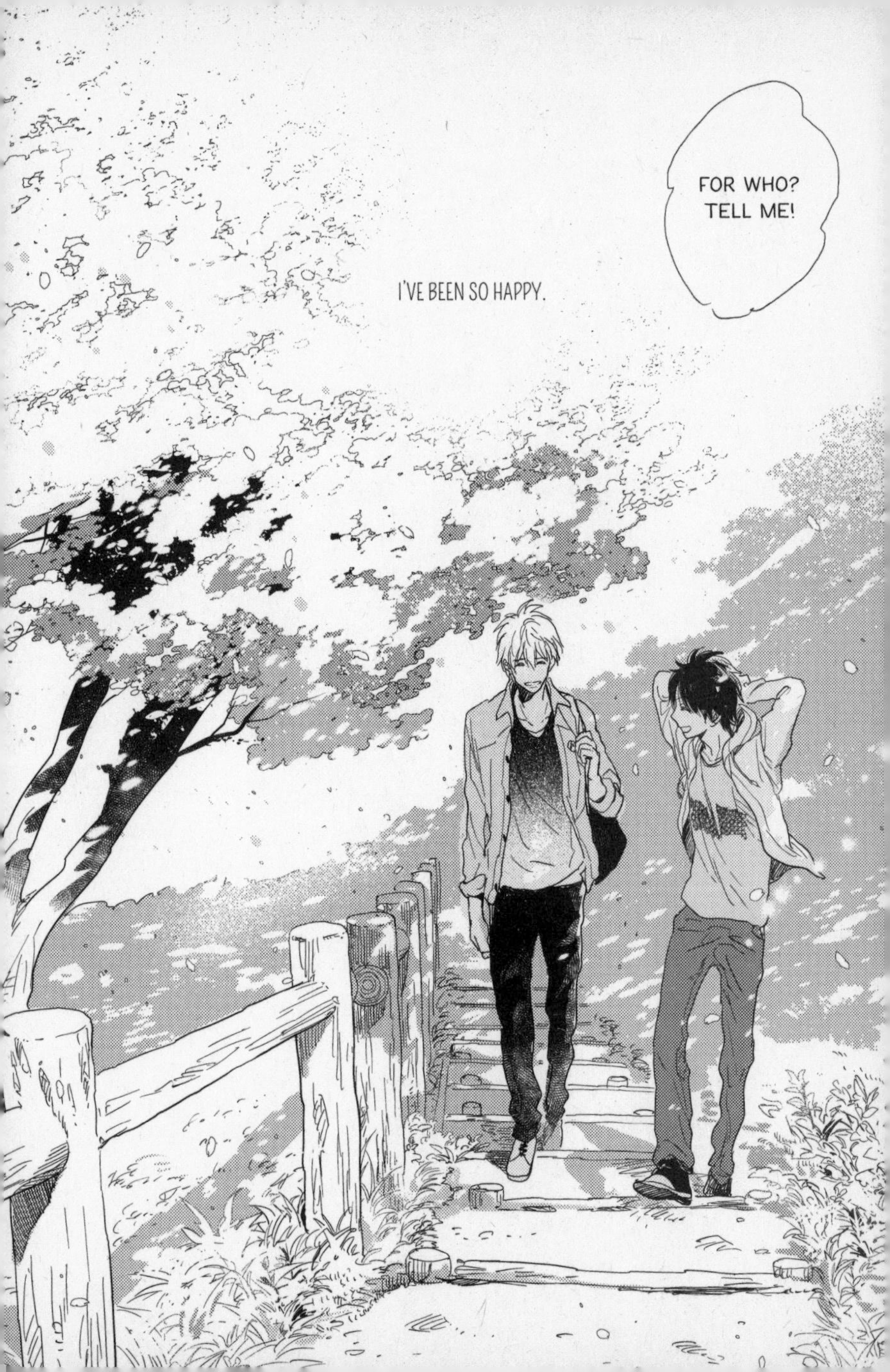
FOR WHO? TELL ME!
I'VE BEEN SO HAPPY.

i hear
the
sunspot

i hear the sunspot

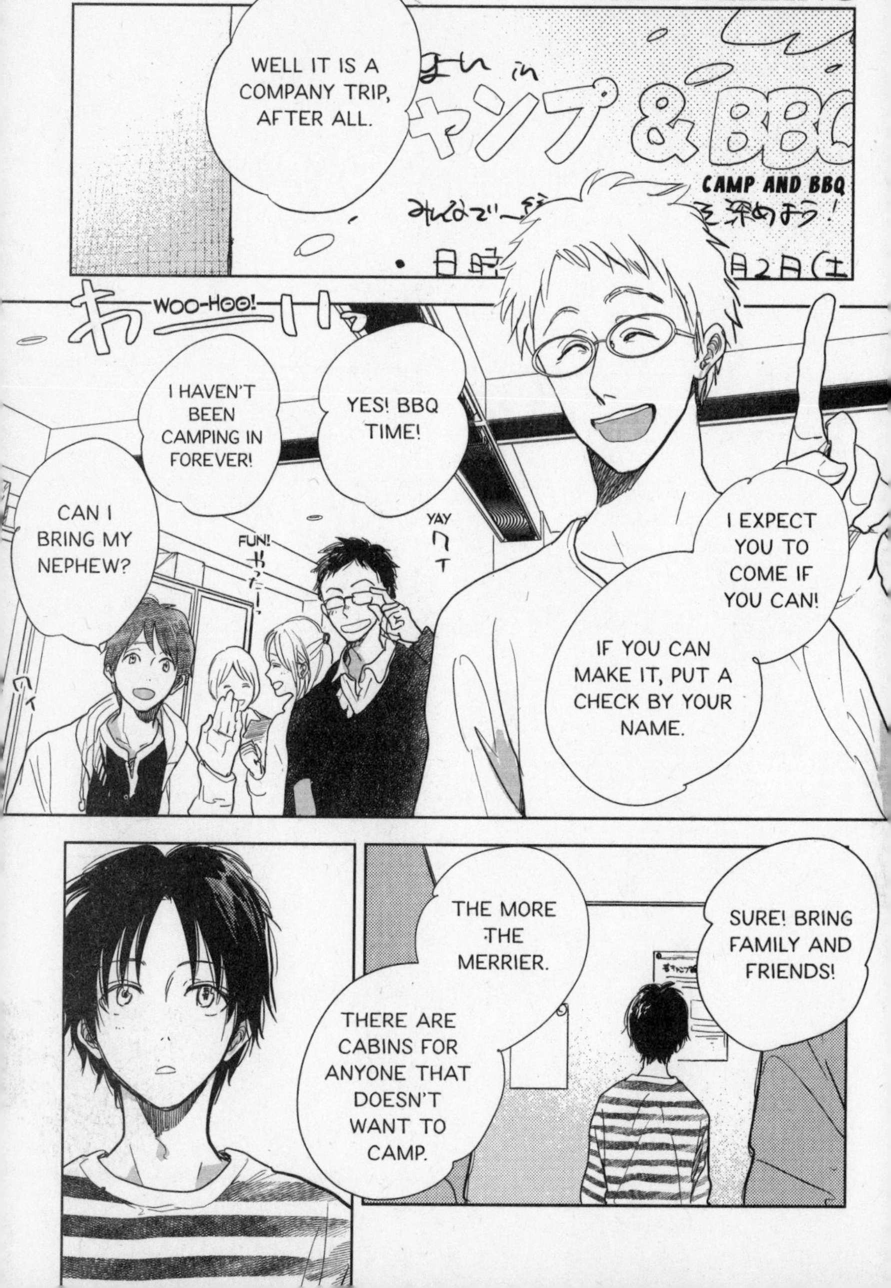
CAMP AND BBQ
WELL IT IS A COMPANY TRIP, AFTER ALL.
I EXPECT YOU TO COME IF YOU CAN!
IF YOU CAN MAKE IT, PUT A CHECK BY YOUR NAME.
WOO-HOO!
YES! BBQ TIME!
YAY
I HAVEN'T BEEN CAMPING IN FOREVER!
FUN!
CAN I BRING MY NEPHEW?
SURE! BRING FAMILY AND FRIENDS!
THE MORE THE MERRIER.
THERE ARE CABINS FOR ANYONE THAT DOESN'T WANT TO CAMP.

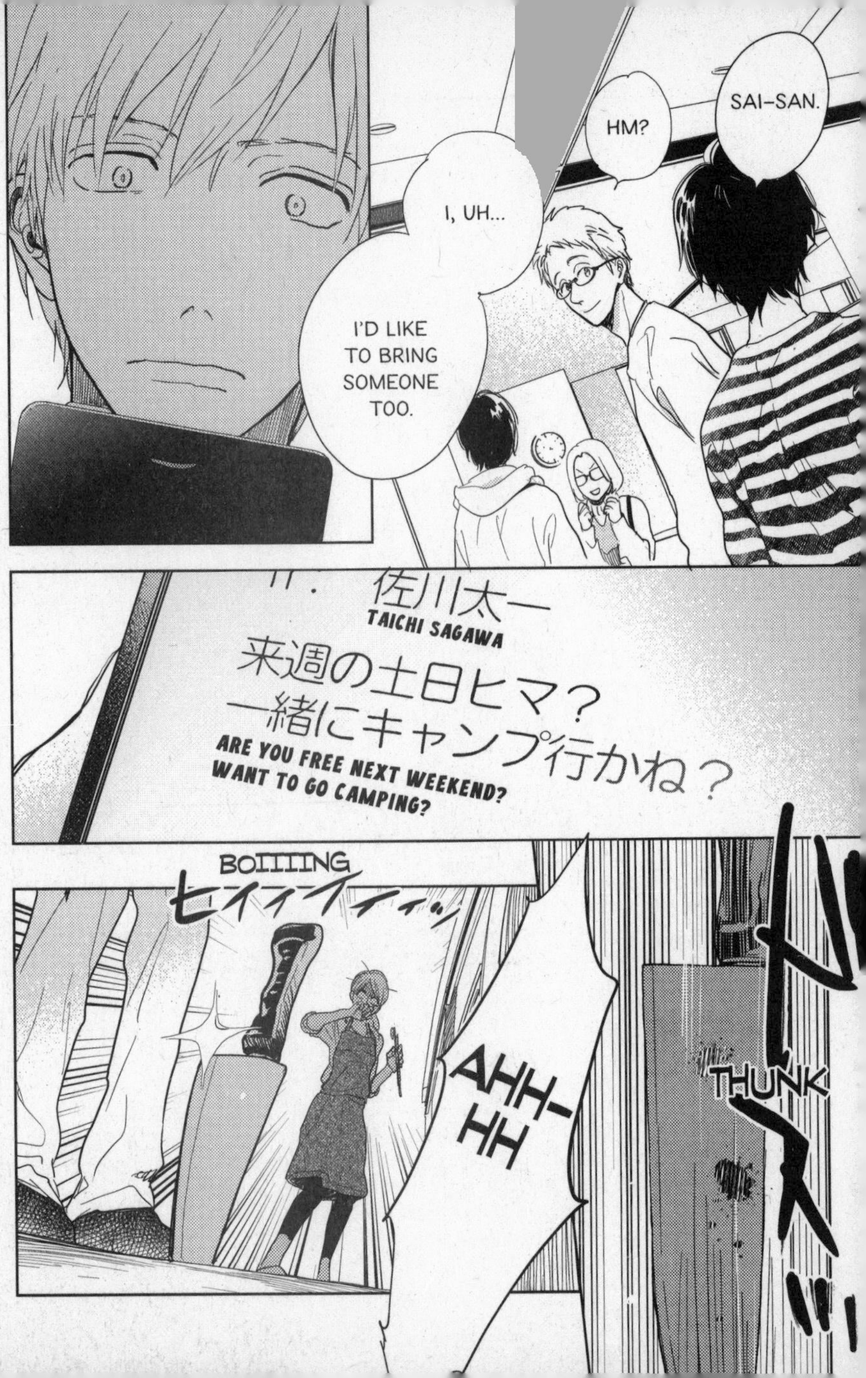

SAI-SAN.
HM?
I, UH...
I'D LIKE TO BRING SOMEONE TOO.
佐川太一
TAICHI SAGAWA
来週の土日ヒマ？
一緒にキャンプ行かね？
ARE YOU FREE NEXT WEEKEND? WANT TO GO CAMPING?
THUNK
BOIIIING
AHH-HH

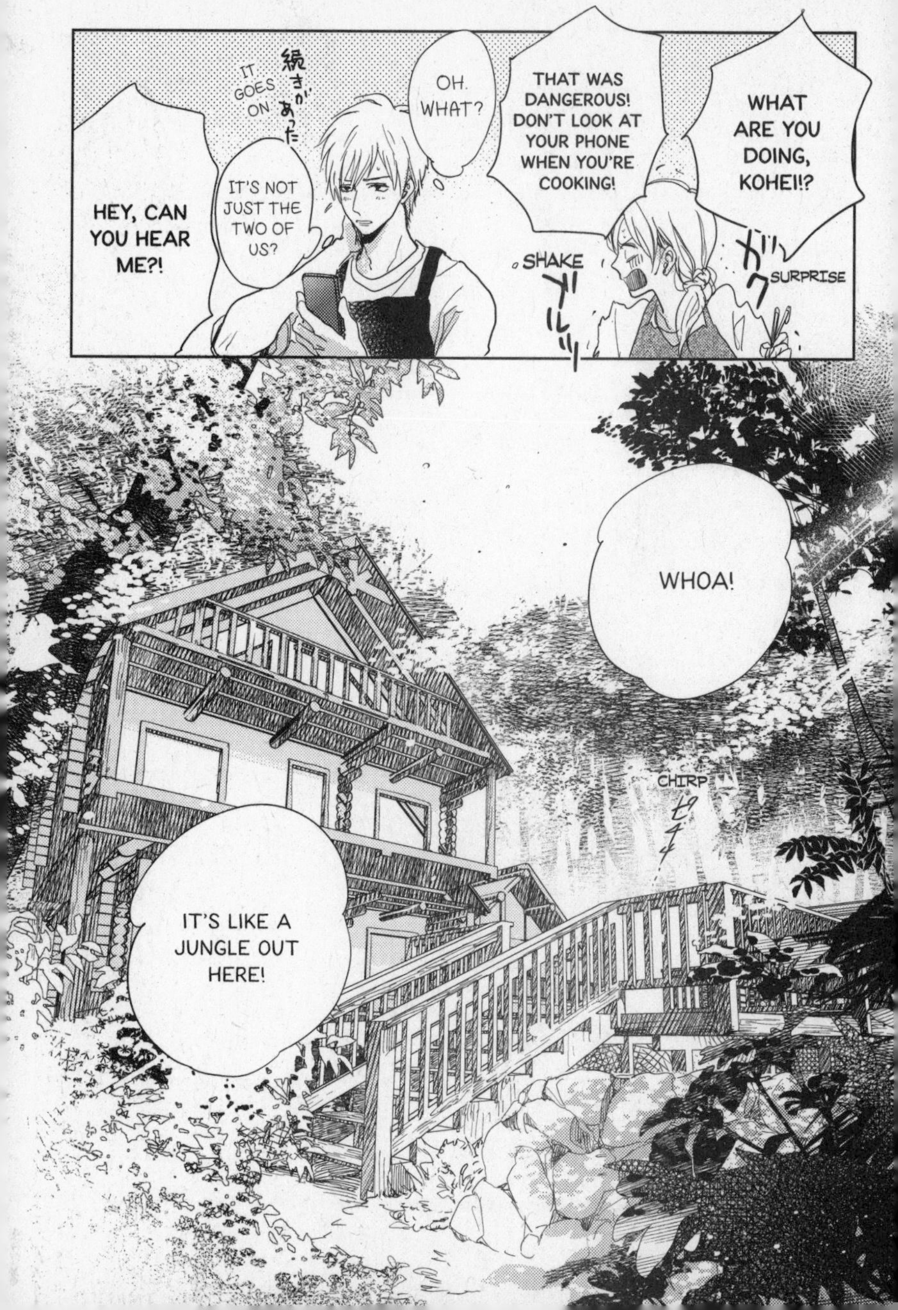
WHAT ARE YOU DOING, KOHEI!?
SURPRISE
THAT WAS DANGEROUS! DON'T LOOK AT YOUR PHONE WHEN YOU'RE COOKING!
SHAKE
OH. WHAT?
続きがあった
IT GOES ON
IT'S NOT JUST THE TWO OF US?
HEY, CAN YOU HEAR ME?!
WHOA!
CHIRP
IT'S LIKE A JUNGLE OUT HERE!

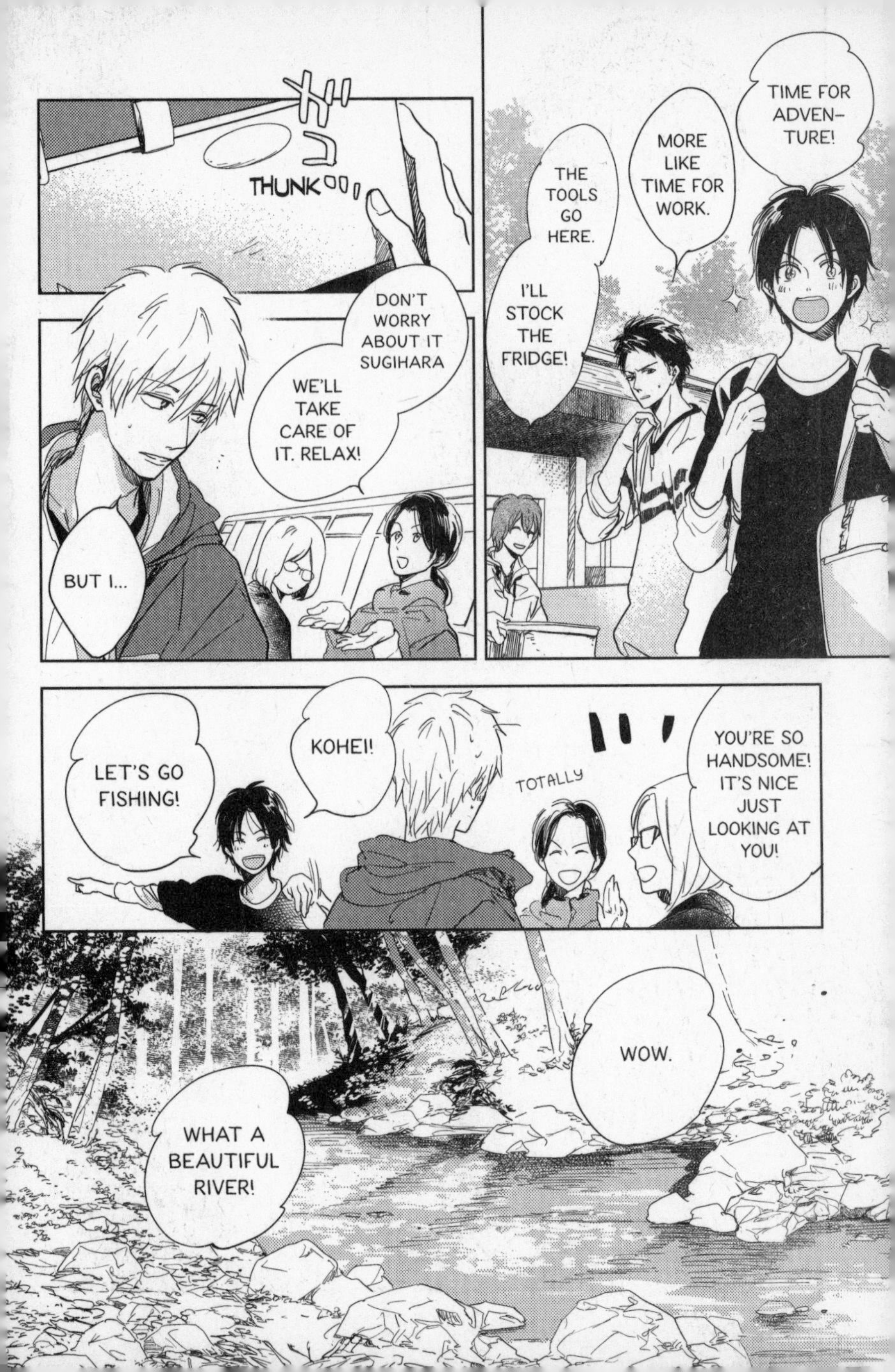
TIME FOR ADVEN- TURE!
MORE LIKE TIME FOR WORK.
THE TOOLS GO HERE.
I'LL STOCK THE FRIDGE!
THUNK
DON'T WORRY ABOUT IT SUGIHARA
WE'LL TAKE CARE OF IT. RELAX!
BUT I...
YOU'RE SO HANDSOME! IT'S NICE JUST LOOKING AT YOU!
TOTALLY
KOHEI!
LET'S GO FISHING!
WOW.
WHAT A BEAUTIFUL RIVER!

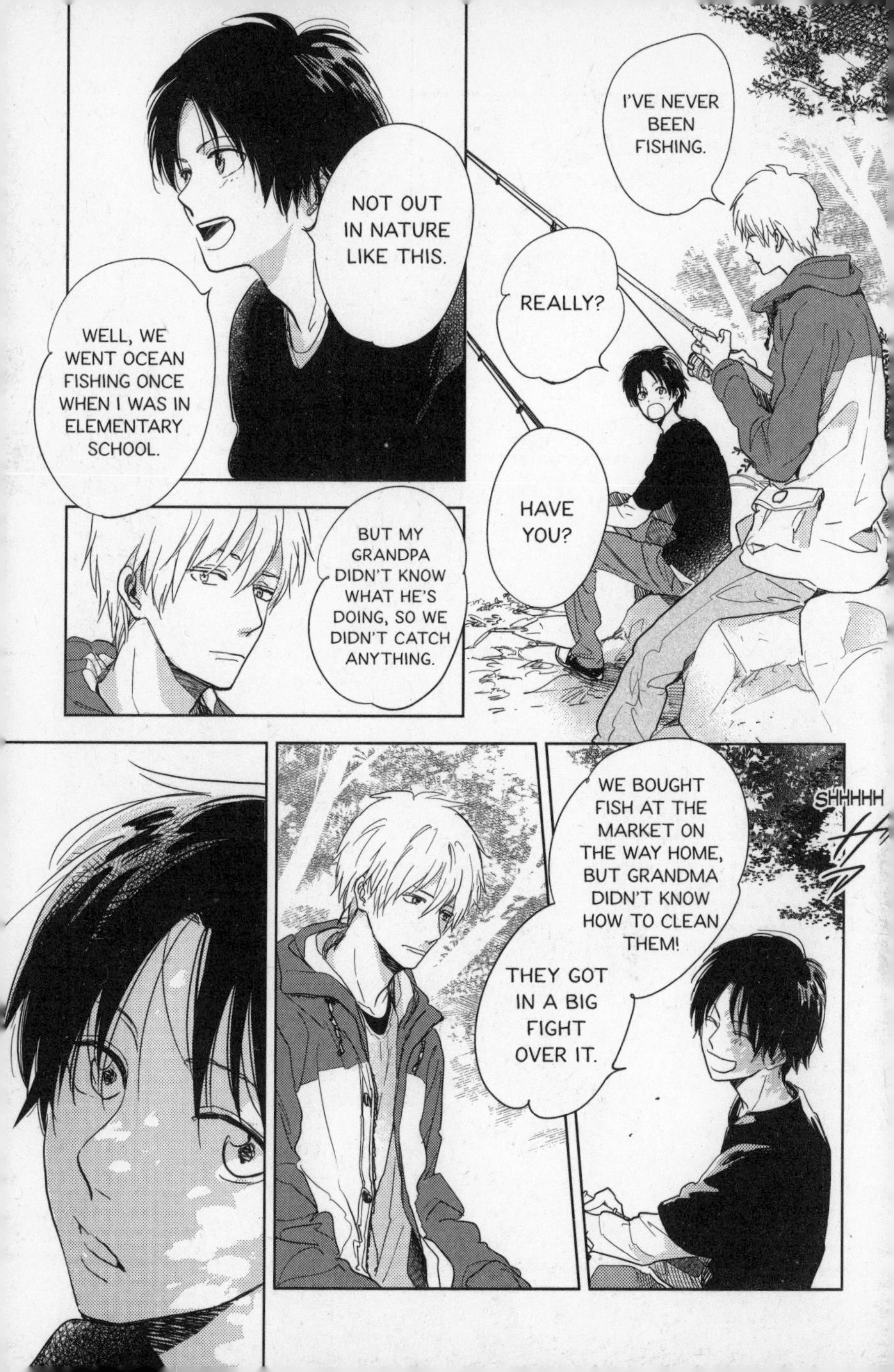
I'VE NEVER BEEN FISHING.
REALLY?
HAVE YOU?
NOT OUT IN NATURE LIKE THIS.
WELL, WE WENT OCEAN FISHING ONCE WHEN I WAS IN ELEMENTARY SCHOOL.
BUT MY GRANDPA DIDN'T KNOW WHAT HE'S DOING, SO WE DIDN'T CATCH ANYTHING.
SHHHHH
WE BOUGHT FISH AT THE MARKET ON THE WAY HOME, BUT GRANDMA DIDN'T KNOW HOW TO CLEAN THEM!
THEY GOT IN A BIG FIGHT OVER IT.

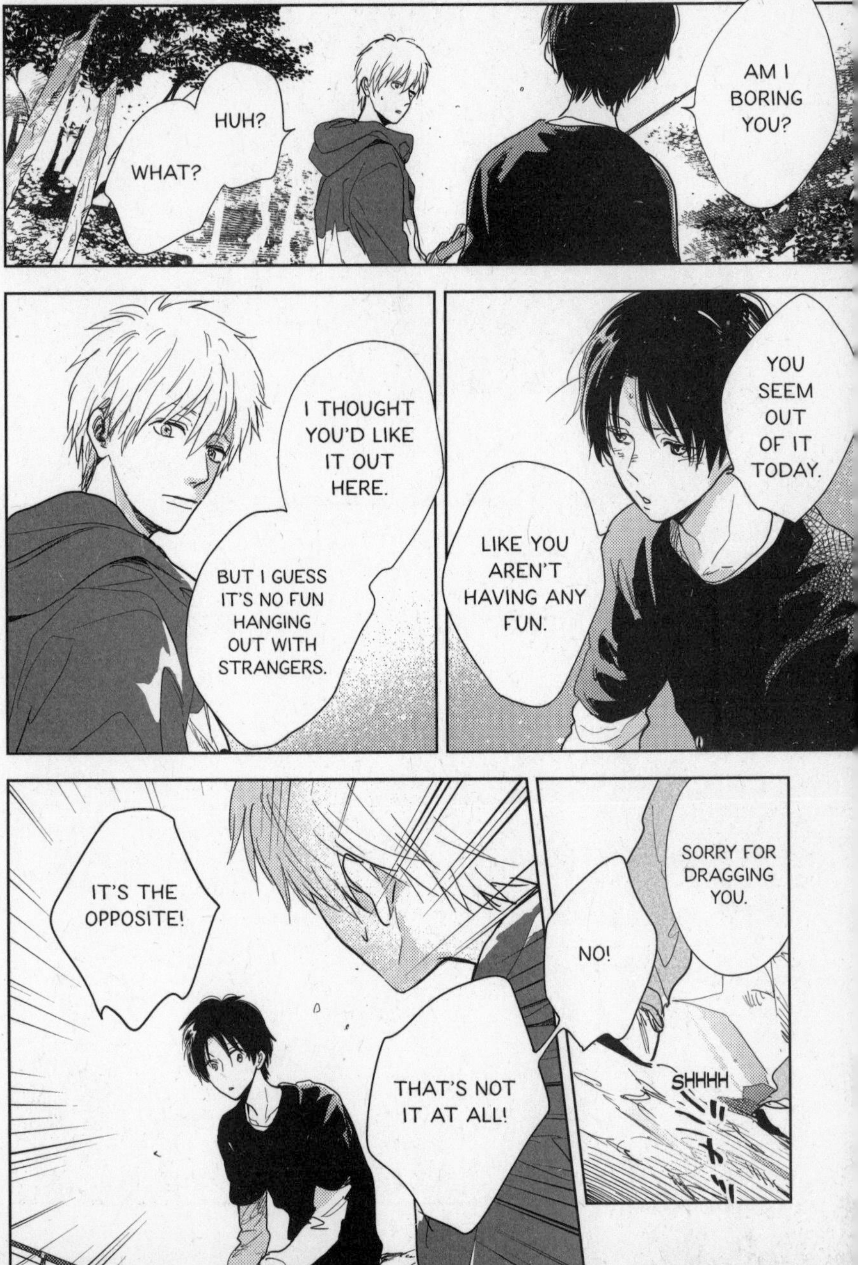
AM I BORING YOU?
HUH?
WHAT?
YOU SEEM OUT OF IT TODAY.
LIKE YOU AREN'T HAVING ANY FUN.
I THOUGHT YOU'D LIKE IT OUT HERE.
BUT I GUESS IT'S NO FUN HANGING OUT WITH STRANGERS.
SORRY FOR DRAGGING YOU.
SHHHH
NO!
THAT'S NOT IT AT ALL!
IT'S THE OPPOSITE!

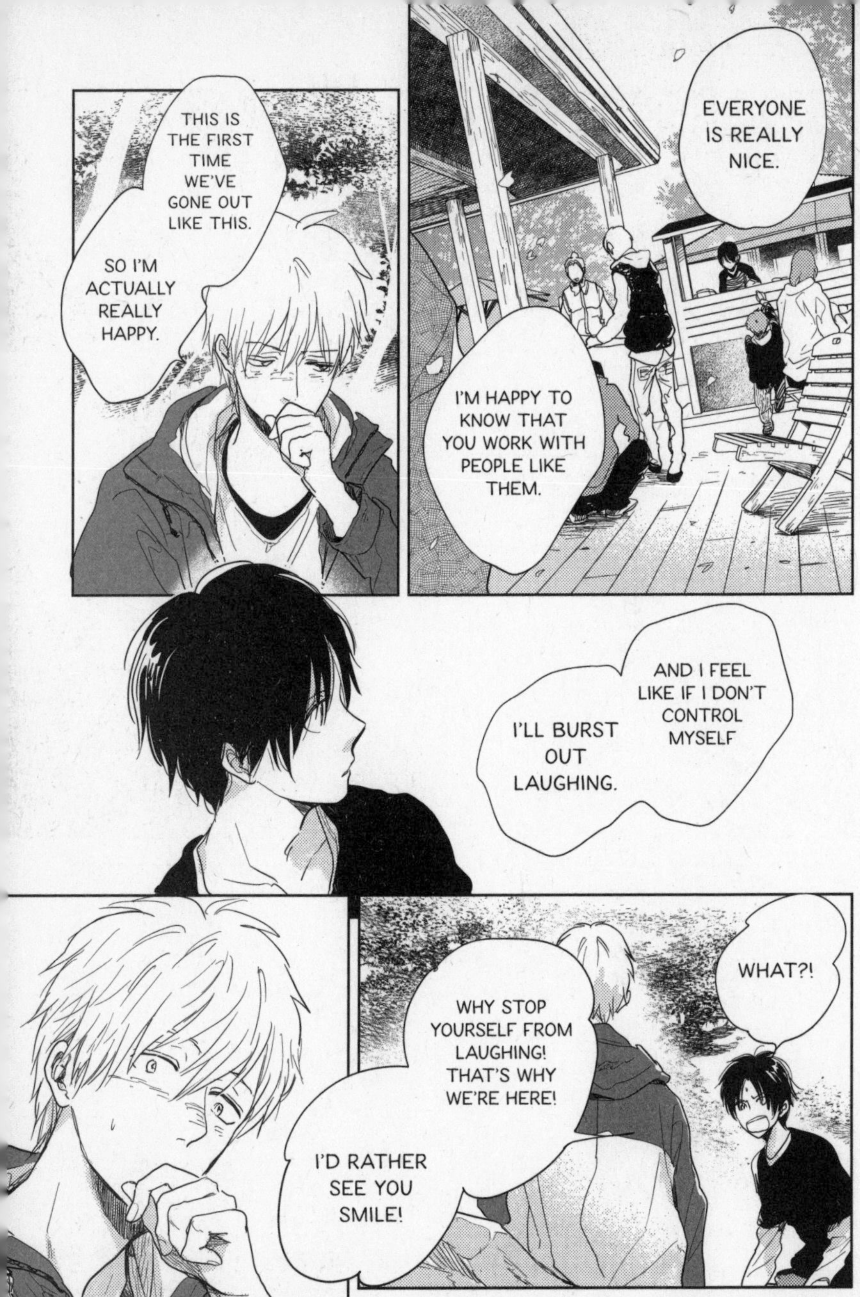
EVERYONE IS REALLY NICE.
I'M HAPPY TO KNOW THAT YOU WORK WITH PEOPLE LIKE THEM.
THIS IS THE FIRST TIME WE'VE GONE OUT LIKE THIS.
SO I'M ACTUALLY REALLY HAPPY.
AND I FEEL LIKE IF I DON'T CONTROL MYSELF
I'LL BURST OUT LAUGHING.
WHAT?!
WHY STOP YOURSELF FROM LAUGHING! THAT'S WHY WE'RE HERE!
I'D RATHER SEE YOU SMILE!

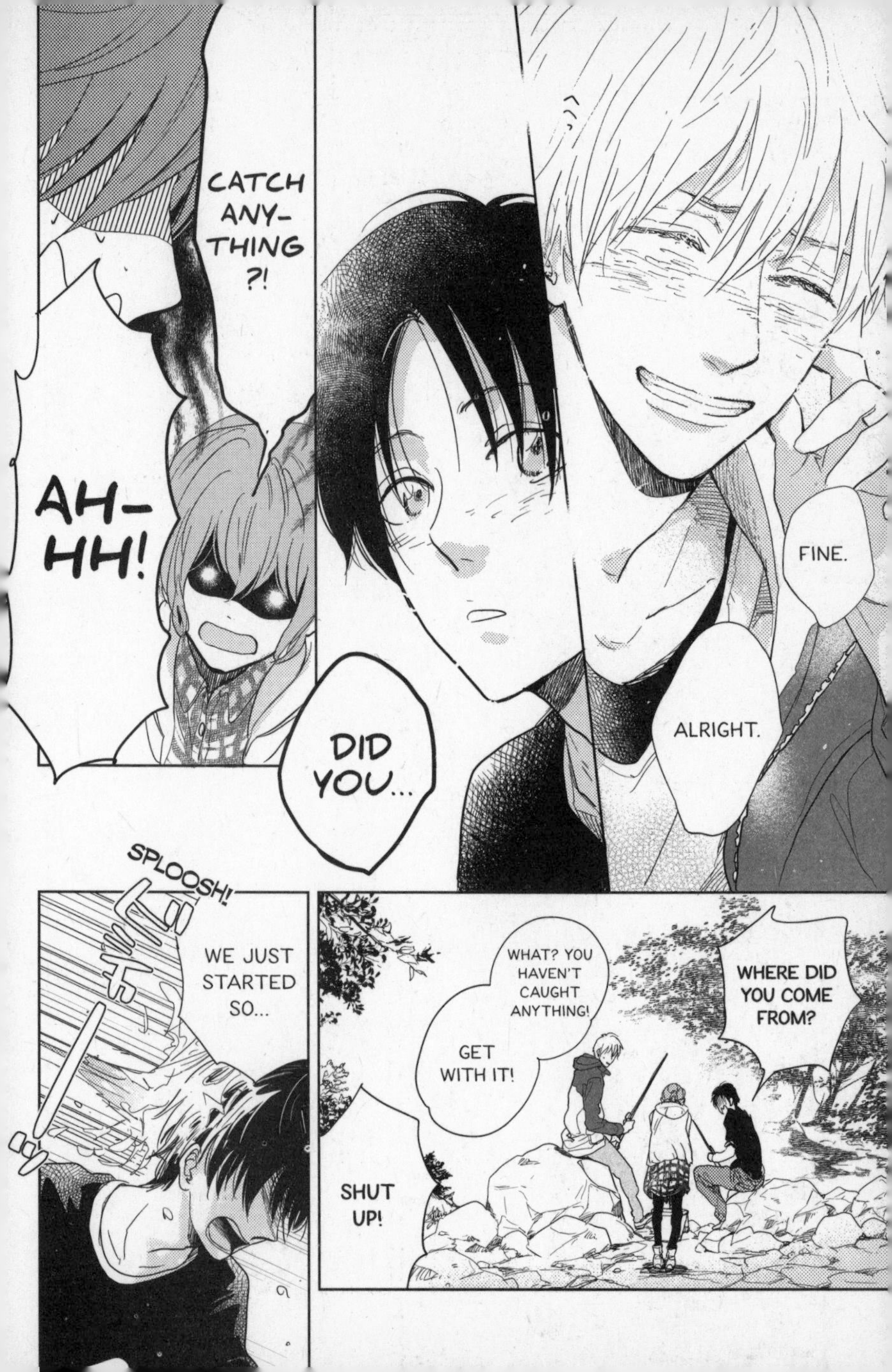
FINE.
ALRIGHT.
DID YOU...
CATCH ANY-THING ?!
AH-HH!
WHERE DID YOU COME FROM?
WHAT? YOU HAVEN'T CAUGHT ANYTHING!
GET WITH IT!
SHUT UP!
SPLOOSH!
WE JUST STARTED SO...

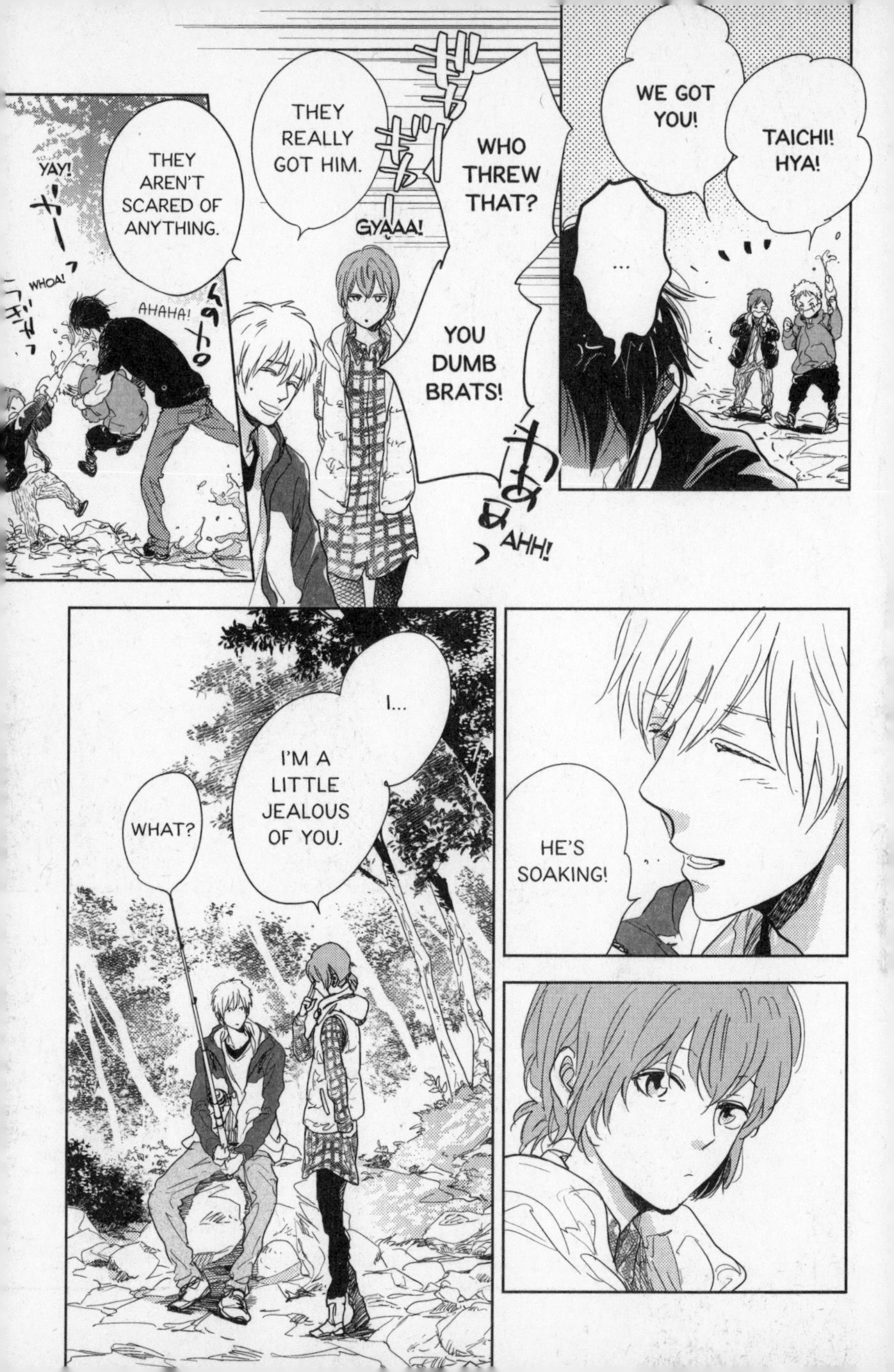

TAICHI! HYA!
WE GOT YOU!
...
WHO THREW THAT?
YOU DUMB BRATS!
AHH!
GYAAA!
THEY REALLY GOT HIM.
THEY AREN'T SCARED OF ANYTHING.
YAY!
AHAHA!
WHOA!
HE'S SOAKING!
I...
I'M A LITTLE JEALOUS OF YOU.
WHAT?

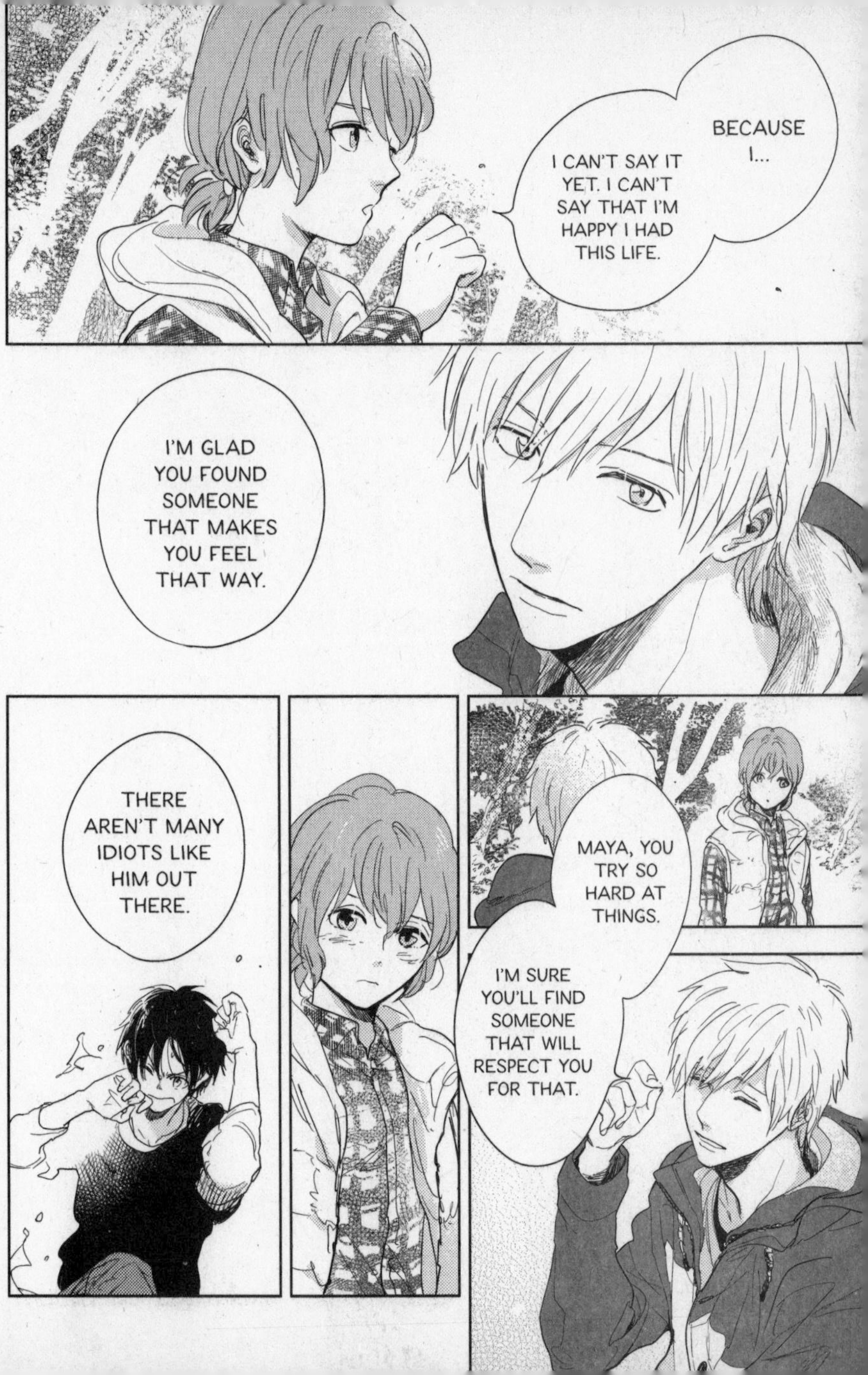
BECAUSE I...
I CAN'T SAY IT YET. I CAN'T SAY THAT I'M HAPPY I HAD THIS LIFE.
I'M GLAD YOU FOUND SOMEONE THAT MAKES YOU FEEL THAT WAY.
MAYA, YOU TRY SO HARD AT THINGS.
I'M SURE YOU'LL FIND SOMEONE THAT WILL RESPECT YOU FOR THAT.
THERE AREN'T MANY IDIOTS LIKE HIM OUT THERE.

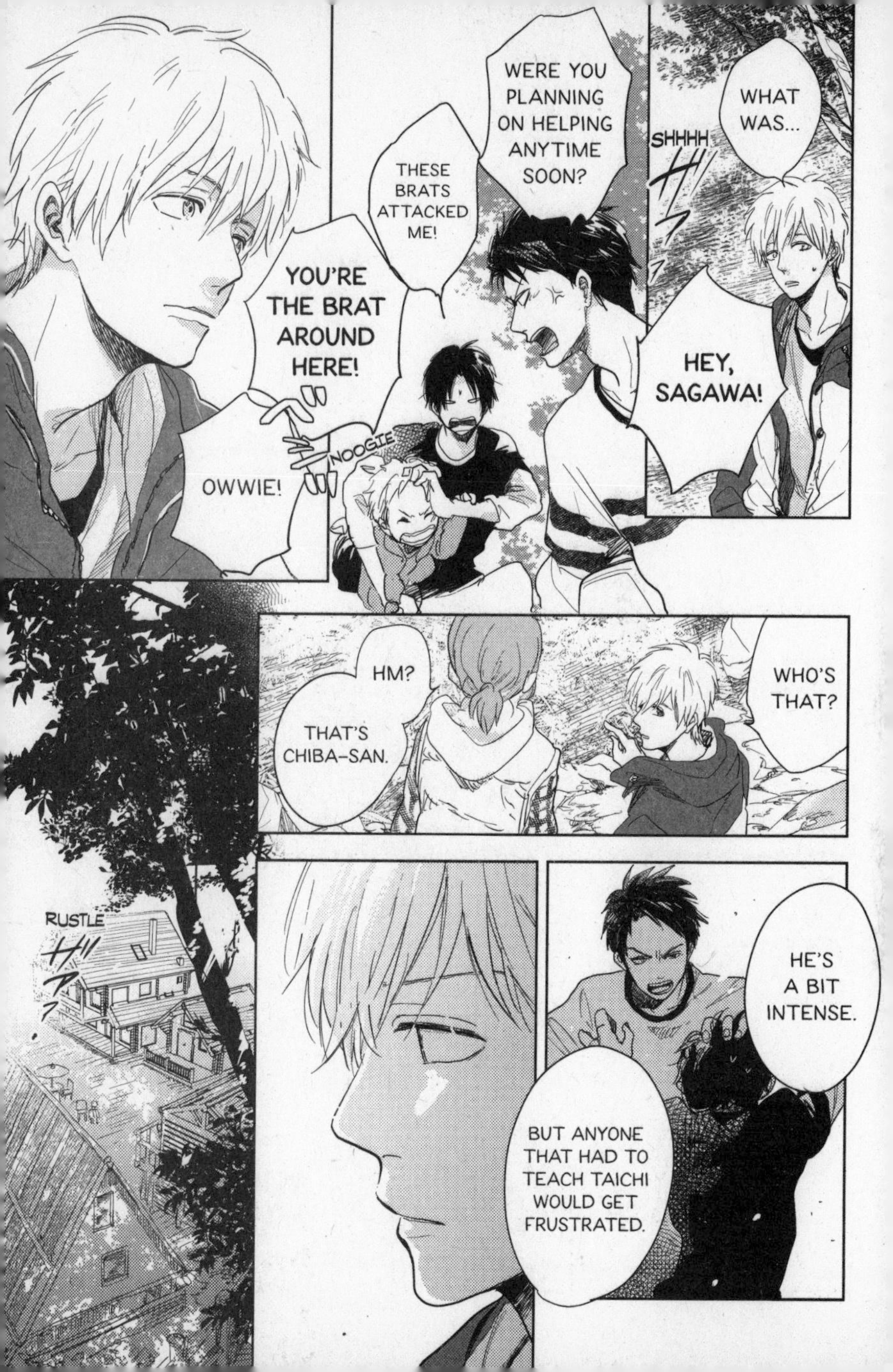
WHAT WAS...
SHHHH
HEY, SAGAWA!
WERE YOU PLANNING ON HELPING ANYTIME SOON?
THESE BRATS ATTACKED ME!
YOU'RE THE BRAT AROUND HERE!
NOOGIE
OWWIE!
WHO'S THAT?
HM?
THAT'S CHIBA-SAN.
HE'S A BIT INTENSE.
BUT ANYONE THAT HAD TO TEACH TAICHI WOULD GET FRUSTRATED.
RUSTLE

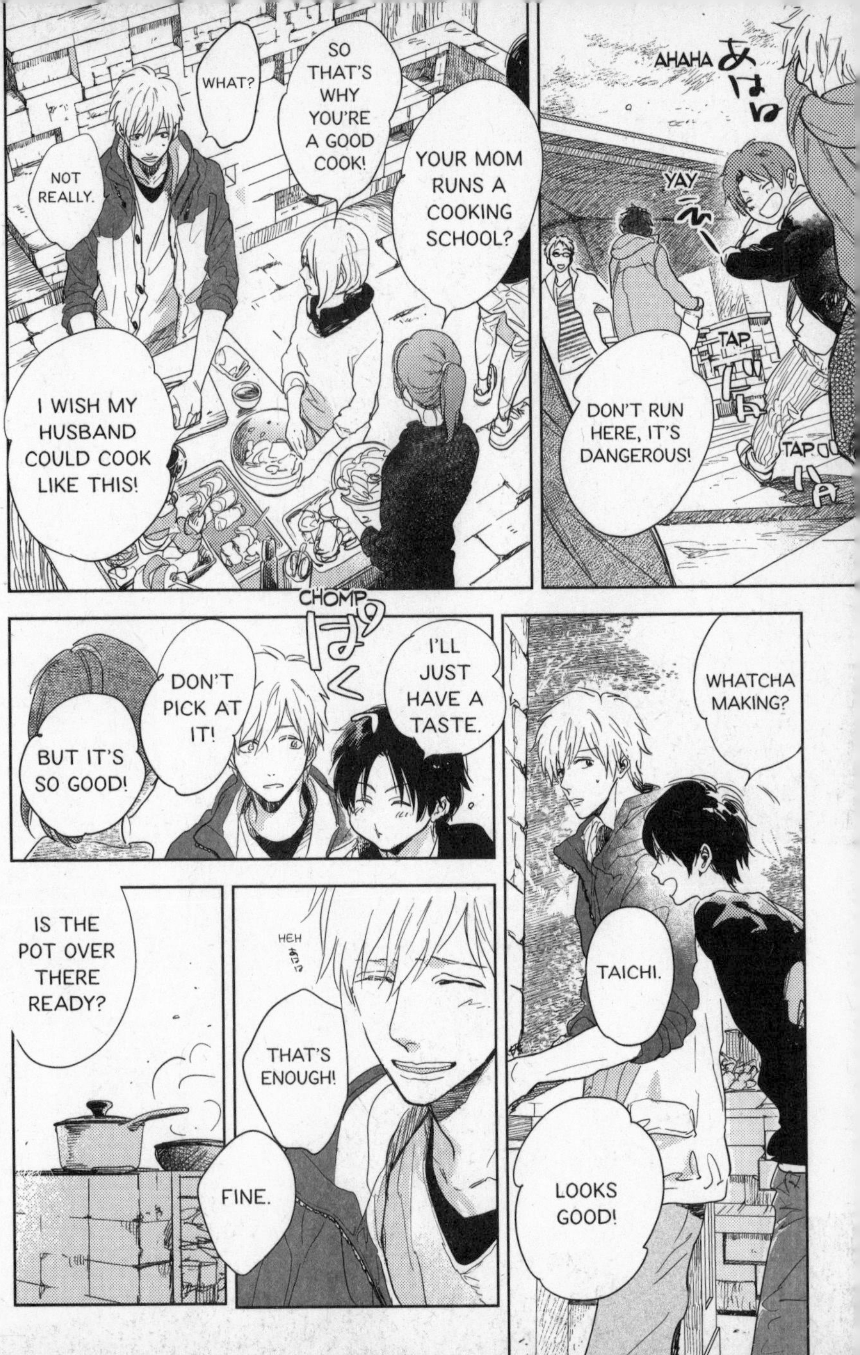
AHAHA
あはは
YAY
TAP
TAP
DON'T RUN HERE, IT'S DANGEROUS!
YOUR MOM RUNS A COOKING SCHOOL?
SO THAT'S WHY YOU'RE A GOOD COOK!
WHAT?
NOT REALLY.
I WISH MY HUSBAND COULD COOK LIKE THIS!
WHATCHA MAKING?
TAICHI.
LOOKS GOOD!
CHOMP
ぱく
I'LL JUST HAVE A TASTE.
DON'T PICK AT IT!
BUT IT'S SO GOOD!
HEH
あはは
THAT'S ENOUGH!
FINE.
IS THE POT OVER THERE READY?

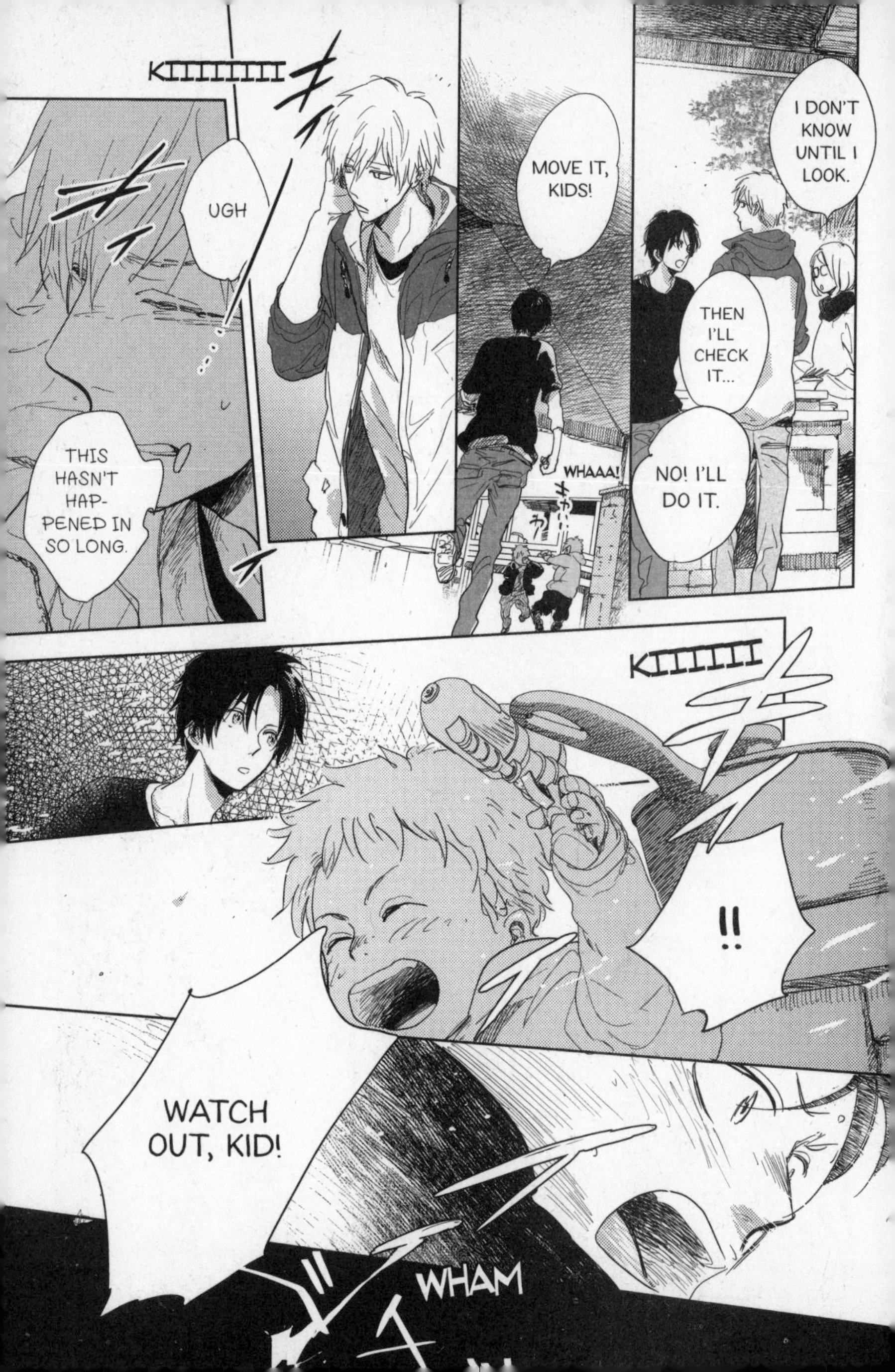

I DON'T KNOW UNTIL I LOOK.
THEN I'LL CHECK IT...
NO! I'LL DO IT.
MOVE IT, KIDS!
WHAAA!
KIIIIIII
UGH
THIS HASN'T HAPPENED IN SO LONG.
KIIIIII
!!
WATCH OUT, KID!
WHAM

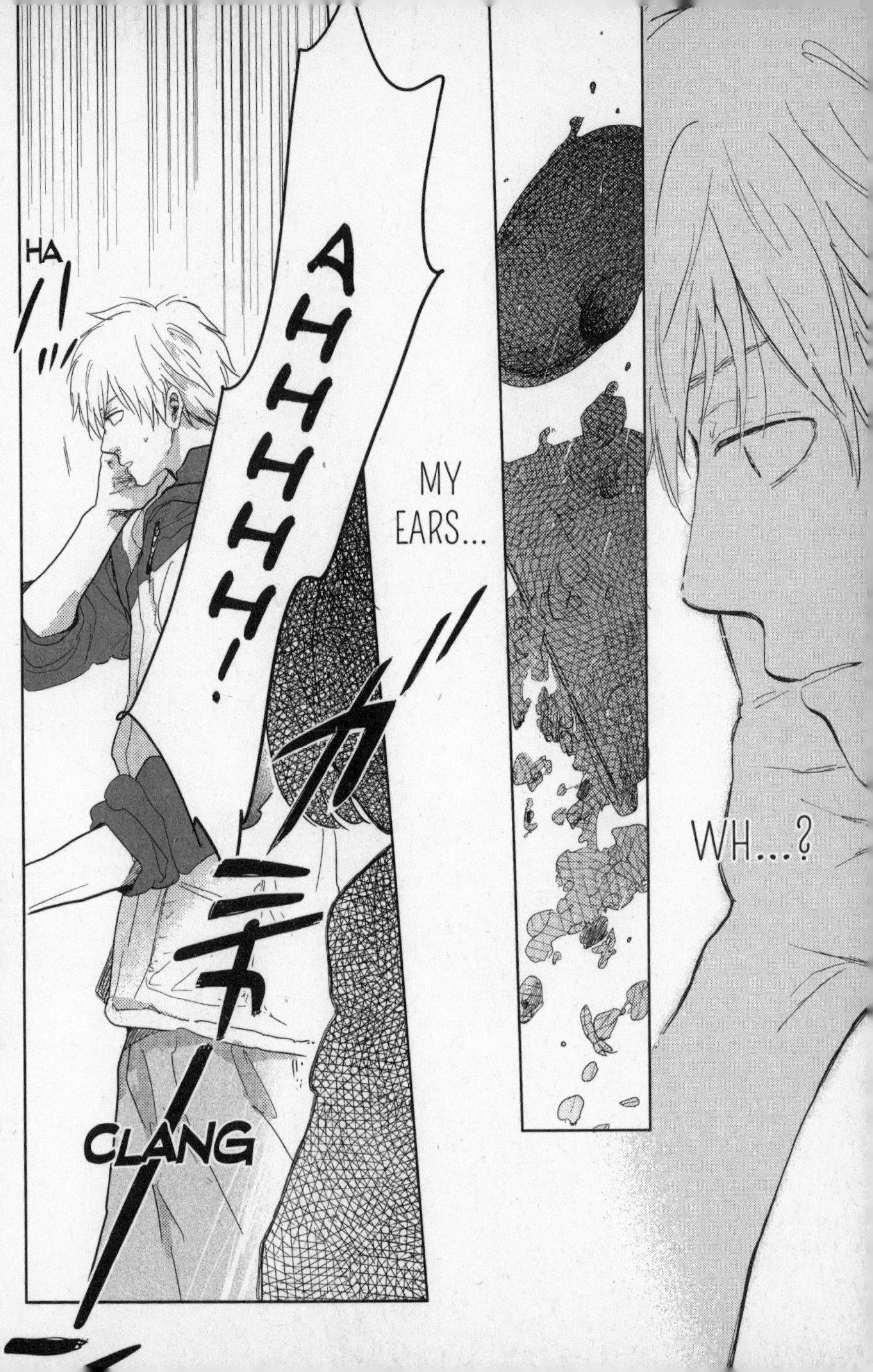
WH...?
AHHHHH!
MY EARS...
HA
CLANG

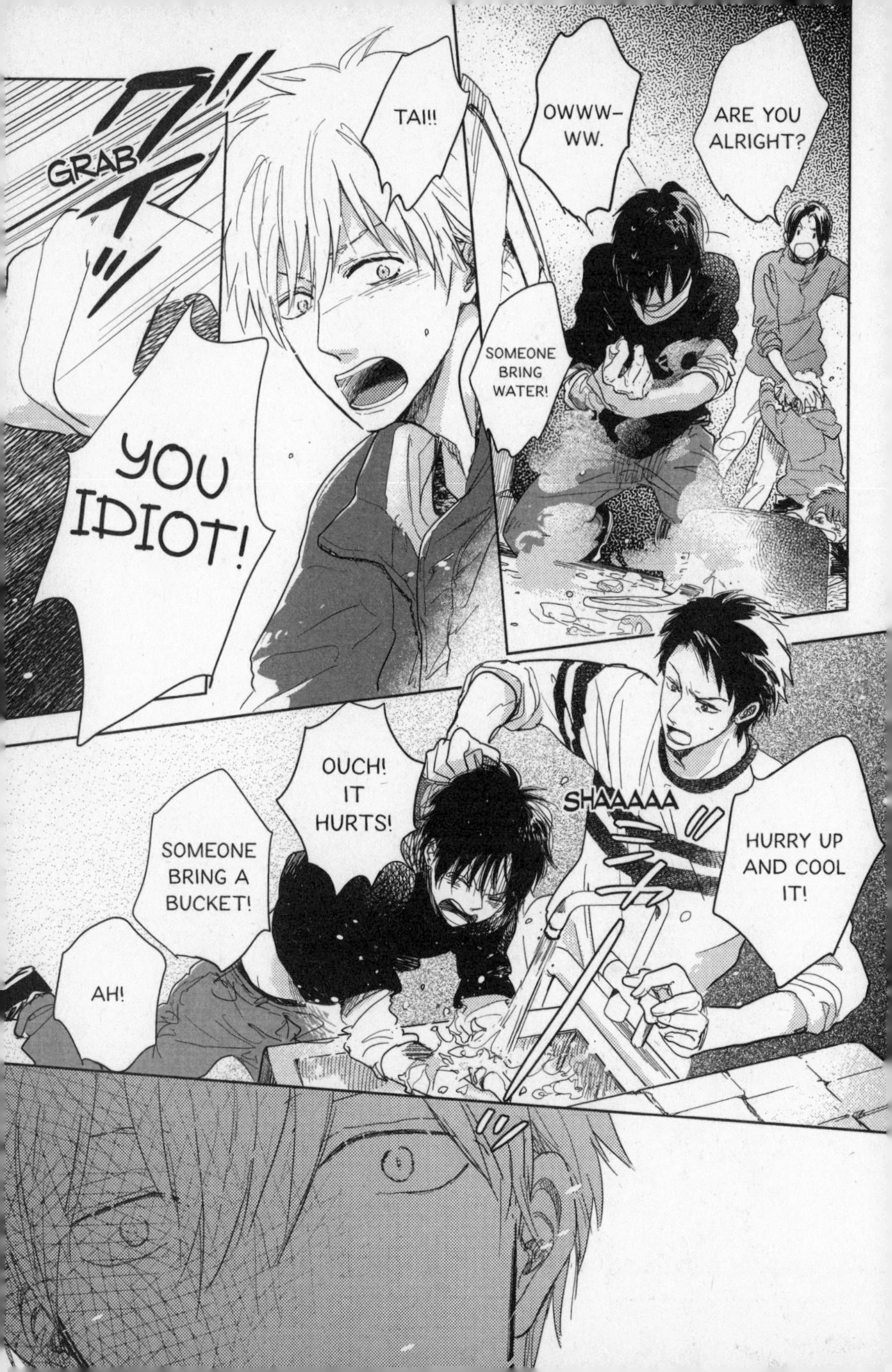
ARE YOU ALRIGHT?
OWWW-WW.
SOMEONE BRING WATER!
TAI!!
GRAB
YOU IDIOT!
HURRY UP AND COOL IT!
SHAAAAA
OUCH! IT HURTS!
SOMEONE BRING A BUCKET!
AH!

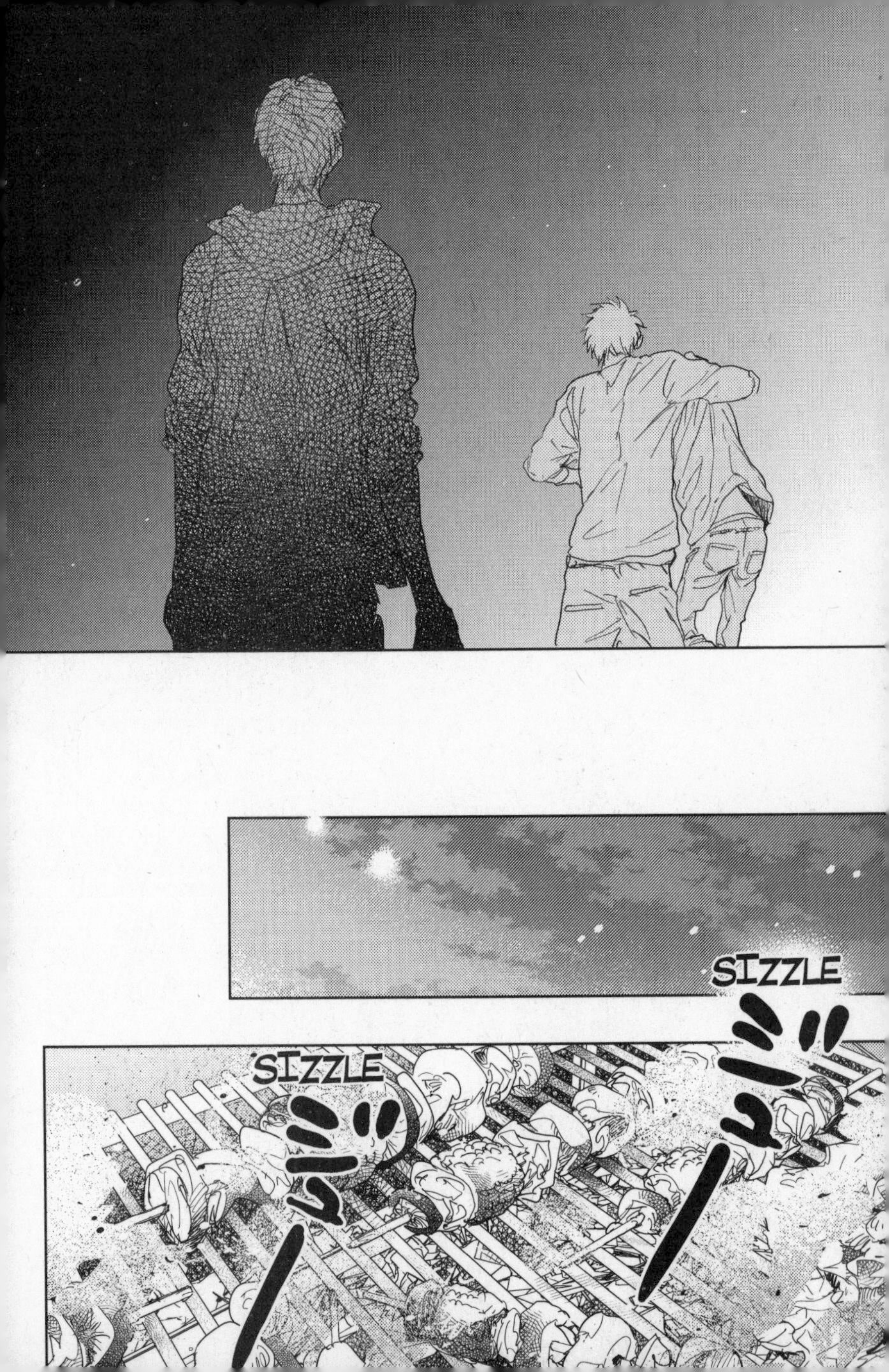
SIZZLE
SIZZLE

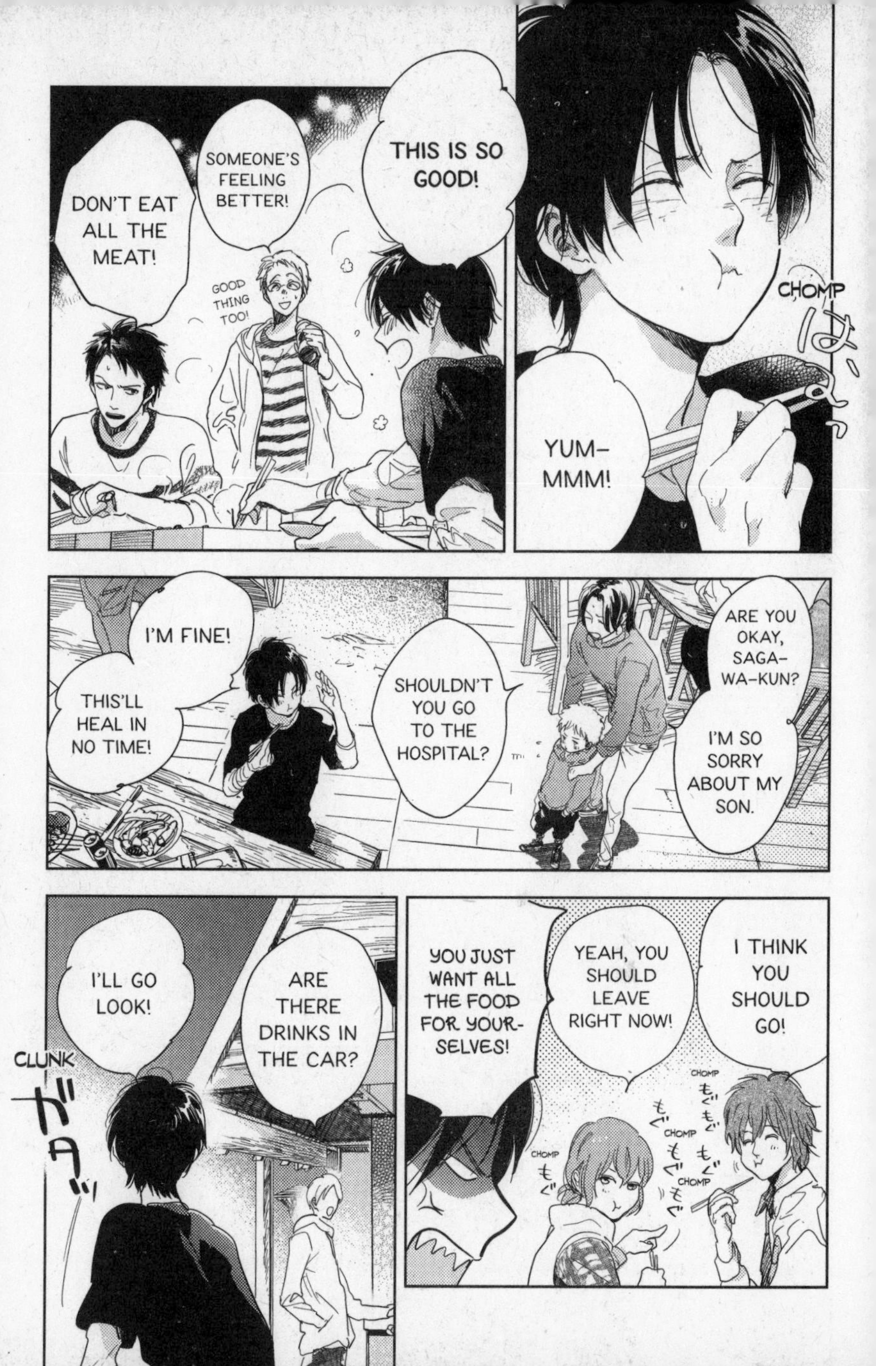
CHOMP
YUM-MMM!
THIS IS SO GOOD!
SOMEONE'S FEELING BETTER!
GOOD THING TOO!
DON'T EAT ALL THE MEAT!
ARE YOU OKAY, SAGA-WA-KUN?
I'M SO SORRY ABOUT MY SON.
SHOULDN'T YOU GO TO THE HOSPITAL?
I'M FINE!
THIS'LL HEAL IN NO TIME!
I THINK YOU SHOULD GO!
YEAH, YOU SHOULD LEAVE RIGHT NOW!
YOU JUST WANT ALL THE FOOD FOR YOUR-SELVES!
CHOMP
CHOMP
CHOMP
CHOMP
ARE THERE DRINKS IN THE CAR?
I'LL GO LOOK!
CLUNK

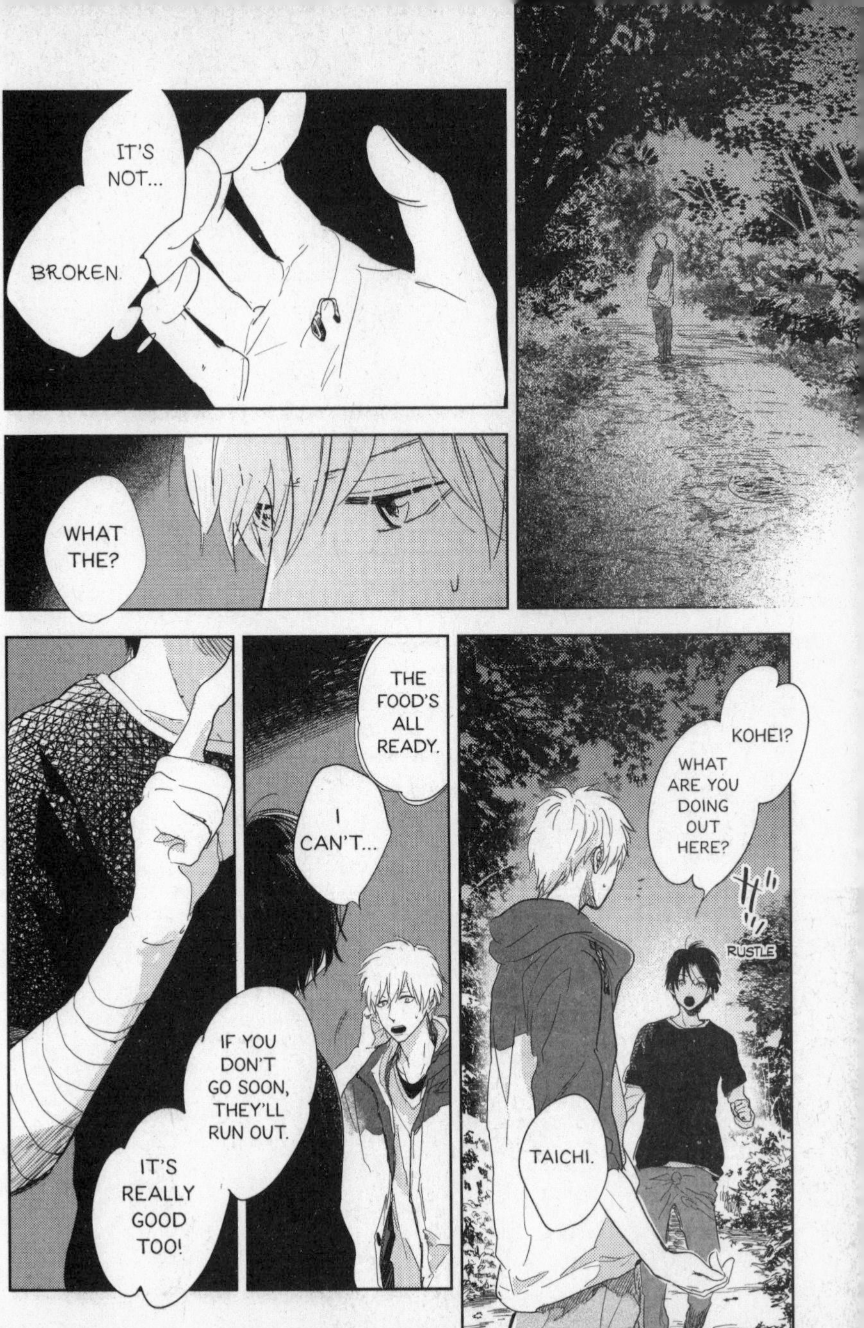
IT'S NOT...
BROKEN.
WHAT THE?
KOHEI? WHAT ARE YOU DOING OUT HERE?
RUSTLE
TAICHI.
THE FOOD'S ALL READY.
I CAN'T...
IF YOU DON'T GO SOON, THEY'LL RUN OUT.
IT'S REALLY GOOD TOO!

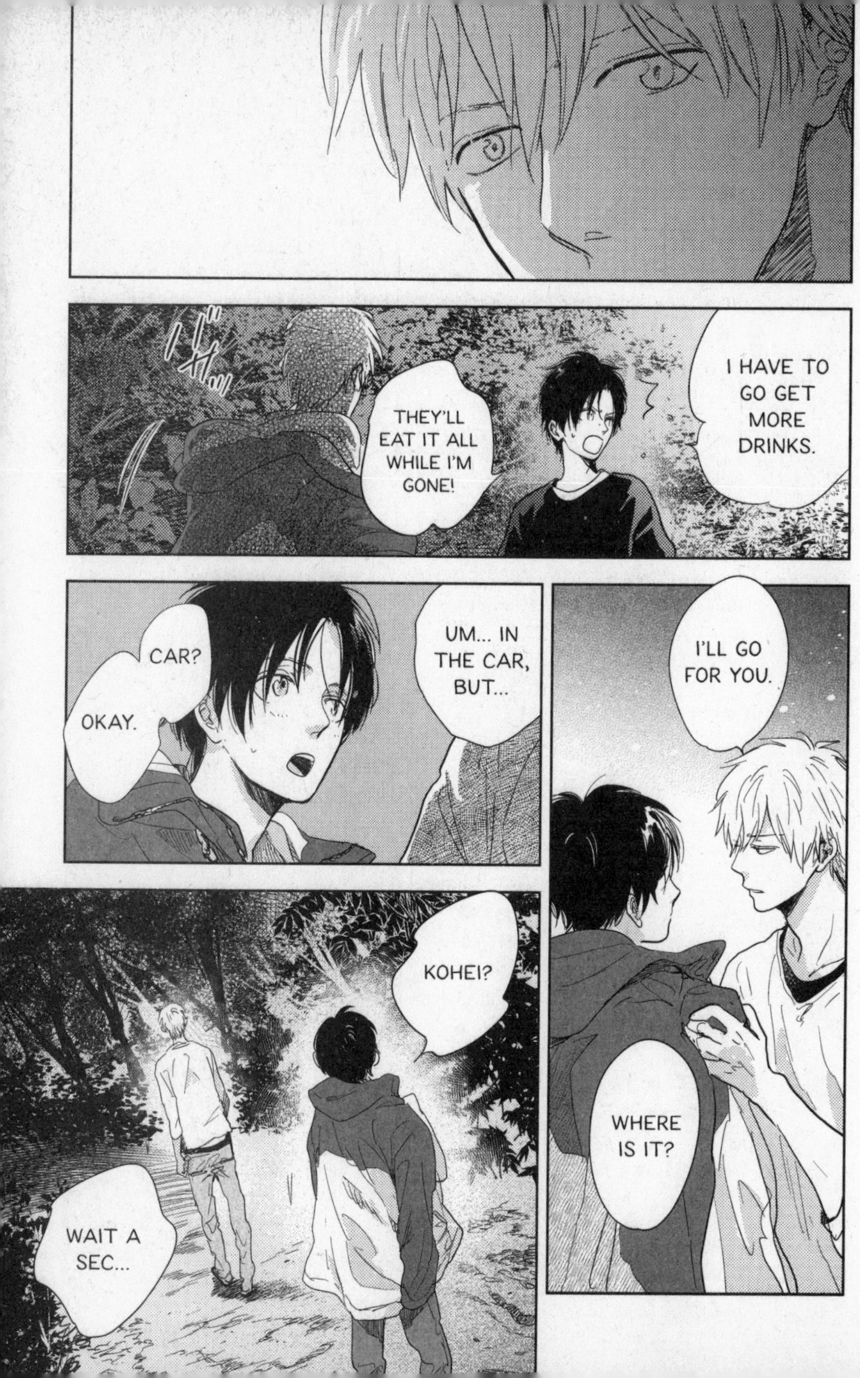
I HAVE TO GO GET MORE DRINKS.
THEY'LL EAT IT ALL WHILE I'M GONE!
I'LL GO FOR YOU.
WHERE IS IT?
UM... IN THE CAR, BUT...
CAR?
OKAY.
KOHEI?
WAIT A SEC...

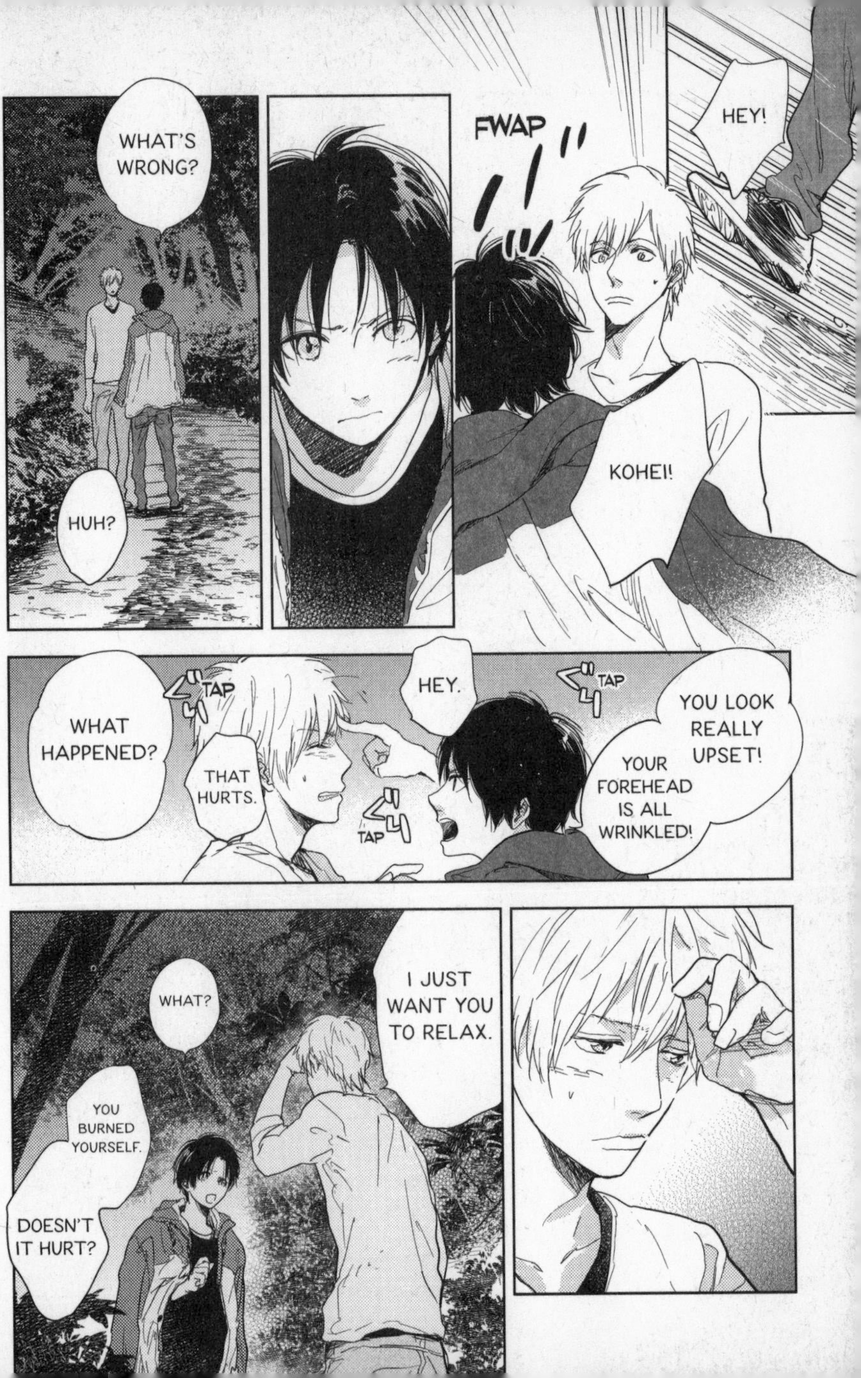
HEY!
FWAP
KOHEI!
WHAT'S WRONG?
HUH?
YOU LOOK REALLY UPSET!
TAP
YOUR FOREHEAD IS ALL WRINKLED!
HEY.
TAP
THAT HURTS.
TAP
WHAT HAPPENED?
I JUST WANT YOU TO RELAX.
WHAT?
YOU BURNED YOURSELF.
DOESN'T IT HURT?

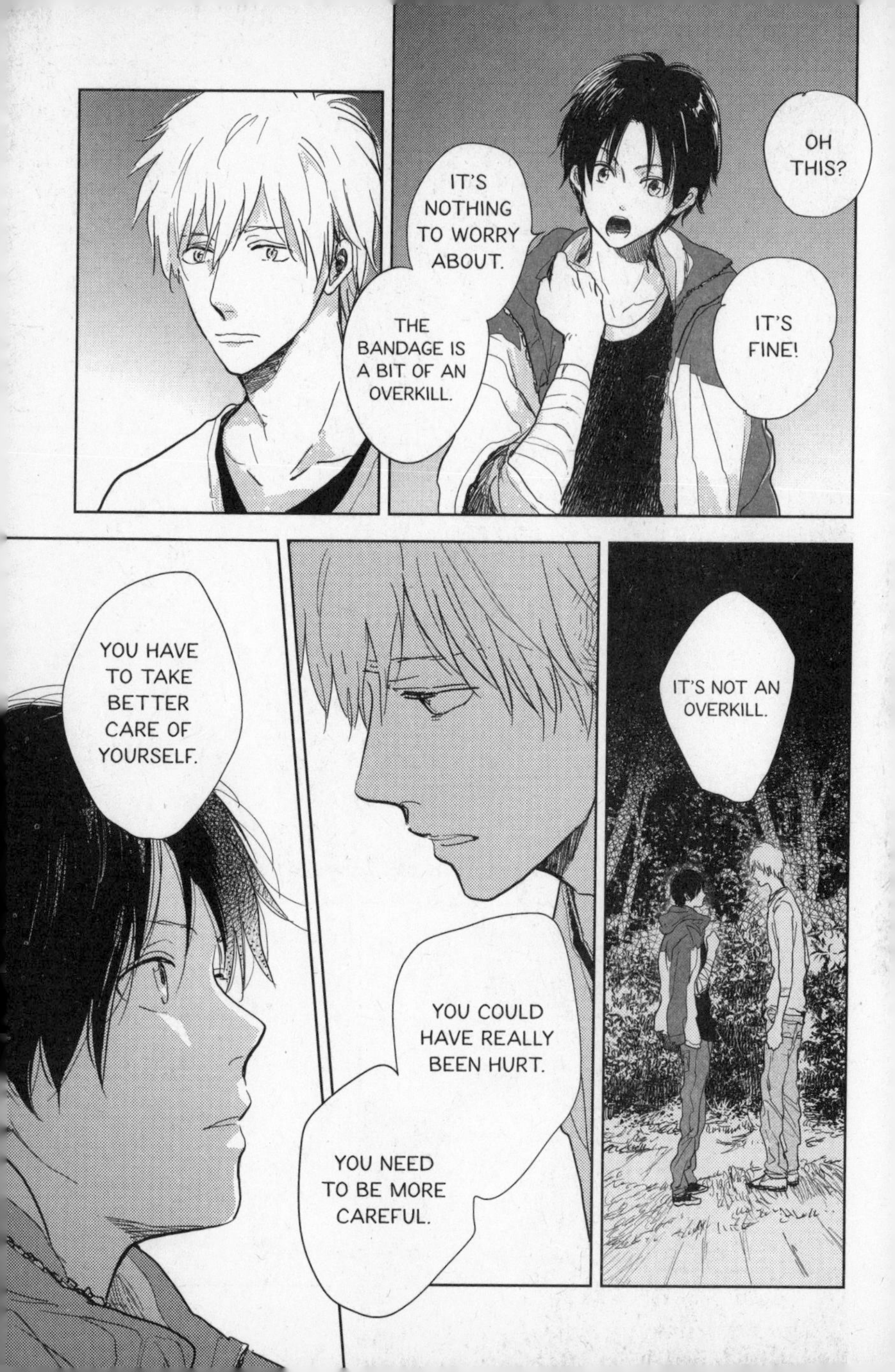
OH THIS?
IT'S FINE!
IT'S NOTHING TO WORRY ABOUT.
THE BANDAGE IS A BIT OF AN OVERKILL.
IT'S NOT AN OVERKILL.
YOU COULD HAVE REALLY BEEN HURT.
YOU NEED TO BE MORE CAREFUL.
YOU HAVE TO TAKE BETTER CARE OF YOURSELF.

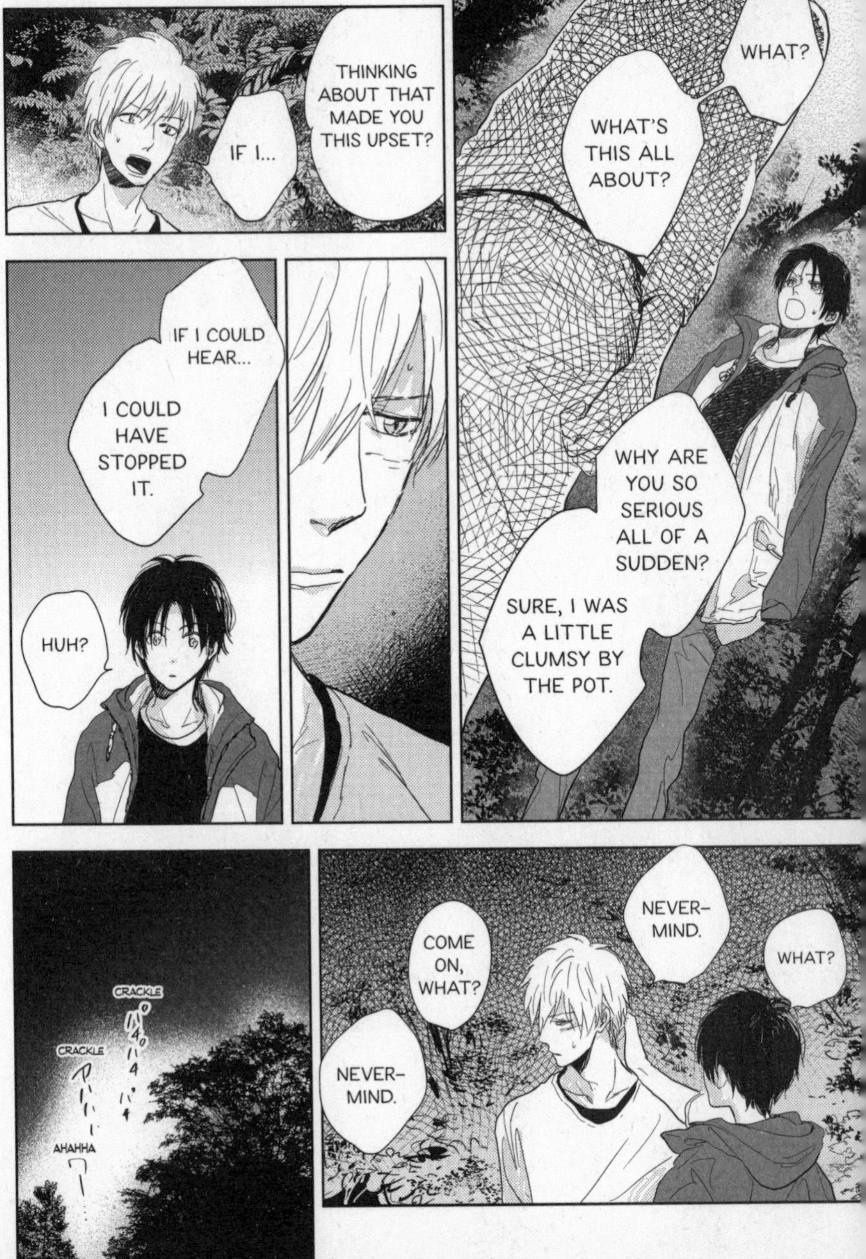
WHAT?
WHAT'S THIS ALL ABOUT?
WHY ARE YOU SO SERIOUS ALL OF A SUDDEN?
SURE, I WAS A LITTLE CLUMSY BY THE POT.
THINKING ABOUT THAT MADE YOU THIS UPSET?
IF I...
IF I COULD HEAR...
I COULD HAVE STOPPED IT.
HUH?
WHAT?
NEVER-MIND.
COME ON, WHAT?
NEVER-MIND.
CRACKLE
CRACKLE
AHAHHA

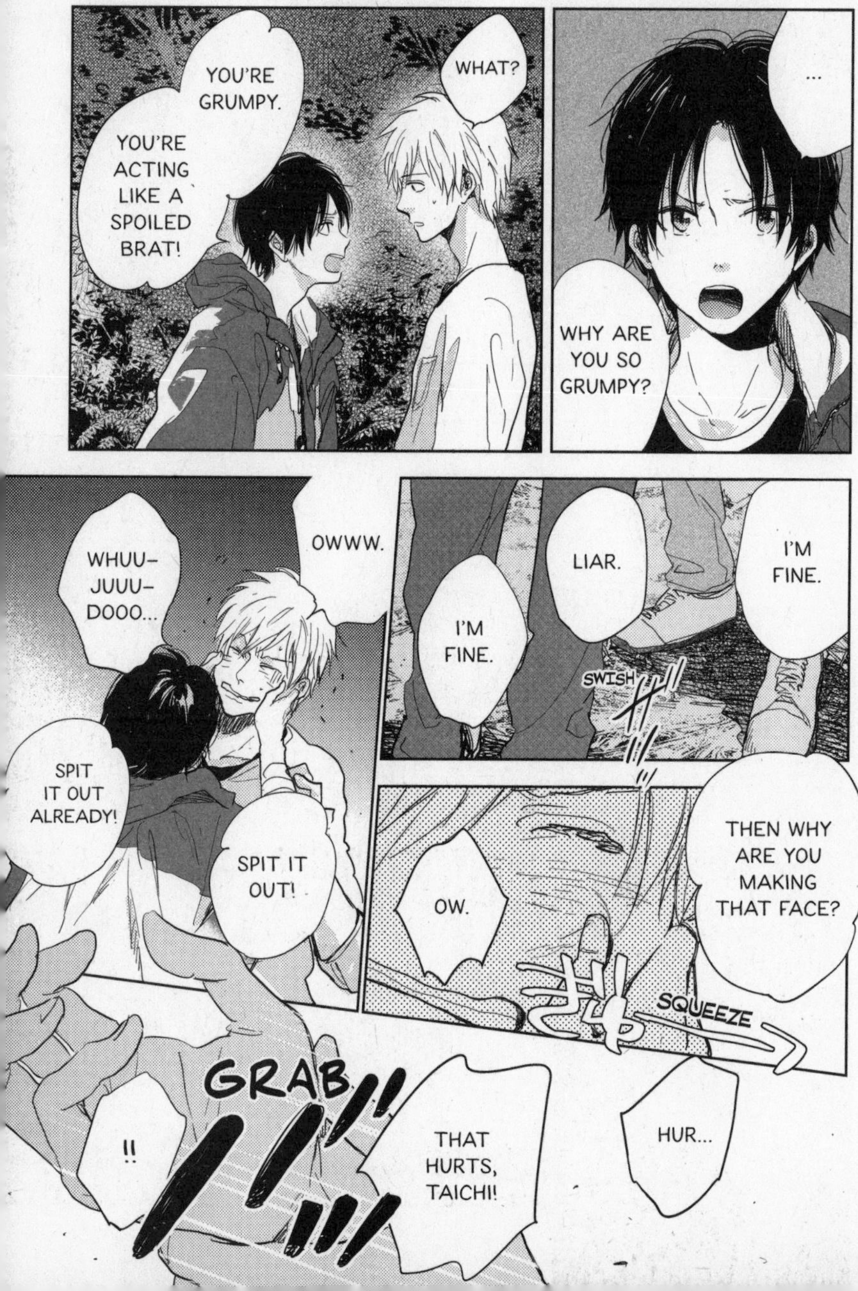
...
WHY ARE YOU SO GRUMPY?
WHAT?
YOU'RE GRUMPY.
YOU'RE ACTING LIKE A SPOILED BRAT!
I'M FINE.
LIAR.
I'M FINE.
SWISH
THEN WHY ARE YOU MAKING THAT FACE?
OW.
SQUEEZE
OWWW.
WHUU-JUUU-DOOO...
SPIT IT OUT!
SPIT IT OUT ALREADY!
HUR...
THAT HURTS, TAICHI!
GRAB
!!

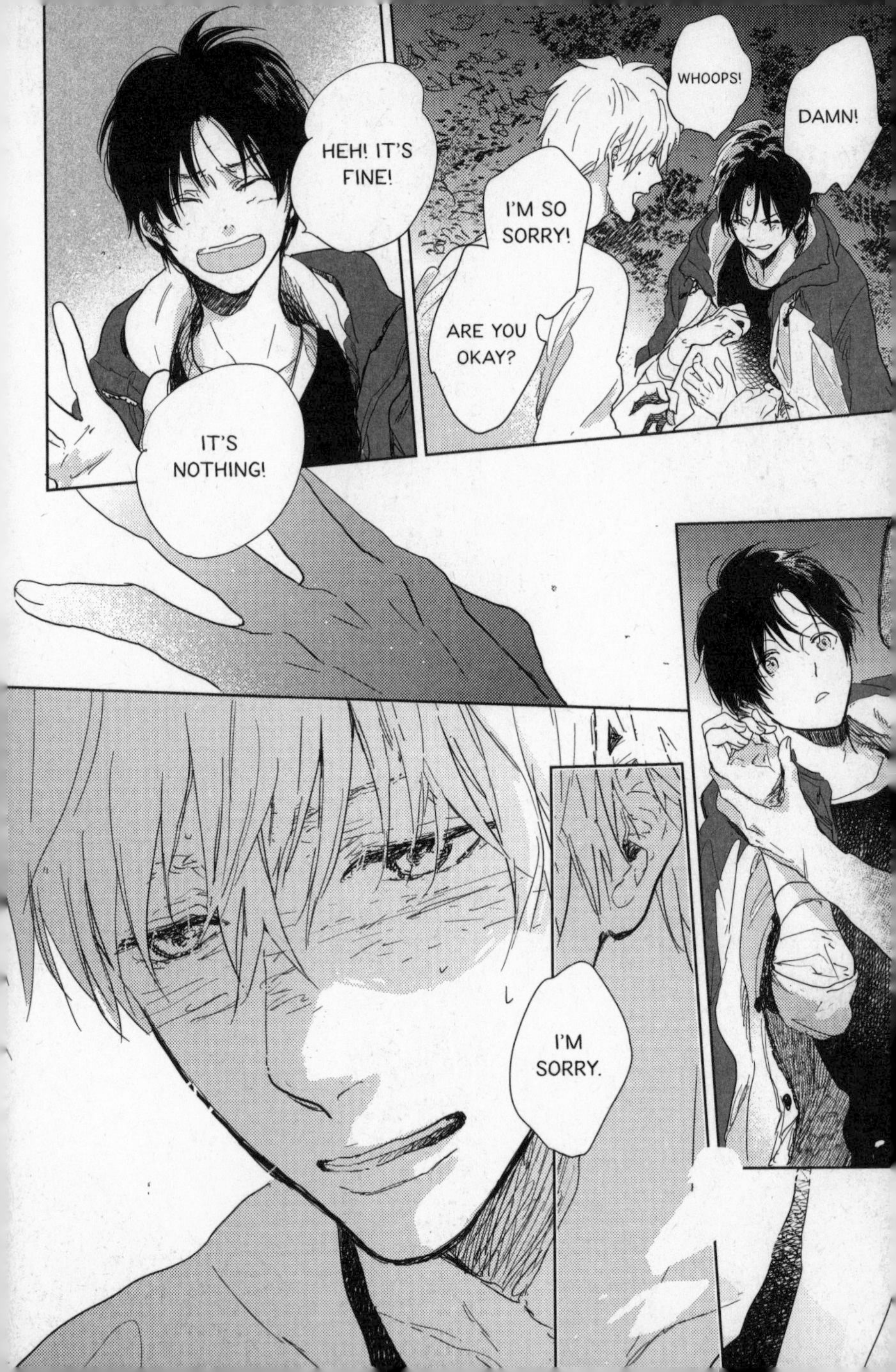
DAMN!
WHOOPS!
I'M SO SORRY!
ARE YOU OKAY?
HEH! IT'S FINE!
IT'S NOTHING!
I'M SORRY.

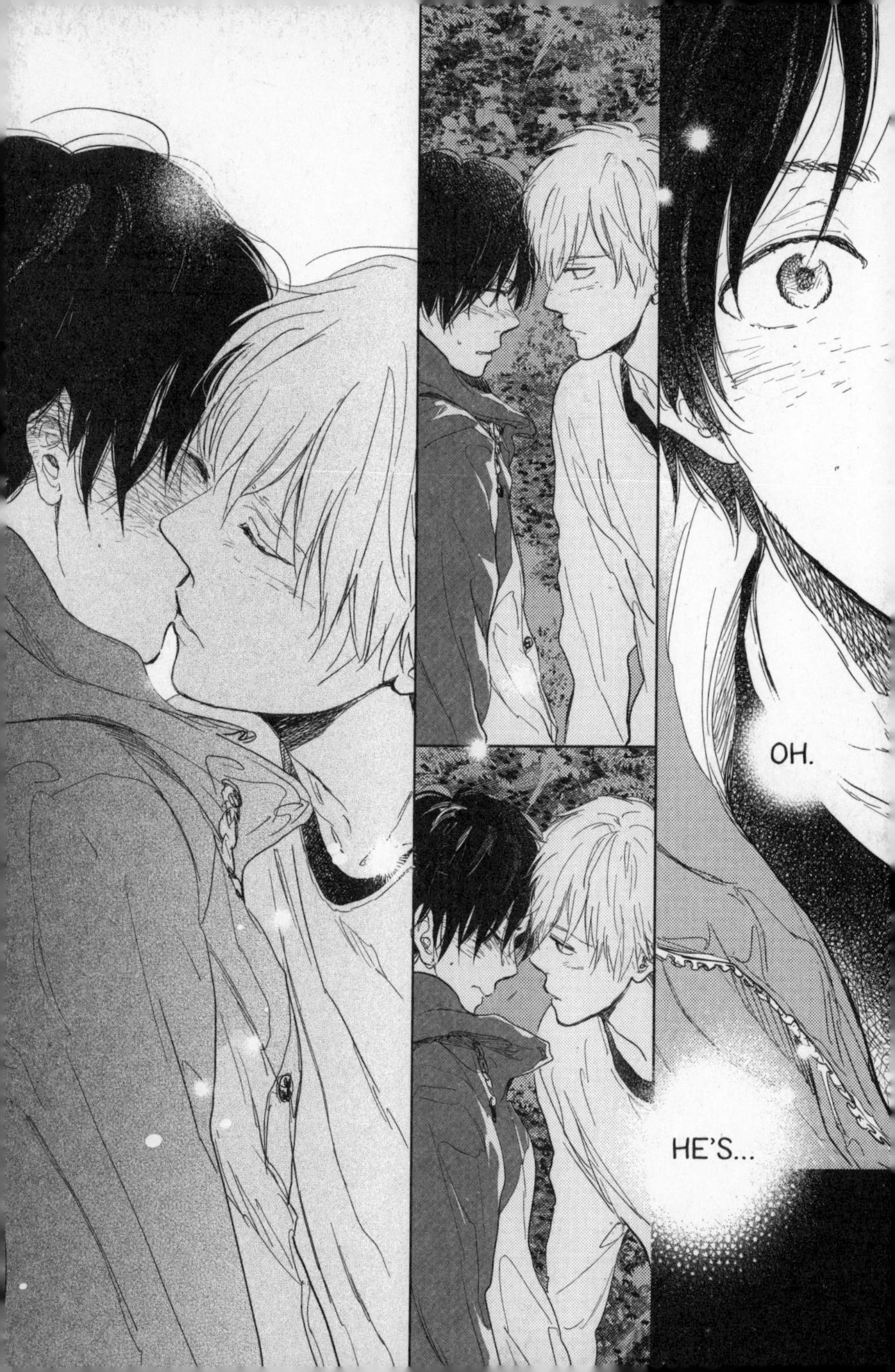
OH.
HE'S...

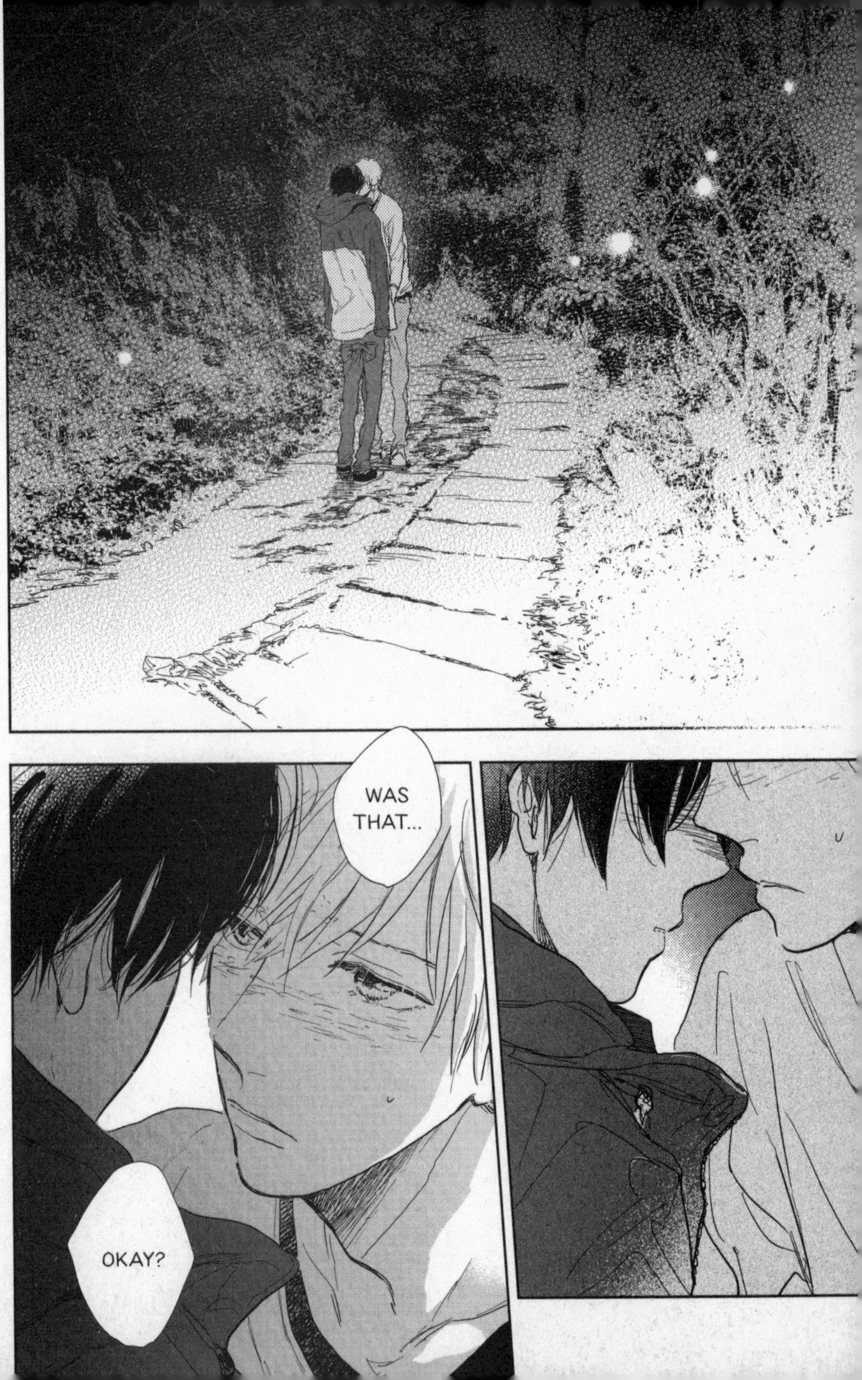
WAS THAT...
OKAY?

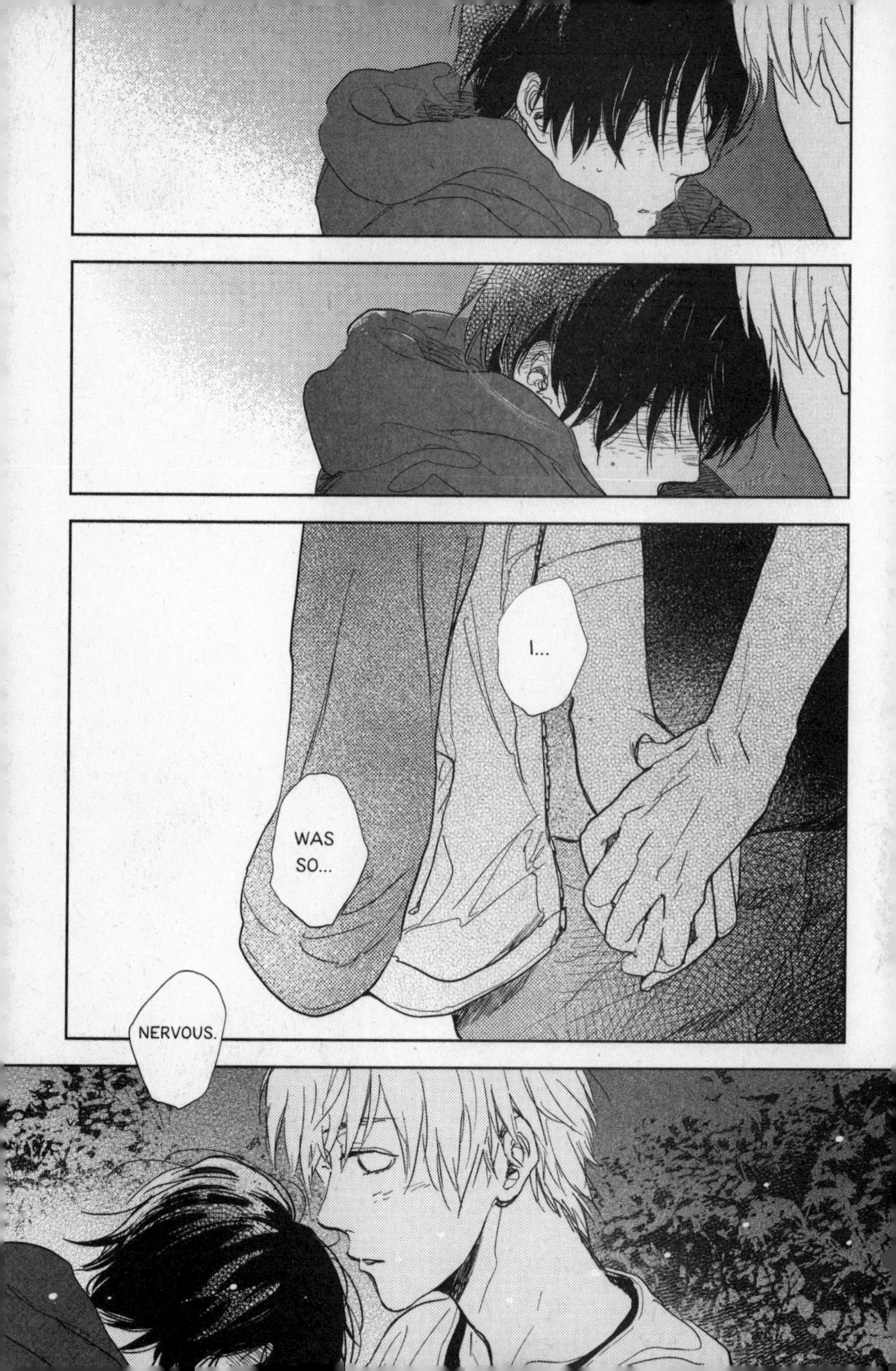
I...
WAS SO...
NERVOUS.

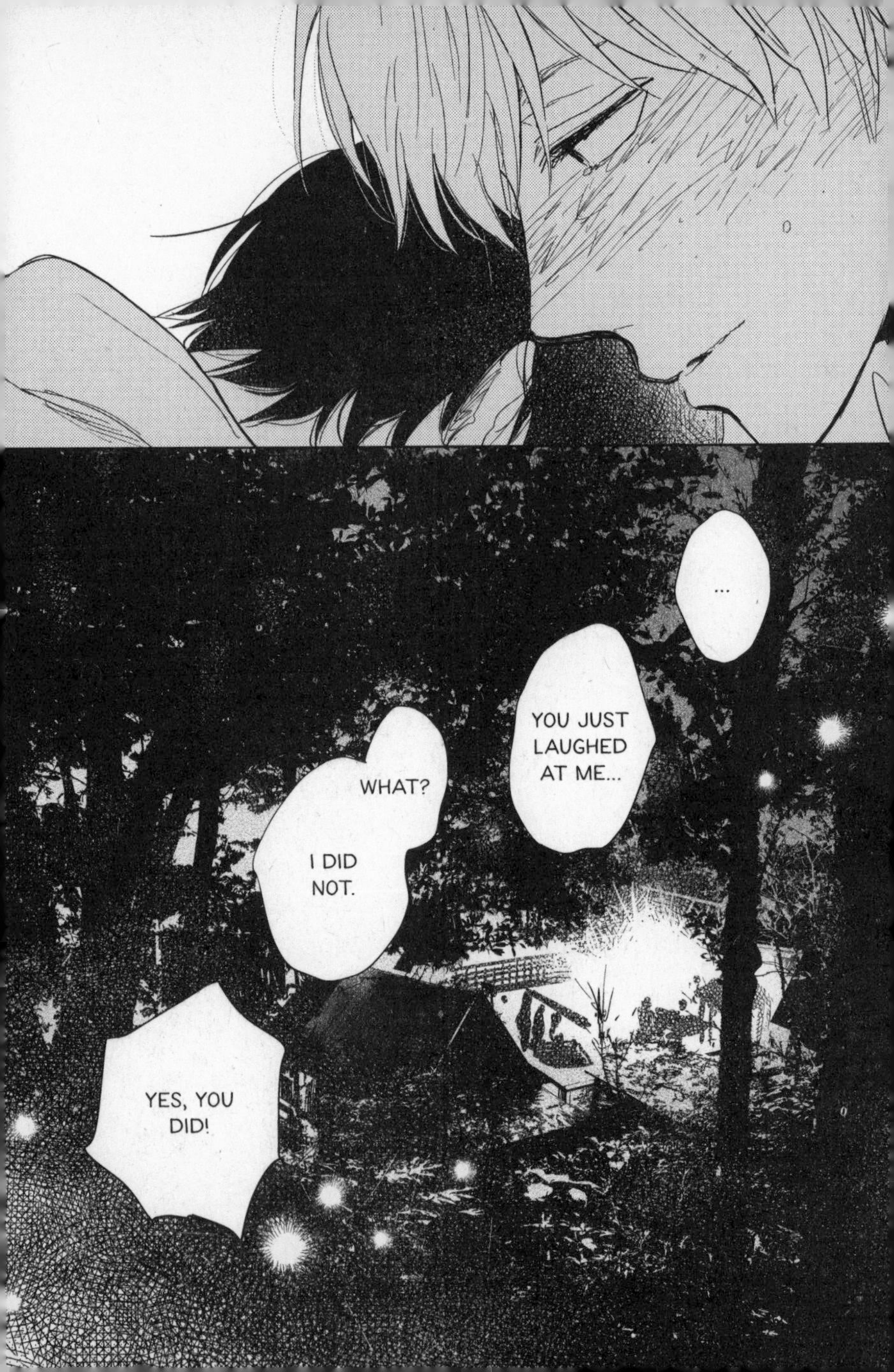
...
YOU JUST LAUGHED AT ME...
WHAT?
I DID NOT.
YES, YOU DID!

SOMETHING LIKE AN AFTERWORD

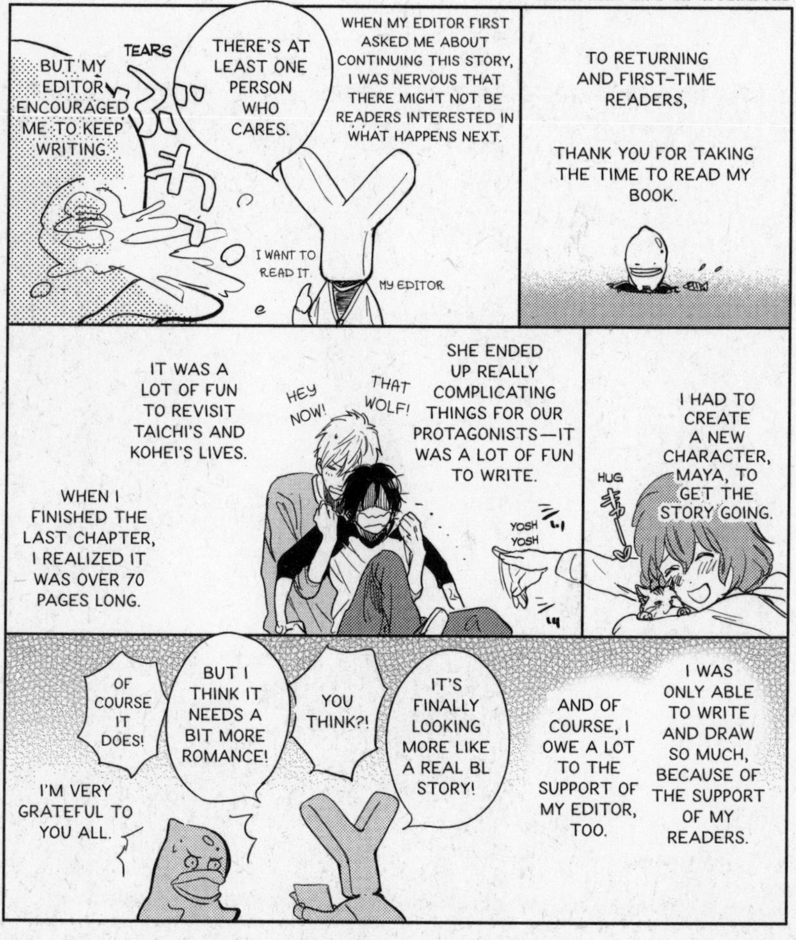
TO RETURNING AND FIRST-TIME READERS,
THANK YOU FOR TAKING THE TIME TO READ MY BOOK.
WHEN MY EDITOR FIRST ASKED ME ABOUT CONTINUING THIS STORY, I WAS NERVOUS THAT THERE MIGHT NOT BE READERS INTERESTED IN WHAT HAPPENS NEXT.
THERE'S AT LEAST ONE PERSON WHO CARES.
TEARS
BUT MY EDITOR ENCOURAGED ME TO KEEP WRITING.
I WANT TO READ IT.
MY EDITOR
I HAD TO CREATE A NEW CHARACTER, MAYA, TO GET THE STORY GOING.
HUG
SHE ENDED UP REALLY COMPLICATING THINGS FOR OUR PROTAGONISTS—IT WAS A LOT OF FUN TO WRITE.
THAT WOLF!
HEY NOW!
YOSH YOSH
IT WAS A LOT OF FUN TO REVISIT TAICHI'S AND KOHEI'S LIVES.
WHEN I FINISHED THE LAST CHAPTER, I REALIZED IT WAS OVER 70 PAGES LONG.
I WAS ONLY ABLE TO WRITE AND DRAW SO MUCH, BECAUSE OF THE SUPPORT OF MY READERS.
AND OF COURSE, I OWE A LOT TO THE SUPPORT OF MY EDITOR, TOO.
IT'S FINALLY LOOKING MORE LIKE A REAL BL STORY!
YOU THINK?!
BUT I THINK IT NEEDS A BIT MORE ROMANCE!
OF COURSE IT DOES!
I'M VERY GRATEFUL TO YOU ALL.

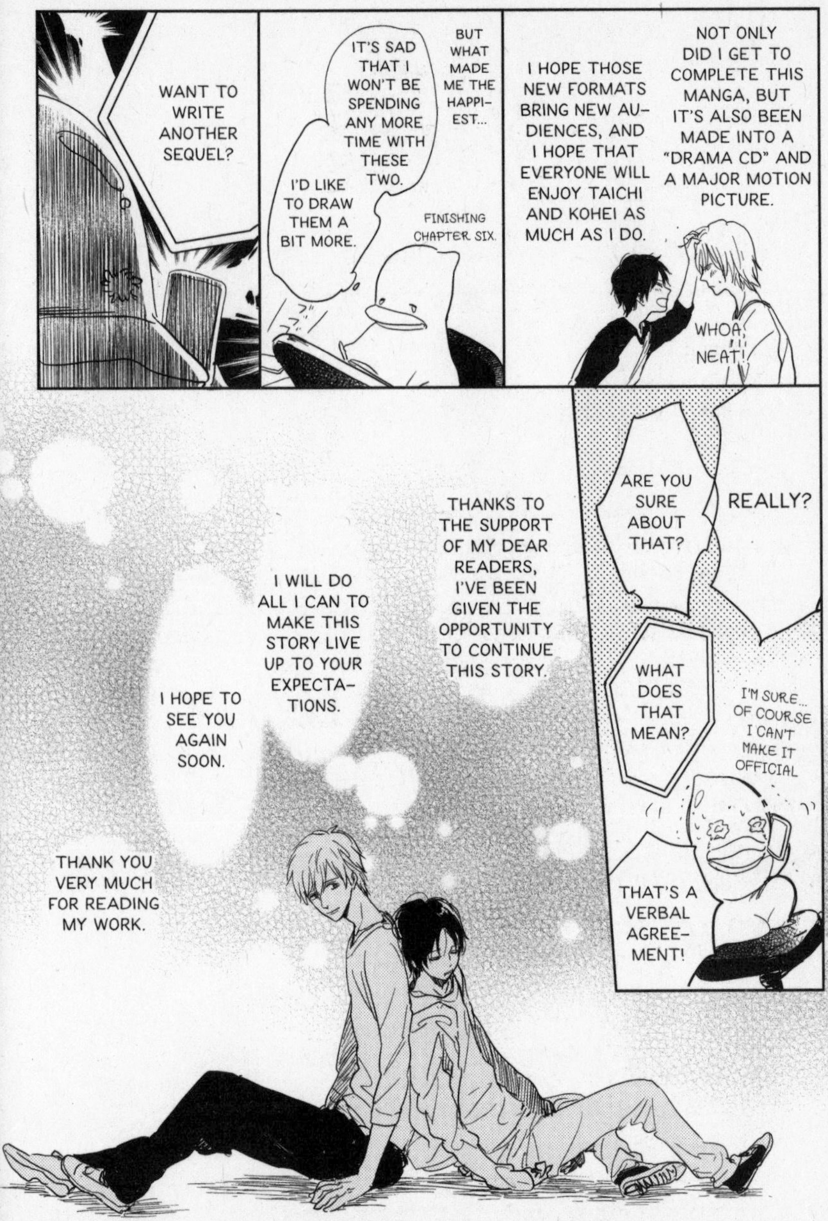
NOT ONLY DID I GET TO COMPLETE THIS MANGA, BUT IT'S ALSO BEEN MADE INTO A "DRAMA CD" AND A MAJOR MOTION PICTURE.
I HOPE THOSE NEW FORMATS BRING NEW AU-DIENCES, AND I HOPE THAT EVERYONE WILL ENJOY TAICHI AND KOHEI AS MUCH AS I DO.
WHOA, NEAT!
BUT WHAT MADE ME THE HAPPI-EST...
IT'S SAD THAT I WON'T BE SPENDING ANY MORE TIME WITH THESE TWO.
I'D LIKE TO DRAW THEM A BIT MORE.
FINISHING CHAPTER SIX.
WANT TO WRITE ANOTHER SEQUEL?
REALLY?
ARE YOU SURE ABOUT THAT?
WHAT DOES THAT MEAN?
I'M SURE... OF COURSE I CAN'T MAKE IT OFFICIAL
THAT'S A VERBAL AGREE-MENT!
THANKS TO THE SUPPORT OF MY DEAR READERS, I'VE BEEN GIVEN THE OPPORTUNITY TO CONTINUE THIS STORY.
I WILL DO ALL I CAN TO MAKE THIS STORY LIVE UP TO YOUR EXPECTA-TIONS.
I HOPE TO SEE YOU AGAIN SOON.
THANK YOU VERY MUCH FOR READING MY WORK.

I Hear the Sunspot: Theory of Happiness
(original Japanese title: Hidamari Ga Kikoeru: koufukuron)

Copyright © 2016 Yuki Fumino
English translation rights arranged with France Shoin
through Japan UNI Agency, Inc., Tokyo

ISBN: 978-1-944937-41-6

Written and illustrated by Yuki Fumino
English Edition Published by One Peace Books 2018

Printed in Canada

1 2 3 4 5 6 7 8 9 10

One Peace Books
43-32 22nd Street STE 204 Long Island City New York 11101
www.onepeacebooks.com